DATE DUE MAY 04

AUG 2 4 '04			
GAYLORD			PRINTED IN U.S.A.

THE CHRONICLE OF UNITED STATES THEATER SINCE 1920

BEST PLAYS
THEATER
YEARBOOK

FOUNDED BY BURNS MANTLE

THE BEST PLAYS OF 2002–2003

JEFFREY ERIC JENKINS
Editor

EDITORIAL BOARD
ROBERT BRUSTEIN
TISH DACE
CHRISTINE DOLEN
MEL GUSSOW
ROBERT HURWITT
JOHN ISTEL
CHRIS JONES
JULIUS NOVICK
MICHAEL PHILLIPS
CHRISTOPHER RAWSON
ALISA SOLOMON
JEFFREY SWEET
LINDA WINER
CHARLES WRIGHT

PAST EDITORS
(1919-2000)
BURNS MANTLE
JOHN CHAPMAN
LOUIS KRONENBERGER
HENRY HEWES
OTIS L. GUERNSEY JR.

CONSULTING EDITOR
HENRY HEWES

PHOTO EDITOR
ROBERT KAMP

ASSISTANT EDITORS
RUE E. CANVIN, PAUL HARDT, VIVIAN CARY JENKINS

THE BEST PLAYS
THEATER YEARBOOK

THE BEST PLAYS OF 2002–2003

EDITED BY

JEFFREY ERIC JENKINS

Illustrated with production photographs

○○○○○

LIMELIGHT EDITIONS

Distribution of *The Best Plays of 2002–2003* is generously underwritten by a grant from the Harold and Mimi Steinberg Charitable Trust.

The Best Plays of 2002–2003 is dedicated to Henry Hewes.

Tireless advocate, dedicated mentor and exceptional friend,
Henry Hewes is a true gentleman of the theater. For more
than 50 years, he has labored on behalf of theater
in this country. All who care for its future
owe him their gratitude.

INTRODUCTION

Hairspray is not among the plays chosen as the best of 2002-2003?
You might want to rethink that—seriously.

—Michael Portanticre

T HE DAY WE released the list of the Best Plays of 2002–2003, the e-mail
quoted in total above landed in our "In" box with that musical "plink"
to which we've become accustomed in the 21st century. It wasn't the first
comment we've received about choices for honors in this series—in three
years, there have been more than a few—but it was the first one to make us
laugh. Portantiere, who is editor of the terrific website called
TheaterMania.com, has been our acquaintance for the better part of the
past decade as a professional colleague. We know his incisive style of
argument and criticism, so it was easy to tell that his brief message came
from a supportive place—besides which he signed his e-mail "Yours
supportively."

But our amusement came from a recollection of a conversation between
the founder of this series, Burns Mantle, and the legendary producer-director
Arthur Hopkins exactly 80 years ago. It was for the 1922–1923 season that
a play produced by Hopkins, *The Old Soak* by Dan Marquis, was named
one of the 10 Best Plays. And yet, it would seem, Hopkins was not satisfied
with Mantle's choices. "Why 10?," Mantle quotes Hopkins as asking, "Why
not 9? Or 12?"

> To which we could make no more reasonable answer than to say
> that, having started with 10, we disliked to break the habit, also that
> unless a specified number was agreed upon the selection would lose
> its zest as a game. "Why should it be a game?" continued Arthur. He
> is a most persistent person.

Hopkins's instinct, of course, was dead right: it shouldn't be a game and we
daresay—Mantle's comment aside—it never has been.

A few days after we received Portantiere's message, we were notified
by Ann Miner of Talkin' Broadway, the popular theater-forum on the web,
that there had been a great deal of discussion on her site about the Best
Play choices. A features editor for a daily newspaper had sparked a discussion
on the website by deploring the lack of musicals on this year's list with a

posting that included the provocative line: "Musicals need not apply." Ms. Miner suggested that we might wish to respond.

At first oblivious to the controversy, we read through the dozen or so messages posted about the Best Plays and, at Miner's invitation, responded to the questions raised, which seemed to satisfy all concerned. We think it bears repeating in edited form:

> We certainly do not have a policy of exclusion when it comes to musicals. In my first year as editor of the series . . . there were two musicals picked as *Best Plays*. . . .
>
> The procedure for picking the *Best Plays* changed when we changed editors in 2001. We believed that the editor of the series needed the input of others in selecting the *Best Plays*, so we created an editorial board and picked a fine group of theater writers and critics from around the United States to offer advice. There are 14 members on the editorial board and their names are listed in all of our press releases and on the masthead of the book.
>
> We provide the editorial board with a list of 30 or so productions— plays and musicals—from the hundreds we see each year. We figure that the board and editor see somewhere in the neighborhood of 2,000 performances each year. Each member of the board is invited to select up to 12 productions to be considered for inclusion. We carefully track the board's selections and invite the board members to suggest productions that may have been overlooked for one reason or another. Once all of the input has been offered, though, it's the editor's choice. . . .
>
> The number of musicals included in *Best Plays* begins to increase with *Oklahoma!*—which is understandable. In the first 23 years of *Best Plays*, there were only 3 musicals chosen. Since that time *Best Plays* has averaged approximately one per year. But we do not have a quota. (And, for those who are still with us, *Imaginary Friends* was not treated as a musical.)
>
> As many of your members know, and some have articulated, choosing 10 works for inclusion is ultimately purely subjective. But we like to think that our choices are solidly based on opinions formed during many years of work in and around the theater. We can tell you that *Hairspray, Avenue Q* and, even, *Movin' Out* were considered for inclusion. And we can tell you that the choices are never made glibly. . . .

And we wrote all of this while mindful of Burns Mantle's glib replies to Arthur Hopkins 80 years ago. Still, though, we have offered no answer to the plaintive cry of "Why no *Hairspray?*"

As we indicated in our posting, *Hairspray* and other musicals were considered for the book. In the case of *Hairspray*, specifically, there was an authorship issue. As fans of John Waters's film, it seemed unclear to us that Mark O'Donnell and Thomas Meehan's Tony Award-winning book was a completely original departure from the film. Had Waters been credited as part of the bookwriting team, it might have made more sense. Finally, though, what made *Hairspray* the wiggly, giggly success it became seemed to have less to do with the narrative and more to do with its confluence of music (thanks to Marc Shaiman and Scott Wittman), casting (Harvey Fierstein and the self-described "chubby girl," Marissa Jaret Winokur) and press agentry (Richard Kornberg and Associates).

In addition to the plays celebrated in these essays, we also hope that readers enjoy the volume's expanded statistics and index. Whenever possible we track all Broadway and Off Broadway revivals back to their original presentations in New York and abroad. In the case of William Shakespeare and others of his ilk, we employ George C.D. Odell's *Annals of the New York Stage*—which links with the *Best Plays* series to chronicle New York theater back to the 18th century—back issues of the *New York Times* and other source materials in an attempt to locate plays in their original context.

If a particular dramatic work was honored by *Best Plays* in the past, we also note that fact. The careful reader may then discover that *Hairspray* is not the only musical mother-daughter act to be overlooked by this series. (Long after the Best Plays were announced for this season, we noticed that the original production of a well-known musical revived this season had been similarly ignored. You can look it up.)

II

AS WE MOVE forward with our 84th volume of this chronicle of theater in the United States, it's important that we consider not only the process we undertake when choosing plays but also the filters through which we present those choices. By filters, we mean the essayists who interpret and contextualize the Best Plays for our readers now and in the future.

In each of the three years since we made our last change of editors, a cloud has hung over our culture. We refer, of course, to the insecurity and instability that came to our shores in the form of the 2001 terrorist attacks, and that transformed into an ever-widening depletion of human and financial resources as war became a tool of cynical political manipulation. Hundreds of thousands—perhaps millions—of people around the world marched to protest a possible war with Iraq, but United States leaders ignored them (and the United Nations) and the battle was engaged. Although the dictator of Iraq, Saddam Hussein, was chased from power and finally captured, casualty totals continue to mount: More US soldiers have died since the cessation of major combat operations than died *during* those operations. Families are asked to sacrifice their children to a cause that has no end in sight and, despite some successes in rebuilding that country's infrastructure, corporations with close ties to the current administration profit handsomely. The term "quagmire" is bandied about and those of us who recall Vietnam think we may hear a familiar tune.

The terrorist attacks in 2001 occurred after the conclusion of our first season, disrupting our editorial and production processes; there was, however, little impact on the essays that year. Last season's essayists began to think about issues of violence and gender in response to the chosen plays, but they also explored how those projects reflected the post-September 11 world. With this season's essays, we see a sharpening focus on US culture as it now exists—even when reflected by plays that may predate that horrible September morning.

Lanford Wilson's *Book of Days* made its New York debut during the season under review, but proved too Middle America for most midtown critics. One of the most popular plays on the resident circuit for the past several years, *Book of Days* was honored in 1999 by the American Theatre Critics Association for its clear-eyed perspective on American values as they relate to corruption in business, politics and religion. For those who found Wilson's critique too dark, we offer Tish Dace's reasoned (and passionate) discussion of the parallels between the playwright's world and the "real" one just beyond the theater's doors.

Charles Wright finds similar parallels between art and culture in Nora Ephron's *Imaginary Friends*. In common with the editor, Wright believes that critics read Ephron's comic fiction as documentary. Coming at a time when fictional constructs dominated every facet of what passed for news in a culture gone mad for "reality television," the critics—themselves part of the machine that generates "reality"—just didn't get it. For the record, none of us at *Best Plays* believes Ephron's play to be a work of dramatic perfection, but for something so rich in commentary about the nature of "reality" to be so misunderstood was indeed dispiriting.

For a topic relating more specifically to September 11, we turn to Neil LaBute's *The Mercy Seat*, which mines themes familiar to those who have followed the writer-director's career in independent film and Off Broadway. As John Istel deatils, *The Mercy Seat* is a two-character study in power and seduction set against the backdrop of the World Trade Center collapse. LaBute's play ultimately has little to do terrorism—except perhaps the small terrors men and women inflict upon one another—but it is a worthy drama nonetheless.

Jennifer de Poyen finds Stephen Adly Guirgis a compelling young playwright in her essay on *Our Lady of 121st Street*. Although he shows a certain mastery in creating interesting New York characters and a powerful sense of community at the margins of society, she argues, there remains a roughness, an incompleteness to his work that she hopes further experience will give sharper focus.

Another young voice is celebrated in an essay by the editor on Adam Rapp's powerful family drama, *Stone Cold Dead Serious*. One of the most prolific playwrights working today—some argue that he's too prolific for his own good—Rapp builds on the familial studies of Eugene O'Neill, Arthur Miller and Sam Shepard with a tale sounds the dark waters of a culture driven by consumerist impulse and reality television.

Nowhere is American culture more broadly reflected than in notions surrounding race and the importance of sports to our society. We're fortunate to have essays on two fine plays from the 2002–03 season: Dael Orlandersmith's *Yellowman* and Richard Greenberg's *Take Me Out*. Both plays were finalists for the Pulitzer Prize, *Yellowman* in 2002, *Take Me Out* in 2003. Noted dramaturg Michele Volansky opens a discusssion on the internecine battles for primacy among African Americans of different shades, which Orlandersmith takes as the topic of her play. Pitting darker African Americans against those with lighter complexions, the playwright's powerful work has mesmerized audiences—even if some audiences would rather that she explore the institutional causes of this type of racism.

Greenberg's play, which premiered in London, summons the grandeur of the all-American sport of baseball while it makes only cursory stabs at exploring darker forces in our culture: homophobia, racism, class conflict. Christopher Rawson, a major-league baseball fan (who loves to see the New York Yankees lose—and is frequently disappointed) provides a thoughtful look at the national game and the Tony Award-winning play inspired by it.

Our remaining Best Plays "cross the pond" in subject matter and authorship, but they too remind us of what it means to be human. *Dublin Carol* is master storyteller Conor McPherson's latest verbal canvas on which he paints a life stunted by fear and drink. As Charles Isherwood tell us, though, the story ultimately encourages us to look past the fear and see what is possible beyond its painful grasp. In *I Am My Own Wife*, playwright Doug Wright follows the remarkable trajectory of Charlotte von Mahlsdorf, a man who lived his life as a woman—first in Nazi Germany and later under Communist rule. Essayist Julius Novick wends his way through some of the dark passages that both author and subject passed on the way to constructing an affecting dramatic identity. Finally the elder statesman among our Best Plays is Alan Bennett's *Talking Heads*, which certainly isn't a play in a conventional sense. Indeed, Bennett created a dozen monologues that fit under the collective title—the first (*Bed Among the Lentils*) starred Maggie Smith and premiered on BBC television in 1987. But the collected pieces— seven were done in repertory fashion during the Off Broadway run—provide a glimpse of a particular kind of life in a particular area of England (around Leeds, in the north). The monologues practically speak to one another and Jeffrey Sweet tells how that works in his essay.

Honorees for the 2003 American Theatre Critics/Steinberg New Play Award and Citations include Nilo Cruz's *Anna in the Tropics*, which received the Pulitzer Prize ($7,500) two days after it won the Steinberg top prize ($15,000). Cruz's play, which continued to be developed after it won the Pulitzer, is discussed by Christine Dolen. The 2003 American Theatre Critics/ Steinberg New Play Citations (along with $5,000 each) went to Arthur Miller for *Resurrection Blues* (detailed here by Claudia W. Harris), and Craig Wright for his September 11-inspired *Recent Tragic Events* (Alec Harvey).

III

BY NOW, THOUGH, the wise reader of the *Best Plays* series knows that Broadway theater is often more about economics than a regenerative experience of the mind and spirit. Indeed, 4 of the Best Plays for this season played Off Off Broadway, which is increasingly the home for much of our finest writing. Of the other 6, all started in resident theaters or Off Broadway, none began on Broadway and only 2 made it to that level.

With our colleagues in the American Theatre Critics Association, we also keep close tabs on the developing new plays that arise in theaters across the US. Through the good offices of the Harold and Mimi Steinberg Charitable Trust, we recognize the honorees and finalists of the American Theatre Critics/Steinberg New Play Award and Citations. The Steinberg Charitable Trust also supports the *Best Plays* series through a gift program in which the Trust distributes copies of the book to theater leaders and supporters. We extend our deepest thanks to the Trust and its board (William D. Zabel, Carole A. Krumland, James D. Steinberg, Michael A. Steinberg and Seth M. Weingarten) for making the *Best Plays* a priority for their support.

The collection of data for a volume such as this relies on the labors of many people. Our thanks to Paul Hardt (Cast Replacements and Touring Productions), and to Mel Gussow for his expanded essay of the Off Off Broadway theater. Rue E. Canvin, who has worked on the *Best Plays* series since the early 1960s, has expanded her duties with this volume and made the USA section a more comprehensive study of the year in theater around the country. Jonathan Dodd, the longtime publisher of the *Best Plays* series, continues to provide important background information and good advice. My good friend Henry Hewes, himself a former editor of this series and my invaluable consulting editor, never stops thinking of ways to help improve the series.

We are also deeply indebted to all of the press representatives who assisted in the gathering of information for this volume, but we particularly want to acknowledge Adrian Bryan-Brown and Chris Boneau of Boneau/ Bryan-Brown for their unflagging support of the series and its editors.

Thanks also are due to the members of the *Best Plays* editorial board, who give their imprimatur to our work by their presence on the masthead. Thanks as well to those who have offered and provided extra support and assistance to this edition: Robert Brustein, Charles Wright, John Istel, Christopher Rawson, Caldwell Titcomb (Elliot Norton Awards), David A. Rosenberg (Connecticut Critics' Circle Awards), Alec Harvey (American Theatre Critics/Steinberg New Play Award and Citations), Edwin Wilson (Susan Smith Blackburn Prize), Michael Kuchwara (New York Drama Critics Circle Awards), Henry Hewes (Theater Hall of Fame Awards) and Ralph Newman of the Drama Book Shop (New Plays and Publications).

We congratulate and thank all of the Best Plays honorees who made the 2002–03 season so invigorating to contemplate. Alan Bennett, Nora Ephron, Richard Greenberg, Stephen Adly Guirgis, Neil LaBute, Conor McPherson, Dael Orlandersmith, Adam Rapp, Lanford Wilson and Doug Wright all enriched our lives during the season under review. The photographers who capture theatrical images on film and help keep those ephemeral moments alive for historical perspective are also due thanks for their generous contributions to the greater body of theatrical work. Building on our work from last year, we have included credits with each photograph and indexed the photographers' names for easier reference. Similarly, we continue offering biographical information about each of this volume's essayists and editors in a brief section at the back of the book.

A personal note: In addition to serving as editor of this book, I teach full-time in the Drama Department at New York University's Tisch School of the Arts. During my career, I have taught at several of the best training programs in this country, but I have never been so blessed as I am at NYU. In addition to superb students who inspire me to strive for excellence in my teaching, research, editing and writing, I have the support and friendship of as fine a faculty as I have known. Each of them has, in ways large and small, provided the kind of encouragement one needs to do an annual compendium of critical perspective and historical reference that runs nearly 500 pages. My thanks to Awam Amkpa, Una Chaudhuri, Laura Levine, Carol Martin, Robert Vorlicky and Edward Ziter. For the season under review, I especially want to thank our department chair, Kevin Kuhlke, and our director of theater studies, Jan Cohen-Cruz, for providing me with teaching assistance in the person of Karmenlara Brownson (whose name appears, as a performer, elsewhere in this volume).

My wife, Vivian Cary Jenkins, continues to serve the theater and the *Best Plays* series as a tracker and editor of what's happening in the New York theater. A professor in the health care professions, she continues to help assemble, collate and check the reference information in this book. Although I repeat these thanks each year, one thing remains true: It is largely through her efforts, and her love and support, that *Best Plays* continues to appear.

And one thing more: we all miss our late friend Al Hirschfeld.

JEFFREY ERIC JENKINS
NEW YORK

Contents

INTRODUCTION   III

THE SEASON ON AND OFF BROADWAY 1

  Broadway and Off Broadway 3
    Essay by Jeffrey Eric Jenkins
      Broadway Season (summary and chart) 4
      Off Broadway Season (summary) 14
      Off Broadway Season (chart) 15

THE BEST PLAYS OF 2002–2003: ESSAYS 39
  Book of Days by Lanford Wilson 41
    Essay by Tish Dace
  Dublin Carol by Conor McPherson 51
    Essay by Charles Isherwood
  I Am My Own Wife by Doug Wright 59
    Essay by Julius Novick
  Imaginary Friends by Nora Ephron 69
    Essay by Charles Wright
  The Mercy Seat by Neil LaBute 79
    Essay by John Istel
  Our Lady of 121st Street by Stephen Adly Guirgis 85
    Essay by Jennifer de Poyen
  Stone Cold Dead Serious by Adam Rapp 93
    Essay by Jeffrey Eric Jenkins
  Take Me Out by Richard Greenberg 103
    Essay by Christopher Rawson
  Talking Heads by Alan Bennett 111
    Essay by Jeffrey Sweet
  Yellowman by Dael Orlandersmith 119
    Essay by Michele Volansky

PLAYS PRODUCED IN NEW YORK 125
  Plays Produced on Broadway 127
  Plays Produced Off Broadway 169
  Cast Replacements and Touring Companies 215

THE SEASON OFF OFF BROADWAY 231
    The Season Off Off Broadway 233
        Essay by Mel Gussow
    Plays Produced Off Off Broadway 243

THE SEASON AROUND THE UNITED STATES 275
    American Theatre Critics/Steinberg
        New Play Award and Citations 277
    Anna in the Tropics by Nilo Cruz 279
        Essay by Christine Dolen
    Recent Tragic Events by Craig Wright 287
        Essay by Alec Harvey
    Resurrection Blues by Arthur Miller 293
        Essay by Claudia W. Harris
    A Directory of New-Play Productions 299

FACTS AND FIGURES 357
    Long Runs on Broadway 359
    Long Runs Off Broadway 363
    New York Drama Critics Circle 365
    Pulitzer Prize Winners 368
    Tony Awards 369
    Lucille Lortel Awards 373
    American Theatre Critics/Steinberg Awards 374
    Additional Prizes and Awards 375
    Theater Hall of Fame 381
    Margo Jones Citizen of the Theater Medal 385
    2002–2003 Publication of Plays, Translations
        and Adaptations 387
    In Memoriam 391
    The Best Plays and Major Prizewinners, 1894–2003 395

CONTRIBUTORS TO BEST PLAYS 421

INDEX 425

THE SEASON
ON AND OFF
BROADWAY

THE SEASON:
BROADWAY AND OFF BROADWAY

○ ○ ○ ○ ○ *By Jeffrey Eric Jenkins* ○ ○ ○ ○ ○

A S THE THEATER season got underway in June 2002, Times Square touts and other ne'er-do-wells spent the days following the 2002 Tony Awards ceremony sniping about Elaine Stritch's ill-advised acceptance speech for her one-woman show, *Elaine Stritch: At Liberty*. It took so long for Stritch and her producers to get onstage that she was "played off" by the orchestra before she could finish thanking the theater community for recognizing her work. The angry quality of Stritch's response rose with the music from the pit of the stage at the Radio City Music Hall and she expanded her remarks when she met with the press backstage a few minutes later.

By the next morning, some uncharitable theater folks—yes, there are a few—were suggesting that she shouldn't even have been accepting the award because it was given to the *production*, not the performer (and never mind that all of the entries in her category were solo acts). Stritch, who has often been her own worst enemy, had complained, as reported by *Variety*'s Robert Hofler, "To be cut down like that has spoiled it for me. For a woman my age, to win her first Tony, it has spoiled it for me." Although the 77-year-old legend later apologized, the entire incident imparted a bitterness that made the season ahead seem as though it might be a long stretch to the next celebration.

But that was before *Hairspray*, the first musical of the season, brought the sweet chorus of beeping credit-card approvals with its August 15 opening. Indeed, *Hairspray* bounced into town with high expectations after its successful tryout at Seattle's 5th Avenue Theatre in June 2002. Featuring Harvey Fierstein as Edna Turnblad—she a massive mama with a heart of gold—the show got good enough reviews to make it the early favorite for the 2003 awards season. Based on John Waters's film, the bubbly stage version lacked the earthy, freewheeling quality that Ricki Lake brought to the screen in the role of Tracy Turnblad. Marissa Jaret Winokur was a spunky fire-hydrant of a diva as the show's Tony Award-winning leading lady.

BROADWAY SEASON 2002–2003

Productions in a continuing run on May 31, 2003 in bold

Productions honored as Best Plays *selections in italics*

NEW PLAYS (6)

Hollywood Arms
Imaginary Friends
Take Me Out
Vincent in Brixton
    (Lincoln Center Theater)
Life (x) 3
Enchanted April

NEW MUSICALS (6)

Hairspray
Amour
Movin' Out
Dance of the Vampires
Urban Cowboy
A Year With Frog and Toad

PLAY REVIVALS (10)

I'm Not Rappaport
Frankie and Johnny
    in the Clair de Lune
Our Town
    (Westport Country Playhouse)
Medea
Dinner at Eight
    (Lincoln Center Theater)
Tartuffe
    (Roundabout Theatre Company)
Ma Rainey's Black Bottom
A Day in the Death of Joe Egg
    (Roundabout Theatre Company)

PLAY REVIVALS (*cont'd*)

Salome
Long Day's Journey Into Night

MUSICAL REVIVALS (6)

The Boys From Syracuse
    (Roundabout Theatre Company)
Flower Drum Song
Man of La Mancha
La Bohème
Nine
    (Roundabout Theatre Company)
Gypsy

SOLO PERFORMANCES (6)

Robin Williams: Live on Broadway
Say Goodnight, Gracie
Prune Danish
Celebrating Sondheim
As Long As We Both Shall Laugh
    (Roundabout Theatre Company)
Bill Maher: Victory Begins at
    Home

SPECIALTIES (3)

Russell Simmons's Def Poetry Jam on
    Broadway
The Play What I Wrote
The Look of Love
    (Roundabout Theatre Company)

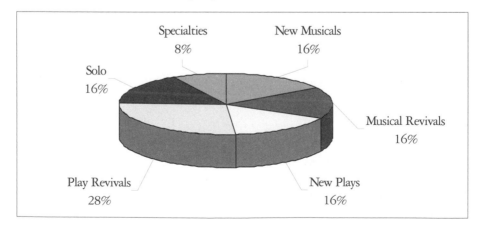

Category	Percentage
Specialties	8%
New Musicals	16%
Solo	16%
Musical Revivals	16%
Play Revivals	28%
New Plays	16%

Although the Waters film was a celebration of the possibilities of music and youth in the pre-assassination 1960s, the stage musical looked (and sounded) like a high-school production done by Broadway professionals—and perhaps that was the intent. The sweetest, most honest moment in the show was a loving duet between Fierstein and Dick Latessa as the parents of Tracy Turnblad. A smooth vaudevillian sketch by a pair of old pros, it was a show-stealing scene. Marc Shaiman and Scott Wittman (music and lyrics) paired amiably with Mark O'Donnell and Thomas Meehan (book), but it was odd that Waters wasn't listed as a co-writer. As noted in the Introduction, Richard Kornberg deserved a great deal of credit for orchestrating the media buzz: there were nearly 600 mentions in the Lexis-Nexis database in the six months leading up to the opening. Buzz oftens leads to a hangover, but *Hairspray* thrived and snagged eight Tony Awards making it the big winner of the Broadway season.

The big losers of the Broadway season were thousands of people—many tourists, some visiting theater critics—who happened to have tickets for musicals during a brief strike by members of the American Federation of Musicians Local 802 (the Broadway musicians' union) in March 2003. There was also the small matter of losses in the range of $10 million at box offices, in restaurants, wages, etc. (The city's tourism bureau estimated the daily loss to the local economy at $7 million—which may be seen as somewhat inflated). Eighteen musicals were closed for four performances over the weekend beginning Friday evening, March 7, when Actors' Equity members and International Alliance of Theatrical Stage Employees (the stagehands' union) joined the musicians' picket lines. At issue were minimum numbers of union musicians for Broadway musicals. Producers wanted no minimums—although they gradually increased their acceptable minimums in the days before the strike—and were prepared to use "virtual orchestras," which are computerized musical tracks.

Actors had been required to rehearse with the mechanical music in anticipation of the strike and their reaction to it was extremely negative. Harvey Fierstein (*Hairspray*) told the *New York Times*'s Robin Pogrebin that the synthesized music was unacceptable. "It's a computer made to sound like a roller rink—it was not a pretty sound," he said. "We're professionals, we're artists—a machine is a dead thing. That's not why people go to live theater. It's not why I want to be in live theater." *Variety*'s Robert Hofler reported that the performers "balked at the reportedly 'Nintendo' sound of the new technology." Producers had been assured by the national leadership of the stagehands' union that they would not honor the strike—but IATSE's Local 1 had other ideas.

Mayor Michael Bloomberg asked Frank J. Macchiarola, a college president and former chancellor of the New York City school system, to mediate in an overnight session that ultimately created terms acceptable to both sides. The next big contract challenge facing the producers will be the Actors' Equity production contract, which expires in June 2004. Equity can probably count on similar solidarity from other theatrical unions as the groups coordinate their efforts more closely. In January 2003, two months before the strike, the various unions and craft guilds working on Broadway formed the Coalition of Broadway Unions and Guilds to foster cooperation and solidarity among its constituent groups. A precedent for communication among these memberships had been set during the serious economic setback experienced in the weeks following September 11, 2001, when IATSE formed a Broadway Council to make certain that its wide-ranging theatrical unions were in communication during discussions with producers.

The result of this contretemps was that producers received concessions reducing mandated minimums of orchestra members—which vary by theater size—and musicians were able to hold the line on job losses (based on a chart published by *Variety*, more than 100 Broadway orchestra positions had been lost overall). Why does it matter? Musicians—in addition to composers such as John Kander, Jerry Herman and Jason Robert Brown, who spoke against the changes—believe that reducing minimums not only costs them jobs but also undermines the richer, more luxurious sound provided by a larger orchestra. Producers, on the other hand, who need to cut costs and recoup their investments, saw the old minimums as "padding" or "featherbedding." Musicians and their allies fear that the new minimums will now become maximums and live music will further recede from the Great White Way. The saddest irony in the settlement was that the Richard Rodgers Theatre—named for one of our greatest composers—lost the largest number of musicians. The Rodgers went from a minimum of 24 to 14, a loss of 10.

As both the *New York Times*'s Anthony Tommasini and *Variety*'s Charles Isherwood wrote in the wake of the strike, the problem in Broadway music isn't minimum numbers of musicians: it's the exploding growth of amplified and/or "enhanced" live music. On March 11, 2003, Tommasini wrote:

> Today sheer, bombastic volume makes most Broadway orchestras already sound quite surreal. I'll never forget the overamplified revival of *Damn Yankees* in 1995 at the Marquis Theatre, with Jerry Lewis as the Devil (Mr. Applegate). The first flourish of the orchestra during the overture was a raucous, deafening blast of brass. Why should brass instruments need amplification? And it's only gotten worse since.

Just listen to the aggressively hyper, aggressively amplified orchestra for *Thoroughly Modern Millie*. And scores that blend elements of pop, like Elton John's *Aida*, are out of control.

Isherwood offered a suggestion in a piece the next day that is sure to tug at the heart of every lover of the Broadway musical:

> [W]hile the union won a clear victory in keeping minimums in place, the lowered minimums are still a measure of a decline that began decades ago, when amplification began to be acceptable—and then *de rigueur*—in Broadway theaters. The sad truth is that most Broadway music is so electronically processed, and amplified, that it's really impossible to tell whether it is being performed live or not. My fantasy solution to the strike was a more radical compromise: Eliminate the minimums, but yank out the sound systems.

Wouldn't it be loverly? Ah, but who among our pop-trained vocalists these days could fill a 1,200-seat hall with the powerful sound of an Ethel Merman or a John Raitt?

Back to the Summer

BEFORE *HAIRSPRAY* ARRIVED with every strand firmly in place, the usual post-Tony Awards closings cleared space in the Theater District. Robin Williams played four performances in the Broadway Theatre for an HBO special, but for our purposes the season began with a pair of summer revivals. Daniel Sullivan's delightful production of *I'm Not Rappaport* got

Fast friends? Judd Hirsch and Ben Vereen in I'm Not Rappaport. *Photo: Carol Rosegg*

Star power: Stanley Tucci and Edie Falco in Frankie and Johnny in the Clair de Lune.
Photo: Robert Maxwell

the season rolling with Judd Hirsch and Ben Vereen as a pair of old men
who bicker and bond on a bench in Central Park. Critically underappreciated
when it opened July 25, 2002, the production never got the audiences it
deserved and closed September 8 after 53 performances.

Two weeks after *Rappaport* opened, another play revival bowed on
Broadway—although it had actually played Off Broadway (533
performances) in its earlier run. *Frankie and Johnny in the Clair de Lune*
by Terrence McNally starred Edie Falco and Stanley Tucci as a pair of
middle-age lovers negotiating the rocky shoals of modern relationships. As
one performance drew to a close at the Belasco Theatre, a wise guy two
rows back muttered "Oh, it has two first acts." The implication that McNally's
naturalist project, under the steady directorial hand of Joe Mantello, was
too evenly modulated, too lacking in a narrative arc rang true. Nevertheless,
Falco (a respected stage veteran who attained stardom on HBO's hit series
The Sopranos) and Tucci (a well-known film actor and producer) attracted
audiences—and a widely reported nude scene probably didn't hurt ticket
sales. The actors, who also began a relationship offstage, left the show in
January 2003 and were replaced by Rosie Perez and Joe Pantoliano. Stories
emanating from the replacement cast's rehearsal hall sounded less than
promising with tales of emotional meltdowns (not unheard of in the theater)
and lines unmemorized as the first performance neared. Six weeks after
Perez and Pantoliano opened, the *New York Times*'s Ben Brantley, wrote "I

felt as if I were watching an acting-class assignment." On March 9, 2003, the show closed after 243 performances.

Even before those first summer openings, though, a handful of productions from the 2001–02 season folded: *The Elephant Man*, *The Crucible*, *Sweet Smell of Success*, *QED*, *The Man Who Had All the Luck* and *Fortune's Fool*. *QED* had played only on Sundays and Mondays at Lincoln Center Theater's Vivian Beaumont Theater. It made room for the return of Barbara Cook's *Mostly Sondheim* concerts, which had taken a hiatus from February 11 to June 22, 2002. *Fortune's Fool* won Tony Awards for actors Frank Langella and Alan Bates, but those wins never translated into capacity crowds. As the dog days of summer approached, *Morning's at Seven* and *Topdog/Underdog* dimmed their lights—the latter managing to earn a profit. By Labor Day 2002, gone and going were the long-running *Contact*, *The Full Monty*, *Noises Off* and *The Tale of the Allergist's Wife*. There were no closings between September 15 and December 15, when the Tony Award-winning *The Goat, or Who is Sylvia?* closed with its replacement cast of Sally Field and Bill Irwin. Despite more stable business during the fall, *Hairspray* received the lion's share of media (and box office) attention as the traditional post-Labor Day season got a slow start.

Before summer's end, though, Roundabout Theatre Company revived *The Boys From Syracuse* August 18 (three days after *Hairspray*) for a limited run at the former Selwyn Theatre. The book of the musical by Richard Rodgers (music), Lorenz Hart (lyrics) and George Abbott (book) was extensively rewritten by Nicky Silver into a charming update of the tale of twins separated at birth who are comically reunited. It must be noted, though, that "charming" was not the majority opinion. Although New York critics enjoyed the songs, the production itself—filled with strapping men and sexy women—took it on the chin. The *New York Times*'s Ben Brantley compared it to Las Vegas fare and *Variety*'s Charles Isherwood wrote that director Scott Ellis's staging was "unfortunate" and squandered "the show's potential charms." It probably didn't help the production that City Center's Encores! series staged a well-received concert version in 1997—to which the Roundabout production was repeatedly compared.

What's New?

AS PRODUCERS JOCKEY to position productions closer to spring awards' deadlines, fewer and fewer productions open in the first half of the season. Taking June 1 as the beginning of the season, less than one-third of all new productions—12 of 37—opened on Broadway in the first six months of the season. And slightly more than a third—14 of 37—opened in the last two months of Tony Award eligibility. But the most disturbing statistic further confirms Broadway's diminishing importance as a home to new plays. In the first half of the season, only one new play (*Hollywood Arms*) opened on Broadway—and it didn't open until the end of the fifth month (October 31).

Co-authored by Carrie Hamilton and Carol Burnett, *Hollywood Arms*—which is based on Burnett's memoir *One More Time*—had its first presentation at Chicago's Goodman Theatre after development at the Sundance Theatre Laboratory in Utah. Hamilton, who died not long before the play's premiere in Chicago, was Burnett's daughter and had convinced her mother of the stageworthiness of her autobiography. Directed by Harold Prince and featuring a strong cast in Linda Lavin, Michele Pawk, Donna Lynne Champlin and Frank Wood, the production's pedigree helped it to receive respectful reviews. Pawk even won a Tony Award five months after the show closed. But the story of a young girl who overcomes her family's dysfunction to launch a career in show business seemed not to resonate with prospective audiences—it closed January 5 after 76 performances.

The next two new plays to open—*Imaginary Friends* and *Take Me Out*—were chosen Best Plays, but neither started on Broadway. *Imaginary Friends*, Nora Ephron's "play with music"—lyrics by Craig Carnelia, music by Marvin Hamlisch—premiered at San Diego's Old Globe before its Broadway stand and Richard Greenberg's play about sex and democracy, *Take Me Out*, opened (oddly) at the Donmar Warehouse in London before an Off Broadway run at the Joseph Papp Public Theater. Charles Wright and Christopher Rawson, respectively, elucidate the qualities of these plays in the next section—suffice to say that their perspectives are near to our own. (The exception being Rawson's gratuitous denigration of the New York Yankees.)

Ephron's play may require more knowledge of its subjects—Lillian Hellman and Mary McCarthy—than audiences and critics generally bring to the theater. Some seemed to think the play was a documentary. It is, in fact, a comic meditation on the nature of public "reality" and its construction. Others saw the play as postfeminist propaganda, even though it shows clearly how women (smart, powerful women) are often pitted against one another for the only female seat at the "big boys' table." (Despite the play's historical bent, statistics show that women still are not well represented at "the top.") And this theatrical conversation is rejected in a time when many college-age people think the battles for equality are won.

After invoking drag queens to help describe the production, the *Times*'s Brantley ended his review by writing that *Imaginary Friends* "never generates much heat." *Variety*'s Charles Isherwood found it a "superficial, theatrically lifeless text." The Associated Press's Michael Kuchwara called it "fanciful speculation that is only intermittently entertaining." Critics consistently praised the show's principals, Swoosie Kurtz (as Hellman) and Cherry Jones (as McCarthy), and the production team. It seemed as though the target of critical scorn was Ephron—an extremely successful writer of romantic comedies for Hollywood—which was ironic, considering her topic. Her show closed February 16 after 76 performances.

Greenberg's Tony Award-winning *Take Me Out*—the story of what happens when a baseball superstar announces that he is homosexual—was well received when it opened Off Broadway at the Public. The playwright hit a home run with a narrative exposing the cracks in our democratic system: the divisions caused by class, race, language, nationality, sexual preference. Before its Broadway bow, *Take Me Out* was a three-act play that celebrated baseball and its intersections with the ideals of democracy—even if many of those ideals remain unrealized. Greenberg shortened the play for Broadway, making it into two acts, but he never resolved questions raised by making his primary narrator—there are two—a white heterosexual male who (mis)translates and clumsily negotiates the differences of class, race, language, nationality, sexual preference. Still, it was a pleasure to see (twice) and even at the end of the longer version, there was a longing for more. Joe Mantello won the Tony Award for play direction for his work on *Take Me Out* and his ensemble (Denis O'Hare, Daniel Sunjata, Neal Huff, Frederick Weller, Joe Lisi and others) was superb. O'Hare received the Tony Award for featured actor (he was also one of the few who did not have a nude scene).

The three other new plays on Broadway (*Vincent in Brixton*, *Life (x) 3* and *Enchanted April*) also originated elsewhere. The first two came from London and the last premiered at Hartford Stage in Connecticut in February 2000. *Vincent in Brixton*, by Nicholas Wright, marked a star turn for Clare Higgins as the lonely older woman who serves as muse and caretaker for the artist Vincent van Gogh (Jochum ten Haaf) when he lives in England for a short time. A solemn dirge of a play, it won Olivier Awards for best play and for Higgins. New York audiences, though, were not similarly enamored of the play. The Lincoln Center Theater production (in association with the Royal National Theatre) closed after 69 performances and returned to London where the company played a few more weeks.

Hell night: Linda Emond and Helen Hunt in
Life (x) 3. *Photo: Joan Marcus*

Yasmina Reza, author of *Art* and *The Unexpected Man*, returned to New York with her latest play, *Life (x) 3*. Directed by Matthew Warchus and translated from the French by Christopher Hampton, the play is a study in how small shifts of choice can alter our lives. Featuring Helen Hunt, John Turturro, Brent Spiner and Linda Emond, the variations played—however amusing—showed little difference of substance, which lowered the stakes for making alternative choices (and confused Broadway critics and audiences). The wittiest moment was the beginning of the show when, via laser lighting effect, a square box filled the circular stage area of the Circle in the Square Theatre. It made a square in the circle. Get it?

Matthew Barber's *Enchanted April* is an adaptation of a novel about a pair of frustrated Englishwomen who break out of their stultifying lives by renting an Italian villa for a vacation. Based on the 1923 book by Elizabeth von Arnim, the play featured Elizabeth Ashley as a grumpy older resident of the villa with Jayne Atkinson and Molly Ringwald as the women trying to reinvigorate their lives. The perfectly suitable cast also included Dagmara Dominczyk, Michael Cumpsty, Daniel Gerroll and Michael Hayden. Kane Campbell wrote an earlier stage adaptation that played a brief run (32 performances) in 1925—he also wrote the first film version (1935). The story is best known (deservedly) for a 1992 film version with Joan Plowright, Miranda Richardson, Alfred Molina and Jim Broadbent.

By the Numbers

THERE WAS AN odd symmetry among the various Broadway production categories during the 2002–03 season. Six was the operative number, apparently, as that was the number of new plays, new musicals, musical revivals and solo performances (see chart on page 4). The other two categories, play revivals and specialties, had 10 and 3 productions respectively.

What this means is that Broadway continued its march down memory lane, a safer, more profitable proposition. Although there were two more productions on Broadway this season (37) than last (35), revivals accounted for a larger percentage of the seasonal pie. Last year (2001–02) there were 15 revivals, comprising 43 percent of the season's productions, this year that number was 16 (44 percent). Although this is only one more revival accounting for approximately one percentage point of increase, the 2002–03 figure is up 8 percent from just two years earlier when revivals accounted for approximately 36 percent of Broadway production. Similarly, two years ago (2000–01), which was the last season before the terrorist attacks on September 11, 2001, productions of new plays and new musicals accounted for 50 percent of Broadway production—they now account for 32 percent (last season the figure was 40 percent).

It's important to note, as we ponder the percentages, that Broadway production has increased in each of the past three years we are comparing. There were 28 productions in 2000–01, 35 in 2001–02 and 37 in 2002–03. Clearly, producers are interested in mounting new Broadway shows—but there is an increasing emphasis on minimizing risk by presenting plays and musicals that are proven successes. Plays and musicals, though, aren't the only shifting categories that concern the theater community: solo performance and specialty acts are becoming a larger part of the Broadway landscape. Of the 100 new productions on Broadway over the past three seasons, 19 have been solos and specialties (15 solos, 4 specialties)—and these numbers are bound to continue to rise because these categories have lower production costs.

Partly due to producers' conservative programming (and ticket-price inflation), the 2002–03 season was another banner year for box-office revenues. Bouncing back from the Season of September 11—which, given the circumstances, showed only a minor dip in revenue and attendance

OFF BROADWAY SEASON 2002–2003

Productions in a continuing run on May 31, 2003 in bold

Productions honored as Best Plays *selections in italics*

NEW PLAYS (30)

Endpapers
Play Yourself (NYTW)
Spanish Girl (Second Stage)
Take Me Out (Public)
The World Over (Playwrights)
My Old Lady
Yellowman (MTC)
Far Away (NYTW)
Temporary Help (Revelation Theater)
Tuesdays With Morrie
Boston Marriage (Public)
Blue/Orange (Atlantic)
Crowns (Second Stage)
What Didn't Happen (Playwrights)
Adult Entertainment
Gone Home (MTC)
Kimberly Akimbo (MTC)
Sleeping With Straight Men
Dublin Carol (Atlantic)
Observe the Sons of Ulster Marching
    Towards the Somme (LCT)
Barbra's Wedding
Our Lady of 121st Street
Fucking A (Public)
Polish Joke (MTC)
Talking Heads
The Last Sunday in June
She Stoops to Comedy (Playwrights)
Cavedweller (NYTW)
Writer's Block (Atlantic)
Humble Boy (MTC)

NEW MUSICALS (11)

The Prince and the Pauper
Thunder Knocking on the Door
Little Ham
Jolson and Company
A Man of No Importance (LCT)
Debbie Does Dallas
Little Fish (Second Stage)
Radiant Baby (Public)
My Life With Albertine (Playwrights)
Zanna, Don't!
Hank Williams: Lost Highway

PLAY REVIVALS (11)

Maria Stuart (BAM)

PLAY REVIVALS (*cont'd*)

All Over (Roundabout)
Comedy of Errors (Aquila)
Twelfth Night (NYSF)
Burn This (Signature)
The Resistible Rise of Arturo Ui (NAT)
Antigone (National Theater of Greece)
Uncle Vanya (BAM)
Twelfth Night (BAM)
The Island (BAM)
As You Like It (Public)

SOLO (14)

In Real Life (MTC)
Dudu Fisher: Something Old, Something
    New
Bewilderness
Bartenders
The Love Hungry Farmer (Irish Rep)
One Million Butterflies (Primary Stages)
Tea at Five
Bexley, Oh(!) Or, Two Tales of One City
    (NYTW)
Foley (Irish Rep)
Golda's Balcony (Manhattan Theater
    Ensemble)
Broad Channel
Mary Todd . . . A Woman Apart
    (Centenary Stage)
Down a Long Road
I Am My Own Wife (Playwrights)

SPECIALTIES (7)

The Exonerated (Culture Project)
House of Flowers (Encores!)
Hashirigaki (BAM)
Midnight's Children (Columbia)
Elegies (LCT)
The New Moon (Encores!)
No Strings (Encores!)

REVUES (6)

Harlem Song
Water Coolers
Tommy Tune: White Tie and Tails
Showtune: The Words and Music of Jerry
    Herman
The Jackie Wilson Story
Boobs! The Musical

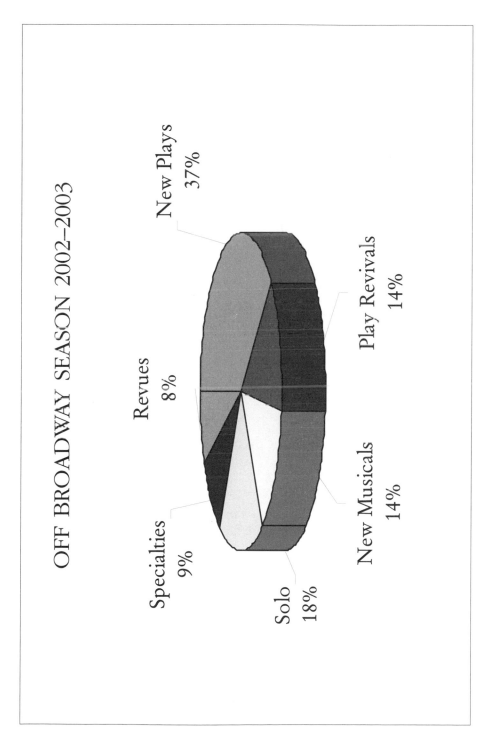

OFF BROADWAY SEASON 2002–2003

New Plays
37%

Play Revivals
14%

New Musicals
14%

Solo
18%

Specialties
9%

Revues
8%

(3.4 percent in revenues, 8 percent in attendance)—Broadway collected a record $720 million at the box office in 2002–03, an increase of nearly $80 million over 2001–02 (slightly more than 12 percent). But most of the surge came from increased ticket prices, which according to *Variety* increased $4.64, on average. Attendance this season was up 430,000 to 11.3 million, but fell short by more than half a million of the nearly 12 million Broadway patrons in 2000–01.

Although the four-day strike certainly cut into the final totals, even without it Broadway could not have reached its 2000–01 attendance figures. As soon as the strike was over, everyone returned to work—with the unions relieved that they weren't forced into a prolonged strike, which doubtless would have severely tested their solidarity. Just as it was back to business as usual and it looked as though the strike was a mere speed bump in an otherwise promising year, the United States and its "coalition of the willing" invaded Iraq March 19, 2003, in a move to unseat Saddam Hussein. According to *Variety*, though, Broadway managed to avoid the 20 percent drop it experienced in 1991 when the first Bush administration went to Iraq and, in fact, saw a slight lift in revenues that week.

More on Musicals

THE NUMBER OF new musicals on Broadway held steady this season. Two months after *Hairspray*'s opening, two more new musicals opened. But they followed a much-anticipated revival (and revisal) of *Flower Drum Song*, whose book was overhauled by David Henry Hwang. The fine cast included the remarkable Lea Salonga—who should be working on a Broadway stage every night—along with Randall Duk Kim, Sandra Allen and Jodi Long. The music was touching and memorable, but even with revisions the show skated the razor's edge of Asian minstrelsy in characters created by Richard Rodgers, Oscar Hammerstein II and Joseph Fields.

The two new musicals to open in October 2002 couldn't have been more different from one another. At one end of the spectrum was Michel Legrand and Didier van Cauwelaert's *Amour*, a sung-through musical about a petty bureaucrat who gains the ability to pass through walls. The music was a throwback to the simple melodies of 1960s pop music and was terribly reminiscent of well-known American tunes. The considerable talents of actors Malcolm Gets and Melissa Errico had little impact: the show closed after 17 performances.

Twyla Tharp and Billy Joel's *Movin' Out* came to town on a wave of negative press from its Chicago tryout. Critics there found the piece nearly

Tasty morsel: Mandy Gonzalez and Michael Crawford in Dance of the Vampires. *Photo: Paul Kolnik*

incomprehensible when they reviewed it, but Tharp continued to work on the narrative—told through Tharp's choreography set to Joel's anthems on life among the Baby Boomers. Before the troupe left town for Broadway, Tharp invited the critics back and Michael Phillips of the *Chicago Tribune* praised the improvements. The director-choreographer never stopped working to improve the piece—it's something for which she's well known—and her efforts on this musical will pay dividends for years to come. *Movin' Out* should have been the clear choice for best musical at the Tony Award ceremony, despite its lack of a conventional book—a drawback that certainly didn't hinder *Contact* in 2000. The Tharp-Joel collaboration created the most emotionally powerful musical theater experience offered on Broadway in years. Both Tharp and Joel received Tony Awards: she for choreography, he for orchestrations (with Stuart Malina).

In December, Michael Crawford made his long-anticipated return to Broadway in *Dance of the Vampires*. The opening earlier had been postponed due to technical problems and the critical illness of director John Rando's mother. It was a short-lived run after critics panned it decisively, but still managed to eke out 56 performances. The musical, based on Roman Polanski's film *The Fearless Vampire Killers*, was a big hit in Germany. But when the American team of David Ives (book) and Rando attempted to ironize the show's over-the-top Gothic quality, they hit a creative wall. The show was a $12 million hulking mass of design run wild with some bits of fun, but also had its share of "Did he just say that?" moments.

After *Vampires* opened, it was nearly four months until the next musical opened on Broadway, but a pair of revivals opened just days before it. *Man of La Mancha* starring the incomparable Brian Stokes Mitchell and filmmaker Baz Luhrmann's production of the opera *La Bohème* heated the rainy December days and nights. Mitchell was joined by Mary Elizabeth Mastrantonio, who acquitted herself admirably. The production itself was a loud, clanking machine that overwhelmed the musical even if it never dominated its star. The question in the Theater District: Why do *La Mancha* again now? Answer: Because "Stokes," as Mitchell is commonly known, wants to do it. It's a good enough answer, even if most audience members would rather see him in a different show—almost any other show.

Luhrmann—he of the teen-friendly 2001 musical film *Moulin Rouge* (with Nicole Kidman) and the 1996 film update of *Romeo and Juliet* (with Leonardo DiCaprio)—first directed *La Bohème* in his native Australia in 1990. The Broadway production employed the same sort of lavish eye-candy designs (by his wife and creative partner, Catherine Martin) that helped make *Moulin Rouge* popular. Even though a rotating cast was employed in the principal roles to preserve voices, the opera was amplified—which undermined the lyrical textures of the singing. The English titles projected on the stage were rendered in "dramatic" fonts and showed little sensitivity to the poetry of the Italian original. The idea, apparently, was to make the opera more relevant by using 1950s slang and making the bohemian characters beatnik-ish. Critics praised the production and young audiences turned out, but it felt (weirdly) too small for the Broadway Theatre—and opera houses are generally much larger than legitimate theaters. Luhrmann's original production, it's worth noting, played in the Sydney Opera House, which made some wonder how (or if) this *La Bohème* worked well in a real opera house. The show managed to run through the end of the season and its performance ensemble received special Tony honors.

Two weeks after the musicians' strike was settled, the musical version of the 1980 John Travolta-Debra Winger film *Urban Cowboy* opened at the Broadhurst Theatre to unanimous critical pans. The producers announced that they would close after four performances, but changed their minds when angels offered extra cash to keep the show running while it tried to find an audience. A musical pastiche of well-known country songs and new numbers (several by Jason Robert Brown), *Urban Cowboy*'s book made its characters into wince-inducing cartoons once found in 19th-century local-color dramas. It closed May 18 after 60 performances.

In the final month before the deadline for Tony Award consideration, three musicals (two revivals, one new) opened on Broadway. Roundabout Theatre Company revived the Arthur Kopit (book) and Maury Yeston (music and lyrics) musical, *Nine*, with Spanish heartthrob Antonio Banderas as filmmaker Guido Contini. Based loosely on Federico Fellini's autobiographical film *8½*—from a translation by the erudite Mario Fratti—the musical tracks the influences of women on an artist's life: how they inspire, titillate, oppress. Raul Julia played the original Guido in the 1982 Tommy Tune production which was a 1981–82 *Best Plays* choice. For this revival, David Leveaux gathered a cast that included Mary Stuart Masterson, Jane Krakowski, Mary Beth Peil, Saundra Santiago, Laura Benanti, Chita Rivera and other exceptionally talented women who emotionally teased and tortured the artistic genius. Banderas was a compelling presence, if a bit diminutive onstage at the Eugene O'Neill Theatre. But the problem with this musical in 2003 is the subtle misogyny in which it indulges. All of the women are stereotypes intended to serve Guido's needs—even if those needs include spiritual self-flagellation. They are expressionistic products of Guido's consciousness, but Leveaux's staging is less interested in consciousness than in showing how women overwhelm the man. Krakowski received a Tony Award for her deliciously inviting portrayal of Guido's mistress, Carla, and the production received the award for best revival.

Arnold Lobel's beloved children's stories about Frog and Toad came to life at the Cort Theatre in the musical *A Year With Frog and Toad* by brothers Willie Reale (book and lyrics) and Robert Reale (music). The show was developed at the Tony Award-winning Children's Theatre Company in Minneapolis and had a brief run at the New Victory Theater before moving to Broadway. Designer Adrianne Lobel, daughter of the late author, designed scenery and coproduced. Her husband, Mark Linn-Baker, played the indolent Toad in this true family affair, with Jay Goede as the industrious Frog. It was a charming production about a pair of amphibians of middle age who, though quite different, are truly the very closest of friends. A trio of performers (Danielle Ferland, Jennifer Gambatese and Frank Vlastnik) played a variety of cleverly rendered supporting characters—birds, squirrels, moles, etc.

The big Broadway story at season's end was the saga of *Gypsy*, starring Bernadette Peters. When it was announced that Peters would go for the gusto as Mama Rose, those same ne'er-do-wells who eviscerated Elaine Stritch's performance at the Tony Awards began to sharpen their paring knives, daggers and axes. Could the tiny cutie-pie tread where dynamos such as Ethel Merman, Angela Lansbury and Tyne Daly had once strode? The smart money was betting against Peters's success in the Arthur Laurents (book), Jule Styne (music) and Stephen Sondheim (lyrics) musical. Yet another British director, Sam Mendes, was hired to tinker with an American musical—he created the dark 1998 revival of *Cabaret* that continues to play on Broadway. (Are American directors in demand in England? Is there an exchange program? Are the Brits really that much better than our stage artists? Or is this continuing trend the result of past critical genuflection and an Anglophilial inferiority complex?)

There were tales of trouble in paradise and reports that the 84-year-old Laurents had complained bitterly to producers at the first preview. Laurents later denied the story to the Associated Press, saying, "Sam and I have had a terrific working relationship." Then vocal problems, predicted by the naysayers, started when Peters caught cold and missed a few performances in the days just before the New York critics' previews. When she finally opened the show, critics were charitable, if mixed in their appraisal. Two weeks after the show's opening—when Peters was presumably over her cold, even if she hadn't had sufficient vocal rest—a matinee audience filled with theater writers seemed genuinely to root for Peters to make it through the performance. But there were moments when it wasn't clear whether she would make it through a song and the audience seemed as relieved as the cast during the curtain call. The instability of Peters's performance was nowhere as obvious as it was during the Tony Awards broadcast when she performed "Rose's Turn." Her vulnerability made the audience wonder not only if she'd make it through the song, but whether it was Peters or her character about to crack. It was discomfiting to watch; a tribute to the power of the "little assassins" who troll the Rialto for gossip and undermine art by emphasizing personality.

One More Time

PLAY REVIVALS ACCOUNTED for the largest single production category on Broadway this season (10 plays; 28 percent)—although there were two fewer than last season. It was four months after the opening of *Frankie and Johnny in the Clair de Lune* that the most-anticipated revival of the season—in a season with four big-name revivals—bowed December 4. Although the Westport Country Playhouse production of Thornton Wilder's

Past perfect: Maggie Lacey, Paul Newman and Ben Fox in Our
Town. *Photo: Joan Marcus*

Our Town received generally lukewarm notices during its June 2002 run in
Connecticut, the mere fact that this community-theater project was covered
by the *New York Times*, the Associated Press, *Variety* and *USA Today* gives
clues to its significance.

Westport Country Playhouse is the community theater that Joanne
Woodward serves as artistic director—and she cast her husband, Paul
Newman, in the pivotal role of the Stage Manager. James Naughton, the
two-time Tony Award-winning actor, directed a stellar cast that included
Frank Converse, Jayne Atkinson, Jane Curtin, Jeffrey DeMunn, Stephen
Spinella and Mia Dillon. When the production came to Broadway, it received
respectful, if not glowing reviews. Critics found the acting to be a bit too
busy for a play meant to be kept simple. It was also clear that life in front
of the camera had taken a toll on Newman, who seemed to have little vocal
energy and at times appeared to be working to recall his next line. The
production earned a profit before it closed January 26 (59 performances).

Actor Fiona Shaw and director Deborah Warner, who are frequent collaborators, brought their powerful production of *Medea* to Broadway after a run at the Brooklyn Academy of Music. A modern-dress production set on a construction (or destruction) site with a shallow pool of water in its midst, Warner's *Medea* made horrifyingly clear why the title character loses her grip and murders her children. Coming at a time when stories of parents killing their children have become all-too-common, this production had an overwhelming emotional impact. Shaw's emotional virtuosity demonstrated Medea's hatred for her husband as well as her unquenchable desire for him. Particularly potent was a scene when one of the children attempted to escape and was dragged out of sight by Medea—it was a wrenching reminder of a Texas woman who drowned her five children in 2001 and later told authorities how she had struggled to subdue them. The production originated in 2000 at the Abbey Theatre in Dublin before moving to London's Queen's Theatre in January 2001. The Broadway production closed after 78 performances.

Lincoln Center Theater revived George S. Kaufman and Edna Ferber's *Dinner at Eight* in a sumptuous production directed by Gerald Gutierrez and designed by John Lee Beatty (scenery) and Catherine Zuber (costumes). Christine Ebersole, James Rebhorn, Marian Seldes, Kevin Conway and Emily Skinner led a glittering cast through the well-known comedy about the mores of the aspiring rich. Although it was delightfully stylish, one leading critic dismissed the production out of hand. This cultural channel-surfer—always trying to catch the next wave—has far too much power for his *fashionista* taste. It lasted only 45 performances.

Roundabout Theatre Company united Brian Bedford and Henry Goodman for a turn in Molière's *Tartuffe*. Another lush setting by Theater Hall of Famer John Lee Beatty and luxurious costumes by Jane Greenwood created a rich canvas for Joe Dowling's clear, elegant staging. It was a triumphant return for Goodman, who was hired to replace Nathan Lane as Max Bialystock last season and fired before the critics saw him. (Some who saw him in previews back then say he wasn't funny, others say he wasn't enough like Lane.) As the unctuous hypocrite of the title, Goodman sounded just the right notes in a city wondering about the place of religious zealots—of all stripes—in civil discourse. Bedford was a perfectly detailed dupe as the hypocrite's victim. Others of note in the cast included Kathryn Meisle, J. Smith-Cameron, Bryce Dallas Howard and John Bedford Lloyd.

After it was announced that Whoopi Goldberg would play the title role in *Ma Rainey's Black Bottom*, with Charles S. Dutton reprising the starmaking role of Levee, two of the show's original producers—Robert Cole and Frederick M. Zollo—claimed that they owned the Broadway rights to the play (and they did). After Cole and Zollo were compensated, the production moved forward but not without a few more bumps in the road. After rehearsals were well underway, Goldberg and Dutton complained about their producers and director Marion McClinton in an interview published in *Time Out New York*. In an odd move, Dutton had earlier said that the original had been the definitive production. (So why do this one?) Then there were several cast changes made for "personal reasons," an actor's burst blood vessel forced the show to cancel performances and the embattled director was hospitalized for low potassium. When the show finally opened February 6, it was a shadow of a great play by a great author. Dutton seemed a bit too well-fed to play the edgy, hungry Levee and Goldberg appeared to be "phoning it in." It made for a long evening at the theater and a short run for the production (68 performances).

With due respect to the play revivals mentioned above, Broadway producers saved the three most fascinating of the season for last. Could that timing have had something to do with the awards season? If so, it had no benefit for the staged reading of Oscar Wilde's *Salome*, which starred Al Pacino as Herod, with Marisa Tomei as the titular temptress, Dianne Wiest as Herodias and David Strathairn as the tortured prophet. Pacino played the same role in a 1992 production at Circle in the Square, but this production was developed at Actors Studio before runs in Upstate New York and at St. Ann's Warehouse in Brooklyn. Estelle Parsons directed the reading, which seemed to be acted in several styles at once: ultrarealism (Tomei), poetic realism (Strathairn), realism (Wiest) and Pacino (Pacino). As it unfolded, the production developed a sensualist edge thanks to Tomei's lack of self-consciousness in her passionate dance (and its torso-baring climax at some preformances). Although Pacino seemed to be using a gangster voice when whining Salome's name, he was perfectly annoying as a dirty old man whose unlimited power allows him to flirt with his stepdaughter.

The high points among this season's play revivals opened a few weeks apart and slugged it out at the Tony Awards with *Long Day's Journey Into Night* winning three (best play revival, best actor and best actress) and *A Day in the Death of Joe Egg* departing empty-handed. The improvisational nature of *Joe Egg*, which was imported from London by Roundabout Theatre Company, and its leading man's reputation as a comedian probably didn't help audiences understand the virtuosity of Eddie Izzard's performances. Izzard turned in a brilliant Tony-caliber performance as the jocular, role-playing father of a disabled child. His character, Bri, laughs to lighten his load and to stave off his pain. Izzard's performance had an ad-libbed quality that kept his audience waiting dizzily for a crash—that it never came made the performance electric.

Even Brian Dennehy, who played James Tyrone in *Long Day's Journey*, seemed surprised that he won over Izzard. But no one was surprised when the iconic Vanessa Redgrave received the Tony Award instead of Victoria Hamilton. Despite what some saw as a mannered portrayal of Mary Tyrone in Eugene O'Neill's masterwork, icons are often given their due on Broadway. Hamilton, who was making her Broadway debut as the anguished mother of a disabled child, never had a chance. As for Dennehy, he was an acceptable Tyrone, but he might have shown more of the bluff, ham-actor in the early going to counterpoint his later vulnerability. It's a character well within the actor's range: he did something near to it as Lopakhin in Peter Brook's 1988 *The Cherry Orchard*. Dennehy has hinted that he and director Robert Falls (who directed *Long Day's Journey*) may next tackle *King Lear*. But an announced production starring Christopher Plummer might place that plan on hold.

All by Themselves

SOLO PERFORMANCE SEEMS to be a growth industry on Broadway for reasons outlined above: lower overheads in production design and salaries. Over the past two seasons there have been six solo shows each season. Some of these productions have been billed as "plays," and *Best Plays* has occasionally honored high-quality solo shows with engaging dramatic narratives and conflicts. But we do not count one-person plays in our new-play numbers so that we can accurately track solo shows and plays with two or more characters.

Of this season's solos, only one truly engaged a dramatic narrative, *Say Goodnight, Gracie* by Rupert Holmes. Based on the lives of the great comic team of George Burns and Gracie Allen, the show begins with the departed Burns waiting for admission to Heaven. Frank Gorshin, the talented mimic and actor, played Burns and Didi Conn—whom the audience never saw—was the voice of Allen at crucial times. The play was a gentle, often hilarious reminiscence of their careers in vaudeville, radio, film and television. Allen's heart condition caused her to retire in 1958; she died in 1964 at age 69. Burns lived for 32 more years and had the equivalent of two more careers in show business. He died a few weeks after his 100th birthday in 1996.

Jackie Mason returned with another of his standup routines, *Prune Danish*, which relied on the comic's trademark comparisons of Jews and gentiles, jabs at politicians on both ends of the spectrum and other aging gems of observational humor. For years, theater critics have responded to Mason with something like, "Jackie Mason's back and his fans will be thrilled to see him again." This season, though, the *New York Times*'s Bruce Weber reacted negatively to Mason's verbal onslaught, writing that some of his jokes were "idiotically, hypocritically reactionary," "nasty and diminishing" and concluded "it isn't funny." Mason declared war on Weber calling him a "sick bastard" and was photographed destroying a copy of the *Times*. *Prune Danish* closed December 1 after 39 performances, but you can bet Mason's not finished taking shots at Weber and the *Times*.

Mandy Patinkin performed a limited run of concerts, *Celebrating Sondheim*, at the Henry Miller Theatre on Sunday and Monday evenings when *Urinetown* was dark. Patinkin was joined by Paul Ford on the piano as he worked his way through his own personal relationship with nearly three dozen songs by Stephen Sondheim. We often hear that young composers today have been influenced by Sondheim's work. But how many of them are writing songs—as opposed to dark, complex compositions—that people want to sing? Patinkin, Barbara Cook, Elaine Stritch and others have enhanced their careers (and Sondheim's) by singing his songs. *Celebrating Sondheim* closed, as planned, after 10 performances.

The Russian comedian Yakov Smirnoff performed a limited run at Roundabout Theatre Company's Broadway theater. *As Long As We Both Shall Laugh* was rooted in the sort of humor for which Smirnoff was celebrated in the 1980s when the difference between US and Russian lifestyles was more stark. Nowadays, Russians are trying to outcapital the capitalists—they even have organized criminals who make ours look soft. Based in Branson, Missouri, where he owns his own theater, Smirnoff has made a successful career by celebrating a flag-waving, patriotic American way of life and his place in it. He even created his own catch phrase: "What a country!"

In a completely different vein was the solo show performed by the acerbic Bill Maher, *Victory Begins at Home*. Maher's television program, *Politically Incorrect*, was cancelled by ABC Television after he made remarks that offended people (especially advertisers) in the wake of the September 11, 2001, terror attacks. He later resurfaced on HBO in *Real Time With Bill Maher* and brought some of that program's material to his Broadway show. Maher delights in tearing holes in the balloons of liberals and conservatives alike. Working with a teleprompter located on the front of the balcony,

Maher made his way through a libertarian rant that veered from politics, terrorism and the war in Iraq to relations between the genders (which earned some negative responses). At the end of his show, Maher, spoiled by programmed television-studio audiences, seemed annoyed by the reluctance of New York theatergoers to give him a standing ovation.

There were three specialty productions in the 2002–03 season, *Russell Simmons's Def Poetry Jam on Broadway*, *The Play What I Wrote* and *The Look of Love*. The 2003 Tony Award for special theatrical event was given to *Def Poetry Jam*, an all-star stage version of hip-hop mogul Simmons's HBO series. Both televised and stage versions of the show feature diverse poets using rhyme and meter to explore the nature of the human condition. Despite the fact that there were no fewer than eight major articles in the *New York Times* celebrating the show, its energy and its cast, attendance generally hovered in the 30 to 40 percent range with the average ticket price remaining at 50 percent of the top price. The show's best week also coincided with Broadway's best week of the season (December 23–29, 2002), when *Def Poetry Jam* did almost 75 percent attendance at a little better than 50 percent of the top ticket price ($38/$65). Even during the strike week, the show couldn't break 50 percent attendance.

Does this mean that the "Gray Lady," the *Times*, has lost some of her influence over ticket buying? Perhaps. One of the best weeks for the show—Valentine's Week (February 10–16, 2003; 61 percent)—was the week *before* three separate articles mentioned the show. February 19, a lengthy feature (1,800 words) on Arab-American writers led with an interview of poet-performer Suheir Hammad, but ticket sales the following week stayed in the 40s. After an upbeat feature dedicated to *Def Poetry Jam* (more than 3,000 words) appeared April 18 on the front page of the Friday arts section, ticket sales for the following week dropped 2 percent. The show closed May 4 after 198 performances.

The sluggish ticket sales may also have had something to do with a perception on the part of theatergoers that there was a fair amount of angry rant coming from the stage, which director Stan Lathan addressed in the April 18 article. But after five months on Broadway, word of mouth (and the weight of the *Times*) should have built more support. The problem with a poetry jam on Broadway is that it undermines the performance intimacy of a club or a small theater. Simmons's television program has performers practically surrounded by their audience and there is a sense of commonality, of community. The 1,100-seat Longacre Theatre, with one performer at a time representing the "next America," constructed a paradigm

of "us against them"—instead of "We're all in the next America together."
And some audience members surely found themselves thinking, "When is
that charismatic performer named Poetri coming back onstage?" and "Why
is this overweight woman on a pathetic run about junk food filling in for
love in her life?" To counter one of the *New York Times*'s critics: That's *not*
entertainment—it's public therapy for performers and the audience foots
the bill (even though it's half price).

    The Play What I Wrote is an English music-hall entertainment with a
story line (of sorts) that involves a lot of puns and foolishness leading up to
a mystery-guest celebrity—often Roger Moore (who collapsed during one
performance and had to be hospitalized). It has its partisans and continued
to run at season's end. *The Look of Love*, a musical revue celebrating the
careers of Burt Bacharach and Hal David, was produced by the Roundabout
Theatre Company at the Brooks Atkinson Theatre. Simply the performance
of song after song with no narrative, the point of the entire exercise was
elusive—except, perhaps, that love is a good thing.

Where's Off Broadway?

DURING THE MUSICIANS' strike, Off Broadway entrepreneurs distributed
fliers in Times Square directing disappointed Broadway ticket holders to
their theaters. One tourist from Canada told the *New York Times*'s Robin
Pogrebin, "Some shows are going on, but I don't even know where Off
Broadway is." The short answer, of course, is that it's everywhere in New
York City—even on Broadway (the street). "Off Broadway," of course, refers
to a certain size of theater and a certain type of union contract. It has
nothing to do with the real estate mogul's favorite cliché about location.
But there is a simple truth in the Canadian tourist's confusion: Broadway
(the street) and Times Square can be found on a map. Off Broadway,
though, is a bit more elusive. For those adventurous souls who wandered
Off Broadway, 2002–03 had some pleasant surprises. Six of the Best Plays
had their New York debuts Off Broadway (three others had Off Off Broadway
runs and one came to Broadway from a resident theater).

    Off Broadway saw a slight lift in the number of productions this season.
Seventy-nine productions opened Off Broadway in the 2002–03 season,
two more than in the previous season. The biggest shift Off Broadway,
though, was a sharp decline in the number of new plays produced. New-play
production was down 32 percent (44 plays to 30) from the 2001–02 season.
And that number includes three productions at Atlantic Theater Company,
which is usually listed in Off Off Broadway because the group generally

does not run 8 performances per week. The largest decrease was in commercial production, with 5 fewer commercial productions of new plays Off Broadway this season. The other decline was in the specialty-act category, which was down from 9 to 7 this season. Musical revues tripled their previous season's work, with shows focused on individual personalities such as Tommy Tune, Jerry Herman, Jackie Wilson and Ruth Wallis. Solo performances doubled their 2001–02 output and play revivals increased to 11 from 6.

Without Tony Award consideration to tempt Off Broadway producers, there is a tendency to make fuller use of the calendar. It is fair to note, however, that nearly a third of Off Broadway productions (31) opened in the final three months of the season and March was the single busiest month with 16 openings. Off Broadway has its own share of awards and honors to confer. Although commercial production of new plays was lower Off Broadway this season, those investors may have moved into other categories: there were more commercial productions Off Broadway in 2002–03 (27) than in 2001–02 (26). Most new musicals were commercially produced (7 of 11), as were all revues and half of all solo performances (see statistics on pages 14 and 15 for details). Interestingly, all play revivals, all specialty programs and 70 percent of all new plays were produced by nonprofit companies. How should we read these numbers? It seems obvious that commercial producers are staying close to certain axioms in the theater business: musicals and low-overhead shows (solo acts) are safer bets to return a profit. Solo performances, by the way, have tripled as a percentage of Off Broadway productions over the past three years.

Right Over Here . . .

AMONG THE COMMERCIAL productions, there were eight new plays: *Endpapers* by Thomas McCormack, a retired insider's comedic look at the publishing world; *My Old Lady* by Israel Horovitz, a midlife crisis drama about a man who inherits a Paris apartment from his estranged father and becomes romantically involved with his half-sister; *Tuesdays With Morrie* by Jeffrey Hatcher and Mitch Albom, which offers life lessons from a dying man to a man of middle age; *Adult Entertainment* by Elaine May, a comedy about artistic aspiration among porn stars; *Sleeping With Straight Men* by Ronnie Larsen, a reality-based comedy about "straight" men who are seduced by a gay man and the tragic outcome; *Barbra's Wedding* by Daniel Stern, in which a C-list television actor of middle age becomes addled by his proximity to Barbra Streisand's glowing celebrity; *Our Lady of 121st Street* by Stephen

Adly Guirgis, a drama about friends revisiting their past and coming to terms with their present (a 2002–03 *Best Plays* choice); *Talking Heads* by Alan Bennett, a collection of monologues that surveys the terrain of middle age near Leeds, England (a 2002–03 *Best Plays* choice); and *The Last Sunday in June* by Jonathan Tolins, a comedy in which gay men ponder their places in society.

Does a pattern emerge? Maybe all theater is ultimately navel-gazing, but it is striking to see the amount of midlife crisis played out in these commercial productions. Of course, theater audiences are largely of middle age—as are theater producers—but even Guirgis's Best Play about 30-somethings and Tolins's play about youngish gay men have a hint of existential desperation. (And both of these plays were Off Off Broadway hits before making the commercial transfer.) It is instructive, too, to note that in all except Bennett's *Talking Heads*, whose characterizations are almost all women, these plays never address women as subject—or object for that matter. Even May's condescending and unfunny play—did Ben Brantley *really* see it?—constructs all of its characters as if they were of less than one dimension. Who knew you could do that? It must have been a dramaturgical breakthrough.

In fairness to the commercial producers, it must be admitted that theater explores the nature of humanity, shows us what it means to be human and reminds us that "human being" is really "human becoming." We are all works in progress and part of that progress is the inevitable examination of our lives as we draw nearer to mortality in our middle years. Although these types of stories also arise from the nonprofit arena, what we hope to find there is less likely to resemble a kit used to make next month's television movie of the week.

When it came to the new in musicals, musical revues and solo performances, commercial productions showed more spirit. The musical season got underway with *The Prince and the Pauper*, a show oriented toward family audiences that ran into the fall, took a hiatus and reopened for a holiday run. Keith Glover's award-winning *Thunder Knocking on the Door* brought Chuck Cooper and Leslie Uggams together in a bluesy tale about a family caught between the natural and the supernatural. Eric Krebs finally brought his musical version of Langston Hughes's, *Little Ham*, to a commercial production after nearly 20 years of trying. Choked with racial, sexual and comic stereotypes—some that bordered on offensive—the production never caught on with audiences. Krebs publicly complained when the *New York Times*'s Bruce Weber panned the production after giving a positive review to a similar production Off Off Broadway in the previous season. Krebs told TheaterMania.com's Michael Portantiere that he was able to raise money largely on the strength of Weber's review. Weber, for his part, couldn't explain to TheaterMania.com why he didn't like the production in the Off Broadway space, but he noted that the shift in critical opinion about the show was widespread. *Best Plays* did not shift its position: some works resist adaptation and should be allowed to rest in peace.

While we're on the topic of resting in peace, Stephen Mo Hanan brought Al Jolson back to life in *Jolson and Company*, which used songs popularized by the singer to tell an unhappy life story. Although Jolson was hugely popular and preferred to be called the "World's Greatest Entertainer"—he was not, shall we say, a man with many friends in show business. But the show had many friends for 97 performances at the Century Center for the Performing Arts. Looking for the next *Urinetown*, producers overhauled *Debbie Does Dallas*, a musical that was a hit at the New York International Fringe Festival, and took it to Off Broadway's Jane Street Theatre. Spoofing a well-known porno film from the 1970s—without the sex—the musical lasted 127 performances. *Zanna, Don't!*, by Tim Acito, played at Amas Musical Theatre before its Off Broadway bow at the Kirk Theatre. Starring Jai Rodriguez as Zanna, this clever musical inverts the world for a group of high-school students. In *Zanna, Don't!*, homosexuality is the norm and the queer ones are straight. *Hank Williams: Lost Highway* finally came to New York, years after it premiered in Denver (1987). It was just the latest appearance of a biographical musical by Randal Myler (written with Mark Harelik). Myler has also helped to create similar shows about Janis Joplin and John Denver.

George C. Wolfe's *Harlem Song* opened at the Apollo Theater August 6 for a bumpy run to the end of the year. Designed as a tourist attraction, the revue (with music by Zane Mark and Daryl Waters) had a hard time attracting audiences to its uptown location. The show closed December 29 after 146 performances. *Water Coolers*, which opened in the back room of Dillon's on West 54th Street, rewrote the lyrics to popular songs well known to Baby Boomers for a two-act revue about the lives of yuppie office workers. *Tommy Tune: White Tie and Tails* surprised the theater community when it opened at the new Little Shubert Theatre on West 42nd Street. The surprise wasn't the new theater, which the community had eagerly awaited, and it wasn't Tune's overdue return to the New York stage. What caught folks off-guard was that Tune's show lacked the crispness they had come to expect from him—some chalked it up to too much time in Las Vegas.

Whatever the reason, the show lasted just 23 performances. *Showtune: The Words and Music of Jerry Herman* performed a bit better as a celebration of the legendary composer's work. Opening February 27, 2003, *Showtune* ran 53 performances at the Theatre at St. Peter's. The Black Ensemble Theater of Chicago brought its touring production of *The Jackie Wilson Story* to the Apollo Theater in April for a two-week run. And just as the season was ending, *Boobs! The Musical*—a tribute to the risqué party songs of Ruth Wallis—opened at the Triad Theater.

The seven commercial solo shows included *Dudu Fisher: Something Old, Something New*, which featured the popular Israeli singer recounting his career in musical theater; *Bewilderness*, in which British comic Bill Bailey returned to soak in the appreciation of New York theatergoers; *Bartenders*, Louis Mustillo's survey of the nobility of the drink-pouring profession (197 performances and still playing at season's end); *Tea at Five*, Kate Mulgrew's astonishingly nuanced impersonation of the great Katharine Hepburn at the Promenade Theatre; *Broad Channel*, a one-man (Doc Dougherty) recreation of a 1977 group of working class kids in Queens; and *Down a Long Road*, David Marquis's wide-eyed wonder about the marvels on life's pathways.

. . . And Over Here . . .

AS THE SEASON developed at New York Theatre Workshop, themes of family played an important role in the company's dramatic explorations. The New York premiere of the late Harry Kondoleon's *Play Yourself* (1986), directed by Craig Lucas with the delicious Marian Seldes and the trenchant Elizabeth Marvel, probed the weakness we all have for a voyeuristic peek at the fabulous (who probably aren't all that fabulous). Seldes and Marvel were a fascinating pair as a mother-daughter team. They were two raw nerves: one fading from glory, the other never to shine. Caryl Churchill's *Far Away*, directed by Stephen Daldry with Frances McDormand and Marin Ireland, caused a stir with its view of a world gone mad for violence—a madness that starts at home. The 50-minute play seemed to divide viewers among ardent champions and those who found it heavy-handed (and lacking drama). We tended to the latter view, but were stunned (with everyone else) by designer Catherine Zuber's remarkable *coup de théâtre* in a "hat parade" of some 60 prisoners about to be executed. It created a powerfully ironic moment of pleasure layered with disgust. In *Bexley, Oh(!) Or, Two Tales of One City*, Prudence Wright Holmes settled scores with her hometown (and family) in a one-woman show about life in

Touching scene: Ann Guilbert and Marian Seldes in Play Yourself. *Photo: Joan Marcus*

the Midwest. In *Cavedweller*, Kate Moira Ryan's adaptation of a Dorothy Allison novel, a hard-living rock star returns to her hometown to resume the care of two daughters left behind. She brings along another daughter, by another man, and tries to make a life with her family. The family was in for a hard slog, as was the audience for the unfocused adaptation. Whenever director Michael Greif needed to bridge action, text was projected on a wall and rock music blasted from the sound system. However much it may have helped the narrative, it still left the production a bit of a jumble.

Second Stage Theatre opened Hunt Holman's *Spanish Girl* for a brief run at the McGinn/Cazale Theatre uptown. A coming-of-age story about adult responsibility and the cravenness of youth, it was withdrawn after 9 performances. At the mainstage on West 43rd Street, the company extended *Ricky Jay on the Stem*, which was heldover from the previous season, until October 20, 2002, when it closed after 81 performances. Next up was Regina Taylor's *Crowns*, a celebration of hat-wearing African-American church women. An exuberant production with music and singing, it ran 40 performances. The final production of the Second Stage season was Michael John LaChiusa's latest musical, *Little Fish*. A dark exploration of contemporary urban life and its dislocating, isolating influence on the spirit, the musical ran 29 performances.

Brian Kulick's all-star production of Shakespeare's *Twelfth Night* at the New York Shakespeare Festival's Delacorte Theater gave audiences a rollicking good time as they ogled stars such as Jimmy Smits, Julia Stiles, Kristen Johnston, Oliver Platt and Christopher Lloyd—a somewhat more thoughtful version of the play would arrive at the Brooklyn Academy of Music in the spring. Kulick's *Twelfth Night* was the festival's only production in summer 2002 as a cost-cutting move. *Take Me Out* (a 2002–03 *Best Plays* choice) gave the Joseph Papp Public Theater a nice bounce into the fall season when it opened September 5. The exciting three-hour, three-act play about baseball, sexuality, democracy and other things American ran 94 performances and later transferred to Broadway. Kate Burton and Martha Plimpton were centerstage in David Mamet's *Boston Marriage*. The title refers to an archaic euphemism for two lesbians who live together, although Mamet—the linguistic prankster—doesn't stop at an obsolete title. Apparently smarting from critical comments—due to the profanity in his work—about the breadth of his vocabulary, he punished audiences with language that few are likely to understand. It closed after 39 performances. In *Radiant Baby*, Stuart Ross, Debra Barsha and Ira Gasman tried to create a musical with the raw spirit of adventure that marked the life and work of pop artist Keith Haring. Unfortunately, not even the directorial flair of George C. Wolfe could make the musical more than a pop-inflected memorial. *Fucking A*, Suzan-Lori Parks's first play since winning the 2002 Pulitzer Prize for *Topdog/Underdog*, was exciting for the first 20 minutes or so as she created a new language and paid dramatic homage to Bertolt Brecht through clever use of text and song. Finally, though, the unrelenting brutality of the play—and its dark outlook about what it is the meek actually inherit—caused the audience to disconnect. It's possible that someone other than Michael Greif might be able to draw the strings more tightly, avoid pounding the audience so mercilessly and make a clearer production (George C. Wolfe would be a great candidate for the job). Erica Schmidt's production of *As You Like It* finished the season at the Public with a lively, acrobatic version of the pastoral comedy. Just six actors performed the various roles in the play: Drew Cortese, Johnny Giacalone, Bryce Dallas Howard, Jennifer Ikeda, Lethia Nall and Lorenzo Pisoni. Pisoni was particularly impressive for his physical skill.

The 2002–03 season was the year that Playwrights Horizons moved into its lovely new home after a couple of seasons during which the company rented from other institutions. With *The World Over* by Keith Bunin, which played at the Duke on 42nd Street, the theater seemed to misjudge what makes a play. Bunin created a story that is the seed of every fairy tale ever told: every man is a king. The story then proceeds on journey after journey as 34 characters enact variations of what was heard in the first 15 minutes. In *What Didn't Happen*, Christopher Shinn constructs a talky, intergenerational battlefield—at a country home—where members of the intelligentsia attempt to thrash out what is possible and what is not. A writer to watch, Shinn couples a flair for dramatic tension with an almost philosophical alienation. Speaking of philosophy, Richard Nelson and Ricky Ian Gordon's musical, *My Life With Albertine*—based on the work of Marcel Proust—has its own share of rumination. Nelson, a prolific and adept writer, seems mired in this topic. Fascinating as a dramatic exercise—emphasis on exercise—Proust's consciousness may exist beyond the theater's essential nature. David Greenspan's *She Stoops to Comedy* demonstrates again the playwright's interest in the transformative power of art and the transformational nature of human beings. Reality and illusion collide as William Shakespeare's *As You Like It* becomes background and foreground for Greenspan's characters and for the playwright himself. Transformation is everything in Doug Wright's *I Am My Own Wife*. As played by Jefferson Mays, a variety of characters construct a narrative about an elderly German man who lived his adult life as a woman. A 2002–03 *Best Plays* choice, Wright's play is a superb meeting place for reality and illusion—which is what Playwrights Horizons appears to have had in mind this season.

As Manhattan Theatre Club, too, moved closer toward occupying a new space in 2003—in its case adding a Broadway venue (the Biltmore Theatre)—the company presented a mixed bag that ranged from the passions of Charlayne Woodard's *In Real Life* and Dael Orlandersmith's *Yellowman* to John Corwin's darkly allusive play about dying young (*Gone Home*) to comedies by David Lindsay-Abaire (*Kimberly Akimbo*), David Ives (*Polish Joke*) and Charlotte Jones (*Humble Boy*). Woodard's solo stand as a young actor who comes to New York was a marvel of life dramatized. The third of her monologues about life's trials and triumphs, *In Real Life* tells the tale of a classically trained actor planning to play all of the great roles—but she's hasn't reckoned on the scarcity of those roles or how her color (she's African American) will affect her casting. She eventually has a Broadway success in *Ain't Misbehavin'* and relates a few amusing anecdotes about Nell Carter as she discusses that experience. (Carter died a few months after the show closed.) Ultimately, Woodard brings a vigorous life-energy to her performance and makes us long to see those classical roles she has yet to perform. Orlandersmith's *Yellowman*, which was a finalist for the Pulitzer Prize in 2002, explores the landscape of intraracial discrimination with a vividness that made it a 2002–03 *Best Plays* choice. With Howard W. Overshown playing the "yellow man" (or light-skinned African American) and all of the other male roles, Orlandersmith acted all of the female roles to create a painful story of racism's often unspoken legacy. Of the other MTC shows, Lindsay-Abaire's *Kimberly Akimbo* was a clever, if tame comedy about a girl who ages at four times the normal rate (she's 16 with the body of a 64-year-old). This is Lindsay-Abaire's third comedy in recent years about kooky females in kooky families, which is probably why it seemed so familiar. *Polish Joke* and *Humble Boy* each covered terrors of family and identity that have been well mined elsewhere.

With three productions Off Broadway during the 2002–03 season, Atlantic Theater Company made a significant contribution to serious drama in New York—the fourth production, *The Butter and Egg Man* is listed under Off Off Broadway because it played 7 performances per week. It seemed, though, that the company took its name seriously with two plays from "across the pond." Atlantic's productions of Joe Penhall's *Blue/Orange* (an Olivier Award-winner in London) and Conor McPherson's *Dublin Carol* (a 2002–03 *Best Plays* choice) were wrenching tales about men struggling with identity, memory, lunacy. Director Neil Pepe, a consistent talent, struggled to keep the pace of Penhall's play about power and perception from flattening into ennui. The performances by the estimable Glenn Fitzgerald, Harold Perrineau Jr. and Zeljko Ivanek were so carefully modulated that the play never quite took flight. McPherson's *Dublin Carol*, on the other hand, was a searing portrayal of an alcoholic undertaker who drifts through life, seeking nothing, finding nothing and hoping to keep it that way. Jim Norton, Keith Nobbs and Kerry O'Malley provided the harrowing performances under the playwright's direction. The final production of the Atlantic season was Woody Allen's *Writer's Block*, two one-act plays connected by the theme of writers' struggling. Featuring a terrific cast of Paul Reiser, Kate Blumberg, Bebe Neuwirth and others, the plays survey Allen's usual fascinations with marital relationships, infidelity and the challenges of creativity.

Lincoln Center Theater's Off Broadway season included the New York debut of Frank McGuinness's *Observe the Sons of Ulster Marching Towards the Somme*, which wins the longest-title award for the season; *A Man of No Importance* by Terrence McNally (book), Stephen Flaherty (music) and Lynn Ahrens (lyrics); and *Elegies*, a song cycle by William Finn. The McGuinness play focuses on young Irishmen who bond in the World War I British military as they prepare for a great assault that leads to their slaughter. Despite the production's proximity to US involvement in the conquest of Iraq—and Nicholas Martin's steady direction of a cast that included Richard Easton, Justin Theroux, Scott Wolf, Jeremy Shamos and others—the playwright's studied dramaturgy holds the audience at arm's length. *A Man of No Importance*, the musical version of a 1994 Albert Finney film, was a modest entry to the season that told an almost-sweet tale of a simple bus driver (Roger Rees) who aspires to create art and literature. Joe Mantello directed the fine cast of Rees, Faith Prince, Charles Keating, Katherine McGrath, Sally Murphy and others; it played 93 performances. William Finn's *Elegies* offered paeans to friends and mentors he has lost along the path of his full, artistic life.

. . . And Here

AMONG THE SEASON'S Off Broadway revivals, it's difficult to decide which was most anticipated. For fans of Ingmar Bergman, whose "magic lantern" always lights the theatergoer's way, there was Friedrich von Schiller's *Maria Stuart* at the Brooklyn Academy of Music. Or perhaps you would prefer to see a couple of *grandes dames* (Rosemary Harris and Michael Learned) simmer—and sizzle—in Edward Albee's *All Over*. There was also Robert Richmond's clever adaptation of William Shakespeare's *The Comedy of Errors* for Peter Meineck's Aquila Theatre Company. For the young and impressionable, film stars Edward Norton and Catherine Keener sauntered through Signature Theatre Company's production of *Burn This* by Lanford Wilson. Al Pacino began his busy New York season with an all-star cast in Bertolt Brecht's *The Resistible Rise of Arturo Ui* for Tony Randall's National Actors Theatre. Directed by Simon McBurney of Complicite, this far underrated production featured Charles Durning, Billy Crudup, John Goodman, Steve Buscemi and other noted actors. The National Theater of Greece brought *Antigone* to City Center and the Donmar Warehouse brought sensitive, nuanced productions of *Uncle Vanya* and *Twelfth Night*—with Emily Watson and Simon Russell Beale—to the Brooklyn Academy of Music. BAM also hosted a return of Athol Fugard, John Kani and Winston Ntshona's *The Island*. This list alone demonstrates why revivals are so popular with producers, who wouldn't want to see these shows? But all of these productions were presented by nonprofit entities.

As we draw near to the end of our Off Broadway overview, a few stragglers need to be brought into the herd. Revelation Theater came into existence this season with plans for a full season of plays, but ground to a halt after 23 performances of its first production, *Temporary Help* by David Wiltse. Margaret Colin and Robert Cuccioli played a farm couple who kill hired hands. The company started with big plans, but cost overruns and a building project slowed the group's progress considerably. The Irish Repertory Theatre had a pair of solo shows that were well received in the 2002–03 season—most Irish Rep productions are included in our Off Off Broadway listings due to the company's playing schedule. Des Keogh adapted and performed writings by John B. Keane in *The Love Hungry Farmer*, which recounts a lonely man's struggle to come to terms with his fate. The company also presented *Foley* by Michael West, with Andrew Bennett in the title role, which details the declining life of a member of Ireland's gentry and how he got that way (*pace* Frank McCourt). The widely circulated production began at the Corn Exchange in Dublin (2000) and was later a hit at the Edinburgh Festival. Primary Stages presented *One Million Butterflies* by Stephen Belber, with Matthew Mabe as a man who muses about life as he makes a solitary journey. Manhattan Theater Ensemble, a company of rising importance on the downtown theater scene, presented the potent performance of Tovah Feldshuh as Golda Meir in *Golda's Balcony* by William Gibson. Feldshuh continued in the role into the summer and there were discussions about a move to Broadway. Near the season's end, Centenary Stage Company from New Jersey brought its production of *Mary Todd . . . A Woman Apart* to Off Broadway for a three-week run at the Samuel Beckett Theatre. Featuring Colleen Smith Wallnau, the play was written and directed by Carl Wallnau.

The Off Broadway specialties this season included, as ever, the superb City Center Encores! series, which spotted a rising new star in Nikki M. James in *House of Flowers*. Other Encores! productions included *The New Moon* and *No Strings*. The Brooklyn Academy of Music presented *Hashirigaki*, a haunting music-theater piece that blended text from Gertrude Stein with music by Beach Boy Brian Wilson and Heiner Goebbels. Goebbels created and directed the piece. Way uptown at the Apollo Theater, Columbia

University joined with the Royal Shakespeare Company to present *Midnight's Children*, a multimedia extravaganza about the birth of the Indian nation. Based on an epic novel by Salman Rushdie, who assisted in the adaptation, the piece was first presented at the Barbican in London a few weeks before it came to New York. But the most important specialty of the season was the reading of *The Exonerated*, a collection of interviews of former death-row inmates edited into a dramatic narrative by Jessica Blank and Erik Jensen. Directed by Bob Balaban, the reading featured Richard Dreyfuss, Jill Clayburgh, Sara Gilbert, Jay O. Sanders, Charles Brown and other noted actors. As the series continued to run, actors changed frequently—similar to the casting changes done in Off Broadway's *The Vagina Monologues*—and the piece had a powerful impact on politicians who employ the death penalty. The piece continued to run well into the next season.

Looking Back

IT SEEMS FITTING that the 2002–03 season in New York became the year of *Hairspray* and *Movin' Out*. With all of the insecurity that comes from worrying about possible attacks at home and probable war abroad, these two musicals made provocative bookends around our cultural discourse. In *Hairspray*, an outsider battles the entrenched status quo in order to do what is morally correct—even though polite society rejects her open, democratic approach to human relationships. Tracy Turnblad is an agent of change for her mother, her friends and her community. In her fairy tale, good triumphs.

But in *Movin' Out*, the music of a more recent time reminds us—enhanced by its virtuosic physical narrative—that sometimes being good and being right isn't enough. Sometimes there is a struggle for survival, but we cannot overcome what is larger than ourselves. The great lesson of sitting in a theater, watching a performance, is that in human connection, in community we are not alone. And when we know we are not alone, when we refuse to be alienated, the challenges we face are easier to handle—and overcome.

It's a good start for the next theater season and it's probably not a bad way to live.

THE BEST PLAYS
OF 2002–2003

2002–2003 Best Play

BOOK OF DAYS

By Lanford Wilson

○ ○ ○ ○ ○

Essay by Tish Dace

RUTH: A clean

WALT: Quiet

SHERIFF ATKINS: Wide awake

REVEREND GROVES: Prosperous town

ALTHOUGH DIRECTOR WENDY C. Goldberg told the *Washington Times* that her February 2003 Arena Stage mounting of Lanford Wilson's *Book of Days* was "only its second production," at least 54 other theaters had previously staged it. Indeed, it's currently one of the most frequently produced plays in America. Yet when it opened at Signature Theatre in November 2002, its New York viewers, like Goldberg, didn't know how popular the play had already become. The program acknowledged only a typical developmental process: Purple Rose Theatre commissioned it, then presented it in April 1998. In fall 1999, Repertory Theatre of St. Louis and Hartford Stage co-produced it. There, director Marshall W. Mason, Wilson and their cast—plus their favorite design team—prepared it for what they hoped would be an immediate Broadway transfer.

But despite winning the 1999 American Theatre Critics Association's New Play Award—even before it headed to St. Louis and Hartford—the work did not tempt New York producers. Perhaps they passed due to the expense 12 actors entail or because the play lacks a big role to attract a star. They might also have worried about its nearly three hours of running time and its bleak conclusion.

In 2000, though, both Grove Press and Dramatists Play Service prepared to publish the award-winning drama. The script's release prompted theaters outside New York to rush into production, resulting in a litany of pre-New York mountings. In spring 2001, People's Light and Theatre in Pennsylvania led the way. Then theaters from Georgia to Maine, from Illinois to California, from Toronto to Texas produced *Book of Days*. By the time Signature opened the play in November 2002, it became not the second or third presenter, as

Brotherly love: Boris McGiver, Alan Campbell and Matthew Rauch in Book of Days.
Photo: Rahav Segev

we would expect of the usual new play, but, at best, number 44. And before the end of that month at least five more productions had opened elsewhere.

Why did this happen? Why did Hillsboro, Missouri (population 1,625), and Valley City, North Dakota (population 8,000), see *Book of Days* before the theater capital of America? What did directors at high schools, junior colleges, and community theaters all across America understand that New York producers did not?

Wilson grew up in the town of Ozark, in southwest Missouri (or "Missoura" as he pronounces it) in the rolling hills that he describes in *Book of Days*. There in the Ozark Bible belt, farm boy Wilson milked cows by hand at 5 a.m. His stepfather even worked in—and lost his job at—the local cheese plant, which accounts for the accuracy of all things concerning cheese production in *Book of Days*. The playwright took from life the story of the plant owner dying in an accident—in that case not a faked accident. He derived a still more important element from his own experience: the play's authentic speech and dramatis personae. Because he takes notes on how the home folks talk, he can write lines like "Oh, drag your mind up

out of the gutter, James, if you can find it" and "What in the devil's work is
he doing here, is what I'd like to know." His rhythmic dialogue likewise
rings true, as in this exchange:

> JAMES: Mom's afraid I'll disgrace her. Look low-class.
>
> SHARON: Don't be ridiculous, this is America, we don't have classes
> here.

Wilson also knows fundamentalist Christians who refuse to attend a
play, but at home watch David Lynch's *Blue Velvet*—and he uses that intimate
knowledge to paint an ugly portrait. Only initially does *Book of Days* bear
comparison to Thornton Wilder's idyllic *Our Town*. In contrast to Wilder's
version of birth, love and death, we get a pregnancy caused by adultery, a
wife who shrieks divorce threats at her cheating husband and two murders,
one a patricide by proxy.

SOUTHWEST MISSOURI QUALIFIES as both Midwest and South, and it's
those areas that have presented many of the play's 80 or more productions.
Wilson recreates the lives of people in the heartland: their jobs, their
churches, their recreation—all in the context of their families. Although he
writes in a presentational style, which reminds us it's a play and we're in a
theater, he dramatizes lives recognizable to the audience. And they could
care less what New York producers think. They know what they like, and
they like this portrait of Middle America. No, "like" doesn't fit.

"Recognize" and "identify with" are more apt since Wilson asks us to
object to some of his characters' behavior. He shows us lies and hypocrisy.
He makes us cringe at greed masquerading as Christian capitalism. Wilson,
who grew up Baptist, skewers fundamentalist Christianity in *Book of Days*,
which could have scared off theaters. Instead, four Lutheran colleges, another
college that accepts only Christian Scientists, a United Methodist college,
many small-town high schools, and the University of West Alabama added
Book of Days to their seasons. So did other school and community theaters
in 26 states, which cut a wide swath into the Midwest. One group mounted
a production in its local Congregational Church. Despite the liberal take on
fundamentalist politics, when the play finally appeared at Signature, the
online edition of *Christianity Today*—without editorial comment—provided
a link to the *New York Times* review.

Familiar Middle American characters in *Book of Days* populate the
fictitious, but recognizably real town of Dublin, county seat of Chosen
County. Three institutions dominate the village: the cheese plant, the
fundamentalist church, and the community theater. The latter imports a

Broadway-Hollywood director to stage George Bernard Shaw's *Saint Joan*, a play that even the local preacher knows challenges church authority. Ruth, the bookkeeper at the cheese plant, attends auditions thinking the show's a musical. Somebody has told her Shaw wrote *My Fair Lady*, so she prepares "You're a Queer One, Julie Jordan" from *Carousel*, then finds herself trying to remember—from a college class—Juliet's lines in her balcony scene. As in much of the first act, this scene keeps us laughing, but it also leads us to a parallel between Joan and Ruth, which sets up Ruth's unswerving pursuit of justice when she believes an accidental death was no accident. In the second-act Ruth exhibits Joan's passion, stubbornness and courage—she likewise is pilloried.

ALL 12 CHARACTERS are interesting and well developed. More importantly, though, they interest potential directors. They provide a terrific opportunity to create acting ensembles, a chance to learn choral performance techniques and they showcase a diverse group of ages and physical types. They also offer five good roles for women, something school and community theaters crave. But all of the roles offer actors terrific, sometimes poetic dialogue, a few flashy moments and a lot of chances to learn they're part of a team—not 12 egos seeking stage glory.

Wilson and director Mason—who staged the play at three theaters—have been joined at the hip since 1964, the year they teamed up on *Balm in Gilead*. *Book of Days* provides few stage directions, but Mason's connection to the playwright's work helps him to accurately hear each inflection, place each pause, locate each actor. The depth of his rehearsal process makes each performer pitch perfect, so by Signature's run even the new people proved flawless.

Although Wilson wrote Ruth for Suzanne Regan, Miriam Shor made the amateur sleuth's role her own, capturing her humor, spirit, and intuitive nature. In a lesser actor's hands, Ruth's interruption of the church service to insist on Earl's arrest would have rung false, but her intensity made us overlook its implausibility. Nancy Snyder returned to the stage after a long absence to act the prim but elegant matriarch, Sharon, who castigates people who criticize America. Susan Kellermann made credible the oxymoron of the dean of a Christian junior college who conceived her son at Woodstock. Among the several excellent men who remained in their roles from an earlier production, Alan Campbell as the suave, philandering James especially excelled by hinting at menace without signaling villainy.

John Lee Beatty designed a bleacher-and-panel set to serve as a high school, a theater, a cheese factory, a church, several homes and a creepy forest. He also does his part to produce a tornado. His wood flaps shake to accompany Dennis Parichy's "ominous green" lighting (and lightning) as well as Chuck London and Stewart Werner's thunder and "deafening roar." As if that were not design marvel enough, Beatty's upstage wall slides open to reveal a murky woods at the play's climax.

WILSON'S TITLE REFLECTS his process: He constructs the plot in segments often denoted by dates. Beginning at the end, he flashes back to May 15,

Proof positive: Alan Campbell and Matthew Rauch in Book of Days. *Photo: Rahav Segev*

further back to May 1, forward to May 23, then back two years, forward to May 23, and thereafter moves mostly forward, until he reaches his starting point. His chorus (comprised of all the actors, who speak individually) announce the dates or other section titles. The device resembles a medieval "book of days" each designated by a saint's name—an appropriate reference for a play that employs Joan of Arc as a plot device.

The playwright also creates a play within the play. He virtually merges Ruth with Joan after she opens in that role. He employs Boyd, the *Saint Joan* director, as the townspeople's director when Sharon, after her husband dies, suddenly disavows her character's breakdown and her use of four-letter words. Boyd instructs Ginger, his assistant, to play Sharon's role in that scene.

In the larger plot, Boyd likewise appears to guide the characters in restaging events that have already happened. In other words, the character Boyd plays Marshall W. Mason or whoever directs a particular production.

Wilson's tightly constructed events amuse, intrigue and, finally, appall us. They show why Ruth and Len chose to leave Dublin—which has happened before the play begins, but we learn about it only at the end. Wilson adroitly plots his "days" in tiny one-, two-, three- or four-minute scenes, speeding up the action by shortening some sequences to mere seconds, and expanding a couple of key scenes to five or six minutes. A recognition scene, when Ruth realizes Walt didn't die accidentally, ends Act I. Later, Wilson repeats and expands this life-altering anagnorisis. He frequently foreshadows important actions; we hear the gun shot three separate times. Before significant events occur, he has already planted the shotguns, the violent death, the tornado, James's hatred of the cheese business, his infidelity, his bond with Bobby—the manipulative preacher—Boyd's problems with the law, Martha's vulnerability to blackmail, Len's commitment to his cheeses and Ruth's knowledge of firearms. This device helps us either to anticipate something or to recall a detail later and therefore understand subsequent events.

All of this foreshadowing propels the play's action with the inevitability of tragedy. Ruth's cat killing a bird, for instance, horrifies her because he murders without compunction: "It's just sport to him." We hear this, we see Earl and Walt cleaning their shotguns and we hear the distant gunshot for the first time. Ten minutes later, Walt provides James and Earl a motive for murdering him, and immediately the chorus announces "the night of Walt's death." What on the surface appear as fragmentary scenes add up to an extraordinarily tight plot, every detail carefully selected and ordered—not always chronologically—but in the most dramatically effective sequence.

Wilson's plot indicts American values. Before the play starts, Walt has sold out his pride in his product because he couldn't resist the money Kraft offered, and greed has ruined Boyd's second film. During the play, greed and ambition tempt James to commit two murders. (Wilson especially chills us by making the victims James's friend and his own father.) We eventually perceive that the amoral James will do anything to serve his self-interest. Earl, a corrupt dairy inspector, pays for his greed with his life. Free-spirit Martha will lose her position at a Christian college if she supports Ruth's efforts. LouAnn becomes complicit in defeating her cousin Ruth; we guess she does this to increase her divorce settlement. Len, a good man who takes pride in creating the finest possible product, lets his love of provolone cause him to undermine Ruth's efforts to unmask a killer. Sharon cannot face anything ugly or unpleasant, so she won't confront the mounting evidence of her husband's murder. The sheriff can't be bothered with anything as irksome as a real crime to solve. And the preacher, who ought to serve as his community's conscience, instead covets money that Sharon and James will donate—and he puts his high-school friendship with basketball teammate James ahead of the truth. Not exactly a Norman Rockwell collection!

The town's complacency eventually upsets us more than the murders. "Whodunit" matters less than everyone's collusion in the crimes. Even Ruth diminishes her own nobility by giving up her quest, wallowing in guilt over her indirect responsibility for the second death, and moving away. First, however, she draws the parallel between Joan's society and Dublin's: "They were just hiding behind dogma and power, and they still do."

"RUTH" MEANS COMPASSION or pity, a quality Wilson's protagonist has in abundance but that the villains lack. Wilson dramatizes evil as the absence of that virtue—which resembles the premise of another Wilson drama about community, *Rimers of Eldritch* (1965). Also set in a small Midwestern town, it unfolds in quick scenes spanning spring, summer and fall, concerns a murder and indicts religious hypocrisy. Yet it lacks *Book of Days*'s subtlety. Nobody would ever call Eldritch "clean," "quiet," "wide awake" and "prosperous" (though of course those lines also prove ironic concerning Dublin). *Rimers* exaggerates its characters' ruthlessness and piles on sinister elements to such a degree that we feel Stephen King has rewritten *Our Town*. In *Rimers*, we recognize from the outset the villainous characters.

Wilson's evolved skill in the newer script uncovers the town's moral decay more gradually. *Book of Days* likewise resembles Wilson's *A Tale Told* (1981; later called *Talley and Son*), which excoriates a narrow-minded, ruthless, rural family corrupted by its dealings with a corporation. Both plays, in their turn, echo Lillian Hellman's *The Little Foxes*—and all three works attack greed.

Book of Days cleverly implicates Ruth (whose name also means repentance or regret) in Dublin's moral malaise. Even though she wants the murder acknowledged and the murderer caught, her actions instead lead to a second murder, as the real culprit silences his trigger man. Therefore the villain, James, wins a new wife and daughter, a fortune and an uncontested election for a seat in the Missouri state legislature. Wilson shows us how politicians get away with murder.

The dramatist taps into a well of disgust many people feel when evil prevails and justice fails. If we look to the church for guidance, we can

Murderer and mom: Alan Campbell and Nancy Snyder in Book of Days. *Photo: Rahav Segev*

hardly avoid noticing pedophile priests and abortion-clinic bombings. If we hope statesmen will show the way, we hear our president didn't really win democratic election and his predecessor cheated on his wife, then lied about it under oath. We cannot believe that corporate America will save the day, because we see CEOs who have ruined their companies—and the fortunes of small investors—to line their own pockets. If we hope idealistic young people may rescue the country, we find kids are murdering classmates, teachers and parents. After our government tells us we're invading a country because a tyrant has weapons of mass destruction, we discover there were no weapons. Fanatical religious leaders urge the extermination of followers of other faiths. A man stands trial for killing his pregnant wife on Christmas Eve. And the Attorney General appointed to protect our civil rights is, heaven help us, Missourian John Ashcroft, cut from the same cloth as Wilson's Bobby and James.

Disgusted at all these things we cannot control, we see a play about a small group of people who could have done something about evil in their own community—but failed to do so. Our anger finds a target close to home. "The Midwest is just America," Wilson said to me in 1980. Will this Midwestern saga inspire Americans to fight for their ideals? Theater has the power to do that.

"Sleep well" and "Safe home" the chorus tells us after James murders his friend Earl, yet flourishes. We shudder. After that visceral impact, perhaps our rage will prompt us to don armor, grab our swords, and ride forth to protect the innocent. Today our country needs saviors. The playwright's bleak parable for our times offers that role to his audience.

WILSON INCREASINGLY DISTURBS and motivates us throughout Act II, but he galvanizes us to action in the play's final three minutes. James tells Earl to write Sharon a note. Earl, who appears tipsy on two beers, thinks what James dictates to him concerns the cheese plant. We may be suspicious, but we're not sure what James has in mind regarding the note, until "James folds Earl's note, drops it on the ground beside Earl. Gets the beer can from the ground, takes the other empty can from Earl's hand, and puts them in his briefcase."

> EARL: (*Weakly*) Hey, buddy.
>
> JAMES: You're dead, Earl. (*Earl stares at him.*) You took one mother dose of poison. Out of remorse, I guess. Everyone'll understand. (*Beat*) It wouldn't work, buddy. I tried to make it work for you, but you just talk too d-a-m-n much.

Middle America values *Book of Days* because *Book of Days* values Middle America—while questioning its values. We can do better, it adjures us.

Clearly, Middle America, or rather Middle-American theaters, agree.

2002–2003 Best Play

DUBLIN CAROL

By Conor McPherson

○ ○ ○ ○ ○

Essay by Charles Isherwood

JOHN: There's nothing worse than decorations after Christmas. That's the way I sometimes used to feel putting my clothes on in the morning.

THE DESTRUCTIVE POWER of drink is not a subject new to Irish literature. Nor has the fabled loquacity of the Irish populace gone uncelebrated by playwrights and novelists from the Emerald Isle. The Irish gift of gab and fondness for whiskey might seem to be subjects—or attributes—best banished from the local literature for an indeterminate period of time. But writers of true talent have a way of animating even the hoariest clichés, of scraping the rust from timeworn literary stereotypes and revealing the sturdy metal of truth underneath. Conor McPherson, the young Irish playwright best known for the barroom ghost sonata *The Weir*, seen on Broadway in the 1998–99 season, is a case in point.

His literary gifts lie squarely in what might be called the national tradition. He is a master creator of character revealed through long arias of language—indeed, he has made a specialty of the stand-alone monologue in plays such as *St. Nicholas* and *The Good Thief*. There is an unabashed lyricism in the voices of the people who populate his plays, even as the minutely detailed inflections of their speech root them deeply to a particular time and place—contemporary Dublin for the most part.

There is also a recurring vein of humor, but it is mordant and dark. The outlook is essentially fatalistic—vestiges of deep religious belief cling to even his most volubly atheistic characters. McPherson's characters instinctively search for redemption, even if they no longer believe in the great Redeemer. Their lives are bound by the despair hanging over a populace that believes in salvation as a reward for earthly suffering.

But to acknowledge McPherson's affinity with Irish writers as diverse as Sean O'Casey and Samuel Beckett is not to suggest that his voice is derivative. It is merely to place him as perhaps the most prominent, and

Pipe dreamer: Jim Norton in Dublin Carol. *Photo: Carol Rosegg*

gifted, heir to an idiosyncratic literary tradition. His most recent full-length play, *Dublin Carol*, may be his most accomplished play to date. First seen in London in 2000, the play was produced in New York by the Atlantic Theater Company during the 2002–03 season, and directed by the author himself. (McPherson directed neither the London staging at the Royal Court Theatre nor the play's subsequent Dublin premiere at the Gate.)

DUBLIN CAROL IS a stylistic departure from his other work in at least one significant way. In his one-act, one-character plays and even in *The Weir*, McPherson's use of the monologue form gave his plays a naturally elegiac form. Even when rooted in a specific theatrical present—as in *The Weir*—his characters appear before us to relate past experience, not to enact a drama in theatrical time. The drama in their lives has come to a conclusion; the theatrical form imposed upon it is merely a frame—the paint is dry on these interior landscapes before the plays begin.

On the surface, *Dublin Carol* might seem to be similarly structured. An unsparing portrait of a life ravaged by alcoholism, the play takes place in the cozy, decrepit office of a funeral home in the city of the title (realized with impressively grimy detail by designer Walt Spangler). It is the morning of Christmas Eve, and John Plunkett (exquisitely played by Jim Norton in the New York production) is just arriving back from a service with his young helper, Mark (Keith Nobbs), in tow. John puts a kettle on for Mark, but quickly pours himself a drop of whiskey: "I'm old. I'll die if I don't drink this," he jokes. But as they convivially discuss the day's work, and the illness of Mark's uncle, Noel (John's employer, who is languishing in the hospital), a bitter truth becomes inescapable: John is late for his own funeral. He's dead already, and it is whiskey itself that killed him.

But the play is not merely an elegy for a wasted life. It moves, subtly but ineluctably, toward a conclusion that has not been predetermined. The action it describes is a man's quiet but distinct moral regeneration—*Dublin Carol* culminates in John's small but determined step toward salvation. It is in this that the play departs from McPherson's prior *oeuvre*: Here the interaction of three characters results in a quiet revolution in the soul of at least one.

At first redemption might seem impossible, and to John, at least, it appears irrelevant. He tells his story in parcels of monologue that reveal a battered heart beating in a body still going through the motions of life—it is writing that illustrates McPherson's incomparable gift for capturing a man's soul in his speech. John's pleasures have been reduced to almost comically childish ones: The day's big event is the opening of a little window on the advent calendar that looks garishly out of place on the office's faded, stained wallpaper. Life's larger rewards—the love of family, the respect of one's self and of others, worldly achievement—he abandoned long ago for the momentary and eternal comfort of drink.

He left his wife and children, and was only saved from a premature death by Noel (the name is of course a playful joke: the play had a few too many Yuletide allusions for some critics, who sniffed sentimental artifice). The proprietor of the funeral home took John home from a pub one day and offered him a job and a place to stay. Now John can barely stand to look back at the wreckage of his past, even if he seems to have made his peace with it, and speaks of wanting to slip away quietly when his time comes, "under cover of darkness."

But ghosts of Christmases past come back to confront him in the play's second scene, when John's daughter, Mary (Kerry O'Malley), arrives to tell him that his wife is now dying of cancer. McPherson doesn't flinch in depicting the depth of John's cravenness, the way the poisonous years of self-abuse and self-justification have left him with just a few shards of conscience left.

John shies away from visiting the hospital; overwhelmed by shame, he becomes belligerent:

> JOHN: I'm not going to say, "I'm sorry," because of the fucking enormity of the fucking things I did!

And when he and Mary begin recollecting a few stray memories from the happy, early years, John's inability to truly face his demons becomes heartbreakingly clear: When Mary suddenly mentions a binge-induced disappearance, out comes a moth-eaten excuse about a locked moviehouse.

Just a drop: Jim Norton and Keith Nobbs in Dublin Carol. *Photo: Carol Rosegg*

"You're still making bloody excuses about a night in Limerick 25 years ago," Mary says. John recoils, awash in further evasions.

IN A PERFORMANCE of wonderful economy and quietly intense feeling, Norton brought alive this tortured, torturing character in all his contradictions. Now gregarious, now morose, bitter and belligerent one moment, gagging with shame and regret seconds later, John is a man who cannot fully face up to the destruction of his life, but can't look away from it either. "I wish

I'd never been born," John says matter-of-factly at one point, and the benumbed look in Norton's clouded blue eyes captured perfectly the despair of a man who simply means what he says.

The actor made agonizingly clear every nuance of this man's anguished wrestling with his misshapen soul: Just watching the way he interacted with the whiskey bottle—eyeing it warily like a wickedly tempting lover at one moment, always remaining anxiously aware of its physical presence in the room—painted a vivid picture of the war that continued to rage inside John, all but obliterating everything else. This was a great, compassionate, unflinchingly honest and deeply moving performance.

Those qualities marked McPherson's writing and directing, too. He drew out a smaller but similarly sensitive performance from O'Malley. Mary bears the wounds of her father's neglect but has survived them to keep alive a small sliver of faith in herself, and in her father. She can tell her father she loves him; he responds not with a similar avowal but a question: "Why do you love me?" Such unanswerable questions echo throughout the dialogue, as do a series of nihilistic outbursts from John: "This is horrible," "This is terrible. . . ." McPherson doesn't supply any handy diagnosis of John's illness. He lightly suggests that the damage is partly a legacy of a pernicious religious upbringing, which taught his generation that "we were all going to hell or somewhere." And John also alludes to the powerful shame of hiding while his father brutally beat his mother.

When Mary asks him why he turned to the bottle, he spills everything out.

> JOHN: I just always felt like people were judging me. I just always felt guilty.
>
> MARY: Why?
>
> JOHN: I don't know. [. . .] I see people my generation. You see them there in their suit jackets. Sitting on some street corner. Begging for money for drink. You think they don't know it's a short-term solution? They know. But the long term is terrifying. Failure reaching up and grabbing you. We were brought up like that a little bit. You know? That we were all going to hell or somewhere. You know?
>
> (Short pause)
>
> My dad used to beat the living daylights out of my mother, you know?
>
> [. . .]
>
> And I let her take it. So he wouldn't hit me. That feeling went away when I got older. He became a little frail old man and stopped all

that shenanigans. And I fucking just generally forgot about it, you know? But then, years later, when you were born, right? I started to feel again like I was a . . . coward. Do you see I thought the world was a bad place and that someone was going to come and attack us.

Some of John's suffering, and the suffering he causes others, has larger dimensions, too—it is of a kind with the nameless, ever-present fear and anxiety that plague Beckett's characters. His is a tale of universal human weakness and cruelty and failure. The demons that hounded John into the bottle are the mundane ones that anyone might greet on certain mornings, and escape with a drink or two on certain evenings:

JOHN: Boredom. Loneliness. A feeling of being out of step with everyone else. Fear. Anxiety. Tension.

Norton's casual recitation of the list, with a bemused shrug and a slight question mark in the voice, was devastating in its simplicity.

BLEAK AS THE play is, it progresses toward a suggestion of hope. Early in the second scene, John accedes to Mary's pleading request that he visit his wife in the hospital, despite his protestations that his transgressions were too grave to be forgiven. She says she'll come by and pick him up at five. But a question hangs in the air for the rest of the play: Will John's shame and fear and embarrassment drive him too deep back into the bottle to

Father's lullaby: Kerry O'Malley and Jim Norton in Dublin Carol. *Photo: Carol Rosegg*

make good on his promise? Will he find the courage to make this small step toward atonement, and redemption, or will he continue to hibernate inside a glass of whiskey, inside a funeral home, a broken man just waiting for his last trip from the mortuary?

At the beginning of the play's last scene, late in the afternoon, it seems as if John's demons have carried the day. He is found in a boozy doze by Mark, and when he tells Mark of his wife's illness, the old uncertainty threatens to win out:

> JOHN: My daughter's coming. I don't have much time. She wants me to go to the hospital and see her. I'm just, I really don't know what to do. Your Uncle Noel would know.

But John's tortured encounter with his daughter, and the reckoning it has inspired in his heart, is given a gentle nudge by a blunt and simple response:

> MARK: You should go.

The play ends in silence. John is left alone to wait for Mary. He washes his face, puts on his jacket and a tie. He combs his hair. As the lights fade he sits patiently in a chair, looking a bit like a boy uncomfortably dressed for his first day at school, anxious with a tense but benign anticipation—the kind that attends all new beginnings.

2002–2003 Best Play

I AM MY OWN WIFE

By Doug Wright

○ ○ ○ ○ ○

Essay by Julius Novick

CHARLOTTE: When families died, I became this furniture. When the Jews were deported in the Second World War, I became it. When citizens were burned out of their homes by the Communists, I became it. After the coming of the wall, when the old mansion houses were destroyed to create the people's architecture, I became it.

ONE MISSION OF modern drama has been to challenge the conventional dichotomies—good and evil (Ibsen, Shaw), true and false (Pirandello, Pinter)—by which we organize our understanding of the world. Gay theater has added two more dichotomies to be challenged: serious and trivial (Wilde), and male and female (Ludlam). To the names in parentheses, of course, many others could be added. The aim in most cases has not been to reject these categories as meaningless, but rather to show us that they are deeply problematic, that the conventional rigid boundaries between them are inadequate to encompass the multiplicity of the world. *I Am My Own Wife*, Doug Wright's biographical play about Charlotte von Mahlsdorf, is a fascinating case in point.

Charlotte von Mahlsdorf really existed (she died in 2002), but who was she *really*? It's a complicated question—not unanswerable, but answerable in various ways—as the play suggests. She was born a boy in 1928 and named Lothar Berfelde, but she spent most of her life in women's clothes as Charlotte von Mahlsdorf. (Sex-change operations were not an option in her generation, but she managed quite well without one.) Living in Mahlsdorf—40 minutes outside of Berlin—she managed to survive both the Nazis and the Communists, she amassed a tremendous collection of old furniture, bric-a-brac, clocks, phonographs, and whatnot, which she displayed lovingly for many years in her house-cum-museum.

DOUG: The rarest artifact she has isn't a grandfather clock or a Beidermeier tall-boy. It's her.

"I GREW UP gay in the Bible Belt," says Doug, the author-character, and *I Am My Own Wife* is clearly an expression of gay pride. But, as the title suggests, it is far subtler, quirkier and stranger, than the usual tales of homophobia and coming out. Wright has previously written about Salvador Dalí, Marcel Duchamp and the Marquis de Sade—three "cultural provocateurs" (his term). (*Quills*, his play about Sade, was made into a film of the same name, with Geoffrey Rush, Kate Winslet, Michael Caine and a

Detailed attention: Jefferson Mays in I Am My Own Wife. *Photo: Joan Marcus*

screenplay by Wright.) Charlotte von Mahlsdorf, too, in her oblique way, was a cultural provocateur, notwithstanding the compromises she made in order to survive.

I Am My Own Wife was years in the making. Wright first met Charlotte in August 1992; Playwrights Horizons in New York commissioned the play in 1996, and finally produced it—to enthusiastic reviews—in May 2003. In an interview distributed with the program at Playwrights Horizons, Wright said:

> [T]he more I discovered about my central character, the more conflicted
> I became about her very nature. [. . .] I realized I needed to find a

dramatic form—a structure for the play—that was as singular as its subject. Charlotte is an endlessly complex figure, and she defies simple biographical storytelling. I also think I was inhibited by this play because it spanned the entire 20th century, and it dealt with the Nazis, and it dealt with the Communists, and realms of oppression that are completely outside my experience. [. . .] Then the dramaturg, Robert Blacker, said to me, "You're correct to have reservations about this play. You have no authority in those departments. But where you do have absolute authority as a writer is in your love affair with a particular character. So don't write a play about the 20th century, write a play about your very personal love affair with Charlotte von Mahlsdorf, and if you're lucky the 20th century will emerge."

So *I Am My Own Wife* became a play about Doug Wright's struggle to come to terms with his enigmatic heroine.

Wright took the tapes of his interviews with Charlotte to the Sundance Theatre Laboratory in Utah, where he worked on them with Moisés Kaufman, the creator-director of *Gross Indecency* and *The Laramie Project,* two impressive works of documentary theater on gay themes, and the protean actor Jefferson Mays. When the play opened at Playwrights Horizons, Kaufman was the director and Mays was the entire cast, making lightning-fast transitions among some 33 characters with astonishing clarity and precision. But why just one actor? Wright said, in the interview quoted above:

> In a play about a character that has to adopt a variety of guises in order to survive, it made astonishing intuitive sense to me to let one actor play all the roles. It just seemed to be thematically correct. I also liked the notion that if the dominant character he was playing for the evening was Charlotte, he would inevitably be in her signature black dress and pearls. So every other character he played would, by default, also be wearing a little black dress. And I thought that becomes a point of unity in the play. Transvestism is the norm not the exception.

In fact, for the record, one character does appear briefly in trousers—but he is the exception, not the norm.

THE ONE-PERSON show, of course, has been with us since long before *The Iliad* and *The Odyssey* took shape as Homer's one-man shows. But in our time the solo show has become a characteristic American genre—partly, at least, for economic reasons: only one actor's salary to pay. Moreover, we are less rigid than we used to be in our thinking about what to expect in the theater, about how many actors are needed to make a play. We no longer demand realism; we are comfortable with performers who switch from role to role, who acknowledge the stage as a stage, as solo performers are almost obliged to do: in real life there is not much of interest to others that one person can do alone.

The solo show appears in many forms, but there are three main ones: the literary/historical, in which the performer, usually not the author, impersonates some figure from the past (Julie Harris as Emily Dickinson); the autobiographical, in which the author-performer talks about himself (Spalding Gray); the journalistic, in which the performer impersonates a series of people she has interviewed (Anna Deavere Smith). *I Am My Own Wife* combines elements of all three forms. It is about the life of Charlotte von Mahlsdorf, who was a real person (historical); it is also about the author (autobiographical); and it is based largely on interviews with Charlotte conducted by the author (journalistic).

More than more populous forms of theater, the solo show naturally tends toward storytelling (cf. Homer). And Charlotte—Wright's Charlotte at least—is a brilliant raconteuse who delights in recalling her colorful past for Doug's tape recorder. Thus Charlotte-as-she-was is filtered through Charlotte-as-she-is, complicating Doug's efforts to understand her. And Doug's inquisitive presence answers the question that bedevils so many one-person shows: Why is the character telling us all this? Meanwhile, Mays creates, vividly, the people who figure in Charlotte's account of her encounters. *I Am My Own Wife* is modestly subtitled, "Studies for a Play about the Life of Charlotte von Mahlsdorf," but unlike some other one-person shows it is truly a play, not just an evening of rambling chat.

As the actor morphs instantaneously from character to character, but is primarily Charlotte, so Derek McLane's setting, under David Lander's exquisite lighting, morphs instantaneously from place to place, but remains primarily Charlotte's museum. The play begins as Charlotte enters through high double doors upstage. She wears a very severe black dress, a strand of pearls, a black cloth on her head, thick black clodhopping shoes; she is obviously a man. She moves slowly, deliberately. She takes a look at the audience, smiles a little smile, opens her mouth to speak, thinks better of it, turns on her heel, and goes out. A moment later she returns, carrying an ancient big-horned phonograph. With a slight touch of mischief she kicks the door closed behind her. She sets down the phonograph and begins to lecture—in her androgynous elderly voice, in intriguingly slightly off English, with a touch of shyness—on the objects she loves so much. Her love is manifest in the way she speaks of them, looks at them, handles them.

Later, she says:

> CHARLOTTE: Museum. Furniture. Men. *This is the order in which I have lived my life.*

And you believe her. In fact, there is very little sex in the play, though there is plenty of gender. She exists at a slight remove from the world.

All of this is conveyed with subtle artistry by the actor—who abruptly turns into a brisk American newspaperman writing to Doug about Charlotte, and then turns instantly into Doug, who turns up in Berlin to see her. The newspaperman is vigorous and blunt; Doug has a soft drawl. As Mays performs them, their ways of speaking, moving, and thinking—like

Divine music: Jefferson Mays in I Am My Own Wife.
Photo: Joan Marcus

Charlotte's—are clearly marked, personal, unforced, and convincing (though they are not strikingly odd, as she is). The actor is a master of self-transformation.

> DOUG (*writing to Charlotte*): [I'm] impressed by the mere fact of your survival. [. . .] The Nazis, and then the Communists? It seems to me, you're an impossibility. You shouldn't even exist.

Soon Doug begins interviewing her. Always when she reminisces, she not only tells but reenacts. When she talks about how she discovered women's clothes, she spreads her skirt in an exquisite moment of self-admiration before an invisible mirror. Her kindly, horse-raising Tante Luise, who always wears men's clothes, says, "Did you know that nature has dared to play a joke on us? You should've been born a girl, and I should have been a man!" Tante Luise gives her a copy of a book, *Die Transvestiten* by Magnus Hirschfeld, saying, "This book is not just any book. This book, it will be your Bible."

Later, Charlotte tells of her narrow escape from being shot by the SS, and about how, menaced by her own brutal Nazi father, she beat him to death with a rolling pin. We begin to be unsure of the boundary between her memory and her imagination.

Periodically we return to her museum, to her collection of old furniture, old phonographs, old clocks. After the wall falls, she receives a medal from the "Cultural Ministry of the *Bundesrepublik Deutschland*" for her "astonishing efforts at conservation."

> CHARLOTTE: The day I received the medal was for me recognition of my work, and I thought—*wie soll ich sagen*—I thought it's good because other people see that a transvestite can work. A transvestite becomes such a medal! [. . .]
>
> JOHN: [. . .] Aw, Doug, I wish you could've been there. Picture it. An elderly man, in a skirt and a string of pearls. Nobody laughed. No cat-calls. And—at the end of the ceremony—the Cultural Minister himself even leaned down to kiss her hand.

By sheer strength of will (and certain other qualities), Lothar Berfelde had imposed him/herself upon the world—even upon the government—as Charlotte von Mahlsdorf.

IN HER FAMOUS essay "Notes on Camp," Susan Sontag writes that "the essence of Camp is its love of the unnatural: of artifice and exaggeration. [. . .] It is the love of the exaggerated, the 'off,' of things-being-what-they-are-not." By this standard, *I Am My Own Wife* is clearly a work of Camp, even though Charlotte—as Wright depicts her—has nothing to do with the exaggerated sexual femininity of the usual drag queen. She is austere; she wears no makeup because she "doesn't need it"; but this man in a dress who lives for her furniture has her own way of exaggerating herself. Sontag says, "Camp is the glorification of 'character.'"

> JOHN: [She's] a true character; [. . .] she may well be the most singular, eccentric individual the Cold War ever birthed.

And yet, according to Sontag, "Camp proposes a comic vision of the world." *I Am My Own Wife* is often exquisitely funny, but its vision is not essentially comic. Charlotte does not ultimately represent laughable "failed seriousness"; ultimately, for Wright, she does not fail. For Sontag, "the Camp sensibility is disengaged, depoliticized—or at least apolitical," and "Camp is a solvent of morality." But *I Am My Own Wife* is deeply engaged, deeply concerned with politics (the Nazis, the Communists), and Doug Wright's sense of morality—both as the author of the play and as a character in the play—is far from dissolved.

Soon after we see Charlotte receiving her medal from the new united Germany, Doug broaches a difficult topic: the rumors of her relationship with the Stasi, the old East German secret police. She acknowledges signing a pledge to work for them, but:

> CHARLOTTE: [. . .] I said to myself, I'll still do whatever I want. [. . .] Meine Tante Luise always said, "Be as smart as the snakes; it's in the Bible." She said, "Never forget that you're living in the lion's den. Sometimes, you must howl with the wolves."

But then:

> JOHN: The German press got its hands on Charlotte's Stasi file. She was an informant, all right. For four years, in the mid-seventies. It says she was "willing." Even "enthusiastic."

The revelations in the Stasi file were big news in Germany. Doug cites some headlines: "Charlotte von Mahlsdorf, Sexual Outlaw and Soviet Spy?" "Mata Hari was Man; the Real Story of Berlin's Most Notorious Transvestite." "Comrade Charlotte: Is the Disguise She's Wearing More Than Just a Dress?"

In a flashback we see Alfred Kirschner, Charlotte's friend, business partner, fellow collector, fellow homosexual, in a Communist prison for selling clocks to American soldiers. (This is the only moment in the play in which the actor wears pants, thus conferring on Alfred a special distinction.) He has been betrayed to the Stasi by Charlotte—at his own urging, she says, to save herself and her museum. Charlotte is assailed by reporters:

> KARL HENNING [REPORTER]: According to the records we've obtained, you valued furnishings torn from the homes of dissidents, of political prisoners, of the wronged and the oppressed—
>
> CHARLOTTE: You are from the West, yes? Did the Stasi ever come to your door? Tell me, I ask you—!
>
> FRANÇOIS GARNIER [REPORTER]: François Garnier, Paris. Did the Stasi really pay you in contraband?
>
> CHARLOTTE: I took nothing!

FRANÇOIS GARNIER: —not even an inkwell, a cigarette box for your museum—

CHARLOTTE (*vehemently*): As a mother would take an orphan child, yes?

The revelation that Charlotte was a Stasi informer is the crux of the play. Her credibility is in ruins. Of all the tales she has told him, what is fact and what is only self-mythologizing?

Shadowy figure: Jefferson Mays in I Am My Own Wife. *Photo: Joan Marcus*

DOUG: [. . .] I need to believe in her stories as much as she does! I need to believe that—a long time ago, in an attic—a generous aunt handed her confused nephew a book and a blessing. That a little boy—*in his mother's housecoat*—survived the *Storm Troopers*. That Lothar Berfelde navigated a path between the two most repressive regimes the Western World has ever known—the *Nazis* and the *Communists*—in a pair of heels. I need to believe that things like that are true. That they can happen in the world.

IN HIS INTERVIEW, Wright speaks of his "sense of betrayal," but he cannot repudiate his heroine. Like Tennessee Williams in his plays, he does not take betrayal lightly, but he can forgive it, and he sees what others call lying as the embrace of a special, subjective reality. (Remember Blanche DuBois: "I didn't lie in my heart . . .") For Wright, Charlotte has a kind of integrity in continuing to be, openly, what the world does not want her to be, and a kind of triumph in getting away with it:

> She was an unequivocal, unapologetic transvestite in the midst of the two most oppressive regimes that the western world has ever forged. I think perhaps at the end of the day, that titanic achievement outweighs the inevitable compromises she made along the way, or at least exempts her from traditional judgment. I think hers was a remarkable and singular life in incredibly oppressive and conformist times.

Cross-dressing as moral heroism. The boundaries between good and bad, true and false, serious and trivial, male and female, all called in question.

In the play itself, he is less explicitly Charlotte's defender. After announcing her death, Doug describes a photograph she has sent him, of Lothar Berfelde, aged ten.

> DOUG: Sitting on either side of him, two tigers. Cubs, sure, but they're still as big as he is. And they're not fond of posing, either. Their eyes are dangerously alert. At any moment they might revolt; they might scratch, or bite.
>
> (*He says with awe*)
>
> But Lothar has one arm around each tiger, and they're resting their forepaws on his knees.

At the end, Doug is, as he was at the beginning, "impressed by the sheer fact of [her] survival," even when she is a boy surrounded by tigers. But now he is reflective rather than emphatic. Then, briefly, we hear Charlotte's voice on tape, and the music in which she found solace, emanating from one of the old Edison phonographs she loved.

The text reads, "Doug stands, listening." We cannot be quite sure what he is thinking.

2002–2003 Best Play

IMAGINARY FRIENDS

By Nora Ephron

○ ○ ○ ○ ○

Essay by Charles Wright

FACT: I'd like to introduce myself
The name is Frankie Fact

FICTION: Hi, I'm Dick Fiction
And frankly, that's a fact

BOTH: At times we tend to tangle
There's friction in the act

FACT: 'Cause "fiction" plays it fast and loose

FICTION: And "fact" is so exact

BOTH: But when we do our number
It's something of an art
And now and then they even say
It's tough to tell us apart

WHEN FIRST-TIME PLAYWRIGHT Nora Ephron's *Imaginary Friends* arrived at the Ethel Barrymore last season, the occasion seemed as much homecoming as debut. Ephron, the eldest, most conspicuous of Phoebe and Henry Ephron's four daughters, is theater royalty. Her mother was impresario Gilbert Miller's production secretary; her father served as stage manager for George S. Kaufman and Moss Hart. From the 1940s to the 1960s, Nora's parents collaborated on stage comedies, beginning with the wartime success *Three's a Family*. Their 1961 Broadway hit, *Take Her, She's Mine*, was even inspired by Nora's student career at Wellesley College.

Ephron comes to the New York stage by way of Hollywood, where she has written and, in some instances, directed romantic comedies, including *When Harry Met Sally, Sleepless in Seattle* and *You've Got Mail*. Her films are reminiscent—in style and structure—of the Broadway confections by writers of her parents' day, such as John Van Druten, F. Hugh Herbert and Jean Kerr. Yet, when *Imaginary Friends* opened on December 12, 2002, it proved an improbable addition to the musical revivals and adaptations of American movies that are the bulk of Broadway's current fare. A duke's

69

Swoosie smolder: Swoosie Kurtz in Imaginary Friends.
Photo: Joan Marcus

mixture of verbal wit and musical fantasia, the play conjures the fireworks that might ensue if Lillian Hellman (1905–84) and Mary McCarthy (1912–89) squared off against each other in the afterlife. Featuring seven songs by composer Marvin Hamlisch and lyricist Craig Carnelia, *Imaginary Friends* was billed not as a musical but as a "play with music."

TWENTY YEARS AGO, playwright Hellman and novelist-critic McCarthy were plaintiff and defendant in a much publicized libel action that never came to trial. The controversy began in 1980 when the 67-year-old McCarthy, appearing on the *Dick Cavett Show*, derided Hellman as "an overrated, a bad writer and a dishonest writer." McCarthy quipped to Cavett that "every word she writes is a lie, including 'and' and 'the.'" Hellman, age 74, slapped McCarthy with a defamation suit, seeking damages of $2.5 million. That case continued, to McCarthy's economic detriment, until Hellman died several years later. Interviewed by the *New York Times*, McCarthy remarked, "I didn't want her to die. I wanted her to lose in court."

What's odd about the Hellman-McCarthy saga—and awkward for a dramatist—is that the two women were only casually acquainted and may not have met more than twice. Hellman, a college dropout, wrote middlebrow dramas, such as *The Little Foxes* and *Watch on the Rhine*. McCarthy was unashamedly highbrow, wearing her privileged education—Annie Wright Seminary and Vassar College—like a suit of armor and brandishing uncompromising intellectual standards like a saber. For instance, as a young critic for the small but influential *Partisan Review*, she turned up her nose at Hellman's "oily virtuosity" as a commercial playwright.

McCarthy was a Trotskyist and, later, a liberal Democrat, who opposed both communism and Senator Joseph McCarthy. Hellman claimed never to have belonged to the Communist Party, but supported Stalin and remained

Mary contrary: Cherry Jones in Imaginary Friends. *Photo: Joan Marcus*

critical, to the end of her days, of those, like Mary McCarthy, who disparaged American Communists. She courted headlines with her dramatic response to a 1952 subpoena from the House Committee on Un-American Activities. "I cannot and will not cut my conscience to fit this year's fashions," she wrote, offering to answer the committee's questions about her own activities but refusing to "bring bad trouble" to others by testifying about anyone else.

McCarthy's comments on the Cavett show were a characteristic response to Hellman's late-career autobiographies. According to critic Elizabeth Hardwick, in a foreword to McCarthy's *Intellectual Memoirs*, "what often seemed to be at stake in Mary's writing and in her way of looking at things was a somewhat obsessional concern for the integrity of sheer fact in matters both trivial and striking." In her books, Hellman aped the crisp, grumpy sentences of her sometime paramour, novelist Dashiell Hammett, and passed off fiction as fact. In a chapter of *Pentimento*, for example, she appropriated the biography of Muriel Gardiner, an American member of the antifascist underground in Central Europe during the 1930s, to create the story of "Julia," her unidentified—and, ultimately, unidentifiable—childhood friend. Hellman also depicted her love affair with Hammett as a marriage of true minds (rather than the love affair it was), and portrayed herself as a heroine of the left, single-handedly defending her principles against a Congressional inquisition. Her prickly nature and reputation for vindictiveness intimidated many who might have contested her tall tales. Since her death, though, biographers and historians have had a field day exposing her as a fabulist.

FRAMED AS A debate between Hellman and McCarthy, *Imaginary Friends* employs a mélange of theatrical and musical styles to depict the feud between the writers and its historical context. Combining dramatic sketches with olios that tie the scenes together and propel the action forward, the show is a near relation of the topical revues that grew out of minstrelsy and 19th-century vaudeville—and were staples of every Broadway season until the late 1950s. *Imaginary Friends* also resembles three plays about historical figures that have recently been successful—or, in one case, a *succès d'estime*—on the New York stage. Claudia Shear's *Dirty Blonde*, which, like *Imaginary Friends,* was produced on Broadway by USA Ostar Theatricals, is about Mae West. The other two, *Gross Indecency: The Three Trials of Oscar Wilde* by Moisés Kaufman and *The Invention of Love* by Tom Stoppard, concern Wilde and other literary lights. Stoppard's play—the *succès d'estime* of the three—doesn't have Wilde as its central figure, but he's the most engaging element of the playwright's concoction.

Writing in the mid-to-late 1990s, Shear, Kaufman and Stoppard defied the conventions of documentary drama, transporting techniques of the postmodern avant-garde into commercial theater. Each in his or her fashion jettisoned linear narrative, reconstructing historical events in a highly theatrical way; juxtaposing scenes from disparate eras—or, in some cases, scenes of reality and scenes of fantasy—against each other to explore the significance of the past to the present.

Imaginary Friends includes a handful of songs which, in New York, were intricately staged, with Jerry Mitchell choreography and a first-rate chorus impersonating southerners, Depression-era radicals, Congressional inquisitors and reporters. But, beneath this show-biz frippery, the action of the play follows an uncomplicated arc. Ephron doesn't specify the setting, calling only for "a bare stage." As the opening dialogue proceeds, the location turns out to be an Aristophanic underworld. For the Broadway production, Michael Levine created a scarlet and velour environment suggestive of some posh mid-century Manhattan *boîte* El Morocco, perhaps, or the Stork Club. Hellman (Swoosie Kurtz) and McCarthy (Cherry Jones) appeared, smoking cigarettes, then adjusting their hair and make-up, apparently in the ladies' room of Limbo (or perhaps, considering the multitude of reds in Kenneth Posner's lighting design, Hell).

> LILLIAN: Did we ever meet?
>
> MARY: Once or twice.

Li'l lecture: Swoosie Kurtz (left), Cherry Jones (far right) and company in Imaginary Friends. *Photo: Joan Marcus*

> LILLIAN: I don't really remember.
>
> MARY: Well, then I don't remember, either.

Act I is devoted to the women's early lives, their associations with radical politics; and their best known sexual alliances. Ephron epitomizes Hellman's New Orleans childhood with an incident in which little-girl Lillian, perched in a fig tree, spots her father consorting with a woman, Fizzy, in a way that leaves no doubt he's unfaithful to her mother. Lillian falls out of the tree, breaking her nose.

> LILLIAN: I went running off to find my old nurse, Sophronia. I told her I'd seen Fizzy and my father kissing each other, and I decided to kill myself. Sophronia bandaged me up and told me that I must never ever tell anyone about Fizzy. I promised her I never would. A few minutes later, as she walked me home, she said, "Don't go through life making trouble for people." I said, "If I tell you I won't tell anyone about Fizzy, I won't."

From Mary's dour Roman Catholic childhood, Ephron selects an incident in which the orphaned girl stands up to her guardian uncle's accusation that she has stolen a toy.

> UNCLE MYERS: [S]omeone took your brother's butterfly and hid it under your plate—
>
> MARY: It wasn't me. Why would I do that?
>
> UNCLE MYERS: You wanted the butterfly—
>
> MARY: But why would I take it and put it under my own plate?
>
> (*Mary starts to run away, and Uncle Myers grabs her.*)
>
> UNCLE MYERS: Admit you took it—
>
> MARY: I will never admit I took it. You can beat me until I'm dead, but I will never admit I took it. Never ever.

The act culminates with conflicting versions, narrated by the feuding writers, of a 1948 literary gathering, where they clashed over an anecdote Lillian told about novelist John Dos Passos. That hostile first meeting is the genesis of antipathies that build for the rest of the play.

In the second act, the women follow a collision course, barreling toward the incident on Cavett's show and the conflagration of *Hellman v. McCarthy*. Ephron's treatment of Mary and Lillian is markedly even-handed; as characters, they are of consonant intelligence and wit, comparably interesting and, at times, equally repugnant. Lillian, with her grudges and lies, is as unsympathetic as one might expect; while Mary, for all of her virtuous rhetoric, is an icily calculating foe. Speaking with a fellow Vassar alumna (Anne Allgood) prior to Cavett's telecast, Mary analyzes the most effective phrasing for the insult she intends to deliver.

> MARY: Do you think I should say, "Everything she writes is false, including 'and' and 'but,'" or should I say, "Everything she writes is false, including 'and' and 'the'"?
>
> ABBY KAISER: Gosh, I don't know. They're not too different.
>
> MARY: [I] think if I say "'and' and 'but,'" people might be confused by the word "but," but if I say "'and' and 'the'"—I mean, obviously I'd have to pronounce it "the"—[Sounding like "thee"]—as opposed to "the"—[Sounding like "thuh"]—so people will be able to hear what I'm saying—[. . .] "The" is better, I think. It's so much more devoid of meaning than "but," if you see what I mean.

AT THE CORE of Ephron's play is a well-made psychological mystery constructed around Lillian's inveterate storytelling and Mary's posturing about "truth." This vein of Ephron's text is a pastiche of the literary styles of Hellman and her intellectual mentor, Hammett. In their respective genres, Hellman and Hammett produced tightly plotted melodramas, doling out clues and efficiently tying up all narrative skeins. Hellman's most successful plays follow the dramaturgical tradition of Scribe, Sardou and Ibsen; even her memoirs display that tidy, melodramatic sensibility. As Mary complains to Lillian in the play:

> MARY: Your plays were [. . . t]oo well made, really—there was way too much of the gun over the mantel in the first act being fired at the end [. . .]

The climax of Act II is the trial, precluded in reality by Hellman's death. This is the *scène à faire* to which Mary and Lillian, as characters in a well-made play, are entitled. Since the trial takes place in the realm of fancy, the rules of civil procedure and all evidentiary niceties are suspended. A single witness provides decisive evidence and serves, also, as judge and jury. That witness, whom Mary describes as "the gun over the mantel," is Muriel Gardiner (Anne Pitoniak), whose efforts in the Central European underground appear to have inspired both *Watch on the Rhine* (1941) and "Julia." Muriel, a psychoanalyst trained in Freud's Vienna, is Ephron's device to identify behavioral patterns that control the lives of the principal characters and account for their unhappy collision.

> MURIEL: Look at you, Mary. Someone once told you a lie, a terrible lie, so you made a religion out of the truth. And it turned out to be your blind spot, because you never understood how subjective and elusive and abstract truth is—you simply thought that if you could

prove someone was telling a lie, you'd won. (*To Lillian*) You, on the other hand, witnessed a traumatic version of the primal scene, and then you were persuaded to lie about it. So you spent your life telling lies and expecting to be applauded for it.

Both Hellman and McCarthy spent considerable time in psychoanalysis, but those real-life experiences don't figure in Ephron's play. Muriel's assessment of Lillian's and Mary's neuroses is a caricature of psychoanalytic methodology; and the climactic diagnosis of *Imaginary Friends* is efficient theater rather than convincing therapy. But however reductive the "obligatory scene," Ephron's theatrical depiction of the two writers steers clear of the kind of caricature that often mars stage impersonations of famous figures—as in, for instance, *Master Class*, Terrence McNally's quick sketch of Maria Callas. In fact, Ephron is so deft at blending research and lively characterization that a surprising number of critics responded to *Imaginary Friends* as though it were a documentary rather than a flight of comic imagination.

Before the play arrived in New York, encouraging word about its San Diego engagement generated anticipation on the East Coast. The excitement was related, in part, to the presence of director Jack O'Brien, whose association with the season's first big hit, *Hairspray*, elevated expectations of both critics and playgoers. Yet, for all the glamour of the production, this work by a first-time playwright always sounded a trifle recherché for the 1,000-plus seats and uneconomic overhead of a midtown playhouse. And so it proved to be.

The New York critics were less impressed than their California colleagues. They praised the professionalism of O'Brien's staging and the comedic virtuosity of Kurtz, Jones and Harry Groener, who played the important men in the writers' lives. They admired Michael Levine's design, with its sumptuous colors and art deco touches; and the way Robert Morgan's costumes evoked the elegance of *couturiers* from five decades. But they dismissed the Hamlisch-Carnelia songs as standard-issue show tunes, insufficiently integrated with the text; and failed to appreciate Ephron's post-September 11 prescience. Some reviewers misconstrued the play as a politically incorrect catfight on the order of Clare Boothe Luce's *The Women*. The comparisons to Luce roused suspicion, at least in some quarters, that *Imaginary Friends* is antifeminist. The production lasted only 76 performances, closing February 16, 2003.

IMAGINARY FRIENDS ISN'T antifeminist. On the contrary, the several appearances of life-sized puppets of Lillian and Mary—a particular annoyance to a number of New York reviewers—signify, however clumsily, the artificial, doll-like expectations that society imposed on women during Hellman and McCarthy's formative years. Ephron's characterization captures the tension of women defying expectations when literature was a men's club and entry appeared—at times—to depend less on talent than on personal association with a man of established position.

Ephron arrived on Broadway at a moment when the industry was preoccupied with self-referential humor (as in *Urinetown* and *The Producers*) and playwrights (or perhaps, producers) were disinclined to soil their hands with politics—unless the political issues were long-settled, as in *Hairspray*. Ephron's play may lack the portentousness of *Idiot's Delight* or *Angels in America*, but it's as much a state-of-the-nation play as they. First performed less than a year after the attacks on the World Trade Center and the Pentagon, it takes place during the Cold War, when the federal government was as heavy-handed regarding civil liberties as it has been of late.

In her denouement, Ephron distills Hellman and McCarthy's disaccord to this: "I believe in the truth," says Mary. "I believe in the story," Lillian replies. Earlier in the play, Mary has derided Lillian for her mythmaking about Hammett.

> MARY: [Y]ou rarely slept together, he was drunk most of the time, and he had the longest writer's block in living memory.
>
> LILLIAN: He loved me and only me.
>
> MARY: [T]his romantic thin man who rode into your life and turned you into a *femme fatale* was a figment of your imagination. He was just a story.

But "stories"—riveting stories—are Lillian's ultimate value, her "truth." Lillian proclaims: "I'm just a story. So are you. The question is, who gets to tell it?" Ephron recognizes that the efficacy of any attempt to capture reality in words depends upon the integrity of the speaker. Consequently, the public is always in danger of being seduced by raconteurs—a panel of justices, for instance, interpreting the 2000 presidential election; a president construing September 11; or a warmongering administration expounding on the likely presence of weapons of mass destruction.

At a time when deceptive rhetoric permeated the American ether, Ephron offered a play about prevarication and truth-telling in public discourse—and delivered a message of skepticism about the objectivity of "truth" and the credibility of those with easiest access to the media. Despite the recent din of political pronouncements designed to confuse the distinction between Al Qaeda and the government of Saddam Hussein; despite the shameless promotion of war by allegations—unsupported by convincing evidence—that Iraq harbored weapons of mass destruction, the New York critics failed to apprehend the timeliness of Ephron's comedy. And they reserved their fiercest execration for "Fact and Fiction," a duet by Frankie Fact (Dirk Lumbard) and Dick Fiction (Peter Marx) with astute lyrics accompanied by a seductively old-fashioned soft shoe.

A LITTLE MORE than two months after *Imaginary Friends* folded, the *New York Times* disclosed that one of its news writers, Jayson Blair, had fabricated at least 36 prominent stories and, a month after that, *Times* executive editor Howell Raines and managing editor Gerald Boyd resigned in disgrace. At that moment, the lyrics of Lumbard and Marx's song—and, in fact, all of Ephron's play—seemed downright prophetic.

2002–2003 Best Play

THE MERCY SEAT

By Neil LaBute

○ ○ ○ ○ ○

Essay by John Istel

ABBY: You call your family, or you don't. You run for the hills, or you don't. You come back in and work on the AmTel account with us or not. Your life's in front of you right now, Ben but *you* have to choose. (*Beat.*) You already made one choice—me— so you can leave the keys on the counter or in your *ficus tree* or wherever . . . and if I see you back at work, that'll be great. It will be. (*She moves toward the door, but hesitates.*) Look, you can't stay here. Uh-uh. I'm not gonna rat you out, whatever you decide, I won't do that. I'll show you some mercy . . . more than you've ever shown me, anyway. . . .

W HO WOULD HAVE thought Neil LaBute even had the word "mercy" in his vocabulary? Sure, characters in other plays often find themselves on the "mercy seat" of the title, which refers to the lid of the Ark of the Covenant, where God manifests Himself—definitely a "Him" in LaBute's work. In fact, you could call LaBute's work "Mercy Seat Theater." After all, his characters are often heinous sinners who find comfort by confessing before the Almighty: the audience. Such religious references aren't unusual in LaBute's work. In *The Shape of Things* the two main characters' names are the Edenic Adam and Evelyn. The title of his first well-known stage success, *bash: the latterday plays*, directly references the playwright's own Mormonism.

But in those previous fierce, no-holds-barred fables (as well as in his first two films *In the Company of Men* and *Your Friends and Neighbors*), the playwright-director lards precious little mercy onto his characters' actions. They are either viciously victorious or sacrificial lamb-like victims. Mercy—as well as faith, hope, charity and other traits that make one proud to be human—are in short supply, and the quality of whatever's left is always strained.

Whether from the suburbs or corporate America or both, LaButian creations dress and look like "normal" people, but in his modern morality plays, they demonstrate mythic-sized, moments of monstrous human

Leaving home: Sigourney Weaver and Liev Schreiber in The Mercy Seat. *Photo: Joan Marcus*

behavior. In LaBute Land, people flash their appetites and sins like badges. They play snarling, sexual, violent games of Life and Domination (to experience the latter fate is often far worse than death or damnation to LaBute's characters). Audiences often leave his plays and films horrified by his characters' abilities to deceive, manipulate and violate each other.

Even if you're not religious, as you step into the daylight, you can't help but mutter a prayer of thanks that you don't know anyone who behaves so badly: Guys who make wooing and dumping a deaf secretary into a betting contest like the cads in *In the Company of Men*. Or the buddy who brags about raping a teammate in a locker room in ecstatic, rapturous tones, as Jason Patric's character does in *Your Friends and Neighbors*. What kind of creature would manipulate, deceive and publicly humiliate a lover in order to complete a master's thesis in fine art, as happens in *The Shape of Things*? And in *The Mercy Seat*, could a young, married father of two really use the chaos caused by the September 11 attacks as a pretext for abandoning his family and running off with his mistress?

As LaBute knows, these enemies *are* us. We can always count on some infamous American citizen to yank away our fairy tale faith and wide-eyed optimism in a beneficent humanity. Witness the suburban Long

Island high school where football team members hazed new teammates by sodomizing them with pine cones. Or the long, public rise and fall of righteous moralizers like William Bennett and Rush Limbaugh. Who can you believe?

LaBute's theatricalizes this loathsome side of humanity in very simple physical and dramatic structures. *bash* consists of a series of monologues on a bare stage addressed directly at the audience. Earlier works used similarly spartan sets and situations, daring audiences to be outraged or titillated solely by the power of the spoken word.

THE MERCY SEAT, which opened in December 2002 in a fine production by MCC Theater, is similar in scenic style to LaBute's earlier efforts in its spare setting, which keeps the focus on what the characters are actually saying to each other. Yet, *The Mercy Seat* is the most developed play LaBute has produced in New York. For one, his characters, Ben Harcourt and Abby Prescott, actually have last names, which in the introduction to the published script the playwright points out as a peculiarity in his opus. They are co-workers at some unnamed business who happen to be carrying on an affair that breaks moral law and corporate ethics (he's married, she's his boss). The play unfolds in real time over the course of about 80 intermissionless minutes. Unlike much of LaBute's other work, the play is not set in some nameless Everyland, like the Midwest campus where *Shape of Things* occurs or the sterile office cubicles haunted by the characters in *In the Company of Men*. Instead, the "action" occurs during what LaBute calls in his introduction, "a long, dark morning of the soul" on the day after September 11, 2001, when most of the world played witness to the heroism lying beneath the wreckage and grief.

The setting is Abby's downtown New York loft apartment, not far from the smoldering, hellish inferno that once was the World Trade Center towers. *Mercy Seat* takes a dramaturgical step forward by making neither Ben nor Abby the clear victor or victim. As played by Liev Schreiber, Ben is the better acting role because his character is the one firmly on the "mercy seat," a reference that LaBute was "bandying around for years," according to one interview. As described in the Bible, the actual object is an ornate gold-covered lid, topped by two winged angels or cherubim, facing each other across the top of the holy box, purported to contain tablets with the Ten Commandments. For much of the play Schreiber didn't move from the couch, but his commanding emotional life was on full gymnastic display, making Ben's inner fortitude spin, tumble, squirm, and wriggle like a fish out of water.

Ben and Abby (played with typically smoldering *sang-froid* by Sigourney Weaver) are neither angels nor insects. They face off in a wrestling match for the soul worthy of Jacob, from the opening to the final bell (both of which are symbolized by the ringing of Ben's cell phone). Ostensibly, Ben had come to Abby's apartment just before the attack in order to call home and finally tell his wife the truth about his affair. Abby had been urging her lover and office subordinate to be truthful for months. She even

Cool customer: Sigourney Weaver and Liev Schreiber in The Mercy Seat. *Photo: Joan Marcus*

offered sexual gratification as incentive "to screw his courage to the sticking place" and was apparently performing fellatio when the immediate world outside blew up.

THE PLAY BEGINS about 24 hours later. Ben's a puddle of misery, cowardice, and moral wavering on Abby's couch. As clear from the epigraph, his vacillations continue through to the end of the play.

The ringing cell phone that brings up and down the lights is not only a reminder of Ben's frantic family trying to reach him to see if he's alive, but of his previous inability to own up to the truth of his affair or to his own self-obsessed narcissism. The first beat plays almost like Beckettian comedy as he decides whether to answer the incessantly ringing cell phone to tell his family he's alive.

> BEN: Should I . . . ?
>
> ABBY: Answer it or keep it off. It's up to you.
>
> BEN: Maybe I should . . . I mean . . .
>
> ABBY: Yeah, maybe you really, really should. Go ahead.
>
> BEN: . . . just say I'm doing all right or . . . / You know . . .
>
> ABBY: Go ahead. / Do it.
>
> BEN: Yeah . . . I probably should.
>
> ABBY: An-swer! (*Just then the phone stops ringing. Dead quiet . . .*)

Ben's vacillations begin to frustrate Abby as much as his seeming apathy in the face of the tragic events outside their window. He claims that just because he's not answering his phone, it doesn't mean that he's "not torn up about this, that it doesn't you know, cover my soul." She mocks his attempts at feeling, at his attempts to be human. She jeers his inability to recognize cultural references to the Amazing Kreskin or the World War II hero Audie Murphy, to whom Ben pales in Abby's comparison.

The couple's jousting reveals the power struggle on which their relationship is based. In much of LaBute's earlier work, sex is but a tool. In *The Mercy Seat*, this fact is explicit. In fact, skip this paragraph if frank sexual language bothers you. Although she's his boss now, she points out that he only started flirting with her after she was promoted to a position that he, too, coveted. Ben describes her at one moment as the one who "wears the Haggar slacks" and tells her that she doesn't have to be such "an overdominating cunt about it." As the play unfolds their emotional armor and guard break down, Abby complains that they always fuck without looking at each other—doggie-style. To really irk him, she confesses that she fantasizes while he's going at her, the most recent imaginary turn-on being that she's being fucked by his wife with a strap-on.

This autopsy of the soul finally uncovers Ben's core. Under Abby's probing he comes clean about who he is.

> BEN: You know what? I take that back . . . This *is* me. I've screwed
> up every step of my life, Abby, I'm not afraid to admit it. Happy to,
> actually, I am happy to sing it out there for anybody who wants to

hear. I always take the easy route, do it faster, simpler, you know, whatever it takes to get it done, be liked, get by. That's me. Cheated in school, screwed over my friends, took whatever I could get from whomever I could take it from.

THE FINAL QUESTION Abby puts forth is the most telling. Does he really love her? More important, if the roles were reversed, would he do the same for her and leave his job and life to run off and disappear with a lover? Everyone, onstage and off, knows the answer by now. At the end, when Ben actually makes a decision to act, he picks up his cell. Abby begins to leave to give him privacy. But he insists she stay. She watches warily. Then her cell phone rings and she panics. Ben urges her to answer it and when she does, she hears his voice. His final confession—delivered over the phone to his lover who is in the same room—is that he'd never intended to tell his wife about Abby; he'd come over to tell Abby that he was breaking off the affair.

It's a typical LaButian reversal via personal betrayal. This time, however, you can't help but feel that Ben's decision is a merciful one. His daughters will get their father back, while Abby is probably better off without the cad. That probably best explains her reciprocal modicum of "mercy." It almost seems like the end of some Greek cycle of revenge.

Some may question the need to play witness to LaBute's Machivellian character manipulations. LaBute's stage and screen efforts often feel like a sort of moral cleanser—or is it abrasive?—and he has little use for that opiate called "hope" that all theatergoers crave. If hope is that thing with feathers that Emily Dickinson once wrote about, in LaBute's harrowing and lyrical landscapes they clearly fall from a dead bird.

Other critics could claim that in *The Mercy Seat* LaBute exploits September 11 in a way not dissimilar from Ben's idea to take advantage of it and escape. But in this ultimately soulful instead of soulless play, forgiveness—especially for one's own sins—actually seems possible. Considering the anger and grief that the World Trade Center attacks caused, LaBute comes up with an ending that, for him, seems a radical notion: forgiveness may be the best—and only—response humans should offer in the face of brute cruelty.

2002–2003 Best Play

OUR LADY OF 121ST STREET

By Stephen Adly Guirgis

○ ○ ○ ○ ○

Essay by Jennifer de Poyen

ROOFTOP: I'm a make this call 'cuz I have to, but I need you to think on this till I get back: Ain't my fault about your husband, dass on you. And it ain't my fault 'bout your scorched up heart—you married me juss like I married you. And I got no choice but to try and forgive myself for everything I done to you, cuz, what's the fuckin' alternative, Inez? I usta think there was some other option, some way 'round it, but there really ain't.

IN STEPHEN ADLY Guirgis's *Our Lady of 121st Street*, a diverse group of friends return to their old neighborhood for the funeral of a beloved teacher, Sister Rose—and all hell breaks loose. In fact, it breaks loose before the curtain rises, when the nun's corpse disappears, but unless the connection is cosmic (or symbolic), that hell bears little relationship to what happens in the rest of the play. In Guirgis's world, as in the real one, causation is hard to trace, motivation is uncertain and life is often just a function of what comes next.

That may be because Guirgis (pronounced GEAR-gis) is an accidental playwright, a talent whose speedy ascent through the ranks of his generation has been a surprise—to himself, to the company for which he writes, and to audiences and critics who have responded to his "stories about people in pain in New York." Guirgis's plays tap a tradition that stretches back to the origins of Western theater. His ambition is not simply to tell stories of individuals, but to put an entire community onstage. And the lifeblood of Guirgis's theater is empathy, as it was with the Greeks.

In a sense, *Our Lady* is more a collection of stories than a fully realized dramatic work, a flaw that is easy to overlook because his characters have such vitality, energy and immediacy. Set in Harlem, not far from the neighborhood in which the half-Irish Catholic, half-Egyptian Guirgis grew up, the play offers an intriguing portrait of a community and bears the marks of an exuberant, still forming talent—*Our Lady* is his third full-length work. Guirgis's flaws are flaws of craft, which can be learned; if he continues

Looking out: David Zayas and Al Roffe in Our Lady of
121st Street. *Photo: Joan Marcus*

to write for the theater—and let's hope he does—his sense of dramatic
structure will improve. What Guirgis has—what no great playwright is
without—is an ear for dialogue, the ability to put words in the mouths of
characters in such a way that the audience is made to feel that something
honest is at stake on the stage.

Guirgis came to the task of writing kicking and screaming, and he's
still reluctant to treat his work as a profession, prone to missing deadlines
and writing second acts with the actors already in rehearsals. After graduating
from college (it took him more than seven years to complete a bachelor's
degree), he joined LAB (or Latino Actors Base, now the hotshot
multi-ethnic LAByrinth Theater Company), which was founded to provide
a gym, classes and playwriting workshops for Latino actors. It was only at
the urging of his fellow LAB actor John Ortiz that Guirgis began to write at all.

HIS FIRST FULL-LENGTH play, *In Arabia We'd All Be Kings*, announced the
seriousness of his intentions. He sought, perhaps instinctively, to create a

play that told the story of his community. Set in and around an 8th Avenue bar during Mayor Giuliani's aggressive cleanup campaign in the 1990s, the play offers a panorama of citizens not welcome in the new New York—drunks, a couple of crackheads, a single mom who hooks on the side and a learning-disabled barman who provides the fuel for their disillusionment. Most notable in that 1999 play, as in *Our Lady*, were Guirgis's lively, sympathetic characters.

With his second full-length play, *Jesus Hopped the 'A' Train*, came the kind of critical acclaim that can make a career. The influential and all-important *New York Times* review said "plays of this ilk automatically raise the body—and mind—temperature of New York theater," and a London production persuaded critics there to nominate it for the prestigious Olivier Award. Set at the famously hellish Rikers Island jail, it follows the fate of two prisoners: a street-smart rebel who is locked up for the accidental killing of a religious charlatan and a serial killer who has found God. As the title suggests, *Jesus* deals with spiritual yearning and strife, themes that return with a vengeance in Guirgis's breakthrough tragicomedy *Our Lady*, which debuted Off Off Broadway in fall 2002 and transferred to the Union Square Theatre for a commercial Off Broadway run the following spring.

On opening night Off Broadway, *Our Lady* was launched with a jolt of electricity, and a startling image: A man standing, minus his pants, bathed in designer James Vermeulen's fluorescent light. In an ugly, spacious, sterile room, the man ranted about the lousy state of the world to a laconic, fully clothed man at his side. As the script makes clear, the semi-clad Vic (Richard Petrocelli) is not so upset about his missing pants as he is about the terrible fate of the late Sister Rose—whose misfortune began in childhood with a violent drunk of a father and continues even after her death. Her remains, along with Vic's pants, have been pinched from the funeral parlor where Vic has spent the night in a coffin-side vigil.

In his plangent opening speech addressed to detective Balthazar (the wonderfully world-weary Felix Solis)—himself a former student of the good Sister—Vic sets the tone for the play with his raging, sorrowful incomprehension of life's cruelty and capriciousness.

> VIC: Why you think she became a nun anyway, beautiful girl like that? All this "needle exchange," "alcoholic drunk tank" she had runnin' up here? "Gangs" this, "stop the violence" that? All that thankless shit she did? Was it because she was a good person? Sure. But if ya look underneath it all, it's two things: she donned the habit because she was terrified of intimacy, and all them programs was a way to atone for the sins of her fuckin' piece of dirt Shanty-Irish Mick-fuck father!

Balthazar, already nipping at a bottle and too beaten-down in any case to summon a similar righteous indignation, tells his own tale of horror—about a man whose son was raped and killed in a playground—and then declares the main viewing room a crime scene. From there, the dramatic focus shifts to the gaggle of mourners who have arrived to attend Sister Rose's wake. With no body to bury, and a desire to see if it turns up, they pass the time picking at each other's (and their own) old wounds. Like Vladimir and Estragon, Beckett's famous duo, they await something—salvation, redemption, explanation—that never arrives. As the play ends, less than a day later, there is no answer to questions surrounding Sister Rose's disappearance, though half of her corpse is found in a suitcase and will be prepared for an unsettled burial. Likewise, the simmering conflicts and checkered histories of the mourners are not resolved in a satisfying way. With its sudden, fleeting joy, arbitrary pain and bewildering uncertainty, life will simply go on.

IN GUIRGIS'S WORLD, life would be futile if it weren't the only one we get—as it is, you might as well play. So his characters don't wait passively for the next thing to happen: they rail against their fate; they seek forgiveness for their failings; they try, sometimes witlessly, to make the best of things.

First sight: Elizabeth Canavan and David Zayas in Our Lady of 121st Street. *Photo: Joan Marcus*

Catharsis, for the characters and audience alike, arrives in the expression of long-unarticulated emotion, of each person finally speaking his piece. Sometimes, that's enough; sometimes, that's all you get.

After the confrontation between Vic and Balthazar in the funeral's main viewing room, the action shifts to the nearby church, where the hip-looking, smooth-talking Rooftop (Ron Cephas Jones) is confessing his sins for the first time since his First Confession, to a legless priest, Father Lux (Mark Hammer). As Jones's detailed performance revealed, Rooftop is a man whose status as a Los Angeles radio personality and whose high-rolling lifestyle can't fill the void in his soul. His long, meandering—often hilarious—confession, occurs over a series of interspersed scenes with Father Lux. We finally discover that the source of his malaise is his shoddy treatment of other people—in particular, his ex-wife, Inez (affectingly portrayed by the actress Portia), whom he betrayed. After digressing to discuss his multiple offenses and to reminisce about his childhood pajamas, he finally admits to his fear that he is a failed human being:

> ROOFTOP: Goddamnit, Father, I'm afraid a everything, ok?! Is that what ya wanna hear?! Afraid I'm never gonna be the person I thought I'd be, back when I thought I had all the time in the world to get there! Afraid I'll never learn ta be happy wit juss one woman. I'm afraid to go next door ta pay my respects to ol' Sister Rose. My ex-wive Inez, she's prolly right next door over there at the wake. I'm afraid of her too. Real afraid . . . Mostly, I'm afraid that the person I like least? wherever I go? will always be me . . . Okay?! You happy?!

It isn't until the end of the long night's vigil, when Rooftop finally faces the angry, heartbroken Inez that he comes to terms with all he has done and been. In his resolution to forgive himself, we feel a commitment to try to live a better life, even though his true love is forever lost.

LOSS IS ALSO at the heart of the story of Edwin (David Zayas, in a moving performance). He's a softhearted superintendent who is sole caretaker of his mentally disabled brother, Pinky (Al Roffe, a model of performative honesty). As it turns out, Pinky was a normal kid before Edwin dropped a brick on his head, a fateful mistake that has haunted Edwin ever since. Edwin mourns Sister Rose, who went out of her way to help Pinky, but most of all he mourns the life he might have had if not for that horrible accident and his decision to shoulder the burden of Pinky's "24-7-365" care. When he meets Rose's niece Marcia (Elizabeth Canavan), he feels the stirring of romance, but he feels helpless to change his lot. After an initial stab at forming a bond with her, he explodes in a hopeless rage.

> EDWIN: So, you wanna love me? Decide to love me right now? Marry me tomorrow? Move in with me and my brother? Love him too? Stay here in this neighborhood for as long as it takes? You wanna do that, I'll give it a shot.
>
> MARCIA: . . . That is so unfair.
>
> EDWIN: Welcome to my life that ain't gonna change.

Like a choreographer who shapes work around certain dancers' strengths and weaknesses, Guirgis writes with particular actors in mind, and his best writing seems to come from his imaginative extrapolation of an actor's personality. (Of Zayas, a former policeman, he once told an interviewer: "I know what words sound good coming out of his mouth.") Guirgis also created an uncommonly memorable character for Zayas's wife, the fiercely talented Liza Colón-Zayas. Her Norca was a truly nasty young woman, so emotionally damaged that she can't understand why old friend Inez is angry at her for sleeping with Inez's ex. When we hear a litany of Norca's failures from Balthazar—who targets her as the body snatcher—or when she attacks an innocent witness (played by Melissa Feldman) to her alcohol-fueled confrontation with Inez, it is easy to paint her as a bad seed. And yet Guirgis gives her a short, uncomprehending speech that reveals how little equipped she is to deal with life.

> NORCA: Doncha "Norca" me; You takin her side!! Why you gotta take her side??!! Everywhere I go, someone tryin' ta take the other person's side!! Why can't someone take my damn side for once in a while!! You juss like my mother, my kids, my P.O., my everybody!!! Everybody always wanna gang up on me, well, what the fuck did I do, huh?! What the fuck I did so bad that you gotta take the side a some bug-eyed bitch you never met before 2 minutes ago instead a me who you know practically from fuckin' birth??!!

For all of his empathy, Guirgis doesn't let his characters off the hook. He lets us know that Edwin's refusal to take a chance on love is an expression of fear, and not just a function of his virtue. And Norca follows up her pitiable speech with a truly outrageous act. She cons poor Pinky out of a hundred bucks and his government check to get high with her friends and Pinky, whose tardy return home provokes a terrifying tirade from Edwin.

SO FAR, ALL of Guirgis's plays have been written for members of the LAByrinth Theater Company, which has evolved into a much-admired producing organization assiduously nurtured by actor Philip Seymour Hoffman—its co-artistic director and chief fundraiser. It is perhaps this intimate association with a consistent company of actors, playwrights and directors—a rare enough phenomenon in today's institutionally driven theater culture—that has given Guirgis the chance to discover his playwriting muse. Hoffman's persistent support, too, has helped. As a star, he keeps the money and attention flowing toward LAByrinth. And he has assigned himself the task of directing all three of Guirgis's full-length plays.

Despite the impact of Guirgis's writing, not all of the characters and narrative threads in *Our Lady* are equally strong. The relationships between Rooftop and Inez, and Edwin and Pinky, are clearly and thoughtfully delineated, and Norca is a haunting creation. Yet we learn (and care) much less about other characters, such as the highly neurotic Marcia, the pantsless Vic or Sonia, who inexplicably hangs around (though never with her friend Marcia). The legless Father Lux is heavier on symbolism than humanity, even when he reveals himself as a bigot, coward and disbeliever. And Balthazar has a whiff of the stockroom about him, despite Solis's nuanced portrayal. (Though there's a terrible moment during Balthazar's interrogation of Norca when she goads him about his son's rape and murder, and we understand that the horror story he has told Vic is his own, tragic tale.) Finally, Guirgis's treatment of a gay couple comes close to flagrant stereotype: For the semi-closeted, from-the-hood Flip (Russell G. Jones), Guirgis creates a flaming-queen boyfriend Gail (Scott Hudson) that is unworthy of his talent for conjuring a real person from a few, well-chosen details. The conflict between Flip, who wants to pass as straight with his old friends, and Gail, a would-be actor whose chief concern is how gay he looks, doesn't resonate.

Sometimes, too, the play's structure works against its bid for psychological realism. The stories are often connected only by the characters' mutual mourning of Sister Rose, and they are fragmented into a series of short—sometimes too-short—scenes. In performance, they were rendered more fragmentary and disconnected by Hoffman's fast-paced, scene-blackout-scene direction. Famous for his nuanced roles on stage and screen, Hoffman is less skilled as a director—Guirgis's *Arabia* was his first directorial assignment—and his pacing in *Our Lady* emphasized the playwright's dramaturgical weaknesses. And Narelle Sissons's set—perfectly proper, perfectly forlorn—was a shade too realistic to encompass all the changes in scene. Although the action moved from the funeral home to a church to a bar, Sissons's design never really let us leave the waiting room. While this helped remind us why the characters have assembled—the script goes for long stretches without any reference to Sister Rose—it also inhibited the visual portrait of the neighborhood.

IF *OUR LADY* doesn't yield an entirely satisfying resolution, it's because the audience is subjected to the same bait-and-switch that the characters experience. The author introduces Sister Rose's pilfered body, and we expect that sorry event to spur on the story. Instead, we get another plot—centered on a funereal reunion—and then that story unfolds in a series of vignettes: mostly two-way conversations and arguments that end when half of Sister Rose's body has been recovered. Seeing *Our Lady* is a little like sitting on the subway, eavesdropping on a series of intense conversations among strangers, who get off before you have a chance to take the measure of their lives.

We are not, however, indifferent to their fates. Indeed, it is remarkable how much we come to care about these characters and to see the connections between their lives and our own. This is the great gift of theater, and Guirgis has it.

2002–2003 Best Play

STONE COLD DEAD SERIOUS

By Adam Rapp

○ ○ ○ ○ ○

Essay by Jeffrey Eric Jenkins

CLIFF: Who're you, anyway?

WYNNE: Who *am* I?

CLIFF: I ain't never seen you before

WYNNE: Dude, I'm your son.

CLIFF: My son don't got blue hair. His hair's black. Blackest hair I ever seen. His name is Wynnewood. Wynnewood Jericho Ledbetter. Who're you—Fuckhead Joe?

WYNNE: Pop, it's me, man—Wynne.

WHO AM I? It's the classic teenage existential question and it is scrawled throughout the text of Adam Rapp's *Stone Cold Dead Serious*, which had its New York premiere April 7, 2003, by the Edge Theater Company at Chashama. What makes Rapp's inscription of it as compelling as some of his dramatic forebears—Eugene O'Neill, Arthur Miller and Sam Shepard come immediately to mind—is the path his hero takes as he seeks to define himself. It's a journey of discovery with a dark, violent overtone in which the audience bears witness to a blistering fairy tale for the new century.

That the play bears some similarity to earlier dramatists of the family dynamic should come as no surprise. Throughout the 20th century, young people constructing identities in relation to family—or in contradistinction to it—became the all-American way of achieving autonomy (and creating drama). And Wynne Ledbetter in *Stone Cold Dead Serious* is, for good and ill, a disaffected 16-year-old finding his way. Whether Rapp intended it or not, Alexis de Tocqueville's vision of American democracy runs through the play like the electric current from Wynne's taser gun. The play reflects, tellingly, an American attitude about identity that Tocqueville observed:

> It is in the West that one can see democracy in its most extreme form. In these states, in some sense *improvisations of fortune*, the inhabitants have arrived only yesterday in the land where they dwell. They hardly know one another, and each man is ignorant of his nearest neighbor's history. [emphasis added]

Pretty knives: Guy Boyd and Matthew Stadelmann in Stone Cold Dead
Serious. *Photo: Steven Freeman*

With this country's official rejection of aristocratic ties and the aggrandizement
of continuous personal reinvention, the lingering "American ideal" leads
almost inexorably to modern examinations of family and self. "Who am I?,"
indeed.

THE "IMPROVISATIONS OF FORTUNE" to which Tocqueville refers imply
a metatheatricality in everyday life: an acting out or creation of who we
think we might become that is a fetish of American identity. In *Stone Cold
Dead Serious*, Wynne (honestly rendered by Matthew Stadelmann) is about
to start on his path when the play's action begins. He plans to travel from
his Illinois home to New York—reversing the typical westward flow—where
he will compete as a finalist in the live-action version of a video game he
has mastered. Three finalists—Wynne and two others—will challenge three
Kung Fu masters in a fight to the death that will be televised as a live event.
The prize? The capitalist dream of $1 million.

But before Wynne can begin his excellent adventure, he must first
deal with the quotidian details of his existence: his semi-comatose father,
Cliff, is incontinent and he's addicted to painkillers and to the home-shopping
channel on television; his depraved sister, Shaylee, comes looking for money,
offering him sex in exchange; and his mother, Linda, tries to hold everything
together by waiting tables for a living and serving takeout lasagna on trays

parked before the television set. (It's no accident that the television is centerstage and huge—its blue light is the flicker of life to these folks.)

> CLIFF: Four-fifty for a Tiger Woods rookie card. Must be blue book value.
> WYNNE: It's *two payments* of four-fifty.
> CLIFF: Two payments?
> WYNNE: Yeah, man—it's called the Flexplan. That's nine hundred bucks.
> CLIFF: Well, I can't afford that.
> WYNNE: Nobody can afford that. The Flexplan is fuckin' larceny.

In Rapp's play, the "reality" on television is a counter-world from which its characters can scarcely avert their eyes. Home shopping becomes the lottery you might actually win: "There is a limited number of units available and time is running out. Call now!" Cliff, Wynne's confused father, is always ready to go for the goods offered on the airwaves. And the family expends its efforts trying to keep him from amassing credit card bills while he convalesces from a job-related injury.

> CLIFF: When I was sixteen I joined a band of glaziers.
> WYNNE: I know. There were hundreds of you and you'd follow tornadoes around on a tour bus.
> CLIFF: That's right. We'd follow the tomatoes around.
> WYNNE: Tornadoes.
> CLIFF: We'd fix all the greenhouses. I used to read the weather maps. Look for the tomatoes. [. . .]

This father figure is a Midwestern malapropist who confuses Muhammad Ali with Mahatma Gandhi ("Mahatma Gandhi was the greatest fighter that ever lived! Float like a bumble bee sting like a sticka butter! Mahatma Gandhi!"), calls a willow tree "wilma" and refers to mercenaries as "macaronies." The playwright uses him as a kind of comic foil—and he is funny (particularly in Guy Boyd's detailed performance). But Cliff's addiction and his addled behavior are partly due to finding himself lacking control over his body and without resources for treatment—which echoes Willy Loman's struggle in *Death of a Salesman*:

> WILLY: [. . .] You mustn't tell me you've got people to see—I put 34 years into this firm, Howard, and now I can't pay my insurance! You can't eat the orange and throw the peel away—a man is not a piece of fruit! [. . .]

But Willy's befogged consciousness (and his anger) aren't pharmaceutically induced—Cliff's misery is almost beyond his own comprehension.

The struggles of the working class run throughout this play, but Rapp doesn't indulge in victimology. These characters never feel sorry for themselves and neither do we. The Ledbetters are members of a permanent underclass in US society who work hard and hope for the best when obsolescence applies to people as well as goods. These people buy what they can (and cannot) afford. The parents turn for solace to religion or the mind-numbing pleasure of the television set. The children see their parents' lives awaiting them in adulthood so they tunnel into fantasy, substance abuse, prostitution. Through it all, though, even when spouting foul language, there is an easy bond, a pleasure in one another's company.

As families do, they employ their own tropes to foster communication. In one of these configurations, Cliff responds to a jibe or a critical comment from Linda or Shaylee with a dismissive "Ha." The comeback is the same:

> LINDA: Excuse you.
> CLIFF: Ha.
> LINDA: You're the Ha.

Later, when Shaylee is in the hospital, she and her father comfort each other by replaying this childish word game just like old times:

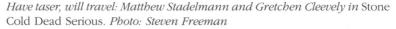

Have taser, will travel: Matthew Stadelmann and Gretchen Cleevely in Stone Cold Dead Serious. *Photo: Steven Freeman*

> SHAYLEE: Why you so dressed up, you goin' to the prom or somethin'?
> CLIFF: Ha.
> SHAYLEE: You're the Ha.

What's a "Ha"? In this case it's a familial code that gently cinches the ties that bind, the verbal equivalent of comfort food in a society that provides little ease.

WHEN SHE COMES home from work with dinner, Linda is skeptical about the source for the wad of cash her son offers to help with the bills. Wynne tells her that he fixes computers in his spare time, but she suspects something darker at work:

> LINDA: You didn't go in his Lexus with him, did you?
> WYNNE: I told you I fixed his hard drive. It wouldn't spin down right, I fixed it.
> LINDA: You're tryin' to tell me he gave you four hundred bucks for fixin' his computer.
> WYNNE: Just take the money, Ma.
> (She takes it, folds it into her bra. She starts to cry.)
> WYNNE: Ma.

Throughout the first section of the play, there are several references to Wynne working on computers—he even fantasizes about having his own computer business with his mom working for him—so we're inclined to think that Linda is just being a too-protective mother. (Undermining Linda's position as protector, though, is her ultimate willingness—even if reluctant—to let her 16-year-old son hitchhike to New York where he will battle to the death for money.)

After Wynne departs for New York there is a clever scene shift performed—as are others—by a group of black-clad, hooded "ninjas" who both lighten the mood and create a sense of destiny at work. When the change is complete, we see Wynne seated in an automobile driven by the actor who plays his father. At first, this casting seems innocuous—the play premiered Off Off Broadway where double casting is often the norm—but a shuddery creepiness arises as the scene unfolds.

Jack, the driver, is a traveling knife salesman who likes to listen to Chuck Mangione and smoke pot as he tools down the highway. Indeed, he sells "Cutco" products, which, it happens, is the brand Wynne's father bought from the home-shopping channel. The travelers discuss knives, *seppuku* (ritual disembowelment) and women before Jack proposes that Wynne perform oral sex on him. Although Wynne isn't eager to do it, neither does he react strongly to the suggestion—after all, it is rainy, cold and dark out on the highway. He agrees to go along with Jack's idea for $100, but the older man is warned "if you blow your load in my mouth, I'll Cutco your fuckin' balls off." As the lights fade to black, we realize that Linda's fears about where her son got his money might not be baseless—and we begin to ponder the darker psychological implications of doubling Cliff and Jack.

We're not allowed to think for long, though, because the ninjas appear suddenly to make another clever set change while Linda works in the Ledbetters' kitchen. The development of this amusing scenic technique by Rapp, scene designer David Korins and director Carolyn Cantor, disrupts the play's bleak psychological underpinnings.

Following the set change, Linda (Betsy Aidem in a rich performance) speaks from the tiny kitchen about her newfound fascination with saints while Cliff seems transported into a fantasy where his folded bathrobe is his baby daughter, Shaylee. He finally lies on the sofa and passes out just before the real Shaylee enters wearing a nightgown, bleeding profusely from cuts she has made with one of her father's knives. She had gone upstairs earlier, when Wynne was still at home, and apparently never left. Shaylee (played with gritty honesty by the versatile Gretchen Cleevely) lies atop her father as she, too, loses consciousness in a tragic, sacrificial image that counterpoints Linda's monologue on the beauty of the saints.

THE SECOND ACT opens in a tiny room in New York's East Village that Wynne shares with Sharice, a mute young woman who is also a contest finalist. She and Wynne have traveled to New York together from her home in Indiana. Before they even met in person, though, Wynne had fantasized that she would be his dream girl: Because she can't talk? Because she's a video-game whiz? Just because? We never find out why Wynne decides that she's "the one," but we suspect it's because she's from somewhere beyond his family.

As it turns out, Wynne and Sharice have an affinity for one another, but the character is played by the same actor (Cleevely) who plays his sister. There are distinct differences between Sharice and Shaylee: one mute, the other vociferous; one competent, the other a wreck. Despite the limitations of her voiceless role, Cleevely makes Sharice a force onstage. And we begin to further appreciate the inversions Rapp has located throughout his play. Just as we begin to consider, again, the playwright's intentions regarding character doubling, in walks Snake Lady—played by the same actor who plays Linda (Aidem). Snake Lady is a walking, talking

Like happy families? Betsy Aidem, Matthew Stadelmann and Guy Boyd in Stone Cold Dead Serious. *Photo: Steven Freeman*

freak show covered in tattoos and oozing sexual adventure. She's a temptress who invites the young couple to "get a little freaky":

> SNAKE LADY: [. . .] You know what freaky is?
> WYNNE: Um. Yeah.
> SNAKE LADY: Yeah, I bet you do. You ever been freaked?
> WYNNE: I've been freaked.

After Snake Lady leaves, Sharice and Wynne get involved in lovemaking—although he nervously postpones it with a phone call to his mother and a check of the television channels. It's apparent that despite how he earns money, he is a novice when it comes to his own pleasure. The playwright, though, isn't finished making us question Wynne's forming identity. While flipping through the channels, Wynne happens on pornography and they watch for a few moments. He tells Sharice about another film that we recognize as parallel to his own experience:

> WYNNE: There's this one where this chick drives around in a Lamborghini and picks up hitchhikers and sucks their dicks for gas money. The weird thing is, you can't tell if she's suckin' dick 'cause she likes it or if she really needs gas money. But on a symbolic level that's what sorta makes the movie work. Metaphors, you know? [. . .]

THIS IS QUITE a journey. Wynne travels an adventurous path aimed at making his own way while battling to win enough money to start a company, employ his mom, get surgery for his dad, help his sister get "clean" and buy central air conditioning for the home. In short, he leaves his family not merely to remake his life but to remake the world. Along the way, he also enacts a little Freudian drama. Think of it: sex with older men, a voiceless girl, all those knives and Kung Fu swords—as Wynne says in the speech above, "Metaphors, you know?"

In an e-mail exchange, I asked Rapp about the doubling. He responded:

> I had always intended for the parents and the sister to double in a kind of *Wizard of Oz*-like picaresque journey. So at the end Wynne would almost feel like "you were there, and you were there," etc. I also wanted that to happen because of the notion that you can't ever really escape your family.

Click your heels three times and repeat after me: Sigmund Freud meets L. Frank Baum. (Interestingly, Freud and Baum were born in the same year, 1856, and the original version of *The Interpretation of Dreams* appeared in 1900—as did *The Wonderful Wizard of Oz*.) Rapp, though, seems not to subscribe to Tocqueville's vision of the individual moving beyond family identity to reinvent himself. His character seems determined to reinvent himself *within* the family.

Where Rapp draws obvious influence is from the plays of Sam Shepard that deal with identity and its inversion—particularly in *Buried Child* and *True West*. In each of these Shepard plays, characters face the familial Other and become it—or fail. Cliff's inability to recognize Wynne, as quoted in the epigraph, could have been taken from a scene between Vince and Dodge (grandson and grandfather) in *Buried Child*. Indeed, Dodge's lack of recognition when he sees his grandson—along with other bits of disorienting family behavior—causes Vince to get into his car and drive away. But he returns:

> VINCE: [. . .] I could see myself in the windshield. My face. My eyes. I studied my face. Studied everything about it as though I was looking at another man. [. . .] In the windshield I watched him breathe as though he was frozen in time and every breath marked him. [. . .] His face became his father's face. [. . .] And his father's face changed to his grandfather's face. [. . .] Clear on back to faces I'd never seen before but still recognized. Still recognized the bones underneath. [. . .] I followed my family clear into Iowa. [. . .] Straight back as far as they'd take me. Then it all dissolved. Everything dissolved. Just like that.

When Vince returns in *Buried Child*, he has become the thing that he fled—the new head of the family. And that's where Rapp seems to lead Wynne.

FOLLOWING THE LOVE scene between Wynne and Sharice, we are whisked solemnly (via a ritualized ninja change) into a brilliant white hospital room where Shaylee lies in a bed. Cliff—whose hands are bandaged—watches television and shifts uncomfortably. A scene of reconciliation gradually evolves between the father and daughter; when Linda arrives a quiet momentum toward family healing builds—though not without tension.

Suddenly, Linda realizes that it's time to watch Wynne battle in the "Tang Dynasty Superchampionship." The family focuses on a small hospital television as a brutally violent battle unfolds—complete with blood, gore and beheadings. Wynne and Sharice engage the three Kung Fu masters without help because the third finalist has backed out. But the audience only hears about the carnage from an announcer with an Australian accent (played by the author's brother, Anthony Rapp). The young lovers hold their own until Sharice hesitates to kill one of the masters, leading to her gruesome death. Wynne ultimately finishes off the men who beheaded his beloved, is pronounced the winner and proceeds to attempt *seppuku*.

In the final scene, we see Wynne in the same hospital bed that his sister previously occupied. His head is shaved and tattooed with the blue star that marks him as a champion. Shaylee tells him that the house is paid off, Cliff is seeing a doctor and that she is staying clean and about to go back to school. A tube prevents Wynne from speaking, but he writes notes and begs his sister to smother him. She regards his misery, braces his pillow and considers killing him. Finally, though, she lies next to him on the bed and tries to revivify old times. This family has been through much and Shaylee wants Wynne—the warrior who has won and lost—to be around for the story about to be constructed:

> SHAYLEE: 'Cause I just want us to be happy again. And not just not-sad. Happy.

STONE COLD DEAD SERIOUS sets the American Dream on its ear. Through pungent imagery, stark humor and language ranging from the vulgar to the poetic, Rapp reminds his audience that self-actualization celebrated by the privileged is merely the "pipe dream" of the growing underclass. There is no "Tang Dynasty Superchampionship"—though with the direction television is headed there may be someday soon—and the struggles of the working poor tend to keep them working and poor.

If we look closely, Rapp seems almost to mock the American Dream of creating one's own life and identity—but he doesn't mock the people who are denied it. With 13 plays to his credit, Rapp's families—and there is often a family even if no one is related by blood—are connected by mutual need. His characters and situations tend to the bleak: a production of *Finer Noble Gases* at the 2002 Humana Festival of New American Plays in Louisville saw people head for the exits when bodily functions became part of the performance. Beneath the surface, though, his work consistently glimmers with a ray of hope for the possibility of survival against the odds.

Those who suggest that Rapp—now in his mid-30s—writes too many plays filled with too many ideas (you know who you are), should try to recall that Eugene O'Neill was a writing machine in his early career. Remember *Abortion* or *The Movie Man*? But the capstone of O'Neill's career, *Long Day's Journey Into Night*, wasn't written until he was in his 50s.

This isn't to say that Rapp is the next O'Neill, but he is the next Rapp. And it'll be interesting to see what kind of American identity he creates on his own journey. Let's hope he keeps writing too many plays with too many ideas—it's preferable to most of the alternatives.

2002–2003 Best Play

TAKE ME OUT

By Richard Greenberg

○ ○ ○ ○ ○

Essay by Christopher Rawson

KIPPY: The whole mess started in eighteen something-something when Abner Doubleday (this never happened) gathered a group of friends into a sylvan vale and mapped out a diamond made of four bases set ninety feet apart . . . No

The whole mess started with a really beautiful *park*. And in the park were a man, a woman, a serpent, and this *tree*.

THAT'S THE BACKGROUND proposed jokingly, but seriously, too, by Kippy Sunderstrom, brainy shortstop of the New York Empires in Richard Greenberg's sharp, Tony Award-winning comedy, *Take Me Out*. Kippy is the play's chief narrator, described with only a hint of irony by the central figure, superstar Darren Lemming, as "the most intelligent man in major league baseball." So, in setting up the story right at the play's start, Kippy archly calls for the "*back*-story" and takes us back . . . and then *way* back. It's a literary joke about how to tell a story, but it also effectively introduces the Eden image that is central to baseball mythology and to the expulsion from Eden motif in *Take Me Out*. And the flashiness of Kippy's joke does something else: Even while giving us reason to respect him as a witty narrative guide, it should remind us he is also a character. Can we trust him?

Heady stuff, baseball. Theater, too. Like theater, sports can be a simple pastime but also passion, craft, business and sometimes art. And among American sports, the preeminent locus of nostalgia, tradition and history is baseball, with a structure of meaning capable of ingenious expansion. So surely does baseball seem one big extended metaphor for American culture that we might imagine its entire institutional history and structure have evolved just to give writers a rich field of dreams within which to luxuriate. As declared by the title of a traveling exhibit from the Baseball Hall of Fame in Cooperstown, now making its leisurely progress around the country, Baseball Is America.

Leading man: Daniel Sunjata in Take Me Out. *Photo: Joan Marcus*

The best proof of that proposition is the distinguished array of novels celebrating the metaphoric riches of baseball. Oddly, though, there have been few successful plays with baseball as their subject, so *Take Me Out* is able to draw on theatrically underused emotional and conceptual material. But to the extent that "baseball is America" is true (or true enough), it seems perverse that *Take Me Out* premiered in London. It appeared in a five-play "American Imports" series at the Donmar Warehouse in summer 2002, directed by Joe Mantello with an American cast—pretty much the production that went to Broadway after a run at Off Broadway's Joseph Papp Public Theater. And in spite of their disbelief that baseball provides a sufficiently capacious metaphor for America, the British critics, judging by 16 reviews I read in a marathon of cross-cultural mirror-gazing, generally loved it.

This is because, although some of the play's fun does draw on what one knows about baseball, *Take Me Out* is about baseball only in the important but partial way that *Copenhagen* is about physics or *Angels in America* about AIDS. It's the people that matter. Structurally, *Take Me Out* is an old-fashioned three-act play (though with just one intermission on Broadway) with suspenseful curtain lines and lots of plot twists. Its chief dynamic is the evolving relationship among the central characters; its chief pleasure is the considerable snap and crackle of Greenberg's comic writing. But *Take Me Out* is also about democracy, race, culture wars, sexual anxiety, political correctness, celebrity and the intersection of all this with self, sport and art.

THE CENTRAL FIGURE is Darren Lemming, handsome and effortlessly successful half-black superstar outfielder for the "world champion Empires"—i.e., pretty transparently, the historically dominant and endlessly self-regarding New York Yankees. Kippy describes Darren as "a five-tool player of such incredible grace he made you suspect there was a sixth tool," which introduces the mystical dimension toward which baseball and its heroes inevitably tend. But as the play starts, Darren casually and obliquely lets it be known he is gay. Apparently he has no specific agenda for this revelation, not even a lover. He tells the philosophical Kippy: "If I'm gonna have sex—and I *am* because I'm young and rich and famous and talented and handsome so it's a *law*—I'd rather do it with a guy, but when all is said and done, Kippy? I'd rather just play ball."

If Darren's revelation does have a motive, it seems to be self-confident honesty, triggered (we later learn) by a black superstar from another team. Clearly, Darren's invincible ego is involved. "I don't mean for this to be a distraction," he says. "I'm hoping this is gonna ward off distraction." He even handles what he should realize will become a media sensation with a light touch: "I hope this sends a message that it's okay. [. . .] Any young man, creed, whatever, can go out there and become a ballplayer. Or an interior decorator. (*He smiles beguilingly.*)" But Greenberg does not focus on the media. Instead, he takes the harder path and features the team. The male Eden of the locker room has now been shattered. "And they knew that they were naked," Genesis says, and the team members certainly do in a mass shower scene in which none of them now knows where to look. The audience, of course, looks everywhere.

Kippy narrates the twists and turns that follow, including a media frenzy, dissension on a multi-ethnic team where players (literally) don't speak the same language, bigoted remarks by a mullet-maned relief ace and the intervention of the other black superstar. More comic narrative intervention comes from Mason Marzac, a repressed gay accountant who becomes Darren's new business manager and waxes ecstatic over the new (to him) riches of baseball. Here's a taste of Mason's new-found infatuation:

> MASON: [B]aseball is better than Democracy—or at least than Democracy as it's practiced in this country—because unlike Democracy, baseball acknowledges loss.
>
> While conservatives tell you, leave things alone and no one will lose, and liberals tell you, interfere a lot and no one will lose, baseball says: someone will lose. Not only *says* it—insists upon it!
>
> So that baseball achieves the tragic vision that Democracy evades. Evades *and* embodies.
>
> Democracy is lovely, but baseball's more mature.

In this and other paeans to baseball, Mason recapitulates Greenberg's own enraptured discovery. As Greenberg told *American Theatre*:

> That sort of Wordsworthian experience of baseball being unconsciously lodged in us—it certainly happened to me. And that's what I uncovered writing this play. It was almost an enormous relief coming to baseball so late in my life—it conjured up these memories I didn't even know I had, but of course I did. It's like that closing sentence in Jim Bouton's *Ball Four*: "You spend a good piece of your life gripping a baseball, and in the end it turns out that it was the other way around all the time."

The arrival of Mason as a quasi-narrative, passionate authorial voice naturally problematizes Kippy's position in the audience's mind. But more immediately, Mason opens up the gay theme, telling us Darren is the new gay poster guy:

> DARREN: Oh. That wasn't why I did it.
>
> MASON: Even so, it was tremendously brave.
>
> DARREN: It's only brave if ya think somethin' *bad*'s gonna happen. They don't . . . to me.
>
> MASON: . . . Never?
>
> DARREN: Pretty much.
>
> MASON: Why is that?
>
> DARREN: Because I'm in baseball. And so is God, Mason. So is God.
>
> MASON: That's more-or-less your all-purpose punch line, isn't it?
>
> DARREN: No, I *mean* it this time. Look around you: Typhoons, earthquakes, avalanches. War. He's absent. The Holocaust. Nowhere. That's not how He works. He's got a whimsical nature. He makes Himself known in stupid stuff. Trivia. Baseball. The Grammys. But especially baseball.

With their new distraction, the Empires start losing, until they bring up the eccentric relief pitcher, Shane Mungitt, whose provocative name suggests both mythic lone hero and white trash mongrel. "And He Came Unto Us," says Kippy, with ironic religious overtones. Shane is a closer who, in one of the oddest stage directions since "exit, pursued by a bear," Greenberg tells us "throws like a dybbuk." Shane is also a taciturn puzzlement. Kippy goads him and then, the thoughtful liberal, says he understands that Shane's lack of words is due to educational deprivation. But in a television interview, the words come: Describing the Empires clubhouse, Shane says, "I don't mind the colored people—the gooks an' the spics an' the coons an' like that. But *every night* t'have'ta take a shower with a *faggot*!?" It's a great first-act curtain.

THE SNAKE IS loose in Eden. The first response is smothering, knee-jerk support for Darren, which he takes as an insult: "Don't you have compassion for me, you *envy* me, this is how it is with me, this is how it's always been," he insists.

> DARREN: . . . I don't *have* a secret, Kippy.
> I *am* a secret.
>
> KIPPY: Even from me?
>
> (*A beat. The question slides away.*)

That proves important, of course. Kippy cannot hide in narrative privilege forever. Reminiscent of the guilty Gene in John Knowles's *A Separate Peace*, his own love for and jealousy of Darren remains slippery, unplumbed.

You did what? Daniel Sunjata, Neal Huff and Frederick Weller in Take Me Out. *Photo: Joan Marcus*

Meanwhile, the multi-ethnic Empires, including two Hispanics and a Japanese, get antsy. Greenberg indulges in some dialogue in Spanish and Japanese, complete with funny "translation" by the ever-condescending Kippy. Then Kippy continues with his self-appointed documentary role, describing, "The Letter. The famous letter that changed everything," in which Shane pleads his own ignorance. "The spelling was so horrible—it was *authentic* somehow," Kippy says. Greenberg supplies a funny scene between Darren and Skipper, the team manager, who could be modeled on one of the witless enigmatics in Bouton's book. Then there's a climactic game against Davey Battle's team—he's the other black superstar—filled with improbabilities, which ends with Shane throwing a pitch that kills Battle. End of Act II.

TALK ABOUT YOUR well-made play! The third act begins with one of those great Greenberg moments where balanced expression meets incisive content. The Japanese pitcher Kawabata soliloquizes about the tragedy:

> KAWABATA: Why must things have meanings?
> *This* is how I try to be an American. I make my mind a prairie.
> I think nothing. I think of great flat stretches of nothing.

But lest we begin to think metaphor and parable are paramount, the plot clamors back into focus. Under Kippy's guidance, we get further backstory and sidestory. Before the lethal game, after being taunted in the shower by Darren, Shane had been heard to say, "I'm gonna *kill* somebody—I'm gonna take somebody out." And there's a further complicating flashback: a pre-game scene between Darren and a Davey full of himself and his pompous locutions, who calls Darren a pervert.

"So now we start the Kafkaesque portion of the evening," says Kippy. "Well, Kafka-lite, anyway . . . Dekaf-ka." He and Darren visit Shane, who is suspended from baseball but remains clueless and unregenerate. Here, we're tangled in an impossible situation and messy emotions. Kippy learns about Darren's final scene with Davey and his subsequent provocation of Shane, while Darren and the audience are astonished to learn that Kippy actually wrote Shane's "famous letter." Everyone is implicated and everyone must confront the guilt of his unplumbed desires. "And, yeah, we won the World Series."

But what of Mason? As the baseball events spiral down into tragedy, the repressed accountant has been spiraling upward into rejuvenating comedy, dizzied by his delight in baseball, which is at least partly sublimation of his inevitable love for the beautiful, nonchalant (to him) Darren. Mason's self-deprecation isn't fully believable, except as passive-aggressive stance. But he has great charm, especially as performed by the very likable Denis O'Hare, who won a Tony Award for the role. And since he is Greenberg's alter ego, it fits the play's inner creative propulsion to contrive an upbeat ending to trump the tragic events. So Darren begins to notice Mason. There's even a ring exchanged, hinting of the marriage with which comedy traditionally ends. This audience-friendly ending may be a bit of a cop-out, but it doesn't compromise the central enigmas of human character.

And what of Kippy, played with wiry intelligence by Neal Huff? He starts out smarter than we expect, with his references to social psychology and *Billy Budd*—suggesting Greenberg's analogous moral seriousness—as well as insights into the team. "Everybody loves Darren but with the Skipper it's different," Kippy explains: "He thinks he *invented* Darren." Kippy may think he's invented Darren, too, but how can we doubt his persuasive voice? Gradually, of course, we do: Kippy continues his documentary role, but Mason attracts our affection. And when Kippy's manipulation becomes clear, the thoughtful audience must reevaluate. Initially, Kippy serves to rebuke our own condescension toward ballplayers. But he is gradually revealed as unreliable, the storyteller who is an interested party to the story he tells. We may question his narrative, especially the way he speaks for the players of color—providing his own translations for the Hispanics and a joke translation for the Japanese. But above all, Kippy's own relationship with Darren remains an area of squeamish avoidance. Is that a fault in the play or (my choice) in Kippy?

Kippy and Mason, the two intellectualizing narrators, make fable instructive, even as they participate in the ongoing story that exemplifies or undercuts the moral they imagine. Kippy and Mason may seem too articulate and Darren too little, but articulation, the play teaches, is not always truth. For example, Mason's praise of baseball clearly goes over the top. Its emotional energy is captivating, but baseball is not the democratic leveler its apologists suggest. It is racist, it privileges wealth and it stigmatizes the uneducated. Baseball is America.

Though Darren is often silent, in his interaction with Kippy, Davey and Mason, we see how insightful he can be—though he doesn't much want to be insightful, he just wants to *be*. Maybe that's why he's more trustworthy. His riffs are shorter than the others, as when he complains about financial contributions made as gifts:

> DARREN: 'Stead of another meaningless, pretty *object*, they're givin' you the gift of phony concern. I don't want that. 'f I do some big charitable thing, I want it to be somethin' I give a shit about."

MASON: Absolutely.

(*Beat.*)

So what do you give a shit about?

(*Pause.*)

(*Longer pause.*)

DARREN: Let me get back to ya on that one.

This is Darren's flaw. Maybe Mason helps him grow out of it. But Darren, played with effortless charisma by Daniel Sunjata, remains the central enigma that asks how we know who we are and how we make that known.

ARTICULATENESS MAY NOT always demonstrate truth in characters, but it certainly attracts an audience. Greenberg's writing and Joe Mantello's direction are so smart that they engage us independent of the plot. Baseball, Kippy tells us, is "one of the few realms of American life in which people of color are routinely adulated by people of pallor." Describing some of his clients, Mason calls them, "Not even supermodels. The kind that go to restaurants and are barely snide." And Greenberg can also turn demotic when needed.

In the land of instructive fable, it's not surprising that even names suggest meaning: Shane Mungitt, Darren Lemming (he's the reverse of a Lemming), Davey Battle. Kippy's name, Sunderstrom, clearly Swedish in origin, could well mean river-sunderer, a parting of the Red Sea image. Perhaps more interesting are the names of real players who have been suggested as models. Shane immediately brings to mind John Rocker, another relief pitcher with offensive ethnic views, and Darren has been likened to Derek Jeter, though perhaps only by Yankees fans who overrate Jeter's superstardom. Others will have to overlook the oddity of basing a fantasy on having the Yankees' thinly-disguised avatars triumph. Usually fantasies go the other way, as in the most familiar baseball-based stage show, *Damn Yankees*, based on a story in which it's revealed that the Devil is (of course) a Yankees fan.

The play's title is rich with implication as it applies to baseball (take me out of the game or to the game), dating, sexual preference ("outing"), sexual longing (suggesting orgasm) and even fantasies of murder or death, as in Shane's "I'm gonna take somebody out." In response to Darren's intimation that he's contemplating sudden retirement, Mason defends baseball: "Life is so . . . tiny, so *daily*. This [baseball] . . . you . . . take me out of it . . ." Yes, it takes us out of ourselves. As Greenberg has Kippy say to end the play, "What will we do till spring?"

2002–2003 Best Play

TALKING HEADS

By Alan Bennett

○ ○ ○ ○ ○

Essay by Jeffrey Sweet

MISS FOZZARD: I suppose there's a word for what I'm doing, but I skirt around it.

ALAN BENNETT FIRST made a name for himself in the 1960s as one of the quartet of young writer-performers who created *Beyond the Fringe*, a satiric revue that challenged the complacency of postwar Britain. In his signature turn, "Take a Pew," he played a clergyman who chose an obscure text from the Bible ("But my brother Esau is an hairy man, but I am a smooth man") and built on it a sermon comprised of conventional sentiments upholstered in platitudes carried to an absurd length. The clergyman didn't know the audience thought he was a fool (endearing, yes, but a fool nonetheless); he purred away what he thought passed muster as spiritual guidance, and the audience howled.

Much of Bennett's work in *Talking Heads* is built on a similar model. In many of the monologues, a character earnestly relates her thoughts and experiences (10 of the 12 pieces are for women), and the audience sees through her affirmations to make its own evaluations.

THE TITLE *TALKING Heads* is derived from a derogatory term referring to what television producers believe makes boring programming—a camera trained on a single speaker for a long time. Bennett took the challenge implicit in the term and wrote six pieces—roughly a half-hour each—comprised of solo performers facing a camera. First broadcast in 1987 to acclaim, their success led him to return to the form a decade later to write an additional six. Various combinations of the pieces have been produced under the title *Talking Heads* on stages in London, Los Angeles and Chicago. Usually these performances have been made up of three selections. In New York, there were two programs of three pieces each. A seventh piece, *Waiting for the Telegram*, was substituted when the performer of one of the original six was unavailable for a performance.

111

Mama's boy: Daniel Davis in A Chip in the Sugar *from* Talking Heads. *Photo: Carol Rosegg*

What we have here is not a conventional theatrical offering. Material that was originally written for television has been transferred to the stage, and, since the compositions of the programs may vary from production to production, the result can hardly be called a play under the usual definition that qualifies a script for inclusion in this annual.

But rules should not be invoked to exclude first-rate work, and, whatever the composition of a given program under the title *Talking Heads*, Bennett's writing is indeed first rate.

IN *THE HAND of God*, Celia (Brenda Wehle) makes a series of miscalculations, the first of which is that she has our sympathy. She begins, "I won't touch pictures. I make it a rule. I've seen too many fingers get burned." She is an antique dealer and she has standards. She won't—as some struggling colleagues do—capitulate and sell jars of jam and chutney as a sideline. Visiting an ailing elderly neighbor named Miss Ventriss, Celia itemizes the many fine articles about the house and she induces the maid to promise to do what she can to channel the variety of splendid goods through Celia's hands should Miss Ventriss succumb.

When Miss Ventriss does succumb, however, a niece appears and makes an arrangement with another dealer. Tossing a bone to Celia, the niece gives her a box of odds and ends for a token five pounds. Celia sees nothing much in there except a distinctive-looking frame. She figures that if she substitutes a flower print for the smudgy drawing of a finger that's in the frame at the moment, she might be able to sell it for thirty pounds. Soon after, a young man comes into the shop. Celia can see that he's keen for the frame and finds herself making quite a good deal for it—a hundred pounds. He even takes it as is, without the flower print substituted. Not long after, it turns out that the drawing in the frame has been authenticated as a study Michelangelo did for God's finger in *The Last Supper*. A ring on the finger (which doesn't appear in the final painting) is clearly that of Michelangelo's patron, the Pope. "Very satirical apparently on Michelangelo's part," says Celia, "though I don't see the joke." The value? Maybe as much as ten million. To make matters worse, the young man tells the paper that he found it in "a junk shop." In the final lines, Celia reports she has made some chutney and is pleased it's selling. The woman who wouldn't touch pictures because she's seen too many fingers get burned has been burned by the picture of a finger.

The title character of *Miss Fozzard Finds Her Feet* is a woman of later years who has troubles with the feet in question. Her chiropodist is moving out of the area, but feeling a responsibility that her feet not fall into "the wrong hands," he has taken the liberty to scout a replacement. Miss Fozzard (Lynn Redgrave) spends a lot of time standing behind a counter as a saleslady. Or she did, before her brother Bernard had a stroke and she had to take time off to alternate with a part-time nurse to look after him. The new chiropodist turns out to be 70-year-old Mr. Dunderdale who tells her he took up the trade "so that I could kneel at the feet of thousands of women and my wife would never turn a hair." His wife is dead now. Miss Fozzard decides to return to her job and, drawing on some of her brother's money, engages a full-time nurse from Australia to take care of him. With the help of the nurse, Bernard's speech returns as do, apparently, other functions. Bernard recovers sufficiently to consider reopening his tobacconist's shop in partnership with the nurse.

In the meantime, Mr. Dunderdale has moved from caring for Miss Fozzard's feet to outfitting her with shoes for the purpose of her wearing them to walk on his back. He claims this gives him relief, but Miss Fozzard speculates the full truth may lie elsewhere. Bernard's hopes are dashed when the nurse takes off with his money, triggering another stroke that leaves him in worse shape than before. Miss Fozzard tells Mr. Dunderdale that this reversal in the family's fortunes means she can no longer afford his services. He makes a counter-proposal—he will now pay for *her* services. So, at the close of the piece, Miss Fozzard is able to support a full-time nurse for her brother between her earnings as a saleslady and the substantial something extra Mr. Dunderdale conveys to her in an envelope after each of their visits. When she tells him that, if they knew about it, people would find their arrangement a mite peculiar, Mr. Dunderdale responds, "Well, people would be wrong. We are just enthusiasts, Miss Fozzard, you and I and there's not enough enthusiasm in the world these days. Now if those Wellingtons are comfy I just want you in your own time and as slowly as you like very gently to mark time on my bottom." Miss Fozzard notes, "People keep telling me how well I look."

The middle-age man of *A Chip in the Sugar*, Graham (Daniel Davis), lives with his aging Mam who is a little unsteady on her feet and a little vague in her memory. But she's not too vague to remember a certain Mr. Turnbull when they encounter him. "How does he fit in vis-à-vis Dad?" Graham asks her. Mam tells him he was "pre-Dad." Mam and Mr. Turnbull have a good time together, mostly making little jokes at Graham's expense—about his dress, his hygiene, his occupational therapy. "I don't believe in mental illness," Mr. Turnbull says. "Nine times out of ten it's a case of pulling your socks up." To Graham's dismay, the relationship deepens.

Mam goes off on expeditions without Graham and she comes back echoing Turnbull's opinions that what's gone wrong with the world is the fault of various kind of coloreds. The two are talking marriage now. Turnbull speaks of making her home the base of operations and encouraging Graham to return to a hostel. Graham's salvation appears when Turnbull's daughter knocks at the door with the news that her father is already married and his wife is an invalid in a wheelchair. It seems Turnbull has something of a history of making promises to elderly women. Graham relays this to his mother who strikes back by telling him she knows the kind of magazines he hides and the pictures of naked men in them. But the next day, they're having an outing just as in pre-Turnbull days. They exchange professions of love and she puts her arm through his.

Her Big Chance introduces Lesley (Valerie Mahaffey), a self-described actress whose primary talent seems to be taking off her clothes. The tale she tells is of landing a bigger part in a movie than usual—though still with only a line or two and requiring her to take off her top—of the beds of various film people she somehow seems to find herself awakening in and of her cheerful determination to view everything as experience that will deepen what she believes is her art.

The lady in *A Lady of Letters* is a Miss Ruddock (Christine Ebersole), and the letters she posts are to various offices, institutions and authorities articulating her many concerns. Most she quotes sound trivial, but then she begins to write to the authorities about a family new to the neighborhood and her conclusion that the parents' frequent absence and the disappearance of their child must spell child neglect or child abuse. Except that doesn't turn out to be the case at all—the parents have been away to the hospital watching their son die of leukemia.

We discover Miss Ruddock has a history of abusing the post in this manner (she doesn't seem to have much of a life outside her correspondence) and, by not heeding official warnings about this behavior, she has finally crossed the line and made herself vulnerable to legal action. At the end, she is in a women's prison. She's taking a secretarial course (and doing so well the teacher predicts immediate employment after her release), learning from her fellow inmates about the mechanics of sex (not that she expects to indulge, but it's always good to have extra information), and helping some of the other women (including some guilty of crimes of violence) compose letters. And what do you know—she's happy.

Lost opportunity: Brenda Wehle in The Hand of God *from* Talking Heads. *Photo: Carol Rosegg*

Bed Among the Lentils concerns Susan (Kathleen Chalfant), a vicar's wife overcome with the tedium of her circumstance and the life of the vicarage. She finds some relief in the bottle, including some of the spirits used in her husband's sacraments. As oppressive as the dreary duties that come with her position are the aging ladies she nicknames the "fan club" who are ardent acolytes of her husband, Geoffrey.

One day, having sneaked a little more of the communion wine than is good for her, she gets into an argument with some of these women while arranging flowers in the church. She loses her footing and rolls down the altar stairs. The news of her accident as well as speculations as to its cause become the topic of gossip among the parish. Fleeing their shows of concern, she runs to a Mr. Ramesh, the 26-year-old Indian proprietor of a small shop with whom she has occasionally shared conversation on Indian life and religion. This time, the meeting is not for talk. He closes the shop and they go into the back room and make love. She continues to visit him, admitting to us that for the first time she understands what the fuss over sex is about. She continues to drink, however, until Mr. Ramesh asks if she needs to get drunk in order to have sex with a man of his color. This sends her to Alcoholics Anonymous. Seeing that his wife has sobered up, Susan's husband assumes that this is a great victory for his God and their love. He makes a great show of their joint victory and Susan plays wanly along. Then, one day, she learns that Mr. Ramesh has gone back to India. Ultimately, Susan is stuck with attending both church services and meetings of AA, not finding much difference between them.

As noted above, a seventh piece, *Waiting for the Telegram*, was added to the mix as an intermittent substitution. In this monologue, Violet (Frances Sternhagen) is a 95-year-old woman in a nursing home ruminating about her inadvertent exposure to some male equipment. "I saw this feller's what-do-you-call-it today," she says, and we're launched into a gauzy tale that conflates ancient memories of a boy who died in World War I with more recent encounters.

Although the title refers to a message that centenarians receive from the Crown on their 100th birthday, Violet is more fascinated by the quotidian details of her incidental flasher and, more importantly, her loving relationship with a male attendant named Francis. Though she has suffered a stroke, she is aware enough of her surroundings to know when it might be a good time to pretend she is unaware. On one occasion, she decides not to recognize her son. A bit frail at her advanced age, she still manages to offer a kind of dry hope that we can hold our own as time ticks away.

Post mistress: Christine Ebersole in A Lady of Letters *from* Talking Heads. *Photo: Carol Rosegg*

MOST DRAMA IS written about extraordinary people and extraordinary actions. Bennett's achievement here is to make compelling people who, at casual glance, would look mundane. He doesn't entirely suppress his own amusement (particularly in the case of Lesley, the actress) but he never violates the voices of his characters. As the author notes in his introduction to the published edition, "None of the narrators . . . is telling the whole story." Not that they intend to mislead, writes Bennett. "[T]hese narrators are artless. They don't quite know what they are saying and are telling a story to the meaning of which they are not entirely privy."

This strategy—employing an unreliable narrator—allows the audience to come to independent conclusions about the lives being examined. As Bennett observes, "[W]ith the rest of the story pictured and peopled by the viewer more effort is demanded of the imagination." In *A Chip in the Sugar*, for example, we can appreciate the terror the overage boy attached to his elderly mother feels when her affections threaten to drift elsewhere, and we certainly sympathize with him, but we also view him as a comic character.

What makes these works moving instead of simply ironic is the gallantry with which Bennett equips the characters—there is a determination to keep plugging though dogged by little failures. (Their lives aren't big enough for big failures.)

The narratives we most frequently encounter (whether in fictional constructs or in what we call the news) revolve around characters whose significance is pumped up to justify our attention: This criminal has committed the most heinous crime, that performer has won more awards of dubious value, the person over here has been involved in the biggest scandal since . . . the last biggest scandal. It can get numbing to constantly be pummeled with superlatives and hyperbole in relation to so many of the folks who intrude into our consciousness.

Bennett strikes a particular chord, I think, because he commands respect, attention and sympathy for those who belong to that vast majority rarely given the compliment of the attention of a narrative. That these characters with their minor crises can keep audiences rapt provides a welcome corrective to the artificially inflated figures who have become standard diet.

Directed by Michael Engler, all seven performers built characters of specificity, though some who claimed expertise in English vowels challenged the veracity of the American performers' accents. (Sometime they should hear what British actors do attempting a Southwestern American accent!) New York theatergoers are accustomed to getting meticulous work from Kathleen Chalfant, and she didn't disappoint in *Lentils*. Particularly surprising was the elegant Christine Ebersole transformed into the dowdy busybody of *Letters*. Daniel Davis has been a solid supporting actor for decades, and it was satisfying to see him display the accumulated craft of those years in *Chip*. The crowd-pleasing performance was Lynn Redgrave's turn as Miss Fozzard, particularly the perverse wriggle of pride she betrays at having become the most genteel of sex workers.

Bennett does in *Talking Heads* what Thornton Wilder did in *Our Town*—using precise detail and eschewing big effects, he gives respect to (and frequently makes heartbreaking) people whom one would otherwise probably not notice. In a passage in the Wilder play, the Stage Manager talks about artifacts being put into a time capsule to represent the town to the future. In some distant year, Bennett's gems will similarly make vivid the middle-class British life of our time as well as the war against loneliness and despair daily fought in snug rooms.

2002–2003 Best Play

YELLOWMAN

By Dael Orlandersmith

○ ○ ○ ○ ○

Essay by Michele Volansky

ALMA: I don't cast aside what is ugly—I don't wear sunglasses to be cool. I see things for what they are.

WHEN RUSSELL II. CHAMPA'S lights hit Dael Orlandersmith onstage at the Manhattan Theatre Club, the audience leaned forward. Her presence—solid, silent and serious—was a sight to behold. Here was the woman they had heard about: she of *The Gimmick*; of *Monster*; of *Beauty's Daughter*, her 1995 hit at American Place Theatre. They were ready to receive her story.

The first lines belong to the woman Orlandersmith portrays:

> ALMA: [M]y mother / women like her and more than likely her mother before her talked in Gullah/Geechie voices about how (VOICE) "da sun can make ya see tings dat ain't dere" or "dat heat is sumpin ya hear." (ALMA) Her statements always seemed to end in questions. [. . .] The question marks at the end of their statements were from women who knew their place and the fact that they had opinions about something as simple as sunrays pulled them from their place—the fact that they would question ANYTHING made them "uppity" in the eyes of their peers.
>
> [. . . W]omen like my mother and her mother before her toiled / tugged the soil right beside the men. They were dark therefore not considered pretty / they were dark and large—therefore sexless [. . .] they were to be pitied.

What this audience, in that first moment, didn't fully know was that this was not just Orlandersmith's story. The title of the piece implied another participant: a Yellow Man. This time, the story was to be shared.

Soon, Champa's lights shift. Focus is given to Howard W. Overshown as Eugene. We later learn he is Alma's childhood friend and ultimately, her lover.

> EUGENE: Black southern men seemed incredibly big—especially men who labored in heat or knew about that heat / sweat of Black men in

Blue Gene: Howard W. Overshown in Yellowman. *Photo: Joan Marcus*

the south / the sweat dripping off their bodies / their big bodies[. . . .] He was big, dark, handsome—my father? Oh yeah, my father was handsome. He didn't know it—that he was handsome [. . .] he'd turn to—rather on me / he'd turn on me and I was about nine—maybe ten but I think I was nine and he said (ROBERT) "Do you think I'm handsome Eugene?" and I said (EUGENE) "Yeah, Daddy." Then he stood over me / towering over me in all his blackness and said with incredible menace (ROBERT) "Do you think I'd be more handsome if I was high yella like you?"

"High yella." It's a term with which those in the predominantly white Manhattan Theatre Club audience might have been unfamiliar. It's a term that oozes degradation. But it opens the door to the story of *Yellowman*.

DAEL ORLANDERSMITH'S PULITZER Prize-finalist play tackles, on the surface, the trauma and tragedy of the love between Alma and Eugene, and the legacy they both endure due to the color of their skins. Hers is a darker shade than Eugene's—and it is in that difference that the two are drawn to one another.

Once the play begins to unfold, however, the issues become more complex—and startling. Under Blanka Zizka's careful direction of Orlandersmith and Overshown, and through the evolution of Orlandersmith's capable storytelling, *Yellowman* takes on the tone of a mystery—what is to become of these two? To whom do they each pledge allegiance? The fundamental human question of "Who am I?" is raised time and time again, in a myriad of different ways. And, most importantly, is it possible to understand, embrace and move forward from (or with) one's identity?

This notion of identity permeates the text of the play. We learn of difficult childhoods—Alma's mother Odelia clings to the notion of an unknown light-skinned stranger who will bring her out of poverty, while Eugene's father Robert (a dark-skinned man) grapples with having a lighter-skinned wife and son. We hear stories of schoolyard beatings and taunts, of isolation and loneliness, and of a resolution to *get away*—from oneself, from one's family, from one's very existence.

Both Alma and Eugene talk of their mothers' alcoholism, and the probable causes of this disease. Alma's mother, "horse-faced" and dark, yearns for her daughter to be light, delicate and green eyed so that Alma can "catch" a light-skinned man—and therefore move ahead in the world. When Alma's father John leaves, Odelia is left "panting like a dog on the tar road," a state of being that Alma vows never to replicate. Over and over, Alma revisits the torment of her mother—and the scar Odelia's desperation has imprinted upon her.

EUGENE'S OWN SCAR comes in the form of two generations of parental rejection. His maternal grandfather rejects his mother Thelma for marrying the dark-skinned Robert; in time, Robert rejects his son Eugene for being too light. Thelma's distress over this legacy leads her to the bottle and later, to her death. It also leaves a lasting imprint upon Eugene—damage that is revisited when he inherits his grandfather's house.

Maternal alcoholism is just one by-product of what Orlandersmith dubs "internal racism"; that is, the prejudice that takes place within a given race. In a 2002 interview with Kentucky Educational Television, Orlandersmith described this as

> the rift between light-skinned people and dark-skinned people, which has its roots in slavery. So in this particular case, I don't want to let anyone off the hook. The people that have enslaved, and the people

who have taken on being enslaved and taken the very bias that's been done unto us. You know, because it still happens. Every group of people does it. Eastern European Jews vs. Northern European Jews. The rift between blondes and brunettes has nothing to do with hair color. It has to do with what people perceive as racial purity. I wanted to look at how it affects black folks.

In *Yellowman*, both Alma and Eugene struggle to move beyond skin color, to find a solid sense of self, but—as is often the case—they are unable to do so. Moreover, each grapples with larger identity issues: Alma notes that she is not "girl-like," while Eugene is labeled a "faggot." Neither is allowed to experience the joys of childhood, and yet, as they age, each lingers in a state somewhere between adulthood and childhood. From searing familial indictments to tragic events between friends, Alma and Eugene are wholly ill-equipped to navigate their evolution into a couple. Through the portrayals by Orlandersmith and Overshown, we see how much pain such labels inflict—and how they lead to the ultimate tragedy of the play. Alma and Eugene cannot understand, accept or move beyond what they have been told they are, and their union—despite its initial comfort—leads to discord, revenge and death.

ZIZKA'S PRODUCTION OF *Yellowman* embraces the complexity of Orlandersmith's storytelling with a design that is as spare as it is complementary: two chairs sitting in an open space. Designer Klara Zieglerova's set encourages the audience's eyes to rest squarely and completely on the actors—there is no other place to look. Through this effective simplicity of design, we are forced to notice the differences in skin tone between Alma and Eugene. We are as responsible for initial assessments about character and identity—as they relate to skin color—as are Alma and Eugene's childhood friends "Wyce," "Alton White," "Louise" and the "Trinidadian friend." Zieglerova's design uses projections to locate us—a country road, a line of laundry, the New York skyline. Despite these visual references, however, the director keeps the audience on point, employing Elliott Sharp's evocative score to lead us back to Orlandersmith and Overshown.

Yellowman succeeds, in my mind, because of its singular focus on the story. Every good play tells us a compelling tale. And this Best Play spins its story with characters in situations that never release the audience from its grasp.

What Orlandersmith is able to achieve in *Yellowman* is beyond compelling, though. It is a poignant story of two individuals who *should*, for all intents and purposes, be together: They are from a South untouched by the civil rights movement, share a similar struggle to rise above their given circumstances and are black—all of which society tells us are "good enough" reasons for coupling. Look beyond these initial assumptions, though, and there rests the dilemma. Each of the characters responds differently to the historical events of the late 1960s. Each defines "rising above" in a profound way, yet it is a way that is vastly dissimilar to that of the other. Most importantly, we have learned that although they are both "black," they cannot overcome the fundamental difference in their skin tone.

Orlandersmith's power as a playwright lies in her deep investment in portraying the unraveling of their commonality, and the triumph, as it were, of difference. Because their differences run so very deep, and have touched both Alma and Eugene so profoundly—from skin to sexuality to loyalty—they head toward a tragedy that is, upon reflection, inevitable.

Color contrast: Howard W. Overshown and Dael Orlandersmith in Yellowman. *Photo: Joan Marcus*

I noted that *Yellowman* at times takes the tone of a mystery, causing us to ask the "what happens next?" question. Throughout the viewing of *Yellowman*, there is a looming sense of dread, an unsourced anxiety that is never released until the last moments of the play. Zizka's slow reveal of Eugene in a prison cell is a physical representation of what both he and Alma have experienced in the play—and the audience nearly gasps when Alma tells them that he has hung himself. Layer upon layer of skin, layer upon layer of tragedy—there is a deep mystery here, and like all of the best playwrights, Orlandersmith gives us not a single answer.

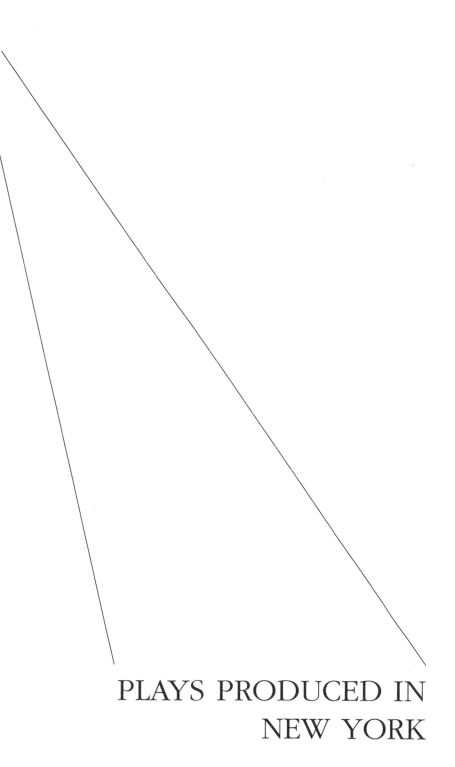

PLAYS PRODUCED IN
NEW YORK

PLAYS PRODUCED ON BROADWAY

○ ○ ○ ○ ○

FIGURES IN PARENTHESES following a play's title give the number of performances. These figures do not include previews or extra nonprofit performances. In the case of a transfer, the Off Broadway run is noted but not added to the figure in parentheses.

Plays marked with an asterisk (*) were still in a projected run June 1, 2003. Their number of performances is figured through May 31, 2003.

In a listing of a show's numbers—dances, sketches, musical scenes, etc.—the titles of songs are identified wherever possible by their appearance in quotation marks (").

HOLDOVERS FROM PREVIOUS SEASONS

BROADWAY SHOWS THAT were running on June 1, 2002 are listed below. More detailed information about them appears in previous *Best Plays* volumes of the years in which they opened. Important cast changes since opening night are recorded in the Cast Replacements section of this volume.

Les Misérables (6,680). Musical based on the novel by Victor Hugo; book by Alain Boublil and Claude-Michel Schönberg; lyrics by Herbert Kretzmer; original French text by Alain Boublil and Jean-Marc Natel; additional material by James Fenton. Opened March 12, 1987. (Closed May 18, 2003)

*The Phantom of the Opera (6,397). Musical adapted from the novel by Gaston Leroux; book by Richard Stilgoe and Andrew Lloyd Webber; music by Andrew Lloyd Webber; lyrics by Charles Hart; additional lyrics by Richard Stilgoe. Opened January 26, 1988.

*Beauty and the Beast (3,719). Musical with book by Linda Woolverton; music by Alan Menken; lyrics by Howard Ashman and Tim Rice. Opened April 18, 1994.

*Rent (2,951). Transfer from Off Broadway of the musical with book, music and lyrics by Jonathan Larson. Opened Off Off Broadway January 26, 1996 and Off Broadway February 13, 1996 where it played 56 performances through March 31, 1996; transferred to Broadway April 29, 1996.

*Chicago (2,723). Revival of the musical based on the play by Maurine Dallas Watkins; book by Fred Ebb and Bob Fosse; music by John Kander; lyrics by Fred Ebb; original production directed and choreographed by Bob Fosse. Opened November 14, 1996.

*The Lion King (2,345). Musical adapted from the screenplay by Irene Mecchi, Jonathan Roberts and Linda Woolverton; book by Roger Allers and Irene Mecchi; music by Elton John; lyrics by Tim Rice; additional music and lyrics by Lebo M, Mark Mancina, Jay Rifkin, Julie Taymor and Hans Zimmer. Opened November 13, 1997.

***Cabaret** (2,125). Revival of the musical based on the play by John van Druten and stories by Christopher Isherwood; book by Joe Masteroff; music by John Kander; lyrics by Fred Ebb. Opened March 19, 1998.

***Aida** (1,324). Musical suggested by the Giuseppe Verdi opera; book by Linda Woolverton, Robert Falls and David Henry Hwang; music by Elton John; lyrics by Tim Rice. Opened March 23, 2000.

Lincoln Center Theater production of **Contact** (1,010). Dance play by Susan Stroman and John Weidman; written by John Weidman. Opened March 30, 2000. (Closed September 1, 2002)

Proof (917). Transfer from Off Broadway of a play by David Auburn. Opened October 24, 2000. (Closed January 5, 2003)

The Full Monty (770). Musical with book by Terrence McNally; music and lyrics by David Yazbek. Opened October 26, 2000. (Closed September 1, 2002)

The Tale of the Allergist's Wife (777). Transfer from Off Broadway of a play by Charles Busch. Opened November 2, 2000. (Closed September 15, 2002)

***The Producers** (875). Musical with book by Mel Brooks and Thomas Meehan; music and lyrics by Mel Brooks. Opened April 19, 2001.

***42nd Street** (861). Revival of the musical based on the novel by Bradford Ropes and the 1933 movie; book by Michael Stewart and Mark Bramble; music by Harry Warren; lyrics by Al Dubin. Opened May 2, 2001.

***Urinetown** (700). Transfer from Off Broadway of the musical with book and lyrics by Greg Kotis; music and lyrics by Mark Hollmann. Opened September 20, 2001.

***Mamma Mia!** (256). Musical with book by Catherine Johnson; music and lyrics by Benny Andersson and Björn Ulvaeus, some songs with Stig Anderson. Opened October 18, 2001.

Noises Off (348). Revival of the play by Michael Frayn. Opened November 1, 2001. (Closed September 1, 2002)

Lincoln Center Theater production of **QED** (40). By Peter Parnell; inspired by the writings of Richard Feynman and Ralph Leighton's *Tuva or Bust!* Opened November 18, 2001. (Closed June 20, 2002)

Lincoln Center Theater production of **Mostly Sondheim** (26). André Bishop artistic director, Bernard Gersten executive producer, at the Vivian Beaumont Theater. Opened January 14, 2002. Production hiatus February 11–June 22, 2002. (Closed August 25, 2002)

Metamorphoses (400). Transfer from Off Broadway of the play by Mary Zimmerman; based on a translation by David R. Slavitt of Ovid's *Metamorphoses*. Opened March 4, 2002. (Closed February 16, 2003)

The Crucible (101). Revival of the play by Arthur Miller. Opened March 7, 2002. (Closed June 9, 2002)

The Goat, or Who Is Sylvia? (309). By Edward Albee. Opened March 10, 2002. (Closed December 15, 2002)

Sweet Smell of Success (109). Musical with book by John Guare; music by Marvin Hamlisch; lyrics by Craig Carnelia; based on the novella by Ernest Lehman, and the MGM/UA motion picture with screenplay by Clifford Odets and Ernest Lehman. Opened March 14, 2002. (Closed June 15, 2002)

Oklahoma! (388). Revival of the musical with book and lyrics by Oscar Hammerstein II; music by Richard Rodgers; based on the Lynn Riggs play *Green Grow the Lilacs*. Opened March 21, 2002. (Closed February 23, 2003)

Fortune's Fool (127). Adapted by Mike Poulton from the play by Ivan Turgenev. Opened April 2, 2002. (Closed July 21, 2002)

The Graduate (380). Adapted by Terry Johnson from the novel by Charles Webb, and the screenplay by Calder Willingham and Buck Henry. Opened April 4, 2002. (March 2, 2003)

Topdog/Underdog (144). Transfer from Off Broadway of the play by Suzan-Lori Parks. Opened April 7, 2002. (Closed August 11, 2002)

The Elephant Man (57). Revival of the play by Bernard Pomerance. Opened April 14, 2002. (Closed June 2, 2002)

*Thoroughly Modern Millie (463). Musical with book by Richard Morris and Dick Scanlan; new music by Jeanine Tesori; new lyrics by Dick Scanlan; based on the story and screenplay by Richard Morris for the Universal Pictures film. Opened April 18, 2002.

Lincoln Center Theater production of **Morning's at Seven** (112). Revival of the play by Paul Osborn. Opened April 21, 2002. (Closed July 28, 2002)

Private Lives (127). Revival of the play by Noël Coward. Opened April 28, 2002. (Closed September 1, 2002)

Into the Woods (279). Revival of the musical with book by James Lapine; music and lyrics by Stephen Sondheim. Opened April 30, 2002. (Closed December 29, 2002)

Roundabout Theatre Company production of **The Man Who Had All the Luck** (70). Revival of the play by Arthur Miller. Opened May 1, 2002. (Closed June 30, 2002)

PLAYS PRODUCED JUNE 1, 2002–MAY 31, 2003

Robin Williams: Live on Broadway (4). Produced by Home Box Office Inc. at the Broadway Theatre. Opened July 11, 2002. (Closed July 14, 2002).

Performed by Mr. Williams.
Standup comedy performance recorded for broadcast on cable television.

I'm Not Rappaport (53). Revival of the play by Herb Gardner. Produced by Elliot Martin, Lewis Allen, Ronald Shapiro, Bud Yorkin, James Cushing, Roy Miller, Mari Nakachi, Tommy DeMaio, Zandu Productions at the Booth Theatre. Opened July 25, 2002. (Closed September 8, 2002)

Nat .... Judd Hirsch   Midge .... Ben Vereen

Danforth	Anthony Arkin	Clara	Mimi Lieber
Laurie	Tanya Clarke	The Cowboy	Jeb Brown
Gilley	Steven Boyer		

Understudies: Mr. Hirsch—David S. Howard; Mr. Vereen—Adam Wade; Mses. Lieber, Clarke—Nurit Koppel; Messrs. Arkin, Brown—Michael Pemberton; Mr. Boyer–Robert McClure.

Directed by Daniel Sullivan; scenery, Tony Walton; costumes,Teresa Snider-Stein; lighting, Pat Collins; sound, Peter Fitzgerald; fight direction, Rick Sordelet; associate producer, Sharon Fallon; casting, Alison Franck; production stage manager, Warren Crane; stage manager, Marlene Mancini; press, Bill Evans and Associates, Jim Randolph.

Time: October 1982. Place: Central Park, New York City. Presented in two parts.

Two elderly men—one African American, the other Jewish—form a bond of friendship amid comic situations in Central Park. A 1985–86 *Best Plays* choice, the original Broadway production opened at Booth Theatre (11/19/1985; 890 performances) after an Off Broadway run (6/6/1985; 181 performances) at the American Place Theatre.

Bosom buds: Judd Hirsch and Ben Vereen in I'm Not Rappaport. *Photo: Carol Rosegg*

Frankie and Johnny in the Clair de Lune (243). Revival of the play by Terrence McNally. Produced by the Araca Group, Jean Doumanian Productions, USA Ostar Productions, in association with Jam Theatricals, Ray and Kit Sawyer, at the Belasco Theatre. Opened August 8, 2002. (Closed March 9, 2003)

Frankie .... Edie Falco   Johnny .... Stanley Tucci

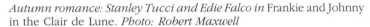

    Understudies: Ms. Falco—Lisa Leguillou; Mr. Tucci—Tim Cummings.

    Directed by Joe Mantello; scenery, John Lee Beatty; costumes, Laura Bauer; lighting, Brian MacDevitt; sound, Scott Lehrer; associate producers, Clint Bond Jr., Aaron Harnick; production stage manager, Andrea J. Testani; stage manager, Bess Marie Glorioso; press, Boneau/Bryan-Brown, Adrian Bryan-Brown, Jackie Green, Amy Jacobs, Martine Sainvil.

    Time: The present. Place: Frankie's small New York apartment in the West 50s. Presented in two parts.

    A working-class couple of middle age forge a relationship amid the emotional insecurities of modern romance. Originally presented by Manhattan Theatre Club (6/2/1987–6/14/1987) at City Center Stage II; reopened for a run at City Center Stage I (10/27/1987–11/29/1987); transferred to the Westside Arts Theatre for a commercial run (12/4/1987–3/12/1989; 533 performances).

Autumn romance: Stanley Tucci and Edie Falco in Frankie and Johnny in the Clair de Lune. *Photo: Robert Maxwell*

Tons o' fun: Marissa Jaret Winokur and Harvey Fierstein in Hairspray.
Photo: Paul Kolnik

*Hairspray (328). Musical with book by Mark O'Donnell and Thomas Meehan; music by Marc Shaiman; lyrics by Marc Shaiman and Scott Wittman; based on the film by John Waters. Produced by Margo Lion, Adam Epstein, the Baruch-Viertel-Routh-Frankel Group, James D. Stern/Douglas L. Meyer, Rick Steiner/Frederic H. Mayerson, SEL and GFO, New Line Cinema, in association with Clear Channel Entertainment, Allan S. Gordon/ Elan V. McAllister, Dede Harris/Morton Swinsky, John and Bonnie Osher, at the Neil Simon Theatre. Opened August 15, 2002.

Tracy Turnblad	Marissa Jaret Winokur	Harriman F. Spritzer	Joel Vig
Corny Collins	Clarke Thorell	Wilbur Turnblad	Dick Latessa
Amber Von Tussle	Laura Bell Bundy	Principal	Joel Vig
Brad	Peter Matthew Smith	Seaweed J. Stubbs	Corey Reynolds
Tammy	Hollie Howard	Duane	Eric Anthony
Fender	John Hill	Gilbert	Eric Dysart
Brenda	Jennifer Gambatese	Lorraine	Danielle Lee Greaves
Sketch	Adam Fleming	Thad	Rashad Naylor
Shelley	Shoshana Bean	The Dynamites	Kamilah Martin,
IQ	Todd Michel Smith		Judine Richard, Shayna Steele
Lou Ann	Katharine Leonard	Mr. Pinky	Joel Vig
Link Larkin	Matthew Morrison	Gym Teacher	Jackie Hoffman
Prudy Pingleton	Jackie Hoffman	Little Inez	Danelle Eugenia Wilson
Edna Turnblad	Harvey Fierstein	Motormouth Maybelle	Mary Bond Davis
Penny Pingleton	Kerry Butler	Matron	Jackie Hoffman
Velma Von Tussle	Linda Hart	Guard	Joel Vig

Denizens of Baltimore: Eric Anthony, Shoshana Bean, Eric Dysart, Adam Fleming, Jennifer Gambatese, Danielle Lee Greaves, John Hill, Jackie Hoffman, Hollie Howard, Katharine Leonard, Kamilah Martin, Rashad Naylor, Judine Richard, Peter Matthew Smith, Todd Michel Smith, Shayna Steele, Joel Vig.

Onstage musicians: Matthew Morrison guitar; Linda Hart keyboard; Joel Vig glockenspiel; Kerry Butler harmonica.

Orchestra: Lon Hoyt conductor, keyboard; Keith Cotton associate conductor, keyboard; Seth Farber assistant conductor, keyboard; David Spinozza, Peter Calo guitars; Francisco Centeno electric bass; Clint de Ganon drums; Walter "Wally" Usiatynski percussion; David Mann, Dave Rickenberg reeds; Danny Cahn trumpet; Birch Johnson trombone; Rob Shaw, Carol Pool violins; Sarah Hewitt Roth cello.

Understudies: Ms. Winokur—Shoshana Bean, Katy Grenfell; Messrs. Fierstein, Latessa—David Greenspan, Joel Vig; Ms. Hart—Shoshana Bean, Jackie Hoffman; Ms. Bundy—Hollie Howard, Katharine Leonard; Ms. Davis—Danielle Lee Greaves, Kamilah Martin; Mr. Reynolds—Eric Anthony, Eric Dysart; Mr. Morrison—Adam Fleming, John Hill; Mr. Thorell—John Hill, Peter Matthew Smith; Ms. Butler—Jennifer Gambatese, Hollie Howard; Ms. Wilson—Judine Richard, Shayna Steele.

Swings: Joshua Bergasse, Greg Graham, Brooke Tansley.

Directed by Jack O'Brien; choreography, Jerry Mitchell; scenery, David Rockwell; costumes, William Ivey Long; lighting, Kenneth Posner; sound, Steve C. Kennedy; orchestrations, Harold Wheeler; music direction, Lon Hoyt; music coordinator, John Miller; assistant director, Matt Lenz; associate choreographer, Michele Lynch; associate producers, Rhoda Mayerson, the Aspen Group, Daniel C. Staton; casting, Bernard Telsey Casting; production stage manager, Steven Beckler; stage manager, J. Philip Bassett; press, Richard Kornberg and Associates, Richard Kornberg, Don Summa, Tom D'Ambrosio, Carrie Friedman.

Time: 1962. Place: Baltimore. Presented in two parts.

Celebration of the liberating power of early 1960s music and dance as filtered through the ironic lens of Mr. Waters's film—although with the customary softer focus of a Broadway musical. Winner of eight Tony Awards: musical, director, lead actor, lead actress, featured actor, book, score and costumes. Originally presented at Seattle's 5th Avenue Theatre (6/14/2002–6/23/2002; 13 performances) after a preview period (5/30/2002–6/13/2002; 17 previews).

ACT I

Prologue: "Good Morning Baltimore" .... Tracy, Company
Scene 1: TV Station WZZT and Turnblad Home
"The Nicest Kids in Town" .... Corny Collins, Council Members
Scene 2: At the Vanities
"Mama, I'm a Big Girl Now" .... Edna and Tracy,
Velma and Amber, Penny and Prudy
Scene 3: TV Station WZZT
"I Can Hear the Bells" .... Tracy
"(The Legend of) Miss Baltimore Crabs" .... Velma, Council Members
Scene 4: Detention
Scene 5: Patterson Park High School Gymnasium
"The Madison" .... Corny, Company
Scene 6: WZZT and Turnblad Home
"The Nicest Kids in Town" (Reprise) .... Corny, Council Members
"It Takes Two" .... Link and Tracy
Scene 7: Turnblad Home and Streets of Baltimore
"Welcome to the '60s" .... Tracy, Edna,
the Dynamites, Company
Scene 8: Patterson Park Playground
"Run and Tell That" .... Seaweed
Scene 9: Motormouth Maybelle's Record Shop
"Run and Tell That" .... Seaweed, Little Inez, Company
"Big, Blond and Beautiful" .... Motormouth, Little Inez,
Tracy, Edna, Wilbur

ACT II

Scene 1: Baltimore Women's House of Detention
"The Big Dollhouse" .... Women
"Good Morning Baltimore" (Reprise) .... Tracy
Scene 2: The Har-De-Har Hut
"Timeless to Me" .... Wilbur and Edna

Scene 3: Tracy's Jail Cell and Penny's Bedroom
"Without Love" .... Link, Tracy, Seaweed, Penny
Scene 4: Motormouth Maybelle's Record Shop
"I Know Where I've Been" .... Motormouth, Company
Scene 5: The Baltimore Eventorium
"Hairspray" .... Corny, Council Members
"Cooties" .... Amber, Council Members
"You Can't Stop the Beat" .... Tracy, Link, Penny, Seaweed,
Edna, Wilbur, Motormouth, Company

Call her madam: Tom Hewitt and Jackée Harry in The
Boys From Syracuse. *Photo: Joan Marcus*

Roundabout Theatre Company production of **The Boys From Syracuse** (73). Revival
of the musical with new book by Nicky Silver; music by Richard Rodgers; lyrics by
Lorenz Hart; based on the original book by George Abbott. Todd Haimes artistic director,
Ellen Richard managing director, Julia C. Levy executive director of external affairs, at
the American Airlines Theatre. Opened August 18, 2002. (Closed October 20, 2002)

A Sergeant .... Fred Inkley	An Apprentice .... Kirk McDonald
The Duke .... J.C. Montgomery	Luce .... Toni DiBuono
Aegean .... Walter Charles	A Sorcerer .... George Hall
A Merchant .... Scott Robertson	Adriana .... Lauren Mitchell
A Soldier .... Davis Kirby	Luciana .... Erin Dilly
Antipholus of Syracuse .... Jonathan Dokuchitz	Madam .... Jackée Harry
Dromio of Syracuse .... Lee Wilkof	Angelo .... Jeffrey Broadhurst
Antipholus of Ephesus .... Tom Hewitt	Courtesans .... Sara Gettelfinger,
Dromio of Ephesus .... Chip Zien	Deidre Goodwin, Milena Govich,
A Tailor .... Joseph Siravo	Teri Hansen, Elizabeth Mills

Orchestra: David Loud conductor; Ethyl Will associate conductor, keyboard; Paul Woodiel, Ella
Rutkovsky, Liuh-Wen Ting violin; Eddie Salkin, Jonathan Levine, Andrew Sterman, Mark Thrasher
reeds; Jon Owens, Matt Peterson trumpet; Charles Gordon trombone; R.J. Kelley, French horn;
Brian Cassier bass; Bruce Doctor drums, percussion.

Understudies: Messrs. Dokuchitz, Hewitt, Charles, Montgomery—Tom Galantich; Ms. Dibuono—
Sara Gettelfinger; Ms. Harry—Deidre Goodwin; Ms. Dilly—Milena Govich, Teri Hansen; Ms.
Mitchell—Teri Hansen, Allyson Turner; Messrs. Broadhurst, Siravo, McDonald, Hall, Robertson—
Tripp Hanson; Mr. Hewitt—Fred Inkley; Mr. Inkley—Tripp Hanson; Messrs. Wilkof, Zien—Scott
Robertson; Mses. Gettelfinger, Goodwin, Govich Hansen, Mills—Allyson Turner.

Directed by Scott Ellis; choreography, Rob Ashford; scenery, Thomas Lynch; costumes, Martin Pakledinaz; lighting, Donald Holder; sound, Brian Ronan; fight direction, Rick Sordelet; orchestrations, Don Sebesky; music direction and vocal arrangments, David Loud; dance music, David Kane; music coordinator, John Miller; casting, Jim Carnahan; production stage manager, Peter Hanson; stage manager, James Mountcastle; press, Boneau/Bryan-Brown, Adrian Bryan-Brown, Matt Polk, Amy Dinnerman.

Time: Thursday. Place: Ephesus, a city in ancient Greece. Presented in two parts.

Updating of George Abbott's updating of William Shakespeare's updating (*The Comedy of Errors*) of Plautus (*The Menaechmi, Amphitryon*). Originally presented at Broadway's Alvin Theatre—now the Neil Simon Theatre—(11/23/1938; 235 performances).

ACT I

Overture .... Orchestra
Scene 1: The Town Square
  "Hurrah! Hurroo! (I Had Twins)" .... Sergeant, Duke, Aegean, Crowd
  "Dear Old Syracuse" .... Antipholus and Dromio of Syracuse
Scene 2: A Tailor's Shop
  "What Can You Do With a Man" .... Luce and Dromio of Ephesus
Scene 3: An Ephesian Street Corner
  "Falling in Love With Love" .... Adriana
Scene 4: The Local Bordello
  "A Lady Must Live" .... The Courtesans
  "The Shortest Day of the Year" .... Antipholus of Ephesus and Adriana
Scene 5: Adriana's Home/The Streets of Ephesus
  "This Can't Be Love" .... Antipholus of Syracuse and Luciana
  "This Must Be Love" .... Antipholus of Syracuse and Luciana

ACT II

Entr'acte .... Orchestra
Prologue: "You Took Advantage of Me" .... The Courtesans
Scene 1: Adriana's Home East Wing
  "He and She" .... Luce, Dromio of Syracuse
  "You Have Cast Your Shadow on the Sea" .... Antipholus of Syracuse
Scene 2: Ephesus's Red Light District
  "Big Brother" .... Dromios of Ephesus and Syracuse
  "Come With Me" .... Sergeant and Policeman
Scene 3: Adriana's Home
  "Oh, Diogenes!" .... Adriana, Luciana, Luce
Scene 4: The Town Square
  "Hurrah! Hurroo!" (Reprise) .... The Crowd
  "Sing for Your Supper" .... Madam, Courtesans, Luce, Adriana, Luciana, the Crowd
  "This Can't Be Love" (Reprise) .... The Company

*Say Goodnight, Gracie (268). By Rupert Holmes. Produced by William Franzblau, Jay H. Harris, Louise Westergaard, Larry Spellman, Elsa Daspin Haft, Judith Resnick, Anne Gallagher, Libby Adler Mages/Mari Glick, Martha R. Gasparian, Bruce Lazarus, Lawrence S. Toppall, Jae French at the Helen Hayes Theatre. Opened October 10, 2002.

George Burns .... Frank Gorshin   Voice of Gracie Allen .... Didi Conn
  Understudy: Mr. Gorshin—Joel Rooks.

Directed by John Tillinger; scenery, John Lee Beatty; lighting, Howard Werner; sound, Kevin Lacy; executive producer, Mr. Franzblau; production stage manager, Tina M. Newhauser; press, Cromarty and Company, Peter Cromarty, Alice Cromarty.

Presented without intermission

Awaiting admission to heaven, George Burns reminisces about his life and career in show business. Originally produced at the Broward Center for the Performing Arts, Ft. Lauderdale, Florida (8/22/2000).

All aboard: Sandra Allen, Jose Llana, Randall Duk Kim, Allen Liu and Jodi Long in Flower Drum Song. *Photo: Joan Marcus*

Flower Drum Song (169). Revival of the musical with new book by David Henry Hwang; music by Richard Rodgers; lyrics by Oscar Hammerstein II; based on the original book by Oscar Hammerstein II and Joseph Fields; from the novel by C.Y. Lee. Produced by Benjamin Mordecai, Michael A. Jenkins, Waxman Williams Entertainment, Center Theatre Group/Mark Taper Forum/Gordon Davidson/Charles Dillingham, in association with Robert G. Bartner, Robert Dragotta/Temple Gill/Marcia Roberts, Kelpie Arts/Dramatic Forces, Stephanie McClelland, Judith Resnick, by arrangement with the Rodgers and Hammerstein Organization, at the Virginia Theatre. Opened October 17, 2002. (Closed March 16, 2003)

Mei-Li	Lea Salonga	Harvard	Allen Liu
Wang	Randall Duk Kim	Linda Low	Sandra Allen
Chin	Alvin Ing	Madame Liang	Jodi Long
Ta	Jose Llana	Chao	Hoon Lee

Ensemble: Rich Ceraulo, Eric Chan, Marcus Choi, Ma-Anne Dionisio, Emily Hsu, Telly Leung, J. Elaine Marcos, Daniel May, Marc Oka, Lainie Sakakura, Yuka Takara, Kim Varhola, Ericka Yang.

Orchestra: David Chase conductor; David Evans associate conductor, keyboard; Janet A. Axelrod flute, bamboo flute, dizi; Lou Bruno bass; Claire Chan violin; Raymond Grappone drums; Richard Heckman woodwinds; Ronald Janelli woodwinds; Christian Jaudes trumpet; Howard Joines percussion; Stu Satalof trumpet; Russel L. Rizner horn; Clay Ruede cello, erhu; Jack Schatz trombone; Andrew Schwartz guitar, pipa; Chuck Wilson woodwind; Julius Rene Wirth viola, violin; Mineko Yajima violin, mandolin.

Standby: Messrs. Kim, Ing—Raul Aranas.

Understudies: Ms. Salonga—Ma-Anne Dionisio, Yuka Takara; Mr. Ing—Eric Chan, Mr. Llana—Rich Ceraulo, Hoon Lee, Telly Leung; Mr. Liu—Marc Oka; Ms. Allen—Emily Hsu; Ms. Long—Kim Varhola; Mr. Lee—Marcus Choi.

Swings: Susan Ancheta, Robert Tatad.

Directed and choreographed by Robert Longbottom; scenery, Robin Wagner; costumes, Gregg Barnes; lighting, Natasha Katz; sound, Acme Sound Partners, orchestrations, Don Sebesky; music adaptation and supervision, Mr. Chase; music coordinator; Seymour Red Press; associate director,

Tom Kosis; associate choreographer, Darlene Wilson; associate producers, Dallas Summer Musicals, Inc., Brian Brolly/Alice Chebba Walsh, Ernest De Leon Escaler; casting, Tara Rubin Casting and Amy Lieberman; production stage manager, Perry Cline; stage manager, Rebecca C. Monroe; press, Boneau/Bryan-Brown, Adrian Bryan-Brown, Jim Byk, Susanne Tighe, Martine Sainvil.

Time: 1960. Place Chinatown in San Francisco. Presented in two parts.

Asian tradition clashes with American innovation in this updated musical romance that seeks to bridge the longings of immigrant Asians and Asian Americans. Originally presented at Broadway's St. James Theatre (12/1/1958–5/7/1960; 600 performances).

ACT I

Prologue: "A Hundred Million Miracles" .... Mei-Li, Company
"I Am Going to Like It Here" .... Mei-Li
"I Enjoy Being a Girl" .... Linda Low, Company
"You Are Beautiful" .... Ta and Mei-Li
"Grant Avenue" .... Madame Liang, Company
"Sunday" .... Ta
"Fan Tan Fannie" .... Linda Low, Company
"Gliding Through My Memoree" .... Wang, Company

ACT II

"Chop Suey" .... Wang, Company
"My Best Love" .... Chin
"Don't Marry Me" .... Madame Liang and Wang
"Love, Look Away" .... Mei-Li
"Like a God" .... Ta
Finale: "A Hundred Million Miracles" .... Company

Passing through: Malcolm Gets in Amour *Photo: Joan Marcus*

Amour (17). Musical with French libretto by Didier van Cauwelaert; English adaptation by Jeremy Sams; music by Michel Legrand; adapted from "Le Passe-Muraille" by Marcel Aymé. Produced by the Shubert Organization, Jean Doumanian Productions, Inc., USA Ostar Theatricals at the Music Box. Opened October 20, 2002. (Closed November 3, 2002)

Dusoleil .... Malcolm Gets	Whore .... Nora Mae Lyng
Isabelle .... Melissa Errico	Policemen .... John Cunningham, Bill Nolte
Claire .... Nora Mae Lyng	Prosecutor .... Lewis Cleale
Bertrand .... Christopher Fitzgerald	Doctor .... John Cunningham
Charles .... Lewis Cleale	Boss .... Bill Nolte
Madeleine .... Sarah Litzsinger	Tribunal President .... John Cunningham
Painter .... Norm Lewis	Advocate .... Christopher Fitzgerald
Newsvendor .... Christopher Fitzgerald	

Orchestra: Todd Ellison conductor, pianist; Antony Geralis associate conductor, pianist; Bill Hayes percussion; Ben Kono woodwinds; Mark Vanderpoel bass.

Understudies: Mr. Gets—Christian Borle; Ms. Errico—Jessica Hendy, Sarah Litzsinger; Messrs. Cleale, Cunningham, Nolte—Matthew Bennett; Messrs. Fitzgerald, Lewis—Christian Borle; Mses. Lyng, Litzsinger—Jessica Hendy.

Directed by James Lapine; choreography, Jane Comfort; scenery, Scott Pask; costumes, Dona Granata; lighting, Jules Fisher and Peggy Eisenhauer; sound, Dan Moses Schreier; orchestrations, Mr. Legrand; musical direction and vocal arrangement, Todd Ellison; associate choreographer, Lisa Shriver; casting, Bernard Telsey Casting; production stage manager, Leila Knox; stage manager, David Sugarman; press, Bill Evans and Associates, Jim Randolph.

Time: Shortly after World War II. Place: Paris. Presented without intermission.

Musical recitative about a lovelorn bureaucrat empowered by a sudden ability to pass through walls. Originally presented in Paris under the title *Le Passe Muraille*, it won the 1997 Prix Molière for Best Musical, the French equivalent of the Tony Award.

Prune Danish (39). By Jackie Mason. Produced by Jyll Rosenfeld and Jon Stoll at the Royale Theatre. Opened October 22, 2002. (Closed December 1, 2002)

Performed by Jackie Mason.

Directed by Mr. Mason, lighting, Traci Klainer; sound, Christopher T. Cronin; stage manager, Don Myers.

Mr. Mason's eighth Broadway comedy. The first was *A Teaspoon Every Four Hours*, presented at the ANTA Playhouse–now the Virginia Theatre–for one performance (6/14/1969) following 97 previews.

*Movin' Out (248). Dance musical based on the songs of Billy Joel; with music and lyrics by Mr. Joel; conceived by Twyla Tharp. Produced by James L. Nederlander, Hal Luftig, Scott E. Nederlander, Terry Allen Kramer, Clear Channel Entertainment, Emanuel Azenberg at the Richard Rodgers Theatre. Opened October 24, 2002.

Eddie .... John Selya	James .... Benjamin G. Bowman
Brenda .... Elizabeth Parkinson	Sergeant O'Leary;
Tony .... Keith Roberts	Drill Sergeant .... Scott Wise
Judy .... Ashley Tuttle	Piano; Lead Vocals .... Michael Cavanaugh

Ensemble: Mark Arvin, Karine Bageot, Alexander Brady, Holly Cruikshank, Ron Dejesus, Melissa Downey, Pascale Faye, Scott Fowler, David Gomez, Rod McCune, Jill Nicklaus, Rika Okamoto.

Wednesday and Saturday Matinees

Eddie .... William Marrié	James .... Benjamin G. Bowman
Brenda .... Holly Cruikshank	Sergeant O'Leary;
Tony .... David Gomez	Drill Sergeant .... Scott Wise
Judy .... Dana Stackpole	Piano; Lead Vocals .... Wade Preston

Uptown gal: Elizabeth Parkinson and company in Movin' Out. *Photo: Joan Marcus*

Orchestra: Michael Cavanaugh piano, lead vocals; Tommy Byrnes leader, guitar; Wade Preston keyboard; Dennis DelGaudio guitar; Greg Smith bass; Chuck Burgi drums; John Scarpulla lead sax, percussion, Scott Kreitzer sax, Barry Danielian trumpet; Kevin Osborne trombone, whistler, vocals.

Swings: Andrew Allagree, Aliane Baquerot, Laurie Kanyok, William Marrié, Meg Paul, Lawrence Rabson, Dana Stackpole, John J. Todd.

Understudies: Mr. Roberts—Ron Dejesus, David Gomez; Ms. Parkinson—Karine Bageot, Holly Cruikshank; Mr. Selya—Andrew Allagree, William Marrié, Lawrence Rabson; Ms. Tuttle—Meg Paul, Dana Stackpole; Mr. Wise—John J. Todd; Mr. Bowman—Scott Fowler, Alexander Brady.

Directed and choreographed by Ms. Tharp; scenery, Santo Loquasto; costumes, Suzy Benzinger; lighting, Donald Holder; sound, Brian Ruggles, Peter Fitzgerald; additional music arrangements and orchestrations, Stuart Malina; music coordinator, John Miller; assisant director and choreographer, Mr. Wise; casting, Jay Binder Casting, Sarah Prosser; production stage manager, Tom Bartlett; stage manager, Kim Vernace; press, Barlow-Hartman, Michael Hartman, John Barlow, Bill Coyle.

Time: 1960s. Place: Long Island, New York. Presented in two parts.

Dance musical that tracks Baby Boomers from coming-of-age through the dawn of middle age with familiar pop music by Mr. Joel to emphasize and counterpoint the tale. Received 2003 Tony Awards for choreography and orchestrations. First presented at Chicago's Shubert Theatre (7/19/2002–9/1/2002; 53 performances).

ACT I

Overture: "It's Still Rock and Roll to Me" .... The Company
Scene 1: Brenda and Eddie Split
   "Scenes from an Italian Restaurant" .... Brenda, Eddie, Tony, James,
Judy, Sergeant O'Leary, Ensemble
Scene 2: Tony Moves Out
   "Movin' Out (Anthony's Song)" .... Tony, Eddie, James, Sergeant O'Leary
Scene 3: James and Judy Are Forever
   "Reverie (Villa D'Este)"/"Just the Way You Are" .... James, Judy, Ensemble

Scene 4: Brenda Is Back
  "For the Longest Time"/"Uptown Girl" .... Brenda, Eddie, Tony, Ensemble
Scene 5: Tony and Brenda Get Together
  "This Night" .... Tony, Brenda, Ensemble
Scene 6: Eddie Knows
  "Summer, Highland Falls" .... Eddie, Brenda, Tony, Ensemble
Scene 7: Off to War
  "Waltz #1 (Nunley's Carousel)" .... Tony, Eddie, James, Drill Sergeant, Ensemble
Scene 8: The Sky Falls
  "We Didn't Start the Fire" .... Judy, Brenda, James, Tony, Eddie, Ensemble
Scene 9: Two Bars: Hicksville/Saigon
  "She's Got a Way" .... Tony, Brenda, Ensemble
Scene 10: Coming Home
  "The Stranger" .... Judy, Ensemble
  "Elegy (The Great Peconic)" .... Judy, Brenda, Tony, Eddie, Drill Sergeant, Ensemble

ACT II

Scene 1: Vets Cast Out
  "Invention in C Minor" .... Eddie, Ensemble
Scene 2: Eddie Rages
  "Angry Young Man" .... Eddie, Ensemble
Scene 3: Tony Disconnects
  "Big Shot" .... Tony, Brenda, Ensemble
Scene 4: A Contest of Pain
  "Big Man on Mulberry Street" .... Tony, Brenda, Ensemble
Scene 5: Eddie Gets High
  "Captain Jack" .... Eddie, Ensemble
Scene 6: Eddie Reaches Out
  "Innocent Man" .... Eddie, Ensemble
Scene 7: Eddie's Nightmares
  "Pressure" .... Judy, Eddie, Ensemble
Scene 8: Eddie's Journey Back
  "Goodnight Saigon" .... Eddie, Judy, James, Tony, Ensemble
Scene 9: Brenda's Lost Dreams
  "Air (Dublinesque)" .... Brenda
Scene 10: Tony and Brenda Reconcile
  "Shameless" .... Brenda and Tony
Scene 11: Judy Releases Eddie
  "James" .... Judy and Eddie
Scene 12: Eddie Attains Grace
  "River of Dreams"/
  "Keeping the Faith"/
  "Only the Good Die Young" .... Eddie, Ensemble
Scene 13: The Reunion Begins
  "I've Loved These Days" .... Tony, Brenda, Eddie, Ensemble
Scene 14: Reunion/Finale
  "Scenes from an Italian Restaurant" (Reprise) .... The Company

Hollywood Arms (76). By Carrie Hamilton and Carol Burnett; based on Ms. Burnett's memoir, *One More Time*. Produced by Harold Prince and Arielle Tepper at the Cort Theatre. Opened October 31, 2002. (Closed January 5, 2003)

Older Helen .... Donna Lynne Champlin	Bill .... Patrick Clear
Young Helen .... Sara Niemietz	Jody .... Frank Wood
Nanny .... Linda Lavin	Cop #1 .... Christian Kohn
Louise .... Michele Pawk	Cop #2 .... Steve Bakunas
Dixie .... Leslie Hendrix	Alice .... Emily Graham-Handley
Malcolm .... Nicolas King	

Understudies: Ms. Lavin—Lucy Martin; Ms. Pawk—Leslie Hendrix; Ms. Miemietz—Sara Kapner; Mr. King–Evan Daves; Mr. Clear—Steve Bakunas; Mr. Wood—Christian Kohn; Messrs. Kohn, Bakunas—Brian Meister; Ms. Champlin—Lindsey Alley; Ms. Graham-Handley—Sara Kapner, Lindsey Alley; Ms. Hendrix—Lucy Martin.

Directed by Harold Prince; scenery, Walt Spangler; costumes, Judith Dolan; lighting, Howell Binkley; sound, Rob Milburn and Michael Bodeen; music, Robert Lindsey Nassif; associate producer, Ostar Enterprises; casting, Mark Simon; production stage manager, Lisa Dawn Cave; stage managers, Brian Meister, Matthew Leiner; press, Barlow-Hartman, John Barlow, Michael Hartman, Wayne Wolfe, Rob Finn.

Time: 1941–1951. Place: Hollywood. Presented in two parts.

Family-dysfunction-to-stardom tale based on Carol Burnett's life and career. 2003 Tony Award for best featured actress. First presented by Chicago's Goodman Theatre (4/29/2002–6/1/2002; 36 performances) after 10 previews (4/19/2002–4/28/2002).

Russell Simmons's Def Poetry Jam on Broadway (198). Poetry performance conceived by Stan Lathan and Russell Simmons. Produced by Mr. Simmons and Mr. Lathan, in association with Kimora Lee Simmons, Island Def Jam Music Group, Brett Ratner, David Rosenberg, at the Longacre Theatre. Opened November 14, 2002. (Closed May 4, 2003)

Performed by Beau Sia, Black Ice. Staceyann Chin, Steve Colman, Mayda Del Valle, Georgia Me, Suheir Hammad, Lemon, Poetri, Tendaji Lathan.

Directed by Mr. Lathan; scenery, Bruce Ryan; costumes, Paul Tazewell; lighting, Yael Lubetzky; sound, Elton P. Halley; production stage manager, Alice Elliott Smith; stage manager, Steven Lukens; press, Pete Sanders Group, Pete Sanders, Glenna Freedman, Terence Womble.

Presented in two parts.

A diverse group of young spoken-word performers celebrate themselves and envision a world they hope to influence. 2003 Tony Award for special theatrical event. Originally produced at San Francisco's Theatre on the Square (6/25/2002–7/28/2002; 40 performances)

Celebrating Sondheim (10). Concert performance of songs by Stephen Sondheim. Produced by Dodger Stage Holding at the Henry Miller Theatre. Opened December 2, 2002. (Closed January 6, 2003)

Performed by Mandy Patinkin, with Paul Ford (piano).

Lighting, Eric Cornwell; sound, Otts Munderloh; arrangements, Mr. Ford.

Presented without intermission.

More than 30 of Mr. Sondheim's songs by performed by Mr. Patinkin during a limited run of Sunday and Monday evenings.

Westport Country Playhouse production of **Our Town** (59). Revival of the play by Thornton Wilder. Joanne Woodward artistic director, Anne Keefe associate artistic director, Alison Harris executive director, at the Booth Theatre. Opened December 4, 2002. (Closed January 26, 2003)

Stage Manager .... Paul Newman	Auditorium Women .... Wendy Barrie-Wilson,
Dr. Gibbs .... Frank Converse	Cynthia Wallace
Joe Crowell .... TJ Sullivan	Auditorium Man .... Reathel Bean
Howie Newsome .... Jake Robards	Simon Stimson .... Stephen Spinella
Mrs. Gibbs .... Jayne Atkinson	Mrs. Soames .... Mia Dillon
Mrs. Webb .... Jane Curtin	Constable Warren .... Stephen Mendillo
George Gibbs .... Ben Fox	Si Crowell .... Travis Walters
Rebecca Gibbs .... Kristen Hahn	Baseball Players .... Kieran Campion,
Wally Webb .... Conor Donovan	Patch Darragh
Emily Webb .... Maggie Lacey	Sam Craig .... Carter Jackson
Professor Willard .... John Braden	Joe Stoddard .... Tom Brennan
Mr. Webb .... Jeffrey DeMunn	

His town: Paul Newman in Our Town. *Photo: Joan Marcus*

Understudies: Mses. Atkinson, Dillon, Curtin—Wendy Barrie-Wilson, Lisa Richards; Messrs. Converse, DeMunn, Spinella—Reathel Bean, Malachy Cleary; Messrs. Fox, Jackson—Kieran Campion, Patch Darragh; Mses. Lacey, Hahn—Erika Thomas; Mr. Robards—Kieran Campion, Patch Darragh, Malachy Cleary; Messrs. Sullivan, Walters, Donovan—Matthew Gusman; Mses. Barrie-Wilson, Wallace—Lisa Richards, Erika Thomas; Messrs. Bean, Braden, Mendillo, Brennan—Martin Shakar.

Directed by James Naughton; scenery and costumes, Tony Walton; lighting, Richard Pilbrow; sound, Raymond D. Schilke; casting, Deborah Brown; production stage manager, Katherine Lee Boyer; stage manager, Jenny Dewar; press, Bill Evans and Associates, Jim Randolph.

Time: The early years of the 20th century. Place: Grover's Corners, New Hampshire. Presented in two parts.

Classic tale of a small town before the first World War and how encroachments of the modern affect the cycle of life. First presented in 1938 by Jed Harris at the McCarter Theatre in Princeton, New Jersey. A 1937–38 *Best Plays* choice, the original Broadway production opened at the Henry Miller Theatre (2/4/1938; 336 performances).

*Man of La Mancha (200). Revival of the musical with book by Dale Wasserman; music by Mitch Leigh; lyrics by Joe Darion. Produced by David Stone, Jon B. Platt, Susan Quint Gallin, Sandy Gallin, Seth M. Siegel, USA Ostar Theatricals, in association with Mary Lu Roffe, at the Martin Beck Theatre. Opened December 5, 2002.

Dancer .... Wilson Mendieta	Pedro .... Gregory Mitchell
Opening Singer .... Olga Merediz	Jose .... Wilson Mendieta
Cervantes;	Maria .... Michelle Rios
Don Quixote .... Brian Stokes Mitchell	Fermina .... Lorin Latarro
Captain .... Frederick B. Owens	Antonia .... Natascia Diaz
Sancho .... Ernie Sabella	Padre .... Mark Jacoby
Governor; Innkeeper .... Don Mayo	Housekeeper .... Olga Merediz
Duke; Carrasco .... Stephen Bogardus	Barber .... Jamie Torcellini
Aldonza .... Mary Elizabeth Mastrantonio	Guard .... Michael X. Martin
Quito .... Andy Blankenbuehler	Guard ....Jimmy Smagula
Tenorio .... Timothy J. Alex	Gypsy Dancer .... Lorin Latarro
Juan .... Thom Sesma	Gypsy Dancer .... Andy Blankenbuehler
Paco ....Dennis Stowe	Prisoner .... Allyson Tucker
Anselmo .... Bradley Dean	Onstage Guitarist .... Robin Polseno

Orchestra: Robert Billig conductor; Cherie Rosen associate conductor, guitar; Braden Toan assistant conductor, bassoon;Wayne duMaine lead trumpet; John Dent trumpet; Dale Kirkland trombone; Douglas Purviance bass trombone; Eva Conti, Patrick Milando, French horns; Kathleen Nester flute; Blair Tindall oboe, Lino Gomez clarinet; Steve Bartosik drums, Randall Landau bass; Robin Polseno guitar; David Yee percussion; Michael Hinton tympani.

Possible dreamer: Mary Elizabeth Mastrantonio and Brian Stokes Mitchell in Man of La Mancha. *Photo: Joan Marcus*

Understudies: Mr. Mitchell—Bradley Dean, Michael X. Martin; Mr. Sabella—Jimmy Smagula, Jamie Torcellini; Ms. Mastrantonio—Natascia Diaz, Allyson Tucker; Mr. Bogardus—Michael X. Martin, Thom Sesma; Mr. Mayo—Michael X. Martin, Frederick B. Owens; Mr. Jacoby—Bradley Dean, Jimmy Smagula; Ms. Diaz—Lorin Latarro, Allyson Tucker; Ms. Merediz—Michelle Rios, Allyson Tucker; Mr. Torcellini—Carlos Lopez, Jimmy Smagula; Ms. Rios—Jamie Karen; Mr. Owens—Timothy J. Alex, Dennis Stowe.

Swings: Jamie Karen, Carlos Lopez, Richard Montoya.

Directed by Jonathan Kent; choreography, Luis Perez; scenery and costumes, Paul Brown; lighting, Paul Gallo; sound, Tony Meola; original orchestrations, Carlyle W. Hall Sr.; original dance music, Neil Warner; new dance music, David Krane; new dance orchestrations, Brian Besterman; music director, Mr. Billig; music coordinator, Michael Keller; associate director, Peter Lawrence; executive producers, Nina Essman, Nancy Nagel Gibbs; casting, Bernard Telsey Casting; production stage manager, Mahlon Kruse; press, the Publicity Office, Bob Fennell, Marc Thibodeau, Candi Adams, Michael S. Borowski.

Time: 1594. Place: A prison in Seville, Spain, and in the imagination of Don Miguel de Cervantes. Presented without intermission.

Musical based on the life and work of Miguel de Cervantes y Saavedra. A 1965–66 *Best Plays* choice, the original Broadway production opened at the ANTA Washington Square Theatre (11/22/1965; 2,328 performances).

MUSICAL NUMBERS

"Man of La Mancha (I, Don Quixote)" .... Don Quixote, Sancho
"It's All the Same" .... Aldonza, Muleteers
"Dulcinea" .... Don Quixote, Muleteers
"I'm Only Thinking of Him" .... Carrasco, Antonia, Padre, Housekeeper
"The Missive" .... Sancho
"I Really Like Him" .... Sancho
"What Does He Want of Me?" .... Aldonza
"Little Bird, Little Bird" .... Anselmo, Pedro, Muleteers
"Barber's Song" .... Barber
"Golden Helmet of Mambrino" .... Don Quixote, Sancho, Barber,
                                                                  Padre, Muleteers
"To Each His Dulcinea (To Every Man His Dream)" .... Padre
"The Impossible Dream (The Quest)" .... Don Quixote
"The Combat" .... Don Quixote, Aldonza,
                                                                  Sancho, Muleteers
"The Dubbing"/"Knight of the Woeful Countenance" .... Innkeeper, Don Quixote,
                                                                  Aldonza, Sancho
"The Abduction" .... Aldonza, Muleteers, Fermina
"The Impossible Dream (The Quest)" (Reprise) .... Don Quixote
"Man of La Mancha (I, Don Quixote)" (Reprise) .... Don Quixote
"Gypsy Dance" .... Don Quixote, Sancho,
                                                                  Gypsy Dancers, Muleteers
"Aldonza" .... Aldonza
"A Little Gossip" .... Sancho
"Dulcinea" (Reprise) .... Aldonza
"The Impossible Dream (The Quest)" (Reprise) .... Don Quixote, Aldonza
"Man of La Mancha (I Don Quixote)" (Reprise) .... Don Quixote, Sancho, Aldonza
"The Psalm" .... Padre
"Finale" .... Company

La Bohème (196). Revival of the opera with libretto by Giuseppe Giacosa and Luigi Illica; music by Giacomo Puccini; based on stories from *Scènes de la Vie de Bohème* by Henri Mürger. Produced by Jeffrey Seller, Kevin McCollum, Emanuel Azenberg, Bazmark Live, Bob and Harvey Weinstein, Korea Pictures/Doyun Seol, Jeffrey Sine/Ira Pittelman/Scott E. Nederlander, Fox Searchlight Pictures at the Broadway Theatre. Opened December 8, 2002.

Naughty Musetta: Jessica Comeau and company in La Bohème. *Photo: Sue Adler*

Marcello .... Eugene Brancoveanu;	Mimi .... Lisa Hopkins;
Ben Davis	Wei Huang; Ekaterina Solovyeva
Rodolfo .... Alfred Boe;	Papignol .... Dan Entriken
Jesús Garcia;	Alcindoro .... William Youmans
David Miller	Musetta .... Jessica Comeau;
Colline .... Daniel Webb	Chlöe Wright
Schaunard .... Daniel Okulitch	Customs Officer .... Sean Cooper
Benoit .... Adam Grupper	Sergeant .... Graham Fandrei

Ensemble: Enrique Abdala, Christine Arand, Janinah Burnett, Gilles Chiasson, Charlotte Cohn, Michael Cone, Vanessa Conlin, Sean Cooper, Patricia Corbett, Evangelia Costantakos, Lawrence Craig, Dan Entriken, Graham Fandrei, Bobby Faust, Katie Geissinger, Jennifer Goode, Paul Goodwin-Groen, Adam Grupper, Joy Hermalyn, Robb Hillman, Adam Hunter, Timothy Jerome, Katherine Keyes, Laurice Lanier, Peter Lockyer, Morgan Moody, Marcus Nance, Daniel Neer, Debra Patchell, Patricia Phillips, Jamet Pittman, Martín Solá, Radu Spinghel, Mark Womack.

Children's Chorus: Ryan Andres, Ellen Hornberger, Joseph Jonas, Antonia Kitsopoulos, Alyson Lange, David Mathews, Suzanna Mathews, Luca Mannarino, Nathan Morgan, Jennifer Olsen, Ben Pakman, Samantha Massell Rakosi, Melissa Remo, Justin Robertazzi, Matthew Salvatore.

Orchestra: Dale Stuckenbruck concert master; Elizabeth Lim-Dutton, Uli Speth, Cecilia Hobbs Gardner, Robert Zubrycki, Sylvia D'Avanzo, Ming Yeh, Katherine Livolsi-Stern, John Connelly violin; Sarah Adams, Maxine Roach viola; Roger Shell, Chung Sun Kim cello; Joe Bongiorno bass; Bob Bush flute, piccolo; Lynne Cohen oboe, English horn; Jon Manasse clarinet; Larry Guy clarinet, bass clarinet; Jeff Marchand bassoon; Carl Albach, Chuck Olsen, Kenny DeCarlo trumpet; Matthew Ingman trombone; Chris Komer, Zohar Schondorf, French horn; Dean Witten timpani, percussion; Warren "Chip" Prince, Karl Mansfield keyboard.

Understudies: Messrs. Brancoveanu, Davis—Graham Fandrei, Joseph Kaiser, Mark Womack; Messrs. Boe, Garcia, Miller—Peter Lockyer; Mr. Webb—Sean Cooper, Morgan Moody; Mr. Okulitch—Graham Fandrei, Joseph Kaiser, Mark Womack; Mr. Grupper—Dan Entriken, Timothy Jerome; Mses. Hopkins, Huang, Solovyeva—Janinah Burnett; Mses. Comeau, Wright—Christine Arand, Jennifer Goode; Mr. Youmans—Adam Grupper, Timothy Jerome.

Ensemble Swing: Joseph Kaiser.

Directed by Baz Luhrmann; scenery, Catherine Martin; costumes, Ms. Martin, Angus Strathie; lighting, Nigel Levings; sound, Acme Sound Partners; orchestrations, Nicholas Kitsopoulos; music director and principal conductor, Constantine Kitsopoulos; music coordinator, John Miller; associate director, David Crooks; executive producers, Noel Staunton, Adam Silberman; associate producers, Daniel Karslake/Coats Guiles, Morton Swinsky/Michael Fuchs; casting, Bernard Telsey Casting; production stage manager, Frank Hartenstein; stage manager, Kelly Martindale; press, Boneau/Bryan-Brown, Chris Boneau, Amy Jacobs, Juliana Hannett.

Time: 1957. Place: Paris. Presented in two parts.

Restaging of a popular Australian production of the famed opera about art, bourgeois values and tragic love—accompanied by supertitles featuring an English translation steeped in 1950s slang. Received Tony Awards for best costume design and best lighting design. 2003 Tony Honors for Excellence conferred on the principal ensemble members. First New York presentation of record at Wallack's Theatre by the Royal Italian Grand Opera Company of La Scala (5/16/1897; 4 performances). Later productions included runs at the Metropolitan Opera House and at first-class theaters such as Gallo Opera House (now Studio 54) and Center Theatre (at Rockefeller Center, later the RKO Roxy; demolished in 1954.

Dance of the Vampires (56). Musical with book by David Ives, Jim Steinman and Michael Kunze; music and lyrics by Jim Steinman; original German book and lyrics by Mr. Kunze; based on a film by Roman Polanski. Produced by Bob Boyett, USA Ostar Theatricals, Andrew Braunsberg, Lawrence Horowitz, Michael Gardner, Roy Furman, Lexington Road Productions, David Sonenberg at the Minskoff Theatre. Opened December 9, 2002. (Closed January 26, 2003)

Sarah .... Mandy Gonzalez	Professor Abronsius .... René Auberjonois
Zsa-Zsa .... Erin Leigh Peck	Alfred .... Max Von Essen
Nadja .... E. Alyssa Claar	Mme. von Krolock ..... Dame Edith Shorthouse
Count von Krolock .... Michael Crawford	Dream Sarah ....Jennifer Savelli
Chagal .... Ron Orbach	Herbert .... Asa Somers
Rebecca .... Liz McCartney	Dream Alfred .... Jonathan Sharp
Magda .... Leah Hocking	Dream Vampire .... Edgar Godineaux
Boris .... Mark Price	

Ensemble: David Benoit, E. Alyssa Claar, Jocelyn Dowling, Lindsay Dunn, Edgar Godineaux, Ashley Amber Haase, Derric Harris, Robin Irwin, Terace Jones, Larry Keigwin, Brendan King, Heather McFadden, Raymond McLeod, Erin Leigh Peck, Andy Pellick, Joye Ross, Solange Sandy, Jennifer Savelli, Jonathan Sharp, Asa Somers, Doug Storm, Jenny-Lynn Suckling, Jason Wooten.

Orchestra: Patrick Vaccariello conductor; Jim Laev associate conductor; Ann Labin concertmaster; Maura Giannini, Victor Heifets, Dana Ianculovici, Fritz Krakowski, Wende Namkung violin; Peter Prosser, Danny Miller, Eileen Folson cello; Tom Hoyt lead trumpet; Larry Lunetta trumpet; Morris Kainuma bass trombone; Roger Wendt, Kelly Dent, Theo Primis, French horn; Helen Campo flute, piccolo; Tuck Lee oboe, English horn; Dennis Anderson reeds; Ray Marchica drums; Dave Kuhn bass; Adam Ben-David keyboard 1; T.O. Sterrett, Jim Laev keyboard; J.J. McGeehan guitar; David Rozenblatt percussion.

Standbys: Messrs. Crawford, Auberjonois—Rob Evan.

Understudies: Ms. Gonzalez—E. Alyssa Claar, Sara Schmidt; Mses. Peck, Claar—Heather McFadden, Sara Schmidt; Messrs. Crawford, Auberjonois—Timothy Warmen, Mr. Orbach—David Benoit, Raymond McLeod; Ms. McCartney—Robin Irwin, Jenny-Lynn Suckling; Ms. Hocking—Jenny-Lynn Suckling; Messrs. Price, Von Essen, Somers–Doug Storm, Jason Wooten.

Swings: Kerrin Hubbard, Nathan Peck, Sara Schmidt, Timothy Warmen.

Blood lust: Michael Crawford and Mandy Gonzalez in Dance of the Vampires. *Photo: Paul Kolnik*

Directed by John Rando; choreography, John Carrafa; scenery, David Gallo; costumes, Ann Hould-Ward; lighting, Ken Billington; sound, Richard Ryan; fight direction, Rick Sordelet; orchestrations, Steve Margoshes; music supervision, vocal and dance arrangements, Michael Reed; music direction, Patrick Vaccariello; music coordinator, Michael Keller; associate choreographer, Tara Young, associate producers, Michael Fuchs/Morton Swinsky, LFG Holdings, Clear Channel Entertainment, Kathryn Conway, Arielle Tepper, Norman Brownstein, William Carrick; casting, Bernard Telsey Casting; production stage manager, Bonnie Panson; stage manager, Michael J. Passaro; press, Barlow-Hartman, John Barlow, Michael Hartman, Wayne Wolfe, Rob Finn.

Time: 1880s. Place: Lower Bélabartókovich, Carpathia. Presented in two parts.

Adaptation of a popular German musical that takes its cues from Mr. Polanski's tongue-in-cheek horror film about the romantic lure of the vampire "life."

ACT I

Overture .... Orchestra
Scene 1: A Graveyard in the Woods
  "Angels Arise" .... Sarah, Nadja, Zsa-Zsa
  "God Has Left the Building" .... Vampires, Sarah, Nadja, Zsa-Zsa

"Original Sin" .... Krolock, Sarah, Vampires
Scene 2: An Inn
"Garlic" .... Chagal, Rebecca, Magda, Boris, Peasants
"Logic" .... Abronsius, Alfred, Chagal, Magda, Rebecca
Scene 3: Sarah's Room, upstairs at the Inn
"There's Never Been a Night Like This" .... Alfred, Sarah, Chagal,
Rebecca, Magda, Abronsius
"Don't Leave Daddy" .... Chagal
"A Good Nightmare Comes So Rarely" .... Krolock
Scene 4: Outside the Inn, next day
"Death Is Such an Odd Thing" .... Rebecca, Magda
Scene 5: Outside the Inn, that evening
"Braver Than We Are" (additional lyrics by Don Black) .... Sarah, Alfred
"Red Boots Ballet" .... Sarah, Company, Krolock
"Say a Prayer" .... Company
Scene 6: The Castle Gate
"Come With Me" .... Krolock

ACT II

Scene 1: The Great Room
"Vampires in Love (Total Eclipse of the Heart)" .... Sarah, Krolock, Vampires
Scene 2: A Hall in the Castle
The Library
"Books, Books" .... Abronsius, Krolock
The Bed
"Carpe Noctem" .... Company
"For Sarah" .... Alfred
Scene 3: The Crypt of the von Krolocks
"Death Is Such an Odd Thing" (Reprise) .... Rebecca, Magda, Chagal
Scene 4: Herbert's Room
"When Love Is Inside You" .... Alfred, Herbert
Scene 5: Sarah's Room
Scene 6: The Castle Graveyard
"Eternity" .... Vampires
"Confession of a Vampire" .... Krolock
Scene 7: The Ballroom
"The Ball: The Minuet" .... Abronsius, Alfred, Herbert,
Boris, Vampires
"Never Be Enough" .... Krolock, Vampires
"Come with Me" (Reprise) .... Krolock
Scene 8: The Wilderness
"Braver Than We Are" (Reprise) (additional lyrics by Don Black) .... Sarah, Alfred
Scene 9: The Finale
"The Dance of the Vampires" .... Company

Medea (78). Transfer of the Off Off Broadway revival of the play by Euripides; translated by Kenneth McLeish and Frederic Raphael. Produced by Roger Berlind, James M. Nederlander, Daryl Roth, Scott Rudin; by arrangment with Max Weitzenhoffer, Nica Burns, Old Vic Productions, Jedediah Wheeler; in association with Jean Stein, True Love Productions, Inc., Wendy vanden Heuvel at the Brooks Atkinson Theatre. Opened December 10, 2002. (Closed February 23, 2003)

Nurse	Siobhán McCarthy	Kreon	Struan Rodger
Medea	Fiona Shaw	Jason	Jonathan Cake
Tutor	Robin Laing	Aegeus	Joseph Mydell
Chorus	Kirsten Campbell,	Messenger	Derek Hutchinson
	Joyce Henderson, Rachel Isaac,	Children	Dylan Denton,
	Pauline Lynch, Susan Salmon		Alexander Scheitinger, Michael Tommer

Empty caress. Fiona Shaw and Jonathan Cake in Medea. *Photo: Joan Marcus*

Directed by Deborah Warner; scenery, Tom Pye; costumes, Jacqueline Durran; lighting, Michael Gunning; sound, David Meschter; production stage manager, Nevin Hedley; stage managers, Patricia McGregor, Laurie Goldfeder; press, Barlow-Hartman, Michael Hartman, John Barlow, Wayne Wolfe.

Presented without intermission.

Ancient tale regarding the furious consequences of a powerful woman betrayed. This 2000 Abbey Theatre production was first presented in New York at the Brooklyn Academy of Music's 2002 Next Wave Festival (see Plays Produced Off Off Broadway section). First New York presentation of record at Wallack's Theatre (2/16/1857; 17 performances) with Matilda Heron and E.A. Sothern; translated by Ms. Heron from an adaptation by Ernest Legouvé.

Imaginary Friends (76). By Nora Ephron; music by Marvin Hamlisch; lyrics by Craig Carnelia. Produced by USA Ostar Theatricals at the Ethel Barrymore Theatre. Opened December 12, 2002. (Closed February 16, 2003)

Lillian Hellman	Swoosie Kurtz	Beguine Dancer; others	Gina Lamparella
Mary McCarthy	Cherry Jones	Fact; others	Dirk Lumbard
The Man	Harry Groener	Fiction; others	Peter Marx
Abby Kaiser; others	Anne Allgood	Vic; others	Perry Ojeda
Leo; others	Bernard Dotson	Fizzy; others	Karyn Quackenbush
Mrs. Stillman; others	Rosena M. Hill	A Woman	Anne Pitoniak

Orchestra: Ron Melrose conductor, piano; Jonathan Smith assistant conductor; Hollis Burridge trumpet; Randy Andos trombone, tuba; Charles Pillow saxophone, woodwinds; Michael Keller drums, percussion; Mary Ann McSweeney bass; Brian Koonin guitar, banjo, ukulele.

Grandes dames: *Swoosie Kurtz and Cherry Jones in* Imaginary Friends. *Photo: Joan Marcus*

Standbys: Mses. Kurtz, Jones—Susan Pellegrino; Mr. Groener—Dirk Lumbard; Ms. Pitoniak—Anne Allgood.

Swings: Male Swing—Jim Osorno; Female Swing—Melanie Vaughan.

Directed by Jack O'Brien; choreography, Jerry Mitchell; scenery, Michael Levine; costumes, Robert Morgan; lighting, Kenneth Posner; sound, Jon Weston; video projection, Jan Hartley; orchestrations, Torrie Zito; music direction and dance arrangements, Ron Melrose; music coordinator, Michael Keller; casting, Tara Rubin Casting; production stage manager, Evan Ensign; stage managers, Jim Woolley, Joel Rosen; press, the Publicity Office, Bob Fennell, Marc Thibodeau, Michael S. Borowski, Candi Adams.

Presented in two parts.

Fantasy play with music explores the intersecting lives of two grande dames of 20th century American letters. Originally presented by the Globe Theatres, San Diego, California (9/28/2002). A 2002–03 *Best Plays* choice (see essay by Charles Wright in this volume).

Lincoln Center Theater production of **Dinner at Eight** (45). Revival of the play by George S. Kaufman and Edna Ferber. André Bishop artistic director, Bernard Gersten executive producer at the Vivian Beaumont. Opened December 19, 2002. (Closed January 26, 2003)

Millicent Jordan	Christine Ebersole	Miss Copeland	Deborah Mayo
Gustave	Simon Jutras	Carlotta Vance	Marian Seldes
Dora	Enid Graham	Dan Packard	Kevin Conway
Oliver Jordan	James Rebhorn	Kitty Packard	Emily Skinner
Paula Jordan	Samantha Soule	Tina	Charlotte Maier
Ricci	Mark Lotito	Dr. J.W. Talbot	John Dossett
Hattie Loomis	Ann McDonough	Larry Renault	Byron Jennings

Eddie, the Bellboy	Rhys Coiro	Mrs. Wendel	Sloane Shelton
Max Kane	Joe Grifasi	Joe Stengel	Peter Maloney
Mr. Hatfield	Karl Kenzler	Mr. Fitch	David Wohl
The Waiter	Philip LeStrange	Ed Loomis	Brian Reddy
Miss Alden	Anne Lange	Musicians	Julian Gamble, Joseph Kamal,
Lucy Talbot	Joanne Camp		Mark LaMura, Philip LeStrange

Understudies: Mses. Ebersole, Mayo, Lange, Shelton—Sherry Skinker; Messrs. Rebhorn, Maloney—Philip LeStrange; Mses. Graham, Soule, Maier—Christy Pusz; Ms. Seldes—Sloane Shelton; Messrs. Conway, LeStrange, Reddy—Julian Gamble; Messrs. Dossett, Jennings, Kenzler—Mark LaMura; Messrs. Lotito, Coiro, Grifasi—Joseph Kamal; Mses. Skinner, Maier, Lange—Natalie Griffith; Ms. Shelton—Deborah Mayo; Ms. Ebersole—Anne Lange; Mses.Camp, McDonough—Charlotte Maier; Musicians—Rhys Coiro.

Directed by Gerald Gutierrez; scenery, John Lee Beatty; costumes, Catherine Zuber; lighting, David Weiner; sound, Aural Fixation; music, Robert Waldman; casting, Daniel Swee; stage manager, Karen Armstrong; press, Philip Rinaldi, Barbara Carroll.

Time: November 1932. Place: Various locations in New York City. Presented in two parts.

Social climbing family in 1930s New York and the bruises their aspirations bring. A 1932–33 *Best Plays* choice, the original Broadway production opened at the Music Box Theatre (10/22/1932; 232 performances).

Class picture (center group, left to right): Emily Skinner, Kevin Conway, Christine Ebersole, James Rebhorn, Marian Seldes and company in Dinner at Eight. *Photo: Joan Marcus*

Roundabout Theatre Company production of **Tartuffe** (53). By Molière; translated by Richard Wilbur. Todd Haimes artistic director, Ellen Richard managing director, Julia C. Levy, executive director of external affairs, at the American Airlines Theatre. Opened January 9, 2003. (Closed February 23, 2003)

Madame Pernelle	Rosaleen Linehan	Cléante	John Bedford Lloyd
Elmire	Kathryn Meisle	Laurent	Erik Steele
Dorine	J. Smith-Cameron	Flipote	Virginia Louise Smith
Damis	T.R. Knight	Orgon	Brian Bedford
Mariane	Bryce Dallas Howard	Valère	Jeffrey Carlson

Tartuffe-ified: Brian Bedford and Henry Goodman in Tartuffe. *Photo: Joan Marcus*

Tartuffe .... Henry Goodman   Officer .... Erik Steele
Mons. Loyal .... Philip Goodwin

Ensemble: Alec Beard, John Nalbach, John Hayden, Melissa Miller, Brandy Mitchell, Robert Thompson.

Standbys: Ms. Linehan—Patricia Kilgarriff; Messrs. Lloyd, Goodwin, Bedford—Anthony Newfield.

Understudies: Messrs. Goodman, Bedford—Philip Goodwin; Mses. Smith-Cameron, Meisle—Virginia Louise Smith; Messrs. Knight, Carlson—Erik Steele; Mses. Howard, Smith—Melissa Miller; Mr. Steele—John Halbach.

Directed by Joe Dowling; scenery, John Lee Beatty; costumes, Jane Greenwood; lighting, Brian MacDevitt; sound and music, Mark Bennett; casting, Jim Carnahan, production stage manager, Jane Pole; stage manager, Kevin Bertolacci; press, Boneau/Bryan-Brown, Adrian Bryan-Brown, Matt Polk, Amy Dinnerman.

Time: 1669. Place: Orgon's house in Paris. Presented in two parts.

A hypocrite worms his way into the home of an ostentatiously pious man and nearly destroys the fervent one's life. First New York presentation of record at the Park Theatre, by the French Company of the New Orleans Theatre (8/23/1826)—believed to be the first Molière in New York.

Ma Rainey's Black Bottom (68). Revival of the play by August Wilson. Produced by Sageworks, Benjamin Mordecai, Robert G. Bartner, Harriet N. Leve, Jennifer Manocherian, Kim Poster, Theatre Royal Haymarket Productions and Whoopi Goldberg, in association with Peg McFeeley Golden/Willa Shalit, Morton Swinsky/James D. Stern, Brian Brolly/Susan Dietz; by special arrangement with Robert Cole and Frederick Zollo, at the Royale Theatre. Opened February 6, 2003. (Closed April 6, 2003)

Sturdyvant .... Louis Zorich   Cutler .... Carl Gordon
Irvin .... Jack Davidson   Toledo .... Thomas Jefferson Byrd

Hittin' it: Carl Gordon, Thomas Jefferson Byrd, Charles S. Dutton, Whoopi Goldberg and Stephen McKinley Henderson in Ma Rainey's Black Bottom. *Photo: Joan Marcus*

Slow Drag .... Stephen McKinley Henderson	Policeman .... Tony Cucci
Levee .... Charles S. Dutton	Dussie Mae .... Heather Alicia Simms
Ma Rainey .... Whoopi Goldberg	Sylvester .... Anthony Mackie

Understudies: Mr. Dutton—Leland Gantt, Anthony Mackie; Ms. Goldberg—Ebony Jo-Ann; Messrs. Gordon, Byrd—Helmar Augustus Cooper; Mr. Henderson—Helmar Augustus Cooper, Leland Gantt; Ms. Simms—Rochelle Hogue; Mr. Mackie—Leland Gantt; Messrs. Zorich, Davidson, Cucci—Joe Zaloom.

Directed by Marion McClinton; scenery, David Gallo; costumes, Toni-Leslie James; lighting, Donald Holder; sound, Rob Milburn, Michael Bodeen; fight direction, David S. Leong; music director, Dwight Andrews; associate producers, Debbie Bisno/Alice Chebba Walsh; casting, Janet Foster; production stage manager, Diane DiVita; stage manager, Cynthia Kocher; press, Barlow-Hartman, Michael Hartman, John Barlow, Jeremy Shaffer.

Time: Early 1927. Place: A band room and a recording studio in Chicago. Presented in two parts.

Aspiration meets frustration in a drama focused on the travails of African Americans in the music business of the 1920s. A *Best Plays* choice for 1984–85, the original Broadway production opened at the Cort Theatre (10/11/1984; 275 performances).

*Take Me Out (108). Transfer from Off Broadway of the play by Richard Greenberg. Produced by Carole Shorenstein Hays and Frederick DeMann at the Walter Kerr Theatre. Opened February 27, 2003.

Kippy Sunderstrom .... Neal Huff	Rodriguez; Policeman .... Gene Gabriel
Darren Lemming .... Daniel Sunjata	Jason Chenier .... Kohl Sudduth
Shane Mungitt .... Frederick Weller	Toddy Koovitz .... David Eigenberg
Skipper;	Davey Battle .... Kevin Carroll
William R. Danziger .... Joe Lisi	Mason Marzac .... Denis O'Hare
Martinez; Policeman .... Robert M. Jiménez	Takeshi Kawabata .... James Yaegashi

Hero worship: Denis O'Hare and Daniel Sunjata in Take Me Out. *Photo: Joan Marcus*

Understudies: Mr. Huff—Paul Sparks; Mr. Sunjata—Michael Duvert; Mr. Weller—Jonno Roberts, Paul Sparks; Mr. Lisi—John Schiappa; Mr. Jiménez—Michael Duvert, Jonno Roberts; Mr. Gabriel— Michael Duvert, Jonno Roberts; Mr. Sudduth—Paul Sparks, Jonno Roberts; Mr. Eigenberg—John Schiappa; Mr. Carroll—Michael Duvert; Mr. O'Hare—Nat DeWolf; Mr. Yaegashi—Musashi Alexander.

Directed by Joe Mantello; scenery, Scott Pask; costumes, Jess Goldstein; lighting, Kevin Adams; sound, Janet Kalas; associate director, Trip Cullman; executive producers, Greg Holland, Pilar DeMann; casting, Jordan Thaler/Heidi Griffiths; production stage manager, William Joseph Barnes; stage manager, C.A. Clark; press, Boneau/Bryan-Brown, Chris Boneau, Amy Jacobs, Juliana Hannett.

Presented in two parts.

A superstar baseball player's announcement of his homosexuality resonates on the field and off. Originally presented by the Donmar Warehouse in London. First presented in New York at Off Broadway's Anspacher Theater at the Joseph Papp Public Theater (9/5/2002; 78 performances— see Plays Produced Off Broadway section in this volume). Received Tony Awards for best play, best director of a play and best featured actor in a play. A 2002–03 *Best Plays* choice (see essay by Christopher Rawson in this volume).

Lincoln Center Theater production of **Vincent in Brixton** (69). By Nicholas Wright. André Bishop artistic director, Bernard Gersten executive producer, by arrangement with the Royal National Theatre, Ambassador Theatre Group Ltd., Maidstone Productions, Robert Fox Ltd., Elliott F. Kulick, Incidental Colman Tod, the Shubert Organization, at the Golden Theatre. Opened March 6, 2003. (Closed May 4, 2003)

Ursula Loyer	Clare Higgins	Sam Plowman	Pete Starrett
Vincent Van Gogh	Jochum ten Haaf	Anna Van Gogh	Liesel Matthews
Eugenie Loyer	Sarah Drew		

Understudies: Ms. Higgins—Sandra Shipley; Messrs. Haaf, Starrett—Louis Cancelmi; Mses. Drew, Matthews—Maggie Baisch.

Directed by Richard Eyre; scenery and costumes, Tim Hatley; lighting, Peter Mumford; sound, Neil Alexander; projections, Wendall K. Harrington; music, Dominic Muldowney; casting, Daniel Swee; stage manager, Michael Brunner; press, Philip Rinaldi, Barbara Carroll.

Time: 1873–76. Place: The kitchen at 87 Hackford Road, Brixton, South London. Presented in two parts.

Drama tracing Vincent van Gogh's young adulthood in England and how it may have helped to form his art. Originally presented by London's Royal National Theatre in the Cottesloe Theatre (5/1–7/27/2002); transferred to Wyndham's Theatre (8/5–10/26/2002).

Urban Cowboy (60). Musical with book by Aaron Latham and Phillip Oesterman; music and lyrics by composers listed below; based on the film by Paramount Pictures. Produced by Chase Mishkin and Leonard Soloway, in association with Barbara and Peter Fodor, at the Broadhurst Theatre. Opened March 27, 2003. (Closed May 18, 2003)

Bud .... Matt Cavenaugh	Bebe Baker .... Michelle Kittrell
Jesse .... Rozz Morehead	Barbie McQueen ... Kimberly Dawn Neumann
Travis Williams .... Michael Balderrama	Candi Cane .... Tera-Lee Pollin
Marshall .... Mark Bove	Billie Wynette .... Kelleia Sheerin
Roadkill .... Gerrard Carter	Sam .... Paula Wise
J.D. Letterlaw .... Justin Greer	Aunt Corene .... Sally Mayes
Baby Boy .... Brian Letendre	Uncle Bob .... Leo Burmester
Trent Williams .... Barrett Martin	Sissy .... Jenn Colella
Luke "Gator" Daniels .... Chad L. Schiro	Pam .... Jodi Stevens
"Tuff" Love Levy .... Nicole Foret	Wes .... Marcus Chait
Bambi Jo .... Lisa Gajda	

Love's flowers: Clare Higgins and Jochum ten Haaf in Vincent in Brixton. *Photo: Joan Marcus*

Texas trouble: Matt Cavenaugh and Jenn Colella in Urban Cowboy. *Photo: Paul Kolnik*

Orchestra: Jason Robert Brown conductor, keyboard; Dave Keyes keyboard; Brian Brake drums; Gary Sieger guitar; Kermit Driscoll bass; Antoine Silverman fiddle; Gordon Titcomb pedal steel guitar, banjo, electric and acoustic guitars.

Standbys: Messrs. Cavenaugh, Chait—Greg Stone; Mses. Morehead, Mayes—Adinah Alexander.

Understudies: Ms. Colella—Nicole Foret, Michelle Kittrell; Ms. Stevens—Nicole Foret, Kimberly Dawn Neumann; Mr. Burmester—Mark Bove; Ms. Mayes—Kimberly Dawn Neumann.

Swings: Cara Cooper, Jennie Ford, Tyler Hanes, Josh Rhodes.

Directed by Lonny Price; choreography, Melinda Roy; scenery, James Noone; costumes, Ellis Tillman; lighting, Natasha Katz; sound, Peter Fitzgerald; fight direction, Rick Sordelet; music direction, orchestrations, arrangements, Mr. Brown; music coordinator, John Miller; assistant choreographer, Chad L. Schiro; associate producer, Barbara Freitag; casting, Jay Binder/Jack Bowdan; stage manager, Heather Fields; press, Pete Sanders Group, Pete Sanders, Terence Womble, Glenna Freedman.

Time: Late 1970s. Place: In and around Houston, Texas. Presented in two parts.

Pastiche musical celebrating a modernized myth of cowboys and girls; based on the 1980 film starring John Travolta and Debra Winger. Originally presented at the Coconut Grove Playhouse (11/16–12/1/2002), Arnold Mittelman, producing artistic director.

ACT I

"Leavin' Home" .... Bud
(Jeff Blumenkrantz)
"Long Hard Day" .... Jesse, Ensemble
(Bob Stillman)
"All Because of You" .... Aunt Corene
(Jeff Blumenkrantz)
"Another Guy" .... Sissy
(Jeff Blumenkrantz)

"Boot Scootin' Boogie" .... Hardhats, Bud, Sissy, Ensemble
(Ronnie Dunn)
"It Don't Get Better Than This" .... Bud
(Jason Robert Brown)
"Dancin' the Slow Ones With You" .... Pam
(Danny Arena and Sara Light)
"Cowboy Take Me Away" .... Sissy
(Marcus Hummon and Martie Maguire)
"Could I Have This Dance?" .... Bud, Ensemble
(Wayland D. Holyfield and Bob Lee House)
"My Back's Up Against the Wall" .... Wes, Cowboys
(Carl L. Byrd and Pevin Byrd-Munoz)
"If You Mess With the Bull" .... Jesse, Ensemble
(Luke Reed and Roger Brown)
"That's How She Rides" .... Wes
(Jason Robert Brown)
"I Wish I Didn't Love You" .... Bud
(Jason Robert Brown)

ACT II

"That's How Texas Was Born" .... Band
(Jason Robert Brown)
"Take You for a Ride" .... Pam, Wes
(Danny Arena, Sara Light and Lauren Lucas)
"Mr. Hopalong Heartbreak" .... Sissy
(Jason Robert Brown)
"T-R-O-U-B-L-E" .... Marshall
(Jerry Chesnut)
"Dances Turn Into Dreams" .... Jesse
(Jerry Silverstein)
"The Hard Way" .... Sissy, Bud
(Clint Black and James Hayden Nicholas)
"Git It" .... Uncle Bob, Jesse, Ensemble
(Tommy Connors and Roger Brown)
"Something That We Do" .... Aunt Corene, Uncle Bob, Ensemble
(Clint Black and Skip Ewing)
"The Devil Went Down to Georgia" .... Marshall, Ensemble
(Charles Daniels, Tom Crain, Fred Edwards, Taz DiGregorio, Jim Marshall, Charlie Hayward)
"It Don't Get Better Than This" (Reprise)/"Lookin' for Love" .... Bud, Sissy, Ensemble
(Jason Robert Brown)/(Wanda Mallette, Patti Ryan and Bob Morrison)

The Play What I Wrote (72). By Hamish McColl, Sean Foley and Eddie Braben. Produced by David Pugh, Joan Cullman, Mike Nichols, Hamilton South, Charles Whitehead, Stuart Thompson at the Lyceum Theatre. Opened March 30, 2003

Sean	Sean Foley	Arthur	Toby Jones
Hamish	Hamish McColl	Mystery Guest Star	Mystery Guest Star

Understudies: Mr. Jones—Jay Russell.

Directed by Kenneth Branagh; choreography, Irving Davies, Heather Cornell; scenery and costumes, Alice Power; lighting, Tim Mitchell; sound, Simon Baker for Autograph; songs, Gary Yershon; musical arrangements, Steve Parry, casting, Juliet Taylor, Ellen Lewis, Patricia Kerrigan; production stage manager, Nancy Harrington; stage manager, Julie Baldauff; press, Boneau/Bryan-Brown, Adrian Bryan-Brown, Jackie Green, Adriana Douzos.

Presented in two parts.

Three's company: Sean Foley, Toby Jones and Hamish McColl in The Play What I Wrote.
Photo: Joan Marcus

English music-hall comedy sketches featuring a mystery guest star such as Roger Moore or Kevin Kline. Originally presented at London's Wyndham's Theatre (11/5/2001–5/4/2002); later returned to Wyndham's (11/5/2002–1/4/2003).

*Life (x) 3 (71). By Yasmina Reza; translated by Christopher Hampton. Produced by Ron Kastner at the Circle in the Square. Opened March 31, 2003.

Sonia	Helen Hunt	Hubert	Brent Spiner
Henry	John Turturro	Inez	Linda Emond

Standbys: Mses. Hunt, Emond—Charlotte Maier; Messrs. Turturro, Spiner—Stephen Lee Anderson.

Directed by Matthew Warchus; scenery, Mark Thompson; lighting, Hugh Vanstone; sound, Christopher T. Cronin; music, Gary Yershon; associate producers, Jerome Swartz, Joseph Smith; casting, Jim Carnahan; production stage manager, David Hyslop; stage manager, James Mountcastle; press, Boneau/Bryan-Brown, Adrian Bryan-Brown, Susanne Tighe, Joe Perrotta.

Time: The present. Place: Henry and Sonia's apartment, Paris. Presented in two parts.

A hellish evening of colleagues and spouses toying with cosmological significance and possibility as a scene is enacted three different ways. Originally presented by London's Royal National Theatre in the Lyttelton Theatre (12/7/2000–1/16/2001); transferred to the Old Vic Theatre (2/12–5/5/2001); later ran at the Savoy Theatre (10/1–12/7/2002).

*Roundabout Theatre Company production of ***A Day in the Death of Joe Egg** (68). Revival of the play by Peter Nichols. Todd Haimes artistic director, Ellen Richard managing director, Julia C. Levy executive director of external affairs, at the American Airlines Theatre. Opened April 3, 2003.

Bri	Eddie Izzard	Pam	Margaret Colin
Sheila	Victoria Hamilton	Freddie	Michael Gaston
Joe	Madeleine Martin	Grace	Dana Ivey

Standbys: Mr. Izzard—Tony Carlin; Ms. Hamilton—Tina Benko; Ms. Martin–Erica Getto; Ms. Colin—Virginia Louise Smith; Mr.Gaston—Rufus Collins; Ms. Ivey–Lucy Martin.

Sunny side: Victoria Hamilton and Eddie Izzard in A Day in the Death of Joe Egg. *Photo: Joan Marcus*

Directed by Laurence Boswell; scenery and costumes, Es Devlin; lighting, Adam Silverman; sound, Fergus O'Hare; casting, Jim Carnahan; production stage manager, Peter Hanson; press, Boneau/Bryan-Brown, Adrian Bryan-Brown, Dennis Crowley, Matt Polk, Juliana Hannett.

Presented in two parts.

A married couple deal with a child's profound disability through fantasy and humor. An earlier version of this production was presented at London's New Ambassadors Theatre 10/1–11/24/2001; transferred to the Comedy Theatre (12/1/2001–2/9/2002). A *Best Plays* choice for 1967–68, the original Broadway production opened at the Brooks Atkinson Theatre (2/1/1968; 154 performances).

Roundabout Theatre Company production of **As Long As We Both Shall Laugh** (15). Solo performance by Yakov Smirnoff. Todd Haimes artistic director, Ellen Richard managing director, Julia C. Levy executive director of external affairs, at the American Airlines Theatre. Opened April 7, 2003. (Closed May 26, 2003)

Performed by Mr. Smirnoff.

Choreographed by Jennifer Werner; scenery, Eric Renschler; lighting, Mike Baldassari; costumes, Robin L. McGee; sound, Fitz Patton; associate producer, Lovely Jewsbury and Grant Niman; casting, Jim Carnahan; production stage manager: Jay Adler; press, Boneau/Bryan-Brown, Adrian Bryan-Brown, Matt Polk, Juliana Hannett.

Presented in two parts.

Comic reminiscence about life in the old country (Soviet Union) and the new.

*Roundabout Theatre Company production of ***Nine** (60). Revival of the musical with book by Arthur Kopit; music and lyrics by Maury Yeston; adapted from the Italian by Mario Fratti. Todd Haimes artistic director, Ellen Richard managing director, Julia C. Levy executive director of external affairs, at the Eugene O'Neill Theatre. Opened April 10, 2003.

Little Guido .... William Ullrich	Olga von Sturm .... Linda Mugleston
Little Guido	Maria .... Sara Gettelfinger
(Wed.; Sat. matinee) .... Anthony Colangelo	Lina Darling .... Nell Campbell
Guido Contini .... Antonio Banderas	Sofia .... Kathy Voytko
Luisa .... Mary Stuart Masterson	Saraghina .... Myra Lucretia Taylor
Carla .... Jane Krakowski	Juliette .... Rona Figueroa
Renata .... Elena Shaddow	Annabella .... Kristin Marks
Guido's Mother .... Mary Beth Peil	Claudia .... Laura Benanti
Stephanie Necrophorus .... Saundra Santiago	Our Lady of the Spa .... Deidre Goodwin
Diana .... Rachel deBenedet	Liliane La Fleur .... Chita Rivera

Orchestra: Kevin Stites conductor, Gregory J. Dlugos associate conductor, keyboard; Martin Agee concertmaster, violin; Conrad Harris violin 2; Liuh-Wen Ting viola; Sarah Seiver cello; Brian Cassier bass; Brian Miller flute; Les Scott clarinet, sax; Marc Goldberg bassoon; Theresa MacDonnell, French horn; Timothy Schadt, Raymond Riccomini trumpet; Randy Andos trombone; Barbara Biggers harp; Bill Miller drums, percussion.

Standby: Mr. Banderas—Paul Schoeffler.

Understudies: Ms. Rivera—Nell Campbell; Ms. Benanti—Elena Shaddow; Mses. Krakowski, Santiago—Sara Gettelfinger; Ms. Masterson–Linda Mugleston, Kristin Marks; Ms. Campbell—Rona Figueroa; Ms. Goodwin—Kathy Voytko; Ms. Peil—Rachel deBenedet; Ms. Taylor—Linda Mugleston;

Phone fantasy: Antonio Banderas and Jane Krakowski in Nine. *Photo: Joan Marcus*

Mses. Shaddow, Gettelfinger, Figueroa, Marks—Stephanie Bast; Mses. deBenedet, Mugleston, Voytko—Jessica Leigh Brown.

Directed by David Leveaux; choreography, Jonathan Butterell; scenery, Scott Pask; costumes, Vicki Mortimer; lighting, Brian MacDevitt; sound, Jon Weston; orchestrations, Jonathan Tunick; music direction, Kevin Stites; music coordinator, John Miller; executive producer, Sydney Davolos; casting, Jim Carnahan and Jeremy Rich; production stage manager, Arthur Gaffin; stage manager, Laurie Goldfeder; press, Boneau/Bryan-Brown, Adrian Bryan-Brown, Matt Polk, Amy Dinnerman.

Time: The early 1960s. Place: A Venetian spa. Presented in two parts.

A brilliant Italian film director muses over the prominence of women in his life and work. This production received Tony Awards for best musical revival and featured actress in a musical. A *Best Plays* choice for 1982–83, the original Broadway production opened at the 46th Street Theatre (5/9/1982; 739 performances).

ACT I

"Overture Delle Donne" .... Company
   "Spa Music"
   "Not Since Chaplin"
"Guido's Song" .... Guido
   "Coda di Guido" .... Company
"My Husband Makes Movies" .... Luisa
"A Call From the Vatican" .... Carla
"Only With You" .... Guido
"The Script" .... Guido
"Folies Bergeres" .... La Fleur, Necrophorus, Company
"Nine" .... Guido's Mother, Company
"Ti Voglio Bene/Be Italian" .... Saraghina, Little Guido, Company
"The Bells of St. Sebastian" .... Guido, Little Guido, Company

ACT II

"A Man Like You"/"Unusual Way" Duet .... Claudia, Guido
"The Grand Canal" .... Guido, Company
   Contini Submits/The Grand Canal/
   Every Girl in Venice/Recitativo/
   Amor/Recitativo/Only You/ Finale
"Simple" .... Carla
"Be On Your Own" .... Luisa
"Waltz di Guido"
"I Can't Make This Movie" .... Guido
"Getting Tall" ....Little Guido
"My Husband Makes Moves"/"Nine" (Reprise) .... Guido

A Year With Frog and Toad (56). Musical with book and lyrics by Willie Reale; music by Robert Reale; based on the children's books by Arnold Lobel. Produced by Bob Boyett, Adrianne Lobel, Michael Gardner, Lawrence Horowitz, Roy Furman, Scott E. Nederlander at the Cort Theatre. Opened April 13, 2003.

Birds	Danielle Ferland, Jennifer Gambatese, Frank Vlastnik	Squirrels	Danielle Ferland, Jennifer Gambatese
Frog	Jay Goede	Young Frog	Jennifer Gambatese
Toad	Mark Linn-Baker	Father Frog	Frank Vlastnik
Snail	Frank Vlastnik	Mother Frog	Danielle Ferland
Turtle	Danielle Ferland	Moles	Danielle Ferland, Jennifer Gambatese, Frank Vlastnik
Mouse	Jennifer Gambatese		
Lizard	Frank Vlastnik		

Orchestra: Linda Twine conductor, piano; Linc Milliman bass, tuba; James Saporito drums, percussion; Brian Koonin guitar, banjo; Eddie Salkin, Dan Block woodwinds; Brian Pareschi trumpet; Art Baron trombone.

Understudies: Messrs. Goede, Linn-Baker, Vlastnik—Jonathan Rayson; Mses.Ferland, Gambatese—Kate Manning.

Directed by David Petrarca; choreography, Daniel Pelzig; scenery, Adrianne Lobel; costumes, Martin Pakledinaz; lighting, James F. Ingalls; sound, Rob Milburn and Michael Bodeen; orchestrations, Irwin Fisch; musical direction, Ms. Twine; music coordinator, Kimberlee Wertz; assistant director, Leland Patton, assistant choreographer, Ginger Thatcher; casting, Cindy Tolan; production stage manager, Michael J. Passaro; stage manager, Michelle Bosch; press, Barlow-Hartman, John Barlow, Michael Hartman, Wayne Wolfe, Rob Finn.

Presented in two parts.

Musical tales of a loving friendship between amphibians based on a children's-book series by Arnold Lobel. Originally presented at the Children's Theatre Company, Minneapolis, Minnesota (8/23/2002). First presented in New York by the New 42nd Street at the New Victory Theater (11/15–12/1/2002). See Plays Produced Off Off Broadway section.

Amphibians' delight: Jay Goede and Mark Linn-Baker in A Year With Frog and Toad. *Photo: Rob Levine*

ACT I

"A Year with Frog and Toad"	Birds, Frog, Toad
"It's Spring"	Frog,Toad, Birds
"Seeds"	Toad
"The Letter"	Snail
"Getta Loada Toad"	Toad, Frog, Turtle, Mouse, Lizard
Underwater Ballet	Orchestra
"Alone"	Frog
"The Letter" (Reprise)	Snail
"Cookies"	Frog, Toad, Birds

ACT II

Entr'acte	Orchestra
"The Kite"	Birds, Frog, Toad

"A Year with Frog and Toad" (Reprise) .... Birds
"He'll Never Know" .... Toad, Frog
"Shivers" .... Young Frog, Father Frog,
Mother Frog, Toad, Frog
"The Letter" (Reprise) .... Snail
"Down the Hill" .... Frog, Toad, Moles
"I'm Coming Out of My Shell" .... Snail
"Toad to the Rescue" .... Toad, Moles
"Merry Almost Christmas" .... Toad, Frog, Moles
Finale .... Birds, Frog, Toad

*Enchanted April (39). By Matthew Barber; from the novel by Elizabeth von Arnim.
Produced by Jeffrey Richards, Richard Gross/Ellen Berman, Raymond J. and Pearl Berman
Greenwald, Irving Welzer, Tonja Walker Davidson, Libby Adler Mages/Mari Glick, Howard
R. Berlin, Jerry Frankel, Terry E. Schnuck, Frederic B. Vogel at the Belasco Theatre.
Opened April 29, 2003.

Lotty Wilton .... Jayne Atkinson	Mrs. Graves .... Elizabeth Ashley
Rose Arnott .... Molly Ringwald	Antony Wilding .... Michael Hayden
Mellersh Wilton .... Michael Cumpsty	Costanza .... Patricia Conolly
Frederick Arnott .... Daniel Gerroll	Servant .... John Feltch
Lady Caroline Bramble .... Dagmara Dominczyk	

Understudies: Messrs.Cumpsty, Hayden, Gerroll—John Feltch; Mses. Ashley, Conolly—Jill Tanner;
Mr. Feltch—Jill Tanner.

Directed by Michael Wilson; scenery, Tony Straiges; costumes, Jess Goldstein; lighting, Rui
Rita; music and sound, John Gromada; associate producers, Jack W. Batman, Lionel Goldfrank III,
Samuel V. Goekjian; casting, Bernard Telsey Casting; production stage manager, Katherine Lee
Boyer; stage manager, Matthew Aaron Stern; press, Irene Gandy, Michelle Patrick, Michael Dressel,
Alana O'Brien.

Time: 1922. Place: London and the coast of Italy. Presented in two parts.

Dissatisfied London wives escape to Italy where they reawaken their passions for life; based
on a 1923 book by Elizabeth von Arnim. First presented at Hartford Stage (2/24/2000). An earlier
play—*The Enchanted April* by Kane Campbell, which was based on the same book by Ms.
Arnim—opened at Broadway's Morosco Theatre (8/24/1925; 32 performances).

*Salome (29) Revival of the play by Oscar Wilde. Produced by Robert Fox, Daryl Roth
and Amy Nederlander at the Ethel Barrymore Theatre. Opened April 30, 2003.

The Young Syrian .... Chris Messina	A Slave .... Jill Alexander
The Page of Herodias .... Timothy Doyle	Herod Antipas .... Al Pacino
First Soldier .... Timothy Altmeyer	Herodias .... Dianne Wiest
Second Soldier .... Brian Delate	Tigellinus .... Chris McGarry
A Cappadocian .... Andrew Garman	Ensemble .... Robert Heller, Owen Hollander,
A Nubian .... Daryl Mismond	Robert Lavelle, Ed Setrakian
Jokanaan .... David Strathairn	Musician .... Yukio Tsuji
Salome .... Marisa Tomei	

Directed by Estelle Parsons; scenery, Peter Larkin; costumes, Jane Greenwood; lighting, Howard
Thies; sound, Erich Bechtel and David Schnirman; music, Mr. Tsuji; production stage manager,
Alan Fox; press, Barlow-Hartman, John Barlow, Michael Hartman, Jeremy Shaffer.

Presented without intermission.

Staged reading version of Mr. Wilde's controversial (in its day) rendering of a biblical tale
centering on power, lust and faith. Production developed at the Actors Studio and previously
performed at St. Ann's Warehouse in Brooklyn, New York, and at the Bardavon 1869 Opera House
in Poughkeepsie, New York. Mr. Pacino also played Herod Antipas in a brief 1992 run at Circle in
the Square Theatre. The first professional New York production featured Mercedes Leigh in the
title role at the Astor Theatre (11/15/1906).

*Gypsy (36). Revival of the musical with book by Arthur Laurents; music by Jule Styne; lyrics by Stephen Sondheim; suggested by the memoirs of Gypsy Rose Lee. Produced by Robert Fox, Ron Kastner, Roger Marino, Michael Watt, Harvey Weinstein, WWLC at the Shubert Theatre. Opened May 1, 2003.

Uncle Jocko .... Michael McCormick	Mr. Goldstone .... Brooks Ashmanskas
Clarence .... Stephen Scott Scarpulla	Miss Cratchitt .... Julie Halston
Balloon Girl .... Molly Grant Kallins	Farmboys .... Matt Bauer, David Burtka,
Baby Louise .... Addison Timlin	Benjamin Brooks Cohen,
Baby June .... Heather Tepe	Joey Dudding, Brandon Espinoza,
Rose .... Bernadette Peters	Tim Federle
Chowsie .... Coco	Cow .... Sarah Jayne Jensen, Dontee Kiehn
Pop .... William Parry	Agnes .... Chandra Lee Schwartz
Newsboys .... Eamon Foley,	Hollywood Blondes .... Jenna Gavigan,
Stephen Scott Scarpulla,	Sarah Jayne Jensen,
Jordan Viscomi	Dontee Kiehn, Ginifer King,
Weber .... MacIntyre Dixon	Julie Martell
Herbie .... John Dossett	Pastey .... Brooks Ashmanskas
Louise .... Tammy Blanchard	Tessie Tura .... Heather Lee
June .... Kate Reinders	Mazeppa .... Kate Buddeke
Tulsa .... David Burtka	Cigar .... Michael McCormick
Yonkers .... Matt Bauer	Electra .... Julie Halston
L.A. .... Brandon Espinoza	Rene .... Cathy Trien
Kansas .... Benjamin Brooks Cohen	Phil .... MacIntyre Dixon
Kringelein .... William Parry	Bougeron-Cochon .... Tim Federle

Ensemble: Matt Bauer, Benjamin Brooks Cohen, MacIntyre Dixon, Joey Dudding, Brandon Espinoza, Tim Federle, Eamon Foley, Jenna Gavigan, Sarah Jayne Jensen, Molly Grant Kallins, Dontee Kiehn, Ginifer King, Gina Lamparella, Julie Martell, Stephen Scott Scarpulla, Chandra Lee Schwartz, Cathy Trien, Jordan Viscomi.

Orchestra: Marvin Laird conductor; Ethyl Will associate conductor, piano; Ann Labin concertmaster; Maura Giannini, Dana Ianculovici violin; Richard Brice viola; Peter Prosser, Eileen Folson cello; Grace Paradise harp; Christian Jaudes lead trumpet; Larry Lunetta, Hollis Burridge trumpet; Bruce Eidem, Michael Seltzer trombone; Morris Kainuma bass trombone; Roger Wendt, French horn; Dennis Anderson, Mort Silver, Ralph Olsen, Charles Pillow, Ron Janelli reeds; Cubby O'Brien drums, Bill Ellison bass, Deane Prouty percussion.

Standby: Ms. Peters—Maureen Moore.

Understudies: Messrs. McCormick (Uncle Jocko), Parry (Parry), Ashmanskas (Goldstone)—MacIntyre Dixon, Wally Dunn; Mses. Tepe, Kallins—Alexandra Stevens; Ms. Timlin—Molly Grant Kallins; Messrs. Foley, Scarpulla, Viscomi—Molly Grant Kallins; Mr. Dossett—Michael McCormick, William Parry; Ms. Blanchard—Ginifer King, Julie Martell; Ms. Reinders—Jenna Gavigan, Chandra Lee Schwartz; Mr. Burtka—Matt Bauer, Tim Federle; Messrs. Parry (Kringelein), McCormick (Cigar), Ashmanskas (Pastey)—Wally Dunn; Ms. Schwartz—Dontee Kiehn; Mses. Halston, Lee, Buddeke—Gina Lamparella, Cathy Trien.

Swings: Graham Bowen, Wally Dunn, Pamela Remler.

Directed by Sam Mendes; original choreography, Jerome Robbins; additional choreography, Jerry Mitchell; scenery and costumes, Anthony Ward; lighting, Jules Fisher and Peggy Eisenhauer; sound, Acme Sound Partners; musical supervisor, Patrick Vaccariello; orchestrations, Sid Ramin and Robert Ginzler; additional orchestrations, Bruce Coughlin; original dance arrangements, John Kander; music direction, additional dance music arrangments, Mr. Laird; music coordinator, Michael Keller; associate director, Peter Lawrence; associate choreographer, Jodi Moccia; casting, Jim Carnahan; stage managers, Richard Hester, Jim Woolley; press, Boneau/Bryan-Brown, Adrian Bryan-Brown, Jim Byk, Jackie Green, Aaron Meier.

Presented in two parts.

The ultimate stage mother pushes her daughters into the limelight she would like to have for herself. The original Broadway production opened at the Broadway Theatre (5/21/1959; 702 performances); transferred during the run to the Imperial Theatre (8/15/1960).

Gleesome threesome: John Dossett, Bernadette Peters and Tammy Blanchard in Gypsy. *Photo: Joan Marcus*

ACT I

Overture .... Orchestra
"May We EntertainYou" .... Baby June, Baby Louise
"Some People" .... Rose
"Travelling" .... Rose
"Small World" .... Rose, Herbie
"Baby June and Her Newsboys" .... Baby June, Baby Louise,
Newsboys
"Mr. Goldstone, I Love You" .... Rose, Ensemble
"Little Lamb" .... Louise
"You'll Never Get Away From Me" Rose, Herbie
"Dainty June and Her Farmboys" .... Dainty June, Louise,
Farmboys
"If Momma Was Married" .... Louise, June
"All I Need Is the Girl" .... Tulsa, Louise
"Everything's Coming Up Roses" .... Rose

ACT II

Entr'Acte .... Orchestra
"Madame Rose's Toreadorables" .... Louise, the Hollywood Blondes

"Together, Wherever We Go" .... Rose, Louise, Herbie
"You Gotta Get a Gimmick" .... Tessie Tura, Mazeppa, Electra
"Small World" (Reprise) .... Rose
"Let Me Entertain You" .... Louise, Company
"Rose's Turn" .... Rose

Roundabout Theatre Company production of *The Look of Love** (32). Musical revue with music by Burt Bacharach; lyrics by Hal David; conceived by David Thompson, Scott Ellis, David Loud and Ann Reinking. Todd Haimes artistic director; Ellen Richard managing director; Julia C. Levy executive director of external affairs, at the Brooks Atkinson Theatre. Opened May 4, 2003.

Performed by Liz Callaway, Kevin Ceballo, Jonathan Dokuchitz, Eugene Fleming, Capathia Jenkins, Janine LaManna, Shannon Lewis, Rachelle Rak, Desmond Richardson.

Pit Singers: Farah Alvin and Nikki Renée Daniels

Orchestra: Mr. Loud conductor; Sue Anschutz associate conductor, keyboard 2; Philip Fortenberry assistant conductor, keyboard 1; Chuck Wilson, Kenneth Dybisz, Mark Thrasher woodwinds; Jon Owens, Matt Peterson trumpet; Stephen Benson guitar; Benjamin Franklin Brown bass; Dave Ratajczak drums; Bill Hayes percussion; Paul Woodiel, Ella Rutkovsky, Jonathan Dinklage violin.

Swings: Allyson Turner and Eric Jordan Young

Directed by Mr. Ellis; choreography, Ms. Reinking; scenery, Derek McLane; costumes, Martin Pakledinaz; lighting, Howell Binkley; sound, Brian Ronan; orchestrations, Don Sebesky; music direction and arrangements, Mr. Loud; music coordinator, John Miller; associate choreography, Debra McWaters; associate producer, James David; casting, Jim Carnahan; production stage manager, Lori M. Doyle; stage manager, Tamlyn Freund Yerkes; press, Boneau/Bryan-Brown, Adrian Bryan-Brown; Dennis Crowley, Matt Polk, Joe Perrotta.

Presented in two parts.

Musical revue of pop music from the 1960s and 1970s.

ACT I

"The Look of Love" .... Capathia Jenkins, Company
"(There's) Always Something There to Remind Me" .... Eugene Fleming,
Jonathan Dokuchitz, Kevin Ceballo
"You'll Never Get To Heaven (If You Break My Heart)" .... Janine LaManna
"I Say a Little Prayer" .... Liz Callaway, Capathia Jenkins,
Janine LaManna
"Promse Her Anything" ....Jonathan Dokuchitz,
Shannon Lewis, Rachelle Rak
"I Just Don't Know What to Do With Myself" .... Liz Callaway
"Raindrops Keep Falling on My Head" .... Eugene Fleming, Desmond Richardson
"Are You There (With Another Girl)" .... Capathia Jenkins
"Another Night" .... Janine LaManna
"Yo Nunca Volveré Amar (I'll Never Fall in Love Again)" .... Kevin Ceballo, Shannon Lewis
"She Likes Basketball" .... Eugene Fleming
"What's New Pussycat?" .... Shannon Lewis,
Janine LaManna, Rachelle Rak
"Walk on By" .... Capathia Jenkins
"A House Is Not a Home" .... Jonathan Dokuchitz
"One Less Bell to Answer" .... Liz Callaway

ACT II

"Casino Royale" .... Orchestra, Farah Alvin, Nikki Renée Daniels
"Wishin' and Hopin'" .... Janine LaManna,
Shannon Lewis, Rachelle Rak
"This Guy's in Love With You"/"This Girl's in Love With You" .... Eugene Fleming,
Capathia Jenkins
"Alfie" .... Liz Callaway

"Trains and Boats and Planes" .... Desmond Richardson
"Do You Know the Way to San Jose?" .... Kevin Ceballo, Jonathan Dokuchitz,
Eugene Fleming, Desmond Richardson
"Twenty-Four Hours from Tulsa" .... Rachelle Rak
"Close to You" .... Janine LaManna, Jonathan Dokuchitz
"Anyone Who Had a Heart" .... Kevin Ceballo
"Wives and Lovers" .... Shannon Lewis,
Desmond Richardson, Eugene Fleming
"Make It Easy on Yourself" .... Capathia Jenkins
"Knowing When to Leave" .... Liz Callaway
"Promises, Promises" .... Liz Callaway, Capathia Jenkins
"What the World Needs Now Is Love" .... Company

Constant comment: Bill Maher in Victory Begins at Home. *Photo: Bruce Glikas*

Bill Maher: Victory Begins at Home (16). Solo performance by Mr. Maher. Produced by Eric Krebs, Jonathan Reinis, CTM Productions, Anne Strickland Squadron, in association with Michael Viner, David and Adam Friedson, Allen Spivak/Larry Magid, M. Kilburg Reedy, at the Virginia Theatre. Opened May 5, 2003. (Closed May 18, 2003)

Scenery and lighting design by Peter R. Feuchtwanger; sound, Jill B.C. DuBoff; executive producer, Sheila Griffith; press, Bill Evans and Associates, Jim Randolph.

Presented without intermission.

Mr. Maher's comic rampage through a herd of sacred cows during a time of war and terroristic threats. Recorded for broadcast on cable television.

*Long Day's Journey Into Night (27). Revival of the play by Eugene O'Neill. Produced by David Richenthal, Max Cooper, Eric Falkenstein, Anthony and Charlene Marshall, Darren Bagert, in association with Kara Medoff, Lisa Vioni and Gene Korf, at the Plymouth Theatre. Opened May 6, 2003.

Night falls: Brian Dennehy and Vanessa Redgrave in Long Day's Journey Into Night. *Photo: Joan Marcus*

James Tyrone .... Brian Dennehy   Edmund Tyrone .... Robert Sean Leonard
Mary Cavan Tyrone .... Vanessa Redgrave   Cathleen .... Fiana Toibin
James Tyrone Jr. .... Philip Seymour Hoffman

Understudies: Mr. Dennehy—Christopher Wynkoop; Mr. Hoffman—C.J. Wilson; Mr. Leonard—Michael Dempsey; Ms. Toibin—Morgan Hallett.

Directed by Robert Falls; scenery and costumes, Santo Loquasto; lighting, Brian MacDevitt; sound, Richard Woodbury; associate producers, Entitled Entertainment, Ergo Entertainment, Anna Ryan Hansen, Toby Simkin; casting, Bernard Telsey Casting; production stage manager, Jane Grey; press, Richard Kornberg, Don Summa, Tom D'Ambrosio, Carrie Friedman, Rick Miramontez.

Time: 1912. Place: The summer home of the Tyrone family. Presented in three parts.

Mr. O'Neill's great drama of dysfunction in a family ravaged by drug and alcohol abuse, Oedipal struggles, secrets, lies and guilt. This production, the fourth major New York revival of record, received Tony Awards for best revival of a play, best actor in a play and best actress in a play. A *Best Plays* choice for 1956–57, the original Broadway production opened at the Helen Hayes Theatre (11/7/1956; 390 performances).

PLAYS PRODUCED OFF BROADWAY
○ ○ ○ ○ ○

FOR THE PURPOSES of *Best Plays* listing, the term "Off Broadway" signifies a show that opened for general audiences in a Manhattan theater seating 499 or fewer and 1) employed an Equity cast, 2) planned a regular schedule of 8 performances a week in an open-ended run (7 a week for solo shows and some other exceptions) and 3) offered itself to public comment by critics after a designated opening performance.

Figures in parentheses following a play's title give number of performances. These numbers do not include previews or extra non-profit performances. Performance interruptions for cast changes and other breaks have been taken into account. Performance numbers are figured in consultation with press representatives and company managements.

Plays marked with an asterisk (*) were still in a projected run on June 1, 2003. The number of performances is figured from press opening through May 31, 2003.

In a listing of a show's numbers—dances, sketches, musical scenes, etc.—the titles of songs are identified wherever possible by their appearance in quotation marks (").

HOLDOVERS FROM PREVIOUS SEASONS

OFF BROADWAY SHOWS that were running on June 1, 2002 are listed below. More detailed information about them appears in previous *Best Plays* volumes of appropriate date. Important cast changes since opening night are recorded in the Cast Replacements section of this volume.

*Perfect Crime (6,672). By Warren Manzi. Opened October 16, 1987.

Tony 'n' Tina's Wedding (4,914). By Artificial Intelligence. Opened February 6, 1988. (Closed May 18, 2003)

*Blue Man Group (Tubes) (5,805). Performance piece by and with Blue Man Group. Opened November 17, 1991.

*Stomp (3,883). Percussion performance piece created by Luke Cresswell and Steve McNicholas. Opened February 27, 1994.

*I Love You, You're Perfect, Now Change (2,836). Musical revue with book and lyrics by Joe DiPietro; music by Jimmy Roberts. Opened August 1, 1996.

Late Nite Catechism (1,268). By Vicki Quade and Maripat Donovan. Opened October 3, 1996. (Closed May 18, 2003)

*De La Guarda (1,952). Spectacle devised by De La Guarda (Pichon Baldinu, Diqui James, Gabriel Kerpel, Fabio D'Aquila, Tomas James, Alejandro Garcia, Gabriella Baldini). Opened June 16, 1998.

*Naked Boys Singing! (1,622). Musical revue conceived by Robert Schrock; written by various authors. Opened July 22, 1999.

*The Donkey Show (1,103). Musical conceived and created by Randy Weiner and Diane Paulus; adapted from William Shakespeare's *A Midsummer Night's Dream*. Opened August 12, 1999.

The Vagina Monologues (1,381). By Eve Ensler. Opened October 3, 1999. (Closed January 26, 2003)

Our Sinatra (1,096). Musical revue conceived by Eric Comstock, Christopher Gines and Hilary Kole; music and lyrics by various authors. Opened December 19, 1999. (Closed July 28, 2002)

The Syringa Tree (586). By Pamela Gien. Opened September 14, 2000. (Closed June 2, 2002)

Love, Janis (713). Musical based on the book by Laura Joplin; adapted and directed by Randal Myler. Opened April 22, 2001. (Closed January 5, 2003)

Puppetry of the Penis (452). By David Friend and Simon Morley. Opened October 5, 2001. (Closed November 3, 2002)

Underneath the Lintel (400). By Glen Berger. Opened October 23, 2001. (Closed January 5, 2003)

Criss Angel Mindfreak (600). By Criss Angel. Opened December 13, 2001. (Closed January 6, 2003)

*Forbidden Broadway: 20th Anniversary Celebration (526). Musical revue created and written by Gerard Alessandrini. Opened February 25, 2002.

Surviving Grace (112). By Trish Vradenburg. Opened March 12, 2002. (Closed June 16, 2002)

Mr. Goldwyn (104). By Marsha Lebby and John Lollos. Opened March 12, 2002. (Closed June 9, 2002)

Lincoln Center Theater presents the Alley Theatre, Guthrie Theater and Hartford Stage production of The Carpetbagger's Children (112). By Horton Foote. Opened March 25, 2002. (Closed June 30, 2002)

The Godfadda Workout (80). Solo performance by Seth Isler. Opened March 25, 2002. (Closed June 2, 2002)

*Menopause: The Musical (512). Musical revue with book and lyrics by Jeanie Linders; music by various popular artists. Opened April 4, 2002.

Second Stage Theatre production of Ricky Jay on the Stem (81). Solo performance by Ricky Jay. Opened May 2, 2002. (Closed June 9, 2003) Reopened June 18, 2003. (Closed July 14, 2003) Reopened September 17, 2003. (Closed October 20, 2003)

The Odyssey (33). By Derek Walcott; adapted from Homer. Opened May 5, 2002. (Closed June 2, 2002)

New York Theatre Workshop production of Vienna: Lusthaus (revisited) (111). By Martha Clarke; music by Richard Peaslee; text by Charles L. Mee. Opened May 8, 2002. (Closed August 11, 2002)

Red Hot Mama (91). Solo performance by Sharon McNight; based on the work of Sophie Tucker. Opened May 8, 2002. (Closed August 4, 2002)

21 Dog Years: Doing Time @ Amazon.com (127). Solo performance by Mike Daisey. Opened May 9, 2002.

Capitol Steps: When Bush Comes to Shove (124). By Bill Strauss, Elaina Newport and Mark Eaton. Opened May 16, 2002. (Closed August 31, 2002)

Primary Stages production of **One Shot, One Kill** (40). By Richard Vetere. Opened May 20, 2002. (Closed June 23, 2002)

Manhattan Theatre Club productions of **House** and **Garden** (80). By Alan Ayckbourn. Opened May 21, 2002. (Closed July 28, 2002)

Playwrights Horizons production of **Boys and Girls** (16). By Tom Donaghy. Opened May 28, 2002. (Closed June 9, 2002)

PLAYS PRODUCED JUNE 1, 2002–MAY 31, 2003

Brooklyn Academy of Music presentation of the **Royal Dramatic Theatre of Sweden** production of **Maria Stuart** (5). Revival of the play by Friedrich von Schiller; English translation by Michael Feingold; Swedish translation by Britt G. Hallqvist. Alan H. Fishman chairman of the board, Karen Brooks Hopkins president, Joseph V. Melillo executive producer, at the Howard Gilman Opera House. Opened June 12, 2002. (Closed June 16, 2002)

Maria Stuart .... Pernilla August	Lord Talbot .... Per Myrberg
Elisabet .... Lena Endre	Lord Paulet .... Ingvar Kjellson
Hanna Kennedy .... Gunnel Lindblom	Melvil .... Erland Josephson
Lord Leicester .... Mikael Persbrandt	Mortimer .... Stefan Larsson
Lord Burleigh .... Borje Ahlstedt	

Directed by Ingmar Bergman; choreography, Donya Feuer; scenery, Göran Wassberg; costumes, Charles Koroly; lighting, Hans Akesson; music, Daniel Börtz; press, Sandy Sawotka, Melissa Cusick, Fateema Jones, Tamara McCaw, Kila Packett.

Presented in two parts.

Female rivals for the English crown maneuver for power and survival in Mr. Schiller's 1800 play, adapted to Mr. Bergman's dramatic purposes. It was the first New York presentation of record in Swedish. The story of Mary Stuart and Elizabeth Tudor has had many theatrical versions on New York stages: *Mary Stuart*, *Mary of Scotland* (versions in 1821 and 1933), *Marie Stuart* (French), *Maria Stuart* (usually German) and *Mary, Queen of Scots*. The first New York presentation of record crediting Mr. Schiller was a German-language production at the Stadt-Theater (10/20/ 1854). The role of Mary Stuart—in diverse versions—became part of the New York repertoire of such 19th century actresses as Charlotte Cushman (1840), Mlle. Rachel (1855), Adelaide Ristori (1866) and Helena Modjeska (1886). Maxwell Anderson's 1933 *Mary of Scotland* was a 1933–34 *Best Plays* choice, its original Broadway production opened at the Alvin Theatre (11/27/1933; 248 performances).

The Prince and the Pauper (194). Musical with book by Bernie Garzia and Ray Roderick; music by Neil Berg; lyrics by Messrs. Berg and Garzia; based on the novel by Mark Twain. Produced by Carolyn Rossi Copeland, Marian Lerman Jacobs and Leftfield Productions at the Lamb's Theatre. Opened June 16, 2002. (Closed October 21, 2002) Reopened November 27, 2002. (Closed January 5, 2003)

Prince Edward .... Dennis Michael Hall	Miles; Charlie; Patch .... Rob Evan
Tom Canty, the Pauper .... Gerard Canonico	Hugh Hendon; Stache .... Stephen Zinnato

Lady Edith; Karyn .... Rita Harvey	Lady Jane; Jamie; Nan .... Allison Fischer
John Canty; King Henry;	Pike; Guard Sergeant .... Wayne Schroeder
Castle Cook .... Michael McCormick	Father Andrew; Woody;
Mary Canty; Maggie .... Sally Wilfert	Soldier; Mr. Ferguson;
Hermit; Grammer;	Richard; Guard .... Aloysius Gigl
Dresser .... Robert Anthony Jones	Annie .... Kathy Brier

Directed by Mr. Roderick; scenery, Dana Kenn; costumes, Sam Fleming; lighting, Eric T. Haugen; sound, One Dream Sound; fight direction, Rick Sordelet; orchestrations, music supervision and arrangements, John Glaudini; press, Cromarty and Company, Peter Cromarty.

Presented in two parts.

Two boys exchange lives and learn important lessons about how others inhabit the world. Abby Sage Richardson wrote the first theatrical adaptation of record—not a musical—which opened at the Broadway Theatre (1/20/1890) with Mark Twain in attendance.

Rumblin': Chuck Cooper and Leslie Uggams in Thunder Knocking on the Door. *Photo: Joan Marcus*

Thunder Knocking on the Door (45). Musical with book by Keith Glover; music and lyrics by Keb' Mo' and Anderson Edwards; additional music and lyrics by Mr. Glover. Produced by Ted Tulchin and Benjamin Mordecai, in association with Mari Nakachi and Robert G. Bartner/Stephanie McClelland, at the Minetta Lane Theatre. Opened June 20, 2002. (Closed July 28, 2002)

Good Sister Dupree .... Leslie Uggams	Marvell Thunder .... Peter Jay Fernandez
Jaguar Senior;	Glory Dupree .... Marva Hicks
Dregster Dupree .... Chuck Cooper	Jaguar Dupree .... Michael McElroy

Musicians: George Caldwell keyboard; Billy Thompson, Billy "Spaceman" Patterson guitar; Toby Williams drums; Anderson Edwards bass; Messrs. Cooper and Fernandez harmonica.

Directed by Oskar Eustis; musical staging, Luis Perez; scenery, Eugene Lee; costumes, Toni-Leslie James; lighting, Natasha Katz; sound, Acme Sound Partners; music supervision, Linda Twine; musical direction, George Caldwell; arrangements and orchestrations, Zane Mark, Ms. Twine, Mr. Caldwell; production stage manager, Diane DiVita; press, Barlow-Hartman, Jeremy Shaffer.

Presented in two parts.

Myth, magic and music converge in an aspiring African-American family. Honored by the American Theatre Critics Association with its 1997 M. Elizabeth Osborn Award. First presented at the Alabama Shakespeare Festival (10/4/1996).

ACT I

"Prologue"	Company
"This House is Built"	Company
"Believe Me"	Dregster and Good Sister
"Big Money"	Jaguar, Good Sister, Glory, Dregster
"Hold On"	Jaguar, Good Sister, Glory, Dregster
"Stranger Blues"	Thunder, Glory, Good Sister
"Hurt Somebody"	Jaguar, Dregster, Thunder
"See Through Me"	Thunder and Glory

ACT II

"Way Down on the Inside"	Jaguar
"I'm Back"	Glory
"I Wish I Knew"	Glory and Good Sister
"Motor Scooter"	Dregster and Jaguar
"Even When You Win, Sometimes You Lose"	Thunder
"Rainmaker"	Glory and Thunder
"That Ain't Right (Cuttin' Contest)"	Glory, Thunder, Company
"Take On the Road"	Jaguar, Thunder, Jaguar Sr.
"Willing to Go"	Good Sister
"Movin' On"	Glory and Company

Endpapers (145). By Thomas McCormack. Produced by Benjamin Mordecai and Griffin Productions at the Variety Arts Theatre. Opened June 23, 2002. (Closed October 27, 2002)

Griff	Bruce McCarty	Kay Carson	Beth Dixon
Cora McCarthy	Pippa Pearthree	John Hope	Alex Draper
Grover Shively	Neil Vipond	Ted Giles	Tim Hopper
Joshua Maynard	William Cain	Ram Spencer	Gregory Salata
Sara Maynard	Maria Thayer	Peter Long	Oliver Wadsworth
Sheila Berne	Shannon Burkett		

Directed by Pamela Berlin; scenery, Neil Patel; costumes, Amela Baksic; lighting, Rui Rita; sound, Ken Travis; production stage manager, Pamela Edington; press, Cohn Davis Associates, Helene Davis.

Presented in two parts.

Literary merit and profit margins collide in an insider's tale of publishing's harsh reality.

Roundabout Theatre Company production of **All Over** (77). Revival of the play by Edward Albee. Todd Haimes artistic director, Ellen Richard managing director, Julia C. Levy executive director for external affairs, in association with the McCarter Theatre, at the Gramercy Theatre. Opened June 27, 2002. (Closed September 1, 2002)

The Wife	Rosemary Harris	The Son	Patrick Garner
The Daughter	Pamela Nyberg	The Best Friend	John Carter
The Mistress	Michael Learned	The Nurse	Myra Carter
The Doctor	Bill Moor		

Newspapermen: Richard Cottrell, Keith Dixon, Chuck McMahon.

Betrayer, betrayed: Michael Learned and Rosemary Harris in All Over. *Photo: Joan Marcus*

Understudies: Mses. Harris, Carter—Mikel Sarah Lambert; Mses. Learned, Nyberg—Alison Edwards; Messrs. Carter, Moor—Fred Burrell; Mr. Garner—Richard Cottrell.

Directed by Emily Mann; scenery, Thomas Lynch; costumes, Jennifer von Mayrhauser; lighting, Allen Lee Hughes; casting, Bernard Telsey Casting; production stage manager, Jay Adler; stage manager, Richard Costabile; press, Boneau/Bryan-Brown, Adrian Bryan-Brown, Matt Polk, Amy Dinnerman.

Time: 1971. Place: The private quarters of a townhouse. Presented in two parts.

Factions battle over the legacy of a man dying in an offstage room. First New York presentation of record at Broadway's Martin Beck Theatre (3/28/1971; 40 performances).

New York Theatre Workshop production of **Play Yourself** (31). By Harry Kondoleon. James C. Nicola artistic director, Lynn Moffat managing director, at the Century Center for the Performing Arts. Opened July 10, 2002. (Closed August 4, 2002)

Selma .... Ann Guilbert	Yvonne .... Elizabeth Marvel
Harmon .... Juan Carlos Hernandez	Jean .... Marian Seldes

Directed by Craig Lucas; scenery, John McDermott; costumes, Catherine Zuber; lighting, Ben Stanton; music and sound, David Van Tieghem; production stage manager, Antonia Gianino; press, Richard Kornberg and Associates, Don Summa.

Presented in two parts.

Faded movie queen and her angry daughter encounter persons as peculiar as they. First New York presentation of record for the 1986 play.

Aquila Theatre Company production of **The Comedy of Errors** (150). Revival of the play by William Shakespeare; adapted by Robert Richmond. Peter Meineck artistic director, at the East 13th Street Theatre. Opened July 11, 2003. (Closed September 1, 2002) Reopened September 3, 2002, at the Harold Clurman Theatre. (Closed November 17, 2002)

Egeon; Balthasar; Pinch .... Alex Webb
Solinus, Duke of Ephesus .... William Kwapy
Both Antipholuses .... David Caron
Adriana .... Lisa Carter
Luciana .... Mira Kingsley
Emilia; Nell .... Marci Adilman
Both Dromios .... Louis Butelli

Directed by Mr. Richmond; scenery, David Coleman and Owen Collins; costumes, Lisa Martin Stuart; lighting, Mr. Meineck; composer and musical director, Anthony Cochrane; press, Pete Sanders Group, Rick Miramontez.

Presented in two parts.

Mr. Shakespeare's comedy about long-lost brothers and mistaken indentity. First presentation of record at Gray's Inn, London, December 1594. First New York presentation of record at the Park Theatre (5/25/1804).

The Joseph Papp Public Theater/New York Shakespeare Festival production of **Twelfth Night** (19). Revival of the play by William Shakespeare. George C. Wolfe producer, at the Delacorte Theater. Opened July 21, 2003. (Closed August 11, 2003)

Orsino .... Jimmy Smits
Curio ....,,,,,,,, Al Espinosa
Valentine .... Andre McGinn
Viola .... Julia Stiles
Captain .... Bill Buell
Sir Toby Belch .... Oliver Platt
Maria .... Kristen Johnston
Sir Andrew Aguecheek .... Michael Stuhlbarg
Feste .... Michael Potts
Olivia .... Kathryn Meisle
Malvolio .... Christopher Lloyd
Antonio .... Sterling K. Brown
Sebastian .... Zach Braff
Fabian .... Kevin Isola
Servant Marsha ....,,,,,,,Stephanie Blake
Priest .... Craig Baldwin

Directed by Brian Kulick; scenery, Walt Spangler; costumes, Miguel Angel Huidor; lighting, Michael Chybowski; sound, Acme Sound Partners; music, Duncan Sheik; production stage manager, James Latus; press, Carol R. Fineman, Tom Naro.

Presented in two parts.

Comedy about the mysteries of sexual attraction. First presentation of record at the Middle Temple, London (2/2/1602). First New York presentation of record at the Park Theatre (6/11/1804).

Fading glory: Ann Guilbert, Elizabeth Marvel and Marian Seldes in Play Yourself. *Photo: Joan Marcus*

Second Stage Theatre production of **Spanish Girl** (9). By Hunt Holman. Carole Rothman artistic director, Carol Fishman managing director, at the McGinn/Cazale Theatre. Opened July 28, 2002. (Closed August 4, 2002)

Skyler	Ari Graynor	Chet	Nate Mooney
Bucky	Joey Kern	Jolene	Jama Williamson

Directed by Erica Schmidt; scenery, Michelle Malavet; lighting Shelly Sabel; costumes, Juman Malouf; sound, Bart Fasbender; production stage manager, Jennifer O'Byrne; press, Richard Kornberg and Associates, Don Summa.

Presented without intermission.

A college student indulges his sexual passion and discovers adult responsibility.

Harlem Song (146). Musical revue by George C. Wolfe; music by Zane Mark and Daryl Waters. Produced by John Schreiber, Margo Lion/Jay Furman, Daryl Roth, Morton Swinsky, Color Mad Inc. and Charles Flateman, in association with Sony Music, Arielle Tepper, Whoopi Goldberg, the Apollo Theater Foundation and Herb Alpert, at the Apollo Theater. Opened August 6, 2002. (Closed December 29, 2002)

Performed by Rosa Evangelina Arredondo, Renee Monique Brown, Gabriel A. Croom, B.J. Crosby, Rosa Curry, Randy A. Davis, Queen Esther, DeLandis McClam, Sinclair Mitchell, Zoie Morris, DanaShavonne Rainey, Stacey Sargent, David St. Louis, Keith Lamelle Thomas, Charles E. Wallace.

Orchestra: Zane Mark conductor, keyboard; John Gentry Tennyson associate conductor, keyboard; Benjamin Franklin Brown bass; Rodney Jones guitar; Jason Jackson brass; Bill Easley, Jimmy Cozior reeds; Brian O. Grice drums.

Directed by Mr. Wolfe; choreography, Ken Roberson; scenery, Riccardo Hernández; costumes, Paul Tazewell; lighting, Jules Fisher and Peggy Eisenhauer; sound, Acme Sound Partners; projections, Batwin and Robin Productions; orchestratrions, Mr. Waters; arrangements and music supervision, Messrs. Mark and Waters; production stage manager, Fred D. Klaisner; press, Carol R. Fineman, Leslie Baden.

Presented without intermission.

Celebration of the African-American life and culture of Harlem in vignettes and songs.

MUSICAL NUMBERS

Opening .... David St. Louis, B.J. Crosby, Gabriel A. Croom,
Randy A. Davis, Charles E. Wallace
Strollin'
"Well Alright Then" .... Queen Esther
Slummin'
"Drop Me Off in Harlem" .... Rosa Curry
"Connie's Inn Kids" .... Rosa Evangelina Arredondo, Renee Monique Brown,
Keith Lamelle Thomas, Sinclair Mitchell
"Tarzan of Harlem" .... Queen Esther, Rosa Evangelina Arredondo,
Renee Monique Brown, Rosa Curry, DanaShavonne Rainey
"Shakin' the Africann" .... Keith Lamelle Thomas, Gabriel A. Croom,
Randy A. Davis, DeLandis McClam, Sinclair Mitchell
"For Sale" .... B.J. Crosby, Charles E. Wallace
"Drop Me Off in Harlem" (Reprise) .... Company
Migration
"Take the 'A' Train" .... Rosa Evangelina Arredondo,
Gabriel A. Croom, Charles E. Wallace
Depression
"Doin' the Niggerati Rag" .... Queen Esther, Gabriel A. Croom, Rosa Curry,
Randy A. Davis, Sinclair Mitchell, Stacey Sargent,
Keith Lamelle Thomas
"Hungry Blues" .... B.J. Crosby, Randy A. Davis
"Miss Linda Brown" .... Rosa Curry

Eviction
  "Here You Come With Love" .... Queen Esther
Visions
  "Time Is Winding Up" .... David St. Louis, Keith Lamelle Thomas,
                                                                                     Stacey Sargent, Charles E. Wallace
The Brown Bomber
  "King Joe" .... Queen Esther, B.J. Crosby
  "Fable of Rage in the Key of Jive" .... David St. Louis, Company
Main Drag of Many Tears
  "Dream Deferred" .... Queen Esther
  "Shake" .... David St. Louis, Rosa Curry, Stacey Sargent
  "Tree of Life" .... B.J. Crosby, Company

The Joseph Papp Public Theater/New York Shakespeare Festival production of
Take Me Out (94). By Richard Greenberg. George C. Wolfe producer, Mara Manus
executive director, in association with the Donmar Warehouse, in the Anspacher Theater.
Opened September 5, 2002. (Closed November 24, 2002)

Kippy Sunderstrom .... Neal Huff
Darren Lemming .... Daniel Sunjata
Shane Mungitt......................... Frederick Weller
Skipper;
  William R. Danziger ....Joe Lisi
Martinez;
  Stadium Announcer ....Robert M. Jiménez

Rodriguez;
  TV Interviewer .... Gene Gabriel
Jason Chenier .... Kohl Sudduth
Toddy Koovitz .... Dominic Fumusa
Davey Battle .... Kevin Carroll
Mason Marzac .... Denis O'Hare
Takeshi Kawabata .... James Yaegashi

Directed by Joe Mantello; scenery, Scott Pask; costumes, Jess Goldstein; lighting, Kevin Adams;
sound, Janet Kalas; associate director, Trip Cullman; associate producers, Bonnie Metzgar and

Fan-attc: Denis O'Hare in Take Me Out. *Photo·
Joan Marcus*

John Dias; casting, Jordan Thaler/Heidi Griffiths; production stage manager, C.A. Clark; press, Carol R. Fineman, Elizabeth Wehrle.

Presented in three parts.

Passions are fanned when homosexuality steps out of the closet and into the baseball locker room. First presented at the Donmar Warehouse, London, July 2002. After a run at the Joseph Papp Public Theater, the play transferred to Broadway's Walter Kerr Theatre (2/27/2003; 108 performances through May 31, 2003)—see Plays Produced on Broadway section in this volume. A 2002–03 *Best Plays* choice (see essay by Christopher Rawson in this volume).

Hot ticket: Edward Norton and Catherine Keener in Burn This. *Photo: Susan Johann*

Signature Theatre Company production of **Burn This** (114). Revival of the play by Lanford Wilson. James Houghton founding artistic director, at the Union Square Theatre. Opened September 19, 2002. Production hiatus November 10–19, 2002. (Closed January 5, 2003)

Anna	Catherine Keener	Larry	Dallas Roberts
Burton	Ty Burrell	Pale	Edward Norton

Understudies: Messrs. Burrell, Roberts, Norton—Quentin Maré; Ms. Keener—Christa Scott-Reed.

Directed by James Houghton; scenery, Christine Jones; costumes, Jane Greenwood; lighting, Pat Collins; sound, Robert Kaplowitz; fight direction, J. Steven White; music, Loren Toolajian; casting, Jerry Beaver and Associates; production stage manager, Michael McGoff; press, the Publicity Office, Bob Fennell, Marc Thibodeau, Candi Adams.

Time: Mid-October and the following three months. Place: New York City

Presented in two parts.

A distraught man and woman find a tenuous love together after the man's gay brother—who was the woman's best friend—dies in a boating accident. First New York presentation of record at Off Off Broadway's Circle Repertory Company (2/18/1987) after a run at the Mark Taper Forum, Los Angeles (1/22/1987). Before its Broadway run at the Plymouth Theatre (10/14/1987; 437 performances), the play was also presented by Steppenwolf Theatre Company, Chicago, September 1987.

Little Ham (77). Musical with book by Dan Owens; music by Judd Woldin; lyrics by Richard Engquist and Mr. Woldin; based on the play by Langston Hughes. Produced by Eric Krebs, in association with Ted Snowdon, Martin Hummel, Entitled Entertainment, Amas Musical Theatre, at the John Houseman Theatre. Opened September 26, 2002. (Closed December 1, 2002)

Clarence	Christopher L. Morgan	Hamlet Hitchcock Jones	André Garner
Lucille	Cheryl Alexander	Tiny Lee	Monica L. Patton
Opal	Joy Styles	Louie "The Nail" Mahoney	Richard Vida
Larchmont	D'Ambrose Boyd	Rushmore	Jerry Gallagher
Leroy	Lee Summers	Jimmy	Joe Wilson Jr.
Mrs. Dobson	Venida Evans	Sugar Lou Bird	Brenda Braxton
Amanda	Julia Lema	Policeman; Bradford	Howard Kaye

Orchestra: David Alan Bunn musical director, piano; Warren Smith percussion; Marcus McLaurine bass; Patience Higgins reeds; Reggie Pittman trumpet.

Understudies: Messrs. Vida, Gallagher—Howard Kaye; Mr. Summers—D'Ambrose Boyd; Messrs. Garner, Morgan, Wilson Jr., Boyd, Kaye—Steven Ward, Morgan, Wilson Jr., Boyd, Kaye, Summers—Donnell Aarone; Mses. Patton, Lema, Evans, Styles—Daria Hardeman; Mses. Braxton, Styles, Lema, Evans—Stacey Haughton.

Directed by Eric Riley; choreography, Leslie Dockery; scenery, Edward T. Gianfrancesco; costumes, Bernard Grenier; lighting, Richard Latta; sound, Jens Muehlhausen; orchestrations and arrangements, Luther Henderson; additional orchestrations and arrangements, Mr. Bunn; associate producer, M. Kilburg Reedy; casting, Jessica Gilburne, Edward Urban; production stage manager,

Harlem hoofin': André Garner (front) and the cast of Little Ham. *Photo: Carol Rosegg*

Brenda Arko; press, Origlio Public Relations, Tony Origlio, Joel Treick, Deena Benz, Richard Hillman, Kip Vanderbilt, Yufen Kung.

Time: 1936. Place: Harlem. Presented in two parts.

Musical version of Mr. Hughes's play about working-class denizens of Harlem who get involved with white mobsters in the numbers racket. Mr. Hughes's play was first presented by the Gilpin Players in Cleveland (3/24/1936). This musical version was first presented at the George Street Playhouse, New Brunswick, New Jersey (2/20/1987). It was later presented by Mr. Krebs at Westport Country Playhouse in Connecticut (8/31/1987). First New York presentation by Amas Musical Theatre, in association with Mr. Krebs, November 2001.

ACT I

"I'm Gonna Hit Today" .... Company
"It's All in the Point of View" .... Ham
"Stick With Me, Kid" .... Louie the Nail
"No" .... Tiny, Sugar Lou, Jimmy
"Get Yourself Some Lovin'" .... Ham, Tiny
"That Ain't Right" .... Company
"Cuttin' Out" .... Sugar Lou, Jimmy
"Room for Improvement" .... Lucille, Leroy
"Get Back" .... Company

ACT II

"Harlem, You're My Girl" .... Ham
"Angels" .... Ham, Mrs. Dobson, Company
"Big Ideas" .... Company
"It's a Helluva Big Job" .... Company
"Wastin' Time" .... Ham, Tiny
"Say Hello to Your Feet" .... Clarence, Company

Jolson and Company (97). Musical with book by Stephen Mo Hanan and Jay Berkow; music and lyrics by various artists listed below. Produced by Ric Wanetik and Crimson Productions at the Century Center for the Performing Arts. Opened September 29, 2002. (Closed December 22, 2002)

Performed by Stephen Mo Hanan, Robert Ari, Nancy Anderson.

Direction and musical staging by Mr. Berkow; scenery, James Morgan; costumes, Gail Baldoni; lighting, Annmarie Duggan; musical direction, Peter Larson; production stage manager, Scott DelaCruz; press, Rubenstein Associates Inc., Thomas Chiodo.

Presented in two parts.

Celebration of the life and work of Al Jolson. First presented by the York Theatre Company, December 1999.

MUSICAL NUMBERS

"Swanee" .... Irving Caesar and George Gershwin
"A Bird in a Gilded Cage" .... Arthur J. Lamb and Harry von Tilzer
"I'm Sitting on Top of the World" .... Ray Henderson, Joe Young and Sam Lewis
"The Little Victrola" .... Billy Murray and Norbert Roscoe
"You Made Me Love You" .... James Monaco and Joseph McCarthy
"Where Did Robinson Crusoe Go With Friday on Saturday Night?" .... George Meyer,
Joe Young and Sam Lewis
"California, Here I Come" .... Joseph Meyer, B.G. DeSylva and Al Jolson
"Sonny Boy" .... Ray Henderson, Lew Brown and B.G. DeSylva
"When the Red, Red Robin Comes Bob-Bob-Bobbin' Along" .... Harry M. Woods
"My Mammy" .... Walter Donaldson, Joe Young and Sam Lewis
"Toot, Toot, Tootsie Goodbye" .... Gus Kahn, Ernie Erdman and Dan Russo
"Hello, Central, Give Me No Man's Land" .... Jean Schwartz, Joe Young and Sam Lewis
"Rock a Bye Your Baby with a Dixie Melody" .... Jean Schwartz, Joe Young and Sam Lewis
"April Showers" .... B.G. DeSylva and Louis Silvers
"You Made Me Love You" (Reprise) .... James Monaco and Joseph McCarthy

Wondrous world: Stephen Largay and James
Urbaniak in The World Over. *Photo: Joan Marcus*

Playwrights Horizons production of **The World Over** (16). By Keith Bunin. Tim Sanford artistic director, Leslie Marcus managing director, William Russo general manager, at the Duke on 42nd Street. Opened October 1, 2002. (Closed October 13, 2002)

The Geographer	James Urbaniak	Tobias, a farmer	James Urbaniak
Xavier, a sailor	Kevin Isola	The Gryphon	Kevin Isola
Vincitore, a sea captain	Stephen Largay	Nurse	Rhea Seehorn
Lorenzacchio, a balladeer	James Urbaniak	Oleandra, Empress	Mia Barron
Adam, a castaway	Justin Kirk	Bartholomew, Prince	Stephen Largay
Ferdinand, King	Matthew Maher	Euralie, Princess	Rhea Seehorn
Anselm, Prince	Stephen Largay	Hanif, a hermit	Matthew Maher
Wilhelm, Prince	Kevin Isola	Old Crone in a cave	Rhea Seehorn
Ulrike, a lass	Rhea Seehorn	Root, an coachman	Matthew Maher
Otto, a physic	Matthew Maher	Nicholeaus, a thief	Kevin Isola
Darkly Jack, a pirate	Matthew Maher	Queen Amarantha	Mia Barron
Isobel, Princess	Mia Barron	Johannes, a Guard	Stephen Largay
Cindra, a maid	Rhea Seehorn	Leocad, Crown Prince	Matthew Maher
Saturnius, Sultan	Stephen Largay	Marguerite, a courtesan	Rhea Seehorn
High Priest	James Urbaniak	Mamillus, a watch	James Urbaniak
Karl, a farmer	Matthew Maher	Red-Winged Hawk	Stephen Largay
Ruselka, Karl's wife	Rhea Seehorn	Mapmaker	James Urbaniak

Directed by Tim Vasen; scenery, Mark Wendland; costumes, Ilona Somogyi; lighting, Michael Chybowski; sound and music, David Van Tieghem; fight direction, J. Allen Suddeth; casting, James Calleri; production stage manager, Jared T. Carey; press, the Publicity Office, Bob Fennell, Marc Thibodeau, Michael S. Borowski.

Presented in two parts.

Epic tale of identity lost and found with many adventures along the way.

Daddy's legacy: Jan Maxwell and Peter Friedman in My Old Lady. *Photo: Craig Schwartz*

My Old Lady (78). By Israel Horovitz. Produced by Richard Frankel, Tom Viertel, Steven Baruch, Marc Routh, Amy Danis/Mark Johannes, Center Theatre Group/Mark Taper Forum/Gordon Davidson at the Promenade Theatre. Opened October 3, 2002. (Closed December 8, 2002)

Mathilde Giffard .... Siân Phillips   Chloé Giffard .... Jan Maxwell
Mathias Gold .... Peter Friedman
    Standbys: Ms. Phillips—Betty Low; Mr. Friedman—Sam Guncler; Ms. Maxwell—Rebecca Nelson.

    Directed by David Esbjornson; scenery, John Lee Beatty; costumes, Elizabeth Hope Clancy; lighting, Peter Kaczorowski; sound, Jon Gottlieb and Matthew Burton; music, Peter Golub; associate producers, Pamela Cooper, Judith Marinoff, Ira Pittelman; casting, Jay Binder and Jack Bowdan; production stage manager, John M. Atherlay; press, Barlow-Hartman, John Barlow, Michael Hartman, Jeremy Shaffer.

    Time: The present. Place: An apartment in Paris. Presented in two parts.

    An American man moves to Paris to claim an inherited apartment, but learns that he has a secret legacy as well. First presentation of record at the Mark Taper Forum, Los Angeles (1/4/2002).

Manhattan Theatre Club production of **In Real Life** (34). By Charlayne Woodard. Lynne Meadow artistic director, Barry Grove executive producer, in association with the Mark Taper Forum, at City Center Stage II. Opened October 8, 2002. (Closed November 10, 2002)

    Performed by Ms. Woodard.
    Standby: Angela Lockett.
    Directed by Daniel Sullivan; scenery, John Lee Beatty; costumes, James Berton Harris; lighting, Kathy A. Perkins; sound, Chris Walker; music, Daryl Waters; production stage manager, Denise Yaney; press, Boneau/Bryan-Brown, Chris Boneau, Jim Byk, Jackie Green, Aaron Meier.
    Presented in two parts.
    Ms. Woodard's musings on a life in the theater. First presented by the Seattle Repertory Theatre in Seattle, Washington, and the Mark Taper Forum/Center Theatre Group in Los Angeles, California, after development at the Sundance Theatre Laboratory.

Lincoln Center Theater production of **A Man of No Importance** (93). Musical with book by Terrence McNally; music by Stephen Flaherty; lyrics by Lynn Ahrens. André Bishop artistic director, Bernard Gersten executive producer at the Mitzi E. Newhouse Theater. Opened October 10, 2002. (Closed December 29, 2002)

Alfie Byrne	Roger Rees	Ernie Lally	Martin Moran
Father Kenny	Jarlath Conroy	Mrs. Patrick	Jessica Molaskey
Mrs. Grace;		Sully O'Hara	Sean McCourt
Kitty Farrelly	Katherine McGrath	Peter; Breton Beret	Luther Creek
Miss Crowe	Barbara Marineau	Lily Byrne	Faith Prince
Mrs. Curtin	Patti Perkins	Carney; Oscar Wilde	Charles Keating
Baldy O'Shea	Ronn Carroll	Robbie Fay	Steven Pasquale
Rasher Flynn; Carson	Michael McCormick	Adele Rice	Sally Murphy

Orchestra: Rob Berman conductor, keyboard; Shawn Gough associate conductor, keyboard, accordion; Kevin Kuhn guitar; Antoine Silverman violin, mandolin, Brian Miller flute; Peter Sachon cello; David Phillips bass.

Directed by Joe Mantello; musical staging, Jonathan Butterell; scenery, Loy Arcenas; costumes, Jane Greenwood; lighting, Donald Holder; sound, Scott Lehrer; vocal arrangements, Mr. Flaherty; music direction, Ted Sperling; music coordinator, John Miller; orchestrations, William David Brohn and Christopher Jahnke; stage manager, Michael Brunner; press, Philip Rinaldi Publicity.

Time: Early 1960s. Place: Dublin. Presented in two parts.

A closeted homosexual in 1964 Dublin attempts to find fulfillment in poetry and amateur theatricals. Based on the 1994 Albert Finney film of the same title.

Woman's grasp: Charlayne Woodard in In Real Life. *Photo: Chris Bennion*

Busman's workday: Roger Rees (standing) in A Man of No Importance. *Photo: Paul Kolnik*

ACT I

"A Man of No Importance"	Alfie, Company
"The Burden of Life"	Lily
"Going Up"	Carney, The St. Imelda's Players
"Princess"	Adele
"First Rehearsal"	Alfie, The St. Imelda's Players
"The Streets of Dublin"	Robbie, Company
"Books"	Carney, Lily
"Man in the Mirror"	Alfie, Oscar Wilde
"The Burden of Life" (Reprise)	Lily
"Love Who You Love"	Alfie

ACT II

"Our Father"	Mrs. Patrick, Company
"Confession"	Alfie, Robbie, Father Kenny
"The Cuddles Mary Gave"	Baldy
"Art"	Alfie, The St. Imelda's Players
"A Man of No Importance" (Reprise)	Mrs. Patrick, Breton Beret, Sully O'Hara
"Confusing Times"	Carney
"Love Who You Love" (Reprise)	Robbie
"Man in the Mirror" (Reprise)	Oscar Wilde, Company
"Tell Me Why"	Lily
"A Man of No Importance" (Reprise)	Company
"Love Who You Love" (Reprise)	Adele
"Welcome to the World"	Alfie

*The Exonerated (268). By Jessica Blank and Erik Jensen. Produced by the Culture Project, Dede Harris, Morton Swinsky, Bob Balaban, Allan Buchman, in association with Patrick Blake and David Elliott, at 45 Bleecker Street. Opened October 10, 2002.

Delbert Tibbs	Charles Brown	Male Ensemble #2	Philip Levy
Robert Earl Hayes	David Brown Jr.	David Keaton	Curtis McClarin
Sunny Jacobs	Jill Clayburgh	Gary Gauger	Jay O. Sanders
Kerry Max Cook	Richard Dreyfuss	Georgia Hayes;	
Sue Gauger; Sandra	Sara Gilbert	Judge; Paula;	
Male Ensemble #1	Bruce Kronenberg	Prosecutor	April Yvette Thompson

Understudies: Messrs. Brown Jr., McClarin—Ed Blunt.

Directed by Bob Balaban; scenery, Tom Ontiveros; costumes, Sara J. Tosetti; music and sound, David Robbins; casting, Eve Battaglia, Nina Pratt, Kim Moarefi; production stage manager, Thomas J. Gates, press, the Jacksina Company Inc., Judy Jacksina, Shawyonia Pettigrew, Jacquie Phillips.

Presented without intermission.

Testimony of former death-row inmates shaped into a dramatic narrative and presented as a reading with a rotating cast of stars. First New York presentation of record was a benefit performance at 45 Bleecker (10/30/2000).

Water Coolers (80). Musical revue by Thomas Michael Allen, Joe Allen, Marya Grandy, David Nehls and E. Andrew Sensenig. Produced by Steven Baruch, Marc Routh, Richard Frankel, Tom Viertel, Pete Herber, Ross Meyerson, Rodger Hess, Ken Gentry at Dillons. Opened October 14, 2002. (Closed December 22, 2002)

Judy	Marya Grandy	Frank	Peter Brown
Steve	Adam Mastrelli	Brooke	Elena Shaddow
Glen	Kurt Robbins		

Standbys: Mses. Grandy, Shaddow—Barbara Helms; Messrs. Mastrelli, Robbins, Brown—Mitchell Jarvis.

Directed by William Wesbrooks; choreography, Timothy Albrecht; scenery, Michael Schweikardt; costumes, Jeffrey Johnson Doherty; lighting, John-Paul Szczepanski; sound, T. Richard Fitzgerald; musical direction and arrangements, Mr. Nehls and Fiona Santos; production stage manager, Jason Brantman; press, Barlow-Hartman, John Barlow, Jeremy Shaffer.

Presented in two parts.

Tales of office politics, relationships, family and survival in the post-postmodern world of computers and instant communication.

ACT I

"Gather 'Round"	The Company
"Panic Monday"	Brooke, Men
"In My Cube"	Judy, Company
"The Paranoia Chorus"	The Company
"PC"	Glen, Steve, Frank
"The Great Pretender"	Glen, Company
"A Song of Acceptance"	Steve
"And Hold Please"	The Company
"The IT Cowboy"	The Company
"In Windows 2525"	Steve, Company

ACT II

"Who Will Buy"	The Company
"One Rung Higher"	Judy
"Chat Room"	Brooke, Company
"A Love Song"	Glen, Steve, Frank
"What You Want"	Brooke, Judy
"Just Another Friday"	The Company
"Many Paths"	The Company

Dudu Fisher: Something Old, Something New (63). Musical revue by Richard Jay-Alexander; based on Mr. Fisher's life. Produced by Elie Landau, Yeeshas Gross, Donny Epstein, in association with Ergo Entertainment, at the Mazer Theatre. Opened October 15, 2002. (Closed December 8, 2002)

Performed by Mr. Fisher; with Jason DeBord (piano) and Michael Blanco (bass).

Directed by Mr. Jay-Alexander; scenery, Michael Brown.

From Israel to Broadway and back in songs and stories about Mr. Fisher's life and career.

National Actors Theatre production of **The Resistible Rise of Arturo Ui** (18). Revival of the play by Bertolt Brecht; adapted by George Tabori. Tony Randall founder and artistic director, in association with Complicite. Opened October 21, 2002. (Closed November 10, 2002)

The Barker	Ajay Naidu	Goodwill	Sterling K. Brown
Flake	Billy Crudup	Gaffles	Robert Stanton
Caruther	Chris McKinney	O'Casey	William Sadler
Butcher	John Ventimiglia	The Actor	Tony Randall
Mulberry	Jack Willis	Giuseppe Givola	Steve Buscemi
Clark	Dominic Chianese	Crocket	John Ventimiglia
Sheet	William Sadler	Greenwool	Chris McKinney
Arturo Ui	Al Pacino	A Wounded Woman	Novella Nelson
Ernesto Roma	Chazz Palminteri	The Defendant Fish	Lothaire Bluteau
Young Inna	Lothaire Bluteau	The Defense Counsel	Billy Crudup
Old Dogsborough	Charles Durning	Prosecutor	Paul Giamatti
Young Dogsborough	Tom Riis Farrell	Judge	William Sadler
Dockdaisy	Jacqueline McKenzie	Court Physician	Ajay Naidu
Arturo Ui's Bodyguards	Michael Goldfinger, Matte Osian	Betty Dullfeet	Linda Emond
		Shorty	Ajay Naidu
Ted Ragg	Paul Giamatti	Ignatius Dullfeet	Paul Giamatti
Emanuele Giri	John Goodman	Pastor	Tom Riis Farrell
Bowl	Ajay Naidu	Reporters; Gunmen; Grocers	Ensemble

Directed by Simon McBurney; scenery, Robert Innes Hopkins; costumes, Mr. Hopkins and Christina Cunningham; lighting, Paul Anderson; sound, Christopher Shutt; projections, Ruppert Bohle; executive producer, Manny Kladitis; casting, Cindy Tolan; production stage manager, Doug Hosney; stage managers, Andrew Neal and Christine Catti; press, Springer/Chicoine Public Relations, Gary Springer, Susan Chicoine, Ann Guzzi, Joe Trentacosta, Michelle Moretta.

Time: Early 1930s. Place: Chicago, Illinois. Presented in two parts.

Parable about the rise of Adolph Hitler as filtered through Mr. Brecht's fascination with Hollywood representations of Chicago gangsters. First presented in Stuttgart (1958). First New York presentation

Riot actor: Al Pacino in The Resistible Rise of Arturo Ui. Photo: Joan Marcus

Worlds apart: Dael Orlandersmith and Howard W. Overshown in Yellowman. *Photo: Joan Marcus*

at Broadway's Lunt-Fontanne Theatre under the title *Arturo Ui* (11/11/1963; 8 performances) with Christopher Plummer in the title role.

Manhattan Theatre Club production of **Yellowman** (64). By Dael Orlandersmith. Lynne Meadow artistic director, Barry Grove executive producer, at City Center Stage I. Opened October 22, 2002. (Closed December 15, 2002)

Alma .... Dael Orlandersmith   Eugene .... Howard W. Overshown

Understudies: Ms. Orlandersmith—Michael Hyatt; Mr. Overshown—Cornell Womack.

Directed by Blanka Zizka; scenery, Klara Zieglerova; costumes, Janus Stefanowicz; lighting, Russell H. Champa; music, Elliott Sharp; casting, Nancy Piccione and David Caparelliotis; production stage manager, Alex Lyu Volckhausen; press, Boneau/Bryan-Brown, Chris Boneau, Jim Byk, Jackie Green, Aaron Meier.

Presented without intermission.

Two actors perform a variety of roles in a study of racial tension among African Americans. A finalist for the 2002 Pulitzer Prize, it was first presented by the McCarter Theatre, Princeton, New Jersey (1/13/2002). A 2002–03 *Best Plays* choice (see essay by Michele Volansky in this volume).

Debbie Does Dallas (127). Musical with book by Erica Schmidt; music by Andrew Sherman; additional music and lyrics by Tom Kitt and Jonathan Callicutt; conceived by Susan L. Schwartz; adapted from the film. Produced by the Araca Group, Jam Theatricals and Waxman Williams Entertainment, by special arrangement with VCX Ltd., at the Jane Street Theatre. Opened October 29, 2002. (Closed February 15, 2003)

Hardwick; others .... Paul Fitzgerald   Greenfelt; Biddle; Kevin .... Del Pentecost
Lisa .... Mary Catherine Garrison   Debbie .... Sherie René Scott
Tammy .... Caitlin Miller   Rick; Hamilton; Bigtime .... Jon Patrick Walker
Donna .... Tricia Paoluccio   Roberta .... Jama Williamson

Directed by Ms. Schmidt; choreography, Jennifer Cody; scenery, Christine Jones; costumes, Juman Malouf; lighting, Shelly Sabel; sound, Laura Grace Brown; music supervision, Mr. Kitt;

associate producers, Ms. Schwartz, Clint Bond Jr., Aaron Harnick; production stage manager, Megan Schneid; press, Boneau/Bryan-Brown, Adrian Bryan-Brown, Jackie Green.

Musical spoof (sans sex) of a 1970s pornographic film about teenage cheerleaders. First presented at the New York International Fringe Festival, August 2001.

Antigone (6). Revival of the play by Sophocles; Modern Greek translation by Nikos Panayotopoulos. Produced by the National Theater of Greece, in association with ICM Artists, Ltd. and Kritas Productions, at City Center. Opened October 30, 2002. (Closed November 3, 2002)

Antigone .... Lydia Koniordou	Tiresias .... Kosmas Fondoukis
Ismene .... Maria Katsiadaki	Messenger A .... Themistoklis Panou
Creon .... Sophoclis Peppas	Eurydice .... Miranta Zafiropoulou
Guard .... Kostas Triantaphyllopoulos	Messenger B .... Thodoros Katsafados
Haemon .... Nikos Arvanitis	

Directed by Niketi Kontouri; choreography, Vasso Barboussi; scenery and costumes, Yorgos Patsas; lighting, Lefteris Pavlopoulos; music, Takis Farazis; assistant director, Yiannis Anastassakis; assistant choreographer, Nina Alkalae.

A woman clashes with state authority when it undermines what she considers a higher calling. First New York presentation of record at Palmo's Opera House (4/7/1845).

Bewilderness (61). Revival of the solo performance by Bill Bailey. Produced by WestBeth Entertainment, Islington Entertainment, Jam Theatricals and BBC America Comedy Live at the 47th Street Theatre. Opened November 7, 2002. (Closed December 29, 2002)

Performed by Mr. Bailey.

Lighting, Josh Monroe; sound, Gregory Kostroff; press, the Jacksina Company Inc., Judy Jacksina, Shawyonia Pettigrew.

Presented in two parts.

Storytelling and songs in a comic solo performance mixing religion, politics and physics. First presented in New York at Westbeth Theatre Center (3/7–3/30/2002).

New York Theatre Workshop production of **Far Away** (79). By Caryl Churchill. James C. Nicola artistic director, Lynn Moffat managing director. Opened November 11, 2002. (Closed January 18, 2003)

Harper .... Frances McDormand	Joan .... Marin Ireland
Joan (child) .... Alexa Eisenstein; Gina Rose	Todd .... Chris Messina

Directed by Stephen Daldry; scenery, Ian MacNeil; costumes, Catherine Zuber; lighting, Rick Fisher; sound, Paul Arditti; associate director, Michael Sexton; production stage manager, Martha Donaldson; press, Richard Kornberg and Associates, Don Summa.

Presented without an intermission.

The terror of the unknown leads to horrifying ends in a short (50 minutes), dark parable of the New World Disorder. First presented at London's Royal Court Theatre Upstairs (11/30–12/22/2000); transferred to the Albery Theatre (1/18–3/10/2001).

Temporary Help (23). By David Wiltse. Produced by Revelation Theater, in association with Eileen T'Kaye, at the Women's Project Theatre. Opened November 17, 2002. (Closed December 8, 2003)

Faye Streber .... Margaret Colin	Vincent Castelnuovo-Tedesco .... Chad Allen
Karl Streber .... Robert Cuccioli	Ron Stucker .... William Prael

Directed by Leslie L. Smith; scenery, Troy Hourie; costumes, Mattie Ullrich; lighting, Chris Dallos; sound, David A. Arnold; production stage manager, Jana Llynn; press, Barlow-Hartman, Michael Hartman, Joe Perrotta.

Presented in two parts.

Cold comfort: Frances McDormand and Alexa Eisenstein in Far Away. *Photo: Joan Marcus*

Stage thriller about the sexually abused and the persons it makes them want to kill. First presentation of record at ACT Theatre, Seattle (8/19/1999).

Tuesdays With Morrie (112). By Jeffrey Hatcher and Mitch Albom; based on the book by Mr. Albom. Produced by David S. Singer, Elizabeth Ireland McCann, Joey Parnes, Amy Nederlander and Scott E. Nederlander, Harold Thau, Moira Wilson, ShadowCatcher Entertainment at the Minetta Lane Theatre. Opened November 19, 2002. (Closed February 23, 2003)

Morrie .... Alvin Epstein   Mitch ....Jon Tenney

Understudies: Mr. Epstein—Yusef Bulos; Mr. Tenney—Daniel Cantor.

Directed by David Esbjornson; scenery, Robert Brill; costumes, Valerie Marcus; lighting, Brian MacDevitt; sound, John Kilgore; casting, Jerry Beaver; production stage manager, Mo Chapman; press, Barlow-Hartman, Michael Hartman, John Barlow, Jeremy Shaffer.

Presented without intermission.

A sportswriter of middle age revisits his dying former college professor to recover the meaning of life. First presented by New York Stage and Film Company and the Powerhouse Theatre at Vassar, June 2002.

The Joseph Papp Public Theater/New York Shakespeare Festival production of **Boston Marriage** (39). By David Mamet. George C. Wolfe producer, Mara Manus executive director, in Martinson Hall. Opened November 20, 2002. (Closed December 22, 2002)

Claire .... Martha Plimpton   Catherine, the maid .... Arden Myrin
Anna .... Kate Burton

Directed by Karen Kohlhaas; scenery, Walt Spangler; costumes, Paul Tazewell; lighting, Robert Perry; production stage manager, James Latus; press, Carol R. Fineman, Elizabeth Wehrle.

Dying words: Jon Tenney and Alvin Epstein in Tuesdays With Morrie. *Photo: Dixie Sheridan*

Presented in two parts.

A Mametian take on the early 1900s, drawing-room comedy and an intimate relationship between women. First presented at the American Repertory Theatre, Cambridge, Massachusetts, June 1999.

*Bartenders (192). Solo performance by Louis Mustillo. Produced by Louis S. Salamone, Janice Montana, Christopher Wright, Edgewood Productions and Jeff Murray at the John Houseman Studio Theatre. Opened November 22, 2002

Performed by Mr. Mustillo.

Directed by Janis Powell; press, the Jacksina Company Inc., Judy Jacksina.

Six bartenders and their stories performed by one man. First New York presentation at the Phil Bosakowski Theatre, September 2002.

Atlantic Theater Company production of **Blue/Orange** (57). By Joe Penhall. Neil Pepe artistic director, Beth Emelson producing director. Opened November 24, 2002. (Closed January 12, 2003)

Christopher .... Harold Perrineau Jr.   Robert .... Zeljko Ivanek
Bruce .... Glenn Fitzgerald

Directed by Mr. Pepe; scenery, Robert Brill; costumes, Laura Bauer; lighting, Brian MacDevitt; sound, Scott Myers; casting, Bernard Telsey Casting/William Cantler; dramaturg, Christian Parker; production stage manager, Darcy Stephens; press, Boneau/Bryan-Brown, Chris Boneau, Susanne Tighe, Adriana Douzos.

Presented in two parts.

Three men—one a patient—struggle for psychological dominance in a modern psychiatric hospital in London. First presented at the Cottesloe Theatre, Royal National Theatre, London (4/13–8/23/2000); transferred to the Duchess Theatre, London, (4/30–12/15/2001). Winner of several best new-play awards including: the 2000 London *Evening Standard* Award, the 2000 London Critics' Circle Award and the 2001 Olivier Award.

True colors? Harold Perrineau Jr. and Glenn Fitzgerald in Blue/Orange. *Photo: Carol Rosegg*

Second Stage Theatre production of **Crowns** (40). By Regina Taylor; based on a book by Michael Cunningham and Craig Marberry. Carole Rothman artistic director, Carol Fishman managing director, in association with the McCarter Theatre. Opened December 3, 2002. (Closed January 5, 2003)

Man	Lawrence Clayton	Wanda	Janet Hubert
Yolanda	Carmen Ruby Floyd	Mother Shaw	Ebony Jo-Ann
Jeanette	Harriett D. Foy	Velma	Lillias White
Mabel	Lynda Gravátt		

Musicians: David Pleasant percussion; Michael Mitchell piano.

Directed by Ms. Taylor; choreography, Ronald K. Brown; scenery, Riccardo Hernández; costumes, Emilio Sosa; lighting, Robert Perry; sound, Darron L. West; musical direction and arrangements, Linda Twine; production stage manager, Alison Cote; press, Richard Kornberg and Associates, Tom D'Ambrosio.

Presented without intermission.

Celebration of the millinarian traditions of church-going African-American women. First presented at the McCarter Theatre, Princeton, New Jersey (10/18/2002).

Playwrights Horizons production of **What Didn't Happen** (16). By Christopher Shinn. Tim Sanford artistic director, Leslie Marcus managing director, William Russo general manager, at the Duke on 42nd Street. Opened December 10, 2002. (Closed December 22, 2002)

Jeff	Matt Cowell	Dave	Steven Skybell
Emily	Suzanne Cryer	Peter	Chris Noth
Scott	Matt McGrath	Alan	Robert Hogan
Elaine	Annalee Jefferies		

Directed by Michael Wilson; scenery, Jeff Cowie; costumes, David C. Woolard; lighting, Howell Binkley; music and sound, John Gromada; production stage manager, Susie Cordon; press, the Publicity Office, Bob Fennell, Michael S. Borowski.

Rakish raconteur: Steven Skybell, Annalee Jefferies and Chris Noth in What Didn't Happen.
Photo: Joan Marcus

Time: 1999; 1993. Place: A country house. Presented in two parts.

Artists and intellectuals survey the detritus of modern culture in a country retreat.

Adult Entertainment (143). By Elaine May. Produced by Julian Schlossberg, Roy Furman, Ben Sprecher, Jim Fantaci, Bill Rollnick and Nancy Ellison, Ted Lachowicz, in association with Aaron Levy, at the Variety Arts Theatre. Opened December 11, 2002. (Closed April 13, 2003)

Guy Akens	Danny Aiello	Gerry DiMarco	Brandon Demery
Frosty Moons	Jeannie Berlin	Jimbo J	Eric Elice
Vixen Fox	Mary Birdsong	Heidi-the-Ho	Linda Halaska

Understudies: Mr. Aiello—Alfred Karl; Messrs. Demery, Elice—Reese Madigan; Mses. Berlin, Birdsong, Halaska—Jen Cooper Davis.

Directed by Stanley Donen; scenery, Neil Patel; costumes, Suzy Benzinger; lighting, Phil Monat; sound, T. Richard Fitzgerald; music, Bryan Louiselle; associate producer, Jill Furman; casting, Stuart Howard/Amy Schecter/Howard Meltzer; production stage manager, Jane Grey, stage manager, Marc Schlackman; press, the Publicity Office, Bob Fennell, Marc Thibodeau, Candi Adams, Michael S. Borowski.

Time: The present; a few weeks later. Presented in two parts.

Stars of second-rate pornographic films aspire to create deeper, more artistic work. Originally presented at Rich Forum, Stamford Center for the Arts, November 2002.

Manhattan Theatre Club production of **Gone Home** (48). By John Corwin. Lynne Meadow artistic director, Barry Grove executive producer, at City Center Stage II. Opened December 17, 2002. (Closed January 26, 2003)

Kate	Chelsea Altman	Anne	Kellie Overbey
Del	Rob Campbell	Suzie	Callie Thorne
Jack	Josh Hamilton		

Directed by David Warren; scenery, James Youmans; costumes, Laura Bauer; lighting, Jeff Croiter; sound, Fitz Patton; casting, Nancy Piccione, David Caparelliotis; production stage manager, Kelley Kirkpatrick; press, Boneau/Bryan-Brown, Chris Boneau, Jim Byk, Jackie Green, Aaron Meier.

Presented in two parts.

A young man remembers the past as he slips, unknowing, toward death. First presented by Wax Lips Theatre Company, Chicago, November 1999.

Tommy Tune: White Tie and Tails (23). Musical revue featuring the works of Fred Astaire, Peter Allen, Irving Berlin, Cole Porter, George Gershwin and others. Produced by Chase Mishkin, Leonard Soloway, Roy Furman, Julian Schlossberg, in association with James M. Nederlander, at the Little Shubert Theatre. Opened December 18, 2002. (Closed January 5, 2003)

Performed by Mr. Tune with the Manhattan Rhythm Kings, Marc Kessler, Brian Nalepka, Hal Shane.

Lighting, Natasha Katz; sound, Peter Fitzgerald; projections, Wendall K. Harrington; arrangements, Wally Harper; orchestrations, Peter Matz, Randall Biagi, Larry Blank, Don Sebesky, Andy Stein; music director, Michael Biagi; press, Pete Sanders Group, Glenna Freedman.

Presented without intermission.

Musical revue featuring Mr. Tune and other performing well-known musical works.

Musical numbers included: "Same Old Song and Dance," "Tap Your Troubles Away," "Everything Old Is New Again," "Puttin' on the Ritz," "When I'm 64," "I'm My Own Grandpa," "Shanghai Lil," "I Can't Be Bothered Now," "Fascinatin' Rhythm," "It's You," "When That Midnight Choo-Choo Leaves for Alabama," "Nice Work If You Can Get It," "Shall We Dance," "They Can't Take That Away From Me," "Nowadays"/"Honey Rag."

Brooklyn Academy of Music presentation of a **Donmar Warehouse** production of **Uncle Vanya** (25). Revival of the play by Anton Chekhov; adapted by Brian Friel. Alan H. Fishman chairman of the board; Karen Brooks Hopkins president; Joseph V. Melillo executive producer, at the Harvey Theater. Opened January 17, 2003. (Closed March 9, 2003)

Alexander Serebryakov	David Bradley	Illya Telegin	Anthony O'Donnell
Marya Voynitsky	Selina Cadell	Vanya	Simon Russell Beale
Yefim	Luke Jardine	Petrushka	Gyuri Sárossy
Yelena	Helen McCrory	Mikhail Astrov	Mark Strong
Marina	Cherry Morris	Sonya	Emily Watson

Orchestra: Caroline Humphris piano; Peter Sachon cello; Frederic Hand guitar.

Directed by Sam Mendes; scenery, Anthony Ward; costumes, Mark Thompson; lighting, Hugh Vanstone, David Holmes; sound, Paul Arditti; music, George Stiles; musical director, Ms. Humphris; assistant director, Orla O'Loughlin; casting, Anne McNulty; stage manager, Marian Spon; press, Sandy Sawotka, Melissa Cusick, Fatima Kafele, Tamara McCaw, Kila Packett.

Time: Late 1800s; summer and early September. Place: The Serebryakov Estate. Presented in two parts.

Indolence is raised to high art in Mr. Chekhov's play about unrequited love, the passing of time and the massing forces of change. The play was first presented by the Moscow Art Theatre in Russia (11/7/1899); the US premiere was by the same company at Jolson's 59th Street Theatre, New York City (1/28/1924). This production was first presented at the Donmar Warehouse, London (9/17–11/20/2002).

Brooklyn Academy of Music presentation of a **Donmar Warehouse** production of **Twelfth Night** (30). Revival of the play by William Shakespeare. Alan H. Fishman chairman of the board; Karen Brooks Hopkins president; Joseph V. Melillo executive producer, at the Harvey Theater. Opened January 18, 2003. (Closed March 8, 2003)

Donmar Warehouse at
Brooklyn
Academy of Music

*Top to bottom: Cherry Morris,
Simon Russell Beale and Anthony
O'Donnell in* Uncle Vanya; *Helen
McCrory and Emily Watson in*
Uncle Vanya; *Mark Strong and
Emily Watson in* Twelfth Night.
Photos: Stephanie Berger

Sir Andrew Aguecheek	David Bradley	Feste	Anthony O'Donnell
Maria	Selina Cadell	Antonio	Gary Powell
Fabian	Luke Jardine	Malvolio	Simon Russell Beale
Sir Toby Belch	Paul Jesson	Sebastian	Gyuri Sárossy
Olivia	Helen McCrory	Orsino	Mark Strong
Lady	Cherry Morris	Viola	Emily Watson

Directed by Sam Mendes; scenery, Anthony Ward; costumes, Mark Thompson; lighting, Hugh Vanstone, David Holmes; sound, Paul Arditti; music, George Stiles; musical director, Ms. Humphris; assistant director, Orla O'Loughlin; casting, Anne McNulty; stage manager, Marian Spon; press, Sandy Sawotka, Melissa Cusick, Fatima Kafele, Tamara McCaw, Kila Packett.

Presented in two parts.

Mr. Shakespeare's comedy about the mysteries (and pains) of sexual attraction. First presentation of record at the Middle Temple (2/2/1602). First New York presentation of record at the Park Theatre (6/11/1804). This production was first presented at the Donmar Warehouse, London (11/22–11/30/2002).

Irish Repertory Theatre production of **The Love Hungry Farmer** (27). By Des Keogh; based on the writings of John B. Keane. Charlotte Moore artistic director, Ciarán O'Reilly producing director. Opened January 22, 2003. (Closed February 16, 2003)

Performed by Mr. Keogh.

Directed by Ms. Moore; costumes, David Toser; lighting, Sean Farrell; production stage manager, Andrew Theodorou; press, Barlow-Hartman, Joe Perrotta.

Forlorn farmer struggles with longing, love and loneliness.

Manhattan Theatre Club production of **Kimberly Akimbo** (72). By David Lindsay-Abaire. Lynne Meadow artistic director, Barry Grove executive director, at City Center Stage I. Opened February 4, 2003. (Closed April 6, 2003)

Kimberly	Marylouise Burke	Pattie	Jodie Markell
Jeff	John Gallagher Jr.	Buddy	Jake Weber
Debra	Ana Gasteyer		

Understudies: Mses. Markell, Gasteyer—Antoinette LaVecchia; Ms. Burke—Patti Perkins; Mr. Weber—Gareth Saxe; Mr. Gallagher Jr.—Daniel Zaitchik

Directed by David Petrarca; scenery, Robert Brill; costumes, Martin Pakledinaz; lighting, Brian MacDevitt; sound, Bruce Ellman; music, Jason Robert Brown; casting, Nancy Piccione and David Caparelliotis; production stage manager, Jason Scott Eagan; press, Boneau/Bryan-Brown, Chris Boneau, Jim Byk, Jackie Green, Aaron Meier.

Time: The Present. Place: Bogota, New Jersey. Presented in two parts.

Comedy about a teenage girl whose rare condition causes her to age at several times the normal rate, and whose family is a cartoonish group of losers from the underclass. First presented at South Coast Repertory, Costa Mesa, California (4/13/2001).

Second Stage Theatre production of **Little Fish** (29). Musical with book, music and lyrics by Michael John LaChiusa; based on stories by Deborah Eisenberg. Carole Rothman artistic director, Carol Fishman managing director. Opened February 13, 2002. (Closed March 9, 2002)

Charlotte	Jennifer Laura Thompson	Cinder	Lea DeLaria
Kathy	Marcy Harriell	John Paul	Eric Jordan Young
Marco	Jesse Tyler Ferguson	Young Girl	Celia Keenan-Bolger
Robert	Hugh Panaro	Mr. Bunder; Bodega Man	Ken Marks

Directed and choreographed by Graciela Daniele; scenery, Riccardo Hernández; costumes, Toni-Leslie James; lighting, Peggy Eisenhauer; sound, Scott Lehrer; music coordinator, Seymour Red Press; production stage manager, Lisa Iacucci; stage manager, Thomas Borchard; press, Richard Kornberg and Associates, Tom D'Ambrosio.

Presented without intermission.

Musical centered on the anxieties, dislocation and loneliness of contemporary New York life.

City Center Encores! presentation of **House of Flowers** (5). Concert version of the musical with book by Truman Capote; music by Harold Arlen; lyrics by Mr. Arlen and Mr. Capote. Judith E. Daykin executive director; Jack Viertel artistic director, Rob Fisher musical director, Kathleen Marshall director in residence, at City Center. Opened February 13, 2003. (Closed February 16, 2003)

Performed by Tonya Pinkins, Armelia McQueen, Maurice Hines, Roscoe Lee Browne, Nikki M. James, Brandon Victor Dixon, Brenda Braxton, Stacy Francis, Alexandra Foucard, Peter Francis James, Desmond Richardson, Wayne W. Pretlow, Everett Bradley.

Ensemble: Sondra M. Bonitto, Lloyd Culbreath, Duane Martin Foster, Darren Gibson, Amy Hall, Francesca Harper, Derric Harris, Danielle Jolie, C. Mingo Long, Monique Midgette, Mayumi Miguel, Maia A. Moss, Herman Payne, Solange Sandy, Laurie Williamson, Michael-Leon Wooley.

Directed and choreographed by Kathleen Marshall; scenery, John Lee Beatty; costumes, Toni-Leslie James; lighting, Peter Kaczorowski, sound, Bruce Cameron; orchestrations, Jonathan Tunick; concert adaptation, Kirsten Childs; music coordinator, Seymour Red Press; guest musical director, David Chase; associate choreographer, Vince Pesce; casting, Jay Binder; production stage manager, Beverley Randolph; press, Rubenstein Associates Inc.

A trade war between competing West Indian madams erupts and a pure romance blossoms amid the rancor. First presentation of record at Broadway's Alvin Theatre (12/30/1954; 165 performances).

Sleeping With Straight Men (41). By Ronnie Larsen. Produced by Great Scott Productions at the Maverick Theatre. Opened February 16, 2003. (Closed March 23, 2003)

Performed by Joanna Keylock, Mink Stole, Paul Tena, Leila Babson, Jared Scott, Hedda Lettuce, Dia Shepardson, Aaron Wimmer.

Directed by Mr. Larsen; scenery, Scott Aronow; lighting, Russel Drapkin and Aaron J. Mason; production stage manager, Lauren A. Oliva; press, KPM Associates, Kevin P. McAnarney, Grant Lindsey.

Presented without intermission.

A gay man, who seduces purportedly heterosexual men, meets an untimely end.

Atlantic Theater Company production of **Dublin Carol** (54). By Conor McPherson. Neil Pepe artistic director, Beth Emelson producing director. Opened February 20, 2003. (Closed April 6, 2003).

John	Jim Norton	Mary	Kerry O'Malley
Mark	Keith Nobbs		

Directed by Mr. McPherson; scenery, Walt Spangler; costumes, Kaye Voyce; lighting, Tyler Micoleau; sound, Scott Myers; production stage manager, Darcy Stephens; press, Boneau/Bryan-Brown, Chris Boneau, Susanne Tighe, Adriana Douzos.

Presented without intermission.

A whiskey-ravaged undertaker encounters his demons at Christmas. First presented the Royal Court Theatre at the Old Vic, London (1/20/2000). A 2002–03 *Best Plays* choice (see essay by Charles Isherwood in this volume).

Lincoln Center Theater production of **Observe the Sons of Ulster Marching Towards the Somme** (56). By Frank McGuinness. André Bishop artistic director, Bernard Gersten executive producer, in the Mitzi E. Newhouse Theater. Opened February 24, 2003. (Closed April 13, 2003)

Kenneth Pyper (in his 80s)	Richard Easton	Kenneth Pyper (in his 20s)	Justin Theroux

Fighting words: Scott Wolf, Justin Theroux and Dashiell Eaves in Observe the Sons of Ulster Marching Towards the Somme. *Photo: Carol Rosegg*

David Craig .... Jason Butler Harner   Martin Crawford .... Christopher Fitzgerald
John Millen ...., Scott Wolf   George Anderson .... Rod McLachlan
William Moore .... Dashiell Eaves   Nathaniel McIlwaine .... David Barry Gray
Christopher Roulston .... Jeremy Shamos

Understudies: Messrs. Theroux, Shamos—Barnaby Carpenter; Messrs. Harner, Eaves, McLachlan—Tom O'Brien; Mr. Easton—Geddeth Smith; Messrs. Wolf, Fitzgerald, Gray—Seth Ullian

Directed by Nicholas Martin; scenery, Alexander Dodge; costumes, Michael Krass; lighting, Donald Holder, sound, Jerry Yager; music, Shaun Davey; casting, Amy Christopher and Daniel Swee; stage manager, Leila Knox; press, Philip Rinaldi Publicity, Barbara Carroll.

Time: 1969; 1915; 1916. Place: Ulster; the Somme.

Presented in two parts.

A group of Northern Irishmen bond with one another before pointless deaths in World War I. This production was first presented by the Williamstown Theatre Festival, August 2001. It was later presented by the Huntington Theatre Company, in association with Broadway in Boston, March 2002. The first presentation of record was at Hampstead Theatre, London, July 1986.

Primary Stages production of **One Million Butterflies** (21). By Stephen Belber. Casey Childs executive producer, Andrew Leynse artistic director. Opened February 24, 2003. (Closed March 16, 2003)

Mike .... Matthew Mabe

Directed by Tyler Marchant; scenery, Narelle Sissons; costumes, Olivera Gajic; lighting, Jane Cox; production stage manager, Nina Iventosch; press, Jeffrey Richards Associates.

Presented without intermission.

A man on a solitary road trip mulls his past, his present and the people he meets along the way.

Showtune: The Words and Music of Jerry Herman (53). Musical revue by Paul Gilger; words and music by Jerry Herman. Produced by Jenny Strome and David Brown at the Theatre at Saint Peter's Church. Opened February 27, 2003. (Closed April 13, 2002)

Performed by Sandy Binion, Paul Harman, Russell Arden Koplin, Thomas Korbee Jr., Karen Murphy, Bobby Peaco, Martin Vidnovic.

Directed and choreographed by Joey McKneely; scenery, Klara Zieglerova; costumes, Tracy Christensen; lighting, Brian Nason; sound, Peter Fitzgerald; musical arrangements, James Followell; press, Keith Sherman and Associates, Brett Oberman.

Presented in two parts.

Celebration of the work and accomplishments of Mr. Herman. First presented at the Helen Hayes Theatre, Nyack, New York (10/12–10/21/2002).

Musical numbers included: "Shalom," "Before the Parade Passes By," "Hello, Dolly!," "It Only Takes a Moment," "It Takes a Woman," "Put on Your Sunday Clothes," "Ribbons Down My Back," "So Long Dearie," "Bosom Buddies," "If He Walked Into My Life," "It's Today," "Mame," "The Man in the Moon," "My Best Girl," "Open a New Window," "That's How Young I Feel," "We Need a Little Christmas," "What Do I Do Now?," "And I Was Beautiful," "Kiss Her Now," "I Don't Want to Know," "One Person," "Big Time," "Hundreds of Girls," "I Promise You a Happy Ending," "I Won't Send Roses," "Look What Happened to Mabel," "Movies Were Movies," "Tap Your Troubles Away," "Time Heals Everything," "Wherever He Ain't," "I'll Be Here Tomorrow," "Just Go to the Movies," "Nelson," "A Little More Mascara," "The Best of Times," "I Am What I Am," "Song on the Sand," "With You on My Arm."

The Joseph Papp Public Theater/New York Shakespeare Festival production of **Radiant Baby** (25). Musical with book by Stuart Ross; music by Debra Barsha; lyrics by Ira Gasman and Mr. Ross; based on *Keith Haring: The Authorized Biography* by John Gruen. George C. Wolfe producer, Mara Manus executive director, in the Newman Theater. Opened March 2, 2003. (Closed March 23, 2003)

Mikayla	Anny Jules	Keith Haring	Daniel Reichard
Jake; Maurice	Gabriel Enrique Alvarez	Carlos	Aaron Lohr
Rini	Remy Zaken	Mr. Haring;	
Amanda	Kate Jennings Grant	Johnny Lounge	Michael Winther
Tseng Kwong Chi	Keong Sim	Mrs. Haring; Andy Warhol	Julee Cruise

Ensemble: Curtis Holbrook, Billy Porter, Angela Robinson, Tracee Beazer, Celina Carvajal, Christopher Martinez, Rhett G. George, Christian Vincent, Christopher Livsey, Jermaine Montell.

Musicians: Kimberly Grigsby conductor, synthesizer; John Roggie, James Sampliner synthesizer; Vincent Henry guitar, saxophone; Konrad Adderley bass; John Clancy drums.

Directed by Mr. Wolfe; choreography, Fatima Robinson; scenery, Riccardo Hernández; costumes, Emilio Sosa; lighting, Howell Binkley; sound, Dan Moses Schreier; projections, Batwin and Robin Productions; orchestrations, Zane Mark; music director, Ms. Grigsby; production stage manager, Rick Steiger; press, Carol R. Fineman, Elizabeth Wehrle.

Time: 1988. Presented in two parts.

Musical treatment of the life and death of pop artist Keith Haring.

*Barbra's Wedding (101). By Daniel Stern. Produced by Dodger Stage Holding, Manhattan Theatre Club at the Westside Theatre. Opened March 5, 2003.

Jerry Schiff	John Pankow	Molly Schiff	Julie White

Understudies: Mr. Pankow—Tony Freeman; Ms. White—Deirdre Madigan.

Directed by David Warren; scenery, Neil Patel; costumes, David C. Woolard; lighting, Jeff Croiter; sound, Fitz Patton; fight direction, Rick Sordelet; executive producer, Dodger Management Group; associate producer, Lauren Mitchell; casting, Jay Binder; production stage manager, Scott Allen; press, Boneau/Bryan-Brown, Adrian Bryan-Brown, Susanne Tighe, Adriana Douzos.

Presented without intermission.

Comedy about an actor who longs for the spotlight focused on Barbra Streisand. First presented by the Philadelphia Theatre Company (6/5/2002).

Cork screwball: John Pankow and Julie White in Barbra's Wedding. *Photo: Joan Marcus*

Killin' time: Melissa Feldman, Portia and Liza Colón-Zayas in Our Lady of 121st Street. *Photo: Joan Marcus*

*Our Lady of 121st Street (100). By Stephen Adly Guirgis. Produced by John Gould Rubin, Ira Pittelman, Robyn Goodman, Ruth Hendel, Daryl Roth, in association with the LAByrinth Theater Company, at the Union Square Theatre. Opened March 6, 2003.

Victor	Richard Petrocelli	Inez	Portia
Balthazar	Felix Solis	Norca	Liza Colón-Zayas
Rooftop	Ron Cephas Jones	Edwin	David Zayas
Father Lux	Mark Hammer	Pinky	Al Roffe
Flip	Russell G. Jones	Marcia	Elizabeth Canavan
Gail	Scott Hudson	Sonia	Melissa Feldman

Directed by Philip Seymour Hoffman; scenery, Narelle Sissons; costumes, Mimi O'Donnell; lighting, James Vermeulen; sound, Eric DeArmon; assistant director, Brian Roff; associate producers, Jack Thomas, Michael Filerman; casting, Bernard Telsey Casting; production stage manager, Monica Moore, stage manager, Jacki O'Brien; press, Barlow-Hartman, John Barlow, Michael Hartman, Wayne Wolfe, Rob Finn.

Presented in two parts.

A diverse group of old friends gather when the body of neighborhood nun mysteriously disappears. Transferred to Off Broadway after a LAByrinth Theater Company workshop (8/20–10/12/2002; 15 performances from the September 28, 2002 press opening). See Plays Produced Off Off Broadway section. A 2002–03 *Best Plays* choice (see essay by Jennifer de Poyen in this volume).

*Tea at Five (84). By Matthew Lombardo. Produced by Daryl Roth, David Gersten, Paul Morer, Michael Filerman, Amy Nederlander and Scott E. Nederlander, in association with Hartford Stage, at the Promenade Theatre. Opened March 9, 2003.

Katharine Hepburn .... Kate Mulgrew

Directed by John Tillinger; scenery, Tony Straiges; costumes, Jess Goldstein; lighting, Kevin Adams; sound, John Gromada; production stage manager, Christine Catti; press, David Gersten.

Presented in two parts.

Reflections on the momentous life of Ms. Hepburn. First presented by Hartford Stage (2/7–3/17/2002).

Tea for one: Kate Mulgrew in Tea at Five. *Photo: Carol Rosegg*

Remember this? Chad Kimball, Brent Carver and Kelli O'Hara in My Life With Albertine. *Photo: Joan Marcus*

New York Theatre Workshop production of **Bexley, Oh(!) Or, Two Tales of One City** (24). By Prudence Wright Holmes. James C. Nicola artistic director, Lynn Moffat managing director. Opened March 10, 2003. (Closed March 30, 2003)

Performed by Ms. Holmes.

Directed by Lisa Peterson; scenery, Riccardo Hernández; costumes, Gabriel Berry; lighting Ben Stanton; sound and music, Robert Kaplowitz; production stage manager, Erika Timperman; press, Richard Kornberg and Associates, Don Summa.

Presented in two parts.

Personal memoir about an uneasy childhood in the Midwest.

Playwrights Horizons production of **My Life With Albertine** (22). Musical with book and lyrics by Richard Nelson; music by Ricky Ian Gordon; based on sections from *Remembrance of Things Past* by Marcel Proust. Tim Sanford artistic director, Leslie Marcus managing director, William Russo general manager. Opened March 13, 2003. (Closed March 30, 2003)

Narrator	Brent Carver	Andree	Caroline McMahon
Marcel	Chad Kimball	Rosemonde	Brooke Sunny Moriber
Albertine	Kelli O'Hara	Pianist	Paul Anthony McGrane
Grandmother;		Mlle. Lea's Girlfriend	Laura Woyasz
Francoise	Donna Lynne Champlin	Three Young Men	Nicholas Belton,
Mlle. Lea	Emily Skinner		Jim Poulos, Paul A. Schaefer

Directed by Mr. Nelson; choreography, Sean Curran; scenery, Thomas Lynch; costumes, Susan Hilferty; lighting, James F. Ingalls; sound, Scott Lehrer; orchestrations, Bruce Coughlin; music direction, Charles Prince; music coordinator, John Miller; associate producer, Ira Weitzman; production stage manager, Matthew Silver; press, the Publicity Office, Bob Fennell, Michael S. Borowski.

Presented in two parts.

Musical journey through parts of Mr. Proust's *Remembrance of Things Past*.

Irish Repertory Theatre production of **Foley** (44). By Michael West. Charlotte Moore artistic director, Ciarán O'Reilly producing director, in association with Richard Wakely and the Corn Exchange. Opened March 13, 2003. (Closed April 19, 2003)

George Foley .... Andrew Bennett

Directed by Annie Ryan; costumes, Suzanne Cave; lighting, Eamon Fox; music, Vincent Doherty; production stage managers, Colette Morris and John Brophy; press, Barlow-Hartman.

Presented without intermission.

A declining member of the Irish gentry tells the dark story of his family's history, which includes his own struggles. First presented by the Corn Exchange in Dublin, where it won the *Sunday Tribune* Award for best new play of 2000; later presented at the Edinburgh Festival and in London.

The Joseph Papp Public Theater/New York Shakespeare Festival production of **Fucking A** (25). By Suzan-Lori Parks. George C. Wolfe producer, Mara Manus executive director, in the Anspacher Theater. Opened March 16, 2003. (Closed April 6, 2003)

Hester Smith	S. Epatha Merkerson	Second Hunter	Manu Narayan
Canary Mary	Daphne Rubin-Vega	Third Hunter	Jesse Lenat
The Mayor	Bobby Cannavale	Jailbait	Chandler Parker
The First Lady	Michole Briana White	Prison Guard	Bobby Cannavale
Freedom Fund Lady	Susan Blommaert	Waiting Woman #1	Manu Narayan
Monster	Mos Def	Waiting Woman #2	Susan Blommaert
Butcher	Peter Gerety	Freshly Freed Prisoners	Full Company
Scribe	Susan Blommaert	Hunter	Chandler Parker
First Hunter	Jojo Gonzalez		

Orchestra: T.O. Sterrett conductor, piano, synthesizer, accordion; Nathan Durham euphonium, trumpet, trombone; Jojo Gonzalez guitar, percussion; Jesse Lenat guitar; Manu Narayan alto, soprano saxophone.

Directed by Michael Greif; scenery, Mark Wendland; costumes, Ilona Somogyi; lighting, Kenneth Posner; sound, Obadiah Faves; music direction, arrangements and orchestrations, Tim Weil; associate producer, Bonnie Metzgar; casting, Jordan Thaler/Heidi Griffiths; production stage manager, Kristen Harris; press, Carol R. Fineman, Elizabeth Wehrle.

Place: A small town in a small country in the middle of nowhere.

Presented in two parts.

Brechtian play with music about the disenfranchised of an unjust (and unspecified) country where relentless brutality leads to certain destruction.

*Zanna, Don't! (84). Musical with book, music and lyrics by Tim Acito; additional book and lyrics by Alexander Dinelaris. Produced by Jack M. Dalgleish, in association with Stephanie Joel, at the John Houseman Theatre. Opened March 20, 2003.

Zanna	Jai Rodriguez	Paige Mike	Enrico Rodriguez
Roberta	Anika Larsen	Tank	Robb Sapp
Buck	Darius Nichols	Kate	Shelley Thomas
Candy	Amanda Ryan	Steve	Jared Zeus

Directed and choreographed by Devanand Janki; scenery and costumes, Wade Laboissonniere and Tobin Ost; lighting, Jeff Nellis; sound, Robert Killenberger; orchestrations, arrangements and musical supervision, Edward G. Robinson; associate producers, Susan R. Hoffman and Lisa Juliano; production stage manager, Jenifer Shenker; press, Origlio Public Relations, Tony Origlio, Richard Hillman, Philip Carrubba.

Presented without intermission.

Musical fantasy about a high school where homosexuality is the norm and heterosexuality is not. First presented in New York by Amas Musical Theatre at the Kirk Theatre (10/17–11/3/2002; see Plays Produced Off Off Broadway Section).

MUSICAL NUMBERS

"Who's Got Extra Love?"	Zanna, Ensemble
"I Think We Got Love"	Steve, Mike
"I Ain't Got Time"	Roberta, Ensemble
"Ride 'Em"	Kate, Roberta, Ensemble
"Zanna's Song"	Zanna

Fantasy high: Jai Rodriguez (center) and the cast of
Zanna, Don't! *Photo: Joan Marcus*

"Be a Man"	Zanna, Ensemble
"Don't Ask, Don't Tell"	Kate, Steve
"Fast"	Bronco, Tex, Loretta
"I Could Write Books"	Mike, Ensemble
"Don't You Wish We Could Be in Love?"	Roberta, Mike, Kate, Steve, Zanna
"Whatcha Got?"	Roberta, Ensemble
"Do You Know What It's Like?"	Steve, Mike, Kate, Roberta
"Zanna's Song" (Reprise)	Zanna
"'Tis A Far, Far Better Thing I Do"/"Blow Winds"	Zanna, Ensemble
"Straight to Heaven"	Tank, Ensemble
"Someday You Might Love Me"	Zanna
"Straight to Heaven" (Reprise)	Ensemble

Manhattan Theatre Club production of **Polish Joke** (40). By David Ives. Lynne Meadow artistic director, Barry Grove executive producer, at City Center Stage II. Opened March 18, 2003. (Closed April 20, 2003)

Jaslu	Malcolm Gets	Magda; others	Nancy Opel
Uncle Roman; others	Richard Ziman	Helen; others	Nancy Bell
Wojtek; others	Walter Bobbie		

Directed by John Rando; scenery, Loy Arenas; costumes, David C. Woolard; lighting, Donald Holder; sound, Bruce Ellman; production stage manager, Heather Cousens, press, Boneau/Bryan-Brown, Chris Boneau, Jim Byk, Aaron Meier.

Presented in two parts.

Comedy in which ethnic jokes plague a man who searches for his identity. First presented by ACT Theatre, Seattle (7/12/2001).

Brooklyn Academy of Music presentation of **Hashirigaki** (5). Music-theater piece with book by Gertrude Stein; music by Brian Wilson; additional music by Heiner Goebbels; based on Ms. Stein's *The Making of Americans* and Mr. Wilson's *Pet Sounds*. Alan H. Fishman chairman of the board, Karen Brooks Hopkins president, Joseph V. Melillo executive producer at the Harvey Theater. Opened March 19, 2003. (Closed March 23, 2003)

Performed by Charlotte Engelkes, Marie Goyette, Yumiko Tanaka.

Directed by Mr. Goebbels; scenery and lighting, Klaus Grünberg; costumes, Florence von Gerkan; sound, Willi Bopp; press, Sandy Sawotka, Melissa Cusick, Fatima Kafele, Tamara McCaw, Kila Packett.

Presented without intermission.

Performance art blending music and text to explore the fluidity, the spirituality of movement—even in stillness.

Columbia University presentation of the **Royal Shakespeare Company** production of **Midnight's Children** (9). By Salman Rushdie, Simon Reade and Tim Supple; based on Mr. Rushdie's novel. Lee C. Bollinger president, in association with the University of Michigan Musical Society, at the Apollo Theater. Opened March 24, 2003. (Closed March 30, 2003)

Performed by Ravi Aujla, Antony Bunsee, Pushpinder Chani, Kammy Darweish, Meneka Das, Neil D'Souza, Mala Ghedia, Kulvinder Ghir, Anjali Jay, Alexi Kaye Campbell, Shaheen Khan, Ranjit Krishnamma, Syreeta Kumar, Selva Rasalingam, Tania Rodrigues, Sirine Saba, Kish Sharma, Zubin Varla, Antony Zaki, Sameena Zehra.

Directed by Mr. Supple; choreography, scenery, costumes and video direction, Melly Still; lighting, Bruno Poet; sound and video design, John Leonard; dramaturg, Mr. Reade; stage manager, Jondon; press, Boneau/Bryan-Brown, Adrian Bryan-Brown, Dennis Crowley.

Presented in two parts.

Multimedia adaptation of Mr. Rushdie's novel about the birth of the Indian nation and how its people's identity (or identities) coalesced. First presented at the Barbican Theatre, London (1/29– 2/23/2003).

Lincoln Center Theater production of **Elegies** (9). Song cycle by William Finn. André Bishop artistic director, Bernard Gersten executive producer at the Mitzi E. Newhouse Theater. Opened March 24, 2003 (Closed March 30, 2003) Reopened April 14, 2003. (Closed April 19, 2003)

Performed by Christian Borle, Betty Buckley, Carolee Carmello, Keith Byron Kirk, Michael Rupert.

Directed by Graciela Daniele; costumes, Toni-Leslie James; lighting, Donald Holder; sound, Scott Stauffer; music director, Vadim Feichtner; vocal arranger, Gihieh Lee; stage manager, Patty Lyons; press, Philip Rinaldi.

Presented in two parts.

Songs in celebration of friends who have passed on. Presented in a limited run on Sundays and Mondays when *Observe the Sons of Ulster Marching Towards the Somme* was dark. Returned for an additional week of performances.

*Manhattan Ensemble Theater production of ***Golda's Balcony** (72). By William Gibson. David Fishelson artistic director, Sandra Garner managing director. Opened March 26, 2003. (Closed July 13, 2003)

Golda Meir .... Tovah Feldshuh

Directed by Scott Schwartz; scenery, Anna Louizos; costumes, Jess Goldstein; lighting, Howell Binkley; music and sound, Mark Bennett; projection design, Batwin and Robin Productions; dramaturg, Aaron Leichter; production stage manager, Charles M. Turner III; press, Bradford Louryk.

Israeli prime minister charts her life as a Jewish patriot and worries over the future of her nation when threatened from without. First presented by Shakespeare and Company, Lenox, Massachusetts (5/18/2002).

*Hank Williams: Lost Highway (65). Transfer of the Off Off Broadway musical with book by Randal Myler and Mark Harelik; music and lyrics based on the work of Mr. Williams. Produced by Cindy and Jay Gutterman, Kardana-Swinsky Productions Inc., Jerry Hamza, Sony/ATV Music Publishing LLC, in association with Manhattan Ensemble Theater, at the Little Shubert Theatre. Opened March 26, 2003.

Hank Williams	Jason Petty	Jimmy (Burrhead)	Myk Watford
Tee-Tot	Michael W. Howell	Leon (Loudmouth)	Drew Perkins
Waitress	Juliet Smith	Fred "Pap" Rose	Michael P. Moran
Mama Lilly	Margaret Bowman	Audrey Williams	Tertia Lynch
Hoss	Stephen G. Anthony	Shag	Russ Wever

Directed by Mr. Myler; scenery, Beowulf Boritt; costumes, Robert Blackman; lighting, Don Darnutzer; sound, Randy Hansen; musical direction, Dan Wheetman; production stage manager, Antonia Gianino; press, Carol R. Fineman, Leslie Baden.

Presented in two parts.

The life and music of Hank Williams as told though his songs. First presented by the Denver Center Theatre Company. First presented in New York at Off Off Broadway's Manhattan Ensemble Theater (12/19/2002–2/23/2003).

ACT I

"This Is the Way I Do"	Tee-Tot
"Message to My Mother"	Hank
"Thank God"	Hank, Mama, Company
"WPA Blues"	Hank
"Long Gone Lonesome Blues"	Tee-Tot, Hank
"Settin' the Woods on Fire"	Hank, The Drifting Cowboys
"Sally Goodin"	Leon
"Honky Tonk Blues"	Hank, The Drifting Cowboys
"I'm Tellin' You"	Audrey, The Drifting Cowboys
"I Can't Help It (If I'm Still in Love With You)"	Hank, The Drifting Cowboys
"I'm So Lonesome I Could Cry"	Tee-Tot
"Jambalaya (On the Bayou)"	Hank, The Drifting Cowboys
"Move It on Over"	Hank, The Drifting Cowboys
"Mind Your Own Business"	Hank, The Drifting Cowboys
"Lovesick Blues"	Hank, The Drifting Cowboys

ACT II

"The Blood Done Sign My Name"	Tee-Tot
"Happy Rovin' Cowboy"	Hank, The Drifting Cowboys
"I'm Gonna Sing, Sing, Sing"	Hank, Audrey, The Drifting Cowboys
"Long Gone Lonesome Blues" (Reprise)	Hank, Tee-Tot, The Drifting Cowboys
"Way Downtown"	The Drifting Cowboys
"I'm So Lonesome I Could Cry" (Reprise)	Hank
"I'm a Run to the City of Refuge"/"A House of Gold" (Medley)	Tee-Tot, Hank
"Hey, Good Lookin'"	Hank, The Drifting Cowboys
"I Saw the Light"	Hank, Hoss
"Lost Highway"	Hank, Tee-Tot
"Your Cheatin' Heart"	Hank, The Drifting Cowboys
"I Saw the Light" (Reprise)	Company

City Center Encores! presentation of **The New Moon** (5). Concert version of musical with book and lyrics by Oscar Hammerstein II, Frank Mandel and Laurence Schwab; music by Sigmund Romberg. Judith E. Daykin executive director; Jack Viertel artistic director, Rob Fisher musical director, Kathleen Marshall director in residence, at City Center. Opened March 27, 2003. (Closed March 30, 2003)

Julie	Lauren Ward	Marianne Beaunoir	Christiane Noll
Monsieur Beaunoir	Simon Jones	Fouchette	David Masenheimer
Butler	Ravil Atlas	Doorkeeper	John Wilkerson
Captain George Duval	Burke Moses	Philippe L'Entendu	Brandon Jovanovich
Le Vicomte Ribaud	F. Murray Abraham	Girl	Anne Allgood
Robert Mission	Rodney Gilfry	Rosita	Mary Ann Lamb
Alexander	Peter Benson	Innkeeper	Jason Mills
Besac	Danny Rutigliano	Clotilde Lombaste	Alix Korey
Jacques	Alex Sanchez	Admiral de Jean	Simon Jones

Ensemble: Anne Allgood, Ravil Atlas, Christopher Eaton Bailey, Tony Capone, Marie Danvers, Colm Fitzmaurice, Ann Kittredge, David Masenheimer, Jason Mills, Morgan Moody, Karyn Overstreet, Devin Richards, Vale Rideout, Rebecca Robbins, Margaret Shafer, Rebecca Spencer, Susan Wheeler, John Wilkerson.

Chorus: Jennifer Chase, Julie Cox, Alexandra de Suze, Cherry Duke, Sherrita Duran, David Gagnon, Cara Johnston, Daniel Judge, Sara Lerch, Kenneth Overton, John Pickle, Douglas Purcell, Katherine Schmidt, Sam Smith, Keith Spencer, J.D. Webster.

Orchestra: Rob Fisher conductor; Suzanne Ornstein, concertmistress, violin. Belinda Whitney, Mineko Yajima, Katherine Livolsi-Stern, Kristina Musser, Eric DeGioia, Robert Zubrycki, Lisa Matricardi, Laura Seaton, Mia Wu, Susan Shumway violin; Jill Jaffe, Ken Burward-Hoy, David Blinn, Crystal Garner viola; Clay Ruede, Lanny Paykin cello; John Beal, Richard Sarpola double bass; Sheryl Henze flute, piccolo; Seymour Red Press flute; William Blount, Lino Gomex clarinet; Blair Tindall oboe, English horn; Russ Rizner, Dan Culpepper, French horn; Domenic Derasse, Lowell Hershey trumpet; Jack Gale trombone; John Redsecker drums; Joseph Passaro percussion; Lise Nadeau harp.

Directed by Gary Griffin; choreography, Daniel Pelzig; scenery, John Lee Beatty; costumes, Michael Krass; lighting, Ken Billington; sound, Scott Lehrer; orchestrations, Emil Gerstenberger, Alfred Goodman, Hans Spialek; musical director, Mr. Fisher; concert adaptation, David Ives; musical coordinator, Mr. Red Press; associate music director and choral preparation, Ben Whiteley; casting, Jay Binder/Laura Stanczyk; production stage manager, Karen Moore; press, Rubenstein Associates Inc.

Presented in two parts.

Musical based on the autobiography of an 18th century French aristocrat who escapes to New Orleans, falls in love, is returned to France in chains and inadvertently joins with pirates. First New York presentation of record at Broadway's Imperial Theatre (9/19/1928; 509 performances); transferred to the Casino Theatre (11/18/1929) near the end of its run.

ACT I

Overture	The Orchestra

Scene 1: Outside the Beaunoir home, near New Orleans, 1792

Opening	Ensemble
"Marianne"	Rodney Gilfry, Peter Benson, Christiane Noll, Ensemble
"The Girl on the Prow"	Christiane Noll, Danny Rutigliano, Ensemble
"Gorgeous Alexander"	Lauren Ward, Peter Benson, Women
"An Interrupted Love Song"	Burke Moses, Christiane Noll
Finaletto, Scene 1	Rodney Gilfry

Scene 2: The Café Creole

"Tavern Song"	Ensemble
"Rosita's Tango"	Mary Ann Lamb, Alex Sanchez
"Softly, as in a Morning Sunrise"	Brandon Jovanovich
"Stouthearted Men"	Rodney Gilfry, Brandon Jovanovich, Men
Finaletto, Scene 2	Rodney Gilfry, Brandon Jovanovich

Scene 3: The Beaunoir home

"One Kiss"	Christiane Noll, Women
"Ladies of the Jury"	Alix Korey, Peter Benson, Lauren Ward, Ensemble
"The New Cotillion Dance"	Ensemble
"Wanting You"	Rodney Gilfry, Christiane Noll
Finale, Act I	Rodney Gilfry, Christiane Noll, Ensemble

ACT II

Intermezzo .... The Orchestra
Scene 1: The deck of the *New Moon*
   "Funny Little Sailor Men" .... Danny Rutigliano, Alix Korey, Ensemble
   "Lover, Come Back to Me" .... Christiane Noll, Rodney Gilfry
   Finaletto, Scene 1 .... Rodney Gilfry, Ensemble
Scene 2: The Isle of Pines
   "Love is Quite a Simple Thing" .... Danny Rutigliano, Lauren Ward,
                                                                            Peter Benson, Alix Korey
Scene 3: The Isle of Pines, one year later
   "Try Her Out at Dances" .... Peter Benson, Lauren Ward, Ensemble
   "Softly, as in a Morning Sunrise" (Reprise) .... Brandon Jovanovich, Men
   "Never for You" .... Christiane Noll
   "Lover, Come Back to Me" (Reprise) .... Rodney Gilfry, Christiane Noll
Scene 4: Marianne's cabin
   "One Kiss" (Reprise) .... Christiane Noll, Rodney Gilfry
Scene 5: Near the shore, just before dawn
   Finale Ultimo .... Christiane Noll, Rodney Gilfry and Company

Brooklyn Academy of Music presentation of the **Royal National Theatre** and **Market Theatre of Johannesburg** production of **The Island** (13). Revival of the play by Athol Fugard, John Kani and Winston Ntshona. Alan H. Fishman chairman of the board; Karen Brooks Hopkins president; Joseph V. Melillo executive producer, at the Harvey Theater. Opened April 1, 2003. (Closed April 13, 2003)

   Performed by Mr. Kani, Mr. Ntshona.
   Directed by Mr. Fugard; lighting, Mannie Manim; press, Sandy Sawotka, Melissa Cusick, Fatima Kafele, Tamara McCaw, Kila Packett.
   Presented without intermission.
   Prison drama focusing on the brutality of South African incarceration and the resilience human beings demonstrate amid adversity. A 1974–75 *Best Plays* choice, the original Broadway production opened at the Edison Theatre (11/24/1974; 52 performances).

The Jackie Wilson Story (19). Musical revue by Jackie Taylor; based on the work of Mr. Wilson with additional songs by Ms. Taylor. Produced by Ms. Taylor and Brian Kabatznick, in association with the Black Ensemble Touring Company, at Apollo Theater. Opened April 6, 2003. (Closed April 27, 2003)

Jackie Wilson	Chester Gregory II	Father; William Davis	Elfeigo N. Goodun III
Eliza	Melba Moore	Shaker; Sam Cooke;	
BB	Rueben D. Echoles	Clyde McPhatter	Lyle Miller
Freda	Katrina Tate	Shaker; Billy Ward; Reporter	Tony Duwon
Roquel "Billy" Davis	Mark D. Hayes	Etta James; Harlene	Valarie Tekosky
Carl Davis	Robert L. Thomas	LaVern Baker; Barbara Acklin	Eva D.

   Directed by Ms. Taylor; musical arrangements, George Paco Patterson; musical direction, Jimmy Tillman and Rick Hall; associate producer, Douglas Gray; production stage manager, Dre Robinson; press, Carol R. Fineman, Leslie Baden.
   Presented in two parts.
   Celebration of the life and work of Jackie Wilson through his music. A touring production of the Black Ensemble Theater, Chicago.
   Musical numbers included: "My Heart Is Crying," "I Am the Man," "We Are the Shakers," "I Ain't Had Your Woman," "When The Sun Refused to Shine," "You Can't Keep a Good Man Down," "Little-Bitty Pretty One," "Move to the Outskirts of Town," "Tweedle Dee," "Reet Petite," "I Can't Help It," "That's Why I Love You So," "To Be Loved," "Tennessee Waltz," "Something's Got a Hold on Me," "Lonely Teardrops," "Shake, Shake, Shake," "Doggin' Me Around," "A Woman, A Lover, A Friend," "Oh, Danny Boy," "Whispers (Getting Louder)," "The Closer I Get," "(Your Love Keeps Lifting Me) Higher and Higher," "To Be Loved" (Reprise), "Baby Workout," "Nightshift," "Higher and Higher" (Reprise).

Homebody ancestor: Kathleen Chalfant in Bed Among the Lentils *from* Talking Heads. *Photo: Carol Rosegg*

*Talking Heads (63). By Alan Bennett. Produced by Tom Hulce and Julia Rask, Ron Kastner, Daryl Roth, Cheryl Wiesenfeld, Margaret Cotter, Amy Nederlander, Scott E. Nederlander, by special arrangement with Roundabout Theatre Company, at the Minetta Lane Theatre. Opened April 6, 2003.

Bed Among the Lentils		*Miss Fozzard Finds Her Feet*	
Susan	Kathleen Chalfant	Miss Fozzard	Lynn Redgrave
A Chip in the Sugar		*Waiting for the Telegram*	
Graham	Daniel Davis	Violet	Frances Sternhagen
A Lady of Letters		*The Hand of God*	
Miss Ruddock	Christine Ebersole	Celia	Brenda Wehle
Her Big Chance			
Lesley	Valerie Mahaffey		

Directed by Michael Engler; scenery, Rachel Hauck; costumes, Candice Donnelly; lighting, Chris Parry; music and sound, Michael Roth; projections, Wendall K. Harrington; associate producers, Jerry Meyer, Joseph Smith; casting, Jim Carnahan; production stage manager, Martha Donaldson; press, Barlow-Hartman, John Barlow, Michael Hartman, Bill Coyle.

Presented in two parts.

Seven solo plays from Mr. Bennett's collection of 12 monologues about life in England. Parts of the work were first televised by the BBC in 1987. A 2002–03 *Best Plays* choice (see essay by Jeffrey Sweet in this volume).

*The Last Sunday in June (61). Transfer of the Off Off Broadway play by Jonathan Tolins. Produced by Ted Snowdon, in association with Rattlestick Theatre, at the Century Center for the Performing Arts. Opened April 9, 2003.

Beefy boy: Matthew Wilkas and Arnie Burton in The Last Sunday in June. *Photo: Sandra Coudert*

Brad	Arnie Burton	James	Mark Setlock
Charles	Donald Corren	Tom	Peter Smith
Michael	Johnathan F. McClain	Joe	David Turner
Susan	Susan Pourfar	Scott	Matthew Wilkas

Directed by Trip Cullman; scenery, Takeshi Kata; costumes, Alejo Vietti; lighting, Paul Whitaker; sound, Jeffrey Yoshi Lee; production stage manager, Lori Ann Zepp; press, Origlio Public Relations, Tony Origlio.

The latest addition to the *oeuvre* in which gay men comment on the current state being gay. First presented at Off Off Broadway's Rattlestick Theatre (2/9–3/16/2003). See Plays Produced Off Off Broadway section in this volume.

Broad Channel (25). By Anna Theresa Cascio and Doc Dougherty. Produced by Helen Maier at the Phil Bosakowski Theatre. Opened April 13, 2003. (Closed May 4, 2003)

Performed by Mr. Dougherty.

Directed by Molly Fowler; scenery, Michelle Malavet; lighting, Greg MacPherson; sound, Elizabeth Rhodes; press, Boneau/Bryan-Brown, Chris Boneau, Juliana Hannett.

Presented without intermission.

Solo performance centered on a group of working-class young people in 1977 Queens.

Playwrights Horizons production of **She Stoops to Comedy** (17). By David Greenspan. Tim Sanford artistic director, Leslie Marcus managing director, William Russo general manager. Opened April 13, 2003. (Closed April 27, 2003)

Alexandra Page	Mr. Greenspan	Kay Fein	E. Katherine Kerr

Jayne Summerhouse .... E. Katherine Kerr   Alison Rose .... Marissa Copeland
Hal Stewart .... Philip Tabor   Simon Lanquish .... T. Ryder Smith
Eve Addaman .... Mia Barron

Directed by Mr. Greenspan; scenery, Michael Brown; costumes, Miranda Hoffman; lighting, Matthew Frey; production stage manager, Beth-Stiegel Rohr; press, the Publicity Office, Bob Fennell, Michael S. Borowski.

Presented without intermission.

A comic take on the nature of reality, identity, love and life in the theater.

The Joseph Papp Public Theater/New York Shakespeare Festival production of **As You Like It** (24). Revival of the play by William Shakespeare. George C. Wolfe producer, Mara Manus executive director, in Martinson Hall. Opened April 14, 2003. (Closed May 4, 2003)

LeBeau; Duke Frederick;   Adam; Phebe; Audrey .... Jennifer Ikeda
  Duke Senior; Silvius .... Drew Cortese   Celia; William .... Lethia Nall
Touchstone; Jaques .... Johnny Giacalone   Orlando; Oliver .... Lorenzo Pisoni
Rosalind .... Bryce Dallas Howard

Direction and costumes by Erica Schmidt; lighting, Shelly Sabel; casting, Jordan Thaler/Heidi Griffiths; associate producer, Bonnie Metzgar; production stage manager, Buzz Cohen; press, Carol R. Fineman, Elizabeth Wehrle.

Presented without intermission.

Revival of Mr. Shakespeare's comedy about injustice, country life, hidden identities and romance. According to our research, the play was presumably written in 1599 but the first presentation of record was a 1723 adaptation by Charles Johnson known as *Love in a Forest*. The first New York presentation of record was at the John Street Theatre (7/14/1786). This production was first presented as part of the Joseph Papp Public Theater's 2001 New Works Now! Festival.

Who's who? Marissa Copeland, T. Ryder Smith and David Greenspan in She Stoops to Comedy. *Photo: Joan Marcus*

Subterranean blues: Merritt Wever and Deirdre O'Connell in Cavedweller. *Photo: Joan Marcus*

Mary Todd . . . A Woman Apart (20). By Carl Wallnau. Produced by the Centenary Stage Company at the Samuel Beckett Theatre. Opened April 29, 2003. (Closed May 17, 2003)

   Performed by Colleen Smith Wallnau.
   Directed by Mr. Wallnau; scenery, Gordon Danielli; costumes, Brenda Lightcap; lighting, Ed Matthews; sound, Joseph Langham.
   Solo portrait of Abraham Lincoln's wife. First presented by Centenary Stage Company, Hackettstown, New Jersey (3/1/2002).

*New York Theatre Workshop production of ***Cavedweller** (28). By Kate Moira Ryan; based on a novel by Dorothy Allison. James C. Nicola artistic director, Lynn Moffat managing director. Opened May 8, 2003.

Delia Byrd	Deirdre O'Connell	Dede Windsor	Jenny Maguire
Rosemary	Adriane Lenox	Amanda Windsor	Shannon Burkett
Cissy Pritchard	Merritt Wever	Clint Windsor;	
Waitress; Louise Windsor;		Deputy Emmet Tyler;	
Marcia Pearlman; Nadine Reitower;		Michael Graham;	
Gillian Wynchester;		Billy Tucker	Stevie Ray Dallimore
Mrs. Caidenhead;		Vocals	Julia Greenberg
Bartender	Lynne McCollough		
Grandaddy Byrd;			
Nolan Reitower	Carson Elrod		

   Directed by Michael Greif; scenery, Riccardo Hernández; costumes, Ilona Somogyi; lighting, Jennifer Tipton; sound, Jerry Yager; projections, Jan Hartley; music, Stephen Trask and Julia Greenberg; production stage maanger, Michael McGoff; press, Richard Kornberg and Associates, Don Summa.
   Presented in two parts.
   Adaptation of a novel about hard knocks experienced by the children of a rock-and-roll singer who stops her high living in order to be a parent.

City Center Encores! presentation of **No Strings** (5). Concert version of musical with book by Samuel Taylor; music and lyrics by Richard Rodgers. Judith E. Daykin executive director, Jack Viertel artistic director, Rob Fisher musical director, Kathleen Marshall director in residence, at City Center. Opened May 8, 2003. (Closed May 11, 2003)

Barbara Woodruff	Maya Days	Mike Robinson	Marc Kudisch
David Jordan	James Naughton	Louis de Pourtal	Len Cariou
Jeanette Valmy	Caitlin Carter	Comfort O'Connell	Emily Skinner
Luc Delbert	Casey Biggs	Gabrielle Bertin	Mary Ann Lamb
Molie Plummer	Penny Fuller	Marcello Agnolotti	Denis Jones

Ensemble: Harry Bayron, Kristine Bendul, John Carroll, Alessandra Corona Lamm, Dylis Croman, Lloyd Culbreath, Naleah Dey, Joey Dowling, Darren Gibson, Melissa Hillmer, Ashley Hull, Darren Lorenzo, Abbey O'Brien, Alex Sanchez, Jennifer Savelli, Patricia Tuthill, Darlene Wilson.

Orchestra: Rob Fisher conductor; Andrew Sterman piccolo, flute, alto flute, clarinet, tenor sax; Roger Rosenberg flute, clarinet, bass clarinet, bassoon, baritone sax; Richard Heckman piccolo, flute, oboe, clarinet, alto sax; Steven Kenyon flute, clarinet, bass clarinet, alto sax; Seymour Red Press flute, clarinet, alto sax; Lawrence Feldman flute, clarinet, alto sax; Alva Hunt flute, clarinet, bass clarinet, tenor sax; John Campo clarinet, bass clarinet, bassoon, baritone sax; John Frosk, Stu Satalof, Kamau Adilifu, Glenn Drewes trumpet; Jack Gale, Jason Jackson, Jack Schatz trombone; Susan Jolles harp; Lawrence Yurman piano; Jay Berliner guitar; John Beal acoustic bass; John Redsecker drums; Erik Charlston percussion.

Directed and choreographed by Ann Reinking; scenery, John Lee Beatty; costumes, Candice Donnelly; lighting, Ken Billington; sound, Scott Lehrer; music director, Mr. Fisher; orchestrations, Ralph Burns; concert adaptation, David Thompson; music coordinator, Mr. Red Press; associate choreographer, Debra McWaters; casting, Jay Binder; production stage manager, Karen Moore; press, Rubenstein Associates Inc.

Presented in two parts.

A May-September musical romance between a blocked writer and a beautiful model in Paris—he's white, she's black. First presented in New York at Broadway's 54th Street Theatre on (3/15/1962; 580 performances); it later transferred to the Broadhurst Theatre (10/1/1962) near the middle of its run.

ACT I

Prologue

"The Sweetest Sounds" .... Maya Days, James Naughton
"How Sad" .... James Naughton, Models
"The Sweetest Sounds" (Reprise) .... James Naughton
"Loads of Love" .... Maya Days
"The Man Who Has Everything" .... Len Cariou
"Be My Host" .... James Naughton, Marc Kudisch, Emily Skinner, Casey Biggs, Mary Ann Lamb, Ensemble
"La-La-La" .... Caitlin Carter, Casey Biggs
"You Don't Tell Me" .... Maya Days
"Love Makes the World Go" .... Penny Fuller, Emily Skinner
"Nobody Told Me" .... James Naughton, Maya Days

ACT II

Entr'acte .... The Orchestra
"Look No Further" .... James Naughton, Maya Days
"Maine" .... James Naughton, Maya Days
Casino Ballet .... Company (Alessandra Corona Lamm, soloist)
"An Orthodox Fool" .... Maya Days
"Eager Beaver" .... Emily Skinner, Marc Kudisch, Ensemble
"No Strings" .... James Naughton, Maya Days
"Maine" (Reprise) .... Maya Days, James Naughton
"The Sweetest Sounds" (Reprise) .... James Naughton, Maya Days

Down a Long Road (6). By David Marquis. Produced by Long Road Productions at the Lamb's Theatre. Opened May 14, 2003. (May 18, 2003)

Performed by Mr. Marquis.

Buddy Mohmed guitar, bass; Gale Hess violin; Kenny Grimes percussion.

Directed by Doug Jackson; choreography, Deanna Deck; costumes, Giva Taylor; lighting, Linda Blasé; musical direction, Mr. Mohmed; press, KPM Associates, Kevin P. McAnarney, Grant Lindsey.

Presented without intermission.

Solo performance focusing on one man's wondrous journeys through life.

*Atlantic Theater Company production of ***Writer's Block** (20). By Woody Allen. Neil Pepe artistic director, Beth Emelson producing director, in association with Letty Aronson. Opened May 15, 2003.

Riverside Drive		Norman	Jay Thomas
Jim	Paul Reiser	Jenny	Heather Burns
Fred	Skipp Sudduth	David	Grant Shaud
Barbara	Kate Blumberg	Hal	Christopher Evan Welch
Old Saybrook		Sandy	Clea Lewis
Sheila	Bebe Neuwirth	Max	Richard Portnow

Being Woody Allen: Skipp Sudduth, Paul Reiser and Kate Blumberg in Riverside Drive *from* Writer's Block. *Photo: Carol Rosegg*

Directed by Mr. Allen; scenery, Santo Loquasto; costumes, Laura Bauer; lighting, James F. Ingalls; sound, Scott Myers; casting, Bernard Telsey Casting/William Cantler; production stage manager, Janet Takami; press, Boneau/Bryan-Brown, Chris Boneau, Susanne Tighe, Joe Perrotta.

Presented in two parts.

Two one-act comedies in which writers struggle with their characters, disenchanted spouses, competitors and other challenges to their work.

*Manhattan Theatre Club production of ***Humble Boy** (15). By Charlotte Jones. Lynne Meadow artistic director, Barry Grove executive producer, at City Center Stage I. Opened May 18, 2003.

Felix Humble	Jared Harris	Jim	Bernie McInerney
Mercy Lott	Mary Beth Hurt	George Pye	Paul Hecht
Flora Humble	Blair Brown	Rosie Pye	Ana Reeder

Directed by John Caird; scenery and costumes, Tim Hatley; lighting, Paul Pyant; sound, Christopher Shutt; music, Joe Cutler; production stage manager, Roy Harris; press, Boneau/Bryan-Brown, Chris Boneau, Jim Byk, Aaron Meier.

Presented in two parts.

A man in early middle age returns home to bury his father and discovers his mother is involved with a neighbor. First presented at London's Cottesloe Theatre (8/9–12/6/2001); later reopened at the Gielgud Theatre (2/5–8/17/2002).

*Boobs! The Musical (The World According to Ruth Wallis) (14). Musical revue with book by Steve Mackes and Michael Whaley; music and lyrics by Ruth Wallis. Produced by SRU Productions LLC, Lawrence Leritz and Mr. Whaley at the Triad Theater. Opened May 19, 2003.

Performed by Kristy Cates, Robert Hunt, Max Perlman, J. Brandon Savage, Jenny-Lynn Suckling, Rebecca Young.

Directed by Donna Drake; choreography, Mr. Leritz; costumes, Robert Pease and J. Kevin Draves.

Musical revue based on risqué party songs from the mid-20th century.

*Playwrights Horizons production of ***I Am My Own Wife** (6). By Doug Wright. Tim Sanford artistic director, Leslie Marcus managing director, William Russo general manager. Opened May 27, 2003.

Charlotte von Mahlsdorf;
  others .... Jefferson Mays

Directed by Moisés Kaufman; scenery, Derek McLane; costumes, Janice Pytel; lighting, David Lander; sound, Andre Pluess and Ben Sussman; casting, James Calleri, production stage manager, Andrea J. Testani; press, the Publicity Office, Bob Fennell, Marc Thibodeau, Michael S. Borowski, Candi Adams.

Time: The Nazi Years; the Communist Years. Place: Various locations in the US and Germany. Presented in two parts.

Solo performance centering on a man who lives as a woman under politically challenging circumstances in what was once known as East Germany. Commisioned by Playwrights Horizons, it was first presented at the La Jolla Playhouse (7/10/2001) after development at the Sundance Theatre Laboratory. A 2002–03 *Best Plays* choice (see essay by Julius Novick in this volume).

CAST REPLACEMENTS
AND TOURING COMPANIES

○ ○ ○ ○ ○

Compiled by Paul Hardt

THE FOLLOWING IS A LIST of the major cast replacements of record in productions that opened in previous years, but were still playing in New York during a substantial part of the 2002–03 season; and other New York shows that were on a first-class tour in 2002–03.

The name of each major role is listed in *italics* beneath the title of the play in the first column. In the second column directly opposite appears the name of the actor who created the role in the original New York production (whose opening date appears in *italics* at the top of the column). Indented immediately beneath the original actor's name are the names of subsequent New York replacements—with the date of replacement when available.

The third column gives information about first-class touring companies. When there is more than one roadshow company, #1, #2, etc., appear before the name of the performer who created the role in each company (and the city and date of each company's first performance appears in *italics* at the top of the column). Their subsequent replacements are also listed beneath their names in the same manner as the New York companies, with dates when available.

AIDA

	New York 3/23/00	*Minneapolis, MN 4/6/01* *Closed 8/24/03*
Aida	Heather Headley 　Maya Days 9/13/01 　Simone 1/29/02 　Saycon Senbloh 6/16/03 　Toni Braxton 6/30/03	Simone 　Paulette Ivory
Radames	Adam Pascal 　Richard H. Blake 6/16/03 　Will Chase 6/30/03	Patrick Cassidy 　Jeremy Kushnier
Amneris	Sherie René Scott 　Taylor Dayne 　Idina Menzel 9/13/01 　Felicia Finley 1/29/02 　Mandy Gonzales 6/30/03	Kelli Fournier 　Lisa Brescia

Mereb	Damian Perkins	Jacen R. Wilkerson
	Delisco	Eric L. Christian
Zoser	John Hickok	Neal Benari
	Donnie Kehr	Micky Dolenz

BEAUTY AND THE BEAST

	New York 4/18/94	*#3 Tulsa 9/7/99* *Closed 8/4/03*
Beast	Terrence Mann Jeff McCarthy Chuck Wagner James Barbour Steve Blanchard	#3 Grant Norman Roger Befeler
Belle	Susan Egan Sarah Uriarte Christianne Tisdale Kerry Butler Deborah Gibson Kim Huber Toni Braxton Andrea McArdle Sarah Litzsinger Jamie-Lynn Sigler Sarah Litzsinger 2/11/03 Megan McGinnis 4/15/03	#3 Susan Owen Danyelle Bossardet Jennifer Shrader
Lefou	Kenny Raskin Harrison Beal Jamie Torcellini Jeffrey Howard Schecter Jay Brian Winnick 11/12/99 Gerard McIsaac Brad Aspel Steve Lavner	#3 Michael Raine Brad Aspel Aldrin Gonzales
Gaston	Burke Moses Marc Kudisch Steve Blanchard Patrick Ryan Sullivan Christopher Seiber Chris Hoch 12/10/02	#3 Chris Hoch Edward Staudenmayer Marc G. Dalio
Maurice	Tom Bosley MacIntyre Dixon Tom Bosley Kurt Knudson Timothy Jerome J.B. Adams 11/12/99	#3 Ron Lee Savin
Cogsworth	Heath Lamberts Peter Bartlett Robert Gibby Brand John Christopher Jones Jeff Brooks 11/12/99	#3 John Alban Coughlan Ron Bagden Tom Aulino Andrew Boyer
Lumiere	Gary Beach Lee Roy Reams Patrick Quinn	#3 Ron Wisniski Jay Russell

Gary Beach
Meshach Taylor
Patrick Page
Paul Schoeffler
Patrick Page
Bryan Batt
Rob Lorey 5/7/02
David DeVries

Babette   Stacey Logan   #3 Jennifer Shrader
             Pamela Winslow   Louisa Kendrick
             Leslie Castay   Sally Ann Tumas
             Pam Klinger   Tracy Generalovich
             Louisa Kendrick
             Pam Klinger

Mrs. Potts   Beth Fowler   #3 Janet MacEwen
                Cass Morgan   Mary Jo McConnell
                Beth Fowler
                Barbara Marineau 11/12/99
                Beth Fowler
                Cass Morgan

BURN THIS

New York, 8/27/02
Closed 1/5/03

Pale   Edward Norton
          Peter Sarsgaard 11/20/02

Anna   Catherine Keener
          Elisabeth Shue 11/20/02

Larry   Dallas Roberts

Burton   Ty Burrell

CABARET

New York 3/19/98   *Los Angeles 2/99*

Emcee   Alan Cumming   Norbert Leo Butz
           Robert Sella 9/17/98   Jon Peterson 1/2/00
           Alan Cumming 12/1/98
           Michael C. Hall 6/8/99
           Matt McGrath10/17/01
           Raúl Esparza 10/26/01
           John Stamos 4/29/02
           Raúl Esparza
           Neil Patrick Harris 1/1/03

Sally Bowles   Natasha Richardson   Teri Hatcher
                  Jennifer Jason Leigh 8/20/98   Joely Fisher 9/4/99
                  Mary McCormack 3/2/99   Lea Thompson 3/19/00
                  Susan Egan 6/17/99   Kate Shindle 7/11/00
                  Joely Fisher 6/2/00   Andrea McArdle 1/23/01
                  Lea Thompson 8/2/00

Katie Finneran 11/21/00
Gina Gershon 1/19–6/17/01
Kate Shindle 6/19/01
Brooke Shields 7/3/01
Molly Ringwald 12/18/01
Jane Leeves 4/29/01
Molly Ringwald
Heather Laws 1/27/03
Deborah Gibson 2/18/03

Clifford Bradshaw	John Benjamin Hickey	Rick Holmes
	Boyd Gaines 3/2/99	Jay Goede 10/16/99
	Michael Hayden 8/3/99	Hank Stratton 1/23/01
	Matthew Greer 1/19/01	
	Rick Holmes	
Ernst Ludwig	Denis O'Hare	Andy Taylor
	Michael Stuhlbarg 5/4/99	Drew McVety 10/16/99
	Martin Moran 11/9/99	
	Peter Benson 1/19/01	
Fraulein Schneider	Mary Louise Wilson	Barbara Andres
	Blair Brown 8/20/98	Alma Cuervo 9/4/99
	Carole Shelley 5/4/99	Barbara Andres 6/08/01
	Polly Bergen	
	Carole Shelley	
	Alma Cuervo 2/18/03	
	Mariette Hartley	
Fraulein Kost	Michele Pawk	Jeanine Morick
	Victoria Clark 5/4/99	Lenora Nemetz 2/20/00
	Candy Buckley	
	Penny Ayn Maas	
	Jane Summerhays	
Herr Schultz	Ron Rifkin	Dick Latessa
	Laurence Luckinbill 5/4/99	Hal Robinson 9/4/99
	Dick Latessa 11/9/99	
	Larry Keith	
	Hal Linden	
	Tom Bosley 12/12/02	

CHICAGO

	New York 11/14/96	*#1 Cincinnati 3/25/97* *#2 Ft. Myers, FL 12/12/97*
Roxie Hart	Ann Reinking	#1 Charlotte d'Amboise
	Marilu Henner	Belle Calaway
	Karen Ziemba	Ann Reinking 4/22/99
	Belle Calaway	Belle Calaway 5/18/99
	Charlotte d'Amboise	Sandy Duncan 4/22/99
	Sandy Duncan 8/12/99	Ann Reinking 5/1/99
	Belle Calaway 1/18/00	Belle Calaway 6/1/99
	Charlotte d'Amboise 3/24/00	Sandy Duncan 7/13/99
	Belle Calaway	Belle Calaway 8/3/99
	Nana Visitor	Nana Visitor 11/16/99
	Petra Nielsen 10/8/01	Tracy Shane 1/4/00
	Nana Visitor 11/19/01	#2 Karen Ziemba
	Belle Calaway 1/13/02	Nancy Hess

	Denise Van Outen 3/18/02
	Belle Calaway 4/22/02
	Amy Spanger 8/6/02
	Belle Calaway
	Tracy Shayne 4/15/03

	Charlotte d'Amboise
	Amy Spanger 11/10/98
	Charlotte d'Amboise 11/24/98
	Amy Spanger 12/1/98
	Chita Rivera 2/2/99
	Marilu Henner 7/6/99
	Charlotte d'Amboise 8/24/99
	Marilu Henner 12/22/99
	Nana Visitor 1/3/00

Velma Kelly

Bebe Neuwirth	#1 Jasmine Guy
Nancy Hess	Janine LaManna
Ute Lemper	Jasmine Guy
Bebe Neuwirth	Donna Marie Asbury
Ruthie Henshall 5/25/99	Stephanie Pope
Mamie Duncan-Gibbs 10/26/99	Jasmine Guy 7/7/98
Bebe Neuwirth 1/18/00	Stephanie Pope 7/14/98
Donna Marie Asbury 3/23/00	Mamie Duncan-Gibbs 1/12/99
Sharon Lawrence 4/11/00	Deidre Goodwin 2/16/99
Vicki Lewis	Ruthie Henshall 4/22/99
Jasmine Guy	Deidre Goodwin 5/18/99
Bebe Neuwirth	Ruthie Henshall 4/22/99
Donna Marie Asbury	Deidre Goodwin 6/1/99
Deidre Goodwin	Donna Marie Asbury 10/12/99
Vicki Lewis	Vicki Lewis 11/16/99
Deidre Goodwin 6/29/01	Roxane Carrasco 1/4/00
Anna Montanaro 7/9/01	Vicki Lewis 3/14/00
Deidre Goodwin 9/14/01	Roxane Carrasco 3/21/00
Donna Marie Asbury	#2 Stephanie Pope
Roxane Carrasco 1/13/02	Jasmine Guy
Deidre Goodwin 3/18/02	Stephanie Pope
Stephanie Pope	Khandi Alexander 8/4/98
Roxane Carrasco	Donna Marie Asbury 9/29/98
Caroline O'Connor 11/8/02	Stephanie Pope 2/2/98
Brenda Braxton 3/3/03	Ute Lemper 2/19/99
	Stephanie Pope 4/5/99
	Mamie Duncan-Gibbs 8/3/99
	Jasmine Guy 8/24/99
	Marianne McCord 12/22/99
	Vicki Lewis 1/3/00

Billy Flynn

James Naughton	#1 Obba Babatunde
Gregory Jbara	Alan Thicke
Hinton Battle	Michael Berresse 8/18/98
Alan Thicke	Alan Thicke 8/25/98
Michael Berresse	Destan Owens 10/13/98
Brent Barrett	Alan Thicke 10/27/98
Robert Urich 1/11/00	Destan Owens 1/26/99
Clarke Peters 2/1/00	Adrian Zmed 2/16/99
Brent Barrett 2/15/00	Hal Linden 8/6/99
Chuck Cooper	Gregory Jbara 8/17/99
Brent Barrett 7/2/01	Robert Urich 10/19/99
Chuck Cooper 8/27/01	Lloyd Culbreath 1/4/00
George Hamilton 11/12/01	Alan Thicke 1/18/00
Eric Jordan Young 1/18/02	Lloyd Culbreath 2/29/00
Ron Raines 3/26/02	Alan Thicke 3/14/00
George Hamilton 5/21/02	Clarke Peters 3/21/00
Michael C. Hall 8/8/02	#2 Brent Barrett
Destan Owens	Michael Berresse 11/3/98

	Taye Diggs	Brent Barrett 11/24/98
	Billy Zane 11/8/02	Michael Berresse 12/1/98
	Kevin Richardson 1/20/03	Ben Vereen 2/19/99
	Clarke Peters	Hal Linden 8/31/99
	Gregory Harrison	Gregory Jbara 1/3/00
		Clarke Peters
Amos Hart	Joel Grey	#1 Ron Orbach
	Ernie Sabella	Michael Tucci
	Tom McGowan	Bruce Winant 12/22/98
	P.J. Benjamin	Ray Bokhour 10/19/99
	Ernie Sabella 11/23/99	P.J. Benjamin 4/4/00
	P.J. Benjamin	#2 Ernie Sabella
	Tom McGowan	Ron Orbach
	P.J. Benjamin	Tom McGowan
	Ray Bokhour 7/30/01	Ron Orbach
	P.J. Benjamin 8/13/01	P.J. Benjamin 11/10/98
	Rob Bartlett	Joel Grey 12/1/98
	P.J. Benjamin 3/3/03	P.J. Benjamin 12/29/98
		Ernie Sabella 2/2/99
		Michael Tucci 8/24/99
		P.J. Benjamin 1/3/00
Matron "Mama" Morton	Marcia Lewis	#1 Carol Woods
	Roz Ryan	Lea DeLaria
	Marcia Lewis	Carol Woods 8/4/98
	Roz Ryan	#2 Avery Sommers
	Marcia Lewis	Marcia Lewis 2/2/99
	Roz Ryan	
	Marcia Lewis	
	Jennifer Holliday 6/18/01	
	Marcia Lewis 8/27/01	
	Roz Ryan 11/16/01	
	Michele Pawk 1/14/02	
	Alix Korey 3/4/02	
	B.J. Crosby 3/3/03	
	Angie Stone 4/15/03	
Mary Sunshine	D. Sabella	#1 M.E. Spencer
	J. Loeffelholz	D.C. Levine
	R. Bean	M.E. Spencer 7/7/98
	A. Saunders	R. Bean 7/28/98
	J. Maldonado	A. Saunders 10/13/98
	R. Bean	R. Bean 10/20/98
	A. Saunders 1/2/02	J. Maldonado 10/27/98
	R. Bean 1/14/02	J. Roberson 2/9/99
	M. Agnes	M. Von Essen 5/12/99
	D. Sabella 3/24/03	J. Maldonado 10/12/99
		M. Agnes 1/4/00
		#2 D.C. Levine
		M.E. Spencer 2/2/99
		D. Sabella 9/7/99

42ND STREET

	New York 5/2/01	*Kansas City 8/4/02*
Peggy Sawyer	Kate Levering	Catherine Wreford
	Meredith Patterson	
	Kate Levering 8/30/02	
	Nadine Isenegger	

Julian Marsh	Michael Cumpsty Michael Dantuono Tom Wopat 7/21/02	Patrick Ryan Sullivan
Billy Lawler	David Elder	Robert Spring
Dorothy Brock	Christine Ebersole Beth Leavel 6/9/02	Blair Ross

FRANKIE AND JOHNNY IN THE CLAIR DE LUNE
New York 8/8/02
Closed 3/9/03

| *Frankie* | Edie Falco
Rosie Perez 1/1/03 |
| *Johnny* | Stanley Tucci
Joe Pantoliano 1/1/03 |

THE GOAT, OR WHO IS SYLVIA?
New York 3/10/02
Closed 12/15/02

Stevie	Mercedes Ruehl Sally Field 9/13/02
Martin	Bill Pullman Bill Irwin 9/13/02
Billy	Jeffrey Carlson Todd Swenson

THE GRADUATE
New York 4/4/02
Closed 3/2/03

Mrs. Robinson	Kathleen Turner Linda Gray Lorraine Bracco 11/19/02
Benjamin Braddock	Jason Biggs Josh Radnor Jason Biggs John Lavalle 11/19/02
Elaine Robinson	Alicia Silverstone Kelly Overton Andrea Anders 11/19/02
Mr. Braddock	Murphy Guyer Mark Blum
Mrs. Braddock	Kate Skinner
Mr. Robinson	Victor Slezak Colin Stinton

HAIRSPRAY
New York 8/15/02

Tracy Turnblad	Marissa Jaret Winokur
Edna Turnblad	Harvey Fierstein
Wilbur Turnblad	Dick Latessa
Amber Von Tussle	Laura Bell Bundy
Velma Von Tussle	Linda Hart Barbara Walsh
Motormouth Maybelle	Mary Bond Davis

Seaweed   Corey Reynolds
                       Chester Gregory II 7/14/03

I LOVE YOU, YOU'RE PERFECT, NOW CHANGE

Jordan Leeds
  Danny Burstein 10/01/96
  Adam Grupper 8/22/97
  Gary Imhoff 2/09/98
  Adam Grupper 4/01/98
  Jordan Leeds 3/17/99
  Bob Walton 10/27/00
  Jordan Leeds 1/30/01
  Darrin Baker 1/29/02
  Danny Burstein 4/12/02
  Jordan Leeds 6/03/02

Robert Roznowski
  Kevin Pariseau 5/25/98
  Adam Hunter 4/20/01
  Sean Arbuckle 9/23/02
  Frank Baiocchi 2/17/03
  Colin Stokes 10/10/03

Jennifer Simard
  Erin Leigh Peck 5/25/98
  Kelly Anne Clark 1/10/00
  Andrea Chamberlain 3/13/00
  Lori Hammel 11/04/00
  Andrea Chamberlain 1/29/01
  Amanda Watkins 8/24/01
  Karyn Quackenbush 1/02/02
  Marissa Burgoyne 8/09/02
  Andrea Chamberlain 12/17/02
  Karyn Quackenbush 2/17/03
  Sandy Rustin 6/13/03

Melissa Weil
  Cheryl Stern 2/16/98
  Mylinda Hull 9/17/00
  Melissa Weil 2/09/01
  Evy O'Rourke 3/13/01
  Marylee Graffeo 6/11/01
  Cheryl Stern 1/18/02
  Marylee Graffeo 3/11/02
  Janet Metz 4/26/02
  Anne Bobby 12/17/02
  Janet Metz 3/03/03

LES MISÉRABLES

	New York 3/12/87	*Tampa 11/28/88*
	Closed 5/18/03	*Closing 6/15/03 (scheduled)*
Jean Valjean	Colm Wilkinson	Gary Barker
	Robert Marien 3/12/97	Gregory Calvin Stone 3/3/97
	Ivan Rutherford 9/9/97	Colm Wilkinson 7/15/98
	Robert Marien 12/12/97	Ivan Rutherford 1/19/99
	Craig Schulman 3/3/98	Randal Keith

Fred Inkley 9/8/98
Tim Shaw 9/7/99
J. Mark McVey 3/7/00
Ivan Rutherford 4/23/01
J. Mark McVey 1/29/02
Ivan Rutherford
Randal Keith

Javert

Terrence Mann
  Christopher Innvar 10/15/96
  Robert Gallagher 12/6/97
  Philip Hernandez 10/27/98
  Gregg Edelman 9/7/99
  Shuler Hensley 11/14/00
  Philip Hernandez 11/19/01
  David Masonheimer
  Terrence Mann 2/4/03
  Michael McCarthy 5/16/03

Peter Samuel
  Todd Alan Johnson 3/31/97
  Stephen Bishop 8/3/99
  Philip Hernandez
  Joseph Mahowald
  Stephen Tewksbury

Fantine

Randy Graff
  Juliet Lambert 3/12/97
  Lisa Capps 4/15/98
  Alice Ripley 9/8/98
  Susan Gilmour 3/9/99
  Alice Ripley 3/23/99
  Jane Bodle 9/7/99
  Jacquelyn Piro 4/23/01
  Lauren Kennedy 11/4/02
  Jayne Paterson 3/18/03

Hollis Resnik
  Lisa Capps 3/24/97
  Holly Jo Crane
  Susan Gilmour 6/2/98
  Joan Almedilla 3/2/99
  Thursday Farrar
  Joan Almedilla
  Jayne Paterson
  Tonya Dixon

Enjolras

Michael Maguire
  Stephen R. Buntrock 3/12/97
  Gary Mauer 12/8/98
  Stephen R. Buntrock 4/6/99
  Christopher Mark Peterson 6/21/99
  Ben Davis 9/10/01
  Christopher Mark Peterson 1/7/02

Greg Zerkle
  Brian Herriott
  Kurt Kovalenko
  Michael Todd Cressman
  Matthew Shepard 12/8/98
  Kevin Earley 1/19/99
  Stephen Tewksbury 2/15/00
  Dallyn Vail Bayles

Marius

David Bryant
  Peter Lockyer 3/12/97
  Kevin Kern

Matthew Porretta
  Rich Affannato 8/12/96
  Steve Scott Springer
  Tim Howar
  Stephen Brian Patterson
  Scott Hunt

Cosette

Judy Kuhn
  Cristeena Michelle Riggs
  Tobi Foster 11/6/98
  Sandra Turley 2/5/01

Jacquelyn Piro
Kate Fisher 9/9/96
  Regan Thiel
  Stephanie Waters
  Amanda Huddleston

Eponine

Frances Ruffelle
  Sarah Uriarte Berry 3/12/97
  Megan Lawrence 6/19/98
  Kerry Butler 12/11/98
  Megan Lawrence 2/25/99
  Rona Figueroa 6/3/99
  Megan Lawrence 6/24/99
  Jessica-Snow Wilson 8/31/99
  Rona Figueroa 9/14/99

Michele Maika
  Rona Figueroa 3/31/97
  Jessica-Snow Wilson 5/19/99
  Sutton Foster 1/19/99
  Diana Kaarina 3/21/00
  Dina Morishita
  Ma-Anne Dionisio
  Jessica-Snow Wilson
  Nicole Riding

Jessica Boevers 12/7/00
Catherine Brunell 8/10/00
Dana Meller 12/13/01
Diana Kaarina 1/13/02

THE LION KING

	New York 11/13/97	*#1 US Tour* *#2 Chicago 4/23/03*
Rafiki	Tsidii Le Loka Thuli Dumakude 11/11/98 Sheila Gibbs Nomvula Dlamini	#1 Futhi Mhlongo #2 Thandazile A. Soni
Mufasa	Samuel E. Wright	#1 Alton Fitzgerald White #2 Rufus Bonds Jr.
Sarabi	Gina Breedlove Meena T. Jahi 8/4/98 Denise Marie Williams Meena T. Jahi Robyn Payne	#1 Jean Michelle Grier #2 Marvette Williams
Zazu	Geoff Hoyle Bill Bowers 10/21/98 Robert Dorfman Tony Freeman Adam Stein	#1 Jeffrey Binder #2 Derek Hasenstab
Scar	John Vickery Tom Hewitt 10/21/98 Derek Smith	#1 Patrick Page #2 Larry Yando
Banzai	Stanley Wayne Mathis Keith Bennett 9/30/98 Leonard Joseph Curtiss I' Cook	#1 James Brown-Orleans #2 Melvin Abston
Shenzi	Tracy Nicole Chapman Vanessa S. Jones Lana Gordon Marlayna Sims	#1 Jacquelyn Renae Hodges #2 Shaullanda Lacombe
Ed	Kevin Cahoon Jeff Skowron 10/21/98 Jeff Gurner Timothy Gulan Thom Christopher Warren	#1 Wayne Pyle #2 Brian Sills
Timon	Max Casella Danny Rutigliano 6/16/98 John E. Brady Danny Rutigliano	#1 John Plumpis #2 Benjamin Clost
Pumbaa	Tom Alan Robbins	#1 Ben Lipitz #2 Bob Amaral
Simba	Jason Raize Christopher Jackson Josh Tower	#1 Alan Mingo Jr. #2 Brandon Victor Dixon
Nala	Heather Headley Mary Randle 7/7/98 Heather Headley 12/8/98 Bashirrah Creswell Sharon L. Young Rene Elise Goldsberry	#1 Kissy Simmons #2 Adia Ginneh Dobbins

MAMMA MIA!

	New York 10/18/01	
		#1 US Tour
		#2 2nd Tour
		#3 Las Vegas
Donna Sheridan	Louise Pitre	#1 Dee Hoty
		#2 Monique Lund
		#3 Tina Walsh
Sophie Sheridan	Tina Maddigan	#1 Chilina Kennedy
		#2 Kristie Marsden
		#3 Jill Paice
Tanya	Karen Mason	#1 Cynthia Sophiea
	Jeanine Morick	#2 Ellen Harvey
		#3 Karole Foreman
Rosie	Judy Kaye	#1 Rosalyn Rahn Kerins
		#2 Robin Baxter
		#3 Jennifer Perry
Sky	Joe Machota	#1 P.J. Griffith
		#2 Chris Bolan
		#3 Victor Wallace
Sam Carmichael	David W. Keeley	#1 Gary Lynch
		#2 Don Noble
		#3 Nick Cokas
Harry Bright	Dean Nolen	#1 Michael DeVries
	Richard Binsley	#2 James Kall
		#3 Michael Piontek
Bill Austin	Ken Marks	#1 Craig Bennett
	Adam LeFevre	#2 Pearce Bunting
		#3 Mark Leydorf

MAN OF LA MANCHA

	New York 12/5/02
Don Quixote	Brian Stokes Mitchell
Aldonza	Mary Elizabeth Mastrantonio
	Marin Mazzie 7/1/03
Sancho	Ernie Sabella

NOISES OFF

	New York 11/1/01
	Closed 9/1/02
Dotty Otley	Patti LuPone
	Jane Curtin 7/16/02
Lloyd Dallas	Peter Gallagher
	Leigh Lawson 7/16/02
Selsdon Mowbray	Richard Easton
	John Horton 7/16/02
Belinda Blair	Faith Prince
	Kaitlin Hopkins 7/16/02
Frederick Fellowes	Edward Hibbert
	Byron Jennings 7/16/02
Brooke Ashton	Katie Finneran
	Kali Rocha 7/16/02
Garry Lejeune	Thomas McCarthy
	Paul Fitzgerald 7/16/02
Tim Allgood	T.R. Knight
	Carson Elrod 7/16/02
Poppy Norton-Taylor	Robin Weigert
	Mandy Siegfried 7/16/02

OKLAHOMA!

	New York 3/21/02
	Closed 2/23/03
Curly	Patrick Wilson
	Stephen R. Buntrock 11/19/02
Laurey	Josefina Gabrielle
	Amy Bodner
Aunt Eller	Andrea Martin
	Patty Duke 12/14/02
Jud Fry	Shuler Hensley
	Merwin Foard 1/5/03

THE PHANTOM OF THE OPERA

	New York 1/26/88	*#1 Los Angeles 5/31/90*
		#2 Chicago 5/24/90
		#3 Seattle 12/13/92
The Phantom	Michael Crawford	#1 Michael Crawford
	Thomas James O'Leary 10/11/96	Franc D'Ambrosio 3/28/94
	Hugh Panaro 2/1/99	#2 Mark Jacoby
	Howard McGillin 8/23/99	Rick Hilsabeck
	Brad Little	Craig Schulman 1/30/97
	Howard McGillin	Ron Bohmer 9/97
	Hugh Panaro 4/14/03	Davis Gaines 8/98
		#3 Franc D'Ambrosio
		Brad Little
		Ted Keegan
		Brad Little
		Ted Keegan
		Brad Little
Christine Daae	Sarah Brightman	#1 Dale Kristien
	Sandra Joseph 1/29/98	Lisa Vroman 12/2/93
	Adrienne McEwan (alt.) 4/21/97	Cristin Mortenson (alt.)
	Adrienne McEwan 8/2/99	Karen Culliver (alt.) 6/3/97
	Sarah Pfisterer (alt.)	#2 Karen Culliver
	Sarah Pfisterer 1/17/00	Sandra Joseph 3/26/96
	Adrienne McEwan (alt.)	Marie Danvers 1/13/98
	Sandra Joseph 10/30/00	Teri Bibb 4/98
	Lisa Vroman (alt.) 10/30/00	Susan Owen (alt.) 9/24/96
	Adrienne McEwan (alt.) 7/9/01	Rita Harvey (alt.) 3/98
	Sarah Pfisterer 8/6/01	Marie Danvers 6/98
	Beth Southard 3/25/02	Susan Facer (alt.) 6/98
	Lisa Vroman 4/22/02	#3 Tracy Shane
	Sandra Joseph	Kimilee Bryant
	Adrienne McEwan (alt.)	Amy Jo Arrington
		Tamra Hayden (alt.)
		Marie Danvers (alt.)
		Megan Starr-Levitt (alt.)
		Rebecca Pitcher
		Kathy Voytko
		Julie Hanson
		Rebecca Pitcher
		Lisa Vroman
		Marni Raab (alt.)
Raoul	Steve Barton	#1 Reece Holland
	Gary Mauer 4/19/99	Christopher Carl 7/2/96

Jim Weitzer 4/23/01
Michael Shawn Lewis 11/2/01
John Cudia

#2 Keith Buterbaugh
   Lawrence Anderson
   Jason Pebworth 1/13/98
   Lawrence Anderson 7/98
#3 Ciaran Sheehan
   Jason Pebworth 1/29/97
   Jim Weitzer
   Jason Pebworth 7/22/98
   Richard Todd Adams 3/31/99
   Jim Weitzer 1/12/00
   John Cudia
   Tim Martin Gleason

THE PRODUCERS

New York 4/19/01

Max

Nathan Lane
   Henry Goodman 3/19/02
   Brad Oscar 4/16/02
   Lewis J. Stadlen

Lewis J. Stadlen
   Jason Alexander 4/21/03

Leo

Matthew Broderick
   Steven Weber 3/19/02
   Roger Bart
   Don Stephenson

Don Stephenson
   Martin Short 4/21/03

Ulla

Cady Huffman
   Sarah Cornell 8/5/03

Angie L. Schworer

Roger

Gary Beach
   John Treacy Egan

Lee Roy Reams
   Gary Beach

Carmen Ghia

Roger Bart
   Sam Harris 7/2/02
   Brad Musgrove 12/17/02

Jeff Hyslop
   Michael Paternostro

Franz

Brad Oscar
   John Treacy Egan
   Peter Samuel

Bill Nolte
   Fred Applegate

PROOF

New York 10/24/00

Robert

Larry Bryggman
   Patrick Tovatt 6/12/01
   Len Cariou 7/2/02

Catherine

Mary-Louise Parker
   Jennifer Jason Leigh
   Anne Heche 7/2/02

Hal

Ben Shenkman
   Josh Hamilton
   Neil Patrick Harris 7/2/02
   Stephen Kunken 10/8/02

Claire

Johanna Day
   Seana Kofoed
   Kate Jennings Grant 7/2/02

RENT

New York 4/29/96

Roger Davis   Adam Pascal
                         Norbert Leo Butz
                         Richard H. Blake (alt.)
                         Manley Pope
                         Sebastian Arcelus 12/30/02

Mark Cohen   Anthony Rapp
                         Jim Poulos
                         Trey Ellett 5/15/00
                         Matt Caplan
                         Joey Fatone 8/5/02
                         Matt Caplan 12/23/02

Tom Collins   Jesse L. Martin
                         Michael McElroy
                         Rufus Bonds Jr. 9/7/99
                         Alan Mingo Jr. 4/10/00
                         Mark Leroy Jackson 1/15/01
                         Mark Richard Ford 2/3/02

Benjamin Coffin III   Taye Diggs
                         Jacques C. Smith
                         Stu James 3/13/00

Joanne Jefferson   Fredi Walker
                         Gwen Stewart
                         Alia León
                         Kenna J. Ramsey
                         Danielle Lee Greaves 10/4/99
                         Natalie Venetia Belcon 10/2/00
                         Myiia Watson-Davis
                         Merle Dandridge 10/28/02
                         Kenna J. Ramsey 3/03/03

Angel Schunard   Wilson Jermaine Heredia
                         Wilson Cruz
                         Shaun Earl
                         Jose Llana
                         Jai Rodriguez
                         Andy Senor 1/31/00
                         Jai Rodriguez 3/10/02
                         Andy Senor 2/17/03

Mimi Marquez   Daphne Rubin-Vega
                         Marcy Harriell 4/5/97
                         Krysten Cummings
                         Maya Days
                         Loraine Velez 2/28/00
                         Karmine Alers 12/31/01
                         Krystal L. Washington 5/15/03

Maureen Johnson   Idina Menzel
                         Sherie René Scott
                         Kristen Lee Kelly
                         Tamara Podemski
                         Cristina Fadale 10/4/99
                         Maggie Benjamin 10/28/01
                         Cristina Fadale 10/28/02

THOROUGHLY MODERN MILLIE

New York 4/18/02

Millie	Sutton Foster
Jimmy	Gavin Creel
	Christian Borle 4/29/03
Mrs. Meers	Harriet Harris
Trevor Grayson	Marc Kudisch
	Christopher Seiber 1/28/03
Muzzy	Sheryl Lee Ralph
	Leslie Uggams 4/22/03
Dorothy Brown	Angela Christian

URINETOWN

New York 9/20/02

Caldwell B.Cladwell	John Cullum
Bobby Strong	Hunter Foster
	Charlie Pollack 4/1/03
	Tom Cavanagh 5/20/03
Hope	Jennifer Laura Thompson
	Anastasia Barzee 12/29/02
Office Lockstock	Jeff McCarthy
Mrs. Pennywise	Nancy Opel
	Victoria Clark
	Carolee Carmello 4/29/03
Little Sally	Spencer Kayden
	Megan Lawrence 8/27/02
	Spencer Kayden 3/25/03

FIRST-CLASS NATIONAL TOURS

JESUS CHRIST SUPERSTAR

La Mirada, CA 11/11/02

Jesus of Nazareth	Sebastian Bach
	Eric Kunze 4/15/03
Judas Iscariot	Carl Anderson
	Lawrence Clayton 7/8/03
Mary Magdalene	Natalie Toro
Caiaphas	Stephen Breithaupt
King Herod	Peter Kevoian
	Barry Dennen
Simon Zealotes	Todd Fournier
Peter	James Clow

SATURDAY NIGHT FEVER

South Charleston, NC

Tony Manero	Ryan Ashley
	Joey Calveri
Stephanie Mangano	Jennifer Mrozik
	Jennie Marshall
Annette	Dena Digiancinto
Bobby C.	Cameron Stevens

SOME LIKE IT HOT

	Houston 6/4/2002
Osgood	Tony Curtis
Sugar	Jodi Carmeli
Jerry	Timothy Gulan
Joe	Arthur Hanket
Sweet Sue	Lenora Nemetz
Spats	William Ryall
Bienstock	Gerry Vichi
	Larry Storch

THE FULL MONTY

	Toronto 5/21/01
Jerry Lukowski	Christian Anderson
	Will Chase
Jeanette Burmeister	Carol Woods
	Jane Connell
Malcolm MacGregor	Geoffrey Nauffts
	Leo Daignault
Ethan Girard	Christopher J. Hanke
Noah T. Simmons	Cleavant Derrick
	Milton Craig Nealy
Dave Bukatinsky	Michael J. Todaro
Harold Nichols	Robert Westenberg

TICK, TICK, BOOM

	Dallas, Tx 1/7/03
	Closing 6/8/03 (scheduled)
Jonathan	Christian Campbell
	Joey Lawrence 5/27/03
Girl	Nicole Ruth Snelson
Michael	Wilson Cruz

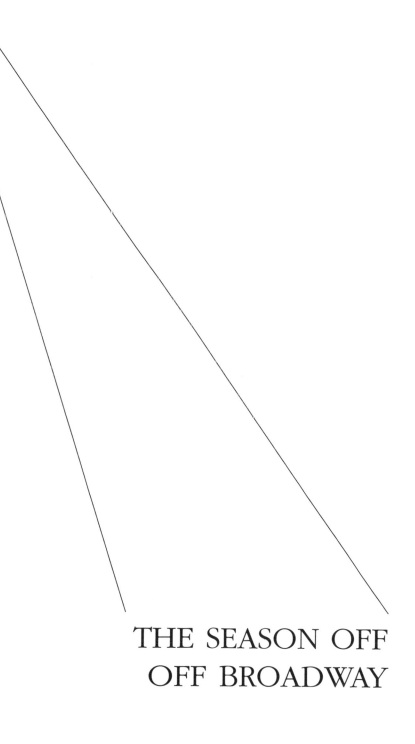

THE SEASON OFF
OFF BROADWAY

THE SEASON OFF OFF BROADWAY

○ ○ ○ ○ ○ *By Mel Gussow* ○ ○ ○ ○ ○

DÉJÀ VU—OR better yet, remembrance of things past—was the principal theme of the season Off Off Broadway, as playwrights and theaters reaffirmed their presence and their significance. Mabou Mines, Samuel Beckett, Richard Foreman, Lanford Wilson, La MaMa, the Ridiculous Theatrical Company, the Open Theater, the Living Theatre were all very much on our minds in a year that made one reflect on what once was and still could be: the excitement and the enticement of Off Off Broadway. Even as some companies confronted difficult times (especially economically), there was a sense of continuity.

Mabou Mines, that paradigm of experimental theater companies, returned in full fervor with *Cara Lucia*, a play about James Joyce's daughter Lucia. As you remember, she was the woman who fell in love with her father's friend Beckett (a love that was not reciprocated), was severely mentally disturbed and confined in an institution for most of her life. Lucia remained a mysterious muse, an inspiration and obsession for her father and, as it turns out, for the playwright Sharon Fogarty. With *Cara Lucia*, an outstanding OOB production (at the Here Arts Center), Ms. Fogarty performed that seemingly impossible task of bringing Lucia to life onstage and evoking a dramatic spirit that was both Joycean and Beckettian in terms of wordplay and theatricality.

In the play, Lucia is trapped in bedlam where she journeys through her mind and memory and, at 69, dreams about leaving the institution and returning to Paris. As elliptical as one might imagine, *Cara Lucia* proved to be striking as a play and even more so as a production (directed by the author). This was a tribute to Ms. Fogarty and to her creative collaborators, beginning with her actresses. Ruth Maleczech incarnated Lucia at an older age and Clove Galilee (Maleczech's daughter) brought a vulnerability and a kind of giddiness to the young Lucia. On and off the sidelines was Issy (a character from *Finnegans Wake*, from which there are occasional excerpts) played by Rosemary Fine. All three became symbiotic aspects of Lucia and her "blinding light." Using dance, music and video—with splendid sets and lighting by Jim Clayburgh, beautiful projections by Julie Archer—the staging added physicality to textuality (part of which was credited to Lee Breuer). At one point, Maleczech, confined to a chair, was magically lifted and flown through time and space.

In a typical exchange a nurse says to old Lucia, "Didn't your father write a story about a little cloud girl who turns into an old woman river. . . . And was it because she cried so much that she rained down a river of tears." And she adds, "Isn't that so Miss Joyce?" and Lucia answers, curtly, "I have no idea as to what you are talking about. No, get me out of this tub!"

In one of her monologues, the young Lucia says:

> My trouble? It is somewhere in my body. When my father visits me here he brings me lots of nice presents . . . a pretty pen and other nice things. Caro Babbo . . . Never forget. If ever I fall for someone, it will not be because I don't love you. I give you my word . . . in fact, I give you all my words. When I speak with my father he frequently takes notes on little bits of paper . . . I found him crying when he could not see to write.

The success of *Cara Lucia* reminded me of the early inventiveness of Mabou Mines—of JoAnne Akalaitis's collage of Colette, *Dressed Like an Egg*; David Warrilow's haunting interpretation of Beckett's *Lost Ones*; Lee Breuer's *The Saint and the Football Players* and *The Gospel at Colonus* and other plays and performance pieces that were such an integral part of Off Off Broadway though the 1970s and 1980s. It was heartening to know that the company continues to be out there searching for and finding new modes of communication, and that Maleczech remains such a daring actress.

IN THE BEST of Off Off, old meets new, also—always—exemplified by Richard Foreman, whose continuing presence and productivity make him a quintessential force in the theater. Consistently, he, too, has enlisted new young performers, indoctrinating them in the principles of being Foreman, which is to say both idiosyncratic and innovative. Every year, he opens a play at his Ontological-Hysteric showplace at St. Marks in the Bouwerie and astonishes us not only with his creativity but with his ability to command an audience. Foreman has fiercely devoted admirers who nightly fill this tiny space, this year for *Panic! (How to Be Happy!)*, another excursion into the imbalances of his mind and metaphor—and an outstanding OOB production. With a hint of pride, Foreman announces, "No story, no message"—and there is none.

Four garishly dressed actors (inmates?), embedded in the "misfits club," twist and turn, climb an imaginary mountain, walk into doors and otherwise cavort. Or, in the author's summary: "A band of eccentric desperados tries to provoke self-enlightenment through ritual sex, magic, mountain climbing and convulsive dancing" to the music of Mahler, Schonberg and punk rock. Sexuality is in the air—and in the scenery and props. As usual, the play is an abstraction, but, this time, it is happily short on pretension, a kind of Foremanesque clown show. As Foreman says in the course of the evening, "A new perspective can only repeat old patterns." With him, as with the Mabou Mines, those patterns remain vibrant.

Then there is Lanford Wilson, the season's playwright in residence at the Signature Theatre Company, which every year honors a writer with a cycle of plays. Janus-like, the Signature looks backward (retrospectively) and forward (plays previously unseen in New York) Wilson's season began auspiciously with an Off Broadway revival of *Burn This*, in which Edward Norton asserted his own identity in a role previously associated with John Malkovich (who created it on Broadway). That was followed by a forceful return of *Fifth of July* (a rich time capsule of the aftermath of the 1960s and the Vietnam war) and two new plays, *Book of Days* and *Rain Dance*. Together these plays—old and new—testified to Wilson's empathetic concern with the humanity of those who have been displaced (by family, war, environment). *Book of Days*, named a Best Play, was the more resonant of the two new works, but *Rain Dance* should not be overlooked, bringing us up close to the tensions of a fateful day of atom bomb testing at Los Alamos. And it reminds us that in plays from *The Mound Builders* onward, Wilson has always been one of our most explorative playwrights into areas of archeology, astronomy and scientific invention.

As is often the case at the Signature (with Sam Shepard, Romulus Linney and others), the season ended there with theatergoers wanting more. Instead of four plays, there could have been more than a dozen, old and new, by Wilson. But the idea of saluting a single playwright and devoting a season to his or her work is one deserving appreciation.

Charles Ludlam brightened Off Off stages for many seasons, and his early death at 44 in 1987—and his absence as playwright, actor-manager and director—is still lamented. Thoughts of his virtuosity returned with the publication of David Kaufman's authoritative biography, *Ridiculous! The Theatrical Life and Times of Charles Ludlam*, and also with a show that could easily have been overlooked. This was *Art, Life and Show Biz: A Non-Fiction Play* by Ain Gordon. In a too-brief run at Performance Space 122, Gordon placed three grand women in the spotlight, and let each tell her story, with the playwright as interviewer and interlocutor providing connective tissue. They were Helen Gallagher, a Broadway babe of the old school; Valda Satterfield, a modern dancer, Off Off actress (and mother of Ain Gordon, wife of David Gordon, both frequent collaborators with their son), and Lola Pashalinski, a queen-pin of Ludlam's Ridiculous Theatrical Company. In this outstanding OOB production, Gallagher, Satterfield, Pashalinski—divas all—traced their lives in theater and dance; their trials, triumphs and work habits. The show was a kind of Stritch Times Three, with a difference: for each of these woman, the struggle continues. All were philosophical and wry about their spiraling careers.

The most pointed—and poignant—was Pashalinski evoking the glory days (but often difficult days) with the Ridiculous, and also speaking about the effects on her own life. As she said: "After I left the Ridiculous company I had a couple of terrific years—stretching myself—working with Richard Foreman, JoAnne Akalaitis, regional theater. Then I did an audition for Joe Papp—for Mabou Mines's production of *The Tempest* at the Delacorte starring Raul Julia. Lee Breuer was directing and he coached me for the audition, because he didn't want me to frighten Mr. Papp—I got the job; I also got my Actors' Equity card—a big deal for me. And I felt good because the Ridiculous had prepared me well for Shakespeare, for everything really."

Performance Space 122, that outpost in the East Village, was also the home for a return of Eric Bogosian's monologue, *Notes From Underground*, and for Mac Wellman's *Bitter Bierce, Or the Friction We Call Grief*, a one-man show reflecting on the life and work of that American original, Ambrose Bierce. Stephen Mellor, a frequent Wellman interpreter, played Bierce.

OF MORE RECENT vintage but significant in the firmament of Off Off are John Kelly and Theodora Skipitares, both of whom had shows on this year. Kelly was represented (at the Kitchen) with *The Paradise Project*, his impressionistic rendering of the film *Children of Paradise*. The play began slowly, then suddenly awakened as Kelly as a character in his play sees *Children of Paradise*, and, overcome by the image of Jean-Louis Barrault, transforms himself into that unforgettable figure. Billed as the first installment of a new Kelly work, the play was raw-edged, not yet on a level with such previous Kelly pieces as *Pass the Blutwurst, Bitte* and *Ode to a Cube*, which may in fact have been a precursor of *The Paradise Project*.

Skipitares's contribution was *Helen* (at La MaMa Annex), in which she uncovered unseen aspects of Helen of Troy, drawing upon Ovid and Stesichorus as well as Euripides. As always, she employed diverse puppetry to tell her story (Bunraku, Bengali and shadow puppets, and a puppet stage within the Trojan horse). The show was both intimate and epic, particularly in the scene of battle. For more than 20 years, Skipitares has been using puppets to investigate the widest range of subjects: Plato, Darwinism, urban mis-planning, Hogarth and, now, the myth of Helen of Troy. In common with Foreman, she very early defined her approach and has held to it with resilience and imagination, in spite of the fact that she has not received the recognition she so clearly deserves.

In contrast, there were proclamations made for the supposed genius of Rezo Gabriadze (from the Republic of Georgia) whose *Battle of Stalingrad* was a feature of the Lincoln Center Festival. The puppetry was artful but the storytelling (in Russian with English subtitles) was defective or at least digressionary, focusing excessively on the love of two horses. The theatrical arm of the festival was a disappointment, coming after previous celebrations of the work of Samuel Beckett and Harold Pinter.

The Brooklyn Academy of Music's Next Wave Festival featured Robert Wilson's version of *Woyzeck*, with a pastiche score by Tom Waits and Kathleen Brennan. The play (or opera) began like a Brecht-Weill musical, with a carnival sideshow atmosphere. Then it settled down to an imaginative parade of Wilson images, fascinating by themselves but missing the edginess of the original play (as previously captured in productions by both Richard Foreman and JoAnne Akalaitis). Yukio Ninagawa brought a new version of *Macbeth* to BAM, longer and less intense than his earlier adaptation.

A vastly different kind of puppetry was represented by *Avenue Q*, a tart take-off on *Sesame Street*, which opened at the Vineyard Theatre and subsequently moved to Broadway at the beginning of the new season. An outstanding OOB production, this musical was the combined handiwork of Robert Lopez and Jeff Marx (music, lyrics and concept), Jeff Whitty (book), Jason Moore (direction) and Rick Lyon (puppets). Have you ever wondered if Bert and Ernie, that closely linked double act of *Sesame* fame, were gay? Or, how truly misanthropic the Cookie Monster was? These and other pressing questions were raised and answered in this delightful show. Mixing puppets with live actors (some Bunraku style) on a pop-up picture book landscape, *Avenue Q* revealed the earthiness behind the innocence. It was of course aimed at adults, especially those with fond memories of seeing *Sesame* with their children. Songs such as "Everybody's a Little Racist" took "It Isn't Easy Being Green" one step further into social consciousness. But mostly *Avenue Q* (Q for quixotic?) was a breezy entertainment.

IN ANTICIPATION OF the 50th anniversary of the premiere of *Waiting for Godot*, PEN presented an evening at Manhattan Town Hall celebrating Samuel Beckett. In the course of that evening, Bill Irwin and John Turturro did scenes from *Godot*, Rosaleen Linehan offered an excerpt from *Happy Days* and Marian Seldes, performing a work of Beckett's for the first time, did

Rockaby. There were also reminiscences and tributes from Edward Albee, Paul Auster, Tom Bishop, this writer and others, all commemorating Beckett's great gift to theater and literature. Along with Jean Genet and Eugene Ionesco, he remains a seminal figure Off Off Broadway. *Elle*, a forgotten oddity by Genet, was rediscovered by the actor Alan Cumming. At the Zipper Theater, he played the central role of the Pope in drag, and was both outrageous and virtuosic. The play, about images and role-playing—was chaotic but far more interesting than many more polished works.

Political subjects were in vogue away from Broadway, with two plays this year dealing directly with the Israeli-Palestinian conflict. At the Flea Theater there was *O Jerusalem* by A.R. Gurney. The formulaic nature of the play was somewhat disguised by the playwright's spontaneity. This was presented as a work in progress, with the playwright occasionally interrupting the action to eliminate a scene before it was staged. Jim Simpson gave the slash-and-burn story a sharp, intimate production. At the center was a government official (Stephen Rowe) thrown into the melee. Gurney, not previously known as a political playwright, earned that mantle with a many-sided view of an irreconcilable problem. At Primary Stages, there was also an updated version of Gurney's 1990 play, *The Fourth Wall*, an artificial attempt at metatheater. John Patrick Shanley's *Dirty Story* covered some of the same territory as *O Jerusalem*, with an approach that was allegorical and at times heavy-handed, with broad satiric brush strokes. Gradually playwrights began dealing with questions arising from the terrorist attack on the World Trade Center, as in *The Mercy Seat* by Neil LaBute (named a Best Play).

There is always room for entertainment, as exemplified by Charles Busch's *Shanghai Moon*, presented by the Drama Dept. A homage and parody of all those old creepy movie melodramas planted in the Far East, the show was brightened by performances by B.D. Wong (as the manipulative General Gong Fei), Daniel Gerroll (two roles for him, a diplomat and a smuggler) and, of course, Busch himself as limpid, lovely Lady Sylvia Allington. The evening was amusing, but not quite up to the level of similar travesties by Ludlam.

Trevor Griffiths's *Comedians*, a probing examination of working-class England (in this case a comedy class in Manchester), was a Broadway hit as directed by Mike Nichols in the 1970s. The play returned in a New Group production starring Jim Dale. In collaboration with the Women's Project and Productions, the New Group also offered *The Women of Lockerbie*, Deborah Brevoort's play about the bombing of the Pan Am plane in Scotland in 1988. The Ensemble Studio Theatre gave Cynthia Nixon an opportunity for an ingratiating performance in Jacquelyn Reingold's *String Fever*. In it she played a woman turning 40 and still trying to find her place in the world. The play itself was overloaded with death, angst and coincidence. In spring, the EST held its annual marathon of one-act plays, highlighted by Deborah Grimberg's *The Honey Makers*, about racism in London.

Classics were represented at several companies. The Mint Theater Company, which specializes in revivals of lost, or at least lesser known plays from the past, unearthed Arthur Schnitzler's *Das Weite Land*, renaming it *Far and Wide*. This provocative end-of-empire drama reached its pinnacle years ago with Tom Stoppard's adaptation *Undiscovered Country* at London's Royal National Theatre. The Pearl Theatre Company presented Shaw's antiwar play *Heartbreak House*, a particularly timely choice during the year of the Iraq conflict, and also lightened the air with a revival of Oliver Goldsmith's *She Stoops to Conquer*.

In the early 1960s, Genet's *The Blacks* was a long running Off Broadway success, giving centerstage to James Earl Jones, Roscoe Lee Browne, Louis Gossett Jr. and many other rising black actors. This season it returned to the Classical Theatre of Harlem and later moved downtown to the East 13th Street Theatre. The Harlem company also offered a revival of Stanislaw Ignacy Witkiewicz's surrealistic comedy, *The Crazy Locomotive*. In his last season as the artistic director of the Classic Stage, Barry Edelstein updated *The Winter's Tale*, with David Strathairn in the central role of Leontes. The CSC also presented Ibsen's *Ghosts*, in a new translation by Lanford Wilson, with a cast headed by Amy Irving and the ever-busy Daniel Gerroll. The Soho Rep brought back María Irene Fornes's barroom play, *Molly's Dream* and also staged a new adaptation of Jim Crace's novel, *Signals of Distress*.

The Irish Repertory Theatre had its usual diversity of plays, many of them of course Irish, Enda Walsh's *bedbound* (brief but endless). In *bedbound*, an insane man and his incapacitated daughter occupy the same bed. The faux Beckett language seemed more in the nature of ranting, although the acting by Brían F. O'Byrne as the father found a certain clarity in the confusion.

OFF OFF, AS always, leaves room for enterprise, and nowhere was it as in evidence as with Tim Martin's *Hamlet*. Martin, a young executive at an antique silver shop in Manhattan, had acted in college and had for many years dreamed about playing Hamlet. Using his own money (a budget of $7,500), he created an Equity showcase production and co-directed with Dave Eisenbach (who also played Horatio). Martin placed an ad in *Back Stage*, and actors turned out in droves even for the promise of only "possible pay." Most of the actors were professionals, although they all had other jobs to pay for their theatrical careers. Gertrude worked at J.P. Morgan, the Player King was a computer consultant, the Gravedigger worked as a tailor and Polonius was a professor of Shakespeare. As Martin said, "You sit on the subway, and so many people look drab on a winter's day. They're going to their jobs, but for all you know, at night they're in a play or they're dancers."

I followed the production from casting through rehearsals and wrote about this venture in the *New York Times*. The article appeared on the front page—under the headline, "To Be Hamlet (But Still Keep the Day Job)." What could have been a vanity production turned out to be quite credible—both energetic and clearly articulated. On an almost bare stage, with basic lighting and everyday clothes for costumes, the production was resourceful, and it featured some admirable performances, including that of Martin in the title role, Frances Chewning as Ophelia and Teige Carroll, who, at 6 foot 8, was probably the tallest Ghost ever to haunt Elsinore. After the opening, Hamlet invited everyone onstage and in the audience to a party at a restaurant around the corner from the theater. It was like Sardi's of Broadway past, except, in this case, no reviews were read aloud (there were no reviews). Emboldened by his success, Martin next planned to tackle *Romeo and Juliet*, while limiting himself to the role of co-director—well, perhaps he would play a small role. The point is that for the adventurous (with $7500 to spend), opportunity awaits Off Off Broadway.

For many years, Andre Gregory has been a stalwart of Off Off Broadway, taking seemingly infinite time to work on a play and sometimes never opening it to the public at large. This happened years ago with his version of *Uncle Vanya*, retitled *Vanya on 42nd Street*, which was eventually seen not in a theater but in a film version by Louis Malle. For Gregory, as for others, the work process is the essential element, as in his ongoing project of *The Master Builder*, adapted by and starring Wallace Shawn. While in process, that production was interrupted by the death of one of the actors, Jerry Mayer, associated with Gregory from *Alice in Wonderland* onward. Mayer was also known for his one-man versions of Albert Einstein and Antonin Artaud.

BRIDGING THE END of this season and the beginning of the next, there were two deaths that brought a close to two of the most significant careers in the experimental theater, those of Jack Gelber and Joseph Chaikin. Each would forever be associated with a company, Gelber with the Living Theatre, Chaikin with the Open Theater. Under the leadership of Julian Beck and Judith Malina, the Living Theatre became the radical conscience of the

American theater and, with Gelber's *The Connection* in 1959, opened the door to plays about the lost and the disenfranchised. In his subsequent career, Gelber continued to write plays and through his teaching also became known as an ardent supporter of new playwrights. In a tribute to Gelber at the New School University, Edward Albee said, "Two plays written in 1958 changed my life. One was mine, *The Zoo Story*, the other was *The Connection*."

The Open Theater was created in 1959 as a laboratory for actors. Soon it also became a nurturing place for playwrights (including Sam Shepard and Jean-Claude van Itallie). Chaikin was its guiding force and most visible presence, leading the company in its original creations of such memorable ensemble plays as *The Serpent, Terminal* and *The Mutation Show*. When asked how Chaikin became the director of the company, Paul Zimet (one of Chaikin's theatrical progeny and head of the Talking Band) said that after every workday the actors would look to him for his opinion and his comments. Chaikin very naturally was the intuitive center of the Open Theater, and after the company disbanded, he went on to work as a playwright in collaboration with Shepard, and as an actor and director.

Following a stroke, he suffered from aphasia, but continued working. In the fall of 2002, he was in residence at the Actors Studio, with Eduardo Machado creating a play about the terrorist attack on the World Trade Center. I sat in on rehearsals as Chaikin, Machado and the actors—who included Estelle Parsons—put together a collage of September 11 experiences. Though that play never achieved fruition, the work process reminded me of the earlier days of the Open and other experimental theaters. Despite his disability, Chaikin never lost his talent to direct or to lead an ensemble. A memorial for him began with a hopeful quotation from Brecht: "You can make a fresh start with your last breath." That, of course, could serve as a motto for Off Off Broadway.

PLAYS PRODUCED OFF OFF BROADWAY
AND ADDITIONAL NYC PRESENTATIONS
○ ○ ○ ○ ○
Compiled by Vivian Cary Jenkins

BELOW IS A comprehensive sampling of 2002–03 Off Off Broadway productions in New York. There is no definitive "Off Off Broadway" area or qualification. To try to define or regiment it would be untrue to its fluid, exploratory purpose. This listing of hundreds of works produced by scores of OOB groups is as inclusive as reliable sources allow. This section pertains to professional theater in New York that is covered by neither Broadway nor full Off Broadway contracts.

The more active and established producing groups are identified in **bold face type**, in alphabetical order, with artistic policies and the names of its leaders given whenever possible. Each group's 2002–03 schedule, with emphasis on new plays, is listed with play titles in CAPITAL LETTERS. Often these are works-in-progress with changing scripts, casts and directors, sometimes without an engagement of record (but an opening or early performance date is included when available).

Many of these Off Off Broadway groups have long since outgrown a merely experimental status and offer programs that are the equal in professionalism and quality (and in some cases the superior) of anything in the New York theater. These listings include special contractual arrangements such as the showcase code, letters of agreement (allowing for longer runs and higher admission prices than usual) and, closer to the edge of the commercial theater, so-called "mini-contracts." In the list below, available data has been compiled from press representatives, company managers and publications of record.

A large selection of developing groups and other shows that made appearances Off Off Broadway during the season under review appears under the "Miscellaneous" heading at the end of this listing.

Amas Musical Theatre. Dedicated to bringing people of all races, creeds, colors and national origins together through the performing arts. Donna Trinkoff producing director.

> ZANNA, DON'T! Musical with book, music and lyrics by Tim Acito; with additional book and lyrics by Alexander Dinelaris. October 17, 2002. Directed and choreographed by Devanand Janki; scenery, Wade Laboissonniere and Tobin Ost; lighting, Jeffrey Lowney; sound, Robert Killenberger. With Adam Michael Kookept, Anika Larsen, Darius Nichols, Amanda Ryan Paige, Robb Sapp, Shelley Thomas, Gregory Treco, Jared Zeus.

> LATIN HEAT. By Ovi Vargas, Maria Torres, Oscar Hernandez, David Coffman. February 18, 2003. Directed and choreographed by Ms. Torres.

Cracking wise: Michael McGrath, Rosemarie DeWitt, Tom Mardirosian, David Turner and Julie Halston in The Butter and Egg Man. *Photo: Carol Rosegg*

Atlantic Theater Company. Produces new plays and reinterpretations of classics that speak in a contemporary voice on issues reflecting today's society. Neil Pepe artistic director, Beth Emelson producing director.

> THE BUTTER AND EGG MAN. By George S. Kaufman. October 2, 2002. Directed by David Pittu; scenery, Anna Louizos; costumes, Bobby Frederick Tilley II; lighting, Robert Perry; music and sound, Fitz Patton; production stage manager, Stephen M. Kaus. With David Turner, Rosemarie DeWitt, Tom Mardirosian, Julie Halston, Michael McGrath, Amelia White, Todd Buonopane, David Cromwell, David Brummel, Robin Skye, Amanda Davies, John Ellison Conlee.

Brooklyn Academy of Music Next Wave Festival. Since 1983, this annual festival has presented hundreds of cutting-edge events, including dozens of world premieres. With its focus on leading international artists, it is one of the world's largest and most prestigious festivals of contemporary performing arts. Alan H. Fishman chairman of the board; Karen Brooks Hopkins president; Joseph V. Melillo executive producer.

> GALILEO GALILEI. An opera with libretto by Mary Zimmerman with Philip Glass and Arnold Weinstein; music by Philip Glass. October 1, 2002. Directed by Ms. Zimmerman; scenery, Daniel Ostling; costumes, Mara Blumenfeld; lighting, T.J. Gerckens; sound, Michael Bodeen, projections, John Boesche; conductor, William Lumpkin. With John Duykers, Andrew Funk, Alicia Berneche, Eugene Perry, Elizabeth Reiter.

> MEDEA. By Euripides; translated by Kenneth McLeish and Frederic Raphael. October 2, 2002. Directed by Deborah Warner; scenery, Tom Pye; costumes, Tom Rand; lighting, Peter Mumford; sound, Mel Mercier. With Siobhán McCarthy, Robin Laing, Fiona Shaw, Struan Rodger, Jonathan Cake, Joseph Mydell, Derek Hutchinson, Dylan Denton. Transferred to Broadway's Brooks Atkinson Theatre (12/10/2002; 78 performances). See Plays Produced on Broadway section.

WOYZECK. By Georg Büchner; adapted by Wolfgang Wiens and Ann-Christin Rommen; music and lyrics by Tom Waits and Kathleen Brennan. October 29, 2002. Direction and scenery by Robert Wilson; codirection, Ann-Christin Rommen; costumes, Jacques Reynaud; lighting, A.J. Weissbard and Mr. Wilson. With Jens Jorn Spottag, Kaya Bruel; Morten Eisner, Marianne Mortensen, Ole Thestrup, Ann-Mari Max Hansen, Morten Lutzhoft, Benjamin Boe Rasmussen, Tom Jensen, Troels II Munk, Joseph Driffield, Jeppe Dahl Rordam, Morten Thorup Koudal, Ivana Catanese, Ryan Hill, Maria Pessino, Matthew Shattuck, Carlow Soto, Kameron Steele.

MERCY. Music-theater work by Meredith Monk and Ann Hamilton; developed in collaboration with Theo Bleckmann, Ellen Fisher, Katie Geissinger, Ching Gonzalez, Lanny Harrison, John Hollenbeck, Louise Smith, Allison Sniffin. December 3, 2002. Music by Ms. Monk; lighting, Noele Stollmack; costumes, Gabriel Berry; sound, David Meschter.

MACBETH. By William Shakespeare. December 4, 2002. Directed by Yukio Ninagawa; scenery, Tsukasa Nakagoshi; costumes, Lily Komine; lighting, Tamotsu Harada; sound, Masahiro Inoue; fight choreography, Masahiro Kunii.

Classic Stage Company. Reinventing and revitalizing the classics for contemporary audiences. Barry Edelstein artistic director, Anne Tanaka producing director.

GHOSTS. By Henrik Ibsen; translation by Lanford Wilson. November 10, 2002. Directed by Daniel Fish; scenery, Christine Jones; costumes, Kaye Voyce; lighting, Scott Zielinski; music and sound, Eric Shim. With Amy Irving, Daniel Gerroll, Lisa Demont, David Patrick Kelly, Ted Schneider.

THE WINTER'S TALE. By William Shakespeare. January 30, 2003. Directed by Barry Edelstein; scenery, Narelle Sissons; costumes, Mattie Ullrich; lighting, Jane Cox; sound, Elizabeth Rhodes; music, Michael Torke. With David Strathairn, Barbara Garrick, Michel Gill, Mary Lou Rosato, Teagle F. Bougere, Tom Bloom, David Costabile, Angel Desai, Mark H. Dold, Gene Farber, Andrew Guilarte, Larry Paulsen, Elizabeth Reaser, Michael Reid, Elizabeth Sherman, Joaquin Torres.

Drama Dept. A collective of actors, directors, designers, stage managers, writers and producers who collaborate to create new works and revive neglected classics. Douglas Carter Beane artistic director, Michael S. Rosenberg.

SHANGHAI MOON. By Charles Busch. January 17, 2003. Directed by Carl Andress; scenery, B.T. Whitehill; costumes, Michael Bottari and Ronald Case; lighting, Kirk Bookman; sound, Laura Grace Brown; fight director, Rick Sordelet; stage manager, John Handy. With Mr. Busch, Becky Ann Baker, Sekiya Billman, Daniel Gerroll, Marcy McGuigan, B.D. Wong.

Ensemble Studio Theatre. Membership organization of playwrights, actors, directors and designers dedicated to supporting individual theater artists and developing new works for the stage. Projects range from readings to fully mounted productions. Curt Dempster artistic director.

MARATHON 2002 (SERIES C). June 10, 2002.
HOPE BLOATS. By Patricia Scanlon. Directed by David Briggs. With Dave Simonds, Ms. Scanlon.
UNION CITY, NEW JERSEY, WHERE ARE YOU? By Rogelio Martinez. Directed by Randal Myler. With Rosie Perez, Felix Solis, Julien A. Carrasquillo.
MY FATHER'S FUNERAL. By Peter Maloney. Directed by Beatrice Terry. With Mr. Maloney, Griffith Maloney.
THE MOON BATH GIRL. By Graeme Gillis. Directed by Eliza Beckwith. With Michael Esper, Alicia Goranson.
CITY OF DREAMS. Musical with book and lyrics by David Zellnik; music by Joseph Zellnik. July 15, 2002. Directed by Michael Alltop; choreography, Janet Bogardus; scenery, Mark Fitzgibbons; costumes, Randall E. Klein; lighting, Hideaki Tsutsui; sound, Ryan Streber. With Ben Nordstrom, Kristin Griffith, D. Michael Berkowitz, Sharron Bower, Alison Fraser, Megan McGinnis, Paul Anthony Stewart, Stephen Bel Davies, Michael Mendiola, John Hellyer.

MASHA NO HOME. By Lloyd Suh. November 30, 2002. Directed by Nela Wagman; scenery, Jennifer Varbalow; costumes, Nan Young; lighting, Greg MacPherson; sound, Robert Gould; music, David Rothenberg. With Cindy Cheung, Kevin Louie, James Saito, Eddie Shin, Samantha Quan.

STRING FEVER. By Jacquelyn Reingold. March 3, 2003. Directed by Mary B. Robinson; scenery, David P. Gordon; costumes, Michael Krass; lighting, Michael Lincoln; sound, Rob Gould. With Cynthia Nixon, Cecilia deWolf, Evan Handler, David Thornton, Tom Mardirosian, Jim Fyfe.

FULL SPECTRUM: A TECHNO-THEATRE EXPERIMENT. Featuring plays by Sarah Ruhl and Susan Kim. March 27, 2003. Directed by Brenda Bakker Harger. With Nate Jones, Serena Lam, Patrick McKiernan, Timothy Price, Christopher M. Spiller, Jennifer R. Spiller.

MARATHON 2003 (SERIES A). May 11, 2003.

OF TWO MINDS. By Billie Aronson. Directed by Jamie Richards. With Geneva Carr, Annie Campbell, Ian Reed Kesler, Brad Bellamy, Conor White.

THE HONEY MAKERS. By Deborah Grimberg. Directed by Tom Rowan. With Thom Rivera, Cori Thomas, Bill Cwikowski, Jake Myers.

CODA. By Romulus Linney. Directed by Julie Boyd. With Thomas Lyons, Joseph Siravo, Helen Coxe, Jane Welch.

A BLOOMING OF IVY. By Garry Williams. Directed by Richmond Hoxie. With James Rebhorn, Phyllis Somerville.

MEMENTO MORI. By Susan Kim. Directed by Abigail Zealey Bess. With Cecilia deWolf, Amy Staats.

Intar. Identifies, develops and presents the talents of gifted Hispanic-American theater artists and multicultural visual artists. Max Ferrá, Michael John Garcés producing artistic directors.

Adoring ayes: Dara Coleman, Christopher Joseph Jones and Derdriu Ring in The Playboy of the Western World. *Photo: Carol Rosegg*

Intimate relations: Kathleen Early, Melissa Hart and Rita Harvey in Peg O' My Heart.
Photo: Carol Rosegg

HAVANA UNDER THE SEA. By Abilio Estévez. March 6, 2003. Directed by Max Ferrá; scenery, Van Santvoord; costumes, Willa Kim; lighting, Ed McCarthy; sound, David M. Lawson. With Doreen Montalvo, Meme Solis.

NEW WORKS LAB SERIES 2003. Costumes, Meghan Healey; lighting, Shawn Kaufman and Kevin Hardy; sound, David M. Lawson. DRAWN AND QUARTERED. By Maggie Bofill. April 18, 2003. Directed by Louis Moreno. With Yetta Gottesman, Carlos Valencia. MEMORIES OF OUR WOMEN. By Arthur Giron; developed in collaboration with Perry Garcia and the actors. April 25, 2003. Directed by Angel David. With Raul Castillo, AnaMaria Correa, Annie Henk, Ana Tulia Ramirez, Joselin Reyes, Letty Soto. WHISPER. By Oscar A. Colón. May 2, 2003. Directed by Jesse Ontiveros. With Melissa Delaney Del Valle, Carlos Molina, Larilu Smith, Michelle Torres. N.E. 2ND AVENUE. By Teo Castellanos. May 9, 2003. Directed by Michael John Garcés. With Mr. Castellanos.

Irish Repertory Theatre. Brings works by Irish and Irish-American playwrights to a wider audience and develops new works focusing on a wide range of cultural experience. Charlotte Moore artistic director, Ciarán O'Reilly producing director.

THE PLAYBOY OF THE WESTERN WORLD. By J.M. Synge. July 2, 2002. Directed by Charlotte Moore; scenery, David Raphel; lighting, Kirk Bookman; costumes, David Toser; sound, Murmod Inc.; music, Larry Kirwan and Black 47. With Clodagh Bowyer, Dara Coleman, David Costelloe, Laura James Flynn, James Gale, Christopher Joseph Jones, John Keating, John Leighton, Aedin Moloney, Heather O'Neill, Derdriu Ring.

BAILEGANGAIRE. By Tom Murphy. October 10, 2002. Directed by Mr. Murphy; scenery, David Raphel; lighting, Brian Nason; costumes, David Toser; sound, Murmod Inc. With Pauline Flanagan, Terry Donnelly, Babo Harrison.

A CELTIC CHRISTMAS. Musical adapted from Dylan Thomas's *A Child's Christmas in Wales*. December 8, 2002. Directed by Charlotte Moore; costumes, Linda Fisher; lighting, Sean Farrell; musical direction, Eddie Guttman. With Rebecca Bellingham, Peter Cormican, Eddie Guttman, Kenny Kosek, Jayne Ackley Lynch, Joyce A. Noonan, Joshua Park.

BEDBOUND. By Enda Walsh. January 23, 2003. Directed by Ms. Walsh; scenery, Klara Zieglerova; lighting, Kirk Bookman; sound, Zachary Williamson. With Brían F. O'Byrne, Jenna Lamia.

PEG O' MY HEART. By J. Hartley Manners; songs by Charlotte Moore. May 22, 2003. Directed by Ms. Moore; scenery, James Morgan; costumes, David Toser; lighting, Mary Jo Dondlinger; sound, Zachary Williamson; musical direction, Eddie Guttman. With Melissa Hart, Jody Madaras, Rita Harvey, James A. Stephens, Jonathan Hadley, Kathleen Early, Don Sparks, J. Kennedy.

The Joseph Papp Public Theater/New York Shakespeare Festival. Schedule of special projects, in addition to its regular Off Broadway productions. George C. Wolfe producer, Mara Manus executive director.

New Work Now! Festival of New Play Readings.

ANNA IN THE TROPICS. Written and directed by Nilo Cruz. April 26, 2003.

MARIELA IN THE DESERT. By Karen Zacarías. April 27, 2003. Directed by Tom Prewitt.

BLIND MOUTH SINGING. By Jorge Ignacio Cortiñas. April 28, 2003. Directed by Ruben Polendo.

A CHINESE TALE. By Aravind Enrique Adyanthaya. April 29, 2003. Directed by Bob McGrath.

TWO LOVES AND A CREATURE. By Gustavo Ott; translated by Heather McKay. April 30, 2003. Directed by Steve Cosson.

EXPAT/INFERNO. By Alejandro Morales. May 1, 2003. Directed by Trip Cullman.

DEMON BABY. By Erin Courtney. May 2, 2003. Directed by Ken Rus Schmoll.

HILDA. By Marie Ndiaye; translated by Erika Rundle. May 3, 2003. Directed by Jo Bonney.

BIRO. Written and directed by Ntare Guma Mbaho Mwine. May 4, 2003.

THE LADIES. By Anne Washburn and Anne Kauffman. May 5, 2003.

JOEY SHAKESPEAR. By Brendan Cochrane and Joseph Assadourian. May 6, 2003. Directed by Michael John Garcés.

BODEGA LUNG FAT. By Mike Batistick. May 7, 2003. Directed by Jo Bonney.

IGGY WOO. By Alice Tuan. May 8, 2003. Directed by Mark Wing-Davey.

THE NEXT EPISODE. By Chris Papagapitos. May 9, 2003. Directed by Robert Milazzo.

THE ARGUMENT. By David Greenspan. May 10, 2003. Directed by Brian Mertes.

New Musicals Now! Festival of Excerpted New Musicals.

ACCIDENTAL NOSTALGIA. By Cynthia Hopkins. May 11, 2003.

TAKING STEPS THREE THIRTEEN. Book, music and lyrics by Matthew Doers. May 11, 2003. Musical direction by Luqman Brown.

NO GOD BUT YEARNING. Book by Donna Di Novelli; music by David Rodwin and others. May 12, 2003.

THE STRANGER. Book and lyrics by Micah Schraft; music by Michael Friedman. May 12, 2003. Directed by Trip Cullman.

La MaMa Experimental Theatre Club (ETC). A workshop for experimental theater of all kinds. Ellen Stewart founder and director.

THE BRONX WITCH PROJECT. By Alba Sanchez. September 19, 2002. Directed and designed by Gary Dini. With Ms. Sanchez.

SLUTFORART A.K.A. AMBIGUOUS AMBASSADOR. By Ping Chong and Muna Tseng. October 3, 2002. Directed by Mr. Chong; costumes, Han Feng; lighting, Mark London; sound, Brian Hallas; projections, Jan Hartley. With Muna Tseng, and the voices of Timothy Greenfield-Sanders, Kristoffer Haynes, Bill T. Jones, Ann Magnuson, Richard Martin, Kenny Scharf, Jenny Yee.

BILLIE. By Roz Nixon. October 10, 2002. Directed by Ms. Nixon. With Madame Pat Tandy.

UE92/02 (an new work in the Undesirable Elements/Secret History series). By Ping Chong and Talvin Wilks. October 17, 2002. Directed by Mr. Chong. With Luanne Edwards, Angel Gardner, Leyla Modirzadeh, Zohra Saed, Tania Salmen, Michelle van Tonder, Mr. Chong.

SURVIVAL OF THE FETUS. Musical with book by Coby Koehl; music and lyrics by Mr. Koehl and Sean Dibble. October 24, 2002. Directed and choreographed by Vic DiMonda; musical direction, Jonah Spidel; arrangements, Mr. Spidel, Erik Reyes and Ken Kincaid. With Mr. Koehl, Cherie Hannouche, Natalie Joy Johnson, Matthew R. Wilson.

CURVE. By Nicholas Devine. October 30, 2002. Directed by Jeffrey Dewhurst. With Mr. Devine.

SPECTACLE OF SPECTACLES: THE CLAIRVOYANT CABARET. By Deirdre Broderick. November 14, 2002. Directed by Ms. Broderick; scenery, Brian P. Glover. With Bill Connington, Mr. Glover, Katherine Gooch.

GENEVA. By Nicholas von Hoffman. November 14, 2002. Directed by Mary Fulham; scenery, Gregory John Mercurio; costumes, Ramona Ponce; sound, Tim Schellenbaum. With Brigitte Barnett, Ari Benjamin, Todd Davis, Steve Hauck, Carol London, John Otis, Michael Quinlan, Kerry Sullivan.

ORPHAN ON GOD'S HIGHWAY. By Josh Fox. November 16, 2002. Directed by Mr. Fox; scenery, David Esler; lighting, Charles Foster. With Sophie Amieva, Mr. Fox, Connie Hall, Gina Hirsch, Ravi Jain, Peter Lettre, Alanna Medlock, Jason Quarles, Bob Saietta, Magin Schantz, Dario Tangelson, Aaron Mostkoff Unger.

STAR MESSENGERS. By Paul Zimet; music by Ellen Maddow. December 2, 2002. Directed by Mr. Zimet; choreography, Karinne Keithley; scenery, Nic Ularu, costumes, Kiki Smith; lighting, Carol Mullins; With Will Badgett, David Greenspan, Christine Ciccone, Ryan Dietz, Court Dorsey, Marcy Jellison, Ms. Keithley, Ms. Maddow, Randy Reyes, Michelle Rios.

H.A.M.L.E.T. By Linda Mussman; in collaboration with Claudia Bruce and Gerald Stoddard. December 5, 2002. Directed by Ms. Mussman; scenery, Jun Maeda; lighting, Ms. Mussman; video, Ms. Mussman and Mr. Stoddard; music, Ms. Bruce and Mr. Stoddard. With Ms. Bruce and Mr. Stoddard.

BLUE SKY TRANSMISSION: A TIBETAN BOOK OF THE DEAD. By Raymond Bobgan and contributing writers Mike Geither, Patricia Hanisame Leebove and Ray McNiece. December 8, 2002. Directed by Mr. Bobgan; scenery, Michael Guy James; costumes, Karen Young; lighting, Trad A. Burns. With Lisa Black, Tracy Broyles, Kishiko Hasegawa, Holly Holsinger, Brett Keyser, Amy Kristina, Karin Randoja, Sophia Skiles, Rebecca Spencer, Chi-wang Yang.

THE DEVILS OF LOUDUN. By Matt Mitler; adapted from Aldous Huxley. January 2, 2003. Directed and designed by Mr. Mitler; costumes, Karen Hatt; musical direction, Bob Strock. With Mr. Mitler.

SSS-T-O-N-E-DDD. By Arthur Maximillian Adair. January 16, 2003. Directed and designed by Mr. Adair; music, S-Dog. With Mr. Adair.

PAINTED SNAKE IN A PAINTED CHAIR. By Ellen Maddow. January 18, 2003. Directed by Paul Zimet; choreography, Karinne Keithley; scenery, Nic Ularu; costumes, Kiki Smith; lighting, Carol Mullins. With Diane Beckett, Gary Brownlee, Randolph Curtis Rand, Steven Rattazzi, Tina Shepard, Louise Smith, "Blue" Gene Tyranny (keyboard).

BAD BUGS BITE. By Andrea Paciotto; based on a fairytale by Ivo Andric and stories by Mr. Paciotto. January 23, 2003. Directed by Mr. Paciotto; lighting, Jasper Buurman; music, Jan Klug. With Charlotte Brathwaite, Monika Haasova, Jelena Jovanovic.

MARGA GOMEZ'S INTIMATE DETAILS. By Marga Gomez. January 30, 2003. Directed by David Schweizer; scenery, Gary Baura; lighting, Arthur Maximillian Adair; sound, Alfredo D. Troche. With Ms. Gomez.

PHILOKTETES. By John Jesurun. February 10, 2003. With Ruth Maleczech.

HELEN: QUEEN OF SPARTA. By Theodora Skipitares. February 13, 2003. Directed and designed by Ms. Skipitares. Music by Arnold Dreyblatt; additional music, Tim Schellenbaum; lighting, Pat Dignan; video, Kay Hines.

A STREET CORNER PIERROT. By Terrell Robinson. February 20, 2003. Directed by Sheila Kaminsky; scenery, Mark Tambella; lighting, Federico Restrepo; music and sound, Joshua Camp. With Mr. Robinson.

THE LAST TWO JEWS OF KABUL. By Josh Greenfeld. February 27, 2003. Directed by George Ferencz; scenery, Tom Lee; costumes, Sally Lesser; lighting, Jeff Tapper; sound, Tim Schellenbaum. With Jerry Matz, George Drance.

BREAD AND CIRCUS 3099. By Jack Shamblin and Nicole Zaray. February 27, 2003. Choreography, Paulo Henrique; scenery, Carlos Diaz; costumes, Tania Sterl and Marika Dadiani; lighting, David Overcamp. With Mr. Shamblin, Ms. Zaray, Hadas Gil Bar.

YOKASTAS. By Saviana Stanescu and Richard Schechner. March 20, 2003. Directed by Mr. Schechner; choreography, Kilbane Porter, scenery and lighting, E.D. Intemann. With Rachel Bowditch, Chris Healy, Tracey Huffman, Ms. Porter, Suzi Takahashi.

THE MOTHER. By Stanislaw Ignacy Witkiewicz. March 27, 2003. Directed by Brooke O'Harra; costumes, Audrey Robinson; lighting, Michael Phillips; music, Brendan Connelly. With Tina Shepard, Jim Fletcher, Suli Holum, Nicky Paraiso, Wilson Hall, Zakia Babb, Barb Lanciers.

THE BOOK OF JOB. Musical with book, music and lyrics by Danny Ashkenasi. April 8, 2003. With Julie Alexander, Mr. Ashkenasi, Ian August, Joel Briel, Ryan Connolly, Allison Easter, Darra Herman, Anita Hollander, Jennie Im, Jamie Mathews.

DIPTERACON, OR SHORT LIVED S*%T EATERS. By Raine Bode; music and lyrics by Felicia Carter Shakman. April 17, 2003. Directed by Ms. Bode; scenery and lighting, Arthur Maximillian Adair. With Kristin Atkinson, John Benoit, Ann Bonner, Antonio Cerezo, Eveleena Dann, Kaori Fujiyabu, Sara Galassini, Mark Gallop, Denise Greber, Nicky Paraiso, Lars Preece, Ramona Pula, Stephanie Rafferty, Peter Schuyler, Shannan Shaughnessy, Shigeko Suga, Mary Ann Walsh.

THE EARTH'S SHARP EDGE. By Thaddeus Phillips. May 1, 2003. Directed by Mr. Phillips. With Tatiana Mallarino, Gareth Saxe, Michael Fegley, Gina E. Cline, Muni Kulasinghe, Kent Davis Packard, Mr. Phillips.

PRIVATE JOKES, PUBLIC PLACES. By Oren Safdie. May 4, 2003. Directed by Craig Carlisle. With M.J. Kang, Fritz Michel, Graeme Malcolm, David Chandler.

GOD'S COMIC. By Oleg Braude; inspired by a novel by Heinrich Böll and Slava Polunin. May 22, 2003. Directed by Mr. Braude; costumes, Kaori Onodera; lighting, Mr. Braude; sound, Tim Schellenbaum. With Amy Kirsten, Daniel Logan, David Tyson, Douglas Allen, Johanna Weller-Fahy, Margaret Norwood, Rachel Diana, Zarah Kravitz.

SLANTY EYED MAMA RE-BIRTH OF AN ASIAN. By Kate Rigg and Leah Ryan. May 22, 2003. Directed by Dave Mowers. With Ms. Rigg, Lyris Hung (violinist).

IT'S A . . . MEXICAN-MORMON. By Elna Baker. May 26, 2003. Directed by Liz Swados. With Ms. Baker.

Lincoln Center Festival 2002. An annual international summer arts festival offering classic and contemporary work.

PACIFIC OVERTURES. Musical with book by John Weidman, music and lyrics by Stephen Sondheim; translated by Kunihiko Hashimoto. July 9, 2003. Directed by Amon Miyamoto; choreography, Rino Masaki; scenery, Rumi Matsui; costumes, Emi Wada; lighting, Yasutaka Nakayama; sound, Kunio Watanabe; fight direction, Akinori Tani; music direction, Kosuke Yamashita. With Takeharu Kunimoto, Norihide Ochi, Ben Hiura, Haruki Sayama, Usaburo Oshima, Shintaro Sonooka, Atsushi Haruta, Yuji Hirota, Akira Sakemoto, Masaki Kosuzu, Kanjiro Murakami, Shuji Honda, Kirihito Saito, Makoto Okada, Shinichiro Hara, Takanori Yamamoto, Kyoko Donowaki, Urara Awata, Shunpo, Mayu Yamada, Takeshi Ishikawa.

THE TA'ZIYEH OF HOR. July 12, 2002. Directed by Mohammad Ghaffari; with Hassan Nargeskhani, Deligani Alaeaddin Ghassemi, Mohammadreza Ghassemi, Hassan Aliabbasi Jazi, Kamal Aliabbasi Jazi, Majid Aliabbasi Jazi, Esmaeil Arefian Jazi, Asadollah Momenzadeh Khoulenjani, Mohammadali Momenzadeh Khoulenjani, Mahmood Moini, Morteza Saffarianrezai.

THE MUTE DREAM. By Attila Pessyani. July 17, 2002. Directed and designed by Mr. Pessyani. With Fatemeh Naghavi, Setareh Pessyani, Khosrow Pessyani and Mr. Pessyani.

Mabou Mines. Established in 1970, the company creates new works based on original and existing texts. The current artistic directorate includes Lee Breuer, Sharon Fogarty, Ruth Maleczech, Frederick Neumann and Terry O'Reilly.

CARA LUCIA. By Sharon Fogarty; additional text by Lee Breuer. April 23, 2003. Directed by Ms. Fogarty; choreography, J'aime Morrison; scenery and lighting, Jim Clayburgh; projections, Julie Archer; music, Carter Burwell. With Ruth Maleczech, Rosemary Fine, Clove Galilee.

MCC Theater. Dedicated to the promotion of emerging writers, actors, directors and theatrical designers. Robert LuPone and Bernard Telsey artistic directors, William Cantler associate artistic director.

THE MERCY SEAT. By Neil LaBute. December 18, 2002. Directed by Mr. LaBute; scenery, Neil Patel; costumes, Catherine Zuber; lighting, James Vermeulen; sound, David Van Tieghem. With Liev Schreiber, Sigourney Weaver. A 2002–03 *Best Plays* choice (see essay by John Istel in this volume).

SCATTERGOOD. By Anto Howard. February 26, 2003. Directed by Doug Hughes; scenery, Hugh Landwehr, lighting, Clifton Taylor; costumes, Linda Fisher; music, David Van Tieghem. With Brian Murray, T.R. Knight, Tari Signor.

Mint Theater Company. Committed to bringing new vitality to worthy but neglected plays. Jonathan Bank artistic director.

Literary valor: T.R. Knight and Brian Murray in Scattergood. *Photo: Dixie Sheridan*

THE CHARITY THAT BEGAN AT HOME. By St. John Hankin. October 7, 2002. Directed by Gus Kaikkonen; scenery, Charles F. Morgan; costumes, Henry Shaffer, lighting, William Armstrong; music, Ellen Mandel. With Christopher Franciosa, Kristin Griffith, Benjamin Howes, Karl Kenzler, Becky London, Lee Moore, Troy Schremmer, Harmony Schuttler, Michele Tauber, Pauline Tully, Bruce Ward, Alice White.

FAR AND WIDE. By Arthur Schnitzler, adapted by Jonathan Bank. February 17, 2003. Directed by Mr. Bank; scenery, Vicki R. Davis; lighting, Josh Bradford; costumes, Theresa Squire; sound, Stefan Jacobs. With Ezra Barnes, Lisa Bostnar, Rob Breckenridge, Lee Bryant, Ann-Marie Cusson, Kurt Everhart, Ken Kliban, James Knight, Victoria Mack, Matt Opatrny, Allen Lewis Rickman, Hans Tester, Pilar Witherspoon.

New Dramatists. An organization devoted to playwrights. Members may use the facilities for projects ranging from private readings of their material to public scripts-in-hand readings. Listed below are readings open to the public during the season under review. Todd London artistic director, Joel K. Ruark executive director.

New Member Event. September 9, 2002. THE TRIPLE HAPPINESS. By Brooke Berman. Directed by Daniel Goldstein. With Michael Chernus, Julie Boyd, Chris McKinney, Susan Pourfar, Jack Wetherall. WAVE. By Sung Rno. Directed by Linsay Firman. With Ron Domingo, Cindy Cheung, Ralph B. Peña. PAPER ARMOR. By Eisa Davis. Directed by David Levine. With Ms. Davis, Duane Boutte, Yvette Ganier. KIT MARLOWE. By David Grimm. Directed by Mr. Grimm. With Michael Stuhlbarg, Ron Riley, Zach Shaffer, Michael Chernus. BYE, BYE. By Victor Lodato. Directed by Tyler Marchant. With Dion Graham, John McAdams. THUNDERBIRD. By Joe Fisher. Directed by Randy White. With Marin Ireland, Michael Stuhlbarg. YELLOWMAN. By Dael Orlandersmith. Directed by Dael Orlandersmith. With Dael Orlandersmith.

LUSCIOUS MUSIC. By Matthew Maguire. September 13, 2002. Directed by Michael John Garcés. With Lourdes Martin, Peter Mele, Edward O'Blenis, Clea Rivera, Donald Silva, Ed Vassallo.

THE ARGUMENT. By David Greenspan. September 30, 2002. Directed by Mr. Greenspan. With David Chandler, Ted Schneider, John McAdams.

DANCING ON MOONLIGHT. By Keith Glover. October 1, 2002. Directed by Mr. Glover. With Cherise Boothe, Chuck Cooper, Yvette Ganier, Leland Gantt, Bryan Hicks, Mike Hodge, Keith Randolph Smith, Stacey Robinson.

CLUBLAND. By Roy Williams. October 10, 2002. Directed by Jo Bonney. With Akili Prince, Leslie Elliard, Yvette Ganier, David Deblinger, Michael Chernus.

BAG OF MARBLES. By Kathryn Ash. October 15, 2002. Directed by Leah Gardiner. With Larry Block, Lynn Cohen, Mia Dillon, Gretchen Lee Krich, Leslie Lyles.

BLOOD WEDDING. By Caridad Svich. October 16, 2002. Directed by Deborah Saivetz. With Jenny Sterlin, Molly Powell, Stacey Robinson, Mercedes Herrero, Gretchen Lee Krich, Lizzy Cooper Davis, Jesse Perez, Robert Alexander Owens, George Heslin, Michael Ray Escamilla, Michael J.X. Gladis.

RAREE. By K.C. Davis. October 17, 2002. Directed by Randy White. With Maria Thayer, Autumn Dornfeld, Florencia Lozano, Siobhán Mahoney, Christopher Evan Welch, Jack Wetherall, Lars Hanson.

Playtime. November 4–16, 2002. SANS CULLOTES IN THE PROMISED LAND. By Kirsten Greenidge. Directed by Seret Scott. With Erika Tazel, Michael Potts, Sandra Daley, Brenda Thomas, Eisa Davis, Cherise Boothe. THE STREET OF USEFUL THINGS. By Stephanie Fleischmann. Directed by Julie Anne Robinson. With Jenny Sterlin, Patrick Husted, Leslie Lyles, Addie Johnson, Molly Powell, Gretchen Lee Krich. SARCOXIE AND SEALOVE. By Sander Hicks. Directed by Peter Hawkins. With Roderick Hill, Sarah Lord, Charles Hyman, Ron Riley, Joseph Goodrich, Ed Vassallo, Gary Perez, John McAdams. PENETRATE THE KING. By Gordon Dahlquist. Directed by David Levine. With Joseph Goodrich, Mary Bacon, Molly Powell, John McAdams, Patrick Husted, Addie Johnson. JUMP/CUT. By Neena Beber. Directed by Leigh Silverman. With Christopher Evan Welch, Mary Bacon, Christopher Duva.

EXPAT/INFERNO. By Alejandro Morales. November 19, 2002. Directed by Scott Ebersold. With Ramon de Ocampo, Justin Bond, Stephen St. Paul, Alma Cuervo, Nathan White, Jeff Bond.

CATARACT. By Lisa D'Amour. November 20, 2002. Directed by Katie Pearl. With Brennan Brown, Brandy Zarle, Paul Sparks, Mia Barron.

UP (THE MAN IN THE FLYING LAWN CHAIR). By Bridget Carpenter. November 21, 2002. Directed by Peter DuBois. With Matthew Maguire, Babo Harrison, Rufus Tureen, Alicia Goranson, Judith Hawking, Ron Riley.

ILLUMINATING VERONICA. By Rogelio Martinez. December 10, 2002. Directed by Lou Jacob. With Lucia Brawley, Gary Perez, Judith Delgado, Ramon de Ocampo, Felix Solis, Vivia Font, Chris DeOni, Joanna Liao.

UNTIL WE FIND EACH OTHER. By Brooke Berman. December 10, 2002. Directed by Randy White. With Michael Chernus, Lennon Parham, Mia Barron, Robert Beitzel, Heather Goldenhersh.

CLEVELAND RAINING. By Sung Rno. December 12, 2002. Directed by Linsay Firman. With Eunice Wong, Louis Galindo, Paul Jun, Deborah S. Craig.

IN LOVE AND ANGER. By Michael Henry Brown. January 6, 2003. Directed by Gordon Edelstein. With Keith David, Curtis McClair, Harriett D. Foy, Linda Powell.

HOMEWRECKER. By Kelly Stuart. January 10, 2003. Directed by Melissa Kievman. With David Chandler, Pamela Gray, Jan Leslie Harding, Ron Riley.

WHORES. By Lee Blessing. January 13, 2003. Directed by Ed Herendeen. With Elizabeth Reaser, Carrie Preston, Karen Ziemba, Jayne Houdyshell, Shawn Elliott.

MESSALINA. By Gordon Dahlquist. January 23, 2003 Directed by David Levine. With Michael Stuhlbarg, Molly Powell, Addie Johnson, John McAdams, Alana Jerins, Robert Alexander Owens.

THE SAVAGES OF HARTFORD. By David Grimm. February 6, 2003. Directed by Mr. Grimm. With Buzz Bovshow, Charles Parnell, Tom Mardirosian, Leslie Lyles, Dan Pintauro, Christopher Duva, Leslie Elliard, Keira Naughton, Martin Rayner.

LOST IN TRANSLATION. By Rogelio Martinez. February 18, 2003. Directed by Ted Sod. With Mimi Lieber, Yul Vazquez, Joseph Siravo, K.J. Sanchez, Ron Riley, Gloria Garayva, Rebecca White.

THE LYSISTRATA PROJECT. March 3, 2003. Directed by Linsay Firman. With Sander Hicks, Arlene Hutton, Honour Kane.

PYRETOWN. By John Belluso. March 11, 2003. Directed by Tim Farrell. With Melissa Leo, Jessica Hecht, Christopher Thornton.

NITA AND ZITA. By Lisa D'Amour. March 12, 2003. Directed by Ms. Amour. With Katie Pearl, Kathy Randals.

MAGNIFICENT WASTE. By Caridad Svich. March 18, 2003. Directed by David Levine. With Jennifer Morris, Nina Hellman, Jonathan Tindle, Jack Ferver, Juliana Francis, Joanna P. Adler, Trevor Williams, John McAdams.

PRECIOUS STONE. By Morgan Allen. March 20, 2003. Directed by Linsay Firman. With David Engel, Mitch Montgomery, Justin Pappas.

MOTHERBONE. Musical with book by Karen Hartman; music by Graham Reynolds. March 27, 2003. Directed by Jason Neulander. With Patricia Phillips, Elan Rivera, Ken Prymus, Adam Michael Kaokept, Olivia Oguma, Rena Strober, Craig Feser, Paul Goodwin-Groen.

SCHOOL FOR GREYBEARDS. By Hannah Cowley. April 3, 2003. Directed by Randy White. With Harding Lemay, Aurora Nonas-Barnes, Caridad Svich, Catherine Filloux, Paul Zimet, Jono Hustis, Mark Bazzone, David Grimm, Dominic Taylor, Karen Hartman, Qui Nguyen, Eisa Davis, Zakiyyah Alexander.

THE ZERO HOUR. By Madeleine George. April 7, 2003. With Colleen Werthmann, Aysan Çelik.

CLANDESTINE CROSSING. By Keith Glover. April 8, 2003. Directed by Mr. Glover. With Michelle Dawson, Trent Dawson, Benim Foster, James Judy, Nicole Orth-Pallavicini, Mark Pinter, Michele Six.

FAIR GAME. By Karl Gajdusek. April 14, 2003. Directed by Robert Milazzo. With Gerry Bamman, Judith Light, Michele Monaghan, Ty Burrell, Jenna Stern.

MEDIA MEDEA. By Tara Welty. April 22, 2003. Directed by Lauren Rosen. With Marin Ireland, Jack Phillips, April Sweeney, David Gravens, David Bennett, Elowyn Castle, Amanda Plattsmier.

TONGUE TIED AND DUTY FREE. By Jim Nicholson. April 22, 2003. Directed by Sturgis Warner. With Yetta Gottesman, Steven Boyer, Christopher Innvar, Molly Powell, Karl Herlinger, Mercedes Herrero, Oliver Wadsworth, Sturgis Warner.

ASCENDING LULU. By Caridad Svich. April 23, 2003. Directed by Linsay Firman. With Carolyn Baeumler, Jennifer Morris, Armando Riesco, Chris Wells, Alfredo Narciso, T.R. Knight.

PHAEDRA IN DELIRIUM. By Susan Yankowitz. May 1, 2003. Directed by Kirsten Brandt. With Shawn Elliott, Maggie Reed, Fiona Scoones, Michael Severence.

THE TROJAN WOMEN. By Ellen McLaughlin; music by Katie Down. May 27, 2003. Directed by Rachel Dickstein. With Jane Nichols, Maggie Gyllenhaal, Seth Kanor, Elena McGhee, Vivienne Benesch, Denis O'Hare, Kerry Chipman, Ruth Coughlin, Stephanie DiMaggio, Tara Good, Briana Mandel, Maria McConville, Concetta Rose Rella, Satomi Yamauchi, Julia Prud'homme.

New Federal Theatre. Dedicated to integrating minorities into the mainstream of American theater through the training of artists and the presentation of plays by minorities and women. Woodie King Jr. producing director.

AMERICAN MENU. By Don Wilson Glenn. April 23, 2003. Directed by Ajene Washington. With Patricia R. Floyd, Sharon Hope, Benja K., Kimberly "Q" Purnell, M. Drue Williams.

WHOSE FAMILY VALUES! By Richard Abrons. May 22, 2003. Directed by Philip Rose; scenery, Robert Joel Schwartz; costumes, Gail Cooper-Hecht; lighting, Shirley Prendergast; sound, Sean O'Halloran. With Glynis Bell, Rosalyn Coleman, Chris Hutchison, Clayton LeBouef, Martha Libman, Ted Rodenborn, Herb Rubens, Gammy Singer.

New Group. Launches fresh acting, writing and design talent and provides an artistic home for artists. Committed to cultivating a young and diverse theater-going audience by providing accessible ticket prices. Scott Elliott artistic director, Geoffrey Rich executive director, Ian Morgan associate artistic director.

COMEDIANS. By Trevor Griffiths. January 15, 2003. Directed by Scott Elliott; scenery; Derek McLane; costumes, Mimi O'Donnell; lighting, Jason Lyons; sound, Ken Travis. With Jim Dale, Raúl Esparza, Max Baker, Ismail Bashey, James Beecher, Gordon Connell, Allen Corduner, William Duell, Jamie Harris, David Lansbury, David McCallum, Marcus Powell.

THE WOMEN OF LOCKERBIE. By Deborah Brevoort. April 6, 2003. Directed by Scott Elliott; scenery, Derek McLane; costumes, Mattie Ullrich; lighting, Jason Lyons; sound, Ken Travis. With Larry Pine, Jenny Sterlin, Angela Pietropinto, Kristen Sieh, Judith Ivey, Adam Trese, Kathleen Doyle. Presented in association with Women's Project and Productions.

Performance Space 122. Exists to give artists of a wide range of experience a chance to develop work and find an audience. Mark Russell artistic director.

JOE. By Richard Maxwell. September 8, 2002. Directed by Mr. Maxwell; scenery, Gary Wilmes; costumes, Tory Vazquez; lighting, Jane Cox. With Richard Zhuravenko, Matthew Stadelmann, Brian Mendes, Mick Diflo, Gene Wynne.

MIGHTY NICE! By Paul Zaloom; additional text by Sean Forrester. January 3, 2003. Directed by Randee Trabitz; scenery, Mr. Zaloom; costumes, Betsey Potter; lighting, Mr. Forrester. With Mr. Zaloom.

BITTER BIERCE, OR THE FRICTION WE CALL GRIEF. By Mac Wellman. February 6, 2003. Directed by Mr. Wellman; scenery and lighting, Kyle Chepulis; costumes, Barb Mellor. With Stephen Mellor.

NOTES FROM UNDERGROUND. By Eric Bogosian. May 1, 2003. Directed by Mr. Bogosian. With Jonathan Ames.

Primary Stages. Dedicated to new American plays. Casey Childs executive producer, Andrew Leynse artistic director.

CALL THE CHILDREN HOME. Musical with book by Thomas Babe; music and lyrics by Mildred Kayden; additional material by J.D. Myers. September 23, 2002. Directed by Kent Gash; choreography, Tanya Gibson-Clark; scenery, Emily Beck; costumes, Austin K. Sanderson; lighting, William H. Grant III; sound, Johnna Doty; musical direction, William Foster McDaniel. With Tamara Tunie, Eugene Fleming, Angela Robinson, Sophia Salguero, Julian Gamble, Caesar Samayoa, Christiane Noll, Sean McDermott.

THE FOURTH WALL. By A.R. Gurney. November 13, 2002. Directed by David Saint; scenery, James Youmans; costumes, David Murin; lighting, Jeff Croiter; sound, Christopher J. Bailey. With Susan Sullivan, Charles Kimbrough, Sandy Duncan, David Pittu.

ROMOLA AND NIJINSKY. By Lynne Alvarez. May 15, 2003. Directed by David Levine; choreography, Robert LaFosse; scenery, Michael Byrnes; costumes, Claudia Stephens; lighting, Lap-Chi Chu; sound, Jane Shaw; music, Brendan Connelly. With David Barlow, Kelly Hutchinson, Allen Fitzpatrick, Michelle Lookadoo, Laura Martin, John McAdams, Daniel Oreskes, Janet Zarish.

Puerto Rican Traveling Theater. Professional company presenting bilingual productions of Puerto Rican and Hispanic playwrights, emphasizing subjects of relevance today. Miriam Colón Valle founder and producer.

BECOMING BERNARDA. By Oscar A. Colón. June 11, 2002. Directed by Sturgis Warner; scenery, Robert Culek; costumes, Karen Flood; lighting, Ben Stanton; With Annie Henk, Nina Polan, Silvia Brito, Blanca Camacho, Adriana Sananes, Maggie Botill, Lourdes Martin, Carlos Molina, Carlos Orizondo, Chaz Mena.

THE MISTRESS OF THE INN (LA POSADERA). By Carlo Goldoni. August 12, 2002. Directed by Dean Zayas; costumes, Elizabeth Wittlin Lipton; sound, Christophe Pierre. With Emanuel Loarca, Hemky Madera, Fior Marte, Coco Nunez, Frank Perozo, Osvaldo Placencia, Pablo Tufino, Fulvia Vergel.

Signature Theatre Company. Dedicated to the exploration of a playwright's body of work over the course of a single season. James Houghton artistic director.

BOOK OF DAYS. By Lanford Wilson. November 3, 2002. Directed by Marshall W. Mason; scenery, John Lee Beatty; costumes, Laura Crow; lighting, Dennis Parichy; sound, Chuck London and Stewart Werner. With Alan Campbell, Hope Chernov, Jim Haynie, Jonathan Hogan, Susan Kellermann, John Lepard, Kelly McAndrew, Boris McGiver, Tuck Milligan, Matthew Rauch, Miriam Shor, Nancy Snyder.

FIFTH OF JULY. By Lanford Wilson. February 3, 2003. Directed by Jo Bonney; scenery, Richard Hoover; costumes, Ann Hould-Ward; lighting, James Vermeulen; music and sound, John Gromada; fight direction, J. Steven White. With Robert Sean Leonard, Michael J.X. Gladis, David Harbour, Parker Posey, Jessalyn Gilsig, Sarah Lord, Pamela Payton-Wright, Ebon Moss-Bachrach.

RAIN DANCE. By Lanford Wilson. May 20, 2003. Directed by Guy Sanville; scenery, Christine Jones; costumes, Daryl A. Stone; lighting, James Vermeulen; sound, Kurt Kellenberger. With Randolph Mantooth, Suzanne Regan, James Van Der Beek, Harris Yulin.

Soho Rep. Dedicated to new and cutting edge US playwrights. Daniel Aukin artistic director, Alexandra Conley executive director.

SIGNALS OF DISTRESS. By the Flying Machine; based on the novel by Jim Crace. November 15, 2002. Directed by Joshua Carlebach; scenery, Marisa Frantz; costumes, Theresa Squire; lighting, Josh Bradford and Raquel Davis; sound, Bill Ware. With Richard Crawford, Jessica Green, Kathryn Phillip, Kevin Varner, Gregory Steinbruner, Jason Linder, Tami Stronach, Matthew Gray.

MOLLY'S DREAM. By Maria Irene Fornes; music by Maury Loeb. May 16, 2003. Directed by Daniel Aukin; choreography, David Neumann; scenery and costumes, Louisa Thompson; lighting, Marcus Doshi; sound, Ken Travis; musical direction, Michael Friedman. With Bo Corre, Dominic Bogart, Erin Farrell, Shannon Fitzgerald, Jessica Hency, Debra Wassum, Casey Wilson, Matthew Maher, Patrick Boll, Toi Perkins.

Theater for the New City. Developmental theater and new experimental works. Crystal Field executive director.

CONNECTIONS. By Vernon Church. September 24, 2002. Directed by Larry Shanet; scenery, Fay Torres-yap; lighting, Mark Hankla; music, Sean Altman. With Rich Egan, Shellee Nicols, Michael S. Rush, Max Goldberg, Sean Devine, Kina Bermudez, Cristy Piccini, Jennifer Maturo, Sonya Tsuchigane, Suzie Moon, Amanita Heird, Franca Vercelloni, Jenny Moss.

AT A PLANK BRIDGE. By Kannan Menon. January 10. 2003. Directed by Tina Chen. With Mano Maniam, Jackson Loo.

THE VOLUNTEER. By Paulanne Simmons. January 30, 2003. Directed by Mary Catherine Burke; choreography, Mary Ann Wall; scenery, Michael V. Moore; costumes, Becky Lasky; lighting, K.J. Hardy; sound, Jake Hall. With Rebecca Hoodwin, Shannon Bryant, Justin Aponte, Victor Barranca, Bill Dealy, Kim Gardner, Frieda Lipp, Amy Silver, Leni Tabb.

THE GOLDEN BEAR. By Laurel Hessing; lyrics by Ms. Hessing; music by Arthur Abrams; based on *Jews Without Money* by Michael Gold. March 13, 2003. Directed by Crystal Field; scenery and lighting, Donald L. Brooks; costumes, Myrna Duarte and Terry Leong; sound, Joy Linscheid. With Alexander Bartenieff, Elizabeth Ruf, Primy Rivera, Mira Rivera, Frank Biancomano, Elizabeth Barkan.

-1 (MINUS ONE). By Gyavira Lasana. May 3, 2003. Directed by David Willinger. With Aja M. Yamagata, Monica Stith, Christopher King, Angelique Orsini, Robert Hatcher, Robert Colston, Shannon Bryant, Robert Lehrer, Jennifer McCabe, Daniel Hicks.

Theatre for a New Audience. Founded in 1979, the company's mission is to help develop the performance and study of Shakespeare and classic drama. Jeffrey Horowitz founding artistic director.

THE GENERAL FROM AMERICA. By Richard Nelson. November 21, 2002. Directed by Mr. Nelson; scenery, Douglas Stein; costumes, Susan Hilferty, lighting, James F. Ingalls; sound, Scott Lehrer; fight direction, Brian Byrnes. With Corin Redgrave, Alice Cannon, Sean Cullen, Jon DeVries, Thomas M. Hammond, Kate Kearney-Patch, Nicholas Kepros, Paul Anthony McGrane, Jesse Pennington, Thomas Sadoski, Yvonne Woods.

JULIUS CAESAR. By William Shakespeare. January 19, 2003. Directed by Karin Coonrod; scenery, Douglas Stein; costumes, Catherine Zuber; lighting, David Weiner; music and sound, Mark Bennett; fight direction, B.H. Barry. With Earl Hindman, Justin Campbell, Hope Chernov, Curzon Dobell, Michael Ray Escamilla, Kristin Flanders, Thomas M. Hammond, Andy Hoey, David Don Miller, Nicholas Mongiardo-Cooper, Simeon Moore, Daniel Oreskes, Michael Rogers, Matt Saldivar, Jacob Garrett White, Graham Winton.

DON JUAN. By Molière; translated by Christopher Hampton. March 23, 2003. Directed by Bartlett Sher; scenery and lighting, Christopher Akerlind; costumes, Elizabeth Caitlin Ward; sound, Peter John Still; fight direction, J. Steven White. With Byron Jennings, John Christopher Jones, Liam Craig, Nicholas Kepros, Sherri Parker Lee, Nicole Lowrance, Dan Snook, Price Waldman, Graham Winton, David Wohl, Anne Louise Zachry.

The Vineyard Theatre. Multi-art chamber theater dedicated to the development of new plays and musicals, music-theater collaborations and innovative revivals. Douglas

Theatre for a
New Audience
2002–2003
Season

Top: Corin Redgrave in The General From
America. *Photo: T. Charles Erickson*

Middle: Kristin Flanders in Julius Caesar.
Photo: Gerry Goodstein

*Bottom: Sherri Parker Lee and Byron
Jennings in* Don Juan. *Photo: Gerry
Goodstein*

Aibel artistic director, Bardo S. Ramirez managing director, Jennifer Garvey-Blackwell executive director for external affairs.

> THE FOURTH SISTER. By Janusz Glowacki. November 21, 2002. Directed by Lisa Peterson; scenery, Rachel Hauck; costumes, Mattie Ullrich; lighting, Kevin Adams; sound, Jill B.C. DuBoff; music, Gina Leishman; fight direction, Rick Sordelet. With Jase Blankfort, Bill Buell, Alicia Goranson, Jessica Hecht, Marin Hinkle, Daniel Oreskes, Lee Pace, Steven Rattazzi, Suzanne Shepherd, Louis Tucci.

> AVENUE Q. Musical with book by Jeff Whitty; music and lyrics by Robert Lopez and Jeff Marx. March 19, 2003. Directed by Jason Moore; choreography, Ken Roberson; scenery, Anna Louizos; costumes, Mirena Rada; lighting, Frances Aronson; sound, Brett Jarvis; puppets, Rick Lyon. With Ann Harada, Natalie Venetia Belcon, Jordan Gelber, Stephanie D'Abruzzo, Rick Lyon, John Tartaglia, Jen Barnhart.

Women's Project and Productions. Nurtures, develops and produces plays written and directed by women. Julia Miles artistic director, Georgia Buchanan managing director.

> CHEAT. By Julie Jensen. October 16, 2002. Directed by Joan Vail Thorne; scenery, David P. Gordon; costumes, Gail Cooper-Hecht; lighting, Michael Lincoln; music and sound, Scott Killian. With Lucy Deakins, Shayna Ferm, Kevin O'Rourke and Karen Young.

> *First Looks Reading Series.*
> BIRDY. By Naomi Wallace, adapted from the novel by William Wharton. February 17, 2003. Directed by Lisa Peterson.

> ELEANORE AND ISADORA: A DUET OF SORROWS. By Diane Kagan. March 10, 2003. Directed by Ms. Kagan.

> BEFORE DEATH COMES FOR THE ARCHBISHOP. By Elaine Romero. March 17, 2003. Directed by Deborah Saivetz.

> BOX OF PEARLS. By Marcie Begleiter. March 24, 2003. Directed by Passion.

York Theatre Company. Dedicated to the development of small-scale musicals, to the rediscovery of underappreciated musicals from the past and to serving the community through educational initiatives. James Morgan artistic director, Louis Chiodo consulting managing director, Scott DelaCruz company administrator.

> PORTERPHILES. Musical revue with book by Judy Brown and James Morgan; music and lyrics by Cole Porter. December 12, 2002. Direction and scenery by Mr. Morgan; musical staging, Barry McNabb; costumes, Margiann Flanagan; lighting, Mary Jo Dondlinger. With Lynne Halliday, Ricky Russell, Stephen Zinnato.

MISCELLANEOUS

ABINGDON THEATRE COMPANY. *Sucker Fish Messiah* by Ryan Michael Teller. June 6, 2002. Directed by Taylor Brooks; with Lori Gardner, Richard Edward Long, Julia Klein, Nicholas Piper. *Teddy Tonight!* by Laurence Luckinbill. October 18, 2002. Directed by Kim T. Sharp; with Mr. Luckinbill. *Uncle Dan* by Joe Byers. December 12, 2002. Directed by William Lipscomb; with Alice Barden, David Rockwell Miller, Mark Willett. *God's Daughter* by Barton Bishop. Janaury 23, 2003. Directed by Alex Dmitriev; with Peter Brouwer, Anne DuPont, Susanne Marley, William Prael. *Daisy in the Dreamtime* by Lynne Kaufman. March 12, 2003. Directed by Kim T. Sharp; with Molly Powell, Jerome Preston Bates, Jodie Lynne McClintock.

ACCESS THEATER. *3 O'Clock in Brooklyn* by Israela Margalit. October 10, 2002. Directed by Margarett Perry; with Jordan Charney, Louisa Flaningam, Jesse Doran, Erica Piccininni, Kim Zimmer, Jeremy Webb. *That Damn Dykstra (The Boxed Set)* by Brian Dykstra. February 10, 2003. Directed by Margarett Perry; with Cynthia Babak, Sarah Baker, Matthew Boston, Mr. Dykstra, Patrick Frederick, Vickie Tanner.

THE ACTING COMPANY. *American Dreams: Lost and Found* by Studs Terkel; adapted by Peter Frisch. May 13, 2003. Directed by Rebecca Guy; with Paul Cosentino, Peter Zazzali, Lamont Stephens,

Joe Osheroff, Jaime St. Peter, Michael Lluberes, Jessica Bates, Siobhan Juanita Brown, Glenn Peters, Fletcher McTaggart, Christen Simon, Kevin Kraft, Evan Zes.

THE ACTORS COMPANY THEATRE (TACT). *Happy Birthday* by Anita Loos. October 13, 2002. Directed by Scott Alan Evans; with Cynthia Darlow, Cynthia Harris, Larry Keith, Jack Koenig, Darrie Lawrence, Margaret Nichols, Scott Schafer, Lynn Wright, Alexander Alioto, James DeMarse, Colton Green, Richard Fromm, Richard Ferrone, Elizabeth Moser, James Prendergast, Kim Sykes, Jenn Thompson, Ashley West. *The Rivals* by Richard Brinsley Sheridan. November 24, 2002. Directed by Scott Alan Evans; with James Murtaugh, Jack Koenig, Rob Breckenridge, Kyle Fabel, Gregory Salata, Scott Schafer, Jamie Bennett, Delphi Harrington, Margaret Nichols, Mary Bacon, Eve Michelson. *The Potting Shed* by Graham Greene. January 26, 2003. Directed by Scott Alan Evans; with James Prendergast, Stina Nielson, Jenn Thompson, Darrie Lawrence, Jack Koenig, Kyle Fabel, Nicholas Krepos, Jamie Bennett, Paddy Croft, Laurinda Barrett, Simon Jones. *Eurydice* by Jean Anouilh. March 3, 2003. Directed by Kyle Fabel; with Kevin Henderson, James Murtaugh, Scott Shafer, Richard Ferrone, Cynthia Darlow, Margaret Nichols, Cynthia Harris, Simon Jones, Denis Butkus, Sean Arbuckle, Gregory Salata, Nick Toren, Richard Ferrone. *USA: A Reading* by Paul Shyre; adapted from the work of John Dos Passos. May 5, 2003. Directed by Scott Alan Evans; with Greg McFadden, Nora Chester, Jamie Bennett, Lynn Wright, Rachel Fowler, Larry Keith.

THE ACTOR'S PLAYGROUND THEATRE. *Victims/Trust* by David Yee. August 3, 2002. Directed by Matthew Landfield; with Heather Aldridge, Mary Holmstrom, Larry Mitchell, April Peveteaux, Nicole Seymour, Guido Venitucci. *Almost Blue* by Keith Reddin. May 11, 2003. Directed by Hal Brooks; with Joe Passaro, Kurt Everhart, James Biberi, Antoinette LaVecchia.

ACTORS PLAYHOUSE. *Rhapsody in Seth* by Seth Rudetsky. March 11, 2003. Directed by Mr. Rudetsky; with Mr. Rudetsky.

ALTERED STAGES. *Last Day* by Daniel Roberts. November 10, 2002. Directed by Samuel Roberts; with Scott Duffy, Michael Hogan, Robert McKay, Heather Raffo, Kate Roe, Alexa Zee. *American Magic* by Gil Kofman. May 8, 2003. Directed by Matthew Wilder, with Lyndsay Rose Kane, Walter Murray, Sonny Perez, Indrajit Sarkar.

AMERICAN GLOBE THEATRE. *Love's Labour's Lost: The Musical*; based on William Shakespeare's play. Adapted by Kenneth Mitchell; music and lyrics by Bob McDowell. March 15, 2003. Directed by John Basil and Mr. Mitchell; with Trent Dawson, Geoffrey Barnes, Julia Cook, Deborah S. Craig, Elizabeth Keefe, Kelley McKinnon, Rainard Rachele, Alyson Reim, Basil Rodericks, Graham Stevens, Ross Stoner, Andrew Thacher, Justin Ray Thompson, Carey Urban.

THE AMERICAN THEATRE OF ACTORS. *Just Us Boys* by Frank Stancati. June 20, 2002. Directed by Thomas Morrissey; with Joe Gulla, Davis Kirby, Gerard Gravellese, Ludis Schnore, Jeffrey Todd.

ARCLIGHT THEATRE. *Big Al* by Bryan Goluboff. November 5, 2002. Directed by Evan Bergman; with Juan Carlos Hernandez, David Thornton, Frank Whaley.

ARS NOVA THEATER. *Julia Sweeney: Guys and Babies, Sex and Gods* by Ms. Sweeney. January 29, 2003. Directed by Mark Brokaw; with Ms. Sweeney.

BANK STREET THEATRE. UNITY FEST 2002. GROWING UP. December 3, 2002. *Overanalysis* by Gabriel Shanks. Directed by Dennis Smith; with Caitlin Barton, John Jay Buol, Matt Gorrek, Bekka Lindström, Jack Merlis, Lawrence Merritt, Karen Stanion. *The Hourglass* by Ryan Mark. Directed by Dennis Smith; with Moe Bertran, Ivan Davila. *Come Light the Menorah* by Rich Orloff. Directed by Courtenay Wendell; with Bekka Lindström, Karen Stanion. *The Mutant Factor of Reconciliation* by Jess Carey. Directed by Donna Jean Fogel; with John Jay Buol, Bekka Lindström, Nicole Longchamp. *Christopher T. Washington Learns to Fight* by Jordan Seavey. Directed by Keith Lorrel Manning; with Caitlin Barton, Moe Bertran, John Jay Buol, Matt Gorrek, Karen Stanion. *The Beginning* by Dan Clancy. Directed by James McLaughlin; with Jack Merlis, Lawrence Merritt. *The Seed* by David Pumo. Directed by Donna Jean Fogel; with Moe Bertran, Bekka Lindström, Tom Johnson, Maxx Santiago. THE GENERATIONS. December 4, 2003. *Madonna and Child* by Kenneth Pressman. Directed by Keith Lorrel Manning; with Lynn Battaglia, Maxx Santiago. *Act of Contrition* by Dan Bacalzo. Directed by Nicholas Warren-Gray; with Moe Bertran, Matt Gorrek. *By Her Side* by Steve Willis. Directed by Donna Jean Fogel; with Ardes Quinn. *Padding the Wagon* by Gary Garrison. Directed by Courtenay Wendell; with Donna Jean Fogel, Keith Lorrel Manning, Gisele Richardson. *Perhaps* by David Pumo. Directed by Karin Bowersock; with Donna Jean Fogel, Mikéah Ernest

Jennings, Bekka Lindström. *What I Missed in the 80s* by David DeWitt. Directed by James McLaughlin; with Matt Gorrek, Tony Hamilton. TRAFFIC. December 5, 2002. *It's a Wonderful Lie* by Tony Hamilton. Directed by Joan Evans; with Mr. Hamilton. *Trafficking in Broken Hearts* by Edwin Sánchez. Directed by Dennis Smith; with Moe Bertran, Ivan Davila, Philip Estrera, Heland Lee, Gisele Richardson, Maxx Santiago, Karen Stanion, Nicholas Warren-Gray. *Red and Tan Line* by Peter Mercurio. March 6, 2003. Directed by Chuck Blasius; with Patrick Davey, Tony Hamilton, Carson Hinners, James McLaughlin. *The Ladies of the Corridor* by Dorothy Parker and Arnaud d'Usseau. May 5, 2003. Directed by Dan Wackerman; with Kelly AuCoin, Ron Badgen, Hal Blankenship, Patrick Boyd, Peggy Cowles, Jo Ann Cunningham, Dawn Evans, Libby George, Astrit Ibroci, Susan Jeffries, Patricia Randell, Andy Phelan, Carolyn Seiff, Susan Varon. *Auntie Mayhem* by David Pumo. May 29, 2003. Directed by Donna Jean Fogel; with Moe Bertran, Ivan Davila, Jimmy Hurley, Randy Aaron, Isaac Calpito, Henry Alberto.

THE BARROW GROUP. *Last Train to Nibroc* by Arlene Hutton. December 5, 2002. Directed by Seth Barrish and Michael Connors; with Jenny Eakes, Emory Van Cleve. *Off the Map* by Joan Ackerman. February 13, 2003. Directed by Eric Paeper; with Lee Brock, Reade Kelly, Rick Pepper, Michael Warren Powell, Melissa Russell, Julie Shain, Wendy vanden Heuvel.

BLUE HERON ARTS CENTER. *Valparaiso* by Don DeLillo. July 24, 2002. Directed by Hal Brooks; with Matthew Lawler, Elizabeth Sherman, Kate Nowlin, Andrew Benator, David Fitzgerald, Carla Harting, Julie Fitzpatrick. *Harlem Duet* by Djanet Sears. November 13, 2002. Directed by Ms. Sears; with Oni Faida Lampley, Gregory Simmons, Walter Borden, Barbara Barnes Hopkins, Nyjah Moore Westbrooks. *Hold, Please* by Annie Weisman. February 28, 2003. Directed by Connie Grappo; with Laura Esterman, Kathryn Rossetter, Emma Bowers, Jeanine Serralles. *Alma and Mrs. Woolf* by Anne Legault; translated by Daniel Libman. March 10, 2003. Directed by Jim Pelegano; with Joan Grant, Nicole Orth-Pallavicini. *The Ontological Detective* by Kenneth Heaton. April 10, 2003. Directed by Mr. Heaton; with Christopher Mattox, Michael Luz, Romi Dias, Mark Sage Hamilton, Charles Paul Holt, Johnny Sparks.

THE BOTTLE FACTORY THEATER COMPANY. *Room 314* by Michael Knowles. March 20, 2003. Directed by Mr. Knowles; with J. Malia Hawley, Mr. Knowles, Anna Lodej, Kate Lunsford, Jared Michalski, Donald Silva, Jennifer Smith, Christopher Trunell. *Territory* by Lawrence Levine. May 21, 2003. Directed by Mr. Levine; with John Good, Amanda Gruss, Grant Varjas.

BOWERY POETRY CLUB. *Door Wide Open* by Joyce Johnson. May 17, 2003. Directed by Tony Torn; with Amy Wright, John Ventimiglia, Adira Amram, Meg Brooker.

CAFÉ A GO GO THEATRE. *Café a Go Go*. Musical by the Heather Brothers. June 5, 2002. Directed by John Hadden; with Jessica Aquino, Jessica Cannon, Wade Fisher, Zachary Gilman, Stacie May Hassler, Matthew Knowland, Jasika Nicole Pruitt, Stephanie St. Hilaire, Juson Williams.

CAP 21 THEATER. *Beach Radio*. Musical with book and lyrics by Drey Shepperd; music by Gerard Kenny. October 29, 2002. Directed and choreographed by Larry Fuller; with Meyer deLeeuw, Ann Hu, Doug Kreeger, Nicole Martone, Meredith McCasland, Rosemary McNamara, Lance Olds, Jonathan Todd Ross, Noah Weisberg, Adrienne Young. *Killing Louise* by Carol Galligan. March 4, 2003. Directed by Michael Montel; with Alexandra Geis, Rosemary Prinz, Brenda Thomas, Eliza Ventura, Van Zeiler. THE BARBARA WOLFF MONDAY NIGHT READING SERIES. *Waiting For My Man (World Without End)* by Tony DiMurro. April 7, 2003. Directed by Anthony Patellis. *Six of One*. Musical with book and lyrics by Scott Burkell; music by Paul Loesel. April 14, 2003. Directed by Lynne Shankel. *Minnesota Fats Is Right Around the Corner* by Tony DiMurro. May 12, 2003. *The Playwright of the Western World* by L.J. Schneiderman. May 19, 2003.

CASTILLO THEATRE. *HamletMachine* by Heiner Müller; translated by Carl Weber; music and lyrics by Fred Newman. Directed by Mr. Newman; with Jeremy Black, Dave DeChristopher, I. Thecia Farrell, Roger Grunwald, Kenneth Hughes, Gabrielle Kurlander, Marian Rich, Anne Suddaby.

CENTER STAGE. *Night Ether* by J. Grawemeyer. February 27, 2003. Directed by Don Jordan; with Gyda Arber, Rosanna Canonigo, Kristina Carroll, Peter Philip Clarke, Paul Daily, Nathan DeCoux, Jeff Pagliano, Malinda Walford. EATFEST: MENU A. April 2–6, 2003. *Almost Full Circle at the Guggenheim* by Dee Sposito. Directed by Tim Herman; with Jeffrey Bateman, Kristin Dubrowsky. *Danger of Strangers* by Glenn Alterman and *V-Day* by Nancy Pothier. *Danger of Strangers* directed by Wesley Apfel; *V-Day* directed by Dawn Copeland; with Ashley Green, Michael Silva, Walker Richards, Tara Perry, Terri Girvin, Johnathan Cedano, Stephanie Ila Silver, Richard Ezra Zekaria,

Ellen Reilly, Brian Letscher, Rochele Tillman, Tim Barke, Chris Lucas, Peter Levine, Amy Bizjak, Bryan McKinley. EATFEST: MENU B. April 2–6, 2003. *The King and Queen of Planet Pookie* by Eric Alter. Directed by Rebecca Kendall; with Jason Hare, Linda Horwatt. *Glimmer of Hope* by Joan Ross Sorkin. Directed by Eric Chase; with Peter Herrick, Lue McWilliams, Jeff Riebe. *The Moment* by Gregg Pasternack. Directed by Chris Wojyltko; with Hal Blankenship, Daniel Gurian, EC Kelly, Sara Kramer, Philippe Cu Leong, Grant Machan, Vivian Meisner. EATFEST: MENU C. April 9–13, 2003. *Counter Girls* by Jonathan Reuning. Directed by Paul Adams; with Jane Altman, Blanche Cholet, Nicola Sheara. *Night Bloomers* by Sarah Morton. Directed by Maryna Harrison; with Marnie Andrews. *Oedipus for Dummies* by Jack Rushen. Directed by Gregory Fletcher; with Jessica Calvello, Jason Cornwell, Bill Dyszel, Glory Gallo, Wayne Henry, Cree Monique, Jason Moreland, Kami Rodgers, Erez Rose, Dayna Steinfeld. EATFEST: MENU D. April 9–13, 2003. *Women in Heat* by Rich Orloff. Directed by Laurissa James; with Wendy Allyn, Daniel Kaufman, Callie Mauldin, Kathy McCafferty. *Nietzsche Ate Here* by Roy Berkowitz. Directed by Christopher Borg; with Wynne Anders, Benjamin Howes. *Sally Smells* by Ted LoRusso. Directed by Ian Marshall; with Scott Clarkson, Margaux Laskey, Jason O'Connell.

CENTURY CENTER FOR THE PERFORMING ARTS. *When We Dead Awaken* by Henrik Ibsen. June 9, 2002. Directed by J.C. Compton; with Tami Dixon, Bruce Barton, Carl Palmer, Tom Knutson.

CHASHAMA. *The Other Side of the Closet* by Edward Roy. September 9, 2002. Directed by Mark Cannistraro; with Vincent Briguccia, Melissa Carroll, Charlene Gonzalez, Willie Mullins, Richard Tayloe. *Stone Cold Dead Serious* by Adam Rapp. April 7, 2003. Directed by Carolyn Cantor; with Betsy Aidem, Guy Boyd, Gretchen Cleevely, Matthew Stadelmann, Anthony Rapp. A 2002–03 *Best Plays* choice (see essay by Jeffrey Eric Jenkins in this volume). CIRCLE EAST 2003 SHORT PLAY FESTIVAL. May 8–May 25, 2003. *Your Call Is Important to Me* by Craig Lucas. *This Will Be the Death of Him* by David DeWitt. *The Long Shot* by Richard Cottrell; directed by Peg Denithorne. *Mermaids on the Hudson* by Anastasia Traina; directed by Mary Monroe. *Lily of the Valley* by Lisa Humbertson; directed by Erma Duricko. *Climate* by Joe Pintauro; directed by Jude Schanzer. *Love* by Betty Shamieh; directed by Janice Goldberg. *Informed Consent* by Paul Knox; directed by Keith Greer. *Soooo Sad* by Ty Adams; directed by Barbara Bosch. *The Fuqua Slone Reisenglass Appraisal* by Lawrence Harvey Shulman; directed by Guy Giarrizzo. *Vert-Galant* by Jon Fraser.

CHERRY LANE THEATRE. *Grasmere* by Kristina Leach. June 8, 2002. Directed by Joseph Arnold; with Darcy Blakesley, Annie Di Martino, Aaron Gordon, Logan Sledge. YOUNG PLAYWRIGHTS FESTIVAL 2002. September 26, 2002. *An Ice Cream Man for All Seasons* by Molly Lambert. Directed by Jeremy Dobrish, with Keith Davis, Jonathan Sale. *Parts They Call Deep* by Lauren Gunderson. Directed by Brett W. Reynolds; with Shannon Emerick, Cynthia Hood, Celia Howard, Nathan Darrow. *Trade* by Caroline V. McGraw. Directed by Valentina Fratti; with Ms. Emerick, Mr. Darrow, Ryan Rentmeester, Adriana Gaviria, Gina Hirsch, Mr. Sale. *Happy Days* by Samuel Beckett. September 29, 2002. Directed by Joseph Chaikin; with Joyce Aaron, Ron Faber. *It Just Catches* by Carol Hemingway; based on stories by Ernest Hemingway; songs by Cole Porter. February 9, 2003. Directed by Edward Hastings; with David Ackroyd, Ann Crumb, Marsh Hanson, Ryan Shively, Daniel Freedom Stewart, Jessica D. Turner. MENTOR PROJECT 2003. *Urgent Fury* by Allison Moore (Marsha Norman, mentor). March 12, 2003. Directed by Richard Caliban; with Patrick Boll, Halley Feiffer, Carol Halstead, Kathryn A. Layng, Peter Scanavino, John Speredakos, Lindsay Wilson. *Slag Heap* by Anton Dudley (Ed Bullins, mentor). April 9, 2003. Directed by Erica Schmidt; with Brienan Bryant, Caroline Clay, Nina Zoie Lam, Andy Powers, Yvonne Woods. *The Parents Evening* by Bathsheba Doran (Michael Weller, mentor). May 7, 2003. Directed by Irina Brown; with Lisa Emery, Ken Marks. *Kiki & Herb: Coup de Théâtre.* Musical by Justin Bond and Kenny Mellman; book by Mr. Bond; musical direction by Mr. Mellman. May 7, 2003. Directed by Scott Elliott; with Messrs. Bond and Mellman.

CLASSICAL THEATRE OF HARLEM. *King Lear* by William Shakespeare. July 12, 2002. Directed by Alfred Preisser; with Paul Butler, Arthur French, April Yvette Thompson, Lawrence Winslow. *Ma Rainey's Black Bottom* by August Wilson. October 4, 2002. Directed by Arthur French; with Leopold Lowe, Charles Turner, Allie Woods, Jerry Matz, Ben Rivers, Henry Bradley, Ronald Rand, Roz Davis, Tamela Aldridge. *The Blacks: A Clown Show* by Jean Genet. January 31, 2003. Directed by Christopher McElroen; with Ty Jones, J. Kyle Manzay, Jammie Patton, Maechi Aharanwa, Yusef Miller, Gwendolyn Mulamba, Erin Cherry, Cherise Boothe, Ron Simons, A-men Rasheed, John-Andrew Morrison, Neil Dawson, Oberon. *The Crazy Locomotive* by Stanislaw Ignacy Witkiewicz.

March 28, 2003. Directed by Christopher McElroen; with Alfred Preisser, Leopold Lowe, Erica Ball, Maria Oliveras, Ross Williams, Michael O'Day, Marissa Tiamfook, Roland Garcia, Yves Rene, Roger Hendricks Simon, Dan Hendricks Simon.

CLEMENTE SOTO VELEZ CULTURAL CENTER (CSV). *A Girl of 16* by Aya Ogawa. April 30, 2003. Directed by Ms. Ogawa; with Karmenlara Brownson, Drae Campbell, Erika Hildebrandt, Peter Lettre, Magin Schantz, Dario Tangelson, Saori Tsukuda, Aaron Mostkoff Unger, Deborah Wallace.

CLUBBED THUMB. *The Typographer's Dream*. By Adam Bock. February 9, 2003. Directed by Drew Barr; with Kate Hampton, Meg MacCary and Dan Snook. SPRINGWORKS 2003. April 11–May 3, 2003. *Somewhere Someplace Else* by Ann Marie Healy. Directed by Annie Dorsen; with Mara Stephens, Laura Heisler, Todd Cerveris, Andrew Weems. *Design Your Kitchen* by Kate Ryan. Directed by Robert Davenport. *Late (A Cowboy Song)* by Sarah Ruhl. Directed by Deborah Saivetz.

CONNELLY THEATRE. *Leonce and Lena* by Georg Büchner. July 11, 2002. Directed by Lenard Petit; with Jonathan Fielding, Carman Lacivita, Keirin Brown, Almeria Campbell, Dalane Mason, Jason Lambert, Drew Hayes, Bryan Fenkart, Leslie Powers, Karen Freer, Alicia Avery, Nick Greco, Lauren Kleiman, Christopher Klinger, Aimee McCabe, Mitchell McEwan, Reyna Decourcy O'Grady, Sebastian Stan, Sylvia Yntena. *La Musica* by Marguerite Duras. September 12, 2002. Directed by Caroline Nastro; with Diana Ruppe, John Sharp, Mercedes Herrero. *Catcall* by Rebeca Ramirez. October 8, 2002. Directed by Ms. Ramirez; with Laine D'Souza, Timothy Hawkinson, Omar Jermaine, Paola Mendoza, Thelma Medina, Rachael Roberts, Jamie Velez, Rolando Zuniga. *Requiem for William*; based on short plays by William Inge. February 8, 2003. Directed by Jack Cummings III; with Dean Alai, Nicole Alifante, Toni DiBuono, Madeleine Jane DoPico, Corinne Edgerly, Taina Elg, Lovette George, Robyn Hussa, Samantha Jumper, Joe Kolinski, Mark Ledbetter, Tom Ligon, Michael Mags, Barbara Marineau, Richard Martin, Sean MacLaughlin, Marni Nixon, Monica Russell, Katie Scharf, Cheryl Stern, Diane Sutherland, Jonathan Uffelman, James Weber, John Wellman, Matt Yeager. *The Lucky Chance* by Aphra Behn. April 25, 2003. Directed by Rebecca Patterson; with Virginia Baeta, Gretchen S. Hall, Jennifer Larkin, Valentina McKenzie, Shauna Miles, Jena Necrason, Shanti Elise Prasad, Jill Repplinger, Gisele Richardson, Ami Shukla and DeeAnn Weir. *The Accidental Activist* by Kathryn Blume. April 30, 2003. Directed by Michaela Hall; with Ms. Blume and live music by Eliza Ladd.

CREATIVE ARTISTS LABORATORY THEATRE. *The Future?* by Tanya Klein. October 26, 2002. Directed by Ms. Klein; with Laurie Ann Orr, Stephen Kelly, Ryan Freeman, Jaime Sheedy, Gayle Pazerski, Michael Fife, Nicholas John Mazza, Tim Loftus.

CULTURE CLUB. *Birdy's Bachelorette Party* by Mark Nassar, Suzanna Melendez and Denise Fennell. June 7, 2002. Directed by Ms. Melendez; with Maria Baratta, Wass M. Stevens, Melissa Short, Jamie Sorrentini, Alice Moore, Michael Gargani, Frank Rempe, Ms. Fennell, Christopher Campbell, Scott Bilecky, Reid Hutchins.

DANCE THEATER WORKSHOP. *Son of Drakula* by David Drake. October 24, 2002. Directed by Chuck Brown; with Mr. Drake. *Antigone* by Sophocles; adapted by Mac Wellman. December 15, 2002. Directed by Paul Lazar; with Didi O'Connell, Molly Hickok, Rebecca Wisocky, Tricia Brouk, Leroy Logan.

DARYL ROTH THEATRE. *Roman Nights* by Franco D'Alessandro. September 12, 2002. Directed by Bick Goss; with Franca Barchiesi, Roy Miller.

DIMSON THEATRE. *Shoppers Carried by Escalators Into the Flames* by Denis Johnson. June 25, 2002. Directed by David Levine; with Gretchen Cleevely, Kevin Corrigan, Emily McDonnell, Betty Miller, Will Patton, Michael Shannon, Adam Trese, James Urbaniak, Kaili Vernoff.

THE DIRECTORS COMPANY. *Addictions* by Tricia Walsh-Smith. October 2, 2002. Directed by Pamela Berlin; with Laila Robins, Robert Cuccioli, Orlagh Cassidy, Julie White, Bernadette Quigley, Redman Maxfield. *Love in the Age of Narcissism* by Brad Desch. November 1, 2002. Directed by Chris Smith; with David Alan Basche, Maddie Corman, Richmond Hoxie, Amy Landecker, Amber McDonald, Alysia Reiner, William Severs. *Blue Heaven* by Raymond Hardie. December 16, 2002. Directed by Judith Dolan; with Colm Meaney, Laila Robins, Mary Bacon, Peter Gerety, Melinda Page Hamilton, James Kennedy. *Minnesota Fats Is Right Around the Corner* by Tony DiMurro. March 7, 2003. Directed by Nancy S. Chu; with John Speredakos, Richard Leighton, Tricia Paoluccio, Amy McKenna, Peter Appel.

DOUGLAS FAIRBANKS THEATRE. *Almost Live From the Betty Ford Clinic* by Michael West. January 16, 2003. Directed by Mr. West; with Mr. West.

DR2 THEATRE. *It's Beginning to Look a Lot Like Murder!* by Kurt Kleinmann. December 6, 2002. Directed by Blake Lawrence; with A. Raymond Banda, Steve Borowka, Darren Copozzi, Tarissa Day, James Gilbert, Shay Gines, Tim Honnoll, Robert Lehrer, Leslie Patrick, Ellen Reilly, John Weigand. *Worm Day* by Matthew Calhoun. February 18, 2003. Directed by Tom Herman; with Miriam Shor, Kelly AuCoin, Will Swenson.

THE FLEA THEATER. *Anything's Dream* by Mac Wellman. January 3, 2003. Directed by Beth Schachter; with Stephen Soroka, Alison Hinks, Jamie McKittrick, Jessica Ball, Jess Barberry, David Bish, Madeline Hoak, Phil Kimble, Goron Ivanovski, Lance Bankerd, Jordan Ahnquist, Liliana Andreano, Justin Brehm, DyShaun Burton, Kevin Cvitanov, Matt Dibiasio, Jared Franzman, Frank Grande-Marchione, Kieran Maroney, Charlotte McIvor, Adam Pinti, Keiko Yoshida. *O Jerusalem* by A.R. Gurney. March 18, 2003. Directed by Jim Simpson; with Priscilla Shanks, Stephen Rowe, Rita Wolf, Mercedes Herrero, Chaz Mena.

45TH STREET THEATRE. *Prince Hal* by Bennett Windheim. March 8, 2003. Directed by Elysabeth Kleinhans; with Bruce Sabath, Deborah Ludwig, Diane Landers, Marc Geller, Simon Feil, Donna Dimino, Jennifer Jiles.

45 BLEECKER. *Evolution* by Jonathan Marc Sherman. September 30, 2002. Directed by Lizzie Gottlieb; with Josh Hamilton, Keira Naughton, Peter Dinklage, Iona Skye, Armando Riesco, Larry Block. *Rapt* by Roland Tec. December 9, 2002. Directed by Mr. Tec. With Chris Arruda, Lisa Barnes, Tom Bozell, Cori Lynn Campbell, Carl Palmer, Bill Tobes, Kate Weiman. *Einstein's Dreams* by Alan Lightman. Adapted by Kipp Erante Cheng. January 10, 2003. Directed by Rebecca Holderness; with Jason Asprey, Amanda Barron, Dunia Bogner, Daniel Brink-Washington, H. Clark, Jared Coscglia, Rebecca DuMaine, Jessma Evans, Tom Knutson, Kate Kohler Amory, Alison Hanson, Puy Navarro, Barrett Ogden, Edward O'Blenis, Malinda Walford. *The Brothers Karamazov, Part 1* by Fyodor Dostoevsky; adapted by Alexander Harrington. February 9, 2003. Directed by Mr. Harrington; with Lisa Altomare, Frank Anderson, Stephen Reyes, Steven L. Barron, Ken Schactman, Joel Carino, David Fraioli, Ken Fuchs, Jennifer Gibbs, Robert Molossi, Gregory Sims, Greta Storace, Yaakov Sullivan, Sorrel Tomlinson, Jim Williams. *American Ma(u)l* by Robert O'Hara. April 14, 2003. Directed by Mr. O'Hara; with Richarda Abrams, Chad Beckim, Colman Domingo, Susan Greenhill, Suzette Gunn, Charles Karel, Greg Keller, Maurice McRae, Lloyd Porter, Ariel Shafir. *Pericles* by William Shakespeare. June 9, 2002. Directed by Jesse Berger; with Dale Soules, Raphael Nash Thompson, Daniel Breaker, Margot White, Wayne Scott, Carol Halstead, Addie Brownlee, Aysan Çelik, Angela Ai, Grant Goodman, Zachary Knower, Alvaro Mendoza, A-men Rasheed, Ashley Strand, Price Waldman.

47TH STREET THEATRE. *Corner Wars* by Tim Dowlin. January 19, 2003. Directed by Mel Williams; with David Shaw, Warren Merrick III, Eric Carter, Joel Holiday, Omar Evans, Christopher Williams, Ray Thomas.

14TH STREET Y. *Lady, Be Good*. Musical with book by Guy Bolton and Fred Thompson; music by George Gershwin; lyrics by Ira Gershwin. May 14, 2003. Directed by Thomas Mills; with Amy Barker, Jennifer Bernstone, Todd Buonopane, Lindsey Chambers, Jeffry Denman, Kurt Domoney, Jennifer Dunn, Leo Ash Evans, Brian Hedden, Nancy Lemenager, Malina Linkas, David McDonald, Andrew Rasmussen, Ginette Rhodes, Tom Sellwood, Doug Shapiro, Jennifer Taylor, Doug Wynn.

GLORIA MADDOX THEATRE. *Prelude to a Kiss* by Craig Lucas. November 16, 2002. Directed by Glenn Krutoff; with Gene Fanning, Rachel Feldman, Lawrence Garello, Eric Hottinger, Elizabeth Hayes, Eric Ilijevich, John Lisanti, Andrea Marshall-Money, Heidi E. Philipsen, Tania Santiago, Peter Sloan.

GROUND FLOOR THEATER. *Part-Time Gods* by Noah Klein. October 14, 2002. Directed by Ben Hodges; with Michael Connors, Renata Hinrichs, Mr. Hodges, Peter Lewis, Nicole Severine, Brant Spencer.

HAROLD CLURMAN THEATRE. *Class Mothers '68* by Eric H. Weinberger. December 9, 2002. Directed by Jeremy Dobrish; with Priscilla Lopez.

HERE ARTS CENTER. QUEER @ HERE FESTIVAL. June 17–June 30, 2002. *Touchscape* by James Scruggs. *In the Realm of the Unreal* by Travis Chamberlain and Kyle Jarrow. *Lesbian Pulp-O-*

Rama! created and performed by Heather de Michele, Anna Fitzwater, Gretchen M. Michelfeld, Beatrice Terry. *The Mystique of Fly* by Leslie Duprey. *A Pair of Hands* by Raymond Luczak. *Cornholed!* by Daniel Nardicio. *Bad Women* by Sidney Goldfarb. June 20, 2002. Directed by Tina Shepard; with Will Badgett, Purva Bedi, Rosemary Quinn, Sonja Rzepski, Jack Wetherall, Connie Winston, Alana Harris, Erica Kelly, Anya Maddow-Zimet, Ruthie Marantz, Tamara Rosenblum. THE AMERICAN LIVING ROOM. July 13–September 1, 2002. *Nine Eleven* by Susanna Speier. Directed by Ms. Speier. *The Franklin Thesis* by Bradley Bazzle. Directed by Alex Timbers. *Snow Angel* by David Lindsay-Abaire. Directed by Jake Hart. *Aloha Flight 243* by Sophia Chapadjiev and Allison Leyton-Brown. Directed by Pamela Seiderman. *The Kingdom of Lost Songs.* By Abhijat Joshi. Directed by Broke Brod. *Public Relations* by Jeff Kellner. Directed by Anthony Castellano. *Noises and Voices* by Michael Schuval. Directed by Hyunjung Lee. *Eighteen* by Allison Moore. Directed by Maryann Lombardi. *Excelsior* by Jay Bernzweig. Directed by Kevin Vavasseur. *Mothergun* by Christine Evans. Directed by Heidi Howard. *Tumor* by Sheila Callaghan. Directed by Catherine Zambri. *Dug Out* by Nicholas Gray. Directed by Mark Armstrong. *White Russian* by Joseph Goodrich. Directed by Isis Saratial Misdary. *Bochenski's Brain* by Gabriel Shanks and Tim Brown. Directed by Messrs. Shanks and Brown. *Out of My Mind* by Suzanne Weber. Directed by Christopher Duva. *Misogamy, or You're So Pretty When You're Unfaithful to Me* by Bronwen Bitetti. Directed by Heather de Michele. *The Death of Tintagiles* by Maurice Maeterlinck. Directed by Joseph Rosswog. *Bronx Casket Company* by Andrea Lepcio. Directed by Ms. Lepcio. *Field of Fireflies* by Jason Mills. Directed by Anna D'Agrossa. *The Basset Table* by Susannah Centlivre. Directed by Rachel Ford. *Last Child* by Rebecca Sharp. Directed by Michele Travis. *Voyage of the Carcass* by Dan O'Brien. July 14, 2002. Directed by Alyse Leigh Rothman; with Michael Anderson, Rebecca Harris, Chris Mason. *Psychotherapy Live!* by Lisa Levy. July 22, 2002. With Ms. Levy. *Mr. Gallico* by Sam Carter. August 8, 2002. Directed by Henry Caplan; with Jason Howard, Karl Herlinger, Tate Henderson. *Ray on the Water* by Edward Allan Baker. September 28, 2002. Directed by Ed Bianchi; with Jessica Alexander, Suzanne Di Donna, Bruce MacVittie, Kirsten Russell, Georgia Strauss. *The Sky Over Nineveh* by Mac Rogers. October 18, 2002. Directed by Boris Kievsky. *Or Polaroids (Version 2.1)* by Ken Urban. November 1, 2002. Directed by Mr. Urban; with Anni Bluhm, Andrew Breving, Kristin Stewart Chase, Maggie Cino. *Fundamental.* Multimedia work created by the company. November 8, 2002. Directed by Brian Rogers; with David Green, Gary Hennion, Mami Kimura, Sheila Lewandowski, James Morss, Stephane Penn. *Iphigenia in Tauris* by Euripides; translated by Witter Bynner. November 13, 2002. Directed by Veronica Newton. CULTURE MART. January 3–11, 2003. *Blue Flower* by Ruth Bauer and Jim Bauer. *Intimate Shift* by Daniel Levy. *Radio Wonderland* by Joshua Fried. *The Dakota Project* by Noah Haidle and Davis McCallum. *Phenomenon* by Alyse Leigh Rothman. *Elegy* by Tiffany Mills; music by John Zorn. *Erendira* by Gabriel García Márquez. February 24, 2003. Directed by Kristin Marting; with Ching Valdes-Aran, Elisa Terrazas, Alex Endy, Janio Marrero, Marc Petrosino. *What's Inside the Egg?* by Lake Simons. March 19, 2003. Directed by Ms. Simons; with Ms. Simons, Harold Lehmann, Erin Eagar, Chris Green, Matthew Acheson. *Saturn's Wake* by Deke Weaver and Michael Farkas. March 23, 2003. Directed by Jill Samuels.

HYPOTHETICAL THEATRE COMPANY. *Almost Grown Up* by Aviva Jane Carlin. September 9, 2002. Directed by Amy Feinberg; with Ms. Carlin.

INTAR 53. *Fuenteovejuna* by Lope de Vega; adapted by Mia Katigbak. October 17, 2002. Directed by David Herskovits; with Konrad Aderer, Yoko Akashi, Pun Bandhu, Joel Carino, Deborah S. Craig, Joel de la Fuente, Andrew Eisenman, Siho Ellsmore, Lydia Gaston, Mel Gionson, Paul Juhn, Ms. Katigbak, C.S. Lee, Tina Lee, Timothy Ford Murphy, Tomi Peirano, Felice Yeh, Aaron Yoo.

IRISH ARTS. *Poor Beast in the Rain* by Billy Roche. November 13, 2002. Directed by Terence Lamude; with Bernadette Quigley, Steve Brady, Tracy Coogan, John Keating and Mickey Kelly. *The Gallant John-Joe* by Tom Mac Intyre. March 17, 2003. With Tom Hickey.

JEAN COCTEAU REPERTORY. *Henry V* by William Shakespeare. September 22, 2002. Directed by David Fuller; with Harris Berlinsky, Christopher Black, Christopher Browne, Stafford Clark-Price, Abe Goldfarb, Edward Griffin, Brian Lee Huynh, Amanda Jones, Marlene May, Rebecca Robinson, Michael Surabian, Jason Crowl. *The Importance of Being Earnest* by Oscar Wilde. September 26, 2002. Directed by Ernest Johns; with Harris Berlinsky, Jason Crowl, Abe Goldfarb, Amanda Jones, Angela Madden, Marlene May, Michael Surabian, Carey Van Driest. *Uncle Vanya* by Anton Chekhov. January 10, 2003. Directed by Eve Adamson; with Harris Berlinsky, Christopher Black, Eileen Glenn, Angus Hepburn, Brian Lee Huynh, Amanda Jones, Marlene May, Craig Smith, Elise Stone. *The Effect of Gamma Rays on Man-in-the-Moon Marigolds* by Paul Zindel. March 7, 2003. Directed by Ernest Johns; with Kate Holland, Angela Madden, Elsie James, Rebecca Robinson, Stefanie Varveris. *The Triumph of Love* by Pierre Marivaux; translated by Rod McLucas. March 21, 2003. Directed by David Fuller; with Amanda Jones, Kate Holland, Michael Surabian, Christopher Black, Edward Griffin, Marlene May, Bill Fairbairn.

JOHN HOUSEMAN THEATRE. *A "Pure" Gospel Christmas* by Leslie Dockery and David A. Tobin. December 17, 2002. Directed and choreographed by Ms. Dockery; with Richard Bellazzin, Ken Boyd, Diane Michelle Buster, Kim Crawford, Brian Dickerson, Arlene Frink, Damon Horton, Sandra Keel-Huff, Delise Jones, Darin Myers, Cypriana Okuzu, Deborah E. Oatman, Kim Pacheco, Romel Robinson, Mr. Tobin.

JOSE QUINTERO THEATRE. *Joe and Betty* by Murray Mednick. June 2, 2002. Directed by Guy Zimmerman. With Annabelle Gurwitch, John Diehl, Shawna Casey, Tom McCleister, Edith Fields, Sharron Shayne, Drago Sumonja. Transferred with cast changes to the Kirk Theatre in the Theatre Row complex for a limited run (12/15/2002). SHAKESPEARE UNPLUGGED: THE HISTORY CYCLE. *Henry V* by William Shakespeare. November 12, 2002. Directed by Joanne Zipay and Ivanna Cullinan; with Laurie Bannister-Colón, Grant Mudge, Jane Titus, Kevin Scott Till, Gail Kay Bell, David Huber, Miriam Lipner, Eileen Glenn, Richard Simon, Eric Aschenbrenner, Joseph Capone, Jovinna Chan, Omri Schein, Irma St. Paule, Jennifer Sherron Stock, Hilary Ward. *Henry VI: Parts 1, 2 and 3* by William Shakespeare. March 27, 2003. Directed by Ivanna Cullinan and Joanne Zipay; with Susan Ferrara, Carey Van Driest, Hilary Ward, Mary Hodges, Miriam Lipner, Michelle Kovacs, Dacyl Acevedo, Alyssa Simon, Lynn Kanter, Corrie McCrea, Angela Liao, Kristen Harlow, Lisa Preston, Sheila Ostadazim, Marie Bridget Dundon, Joseph Capone, Jovinna Chan, Ari Barbanell, Laurie Bannister-Colón, Renee Bucciarelli, John Kinsherf. *The Metamorphosis* by Franz Kafka; adapted by E. Thomalen. January 9, 2003. Directed by Francine L. Trevens; with Peter J. Coriaty, Brandon deSpain, Marcalan Glassberg, David Kornhaber, David Lamberton, Ozlem Turhal, Kevin Whittinghill, Loretta Guerra Woodrull, Alexis Wickwire. *Nurse!* by Lisa Hayes. May 6, 2003. Directed by Annie Levy; with Ms. Hayes.

KEEN COMPANY. *Museum* by Tina Howe. June 9, 2002. Directed by Carl Forsman; with Maxwell L. Anderson, Susan Blackwell, Brennan Brown, Elizabeth Bunch, Jimmon Cole, Teddy Coluca, Chris Denzer, Katie Firth, Jennifer Gibbs, Robyn Goodman, Nathan Guisinger, Tony Hale, Kate Hampton, Chris Hutchinson, Tim Kang, Lael Logan, Jenny Maguire, Marilyn Moore, Christina Parker, Dina Pearlman, Christa Scott Reed, Jordin Ruderman, Andrew Schulman. *Three-Cornered Moon* by Gertrude Tonkonogy. September 8, 2002. Directed by Carl Forsman; with Denis Butkus, Christopher Duva, Yetta Gottesman, Kathleen Kaefer, Maggie Lacey, Mikel Sarah Lambert, Greg McFadden, Andrew McGinn, Nick Toren.

KIRK THEATRE. *Texarkana Waltz* by Louis Broom. November 13, 2002. Directed by Allison Narver; with Tina Benko, Caroline Bottle, Doug Cote, Adrian LaTourelle, Jesse Lenat, Denise Lute, Chuck Montgomery, Annie Parisse, Tom Wiggin. *Heat Lightning*. Musical with book by George Griggs and Paul Andrew Perez; music and lyrics by Mr. Griggs. March 5, 2003. Directed by Mr. Perez; with Laura Marie Duncan, Sean Fri, Nicolette Hart, Jackie Seiden, Coleen Sexton, Will Swenson, Jennifer Waldman. *Meshugah* by Emily Mann; adapted from the novel by Isaac Bashevis Singer. May 15, 2003. Directed by Loretta Greco; with Barbara Andres, Ned Eisenberg, Ben Hammer, Ted Koch, Elizabeth Marvel.

KRAINE THEATER. *The Mayor's Limo* by Mark Nassar. September 25, 2002. Directed by Santo Fazio; with Kevin Alexander, Sharon Angela, Patrick Michael Buckley, James J. Hendricks, Mr. Nassar, Michael Perri, Robert Stevens, Rebecca Weitman, James Wormsworth.

LABYRINTH THEATER COMPANY. *Our Lady of 121st Street* by Stephen Adly Guirgis. September 29, 2002. Directed by Philip Seymour Hoffman; with Elizabeth Canavan, Liza Colón-Zayas, David Deblinger, Melissa Feldman, Mark Hammer, Ron Cephas Jones, Richard Petrocelli, Portia, Al Roffe, Felix Solis, David Zayas. First presented as a LAByrinth Theater Company workshop (8/20–10/12/2002; 15 performances from the September 28, 2002 press opening). Transferred to Off Broadway's Union Square Theatre (3/6/2003; 100 performances through 5/31/2003). See Plays Produced Off Broadway section. *Dirty Story* by John Patrick Shanley. March 2, 2003. Directed by Mr. Shanley; with David Deblinger, Florencia Lozano, Chris McGarry, Michael Puzzo.

LION THEATRE. *Split* by Michael Weller. September 16, 2002. Directed by Drew DeCorleto; with Teresa L. Goding, Leo Lauer, Stephen Brumble Jr., Nina Edgerton, Andrew J. Hoff, Jeremy Koch, Veronica Mittenzwei. *Soar Like an Eagle*. Musical with book by Adam Dick, music and lyrics by

Paul Dick. Directed by Daniel T. Lavender; with Carrie A. Johnson, Nicholas Dalton, Mary Ann Hannon, Paul Straney, Jaye Maynard, Michael Minarik, Seth Golay, Stephanie Girard, Javier Munoz, Patrick Bodd, Michael Shane Ellis. *A Ritual of Faith* by Brad Levinson. March 2, 2003. Directed by Igor Goldin; with Michael Cruz, Laura Fois, Ryan Hilliard, Aaron Feldman, Marilyn Sanabria, Tibor Feldman, Marc Krinsky, Matthew Boston. *New Boy* by William Sutcliffe; adapted by Russell Labey. April 24, 2003. Directed by Mr. Labey; with Neil Henry, Todd Swenson, Lisa Barnes, Dana Powers Acheson, Peter Russo.

MANHATTAN ENSEMBLE THEATER. *Death in Venice* by Robert David MacDonald; adapted from the novella by Thomas Mann; translation by David Luke. June 6, 2002. Directed by Giles Havergal; with Mr. Havergal. *Hank Williams: Lost Highway* by Randal Myler and Mark Harelik. December 19, 2002. Directed by Mr. Myler; with Jason Petty, Michael W. Howell, Juliet Smith, Margaret Bowman, Stephen G. Anthony, Myk Watford, Drew Perkins, Michael P. Moran, Tertia Lynch, Russ Wever. Transferred to the Off Broadway's Little Shubert Theatre (3/26/2003; 65 performances through May 31, 2003).

MA-YI THEATRE. *The Romance of Magno Rubio* by Lonnie Carter; adapted from a story by Carlos Bulosan. October 26, 2002. Direction and scenery by Loy Arcenas; with Art Acuña, Ramon de Ocampo, Ron Domingo, Jojo Gonzalez, Orlando Pabotoy. *Dead Man's Socks* by Ralph B. Peña. March 6, 2003. Directed by Mr. Peña; with Chris Thorn, Rodney To, John Wernke. *Last of the Suns* by Alice Tuan. April 27, 2003. Directed by Chay Yew; with Ching Valdes-Aran, Mia Katigbak, Kathy Kuroda, Tess Lina, Ron Nakahara, Eric Steinberg.

MCGINN/CAZALE THEATRE. *The Notebook* by Wendy Kesselman. June 23, 2002. Directed by Evan Yionulis; with Lisa Harrow, Miles Purinton, Portia Reiners, Peter Van Wagner. *Monsieur Ibrahim and the Flowers of the Koran* by Eric-Emmanuel Schmitt; translated by Stéphane Laporte. January 26, 2003. Directed by Maria Mileaf; with Ed Vassallo. *Buicks* by Julian Sheppard. March 9, 2003. Directed by Brian Kulick; with Olivia Birkelund, Lucia Brawley, Bill Buell, Norbert Leo Butz.

MELTING POT THEATRE COMPANY. *Cookin' at the Cookery* by Marion J. Caffey. January 22, 2003. Directed by Mr. Caffey; with Ann Duquesnay, Debra Walton.

METROPOLITAN PLAYHOUSE. *Sun-Up* by Lula Vollmer. March 7, 2003. Directed by Mahayana Landowne; with Ruthanne Gereghty, Sarah Dandridge, Roy Bacon, John Summerour, Joe Plummer, Scott Ebersold, Tom Richter, T.I. Moore. *Fashion* by Anna Cora Mowatt. April 10, 2003. Directed by Alex Roe; with Henry Afro-Bradley, Erika Bailey, Matt Daniels, Sean Dill, Stephanie Dorian, Jon-Michael Hernandez, Olivia Keister, Sean Kenin, Tod Mason, Sylvia Norman, Karl Williams. *Is There a Doctor in the House?* by Joel Jeske. May 7, 2003. Directed by Mr. Jeske; with Laura Dillman, Bill Edwards, Mr. Jeske, Jeremiah Murphy, Rob Pedini, Juliet Schaefer-Jeske.

MIDTOWN INTERNATIONAL THEATRE FESTIVAL. *All the World's a Stage* by Donna Stearns. *Apple* by Vern Thiessen. Directed by Randy White. *Belles of the Mill*. Musical with book by Rachel Rubin Ladutke; music and lyrics by Jill Marshall-Work. Directed by Arlene Schulman. *Beyond the Veil* by John Chatterton. Directed by Linda Burson. *Boulevard X* by Susan N. Horowitz. Directed by Rajedra Ramoon Maharaj. *Buon Natale, Bruno* by Terianne Falcone. Directed by Gary Austin. *Cirrius, Nebraska* by Nick Vigorito. *City of Dreams*. Musical with book and lyrics by David Zellnik; music by Joseph Zellnik. Directed by Michael Alltop. *Dirty Laundry* by Deborah Louise Ortiz. THE DURANG PROJECT: FIVE SHORT PLAYS by Christopher Durang. *The Doctor Will See You Now*; *DMV Tyrant*; *Funeral Parlor*; *Kitty the Waitress*; *Business Lunch in the Russian Tea Room*. Directed by Michael Klimzak. *Faustus* by Christopher Marlowe; adaptation by Jay Michaels. Directed by Mr. Michaels. *Flack* by Tina Posterli. *Heavy Mettle* by Richard Hoehler. *Heroes* by Jonathan Brady. Directed by Mark Steven Robinson. *I Love Myself* and *Who Are the People in Your Neighborhood?* Two one-man shows with John Tedeschi. *I Love New York—What's Your Excuse?* by David Kosh. Directed by Ann Bowen. *More Bitch Than a Bitch* by John Paul. *Mustard—It's a Gas!* by Ben Murphy. *My Life in the Trenches* by Jill Dalton. *Rubber* by Tom Sleigh. Directed by Dyana Kimball. *Saints and Singing* by Gertrude Stein. *Star Crossed Lovers* by Charles Battersby. Directed by Valentina Cardinalli. *Time Machine 2.0*. Musical with book, music and lyrics by Mark Weiser. Directed by Daniella Topol. *Will and the Ghost* by Aoise Stratford and Conal Condren. Directed by Christian Ely. *Woman vs. Superman* by Kelly Jean Fitzsimmons.

MINT SPACE. *Paddywack* by Daniel Magee. November 3, 2002. Directed by Herman Babad; with Mary Jasperson, Kelly Miller, Declan Mooney, Frank Shattuck, Allan Styer, Carla Tassara. *The*

Uninvited Guest by Michael R. Murphy. January 12, 2003. Directed by Daniel Kuney; with Jane Altman, Jack Garrity, Michael Graves, Rachel Lee Harris, Ryan Hilliard, Sean Matic, Kittson O'Neill, David Runco. *Hallelujah Breakdown* by Ted LoRusso. January 12, 2003. Directed by Gregory Fletcher; with Wynne Anders, David Bell, TJ Gambrel, Jack Garrett, Lue McWilliams, Casey Weaver, Nicholas Wuehrmann. *God and Mr. Smith* by Travis Baker. March 20, 2003. Directed by Marshall Mays; with Brigit Darby, Todd Allen Durkin, Daryl Lathon, Lucy McMichael, Susan Molloy, Marc Moritz, Michael Nathanson, Najla Said, Jim Wisniewski, Jeffrey C. Wolf, Daniel Snow. *Sinfully Rich* by Rich Orloff. March 24, 2003. Directed by Todd Allen Durkin, Nolan Haims, Catherine Baker Steindler, Joseph Ward and Jeffrey C. Wolf; with Ilene Bergelson, Annie Edgerton, William Green, Gavin Hoffman, Daniel Kaufman, Larissa Kiel, Cynthia Posillico, Kim Reed, Sarah Saltzberg, Matty D. Stuart, Jamie Watkins, Gregg Weiner, Marshall York. *Of Mice and Men* by John Steinbeck. April 11, 2003. Directed by Harvey Perr; with John Topping, K. Winston Osgood, Caroline Luft, Paul Barry, Jefferson Slinkard, James Edward Lee, Jason Edwards. *The Novelist* by James Bosley. May 11, 2003. Directed by Rebecca Kendall; with Troy Schremmer, Francisco Lorite, Marilyn Sanabria, Jason Hare, Sean Matic. *Screaming in the Wilderness* by Vanda. May 12, 2003. Directed by Steven McElroy; with Cynthia Brown, Gerald Downey, Barbara J. Spence, Danielle Quisenberry, Tom Dusenbury, Aimee Howard, Marianne Mackenzie, Mark Mears, Billy Rosa, Vanessa Villalobos.

NATIONAL ASIAN AMERICAN THEATRE COMPANY. *Air Raid* by Archibald MacLeish. March 23, 2003. Directed by Stephen Stout; with Michi Barall, Jodi Lin, Han Ong, Eileen Rivera, Joel de la Fuente, Mel Gionson, Jennifer Chang, Gita Reddy, Siho Ellsmore, Geeta Citygirl.

NEW GEORGES. *None of the Above* by Jenny Lyn Bader. March 19, 2003. Directed by Julie Kramer; with Alison Pill, Kel O'Neill.

NEW VICTORY THEATER. *The Junebug Symphony* by James Thiérrée. October 9, 2002. Directed by Mr. Thiérrée; with Mr. Thiérrée, Uma Ysamat, Raphaëlle Boitel, Magnus Jakobsson. *A Year With Frog and Toad*. Musical with book and lyrics by Willie Reale; music by Robert Reale; based on the children's books by Arnold Lobel. November 15, 2002. Directed by David Petrarca; with Jay Goede, Mark Linn-Baker, Danielle Ferland, Kate Reinders, Frank Vlastnik. *Thwak!* by David Collins and Shane Dundas. April 6, 2003. Directed by Philip Wm. McKinley; with Messrs. Collins, Dundas. *A Midsummer Night's Dream* by William Shakespeare; adapted by Robert Richmond. May 2, 2003. Directed by Mr. Richmond; with Kenn Sabberton, Gabriela Fernandez-Coffey, Guy Oliver-Watts, Ryan Conarro, Lindsay Rae Taylor, Andrew Schwartz, Renata Friedman.

NEW YORK THEATRE WORKSHOP. *Details* by Lars Norén. January 23, 2003. Directed by Bille August; with Ole Lemmeke, Benedicte Hansen, Helle Fragalid, Nicolai Dahl Hamilton.

NEW YORK INTERNATIONAL FRINGE FESTIVAL. August 9–25, 2002. *Schedule included: Matt and Ben* by Mindy Kaling and Brenda Withers. Directed by Mses. Kaling and Withers; with Mses. Kaling and Withers. *Marginal Saints* by Lee Gundersheimer. Directed by Donna Sue de Guzman. *Love in Pieces* by Sarah Morton; with Ryan Brack, Lisa Gardner. *The Bizarro Bologna Show* by Dan Piraro; with additional material by Lee Ritchey; music by Steve Powell and Ernie Myers. Directed by Mr. Ritchey. *Medeamachine* by Ian Belton. *Selma's Break* and *Rx* by Matthew Swan. Directed by Mr. Swan and Carlo Vogel; with Jessie Hutcheson, Lisa M. Perry, Jonathan Marc Sherman, Mr. Swan, Linda S. Nelson. *Not Herself Lately* by Neil Genzlinger. *Sherlock Holmes and the Secret of Making Whoopee* by Sean Cunningham. *Five Frozen Embryos* by David Greenspan. Directed by Jon Schumacher; with Ilka Saddler Pinheiro, Ellen Shanman. *The Sleepers* by Christopher Shinn. Directed by Jon Schumacher; with Laura Marks, Russel Taylor, Paul Juhn. *The Way Out* by Timothy Nolan. Directed by Vincent Marano; with Shiek Mahmud-Bey, Tod Engle. *Death of Frank* by Stephen Belber. Directed by Nancy S. Chu; with Raymond James Hill, Alexa Dubreuil, Paul Keany, Tessa Gibbons. *Resa Fantastiskt Mystisk* by Lars Mattsun; adapted by Carolyn Almos, Matt Almos, Jon Beauregard, Joel Marshall, Todd Merrill, Katharine Noon, Victor Ortado, Laura Otis and Selina Smith. Directed by Mr. Almos; with Mr. Beauregard, Mr. Merrill, Mr. Ortado, Ms. Smith, Ms. Otis, Daniel Stewart. *Beat* by Kelly Groves; based on the life and writing of Allen Ginsberg and others. Directed by Mr. Groves; with Dan Pintauro, Andrew Cruse, Todd Kovner, John Jeffrey Martin, Geoffrey Molloy, Ezra Nanes and Glenn Peters. *Him and Her*. Musical with book, music and lyrics by Paul Scott Goodman. Directed by Miriam Gordon; with Paul Scott Goodman, Liz Larsen.

OHIO THEATER. *Rum and Vodka* by Conor McPherson. October 7, 2002. Directed by Samuel Buggeln; with Mark Alhadeff. KOLTÈS NEW YORK 2003: NEW AMERICAN TRANSLATIONS. *West Pier* by Bernard Marie Koltès; translated by Marion Schoevaert and Theresa Weber. May 8, 2003.

Directed by Jay Scheib; with Tom Day, Marina Garcia-Gelpe, Dan Illian, Krassin Iordanov, Ryan Justeson, Aimee Phelan, Michael Stumm, Zishan Ugurlu. *Roberto Zucco* by Bernard Marie Koltès; translated by Daniel Safer. May 11, 2003. Directed by Mr. Safer; with Aubrey Chamberlin, Sean Donovan, Jessma Evans, Emmitt C. George, Jason Lew, Jennie Marytai Liu, Katie Lowes, Mike Mikos, Micki Pellerano, Laura Berlin Stinger. E. Randy Thompson, Raina von Waldenburg, Wendy Meiling Yang, David Cale. *Battle of Black and Dogs* by Bernard Marie Koltès; translated by Michaël Attias. May 14, 2003. Directed by Doris Mirescu; with Joan Jubett, Matt Landers, Leopold Lowe, Eric Dean Scott. *In the Solitude of Cotton Fields* by Bernard Marie Koltès; translated by Lenora Champagne. May 16, 2003. Directed by Marion Schoevaert; with Terrence Bae, Shaun O'Neil.

ONTOLOGICAL THEATRE. *Other Love* by Bill Talen. June 7, 2002. Directed by Tony Torn and Savitri Durkee; with Reverend Billy. *Panic! (How to Be Happy!)* by Richard Foreman. January 9, 2003. Directed and designed by Mr. Foreman; with D.J. Mendel, Elina Löwensohn, Tea Alagic, Robert Cucuzza. *The Autobiography of God as Told by Mel Schneider* by Marv Siegel. May 22, 2003. Directed by Donovan Dolan; with Ron Palillo, Joseph Lee Gramm, Genna Brocone, Rainey Welch, Ward Horton.

PANTHEON THEATRE. *Etta Jenks* by Marlane Meyer. March 8, 2003. Directed by Robert Funaro; with Ruth Aguilar, Neil Barsky, Richard Boccato, Heather Hanemann, Tony Hitchcock, John Koprowski, Ernest Mingione, Susan Mitchell, John Prada, Chesney Snow. *Sealed for Freshness* by Doug Stone. April 2, 2003. Directed by Mr. Stone; with Jeanne Hime, Nancy Hornback, Elissa Olin, Kate VanDevender, J.J. Van Name, Shawn Curran. *That Day in September* by Artie Van Why. April 9, 2003. Directed by Richard Masur; with Mr. Van Why.

PARADISE THEATER COMPANY. *Peter and Vandy* by Jay DiPietro. September 12, 2003. Directed by Mr. DiPietro; with Monique Vukovic, Mr. DiPietro. *I Want You To* by Eric Maierson. March 2, 2003. With Ken Forman, Monique Vukovic. *Fear and Friday Nights* by Lawrence Levine. March 2, 2003. Directed by Mr. Levine; with Jicky Schnee, Grant Varjas. *Losing Ground* by Bryan Wizemann. March 27, 2003. Directed by Mr. Wizemann; with Kendall Pigg, Mark Meyer, Eileen O'Connell, Monique Vukovic, Rhonda Keyser, John Good.

THE PEARL THEATRE COMPANY. *She Stoops to Conquer* by Oliver Goldsmith. September 22, 2002. Directed by Chuck Hudson; with John Camera, Stewart Carrico, Celeste Ciulla, Dominic Cuskern, Sally Kemp, Mary Molloy, Christopher Moore, John Livingstone Rolle, Edward Seamon, Jay Stratton, Scott Whitehurst, Eunice Wong. *Nathan the Wise* by Gotthold Lessing; adapted by Richard Sewell. October 20, 2002. Directed by Barbara Bosch; with John Camera, Celeste Ciulla, Dominic Cuskern, Sally Kemp, Christopher Moore, John Livingstone Rolle, Edward Seamon, Jay Stratton, Scott Whitehurst, Eunice Wong. *The Tempest* by William Shakespeare. December 8, 2002. Directed by Padraic Lillis; with Rachel Botchan, Jonathan Brathwaite, Stewart Carrico, Celeste Ciulla, Dominic Cuskern, Dan Daily, Flannery Foster, Robert Hock, Amy Hutchins, Sean McNall, Christopher Moore, John Newton, Andy Prosky, Edward Seamon, Scott Whitehurst, Brenda Withers. *Heartbreak House* by George Bernard Shaw. February 16, 2003. Directed by Gus Kaikkonen; with Russ Anderson, Rachel Botchan, Robin Leslie Brown, Joanne Camp, Dominic Cuskern, Dan Daily, Robert Hock, George Morfogen, Nada Rowand, Edward Seamon. *Daisy Mayme* by George Kelly. April 13, 2003. Directed by Russell Treyz; with Rachel Botchan, Robin Leslie Brown, Joanne Camp, Dominic Cuskern, Robert Hock, Sean McNall, Carol Schultz, Samantha Soule.

PECCADILLO THEATER COMPANY. *Veronique* by John O'Hara. July 14, 2002. Directed by Dan Wackerman; with Jim Iorio, Jennifer Erin Roberts, Susan Jeffries, Richard Leighton, Meg Brooker, Benjamin Howes, Elizabeth Elson, Jason Cicci. *The Shanghai Gesture* by John Colton; revised by Joanna Chan. October 27, 2002. Directed by Dan Wackerman; with Richard Bekins, Gerald Blum, Nick Bosco, Robert Lee Chu, Briana Davis, Elizabeth Elson, Camilla Enders, Catherine Jhung, Janie Kelly, Brian Linden, Jackson Ning, Frank Perich, Ron Piretti, Jade Wu.

PELICAN THEATRE. *Not Fool the Sun Or Fester 'n Sexx* by Peter Florax. December 9, 2002. Directed by Mr. Florax; with Jason Altman, Randee Barrier, Mike Bocchetti, Dave Durkin, Chris O'Neil, Brian Rush, Steve Tresty.

PHIL BOSAKOWSKI THEATRE. *Baptizing Adam* by David Allyn. August 22, 2002. Directed by Kevin Lee Newbury; with Vince Gatton, Megan Hollingshead, Andrew Glaszek, Philip James Sulsona, Henry Glovinsky. THE ONE FESTIVAL. October 31–November 5, 2002. *Love Arm'd* by Karen Eterovich. *Thieves in the Temple: The Reclaiming of Hip Hop* by Aya DeLeon. *Bang!* by C.C.

Seymour. *Shoes* by Tim Douglas Jensen. *The Poetics of Baseball* by Neil Bradley. *Cirque Jacqueline* by Andrea Reese. *Donna Paradise* by Matthew Wells. November 9, 2002. Directed by Rob O'Neill; with Elissa Lash, Krish Batnagar, Candy Simmons, Jennifer Ward. *Lost and Found* by Paul Harris. May 11, 2003. Directed by Fred Barton; with Leila Martin, Stu Richel, John Kevin Jones.

THE PRODUCERS CLUB. *What's Your Karma?* by Lilith Dove. July 23, 2002. *Johnny 23*. Musical by Jim Doyle. October 5, 2002. Directed by GW Reed; with Bill Tatum, Gerrianne Raphael, Leslie Feagan, Andrew Fitzsimmons, Andrew Horwitz, Jill Kotler, Annie Lee Moffett, Ellen Saland. *Cuban Operator Please* and *Floating Home* by Adrian Rodriguez. October 9, 2002. Directed by Arian Blanco; with Jose Antonio, John C. Cunningham, Emilio Delgado, Omar Hernandez, Mercy Valladares. *Christmas with the Crawfords*. Musical by Mark Sargent and Richard Winchester. November 22, 2002. Directed and choreographed by Donna Drake; with Joey Arias, Kate Botello, Trauma Flintstone, Brant Kaiwi, Joe Levesque, Chris March, Sade Pendarvis, Mark Sargent, Jason Scott. *Kerouac* by Tom O'Neil. January 26, 2003. Directed by Anthony P. Pennino; with Tim Cox, Deanne Dawson, John Kwiatkowski, Kyle Pierson, Gavin Walker, Deirdre Schwiesow, Peter Stewart. *Marathon* by Edoardo Erba; translated by Israel Horovitz. March 7, 2003. Directed by Weylin Symes; with Eric Laurits, Adam Paltrowitz.

PROSPECT THEATER COMPANY. *Spring Awakening* by Frank Wedekind; translated by Ted Hughes. November 2, 2002. Directed by Jackson Gay; with Blake Hackler, Bridget Flanery, Austin Jones. *Taxi Cabaret* by Peter Mills and Cara Reichel. November 5, 2002. Directed by Ms. Reichel; with Alison Cimmet, Christopher Graves, Jason Mills, Katie O'Shaughnessey, Simone Zamore. EXODE. November 11–13, 2002. *The Buccaneer* by Jacob Grigolia-Rosenbaum. *Corn* by Cara Reichel. *Persians* by Andrew Case. *Dido (and Aeneas)* by Roxane Heinze and Cara Reichel; adapted from Virgil; music and arrangements by Daniel Feyer, Richard Hip-Flores and Peter Mills. February 8, 2003. Directed by Ms. Reichel. *The Alchemists*. Musical with book by Peter Mills and Cara Reichel; music and lyrics by Mr. Mills. April 26, 2003. Directed by Ms. Reichel; with Benjamin Eakeley, Damian Long, Tony Valles, Blake Hackler, Kelly Snyder, Jordan Wolfe, Joshua Marmer, Seamus Boyle, Jonathan Demar, Danielle Melanie Brown, Larry Brustofski, Richard Todd Adams, Carol A. Hickey, Erica Wright, Navida Stein, Peter Maris, Greg Horton.

PULSE ENSEMBLE THEATRE. *Alexandra's Web* by H. Richard Silver. June 13, 2002. Directed by Alexa Kelly; with Heather Berman, David Winton, Ezra Nanes, Bill Barnett.

RATTLESTICK THEATRE. *My Special Friend*. Musical with book and lyrics by Philip Courtney; music by PJ Cacioppo. July 4, 2002. Directed by R.J. Tolan; with Eric Axen, Andrew Fetherolf, Lisa Raymond. *Faster* by Adam Rapp. September 8, 2002. Directed by Darrell Larsen; with Robert Beitzel, Mtume Gant, Chris Messina, Fallon McDevitt Brooking, Roy Thinnes. *bliss* by Ben Bettenbender. November 17, 2002. Directed by Julia Gibson; with Johanna Day, Peter Jay Fernandez, Rob Sedgwick. *The Last Sunday in June* by Jonathan Tolins. February 9, 2003. Directed by Trip Cullman; with Arnie Burton, Matthew Wilkas, Johnathan F. McClain, Donald Corren, Mark Setlock, Peter Smith, Susan Pourfar, David Turner. Transferred to Off Broadway's Century Center for the Performing Arts (4/9/2003; 61 performances through 5/31/2003). See Plays Produced Off Broadway section. *Dear Prudence* by Susan Kathryn Hefti. March 27, 2003. Directed by Rosemary K. Andress; with Kristin Stewart Chase, Jerusha Klemperer, Lynn Antunovich, Natasha Piletich, Garth T. Mark, Jim Conroy.

THE RED ROOM. *Match* and *Beep* by Marc Chun. September 2, 2002. Directed by Steven Gridley; with Jessica Calvello, James Mack, Andres Munar, Erin Treadway, Stephen Douglas Wood.

SAMUEL BECKETT THEATRE. *Burning Blue* by D.M.W. Greer. October 16, 2002. Directed by John Hickok; with Jerome Preston Bates, P.J. Brown, Bill Dawes, Matthew Del Negro, Mike Doyle, Sherri Parker Lee, Chad Lowe, Susan Porro.

SANDE SHURIN THEATRE. STAR-CROSSED: A QUINTET OF FIVE SHORT PLAYS. October 11–18, 2002. *Singlish* by Sloan MacRae. *The Tree* by Eric J. Polsky. *Match* by John Cassel. *Salome Sings the Blues* by Sloan MacRae. *The Myth of Moon and Morning Star* by John Cassel. Directed by Stuart Carden and Julie Fei-Fan Balzer. *Jane's Exchange* and *North of Providence* by Edward Allan Baker. November 3, 2002. Directed by Russell Treyz; with Joe Capozzi, Amorika M. Armoroso, Julie Karlin, Tonya Cornelisse, Judy Del Guidice, Mark Belasco. UNRESOLVED: ONE-ACT PLAYS ON LOSS, GRIEF AND RECOVERY. November 21–December 15, 2002. *Ellipsis* by Steven Fechter. *Floating World* by Laren Stover. *Coda* by Romulus Linney. *Rosen's Son* by Joe Pintauro. *Bless Me,*

Father by Jeff Baron. *Cocooning* by R. David Robinson. Directed by Richard Mover; with Wendy Bilton, Ann Carr, Nathan Cline, Eric D'Entrone, Ann Farrar, Alice Gold, Michael J. Lombardi, Allan Mirchin, Mr. Mover, Patricia Randell, Mr. Robinson, Erik Sherr. *Much Ado About Nothing* by William Shakespeare. March 28, 2003. Directed by Jonathan Hadley; with Bill Weeden, Carolyn Younger, Amanda Bruton, Ben Cherry, Todd Faulkner, Sean Griffin, Bob Harbaum, Laura Johnston, Sean Kent, Kasey Mahaffy, Michael Menger, Joey Monacelli, Robyne Parrish, Alex Smith, PJ Sosko, Katrina Thomas.

78TH STREET LAB. *Inside a Bigger Box* by Trish Harnetiaux. January 10, 2003. Directed by Jude Domski; with Caroline Cromelin, Janaki, Nathan Guisinger, Melanie Rey. *Mark of Cain* by Morti Vizki; translated by Jens Svane Boutrup. February 7, 2003. Directed by Mr. Boutrup; with Vincent Sagona, Michael Evans Lopez, Sarah Gifford. *The Chinese Art of Placement* by Stanley Rutherford. March 3, 2003. Directed by Jessica Bauman; with T. Scott Cunningham.

SOURCEWORKS THEATRE. *A Queer Carol* by Joe Godfrey. December 2, 2002. Directed by Mark Cannistraro; with Dan Pintauro, Tim Cross, Kip Driver, Valerie Hill, Michael Lynch, Marc Moritz, Greg Parente, Cynthia Pierce, David Weincek.

STUDIO 42. *redbird* by Clay McLeod Chapman, March 20, 2003. Directed by Isaac Butler; with Hannah Bos, Abe Goldfarb, Bradford Louryk, Alexa Scott-Flaherty, Paul Thureen, Phoebe Ventouras. *Nothing of Origins* by Devon Berkshire, Jackie Kristel, Laura Roemer, Ashley Salmon-Wander and Tella Storey; adapted from Aeschylus. May 1, 2003. Directed by Kate Marks; with Mr. Berkshire, Ms. Kristel, Ms. Salmon-Wander, Ms. Storey.

STUDIO THEATRE. *Anna Christie* by Eugene O'Neill. September 15, 2002. Directed by Mary Catherine Burke; with Barry J. Hirsch, Ben Upham, Duncan Nutter, Craig Rising, Bill Dealy, Dale Fuller, Rebecca Hoodwin, Caroline Strong, William Peden.

SYNAPSE THEATRE. *Silence* by Moira Buffini. June 3, 2002. Directed by Ginevra Bull; with Matthew Maher, Abby Savage, Jessica Claire, Jessica Chandlee Smith, Chan Casey, Jens Martin Krummel. *The Phoenician Women* by Euripides; adapted by David Travis. November 13, 2002. Directed by Mr. Travis; with Michael Arnov, Aysan Çelik, Keith Davis, Will Davis, Curt Hostetter, Robert Kya-Hill, Sybil Lines, Chris Thorn.

THEATRE AT ST. PETER'S. *Modigliani* by Dennis McIntyre. September 22, 2002. Directed by Robert Castle; with William Abadie, Panos Makedonas, Jacob Battat, Amadeo Riva, Marcel Simoneau, Jack Michel-Bernard, Nandana Sen, Bruno Gelormini.

THEATRE 3. *Time and the Conways* by J.B. Priestley. June 13, 2002. Directed by Ron Russell; with Melissa Friedman, James Wallert, Lisa Rothe, Abigail López, Jenny Sterlin, Tom Butler, Craig Rovere, Nilaja Sun. *Only the End of the World* by Jean-Luc Lagarce; translated by Lucie Tiberghien. August 5, 2002. Directed by Ms. Tiberghien; with Michael Emerson, Jennifer Mudge, Stephen Belber, Sandra Shipley, Katie Firth. *The Flashing Stream* by Charles Morgan. April 17, 2003. Directed by Miranda d'Ancona; with Thomas Barbour, Michael Bastock, Glynis Bell, Cameron Francis, L.J. Ganser, Scott Glascock, Steve Groff, Davis Hall, Robert Sonderskov, Jennifer Dorr White. *Habitat* by Judith Thompson. May 22, 2003. Directed by Julia Gibson; with Melissa Friedman, Teri Lamm, Michael Reid, Craig Rovere, Rebecca Schull, James Wallert. *Little Eyolf* by Henrik Ibsen; adapted by Ron Russell. May 29, 2003. Directed by Mr. Russell; with Melissa Friedman, Teri Lamm, Michael Reid, Craig Rovere, Rebecca Schull, James Wallert.

13TH STREET REPERTORY THEATRE. *3 Weeks After Paradise* by Israel Horovitz. September 11, 2002. Directed by Stanley Harrison; with Mel England.

TIMES SQUARE THEATRE. *Blessing in Disguise* by Larry Pellegrini; music by Jason Howland. October 19, 2002. Directed by Mr. Pellegrini; with Patrick Quinn, Ken Prymus, Julio Augustin, Jeffrey Drew, James Grimaldi, Jacob Harran, Allen Hidalgo, Andrew Pang.

TOWN HALL. BRAVE NEW WORLD. September 9–11, 2002. Commemorating the first anniversary of the September 11, 2001, terrorist attacks.

SEPTEMBER 9, 2002: *The Other Line* by Alfred Uhry. Directed by Doug Hughes; with Dana Ivey. "A Song for LaChanze" by Lynn Ahrens and Stephen Flaherty. Sung by LaChanze, who lost her husband, financial trader Calvin Gooding, in the attacks. "Alive," a song by John Patrick Shanley and Daniel Harnett. Directed by John Gould Rubin; with Orfeh. *Nine Ten* by Warren

Leight. Directed by Randal Myler; with Christopher McCann, Jenny McGuire, Brennan Brown, Harriet Harris, Jenna Stern, Timothy McCracken. "I Am Strong in the Face of Everything Except Nuclear War," a poem by Eve Ensler. Read by Isabella Rossellini. Excerpt from *Return to the Upright Position* by Caridad Svich. "Cassandra Song," a song by Ellen McLaughlin; music by Peter Foley. Performed by Melissa Errico. *2001: An Oral History* by Lillian Ann Slugocki. Directed by Erica Gould; with Judith Hawking, Catherine Curtin, Brian Carter, Saidah Arrika Ekulona, Carolyn Baeumler, Steven Rattazzi. "Give Them Wings," an excerpt from *110 Stories* by Sarah Tuft. Directed by Barry Edelstein; with Elias Koteas. *Impact* by José Rivera. Directed by Barry Edelstein; with Kristin Davis, Jason Patric. *Land of the Dead* by Neil LaBute. Directed by Mr. LaBute; with Kristin Davis, Paul Rudd. *A Broken Head* by Andrew Solomon. Directed by Jack Wrangler; with Len Cariou. *Skylab* by Christopher Durang. Directed by Walter Bobbie; with Dana Ivey. *No One You Know* by Neal Bell. Directed by Mark Wing-Davey; with Peter Gallagher, Lorraine Bracco. *The Crazy Girl* by Frank Pugliese. Directed by Mr. Pugliese; with Jill Clayburgh, Lily Rabe. "There Will Be a Miracle," a song by Michael John LaChiusa. Performed by Donna Murphy. *Climate* by Joe Pintauro. Directed by Damian Gray; with Marsha Mason, Austin Pendleton, Peggy Lipton. *Terror Eyes* by OyamO. Directed by Marion McClinton; with Reg E. Cathey. *Adopt a Sailor* by Charles Evered. Directed by Craig Carlisle; with Bebe Neuwirth, Michael Nouri, Neil Patrick Harris. *Elevator* by Rinne Groff. Directed by Edward Stern. *A Prayer* by Terrence McNally. Performed by Frances Sternhagen. "And My Friend," a choral by David Simpatico and Will Todd.

SEPTEMBER 10, 2002: Excerpt from *Return to the Upright Position* by Caridad Svich. *First Day of School* by Lynn Nottage. Directed by Matthew Penn; with Kenajuan Bentley, Catherine Curtin, Judith Hawking, Elias Koteas, Timothy Britten Parker. *The Last One* by Ed Seebald. Performed by Alec Baldwin. "Nun Danket Alle Gott," song by Rinde Eckert. *Exodus* by J. Dakota Powell. Directed by Stephen Wisker; with Maya Gabrielle, Robert Neill, Laura Flanagan, Ninon Rogers, Christen Clifford, Kenajuan Bentley, Ivan Davila, Randy Ryan, Sarah Hayon. "September Morning," a poem by Kathryn Stern. Performed by Frances Sternhagen. *Black Alert in Sarajevo* by Ruth Margraff. Directed by Molly Smith. *Aunt Pitti-Pat in the Tower* by David Simpatico. Directed by Steven Williford; with Mario Cantone. *Throw* by Brian Silberman. Directed by James D. Stern; with Trudie Styler, Matt Servitto, David Bennett. "The Ballad of Mary O'Connor," a song by Greg Kotis and Mark Hollmann. Performed by Rich Krueger. *Passengers* by Betty Shamieh. Directed by Billy Hopkins; with Rosie Perez, Christen Clifford, Jenny Maguire, Sarah Hayon. *Second Skin* by Chay Yew. Directed by John Ruocco. *Haiti* by Keith Reddin, Directed by Mark Brokaw; with Amy Irving, Michael Potts, Boris McGiver. *7-11* by Kia Corthron. Directed by Michael John Garcés; with Rosie Perez, Kenajuan Bentley, Dariush Kashani. *Redesign* by Beth Henley. Performed by Holly Hunter, Elias Koteas, Bud Cort. "That's How I Say Goodbye," a song by Marvin Hamlisch and Craig Cornelia. Performed by Kelli O'Hara. *His Wife* by Romulus Linney. Directed by Penelope Cherns; with Jessica Hecht, Jason Patric, Boris McGiver. *After* by Nicole Burdette. Directed by Ms. Burdette; with Jason Patric. "Hands Holding Hands," a song by Gilles Chaisson and Chris Roberts. Performed by Idina Menzel. *Woman at a Threshold, Beckoning* by John Guare. Directed by Michael Wilson; with John Turturro. "Anthem," a song by John Patrick Shanley.

SEPTEMBER 11, 2002 (MATINEE): Excerpt from *Return to the Upright Position* by Caridad Svich. *The Moon Please* by Diana Son. Directed by Chris Smith; with Gloria Reuben, Frank Wood. *Stop All the Clocks* by Erin Cressida Wilson. Directed by Steve Lawson; with Joel Grey, Ann Reinking. *Exodus* by J. Dakota Powell. Directed by Stephen Wisker; with Maya Gabrielle, Robert Neill, Laura Flanagan, Ninon Rogers, Christen Clifford, Kenajuan Bentley, Ivan Davila, Randy Ryan, Sarah Hayon. "Give Them Wings," an excerpt from *110 Stories* by Sarah Tuft. Performed by Chita Rivera. *Impact* by José Rivera. Performed by Marisa Tomei, Jason Patric. *3 Weeks After Paradise* by Israel Horovitz. Performed by Mr. Horovitz. "I'm Still Here," a song by Stephen Sondheim. Performed by Polly Bergen. "Strong as a Lion, Soft as Silk," a poem by Tyler Wallach. Performed by Eli Wallach. *Adopt a Sailor* by Charles Evered. Directed by Stephen Wisker; with Eli Wallach, Anne Jackson, Craig Williams. *We Never Knew Their Names* by John Henry Redwood. Directed by Amy Saltz; with Brennan Brown, Gina Bardwell, Kate Rigg, James Ascher, James Martinez. *Woman at a Threshold, Beckoning* by John Guare. Directed by Michael Wilson; with John Turturro. *Antigone's Red* by Chiori Miyagawa. Directed by Mary B. Robinson; with performed by Christina Chang, Michi Barall, Brian Nishii, Andrew Garmen, George Sheffey. "Some Other Time," a song by Adolph Green and Leonard Bernstein. Performed by Phyllis Newman. *4/19(/95)* by John Pielmeier. Directed by Shepard Sobel. *The Marriott* by Jacquelyn Reingold. Directed by Michael Warren Powell; with

Michael Nouri, Louise Pitre. *Strange Fish* by Jaye Austin-Williams. Directed by Monika Gross; with Robert McKay, Mylika Davis, Sue Jin Song, Jeff Breckfield, Jeanine Carter, Craig Williams, Haythem Noor, Carl Vitali, Louis Menken. *The Grand Design* by Susan Miller. Directed by Cynthia Croot; with Marlo Thomas, Scott Cohen. "Coming Together," a song by Jason Robert Brown.

SEPTEMBER 11, 2002 (EVENING): Excerpt from *Return to the Upright Position* by Caridad Svich. *Ribbon in the Sky* by Jonathan Marc Sherman. Directed by Michael Wilson; with Ethan Hawke, Amanda Peet. *2001: An Oral History* by Lillian Ann Slugocki. Directed by Erica Gould; with Judith Hawking, Catherine Curtin, Brian Carter, Saidah Arrika Ekulona, Carolyn Baeumler, Steven Rattazzi. *Pops* by Edwin Sánchez. Directed by Dennis Smith; with Ivan Davila. *Lakeera* by Christopher Shinn. Directed by Mark Brokaw; with Armando Riesco. *Land of the Dead* by Neil LaBute. Directed by Mr. LaBute; with Kristin Davis, Liev Schreiber. "Last Year," a song by Michael John LaChiusa. *9-19* by Eric Mendelsohn. Performed by Edie Falco, Stanley Tucci. *The New Rules* by Laurence Klavan. Directed by Robert Knopf; with Erik Jensen, Danny Zorn. *Hands* by Erin Cressida Wilson. Directed by Nela Wagman; with Julianna Margulies. *Steve* by Bill Leavengood. Directed by Lawrence Sacharow; with Fisher Stevens, Dariush Kashani. *Thirty-Fourth and Dyer* by Lee Blessing. Directed by Nela Wagman; with Cynthia Nixon, Keith Nobbs. "Lullaby," music by Geoffrey Menin. Performed by Mr. Menin. *Woman at a Threshold, Beckoning* by John Guare. Directed by Michael Wilson; with John Turturro. *Anonymous Remailers* by Constance Congdon. "I Am Strong In the Face of Everything Except Nuclear War," a poem by Eve Ensler. Performed by Marlo Thomas. "Will the Sun Ever Shine Again?" a song by Alan Menken and Glenn Slater. Performed by Alan Menken. *Skylab* by Christopher Durang. Directed by Walter Bobbie; with Dana Ivey. *Special Price for You, Okay?* by Leah Ryan. Performed by Kate Rigg. *Adopt a Sailor* by Charles Evered. Performed by Liev Schreiber, Sam Waterston, Amy Irving. *Late Night, Early Morning* by Frank Pugliese. Directed by Mr. Pugliese; with Marisa Tomei, Scott Cohen. *Disorderly Conduct* by Tina Howe. Directed by George C. White; with Lorinne Towler, Ned Eisenberg, Kate Rigg, Blake Robbins, Mylika Davis, Charles Montgomery, Kalimi Baxter, Kenajuan Bentley, Ivan Davila, Rana KazKaz, Mather Zickel.

TRIBECA PLAYHOUSE. *Love's Labour's Lost* by William Shakespeare. March 20, 2003. Directed by Kit Thacker; with Katrin Macmillan, Sarah Megan Thomas, Joy Barrett, Amy Groeschel, Michael X. Izquierdo, George Burich, Jordan Dyck, Michael Craig Patterson, Natalie Gold, Vivia Font, Corey Tazmania Stieb, Jessica Chandlee Smith, Nicole Stewart, Matthew R. Wilson.

T. SCHREIBER STUDIO. *The Woman From the Sea* by Spence Porter. February 1, 2003. Directed by Terry Schreiber; with Pete Byrne, Sterling Coyne, Margaret Dawson, A.J. Handegard, Debbie Jaffe, Fred Rueck, Tatjana Vujosevic, David Winton.

29TH STREET REP. *High Priest of California* by Charles Willeford. February 19, 2003. Directed by Leo Farley; with Tim Corcoran, Paula Ewin, Jerry Lewkowitz, David Mogentale, Carol Sirugo, James E. Smith.

URBAN STAGES. *Midwestern Chum* by Sarah Bewley with Cathleen Miller. August 5, 2002. Directed by T.L. Reilly; with Vanessa Quijas, Sam Guncler, Cherene Snow, Maria Cellario, Gabor Morea. *Roses in December* by Victor L. Cahn. February 25, 2003. Directed by T.L. Reilly; with Keira Naughton, Victor Slezak.

THE VILLAGE THEATRE. *Dream a Little Dream* by Denny Doherty and Paul Ledoux. April 23, 2003. Directed by Randal Myler; with Mr. Doherty, Richard Burke, Angela Gaylor, Doris Mason.

WESTSIDE THEATRE DOWNSTAIRS. *Trumbo* by Christopher Trumbo. March 31, 2003. Directed by Peter Askin; with Mr. Trumbo.

WHITE BIRD PRODUCTIONS. BORO TALES: BROOKLYN. March 8–23, 2003. *Twelve Brothers* by Jeffrey M. Jones and Camila Jones. Directed by Page Burkholder. *The Little Matchgirl* by Lynn Nottage. Directed by Miriam Weiner. *Snow White* by Onome Ekeh. Directed by Page Burkholder. *Lucky Hans* by Marjorie Duffield. Directed by Jean Wagner. *The Dancing Princesses* by Creative Theatrics' Performance Team and Marjorie Duffield. Directed by Welker White. With Amie Bermowitz, April Mathis, Robert Hatcher, Joseph Jamrog, C. Andrew Bauer, Corinne Edgerly, Kathryn Velvel.

THE WORKSHOP THEATER COMPANY. *From the Top* by Scott C. Sickles. January 31, 2003. Directed by Max Montel; with Christopher Burke, Rob Cameron, Lori Faiella, Roger Dale Stude, Stephen

Zinnato. *Iphigenia* by P. Seth Bauer, based on Euripides. March 21, 2003. Directed by Elysa Marden; with Shamika Cotton, Carrie Edel, Katherine Freedman, Mark Hofmaier, Brian Homer, Marinell Madden, Greg Skura, Pauline Tully. *Last Stand* by Timothy Scott Harris. May 7, 2003. Directed by Mr. Harris; with Shoshana Ami, Christopher Burke, Dee Dee Friedman, Allan Knee, Gerrianne Raphael, GW Reed, Bill Tatum. SUBWAY SERIES. May 28–31, 2003. *The Subway* by Craig Pospisil. Directed by Keith Teller. *Quick and Dirty (A Subway Fantasy)* by David Reidy. Directed by Greg Skura. *The Local* by Michael Rhodes. Directed by Darleen Jaeger. *Silent Piece* by P. Seth Bauer and Michael Rhodes. *The Attractive Women on the Train* by P. Seth Bauer. Directed by Keith Teller. *Down in the Depths* by Michael Rhodes. Directed by Keith Teller; with Sophie Acadine, Barbara Helms, Mark Hofmaier, Lois Markle, Paul Molnar, Mr. Rhodes, Mr. Skura, Jill Van Note, Hilary Ward.

WORTH STREET THEATER COMPANY. *As You Like It* by William Shakespeare. July 23, 2002. Directed by Jeff Cohen; with Dan Ahearn, Sally Wheeler, Virginia Williams, Dwight Ewell, Devin Haqq, Keith Davis, David Brown Jr., Ron Simons, James Martinez, Matt Conley, Liza Lapira. *The Mystery of Attraction* by Marlane Meyer. January 12, 2003. Directed by Jeff Cohen; with Dan Ahearn, Richard Bekins, Kendra Leigh Landon, Barry Del Sherman, Jefferson Slinkard, Deirdre O'Connell.

ZIPPER THEATER. *Elle* by Jean Genet; adapted by Alan Cumming; translation by Terri Gordon. July 24, 2002. Directed by Nick Philippou; with Stephen Spinella, Anson Mount, Chad L. Coleman, Mr. Cumming, Brian Duguay.

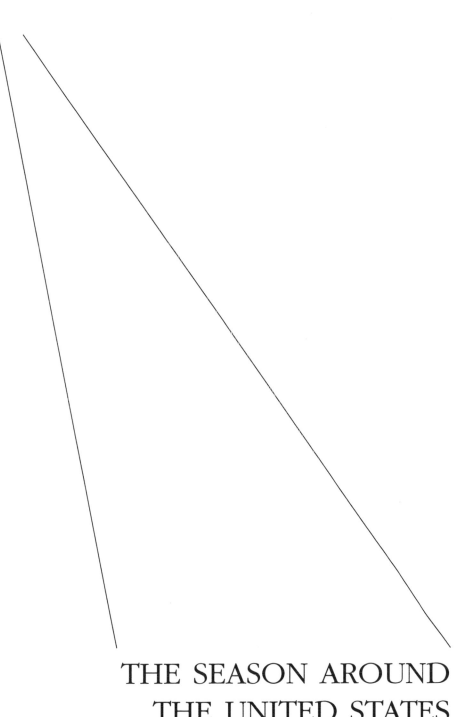

THE SEASON AROUND
THE UNITED STATES

AMERICAN THEATRE CRITICS/STEINBERG
NEW PLAY AWARD AND CITATIONS
○ ○ ○ ○ ○
A DIRECTORY OF NEW
UNITED STATES PRODUCTIONS

THE AMERICAN THEATRE CRITICS ASSOCIATION (ATCA) is the organization of drama critics in all media throughout the United States. One of the group's stated purposes is "To increase public awareness of the theater as a national resource." To this end, ATCA has annually cited outstanding new plays produced around the US, which were excerpted in our series beginning with the 1976–77 volume. As we continue our policy of celebrating playwrights and playwriting in *Best Plays* essays, we offer essays on the recipients of the 2003 American Theatre Critics/Steinberg New Play Award and Citations. The ATCA/Steinberg New Play Award of $15,000 was awarded to Nilo Cruz for his play *Anna in the Tropics*—which also won the Pulitzer Prize a few days later. ATCA/Steinberg New Play Citations were given to Craig Wright for *Recent Tragic Events* and to Arthur Miller for *Resurrection Blues*. Citation honorees receive prizes of $5,000 each.

The ATCA awards are funded by the Harold and Mimi Steinberg Charitable Trust, which supports theater throughout the United States with its charitable giving. The ATCA/Steinberg New Play Award and Citations are given in a ceremony at Actors Theatre of Louisville. Essays in the next section—by Christine Dolen (*Miami Herald*), Alec Harvey (*Birmingham News*) and Claudia W. Harris (*Back Stage*, regional)—celebrate the ATCA/Steinberg honorees.

ATCA's tenth annual M. Elizabeth Osborn Award for a new playwright was voted to John Walch for *The Dinosaur Within*, produced by the State Theatre in Austin, Texas. Mr. Walch received his award during a March luncheon at Sardi's in New York City.

Of the new scripts nominated by ATCA members for the ATCA/Steinberg prizes, six were selected as finalists by the 2001 ATCA

New Plays Committee before making their final citations. Other finalists included: *Across the Way* by Jeff Daniels, produced by Purple Rose Theatre in Chelsea, Michigan; *The Dinosaur Within* by John Walch, produced by the State Theatre in Austin, Texas; and *Good Boys* by Jane Martin, produced at the Guthrie Lab in Minneapolis.

The process of selecting these outstanding plays is as follows: any American Theatre Critics Association member may nominate the first full professional production of a finished play (not a reading or an airing as a play-in-progress) during the calendar year under consideration. Nominated 2002 scripts were studied and discussed by the New Plays Committee chaired by Alec Harvey (*Birmingham News*), Misha Berson (*Seattle Times*) Jackie Demaline (*Cincinnati Enquirer*), Marianne Evett (Cleveland *Plain Dealer*, retired), Bill Gale (Theatre New England) Barbara Gross (freelance, *Washington Post*), Claudia W. Harris (freelance, *Back Stage*), Elizabeth Maupin (*Orlando Sentinel*), Nancy Melich (*Salt Lake Tribune*, retired), Kevin Nance (*The Tennessean*) and Herb Simpson (Rochester *City Newspaper*). These committee members made their choices on the basis of script rather than production. If the timing of nominations and openings prevents some works from being considered in any given year, they may be eligible for consideration the following year if they haven't since moved to New York City.

2003 ATCA/Steinberg New Play Award

ANNA IN THE TROPICS
By Nilo Cruz

○ ○ ○ ○ ○

Essay by Christine Dolen

JUAN JULIAN: [H]ow does one hide behind light?

MARELA: Depends on what you are hiding from.

JUAN JULIAN: Perhaps light itself.

MARELA: Well, there are many kinds of light. The light of fires. The light of stars. The light that reflects off rivers. Light that penetrates through cracks. Then there's the type of light that reflects off the skin. Which one?

JUAN JULIAN: Perhaps the type that reflects off the skin.

MARELA: That's the most difficult one to escape.

EVOCATIVE IMAGERY, BOLD sensuality and smoldering jealousy, all wrapped around a literary classic and a tradition that no longer exists: In *Anna in the Tropics*, Cuban-American playwright Nilo Cruz brings to fruition both the craft he has honed through seven earlier plays and his reputation as a poet of the theater. The gorgeous result, commissioned by the tiny New Theatre of Coral Gables near Cruz's adopted hometown of Miami, won the 2003 ATCA/Steinberg New Play Award and, two days later, the Pulitzer Prize for drama.

When Cruz and New Theatre received a National Endowment for the Arts/Theatre Communications Group Theatre Residency Program for Playwrights grant to support the creation of a new work, the playwright knew only that he wanted to write a piece about the Cuban tobacco workers who settled in Ybor City, a town that blossomed northeast of Tampa, Florida, near the end of the 19th century—his working title, in fact, was *Tobacco Flower (Ybor City)*.

He wanted to bring to life the world of immigrants who had brought with them from Cuba both hopes and traditions—betting on cock fights, casting romantic spells, enduring long days of tedium and enervating heat to create the perfect hand-rolled cigar. And one more now-vanished tradition:

Literary lover: David Perez Ribada and Edna Schwab
in Anna in the Tropics. *Photo: Eileen Suarez*

the *lector*, or reader, who would keep the workers informed and entertained by reading newspapers and novels aloud, enlightening them as they worked.

Because he didn't want to get sidetracked into the politics of early Ybor City—José Martí visited there to find money and men to liberate Cuba from Spain before his death in 1895—Cruz set *Anna in the Tropics* in 1929. The timing itself is poignant: Just before the Great Depression, mechanization was coming to the cigar factories. The machines meant fewer workers, and the machines' noise meant the end of the *lector*, who could no longer be heard above the din.

And once he decided that the book his *lector* would be reading would be Leo Tolstoy's *Anna Karenina*, the tragic masterpiece whose love triangle is reflected in *Anna in the Tropics*, Cruz had his play.

HIS CHARACTERS ARE nearly all members of the same extended family. Santiago is the cigar factory's owner, a man in his late 50s who has a tendency to drink too much and finds himself in the grip of a debilitating depression. His wife Ofelia is his opposite, an energetic woman who sees to it that things get done, even if it means neglecting to tell Santiago that she took money from the factory's safe to bring the new *lector*, Juan Julian, from Cuba.

The couple's elder daughter, Conchita, is married to a fellow worker, Palomo, who has wounded her by having an affair. Conchita's 22-year-old sister Marela is a decade younger, still really a girl given to crushes and dreams—to measure her dreams, she tells her mother, she will need "a very long yardstick. The kind that could measure the sky."

Cheché, Santiago's half-brother, helps run the cigar factory. A later-in-life addition to the family—the result of a union between Santiago's father and an American woman—Cheché is an ambitious and bitter man, the latter because his American wife ran off with a previous *lector*.

Cruz, like August Wilson, writes in a singular dramatic language of his own invention. The words are in English, but the rhythms flow from Spanish as spoken by Cubans. His language is almost tactile, clearly poetic, full of imagery, as when one character speaks of the universality of dreaming:

> MARELA: A bicycle dreams of becoming a boy, an umbrella dreams
> of becoming the rain, a pearl dreams of becoming a woman, and a
> chair dreams of becoming a gazelle and running back to the forest.

Magical realism is clearly one of Cruz's influences, and although plays about Cubans can hardly ignore the political, Cruz focuses on people, their difficulties and their dreams.

ANNA IN THE TROPICS begins with crosscutting scenes, introducing the personalities of the characters as the men wager on a cockfight while the women wait at the seaport for their new *lector* to arrive from Cuba.

Dapperly dressed in long-sleeved, white linen *guayabera* shirts, white slacks and two-toned shoes, Santiago and Cheché drink and wager on the fighting birds. Santiago is losing, getting drunker, anxious to turn his luck around. He asks Cheché for a loan. Cheché hesitates, then relents after Santiago (who can't find a slip of paper) carves his IOU on the sole of his brother's shoe. And still he drinks, loses and asks for more money.

Cheché balks, believing his brother is jinxed, but Santiago changes his mind with a sentence: "If I don't pay you, part of the factory is yours." Cheché bites, then walks home with just one shoe on because "this here is our contract, and I don't want it erased." In the first scene, his covetous, entrepreneurial, self-serving nature is already established—though a bit later, when he shows his "promissory shoe" to Ofelia, she scoffs at his cheek and her husband's foolishness.

Dressed in their best, the family's women clutch white handkerchiefs and gaze at a photograph of Juan Julian, called the "Persian Canary" for his way of transporting the workers to other places. Marela is already half in love with him, a connection enhanced in a post-premiere revision of *Anna in the Tropics*. She confesses to Ofelia that she took a palm reader's advice and put a slip of paper with Juan Julian's name in a glass of water with brown sugar and cinnamon—a spell to summon him.

Conchita warns her sister of the dire consequences of trying to influence fate, recalling a woman who went mad after putting a spell on her lover, who then died. The passage begins to evoke some of the imagery Cruz will use throughout the play—water and tears, as well as sensuality and smoke:

> CONCHITA: They say she couldn't stop crying after her lover's death. That her whole face became an ocean of tears, and the father had to take her back to Cuba, to see if she would get better. But a fever would possess the girl at night. They say she'd run to the sea naked. She'd run there to meet the dead lover.

At the factory, the women explain who's who to Juan Julian, who has already picked up on Cheché's negative attitude toward him. Marela vividly supplies the historical context, about her uncle's wife:

> MARELA: [. . .] She disappeared one day with the lector that was working here. She was a Southern belle from Atlanta and he was from Guanabacoa. Her skin was pale like a lily, and he was the color of saffron. And of course, now Cheché is against all lectors and the love stories they read.

JUAN JULIAN IS soon giving a passionate book his own impassioned reading. He knows how to ride the rhythms of Tolstoy's prose—the *Anna Karenina* passages Cruz uses in the play are woven by the playwright from different translations of the novel—and he knows just where and when to stop each day, leaving the women hungry for more. Though the illicit affair inflames their imaginations, the choice of book and setting works as a kind of aural air-conditioning.

> MARELA: [. . .] I have dreams and they are full of white snow, and Anna Karenina is dancing waltzes with Vronsky. Then I see them in a little room, and all the snow melts from the heat of their bodies and their skin. [. . .]

Alone with her husband in the factory after hours, Conchita presses Palomo to dig beneath the banalities and confront their reality: his infidelity. He dodges her probing, and finally Conchita—who still loves Palomo—says she will take a lover of her own.

Then relationships are repaired, thwarted, begun. Marela plays intermediary in an angry-funny "conversation" between her parents, who aren't officially speaking due to Santiago's gambling debacle. But once their daughter walks out, Ofelia and Santiago *really* talk, drifting from the trivial (discussing the details of *Anna Karenina*, remarking on how much they like Juan Julian's reading) to the critical matter of Santiago's inertia and despair.

Later, Cheché and Marela are by themselves in the factory. Cheché chides his niece for sloppy work, for getting lost in the world of *Anna Karenina*—and in the possibility of the *lector*. He confesses his own desire for her, but Marela haughtily rejects him. Cheché thinks he is losing another woman to a *lector*, which foreshadows the play's ending. But it is Conchita, not dreamy Marela, who soon gives herself to Juan Julian.

THE SECOND ACT begins with the lovers atop a table in the factory, Conchita half-naked as she and Juan Julian finish making passionate, transporting love. They wish for a kind of togetherness that cannot be, hiding their affair from everyone except Palomo—who demands details that Conchita either doles out or withholds. Her lover, she says, tells her:

> CONCHITA: That I taste sweet and mysterious like the water hidden
> inside fruits and that our love will be white and pure like tobacco

Tempestuous triangle: Deborah L. Sherman and Carlos Orizondo with David Perez Rihada (reading) in Anna in the Tropics. *Photo: Eileen Suarez*

flowers. And it will grow at night, the same way that tobacco plants grow at night.

She describes their role-playing as they make love. And then, as Juan Julian reads a passage from *Anna Karenina*, Conchita and Palomo find a new way to surrender to each other.

Cheché begins trying to assert himself in every way. Bringing a rolling machine into the factory, he is the American man, the one drawn to the efficiency and cost-cutting that machines could bring—to modernity. As the others complain and grow anxious, Cheché rails against being forced to give a portion of his pay to hear a *lector* read from a romantic novel he doesn't care to hear.

Juan Julian speaks up for tradition, history and the value of listening; for the ritual and pace of smoking a fine cigar: "The truth is that machines, cars, are keeping us from taking walks and sitting on park benches, smoking a cigar slowly and calmly [. . .] you want modernity, and modernity is actually destroying our very own industry."

The workers applaud, their enthusiasm a slap to Cheché, whose reasons to loathe Juan Julian deepen. After Santiago appears, he calls for a show of hands, and everyone except Palomo and Cheché votes to keep their Persian Canary.

THE HURTLING END of the play begins when Santiago announces that he has decided to launch a new, more expensive cigar called the Anna Karenina, and that he wants Marela to dress as Anna to pose for the label.

Cheché tells Santiago about life since his wife abandoned him:

> CHECHÉ: [. . .] Have you ever seen the tail of a lizard when it's been cut off? The tail twists and moves from side to side like a worm that's been removed from the soil. The thing moves on its own, like a nerve that still has life, and it's looking for the rest of the body that's been slashed away. That's how I feel sometimes. [. . .]

As Cheché speaks, Marela appears, dressed in a white fur coat and hat. Her father leaves to fetch a flower for her hair, and to continue trying to reason with Cheché. Juan Julian enters, looking for his book, compliments her on how good she looks, then leaves. Alone, a wistful Marela says, "I wish you would take a picture of me with your eyes."

And then Cheché destroys almost everything, himself included. As Juan Julian sits alone reading a passage about Anna Karenina and her fear as she rides the train with her angry husband, Cheché follows Marela through a doorway. The sound of a storm and the moving train build, Juan Julian raising his voice as they do. Offstage, as the sounds collide and the lights darken, Cheché is attacking Marela.

Later, at a party to celebrate the new cigar, everyone is getting drunk on rum. Palomo confides his own misery to Cheché: "I can smell him on her skin, her clothes and her handkerchief. I can see him on her face and her eyes." The men ask Juan Julian why Anna's husband doesn't just *shoot* her lover. Then Palomo has a "literary" conversation with the *lector* that is really all about their own situation.

Once everyone except Marela has arrived, Santiago asks Ofelia to light the first Anna Karenina, to begin the ritual of passing it to each person, who weighs in as though describing a wine's bouquet, color and complex taste.

Ofelia says it "burns like a blue dream." Santiago declares that it burns "quietly and mysteriously like embers." To Conchita, it "speaks of forests and orchids." Palomo tastes aged rum and the sweetness of mangoes. And to Juan Julian, it "sighs like a sunset and it has a little bit of cocoa beans and cedar."

Santiago goes to fetch the missing Marela. He exudes a cold fury when he returns and says to Cheché, "Get out and never come back, or I will kill you if you don't." The party, in every sense, is over.

As Cheché is packing, Conchita is describing to Palomo what she and Juan Julian do when they make love. Her husband confesses his pain, wishing for this awful new chapter of his life to end. Haunted, Marela enters, still wearing her warm fur coat, explaining to her sister that she wants to be "layered and still."

Then it ends. As Juan Julian reads a passage about Anna's husband and his fantasies about murdering his rival, Cheché appears. He aims and hesitates. Aims again and shoots. A man dies, and with him a tradition.

CRUZ OFFERS A redemptive coda, one enhanced in his rewrites after *Anna in the Tropics* had its first production: Mourning the silence after Juan Julian's death, Ofelia wonders if someone could read. Palomo picks up *Anna Karenina,* picks it up where Juan Julian left off. And his words, words of determination and reconciliation, are offered to his wife, always there but lost, now found again.

For several decades, playwrights such as Cruz, José Rivera, María Irene Fornes, Eduardo Machado, Edwin Sánchez and so many others have dramatized the experience of being Latino/a and American. As the country's Hispanic population has grown, so too has the audience for these plays, and the understanding of their universality. Nilo Cruz, wedding a story of a lost time in the tropics to a tragic masterpiece covered in Russian snow, shows us how passion and poetry can touch us all.

2003 ATCA/Steinberg New Play Citation

RECENT TRAGIC EVENTS

By Craig Wright

○ ○ ○ ○ ○

Essay by Alec Harvey

WAVERLY: I used to wake up every morning and think "what am I gonna *do?*" Today I woke up and thought, "What's going to *happen* to me?"

AFTER THE BLEAK events of September 11, 2001, playwrights responded in many different ways. Some ignored it, trying to continue with business as usual. Others used their horror and grief to instruct their writing, perhaps creating darker and more thought-provoking work than they had before. Still others—Anne Nelson's *The Guys* comes to mind—wrote work that directly addressed the tragedy.

Few, though, wrote about the terrorism attacks with the disarming mix of comedy and drama that Craig Wright employs in *Recent Tragic Events*, which premiered August 19, 2002, at Woolly Mammoth Theatre Company in Washington, DC.

That Wright could find humor in one of our country's darkest days is hardly surprising to those familiar with his work. The Minneapolis playwright spent 2003 in Los Angeles as story editor for HBO's brilliantly morbid *Six Feet Under*, a television triumph that juxtaposes death, grief and laughs as though they were meant to be together.

Without September 11 in the picture, *Recent Tragic Events* could have been just another situation comedy, and there are times when it comes across as slight and gimmicky: 30-something advertising executive Waverly Wilson meets shy Andrew on a blind date that culminates in a drinking game filled with inebriated pontificating from the couple, her musician neighbor, Ron, his married girlfriend, Nancy, and Waverly's beer-loving great aunt, the author Joyce Carol Oates, a character who in appearance is merely a sight gag but whose dialogue offers much of the meat of Wright's piece.

BUT SEPTEMBER 11 is very much in the picture here, as Waverly and Andrew's date takes place on September 12, 2001. With "Attack on America"

Speed read: Eric Sutton, Holly Twyford and Dori Legg in Recent Tragic Events. *Photo: Stan Barouh*

ever-present on the television, *Recent Tragic Events* becomes a thought-provoking, heartbreaking and, yes, often hysterical look at fate vs. chance and whether we make our own choices in life or they are pre-determined.

Wright begins his play in *Our Town* fashion with the Stage Manager delivering a brief monologue, explaining to the audience that a flip of a coin will determine what actions characters will take during the course of the play. A tone will sound at specific moments in the play, and depending on whether the coin toss comes up heads or tails, he explains, the characters will follow certain paths.

> STAGE MANAGER: You in the audience will know that those particular moments could potentially have occurred differently, or been omitted altogether, with other moments in their place.

Already, the playwright has us wondering if this coin toss will indeed affect the outcome of the play's plot. Only he knows for sure, since the actors continue as if they didn't hear the tone onstage.

The first tone occurs moments into the play, as Andrew first sees Waverly when he enters her Minneapolis apartment. The true import of his surprised reaction will become clear only at the end of the first act. Right now, he's concerned only with trying to make the best of a blind date taking place on perhaps the worst night ever in the history of blind dates.

As with most first dates, Waverly and Andrew engage in awkward small talk. The events of the past 24 hours only make it that much more awkward, and all conversations, as they did across the country in the days and weeks following September 11, tend to lead back to the attacks. Waverly, for instance, is shocked to find out that Andrew knows of no connection he has to anyone in the World Trade Center or on the airplanes, allowing the playwright to break the ice with one of many jokes that will spring out of his characters' nervousness:

> WAVERLY: What are the odds of that, I wonder. Not knowing *anybody?*
> I mean, this must be a really hard day for Kevin Bacon.

Waverly, it turns out, has been trying to reach her twin sister, Wendy, who lives in New York and hasn't been heard from since the attacks. Concern is minimal, since there's no reason she should be near the Trade Center, but it's been nearly a day without a word, and Waverly is becoming increasingly agitated.

Eventually, Waverly's neighbor Ron arrives, as does his girlfriend, the silent but memorable Nancy. Amid Ron's meandering philosophizing and Waverly's unanswered phone calls to reach her sister or mother, the conversation turns to Andrew, a bookstore manager and aficionado of the work of Joyce Carol Oates. In one of the play's many twists of fate, Oates turns out to be Waverly's great aunt and—because of travel problems associated with September 11—she is stuck in Minneapolis. After she calls to say she's on her way to Waverly's apartment, Andrew tries to leave, but Waverly will have none of it.

> WAVERLY: No, it's total fate that you're here! Don't you realize how screwed I'd be if you weren't here. I've never read a single one of those books.

The words fate and choice come up frequently in *Recent Tragic Events*, whether referring to the actual recent tragic events or to the characters onstage. That Andrew happens to be in Waverly's apartment at that particular moment allows him, in one of the play's funniest scenes, to give her a faster-than-Cliffs Notes version of each of Oates's books so that she'll have a passing knowledge of them when her great aunt arrives.

All the while, Wright bounces from the trivial to the life-changing. Eventually, Waverly gets through to Wendy's machine and leaves a message, only to get more upset that she hasn't reached her sister. Ron consoles her, reminding her that Wendy doesn't work in the World Trade Center. And then comes the bombshell from Andrew: "She might."

Two weeks before, he had been in New York and bumped into a girl he now knew was Wendy. She told him that she was a year away from graduating from the Fashion Institute of Technology but had been offered a broadcasting job in the World Trade Center. Again, central to Wright's mission is raising the question of whether Andrew bumped into Wendy simply by chance, or whether he was a cog in an ever-turning, predetermined wheel.

An increasingly frantic Waverly tries to reach her mother as Andrew apologizes for not telling her earlier, and she decides it's best to end the date. But then, as if by fate, Joyce Carol Oates knocks on the door, and Waverly realizes she needs Andrew to be with her.

"OK," she says as the lights fade on Act I. "Everybody try and be normal."

ANY SENSE OF normalcy flies out the window at the beginning of the second act, when the Stage Manager reappears, explaining that nothing previously was an act of chance and that "everything that occurred onstage only happened because that was the only way it ever could have happened." Just when Wright gets a tad too existential on us, he turns back to the frivolous:

> STAGE MANAGER: Just so nobody gets the idea that the "Joyce Carol Oates" portrayed in this play is supposed to be *the* Joyce Carol Oates, the part is going to be played by a sock puppet operated by the actress playing "Nancy."

Sure enough, moments later the group—Andrew, Waverly, Ron, Nancy and, on Nancy's hand, a sock puppet named Joyce Carol Oates—is gathered around Waverly's table playing a drinking game. Waverly's mother calls, confirming that Wendy had taken an internship at WNJY at the World Trade Center but that there was no record of her being there on September 11. Waverly continues to play the game and tries to assure the others, but mainly herself, that everything will be fine. But no one, least of all Waverly, truly believes that, and the game continues, with the conversation taking a decidedly darker turn and tacking the free-will question head on, both in the real world and onstage:

> ANDREW: When I woke up yesterday morning and turned on my computer and saw that picture on AOL, with the planes inside the burning buildings, I don't know why, but all I could think was, "Of course." [. . .] Of course I went to school with Gerald Ittner, right? [. . .] And of course Waverly knows him, too, and of course we have *both* managed to stay friends with him even though he has this

English accent thing which *no one* else can bear [. . .] and of course I went to New York and met Wendy because of course *another* friend had to change his life and teach music after being a stockbroker, *he* had no choice, he was doomed by his own integrity to do that, and now of course I show up tonight, and of course she reads Trollope and is the most perfect girl I've ever met [. . .] I'm saying, I don't know where the chances stop and the choices start anymore!

The game continues, with Waverly eventually realizing she's dealt a Jack, followed by a Queen, followed by a King, an ace, a two, a three, a four, astounded at the pattern the cards are following. And Joyce Carol Oates explains how emotional the man next to her on her flight became when it was announced that their flight, bound for New York, would land in Minneapolis instead:

JOYCE: That's how he felt on *that* plane, and all we were doing was landing in a different city. Imagine how the people must have felt on *those* planes, or in those buildings in those last moments when they saw the planes coming. That's what's terrible. Not that they died; because everybody dies. The terrible part is knowing that it's coming for such an awful reason and you can't do anything to stop it.

That this speech is coming from a character that's actually a sock puppet is *Recent Tragic Events* in a nutshell—absurd, almost slapstick comedy mixed with heartbreaking reality.

Literary linen: "Joyce Carol Oates," Dori Legg and Michael Ray Escamilla in Recent Tragic Events. *Photo: Stan Barouh*

Joyce, Ron and Nancy depart soon after, leaving Waverly and Andrew alone and awkward. A long silence—two or three minutes, according to the script—follows as the two begin cleaning up after the party. The television becomes more audible, still broadcasting news of September 11. The small talk begins again, until Andrew drops another bombshell: He not only met Wendy in New York, but he told her, a complete stranger, that she should take a new job she had been offered at the World Trade Center.

> WAVERLY: You shouldn't have told her what to do, Andrew! You should have told her to call her sister or her mother, or someone who actually cared! [. . .] You shouldn't have said anything! Never say or do anything, ever! It just makes other things happen!

RON HAS RETURNED to Waverly's apartment when, during the final moments of the play, the Stage Manager sits and begins calling cues, as if he's dictating each action that's taking place. Eventually, the phone rings and Waverly answers it off stage. She bursts into tears and Andrew goes into her bedroom to console her.

> STAGE MANAGER: Lights 79.6; go. Sound 125; go. Lights 79.8; go. Time passes. With an air of cosmic disgust, Ron picks up the remote and turns off the TV. Blackout.

Ron remains on stage, and a couple of minutes pass. Then he does exactly as the Stage Manager has directed and the stage fades to black.

That we don't know whether Wendy lived or died is beside the point. Wright has entertainingly forced us to explore many other questions of fate, chance and choice that will linger long after we've seen *Recent Tragic Events*.

2003 ATCA/Steinberg New Play Citation

RESURRECTION BLUES

By Arthur Miller

○ ○ ○ ○ ○

Essay by Claudia W. Harris

> HENRI: The imagination is a great hall where death [. . .] turns into a painting, and a scream of pain becomes a song. The hall of the imagination is really where we usually live; and this is all right except for one thing —to enter that hall one must leave one's real sorrow at the door and in its stead surround oneself with images and words and music that mimic anguish but is really drained of it—no one has ever lost a leg from reading about a battle or died of hearing the saddest song.

LIGHTS COME UP on an idyllic expanse of blue surrounding a bare thrust stage. Silence. More silence. Gradually the sound of flapping wings comes ever closer until a deafening helicopter seems to hover above the theatre. Suddenly, a man hurtles awkwardly across this huge cloud-dappled sky and crashes onto the hard, black surface. Silence. Lights out.

This shocking fall from grace signals the "blues" in Arthur Miller's *Resurrection Blues*, his latest take on contemporary society. As the lights come back up, the corpse is gone and a uniformed character rises magically from an opening in the center of the Guthrie Theater's stage.

The play is set in an unnamed but, no doubt, South American country ruled by a US-backed military junta headed by General Felix Barriaux. But one of Miller's satiric twists is that Felix who rises regally erect into his office from beneath the stage is obsessed with both his actual and symbolic impotence.

As in all of Miller's work, these stunning visual elements are still a distant second to his challenging ideas. He exposes the cynicism of characters who have lost hope in any higher purpose. This biting political satire questions the present world and finds it both alarming and absurd. Miller is singing the blues—loudly—and like a true blues singer, he feels every bit of the hurt. He focuses his clear eye on a world driven by self-interest and devoid of ethics, on a world where real pain and loss have given way to

Where's Messiah? Laila Robins, David Chandler and Jeff Weiss in Resurrection Blues.
Photo: Carol Rosegg

mimicked anguish, and, finally, on an outrageous world of reality television obsessed by the commercial possibilities of broadcasting a crucifixion.

IN THE FIRST scene, Felix is visited by his expatriate cousin, Henri Schultz, who has left the day-to-day running of his inherited pharmaceutical empire and now lives in Munich "lecturing on tragedy." Despite their reminiscences, these cousins share no common ground. Henri confronts Felix over his failure to control the growing pollution and rampant poverty, but Felix counters with "it always amazes me how you gave up everything to just read books and think." Their dialogue shows Miller at his best. From the disintegration of 250-year-old French paintings to dead babies lying in the gutter, each pointed detail is subtly orchestrated into a believable but appalling exchange.

Henri has taken his new wife into the picturesque mountains where they both were struck by a "spiritual phenomenon"; wherever they went, peasants maintained lighted candles before a photograph of a young man whom they refer to as the Messiah. The youth calls himself Ralph or Jack, Vladimir or Francisco, Herby or Charley, apparently changing his name at will, another of Miller's nice twists. After all, why would God's name matter? Felix says he has captured Ralph and "he is history." When Henri protests that Ralph has had no part in the violence and asks about the rumor that he plans "to crucify this fellow," Felix first cagily replies no comment and then rages that he cannot simply shoot him because television has rendered the effect meaningless: "But nail up a couple of these bastards, and believe me this will be the quietest country on the continent and ready for development!"

Henri is the playwright's alter-ego. Miller may have given Henri the earnest speeches, but Felix, the alter-id, has the best lines. To Henri's protest that Ralph is simply preaching justice, comes the reply:

> FELIX: Oh come off it, Henri! Two percent of our people—including you—own 96 percent of the land. The justice they're demanding is your land; are you ready to give it to them? [. . .] No, Henri, it's your common sense telling you that in ten years the land you gave away will end up back in the hands of two percent of the smartest people! You can't teach gorillas to play Chopin.

Despite Henri's obvious angst, his purpose this morning was to bring Felix a distasteful business offer; he has received a letter from the Madison Avenue agency which handles his business. They are offering $25 million for the exclusive rights to televise the crucifixion, complete with commercials every few minutes: "Is there a hole in the human anatomy they don't make a dollar on?" They have calculated their offer based on how many commercials are possible in the five to six hours it would take to die on the cross. When Henri pleads with him not to accept the offer because he will be viewed as a Pontius Pilate or Judas, Felix sneers that Ralph is not even Jewish.

THE OVERWHELMING ABSURDITY but frightening plausibility of such an immodest proposal could lead to the dismissal of *Resurrection Blues* as a one-joke play. Yes, they do propose positioning the cross for the greatest effect—best background and lighting, right height for camera angles. And one of the play's more amusing details is the crew's attention to historical accuracy, referring to paintings of Christ's crucifixion, for example. Nevertheless, Miller uses this aspect of the plot not as the central theme but as a way to confront his audiences. That confrontation is mirrored on stage as his characters struggle over issues of justice, goodness and love. The play is as much about how they treat each other as how they might react if God came to earth again. Miller's is an appropriate and timely question: just how far will materialism drive humanity?

Henri is Miller's perfect construction of a participant-observer, a liberal whose lack of involvement has helped create much of the suffering. A former revolutionary, Henri now spends his time and money on pleasant pursuits far removed from former compatriots who have become drug traffickers. He plans to sell his farms because his managers in his absence have been growing coca. Henri has returned because his daughter Jeanine has leaped or been pushed from a third-story window. He had introduced her to the revolutionary movement and then abandoned it and her. Sitting by Jeanine's side day after day, he realizes the depth of his love for her and finally understands his role in her suffering.

Henri brings Emily Shapiro, the newly arrived American television director, to visit Jeanine and distract her from the pain—they are both Barnard College graduates. When Jeanine gets upset that Emily may film the crucifixion to save her career, Emily protests that she is only a bystander. Jeanine answers: "Really. Well, if you are you're the only one left in the world." Miller's best truths about personal responsibility and the futility of violence are played out between these two young women. Jeanine is another Miller alter-ego. No doubt could remain about his views on war when he has Jeanine say, "[W]hichever side one fought on is partly right no matter how completely wrong it was." Miller claims to have written the play before September 11, 2001, but how does that square with Jeanine's statement to Emily: "A revolution is a comedian wearing a black veil—you don't know whether to laugh or run for your life. . . . I hear they finally believe in death in Manhattan, is that true?"

HOW CAN A play teeming with such lines be character-driven? That is the anomaly of *Resurrection Blues*. The characters dance among the quips, gradually connecting with themselves and with others. Despite how outlandish the plot may appear, Miller has developed characterizations, not caricatures. True, Skip Cheeseboro is worthy of his name: he's the American television producer intent on holding everyone, including Ralph, to the contract. Nonetheless, with Miller's customary skill, he has built ambiguity and complexity into the play's situations and characters; at the same time, he has imbued the roles with terrifying believability. Miller knows humanity. Emily and the rest of her crew are painted with bold comedic strokes, but the portraits are also shaded with nuance and individuality.

Even displaying surprising variation is Felix, whose affair with Emily nearly redeems him. And Stanley, one of Ralph's disciples, may be downright quixotic; he plays Judas, doubting Thomas and Peter the rock, all in one. But then Ralph, at best, is a reluctant Messiah. He waffles. At times he thinks he might be God, but then at other times he is not sure. He does believe, however, that the people may need his crucifixion to show that someone who professes to love them is willing to "go the distance."

Ralph's evasiveness adds to the irony; the play's principal character never speaks or appears on stage except as a bright white light. That light pours out of the dungeon as Henri and Felix approach, but it quickly recedes as Ralph disappears apparently through the walls of the prison. All of his actions and words come through tales shrouded by implication and suggestion. Ralph, in all his elusiveness, is the perfect center for a play about reactions to his innocent manifestations of love. Henri and Jeanine may have reached a halting understanding, but the pure love of the Messiah has saved her. When she regained consciousness after her fall, he was lying in her blood on the pavement "howling like a small child" because he thought she was dead. And she may have been dead. Now he returns to her regularly, blinding her with his light and love. Each visit brings her increased physical and spiritual healing.

This play is clearly a departure for Miller, but then he has always written against expectations. Miller refers to *Resurrection Blues* as both a satiric comedy and a tragic farce. This play, however, is not a calculated stylistic experiment in farce. Instead, it displays an edgy frustration and urgency, exposing well-founded fears, which apparently he has decided can be examined in no better way. And its outrageousness does save it from preachiness. Miller means to counteract the deadening effects of the great "hall of the imagination," waking up all of the emotions, including laughter, which is often the best possible response to the absurd aspects of contemporary life. Even though the play has Brechtian overtones, Miller is in no way standing outside his richly ironical treatment of issues that concern him deeply. He is boldly seeking a cure and has chosen satire as a way to cauterize the gaping wound he sees in society, and to promote healing.

Miller's plays have occupied national and international stages during the past eight decades. His first two productions were in 1934 while a student at the University of Michigan. His first Broadway production was *The Man Who Had All the Luck* in 1944 (revived on Broadway by Roundabout Theatre Company in 2002). Where others may list *Death of a Salesman* (1949) and *The Crucible* (1953) as his career high points, I believe *Resurrection Blues* could be his ultimate morality tale. Now in full voice, Miller sings of pain and loss as no one else can. As a perceptive political commentator, he may recognize that there is frighteningly little time left.

The Guthrie Theater began its 2002–03 season with *Resurrection Blues* (August 3–September 8, 2002), especially appropriate programming since Miller's *All My Sons* (1947) ended the Guthrie's previous season. Having Miller in-house was exhilarating for the company. During his pre-production meetings with director David Esbjornson, Miller continued to revisit the script, showing a characteristic openness to the process.

THE PLAY'S SATIRIC quality should not be misread: this "tragic farce" is not a rant that can be dismissed, but, instead, it is a particularly important work for the writer at this specific time. In *Resurrection Blues*, nothing escapes Miller: from pollution cleanup not being cost effective to poverty being caused by the poor. If the play has a fault, it is this overloaded quality that at times causes a loss of focus. Regardless, there is no detail or comment I would suggest he leave out. Miller makes no pretense at subtlety here; his astute analysis comes across resoundingly. And surely his years give him license just once to say it plainly and to say it all. *Resurrection Blues* is still one of the best plays to occupy a stage in the dawning century, achievement enough for a writer who has given the theatre many memorable characters and much penetrating cultural commentary. Given the widespread despair and escape from reality Miller chronicles, this play demonstrates a surprising hope for theatre as remedy.

Miller's ending is startling. His designation of the play as a tragic farce nearly leaves room for the crucifixion, but not quite. Villages begin vying for the execution site, driven by the possibility of new schools, roads, tourists, a casino or even a theme park. Stanley, the disciple, tells Jeanine that they must convince Charley—the Messiah's latest choice of name—to go away and not come back. The ending undercuts any hope for transcendence, and Esbjornson's staging pushes that hope further outside possibility. The director begins and ends with the empty Guthrie stage: at the beginning, a man is thrown from a helicopter, and at the end, the house lights are brought up, implicating the audience in the final action.

The entire cast gradually gathers on the empty stage. Charley's light begins to appear in the upper reaches of the sky. No silence now. Instead, angry shouts mix with weeping. Arguments come from all sides: go, you must live; no, stay, get up on that cross, do it for the jobs it will bring; no, go, your death will trigger a blood-bath and wreck the economy; yes, go, we love you and will never forget you, but you have to leave. Skip and Felix exit arguing over the money. Slowly Charley's light recedes. Tentative silence. And then from everyone, a weeping, relieved, "Goodbye, Charley!"

A DIRECTORY OF NEW
UNITED STATES PRODUCTIONS
○ ○ ○ ○ ○
Compiled by Rue E. Canvin

T HIS LISTING INCLUDES professional productions that opened during the
June 1, 2002–May 31, 2003 season. Its focus is on new plays—and other
productions of note—by a variety of resident companies around the United
States. Information on casts and credits, which are listed here in alphabetical
order, by state, were supplied by the 73 producing organizations included.
Resident theaters producing new plays and operating under contracts with
Actors' Equity were queried for this comprehensive directory. Active US theater
companies not included in this list may not have presented new (or newly
revised) scripts during the year under review or had not responded to our
query by July 1, 2003. Productions listed below are world premieres, US
premieres, regional premieres, substantial revisions or otherwise worthy of
note. Theaters in the US are encouraged to submit proposed listings of new
works and new adaptations, in addition to the premieres indicated above, to
the editor of the *Best Plays* series.

ALABAMA

Alabama Shakespeare Festival, Montgomery
Kent Thompson artistic director, Alan Harrison managing director

Southern Writers' Project Festival of New Plays. February 14–16, 2003.
THE VENUS DE MILO IS ARMED. By Kia Corthron. February 14, 2003 (world premiere).
Director, Valerie Curtis-Newton; scenery, Ed Haynes; costumes, Elizabeth Novak; lighting,
Liz Lee; sound, Don Tindall; dramaturg, Gwen Orel; production stage manager, Mark
D. Leslie.
    Performed by Richard Allen, Spencer Scott Barros, Quincy Taylor Bernstine, Leo V. Finnie III,
Hope Clarke, Charde Manzy, Margo Moorer, April Yvette Thompson.

AARONVILLE DAWNING. By Linda Byrd Kilian. February 15, 2003 (world premiere).
Director, Kent Thompson; scenery, Ed Haynes; costumes, Elizabeth Novak; lighting, Liz
Lee; sound, Don Tindall; dramaturg, Gwen Orel; production stage manager, Sara Lee
Howell.
    Performed by Carole Monferdini.

THE FULA FROM AMERICA. By Carlyle Brown. February 15, 2003. Director, Louise
Smith; lighting, Mike Wangen; sound, Reid Resja; production stage manager, Tanya J.
Searle.
    Performed by Mr. Brown.

Readings

THE DREAMS OF SARAH BREEDLOVE. By Regina Taylor. February 15, 2003.

SKETCHES OF YUCCA. By Keith Josef Adkins. February 16, 2003.

ART VERSUS LIFE. By Craig Warner. February 16, 2003.

THE ROBESON TAPE. By Vincent Delaney. February 16, 2003.

ARKANSAS

Arkansas Repertory Theatre, Little Rock
Robert Hupp producing artistic director

FRIENDS LIKE THESE. By Tom Dulack. March 14, 2003 (world premiere). Director, Brad Mooy; scenery, Mike Nichols; costumes, Robert A. Pittenridge; lighting, Andrew Meyers; sound, M. Jason Pruzin; fight direction, Mark Hansen; Christine Lomaka, stage manager.

Anthony Powers	Stephen Mendillo	Stanley Roundtree	Curt Hostetter
Gabriella Powers	Lisa Richards	Jessica Evergreen	Rachel Sledd
Belinda Skulnick	Jo Ann Robinson	Adrian Files	Bruce Ward
Theron Skulnick	Tony Hoty		

Time: Memoral day, 1999. Place: The Powerses' home in rural Connecticut. Presented in two parts.

Staged readings of the winners of the Kaufman & Hart Prize for New American Comedy. July 7–13, 2002.

BIG BOYS. By Rich Orloff. Director, Brad Mooy.

Victor	Andrew Boyer	Norm	Steve Wilkerson

STUFF. By Regina Barnett. Director, David Kennedy.

Angela	Casey Sanders	Alex	Jason Plumb
Pam	Mary Ann Pullella	The Wrapper	Ann Hu
Oliver	Andrew Boyer	Waiter; Man	Steve Wilkerson
Eric	Bill Ford Campbell		

FRIENDS LIKE THESE. By Tom Dulack. Director, Brad Mooy.

Gabriella	Jo Ann Robinson	Stanley	Bill Ford Campbell
Anthony	Steve Wilkerson	Jessica	Amy Sabin
Belinda	Mary Ann Pullella	Adrian	Don Bolinger
Theron	Andrew Boyer		

CALIFORNIA

American Conservatory Theater, San Francisco
Carey Perloff artistic director, Heather Kitchen managing director

THE COLOSSUS OF RHODES. By Carey Perloff. January 10, 2003 (West Coast premiere). Director, Ms. Perloff; scenery, Hisham Ali; costumes, Cassandra Carpenter; lighting, Nancy Schertler; sound, Jake Rodriguez; music, Catherine Reid; dramaturg, Paul Walsh; production stage manager, Nicole Dickerson.

Cecil Rhodes .... Allyn Burrows	Randall Pickering .... David Adkins
Barney Barnato .... Paul Vincent Black	Charles Rudd .... Rufus Collins
Ruskin; James; Anderson .... Robert Parsons	Ensemble .... David Stewart Hudson,
Fanny Bees .... Kathleen Antonia	Sidney Burrows Jr.

THE RAMAYANA. By Ruben Polendo; based on the Hindu poem *The Ramayana* by St. Valmiki. February 27, 2003 (Bay Area premiere). Director, Mr. Polendo; scenery and lighting, Ryan Mueller; costumes and masks, Miranda Hoffman; music, Jef Evans.

Prince Rama .... John Patrick Higgins	Prince Bharata; Injarit .... Brud Fogarty
Princess Sita .... Candice McKoy	Prince Shatrughana,
Lava .... D. Matt Worley	Vayu .... David Ryan Smith
Kusha .... Tyler McKenna	Gita; Tataka;
Prince Lakshmana .... Nathan Thomas Wheeler	Rama's Courtesan; Kali .... Camila Borrero
Prince Hanuman .... Ali Baker	Maya; Rama's Courtesan;
King Ravana .... Edward Nattenberg	Angry Mother .... Allison Schubert
King Dasharatha; Samiek .... Jay Randall	Jatayu; Vanara .... Chara Riegel
Queen Kaushalya;	Queen Sumitra; A wise sage;
Princess Shurpa .... Rachel Scott	Rakshasa .... Amanda Hastings-Phillips
Queen Keikeyi;	Dipu; King Janaka .... Jacob Ming-Trent
Princess Nakha .... Elizabeth Raetz	

Aurora Theatre Company, Berkeley
Barbara Oliver artistic director, Tom Ross producing director

THE SHAPE OF THINGS. By Neil LaBute. September 19, 2002 (Bay Area premiere). Director, Tom Ross; scenery, Kate Boyd; costumes, Maggie Whitaker; lighting, Jim Cave; sound, Yvette Janine Jackson.

Jenny .... Arwen Anderson	Adam .... Craig Marker
Evelyn .... Stephanie Gularte	Philip .... Danny Wolohan

Time: Now. Place: A liberal arts college in a conservative midwestern town. Presented without intermission.

PARTITION. By Ira Hauptman. April 17, 2003 (world premiere). Director, Barbara Oliver; scenery and lighting, Richard Olmsted; costumes, Anna Oliver; sound, Matthew Spiro; dramaturg, Jo Perry-Folino; production stage manager, Kevin Johnson.

G.H. Hardy .... David Arrow	Billington .... Chris Ayles
Ramanujan .... Rahul Gupta	Namagiri .... Rachel Rajput
Police Officer; Fermat .... Julian López-Morillas	
Presented in two parts.	

Berkeley Repertory Theatre, Berkeley
Tony Taccone artistic director; Susan Medak managing director

MENOCCHIO. By Lillian Groag. November 6, 2002 (world premiere). Director, Ms. Groag; scenery and lighting, Alexander V. Nichols; costumes, Beaver Bauer; sound, Jeff Mockus.

Menocchio .... Charles Dean	Inquisitor .... Ken Ruta
Menocchio's wife .... Jeri Lynn Cohen	Multiple roles .... Robert Sicular
Bastian .... Dan Hiatt	Father Melchiore .... Peter Van Norden

HAROUN AND THE SEA OF STORIES. By Tim Supple and David Tushingham, from the novel by Salman Rushdie. November 20, 2002 (West Coast premiere). Director, Dominique Serrand; scenery, Wil Leggett and Mr. Serrand; costumes, Sonya Berlovitz; lighting, Marcus Dilliard and Jennifer Setlow; sound, Bill Williams.

Performed by Russ Appleyard, Myla Balugay, Colman Domingo, Katie Kreisler, Jarion Monroe, Jennifer Baldwin Peden, Krisztina Peremartoni, Jennifer Riker, Nora El Samahy, Mr. Serrand, Sky Soleil.

FRÄULEIN ELSE. By Francesca Faridany, from the novella by Arthur Schnitzler. March 5, 2003 (world premiere). Director, Stephen Wadsworth; scenery, Thomas Lynch; costumes, Anna Oliver; lighting, Joan Arhelger; sound, Bill Williams; stage manager, Michael Suenkel. Presented in association with La Jolla Playhouse.

Else	Francesca Faridany	Mother	Mary Baird
Paul	Michael Tisdale	Herr Von Dorsday	Julian López-Morillas
Cissy	Lauren Lovett	Porter	Omid Abtahi

Time: 1912. Place: A spa hotel at the foot of the Cimone mountain in northern Italy. Presented without intermission.

East West Players, Los Angeles
Tim Dang producing artistic director

QUEEN OF THE REMOTE CONTROL. By Sujata G. Bhatt. September 11, 2003 (world premiere). Directors, Ms. Bhatt and Tim Dang; scenery, Akeime Mitterlehner; costumes, Dori Quan; lighting, José Lopez; sound, Nathan Wang; stage manager, Victoria A. Gathe.

Shilpa Shah	Poorna Jagannathan	Divya Shah	Meera Simhan
Padma Rao	Sulekha Naidu	Ashok Shah	Bernard White
Nitin Shah	Kal Penn		

Time: Late December 1999. Place: The home of Ashok and Divya Shah in Calabasas, California. Presented in two parts.

THE TEMPEST. By William Shakespeare; adapted by Andrew Tsao. November 20, 2002. Director, Mr. Tsao; choreography, Nick Erickson; scenery, Victoria Petrovich; costumes, Steven N. Lee; lighting, Rand Ryan; sound and music, Nathan Wang; stage manager, Victoria A. Gathe.

Gonzalo; Spirit	Esther K. Chae	Sebastian; Stephano	Trieu Tran
Prospero	Daniel Dae Kim	Ariel; Miranda	Gwendoline Yeo
Caliban; Ferdinand	Matthew Yang King	Antonio; Trinculo	Ogie Zulueta
Alonso; Spirit	Kipp Shiotani		

Presented without intermission.

THE NISEI WIDOWS CLUB. By Betty Tokudani. May 14, 2003 (world premiere). Director, Tim Dang; scenery, Wayne Nakasone; costumes, Rodney Kageyama; lighting, G. Shizuko Herrera; sound, Kaname Morishita; production stage manager, Anna Woo.

Sumi	Takayo Fischer	Betty	June Kyoko Lu
Michiko	Irene Sanaye Furukawa	Frank	Robert Isaac Lee
Fumiko	Donna Kimura	Tomi	Jeanne Sakata
Hana	Emily Kuroda	Tak	Sab Shimono
Masako	Annabelle M. Lee	Shig	Michael Yama

Place: Home of Sumi Tsuboi in Gardena, California. Presented in two parts.

Geffen Playhouse, Los Angeles
Gilbert Cates producing director, Randall Arney artistic director, Stephen Eich managing director

UNDER THE BLUE SKY. By David Eldridge. September 18, 2002 (West Coast premiere). Director, Gilbert Cates; scenery, Tom Buderwitz; costumes, Joyce Kim Lee; lighting,

Daniel Ionazzi; music, Jef Bek; dramaturg, Amy Levinson Millán; production stage manager, Elsbeth M. Collins. In association with USA Ostar Theatricals and Bob Boyett.

Graham	Willie Garson	Nick	McCaleb Burnett
Anne	Judy Geeson	Helen	Margaret Welsh
Robert	John Carroll Lynch	Michelle	Sharon Lawrence

Time: 1996–98. Place: Three English homes. Presented without intermission.

PEARL. Musical by Debbie Allen, James Ingram and Diane Louie; from the Snow White story by the Brothers Grimm. November 20, 2002 (West Coast premiere.) Director and choreography, Ms. Allen; scenery, Ray Klausen; costumes, Timm Burrow; lighting, William H. Grant III; production stage manager, David Blackwell. Presented in association with the Kennedy Center.

Ringmaster; Dr. Drewdy	Matthew Dickens	Little Pearl	Geffri Hightower,
Ruby	Perris McCracken		Tatianna Barber
The Queen	Debbie Allen	Pearl	Vivian Nixon, Natalie Johnson
Virtual Shirley	Michele Morgan	Q	Buddy Lewis
Seriah	Ashalee Fann	Charm	Rasta Thomas

ROSE AND WALSH. By Neil Simon. February 5, 2003 (world premiere). Director, David Esbjornson; scenery, John Arnone; costumes, Elizabeth Hope Clancy; lighting, Stephen Strawbridge; sound, Jon Gottlieb; dramaturg, Amy Levinson Millán, production stage manager, Elsbeth M. Collins.

Rose	Jane Alexander	Walsh	Len Cariou
Clancy	David Aaron Baker	Arlene	Marin Hinkle

Place: A beach house in East Hampton, New York. Seven scenes, Presented in two parts.

BOY GETS GIRL. By Rebecca Gilman. April 9, 2003 (West Coast premiere). Director, Randall Arney; scenery, Andrew Jackness; costumes, Christina Haatainen Jones; lighting, Daniel Ionazzi; sound and music, Richard Woodbury; dramaturg, Amy Levinson Millán; production stage manager, Elizabeth A. Brohm.

Tony	Mark Deakins	Harriet	Julie Ann Emery
Theresa Bedell	Nancy Travis	Les Kennkat	James Farentino
Howard Siegel	Charles Janasz	Madeleine Beck	Monnae Michaell
Mercer Stevens	Taylor Nichols		

Time: The present. Place: Various locales in New York City. Presented in two parts.

La Jolla Playhouse, La Jolla

Des McAnuff artistic director, Terrence Dwyer managing director

WINTERTIME. By Charles L. Mee. August 18, 2002. Director, Les Waters; scenery, Annie Smart; costumes, Christal Weatherly; lighting, Robert Wierzel; sound, Matthew Spiro; production stage manager, Steven Adler. Presented in association with Long Wharf Theatre.

Dr. Benoit	Michi Barall	Frank	Nicholas Hormann
Maria	Randy Danson	Bertha	Lauren Klein
Ariel	Emily Donahoe	Bob	Bruce McKenzie
Francois	Francois Giroday	Edmund	Tom Nelis
Jonathan	Daoud Heidami	Hilda	Lola Pashalinski

Time: The present. Presented in two parts.

Lamb's Players Theatre, Coronado
Robert Smyth producing artistic director

DEEP RIVER. By David McFadzean. August 9, 2002 (revision). Director, Robert Smyth; scenery, Mike Buckley; costumes, Jeanne Reith; lighting, Karin Filijan; sound, Greg Campbell; music, Deborah Gilmour Smyth; stage manager, Nick Cordileone.

Augusta "Gus" Lambert	K.B. Mercer	Toby Wagner	Allan Heath
Jenise Mckay	Ms. Smyth	Valerie Mckay	Tania Henetz
Lydia Jamison	Maggie Wegener	Frank Mckay	David Cochran Heath
Bud Spivey	Tom Stephenson		

A DIVINE COMEDY. By Dennis Hassell. April 11 2003 (US premiere). Director, Robert Smyth; scenery, Mike Buckley; costumes, Jeanne Reith; lighting, Nathan Peirson; stage manager, Esther Emery.

Bob Shephard	Nick Cordileone	Hellen Dalmation	Kathi Gibbs
Dr. Lobo	Jonathan Dunn-Rankin	Karl Marx	Doren Elias
June Carson	Jennifer Austin	Barbie Marx	Brenda Burke
John Ripley	Paul Eggington	Studley Mudd	Tom Stephenson

Presented without intermission.

Magic Theatre, San Francisco
Larry Eilenberg artistic director, David Gluck managing director

FIRST LOVE. By Charles L. Mee. June 14, 2002 (West Coast premiere). Director, Erin Mee; scenery, Kate Boyd.

Edith	Joan Mankin	Waitress	Lindsay Drummer
Harold	Robert Parnell		

Presented without intermission.

TED KACZYNSKI KILLED PEOPLE WITH BOMBS. By Michelle Carter. October 18, 2002 (world premiere). Director, Bill Peters; scenery, Kate Boyd; costumes, Kira Kristensen; additional costumes, Laura Hazlett; lighting, Jim Cave; sound, Maribeth Back; music, Ms. Carter.

Performed by David Cramer, Anne Darragh, Merle Kessler, Robert Parsons, Celia Shuman, Mark Rafael Truitt.

BODY FAMILIAR. By Joe Goode. January 10, 2003 (world premiere). Director, Mr. Goode; scenery, Mikiko Uesugi; costumes, Fumiko Bielefeldt; lighting, Jack Carpenter; music, Erik Ian Walker; stage manager, Heather Basarab.

Performed by Felipe Barrueto-Cabello, Marit Brook-Kothlow, Elizabeth Burritt, Celia Shuman, Mark Rafael Truitt, Liam Vincent.

8 BOB OFF. By Gary Leon Hill. February 21, 2003 (world premiere). Director, David Dower; scenery, John Mayne; costumes, Kira Kristensen; lighting, Jim Cave; sound, Drew Yerys; fight direction, Christopher Morrison.

Bob Plum	Howard Swain	Bobby	Luis Saguar
Donna	O-Lan Jones		

BLUE SURGE. By Rebecca Gilman. April 4, 2003 (West Coast premiere). Director, Amy Glazer; scenery, Eric Sinkkonen; costumes, Kira Kristensen; lighting, Jim Cave.

Sandy	Kirsten Roeters	Curt	John Flanagan

Beth	Corie Henninger	Heather	Jibz Cameron
Doug	Darren Bridgett		

Mark Taper Forum, Los Angeles

Gordon Davidson artistic director, Charles Dillingham managing director,
Robert Egan producing director

THE HOUSE OF BERNARDA ALBA. By Federico García Lorca, adapted by Chay Yew. July 25, 2002 (West Coast premiere). Director, Lisa Peterson; scenery, Rachel Hauck; costumes, Joyce Kim Lee; lighting, Christopher Akerlind; music and sound, Mark Bennett; production stage manager, Mary K. Klinger.

Maria Josefa	Tsai Chin	Amelia	Lydia Look
Blanca	Shaheen Vaaz	Martirio	Rita Wolf
Poncia	Camille Saviola	Magdalena	Eileen Galindo
Beggar Woman	Christine Avila	Angustias	Marissa Chibas
Girl	Adrianne Avey	Prudencia	Jeanne Sakata
Bernarda Alba	Chita Rivera	Guitar and Oud	Annas Allaf
Adela	Sandra Oh		

Village Women: Adrianne Avey, Christine Avila, Aixa Clemente, Anita Dashiell, Carla Jimenez, Jeanne Sakata.

Time: Late summer, 1936. Place: The courtyard in Bernarda Alba's house. Presented without intermission.

Political squeeze: Eileen Galindo and Ric Salinas in Culture Clash *at the Mark Taper Forum. Photo: Craig Schwartz*

Mark Taper
Forum
2002–2003
Season

Mother, mother (top): Zilah Mendoza and Amy Aquino in Living Out. *Photo: Craig Schwartz*

Pennies, too (bottom): Sharon Lockwood in Nickel and Dimed. *Photo: Craig Schwartz*

NICKEL AND DIMED. By Joan Holden; based on *Nickel and Dimed: On (Not) Getting By in America* by Barbara Ehrenreich. September 8, 2002 (revision). Presented in association with Intiman Theatre Company, Seattle. See Intiman listing for full production information.

LIVING OUT. By Lisa Loomer. January 29, 2002 (world premiere). Director, Bill Rauch; scenery, Christopher Acebo; costumes, Candice Cain; lighting, Lap-Chi Chu; sound, Jon Gottlieb; music, Joe Romano; dramaturgs, Corey Madden and John Glore; production stage manager, Mary Michele Miner.

Ana	Zilah Mendoza	Richard	Daniel Hugh Kelly
Wallace	Kate A. Mulligan	Sandra	Maricela Ochoa
Linda	Elizabeth Ruscio	Zoila	Diane Rodriguez
Nancy	Amy Aquino	Park Maintenance	Richard Azurdia,
Bobby	Carlos Gomez		Dihlon McManne

Time: The present. Place: Los Angeles.

TEN UNKNOWNS. By Jon Robin Baitz. March 27, 2003 (West Coast premiere). Director, Robert Egan; scenery, David Jenkins; costumes, Joyce Kim Lee; lighting, Michael Gilliam; sound, Jon Gottlieb; paintings, Conor Foy; production stage manager, Mary K. Klinger.

Trevor Fabricant	Patrick Breen	Julia Bryant	Klea Scott
Malcolm Raphelson	Stacy Keach	Judd Sturgess	Jonathan M. Woodward

Time: 1992. Place: Oaxaca, Mexico. Presented in two parts.

CHAVEZ RAVINE. By Culture Clash, with music and lyrics by John Avila, Richard Montoya; Randy Rodarte and Scott Rodarte. May 17, 2003 (world premiere). Director, Lisa Peterson; scenery, Rachel Hauck; costumes, Christopher Acebo; lighting, Anne Militello; sound, Dan Moses Schreier; musical director, Mr. Avila; dramaturg, John Glore; production stage manager, James T. McDermott.

Performed by John Avila, Eileen Galindo, Richard Montoya, Randy Rodarte, Scott Rodarte, Ric Salinas, Herbert Siguenza, Robert Alcaraz, Minerva Garcia, Edgar Landa.

Time: 1846–1981, with visits to the deeper past and the present. Place: Locations around Southern California. Presented in two parts.

The Old Globe, San Diego

Jack O'Brien artistic director, Louis G. Spisto executive director, Craig Noel artistic director

PERICLES. By William Shakespeare. August 31, 2002. Director, Darko Tresnjak; scenery, Ralph Funicello; costumes, Linda Cho; lighting, York Kennedy; sound, Jerry Yager; dramaturg, Dakin Matthews; stage managers, D. Adams, Tracy Skoczelas.

Lady of Pentapolis	D'Vorah Bailey	Sailor of Tyre	Brian Ibsen
Marina	Anna Belknap	Helicanus	Charles Janasz
Cleon	Andrew Borba	Fisherman	Michael Kary
Fourth Knight	Jeffrey Brick	Sailor of Tyre	Antonie Knoppers
Lysimachus	Christian Casper	Lychordia	Eleanor O'Brien
Boult	Liam Craig	Fisherman; Cerimon	Gregor Paslawsky
Lord of Tyre	David Raphael D'Agostini	Pericles	Michael James Reed
Diana; Bawd	Dara Fisher	Thaliard; Leonine	Gareth Saxe
Lord of Tyre	Christopher Gottschalk	Gower	Ned Schmidtke
Antiochus; Simonides;		Philoten	Nanka Sturgis
Pander	Wynn Harmon	Thaisa	Emmelyn Thayer
Dionyza	Tracy Hostmyer	Daughter of Antiochus	Michele Vazquez

Time: A period of two decades. Place: Various Mediterranean locales. Presented in two parts.

IMAGINARY FRIENDS. By Nora Ephron; with music by Marvin Hamlisch and lyrics by Craig Carnelia. September 28, 2002 (world premiere). Director, Jack O'Brien; choreography, Jerry Mitchell; scenery, Michael Levine; costumes, Robert Morgan; lighting, Kenneth Posner; sound, Jon Weston; video, Jan Hartley; production stage manager, Evan Ensign; stage managers, Joel Rosen and Jim Woolley.

Lillian Hellman	Swoosie Kurtz	Student; others	Gina Lamparella
Mary McCarthy	Cherry Jones	Fact; others	Dirk Lumbard
The Man	Harry Groener	Fiction; others	Peter Marx
Abby Kaiser; others	Anne Allgood	Vic; others	Perry Ojeda
Leo; others	Bernard Dotson	A Woman	Anne Pitoniak
Smart Woman; others	Rosena M. Hill	Fizzy; others	Karyn Quackenbush

OLDEST LIVING CONFEDERATE WIDOW TELLS ALL. By Martin Tahse; from the novel by Allan Gurganus. February 1, 2003 (world premiere). Director, Don Scardino; scenery, Allen Moyer; costumes, Jane Greenwood; lighting, Kenneth Posner; sound, Peter Fitzgerald; production stage manager, Dianne Trulock.

Lucy Marsden .... Ellen Burstyn

SPLENDOUR. By Abi Morgan. February 8, 2003 (US premiere). Director, Karen Carpenter; scenery, Tony Fanning; costumes, Charlotte Devaux Shields; lighting, Aaron M. Copp; sound, Paul Peterson; stage manager, Raúl Moncada.

Genevieve	Monique Fowler	Micheleine	Gordana Rashovich
Kathryn	Joanna Glushak	Gilma	Chelsey Rives

LOVES AND HOURS. By Stephen Metcalfe. March 29, 2003 (world premiere). Director, Jack O'Brien; scenery and costumes, Robert Morgan; lighting, David F. Segal; sound, Paul Peterson; music, Bob James; projections, Sage Marie Carter; stage manager, D. Adams.

Dan Jr.	Brian Ibsen	Andrea	Nanka Sturgis
Dan Tilney	Brian Kerwin	Tom Houghton	Tom Tammi
Harold Schwabb	David Manis	Linda	Nance Williamson
Sara Houghton	Amanda Naughton	Anne Tripplehorn	Monique Fowler
Julia	Maureen Silliman	Charlotte Walker	Bridget Flanery
Rebecca	Emmelyn Thayer		

Time: Immediate present. Place: Somewhere in Southern California. Presented in two parts.

KNOWING CAIRO. By Andrea Stolowitz. April 5, 2003 (world premiere). Director, Seret Scott; scenery, David Ledsinger; costumes, Jennifer Brawn Gittings; lighting, Chris Rynne; sound, Paul Peterson; stage manager, Raúl Moncada.

Rose	Marilyn Chris	Winsom	Regina Hilliard Bain
Lydia	Susan Wands		

Time: Present. Place: Rose's Upper West Side Apartment, New York City. Presented in two parts.

San Jose Repertory Theatre, San Jose
Timothy Near artistic director, Alexandra Urbanowksi managing director

THE DRAWER BOY. By Michael Healey. August 31, 2002. Director, John McCluggage; scenery, Michael Olich; costumes, B. Modern; lighting, Lap-Chi Chu; sound, Jeff Mockus; stage manager, Jenny R. Friend.

Morgan	Dion Anderson	Miles	Sheffield Chastain
Angus	Bob Morrisey		

THE WIND CRIES MARY. By Philip Kan Gotanda. October 25, 2002 (world premiere). Director, Eric Simonson; scenery and lighting, Kent Dorsey; costumes, Lydia Tanji; sound, Jeff Mockus; dramaturg, Tom Bryant; stage manager, Bruce Elsperger.

Eiko Hanabi	Tess Lina	Raymond Pemberthy	... Thomas Vincent Kelly
Miles Katayama	Stan Egi	Rachel Auwinger	Allison Sie
Dr. Nakada	Sab Shimono	Auntie Gladys	Joy Carlin

Time: 1968. Place: San Francisco. Presented in two parts.

CULTURE CLASH IN AMERICCA. By Culture Clash. January 31, 2003. Director, Tony Taccone; scenery and lighting, Alexander V. Nichols; costumes, Donna Marie; sound, Jeff Mockus; stage manager, Cynthia Cahill.

Culture Clash: Richard Montoya, Ric Salinas, Herbert Siguenza.

Presented without intermission.

HUMPTY DUMPTY. By Eric Bogosian. March 28, 2003 (West Coast premiere). Director, John McCluggage; scenery, Douglas R. Rogers, costumes, B. Modern; lighting, Lap-Chi Chu; sound, Steve Schoenbeck; stage manager, Jenny R. Friend.

Nicole	Elizabeth Hanly Rice	Troy	Louis Lotorto
Max	Saxon Palmer	Spoon	Amy Brewczynski
Nat	Andy Murray		

Time: The present. Place: A vacation home in upstate New York. Presented in two parts.

South Coast Repertory, Costa Mesa

David Emmes producing artistic director, Martin Benson artistic director

THE VIOLET HOUR. By Richard Greenberg. November 8, 2002 (world premiere). Director, Evan Yionoulis; scenery, Christopher Barreca; costumes, Candice Cain; lighting, Donald Holder; music and sound, Mike Yionoulis; dramaturg, Jerry Patch; stage manager, Jamie A. Tucker.

John Pace Seavering	Hamish Linklater	Jessie Brewster	Michelle Hurd
Gidger	Mario Cantone	Rosamund Plinth	Kate Arrington
Denis McCleary	Curtis Mark Williams		

Presented in two parts.

INTIMATE APPAREL. By Lynn Nottage. April 18, 2003. Director, Kate Whoriskey; scenery, Walt Spangler; costumes, Catherine Zuber; lighting, Scott Zielinski; sound, Lindsay Jones; music, Reginald Robinson; dramaturg, Jerry Patch; associate dramaturg, Rhonda Robbins; production stage manager, Randall K. Lum. Presented in association with Center Stage, Baltimore.

Esther	Shané Williams	Mrs. Van Buren	Sue Cremin
Mrs. Dickson	Brenda Pressley	Mr. Marks	Steven Goldstein
George Armstrong	Kevin Jackson	Mayme	Erica Gimpel

THE INTELLIGENT DESIGN OF JENNY CHOW. By Rolin Jones. May 2, 2003 (world premiere). Director, David Chambers; scenery, Christopher Barreca; costumes, Dunya Ramikova; lighting, Chris Parry; sound and music, David Budries; dramaturg, Jennifer Kiger; stage manager, Jamie A. Tucker.

Jennifer Marcus	Melody Butiu	Adele Hartwick;	
Mr. Marcus; Zhang	... William Francis McGuire	Su Yang Zhang	Linda Gehringer
Preston; Terrence;		Todd	Daniel Blinkoff
Col. Hubbard; Dr. Yakunin	JD Cullum	Jenny Chow	April Hong

South Coast Repertory
2002–2003
Season

Above: Mario Cantone and Hamish Linklater in The Violet Hour. *Photo: Ken Howard*

Above: Brenda Pressley and Shané Williams in Intimate Apparel. *Photo: Ken Howard*

Above: April Hong and Melody Butiu in The Intelligent Design of Jenny Chow. *Photo: Ken Howard*

Right: Jimmie Ray Weeks and Hal Landon Jr. in The Drawer Boy. *Photo: Henry DiRocco*

THE DRAWER BOY. By Michael Healey. May 30, 2003. Director, Martin Benson; scenery, James Youmans; costumes, Sylvia Rognstad; lighting, John Philip Martin; sound, Karl Fredrik Lundeberg; dramaturg, Linda Sullivan Baity; stage manager, Scott Harrison.

Angus	Jimmie Ray Weeks	Miles	J. Todd Adams
Morgan	Hal Landon Jr.		

Time: Summer 1972. Place: Kitchen of a Central Ontario farmhouse. Presented in two parts.

6th Annual Pacific Playwrights Festival: Workshop and Readings. May 16–18, 2003.

THE HIDING PLACE (workshop). By Jeff Whitty. Director, Mark Rucker; dramaturg, Jerry Patch; scenery; costumes, Angela Balogh Calin; lighting, JV Jones; stage manager, Ellen Glatman.

Performed by Nancy Bell, Emily Bergl, Bruce Davison, Alan Mandell, Sarah Rafferty, James Waterston.

SAFE IN HELL (reading). By Amy Freed. Director, David Emmes; dramaturg, Kurt Beattie.

Performed by Jeff Allin, JD Cullum, Colette Kilroy, Sal Lopez, Monette McGrath, Megan Obelik, Kimberly Scott, Don Took, John Vickery.

ANNA IN THE TROPICS (reading). By Nilo Cruz. Director, Juliette Carrillo; dramaturg, Jennifer Kiger.

Performed by Karmin Murcelo, Jonathan Nichols, Tony Plana, Geoff Rivas, Onahoua Rodriguez, Adriana Sevan, Jimmy Smits.

SEA OF TRANQUILITY (reading). By Howard Korder. Director, Michael Bloom; dramaturg, Michele Volansky.

Performed by Amy Aquino; Sol Castillo, Kandis Chappell, Casey Collier, Richard Doyle, Anna Gunn, Carlos Sanz, Mandy Siegfried, Joe Spano, Phillip Vaden.

BROOKLYN BOY (reading). By Donald Margulies. Director, Daniel Sullivan; dramaturg, Jerry Patch.

Performed by Lauren Ambrose, Adam Arkin, Mimi Lieber, Todd Lowe, Allan Miller, Paula Newsome, David Paymer.

2002–03 NewSCRipts Readings

THE HIDING PLACE. By Jeff Whitty. November 18, 2002. Director, Mark Rucker.

Performed by Nicholas Hormann, John Michael Higgins, Larry Drake, Susannah Schulman, Gretchen Egolf, Margaret Welsh.

MONTEZUMA. By Davey Holmes. January 13, 2003. Director, Juliette Carrillo.

Performed by Adam Scott, Sarah Rafferty, Ruth Livier, David Barrera, Robert Curtis Brown.

EGG. By Risa Mickenberg. March 3, 2003. Director, Juliette Carrillo.

Performed by Christopher Spencer Wells, Kali Rocha, Meera Shimban, Jeff Sugarman, Ana Ortiz, S.A. Griffin.

PEOPLE BE HEARD. By Quincy Long. April 14, 2003. Director, Doug Wager.

Performed by John-David Keller, Blair Sams, Don Took, Hal Landon Jr., Martha McFarland, Libby West, Erik Johnson, Heather Ehlers.

TheatreWorks, Palo Alto

Robert Kelley artistic director, Randy Adams managing director

THE LEGACY CODES. By Cherylene Lee. March 8, 2003 (world premiere). Director, Amy Gonzalez; scenery, Andrea Bechert; costumes, Chessa Nilsen; lighting and projection, Ethan Hoerneman; sound, Cliff Caruthers; dramaturg, Vicki Rozell; stage manager, Rebecca Muench.

Erling Liu .... Trieu Tran	Richard Fortier .... Michael Keys Hall
Dr. Tai Liu .... Jim Ishida	Minna Fortier .... Susy McInerny
Ming Liu .... Wai Ching Ho	Diane Fortier............................... Sheila Savage

Time: The recent past. Place: Various locations in the San Francisco Bay Area. Presented in two parts.

COLORADO

Denver Center Theatre Company, Denver
Donovan Marley artistic director, Barbara Sellers producing director

BERNICE/BUTTERFLY: A TWO PART INVENTION. By Nagle Jackson. January 23, 2003 (world premiere). Director, Mr. Jackson; scenery, Robert Morgan; costumes, Kevin Copenhaver; lighting, Dawn Chiang; sound, David R. White.

| Bernice .... Kathleen M. Brady | Tommy .... Mark Rubald |
| Randall .... Jamie Horton | |

CONNECTICUT

Goodspeed Musicals, Chester
Michael P. Price executive director, Sue Frost associate producer

THE ROAD TO HOLLYWOOD. Musical with book by Michael Pace and Walter Bobbie; music and lyrics by Rob Preston and Mr. Pace. August 8, 2002 (world premiere). Director, Mr. Bobbie; choreography, Casey Nicholaw; scenery, John Lee Beatty; costumes, David C. Woolard; lighting, Ken Billington; sound, Tony Meola; musical director, Lawrence Yurman; production stage manager, Bethany Ford.

Queen Mother Minnie .... Cynthia Darlow	Baby; Taffy................................... Phillip Huber
Babs .... Jamie Day	Frankie Francado .... Christopher Innvar
Toots .... Kena Tangi Dorsey	Mr. Fritz .... Kevin B. McGlynn
Beau Hartman ....Jeff Edgerton	"Tappy" Butler .... Tom Plotkin
Crown Princess Dorothy .... Laura Griffith	Shiny Eisenberg .... Peter Van Wagner
"The Diva" Rita .... Leah Hocking	

Hartford Stage, Hartford
Michael Wilson artistic director, Jim Ireland managing director

SEASCAPE. By Edward Albee. June 5, 2002. Director, Mark Lamos; scenery, Riccardo Hernández; costumes, Constance Hoffman, lighting, Mimi Jordan Sherin; sound, David Budries; production stage manager, Deborah Vandergrift.

| Nancy .... Pamela Payton-Wright | Leslie .... David Patrick Kelly |
| Charlie .... George Grizzard | Sarah .... Annalee Jefferies |

EDGARDO MINE. By Alfred Uhry; based on the book *The Kidnapping of Edgardo Mortara* by David Kertzer. October 30, 2002 (world premiere). Director, Doug Hughes; scenery, Neil Patel; costumes, Catherine Zuber; lighting, Robert Wierzel; music and sound design, David Van Tieghem; production stage manager, Steve McCorkle.

Pope Pius IX (Nono) .... Brian Murray	Dottore; Card. Antonelli .... Robert LuPone
Marianna Mortara .... Randy Graff	Nina Morisi; Sr. Angelina ...... Spencer Kayden
Momolo Mortara .... Michael Countryman	Edgardo Mortara .... Jesse Schwartz

Lucidi; Scazzocchio .... Brennan Brown   Young Priest ....Johnny Giacalone
    With: Wayne Crow, Walter Corbiere, Jennifer Gawlik, Peter Papadopoulos.
    Time: From the mid- to late 19th century. Place: Bologna and Rome. Presented in two parts.

ELECTRA. By Sophocles; translation by H.D.F. Kitto. January 15, 2003. Director, Jonathan
Wilson; scenery, Scott Bradley; costumes, Linda Ross; lighting, Michael Lincoln; music
and sound, Jim Ragland; fight direction, J. Allen Suddeth; production stage manager,
Carmelita Becnel.

Tutor .... Gustave Johnson   Clytemnestra .... Carmen Roman
Orestes .... Stephen Barker Turner   Aegisthus .... Raphael Nash Thompson
Electra ....Mirjana Jokovic   Attendant .... Sheila McCarthy
Chrysothemis .... Agnes Tsangaridou
    Place: At Mycenae before the palace of Agamemnon. Presented without intermission.

DIOSA. By Edwin Sánchez. April 16, 2003 (world premiere). Director, Melia Bensussen;
choreography, Willie Rosario; scenery, Christine Jones; costumes, Catherine Zuber;
lighting, Robert Wierzel, sound, David Van Tieghem; fight direction, Thom Delventhal;
production stage manager, Jennifer Grutza.

Miguel ....Robert Montano   Chris .... Matthew Mabe
Josefa .... Karina Michaels   Kramer.................................... Edmond Genest
Amber ....Josie de Guzman   Stuart .... Roderick Hill
    Time: In the 1930s and early 1940s. Place: Hollywood. Presented in two parts.

Brand: NEW Readings Festival of New Works. April 25–27, 2003.
ONCE IN ELYSIUM. By David Grimm. Director, Tracy Brigden.
GIZMO LOVE. By John Kolvenbach. Director, Shelley Butler.
LIGHTLY BUILT BRIDGES. By Anthony Giardina. Director, Doug Hughes.
DREAM OF NO WORDS. By Shinho Lee. Director, Victor Maog.

Eugene O'Neill Theater Center, Waterford
James Houghton artistic director, Howard Sherman executive director,
Thomas Viertel chairman of the board, George C. White founder,
Paulette Haupt artistic director of the Music Theater Conference

O'Neill Playwrights Conference. July 5–28, 2002.
AFTER MARSEILLES/IKAMVA. By Janet Neipris.
FASCINATION. By Jim Grimsley.
GEM OF THE OCEAN. By August Wilson.
HINDUSTAN. By William DiCanzio.
KLONSKY AND SCHWARTZ. By Romulus Linney.
LEVEE JAMES. By S.M. Shephard-Massat.
MAE. By Letitia Guillory.
MILLICENT SCOWLWORTHY. By Rob Handel.
MOONTEL SIX. By Constance Congdon.
MOTHERHOUSE. By Victor Lodato.
PRO BONO PUBLICO. By Peter Morris.

THE BALLAD OF BILLY K. By Katherine Griffith and Phill George.

THE BEBOP HEARD IN OKINAWA. By Mat Smart.

THE COLOSSUS OF RHODES. By Carey Perloff.

THE HIGHWAYMAN. By Julia Jarcho; based on the poem by Alfred Noyes.

THE ZERO HOUR. By Madeleine George.

TOTALLY OVER YOU. By Mark Ravenhill.

UNTIL WE FIND EACH OTHER. By Brooke Berman.

WHORES. By Lee Blessing.

Directors: Melia Bensussen, Michael Bloom, Julie Boyd, Tracy Brigden, Liz Diamond, Daniel Goldstein, Suzy Graham-Adriani, Israel Hicks, Marion McClinton, Ethan McSweeny, Jeffrey Miller, Lisa Portes, Craig Slaight, Steven Williford, Harris Yulin.

Featured Artists: Jolly Abraham, David Adkins, Joanna P. Adler, Pascale Armand, Dena Atlantic, Carolyn Baeumler, Noah Bean, Robert Beitzel, Sarah Bishop-Stone, Liz Blocker, Mark Blum, Helen Carey, Michael Chernus, Lloyd Chisholm, Ritchie Coster, Maria Teresa Creasey, Angel Desai, Shawn Elliott, Adam Erdossy, Wayman Ezell, John Feltch, Jesse Tyler Ferguson, Dara Fisher, Kelli Giddish, Letitia Guillory, Hill Harper, Amy Hohn, Paul James, Hannah Kenan, Sean T. Krishnan, Kati Kuroda, Maggie Lacey, Jenna Lamia, Sabrina LeBeauf, Jesse Lenat, Todd Lloyd, Grant MacDermott, Rami Malek, David Margulies, Christopher McCann, Justin McClintock, Bernie McInerney, Chris McKinney, Lizan Mitchell, Peter Morris, Michael Mulheren, Julia Murney, Keith Nobbs, Chris Noth, Deirdre O'Connell, Ramon de Ocampo, Lennon Parham, Jesse Pennington, Paula Pizzi, Brenton Popolizio, Susan Pourfar, Carrie Preston, Elizabeth Reaser, Portia Reiners, Richard Riehle, Dallas Roberts, Taylor Roberts, Daphne Rubin-Vega, David Sajadi, Armand Schultz, Rhea Seehorn, Paul Shaefer, Jeremy Shamos, Anna D. Shapiro, Mat Smart, Samantha Soule, Matthew Stadelmann, Josh Stamberg, Jenna Stern, Sara Tanaka, Tony Todd, Shona Tucker, Mary Tuomanen, Sam Tsoutsouvas, Jason Updike, Colleen Werthmann, Rosalyn Coleman Williams, C.J. Wilson, Fay Wolf, Kevin Wong, Grace Zandarski, Karen Ziemba.

O'Neill Music Theater Conference. August 3–18, 2002.

AVENUE Q. By Jeff Whitty, Robert Lopez and Jeff Marx.

EMBARRASSMENTS. By Laurence Klavan and Polly Pen.

LIL BUDDA. By Stephanie Jones and Janice Lowe.

Directors: Jason Moore, Otis Sallid, Blanka Zizka.

Musical direction: Mary-Mitchell Campbell, Randall Eng, Stephen Oremus.

Featured artists: Norman Daley, Bobby Scott Daye, Stephanie D'Abruzzo, Matt Farnsworth, Jordan Gelber, Nathan Lee Graham, Amanda Green, Ann Harada, Tamra Hayden, Anika Larsen, Jillian Lindsey, Rick Lyon, Lara MacLean, Lauren Mufson, Anika Noni Rose, Peter Samuel, Eric Schroeder, Henry Stram, Steven Sutcliffe, John Tartaglia, Marc Vietor, Lynn Wintersteller, Jason Wooten, Meredith Wright.

Long Wharf Theatre, New Haven
Gordon Edelstein artistic director

GOING NATIVE. By Steven Drukman. October 30, 2002 (world premiere). Director, Greg Leaming; scenery, Nathan Heverin; costumes, Ilona Somogyi; lighting, Dan Kotlowitz; sound, Fabian Obispo; production stage manager, Margaret Cangelosi.

Paul	David Adkins	Jimmy	Jerry Adler
Ed	Billy Porter	Evan	Keith Nobbs
Mother	Jessica Walter	Nick	Jeremy Davidson

Seven Angels Theatre, Waterbury
Semina De Laurentis artistic director

COOKIN' AT THE COOKERY. By Marion J. Caffey. September 26, 2002. Director and choreographer, Mr. Caffey; scenery and lighting, Dale J. Jordan; costumes, Marilyn A. Wall; sound, Asa F. Wember; musical director, James Weidman; production stage manager, David OConnor.

Alberta Hunter	Ernestine Jackson	Narrator	Janice Lorraine

Musical numbers: "My Castle's Rockin'," "My Castle's Rockin'" (Reprise), "Rough and Ready Man," "When the Saints Go Marching In," "The Love I Have for You," "Swing Brother Swing," "Two Cigarettes in the Dark," "Do You Know What It Means to Miss New Orleans?," "When the Saints Go Marching In" (Reprise), "Down Hearted Blues," "Darktown Strutters' Ball," "I'm Having a Good Time," "I'm Having a Good Time" (Reprise), "Sweet Georgia Brown," "I'm Hard to Satisfy," "I've Got a Mind to Ramble," "St. Louis Blues," "My Handy Man Ain't Handy No More," "Nobody Know You When You're Down and Out," "When You Smile (The Whole World Smiles With You)," "The Love I Have For You" (Reprise).

Presented in two parts.

THE BEACON HILL BOOK CLUB. By Susanna Salk. March 27, 2003. Director, Warren Kelley; scenery, Nicole Coppinger; costumes, Renee Purdy; lighting, Susan Kinkade; sound, Asa F. Wember; stage manager, Michele Machalani.

Addy Wolcott	Mimi Bensinger	Rema Angilo	Mia Matthews
Nora Baldwin	Diane J. Findlay	Helen Coolidge	Margery Shaw
George Lapsley	Dane Knell		

Time: Present. Place: The library of a beautiful brownstone in Beacon Hill, Massachusetts.

Westport Country Playhouse, Westport
Joanne Woodward artistic director, Anne Keefe associate artistic director, Alison Harris executive director

A SAINT SHE AIN'T. Musical with book and lyrics by Dick Vosburgh; music by Denis King. August 28, 2002 (US premiere). Director, Eric Hill; choreography, Gerry McIntyre; scenery, Troy Hourie; costumes, David Murin; lighting, Matthew E. Adelson; sound, Domonic Sack. Presented in association with the Berkshire Theatre Festival.

Snaveley T. Bogle	P.J. Benjamin	Willoughby Dittenfeffer	Roland Rusinek
Ray Bagalucci	Joel Blum	Skip Watson	Jay Russell
Faye Bogle	Allison Briner	Columbia; Sign Girl	Caroline Saxe
Trudy McCloy	Lovette George	Stage Hands	John Gray, Devon Higby,
Danny O'Reilly	Jason Gillman		Kathleen Mooney, Eric Thorne
Anna Bagalucci	Christina Marie Norrup		

Musical numbers: "The Technicolor Musical of '43," "Start the Day," "The Navy's In Town," "My All-American Gal," "A Saint She Ain't," "I Love to Hold Rose With the Rolled Hose and the Shing-Shing-Shingled Hair," "I Only Dig That Jive," "You're the Only Star in My Heaven," "Manitowoc," "I Only Dig That Jive" (Reprise), "There Oughta Be a Way," "The Joke's On Me," "Can't Help Dancing," "The Banana For My Pie," "Finaletto," Finale Ultimo.

Time: 1943. Place: Los Angeles. Presented in two parts.

White Barn Theatre, Westport
Vincent Curcio producer, Donald Saddler artistic supervisor

THE ASTRONAUT. By Arlette Ricci. August 2, 2002 (world premiere). Director, Michael Arabian; lighting, Leo B. Meyer; costumes, Tammy Elizabeth McBride; stage manager, Tom Burke-Kaiser.

Dimitri Boisyk .... Robert LuPone
Franz Chasle .... Casey Biggs
Clara Boisyk................................. Denise Lute

Doctor Chasle .... Jerome Kilty
Helena .... Frances Helm

Time: Present day. Place: Paris. Presented in two parts.

COME A LITTLE CLOSER. Musical revue with book by Kimothy Cruse; music and lyrics, John Wallowitch. August 9, 2002. Director, Mr. Cruse; scenery and lighting, Leo B. Meyer; sound, Robert Gould; costume coordinator, Tammy Elizabeth McBride; musical director, Tim Acito; stage manager, Thomas E. Shotkin.

Joan .... Diane J. Findlay
Clarke .... Steve Elmore
Gwen .... Leslie Easterbrook

Alex .... Alden Fulcomer
Lisa .... Kristy Cates

Place: New York. Presented in two parts.

SWANSONG. By Patrick Page. August 16, 2002 (world premiere). Director, Burry Fredrik; scenery and lighting, Leo B. Meyer; costumes, Tammy Elizabeth McBride; production stage manager, Patrick Ballard.

Ben Jonson .... Sam Tsoutsouvas
John Heminges .... Timothy Jerome

Will Shakespeare .... Jack Wetherall

Presented in two parts.

Yale Repertory Theatre, New Haven
James Bundy artistic director, Victoria Nolan managing director,
Mark Bly associate artistic director

MEDEA/MACBETH/CINDERELLA. Conceived by Bill Rauch; adapted by Mr. Rauch and Tracy Young; from the Paul Roche translation of *Medea* by Euripides; from *Macbeth* by William Shakespeare; from *Cinderella* by Richard Rodgers and Oscar Hammerstein II; additional music and lyrics by Shishir Kurup. September 20, 2002 (world premiere). Directors, Mr. Rauch and Ms. Young; choreography, Sabrina Peck; musical direction, Steven Argila; scenery, Rachel Hauck; costumes, David Zinn; lighting, Jennifer Tipton; sound, David Budries; fight direction, Rick Sordelet; dramaturgs, Mark Bly and Christie Evangelisto; stage manager, Karen Quisenberry.

Stage Manager .... Daniel T. Parker
Medea .... Caroline Stephanie Clay
Macbeth .... Stephen Pelinski
Cinderella .... Heather Mazur
Nurse .... Jayne Houdyshell
First Witch; Rebel;
  Murderer; Doctor .... Derek Lucci
Second Witch; Rebel;
  Murderer .... Adam O'Byrne
Third Witch; Rebel;
  Murderer.. Ryan King
Godmother .... Alaina Reed Hall
Banquo .... David Paul Francis
Medea's Son I .... Latrice Hampton
Medea's Son II .... Staysha Liz Silva
Medea's Son
  I, II (alt.) .... Chavon Aileen Hampton

Tutor; Creon;
  Corinthian Woman .... Joan Schirle
Macduff .... Peter Howard
Stepmother .... April Ortiz
Portia .... Stefani Cvijetic
Joy.. Jennifer Lim
Duncan .... Horace A. Little
Malcolm, Duncan's Son .... Peter Macon
Lady Macbeth .... Christopher Liam Moore
Chorus Leader .... Kate A. Mulligan
Jason; Corinthian Woman........ Jennifer Griffin
Fleance, Banquo's Son .... Maulik Pancholy
Queen .... Kimberly Jajuan
Prince .... Peter Kim
King .... Christopher Spencer Wells

Musical numbers: "Cinderella March," "The Prince Is Giving a Ball," I Heard Her Voice," "In My Own Little Corner," "Boys and Girls Like You and Me," "In My Own Little Corner" (Reprise), "Madness Reigns," "Love Is a Dangerous Thing," "It's Possible," "Pray the Gods Forgive," "Gavotte,"

"Ten Minutes Ago," "Murder In Mind," "Stepsisters' Lament," "Waltz for a Ball/Ten Minutes Ago" (Reprise), "Do I Love You Because You're Beautiful?," "A Lovely Night," "Do I Love You Because You're Beautiful?" (Reprise), "Murder Tonight," "Now You're All Alone," "Do I Love You Because You're Beautiful?" (Second Reprise).

Presented in two parts.

BREATH, BOOM. By Kia Corthron. October 25, 2002. Director, Michael John Garcés; scenery, Wilson Chin; costumes, China Lee; lighting, Torkel Skjaerven; sound, Martin Desjardins; fight direction, Rick Sordelet; dramaturg, Emmy Grinwis; stage manager, Elena M. Maltese.

Prix	Opal Alladin	Comet	Afi McClendon
Cat	Donna Duplantier	Pepper, Officer Dray,	
Mother	Saidah Arrika Ekulona	Jo's Friend	Tijuana T. Ricks
Denise	Jan Leslie Harding	Angel	Heather Alicia Simms
Malika; Socks	Carla J. Hargrove	Shondra; Jo	Kellee Stewart
Jupiter	Phyllis Johnson	Fuego; Girl	Marilyn Torres
Jerome;			
Corrections Officer	Billy Eugene Jones		

FIGHTING WORDS. By Sunil Thomas Kuruvilla. November 21, 2003 (US premiere). Director, Liz Diamond; scenery, Marie Davis-Green; costumes, Meredith Palin; lighting, Scott Bolman; sound, Karl Mansfield; dramaturg, Linda Bartholomai; stage manager, Christine Collins.

Peg	Emma Bowers	Mrs. Davies	Jayne Houdyshell
Nia	Meg Brogan		

Time: 1980. Place: Merthyr Tydfil, Wales. Presented without intermission.

THE PSYCHIC LIFE OF SAVAGES. By Amy Freed. February 14, 2003. Director, James Bundy; scenery, Young Ju Baik; costumes, Corrine Larson; lighting, Torkel Skjaerven; sound, Sten Severson; dramaturg, Emily V. Shooltz; stage manager, Laura MacNeil.

Interviewer; Tito;		Rebecca; Kit-Kat;	
Student; Party Guest	Bill Kux	Student; Party Guest	Robyn Ganeles
Ted Magus	John Hines	Sylvia Fluellen	Fiona Gallagher
Dr. Robert Stoner	Will Marchetti	Emily Dickenson; Vera	Phyllis Somerville
Anne Bittenhand	Meg Gibson		

THE BLACK MONK. By David Rabe; based on the novella by Anton Chekhov; translation by Erica Warmbrunn. May 15, 2003 (world premiere). Director, Daniel Fish; choreography, Peter Pucci; scenery, Christine Jones; costumes, Jane Greenwood; lighting, Stephen Strawbridge; sound, Leah Gelpe; musical direction, Vicki Shaghoian; dramaturg, Carrie Hughes; stage manager, Karen Quisenberry.

Yegor Semyonitch Pesotsky	Sam Waterston	Ensemble	Matthew Martin
Andrei Vasilich Kovrin	Thomas Jay Ryan	The Black Monk	Christopher McCann
Nadia	Nancy Anderson	Mikhail	Paul Mullins
Tanya	Jenny Bacon	Varvara Nikolaevna	Pamela Nyberg
Orlov	Leo Leyden	Yakov	Haynes Thigpen
With: Matthew Martin, Jeffrey Withers.			

District of Columbia

Arena Stage, Washington, DC
Molly Smith artistic director, Stephen Richard executive director

ANTHEMS: CULTURE CLASH IN THE DISTRICT. By Richard Montoya, Ric Salinas and Herbert Siguenza. September 4, 2002 (world premiere). Director, Charles Randolph-

Wright; scenery and lighting, Alexander V. Nichols; costumes, Anne Kennedy; sound, Timothy M. Thompson; dramaturg, Michael Kinghorn; stage manager, Pat A. Flora.

Performed by Johanna Day, Bill Grimmette, Nikki Jean, Joseph Kamal, Richard Montoya, Jay Patterson, Psalmayene 24, Ric Salinas, Shona Tucker.

THEOPHILUS NORTH. By Matthew Burnett; based on the novel by Thornton Wilder. January 24, 2003 (world premiere). Director, Mark Cuddy; scenery and costumes, G.W. Mercier; lighting, Ann G. Wrightson, sound, Gregg Coffin; dramaturg, Marge Betley, stage manager, Kathleen Mahan. Presented in association with Geva Theatre, Rochester, New York.

Theophilus North .... Matthew Floyd Miller
Woman 1 .... Siobhán Mahoney
Woman 2 .... Valerie Leonard
Woman 3 .... Lynn Steinmetz
    Presented in two parts.

Man 1 .... Michael Laurino
Man 2 .... Andrew Polk
Man 3 .... Edward James Hyland

BOOK OF DAYS. By Lanford Wilson. February 28, 2003. Director, Wendy C. Goldberg; scenery, Michael Brown; costumes, Anne Kennedy; lighting, Nancy Schertler; sound, Timothy M. Thompson; dramaturg, Michael Kinghorn; stage manager, Pat A. Flora.

Earl Hill .... Jefferson Breland
Rev. Bobby Groves .... David Fendig
James Bates .... Scott James
Len Hoch .... Brian Keane
Ginger Reed .... Susan Lynskey
LouAnn Bates .... Monette Magrath
    Place: Dublin, Missouri.

Ruth Hoch .... Jennifer Mudge
Boyd Middleton .... Mark Pinter
Martha Hoch .... Linda Stephens
Sheriff Conroy Atkins .... David Toney
Walt Bates .... Jack Willis

Readings: Firstglance. October 17–November 2, 2002.

EURYDICE. By Sarah Ruhl. October 17, 2002.

ADVENTURES WHILE PREACHING THE GOSPEL OF BEAUTY. By Craig Wright. October 18, 2002.

BLACKBALLIN'. By Rickerby Hinds. October 19, 2002.

MIGHTY MYTHS. By Wendy Wasserstein. October 20, 2002.

EXPOSED. By Beth Henley. October 25, 2002.

THE MARRIAGE OF MISS HOLLYWOOD AND KING NEPTUNE. By Robert Schenkkan. October 26, 2002.

METHOD SKIN. By Jerome Hairston. November 1, 2002.

HOLD, PLEASE. By Annie Weisman. November 2, 2002.

New Play Readings: Downstairs. April 3–14, 2003.

ARRANGEMENTS. By Ken Weitzman. April 3, 2003.

THE QUICK. By Tanya Barfield. April 4, 2003.

MRS. BOB CRATCHIT'S WILD CHRISTMAS BINGE. By Christopher Durang. April 5, 2003.

PAW PAW PATCH. By Kathleen McGhee-Anderson. April 11, 2003.

COLUMBINUS. By the United States Theatre Project. April 12, 2003.

EXPOSED. By Beth Henley. April 13, 2003.

SHAKESPEARE IN HOLLYWOOD. By Ken Ludwig. April 13, 2003.

AN AMERICAN DAUGHTER. By Wendy Wasserstein. May 2, 2003 (revised version). Director, Molly Smith; scenery, Bill C. Ray; costumes, Gabriel Berry; lighting, John Ambrosone; sound, Martin Desjardins; dramaturg, Michelle T. Hall; stage manager, Brady Poole.

Dr. Lyssa Dent Hughes	Johanna Day	Senator Alan Hughes	Robert Prosky
Quincy Quince	Holly Twyford	Charlotte "Chubby" Hughes	Laurie Kennedy
Judith B. Kaufman	Gail Grate	Jimmy	Tyee Tilghman
Walter Abrahmson	J. Fred Shiffman	Billy Robbins	David Fendig
Morrow McCarthy	Damon Gupton	Television Crew	Tuyet Thi Pham
Timber Tucker	Alex Webb		

The Kennedy Center, Washington, DC
Eric Schaeffer artistic director, Max Woodward producer

MERRILY WE ROLL ALONG. Revival of the musical with book by George Furth; music and lyrics by Stephen Sondheim; based on the play by George S. Kaufman and Moss Hart. July 14, 2002. Director, Christopher Ashley; choreography, Karma Camp; scenery, Derek McLane; costumes, David C. Woolard; lighting, Howell Binkley; sound, Tom Morse; projections, Michael Clark; orchestrations, Jonathan Tunick; musical direction, Eric Stern.

Performed by Anastasia Barzee, Raúl Esparza, Adam Heller, Michael Hayden, Miriam Shor, Emily Skinner.

PASSION. Revival of the musical with book by James Lapine; music and lyrics by Stephen Sondheim. July 21, 2002. Director, Eric Schaeffer; scenery, Derek McLane; costumes, Anne Kennedy; lighting, Howell Binkley; sound, Tom Morse; orchestrations, Jonathan Tunick; musical direction, Patrick Vaccariello.

Performed by Michael Cerveris, Philip Goodwin, Judy Kuhn, Rebecca Luker, John Leslie Wolfe

A LITTLE NIGHT MUSIC. Revival of the musical with book by Hugh Wheeler; music and lyrics by Stephen Sondheim. August 4, 2002. Director, Mark Brokaw; choreography, John Carrafa; scenery, Derek McLane; costumes, Michael Krass; lighting, Howell Binkley; sound, Tom Morse; orchestrations, Jonathan Tunick; musical direction, Nicholas Archer.

Performed by Kristen Bell, Sarah Uriarte Berry, Blair Brown, Barbara Bryne, Natascia Diaz, John Dossett, Randy Graff, Danny Gurwin, Douglas Sills, Erik Sorenson.

Woolly Mammoth Theatre Company, Washington, DC
Howard Shalwitz artistic director, Kevin Moore managing director

RECENT TRAGIC EVENTS. By Craig Wright. August 19, 2002 (world premiere). Director, Michael John Garcés; scenery, Daniel Ettinger; costumes, Lynn Steinmetz; lighting, Lisa L. Ogonowski; sound, Martin Desjardins. (2003 ATCA/Steinberg New Play Citation)

Waverly	Holly Twyford	Nancy	Dori Legg
Andrew	Eric Sutton	Stage Manager	Nehal Joshi
Ron	Michael Ray Escamilla		

JUMP/CUT. By Neena Beber. March 2, 2003 (world premiere). Director, Leigh Silverman; scenery, Erhard Rom; costumes, Michele Reisch; lighting, Dan Conway; sound, Jill B.C. DuBoff. Presented in association with Theater J.

Paul	Eric Sutton	Karen	Colleen Delany
Dave	Michael Chernus		

FLORIDA

New Theatre, Coral Gables
Rafael de Acha artistic director, Eileen Suarez managing director

ANNA IN THE TROPICS. By Nilo Cruz. October 12, 2002 (world premiere). Director, Rafael de Acha; scenery, Michelle Cumming; costumes, Estela Vrancovich; lighting, Travis Neff; music and sound, M. Anthony Reimer; production stage manager, Margaret M. Ledford. (2003 ATCA/Steinberg New Play Award)

Eliades	Carlos Orizondo	Conchita	Deborah L. Sherman
Cheché	Ken Clement	Marela	Ursula Freundlich
Santiago	Gonzalo Madurga	Palomo	Carlos Orizondo
Ofelia	Edna Schwab	Juan Julian	David Perez Ribada

Presented in two parts.

Coconut Grove Playhouse, Coral Gables
Arnold Mittelman producing artistic director, Laura Calzolari executive director

URBAN COWBOY. Musical with book by Aaron Latham and Phillip Oesterman, based on the 1980 film by Paramount Pictures; music and lyrics by various songwriters. November 25, 2002 (world premiere). Director, Lonny Price; choreography, Melinda Roy; scenery, James Noone; costumes, Ellis Tillman; lighting, David F. Segal; sound, Peter Fitzgerald; musical direction, orchestrations, arrangements, Jason Robert Brown; fight direction, Rick Sordelet; production stage manager, Neil Krasnow. Presented by special arrangment with Chase Mishkin and Leonard Soloway.

Jesse	Rozz Morehead	Bebe "Bubbles" Baker	Michelle Kittrell
Travis Williams;		Barbie McQueen	Kimberly Dawn Neumann
Gilley's Regular	Michael Balderrama	Candi Cane	Tera-Lee Pollin
Bubba; Policeman	Mark Bove	Bud	Matt Cavenaugh
Randy Jay Jacobs	Gerrard Carter	Billie "Veruka" Wynette	Kelleia Sheerin
J.D. Letterlaw; Policeman	Justin Greer	Johnnie Wynette	Paula Wise
Johnnie Ray	Brian Letendre	Sissy	Jenn Colella
Trent Williams	Barrett Martin	Uncle Bob	Leo Burmester
Luke "Gator" Daniels	Chad L. Schiro	Aunt Corene	Sally Mayes
Love Levy	Nicole Foret	Pam	Jodi Stevens
Shelby Chevy Tucker	Sarah Jayne Jensen	Wes	Marcus Chait

Musical numbers: "Long Hard Day," "Buckaroo," "I'm Gonna Like It Here," "Corene's Commandments," "Boot Scootin' Boogie, "It Don't Get Better Than This," "Dancing the Slow Ones With You," "Cowboy Take Me Away," "Could I Have This Dance," "My Back's Against the Wall," "If You Mess With the Bull," "I Used to Like It Here," "Honey, I'm Home," "That's How She Rides the Bull," "I Take it Back," 'Houston Hustle," "Take You for a Ride," "Sin Wagon," "T-R-O-U-B-L-E," "Dances Turn Into Dreams," "The Hard Way," "Git It," "Something That We Do," "Better Days," "The Devil Went Down to Georgia," "Lookin' for Love."

Time: 1980. Place: Houston, Texas. Presented in two parts.

ROMEO AND BERNADETTE. Musical with book and lyrics by Marc Saltzman; music adapted from classic Neapolitan songs. January 10, 2003 (world premiere). Director, Mark Waldrop; scenery, Michael Anania; costumes, Miguel Angel Huidor, lighting, F. Mitchell Dana; sound, Steve Shapiro; musical direction and arrangements, Bruce W. Coyle; production stage manager, Naomi Littman. Presented in association with Paper Mill Playhouse, Millburn, New Jersey.

Romeo .... Adam Monley	Camille Penza .... Emily Zacharias
Julie; Bernadette Penza .... Natalie Hill	Sal Penza .... Charles Pistone
Brooklyn Guy;	Tito Titone .... Andrew Varela
Dino Del Canto .... Andy Karl	Lips .... Vince Trani
Brooklyn Girl;	Don Del Canto .... David Brummel
Donna Dubacek .... Rosie De Candia	Enzo; Agent; Priest .... John Paul Almon

Musical numbers: "Oh Woe!/There's More," "Marechiare," "Bernadatte," "My Sweet Verona," "I'm With the Philharmonic," "Boom! In Love," "One Tender Word," "Non La Famiglia," "A World Away," "Moonlight Tonight Over Brooklyn," "The Swan Contessa," "O, For A Song," "Bernadette II," "More Woe!" "That's Love," "That's Love II," "To Be Tito Titone," "One Tender Word II," "When He Looked At Me That Way," "Sal's Toast," "O, For A Song II," "D'Amore."

Presented in two parts.

BOULEVARD OF BROKEN DREAMS. Musical with book by Joel Kimmel; music by Harry Warren. February 14, 2003. Director and choreographer, Kay Cole; scenery, Bradley Kay; costumes, Shon LeBlanc, lighting, Steven Young; sound, Steve Shapiro; production stage manager, Naomi Littman. Presented in association with Corky Productions, LLC.

Al Dubin.. Jordan Bennett	Cab Calloway.................................... Allan Louis
Harry Warren .... Troy Britton Johnson	Roberta .... Mary Jo Mecca
Helen McClay .... Elizabeth Ward Land	Busby Berkeley .... Rick Negron
Patricia Dubin .... Fleur Phillips	Dick Powell;
Ruby Keeler;	Johnny Mercer .... Randy Slovacek
Carmen Miranda .... Beth Curry	

Musical numbers: "'Twas Only Any Irishman's Dream," "For You," "Tiptoe Through the Tulips," "I'll String Along With You," "A Cup of Coffee, a Sandwich and You," "Two Many Kisses in the Summer," "Frankfurter Sandwiches," "O'Brien Is Trying to Learn to Talk Hawaiian," "Mechanical Man," "We're in the Money," "Painting the Clouds With Sunshine," "Forty Second Street," "Lulu's Back in Town," "I Only Have Eyes For You," "Plenty of Money and You," "Tiptoe Through the Tulips" (Reprise), "September in the Rain," "You're Getting to Be a Habit With Me," "South American Way," "Indian Summer," "Boulevard of Broken Dreams," "We Mustn't Say Good-Bye," "Lullaby of Broadway."

Presented in two parts.

SIX DANCE LESSONS IN SIX WEEKS. By Richard Alfieri. March 21, 2003. Director, Arthur Allan Seidelman; scenery, Roy Christopher; costumes, Helen Butler; lighting, Tom Ruzika; sound, Philip G. Allen; production stage manager, Naomi Littman.

Lily Harrison .... Rue McClanahan	Michael Minetti .... Mark Hamill

Time: Present. Place: Lily Harrison's condo in St. Petersburg Beach, Florida. Presented in two parts.

ONCE REMOVED. By Eduardo Machado. April 25, 2003. Director, Michael John Garcés; scenery, Steve Lambert; costumes, Ellis Tillman; lighting, Eric Nelson; sound, Steve Shapiro.

Matriarch .... Lucie Arnaz	Fernando .... Gary Perez
Rolando .... Gilbert Cruz	Rosita .... Lourdes Martin
Barbara .... Fiora Diaz	

Hippodrome State Theatre, Gainesville

Lauren Caldwell artistic director, Mary Hausch producing director

STONES IN HIS POCKETS. By Marie Jones. August 30, 2002. Director, Mary Hausch; scenery, J. Jeffrey Guice; costumes, Marilyn A. Wall; lighting, Robert P. Robins; sound, Rocky Draud; dramaturg, Tammy Dygert; stage manager, Elizabeth Nehls. Presented by arrangement with Paul Elliott, Adam Kenwright and Pat Moylan.

Charlie Conlon .... Mark Ellmore   Jack Quinn .... Paul Taviani
    Place: A small village in County Kerry, Ireland.

GEORGIA

Alliance Theatre Company, Atlanta
Susan V. Booth artistic director, Thomas Pechar managing director

FRAME 312. By Keith Reddin. October 23, 2002 (US premiere). Director, Susan V. Booth; scenery, G.W. Mercier; costumes, Nan Cibula-Jenkins; lighting, Michael Philippi; sound, Clay Benning; dramaturg, Megan Monaghan; stage manager, Kate McDoniel.

Lynette (1960s) .... Rebecca Harris   Lynette (1990s) .... Linda Stephens
Margie; Marie; Doris .... Courtney Patterson   Tom; Roy; Agent Barry;
Graham .... Jim Peck   Conductor .... Greg Stuhr
Stephanie .... Susan Pourfar
    Time: Early 1960s and the mid-1990s. Presented in two parts.

THE BENCH. By Larry Larson and Eddie Levi Lee. November 13, 2002 (world premiere). Director, Jessica Phelps West; scenery, Elaine Williams; costumes, Stan Poole; lighting, Liz Lee; sound, Clay Benning; musical direction and arrangements, Philip DePoy; dramaturg, Megan Monaghan; stage manager, Robert Allen Wright.

Sam Jenkins .... Eddie Levi Lee   Rachel; Finch singer .... Jennifer Courtade
Jeff Carlson .... Larry Larson   Arlene; Finch singer .... Donna Wright
William; Finch singer .... Steve Coulter   Voice of the Mall .... Rosemary Newcott
    Place: Small area of a shopping mall near you. Presented in two parts.

SAINT LUCY'S EYES. By Bridgette Wimberly. February 12, 2003. Director, Billie Allen; scenery, Beowulf Boritt; costumes, Alvin B. Perry; lighting, Brian Nason; sound, Clay Benning, music and sound, Michael Wimberly; dramaturg, Freddie Ashley, stage manager, Kate McDoniel.

Grandma .... Ruby Dee   Young Woman .... Toks Olagundoye
Woman .... Karan Kendrick   Bay .... Roger Robinson
    Time: 1968–81. Place: Memphis, Tennessee. Presented in two parts.

BAT BOY: THE MUSICAL. Musical with book by Keythe Farley and Brian Flemming; lyrics by Laurence O'Keefe. May 23, 2003. Director, Sean Daniels; choreography, Zoetic Dance Ensemble; scenery, Rochelle Barker; costumes, Sydney Roberts; lighting, Elisabeth Cooper; musical direction, Sally Priester; fight direction, Jason Armit; stage manager, Sloane Warren.

Bat Boy .... Clifton Guterman   Sheriff; Pan; Doctor #2Voice .... Travis Sharp
Shelley Parker .... Jill Hames   Rev. Hightower; Mrs. Taylor;
Meredith Parker;   Roy; Forest Creature .... Spencer Stephens
    Forest Puppeteer .... Patty Guenthner   Ruthie/Lorraine (Bud) .... Leslie Truman
Dr. Thomas Parker;   Rick; Ned (Daisy);
    Forest Puppeteer .... Geoff Uterhardt   Institute Man .... Michael Schneider
Mayor Maggie; Ron;
    Forest Creature .... Anne Towns

    Musical numbers: "Hold Me, Bat Boy," "Christian Charity," 'Ugly Boy," "Whatcha Wanna Do?," "A Home For You," "Another Dead Cow," "Dance With Me Darling," "Mrs. Taylor's Lullaby," "Show You a Thing Or Two," "A Home For You" (Reprise), "Comfort and Joy," "A Joyful Noise," "Let Me Walk Among You," "Three Bedroom House," "Children, Children," "Inside Your Heart," "Apology to a Cow," "I Imagine You're Upset," "Hold Me, Bat Boy" (Reprise).

PACIFIC OVERTURES. Musical with book by John Weidman; music and lyrics by Stephen Sondheim; additional material by Hugh Wheeler. May 7, 2003. Director, Kent Gash; choreography, Darren Lee and Francis Jue; scenery, Neil Patel; costumes, Paul Tazewell; lighting, Michael Philippi; sound, Clay Benning; musical direction, M. Michael Fauss; dramaturg, Megan Monaghan; production stage manager, Pat A. Flora.

Second councilor; others	Ronald M. Banks	Tamate; others	Allan Mangaser
Fisherman; others	Eric Bondoc	Lord Abe; others	Tony Marinyo
Kayama	Steven Eng	Third councilor; others	Alan Muraoka
Kurogo	Natalie Gray	Kurogo	Zany Pohlel
Shogun's mother; others	Mikio Hirata	Priest; others	Randy Reyes
Samurai; others	Kenway Hon Wai K. Kua	Reciter; others	James Saito
Manjiro; others	Jason Ma	Shogun's wife; others	Erwin G. Urbi

Musical numbers: "The Advantages of Floating in the Middle of the Sea," "There Is No Other Way," "Four Black Dragons," "Chrysanthemum Tea," "Poems," "Welcome to Kanagawa," "Someone in a Tree," "Lion Dance," "Please Hello," "A Bowler Hat," "Pretty Lady," "Next."

Time: July 1853 to present. Place: Japan. Presented in two parts.

ILLINOIS

Court Theatre, Chicago
Charles Newell artistic director, Diane Clausen executive director

PHÈDRE. By Jean Racine; translated and adapted by Paul Schmidt; additional adaptation by JoAnne Akalaitis. September 5, 2002. Director, Ms. Akalaitis; scenery, Gordana Svilar; costumes, Kaye Voyce and Joel Moritz; sound, Andre Pluess and Ben Sussman; dramaturg, Celise Kalke; stage manager, Laxmi Kumaran.

Phèdre	Jenny Bacon	Theseus	James Krag
Ismene	De Anna N.J. Brooks	Enone	Elizabeth Laidlow
Aricia	Chaon Cross	Theramenes	Scott Parkinson
Hippolytus	James Elly	Panope	Nicole Wiesner

Place: A room in Theseus's palace in Greece; the childhood home of Theseus and Hippolytus.

SCAPIN. By Molière; adapted by Shelley Berc and Andrei Belgrader; music and lyrics by Rusty Magee. October 24, 2002. Director, Christopher Bayes; choreography, David Silverman; scenery, Michael Sommers; costumes, Elizabeth Caitlin Ward; lighting, Diane D. Fairchild; musical direction, Jeff Caldwell; production stage manager, Christine D. Freeburg. Presented in association with Intiman Theatre Company, Seattle.

Nérine	Jeff Caldwell	Musician; others	Matthew Krause
Hyacinte	Chaon Cross	Léandre	Ned Noyes
Silvestre	Sean Fortunato	Scapin	Jeremy Shamos
Argante	Allen Gilmore	Géronte	David Silverman
Octave	Chester Gregory	Porter	Jason Denuszek
Zerbinette	Kimberly Hébert-Gregory		

Presented in two parts.

THE ROMANCE CYCLE. By Charles Newell; adapted from plays by William Shakespeare (Part 1: *Cymbeline*; Part 2: *Pericles*). April 12, 2003 (world premiere). Director, Mr. Newell; scenery, John Culbert; costumes, Linda Roethke; lighting, Michelle Habeck; sound, Joshua Horvath, Lindsay Jones and Andre Pluess; dramaturg, Celise Kalke; production stage manager, Laxmi Kumaran.

British Lord	Guy Adkins	Posthumus	Lance Stuart Baker

Helen	Kati Brazda	Philario	Warren Jackson
Pisanio	McKinley Carter	Cloten	Timothy Edward Kane
Caius Lucius	Chaon Cross	Queen	Kymberly Mellen
Cymbeline	Will Dickerson	Arviragus	Braden Moran
Belarius	Neil Friedman	Guiderius	Chuck Stubbings
Imogen	Kate Fry	Iachimo	Jay Whittaker

Place: Britain, Rome and Wales

Pericles	Guy Adkins	Dionyza	Kate Fry
Simonides	Lance Stuart Baker	Thaliard	Warren Jackson
Cerimon	Kati Brazda	Cleon	Timothy Edward Kane
Thaisa	McKinley Carter	Antiochus's Daughter	Kymberly Mellen
Marina	Chaon Cross	Knight	Braden Moran
Knight	Will Dickerson	Third Fisherman	Chuck Stubbings
Helicanus	Neil Friedman	Antiochus	Jay Whittaker

Place: Various cities along the Mediterranean coast.

Goodman Theatre, Chicago
Robert Falls artistic director, Roche Schulfer executive director

GALILEO GALILEI. An opera with libretto by Mary Zimmerman with Philip Glass and Arnold Weinstein; music by Mr. Glass. June 24, 2002 (world premiere). Director, Ms. Zimmerman; scenery, Daniel Ostling; costumes, Mara Blumenfeld; lighting, T.J. Gerckens; sound, Michael Bodeen; production stage manager, Alden Vasquez.

Performed by John Duykers, Andrew Funk, Mark Crayton, Gregory Purnhagen, Andrew McQuery, Alicia Berneche, Sarah Shepherd, Eugene Perry, Mary Wilson, Elizabeth Reiter, Laurence Di Stasi, Tess Given, Mandi Michalski, Tim Mullaney, Matt Orlando, Peter Scisioli, Zach Gray, Shelby Hyman.

THE BEARD OF AVON. By Amy Freed. October 7, 2002. Director, David Petrarca; scenery, Michael Yeargan; costumes, Jane Greenwood; lighting, James F. Ingalls; music and sound, Rob Milburn and Michael Bodeen; dramaturgy, Tom Creamer; production stage manager, Joseph Drummond.

William Shakespeare	Rob Campbell	Henry Conde;	
Old Colin; Lord Burleigh	Rob Riley	Sir Francis Bacon	Jeffrey Hutchinson
Anne Hathaway	Hollis Resnik	Edward de Vere,	
Geoffrey Dunderbread;		17th Earl of Oxford	Mark Harelik
Lady Lettuce	Ian Brennan	Henry Wriothesley	Jeff Whitty
Richard Burbage;		Fitch, Earl of Derby	Joe Foust
Sir Francis Walsingham	Craig Spidle	Elizabeth, Queen of England	Ora Jones
John Heminge	Greg Vinkler		

LOBBY HERO. By Kenneth Lonergan. November 4, 2002. Director, Robert Falls; scenery, Linda Buchanan; lighting, Michelle Habeck; costumes, Rachel Anne Healy; music and sound, Richard Woodbury; stage manager, Kimberly Osgood.

Jeff	Lance Stuart Baker	Dawn	Julie Granata
William	Rolando Boyce	Bill	Scott Cummins

BY THE MUSIC OF THE SPHERES. By Carson Grace Becker and David Barr III. February 24, 2003 (world premiere). Director, Chuck Smith; scenery, Felix E. Cochren; costumes, Birgit Rattenborg Wise; lighting, Robert Christen; music and sound, Ray Nardelli; dramaturg, Rick DesRochers; production stage manager, Kimberly Osgood.

Katherine	Antoinette Abbamonte	Nicholas	Fred Michael Beam

Goodman
Theatre
2002–2003
Season

Above: Fred Michael Beam and Antoinette Abbamonte in By the Music of the Spheres. *Photo: Eric Y. Exit*

Right: Caitlin Hart in Trojan Women. *Photo: Liz Lauren*

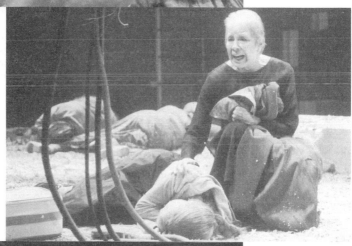

Left: Greta Oglesby and Yvette Ganier in Gem of the Ocean. *Photo: Michael Brosilow*

Doctor Newholm.............................John Lordan	Thomas..Troy West
Ellenore................................Arlene Malinowski	

DINNER WITH FRIENDS. By Donald Margulies. February 24, 2003. Director, Steve Scott; scenery, Geoffrey M. Curley; costumes, Nan Cibula-Jenkins; lighting, Rita Pietraszek; sound, Lindsay Jones; production stage manager, Alden Vasquez.

Beth...Suellen Burton	Gabe..Scott Jaeck
Karen.....................................Mary Beth Fisher	Tom...James Krag

TROJAN WOMEN. By Seneca; translated by Donald Slavitt. April 14, 2003. director, Mary Zimmerman; scenery, Daniel Ostling; costumes, Mara Blumenfeld; lighting, John Culbert; music, Philip Glass; sound and additional music, Andre Pluess.

Chorus.................................Cheryl Lynn Bruce	Astyanax..................................Zachary Leipzig
Soldier..Agustin Buñuel	Polyxena.................................Elizabeth Reiter
Old Servant.................................Nathan Davis	Andromache...............................Wendy Robie
Ulysses..Joe Dempsey	Soldier...Brad Stevens
Chorus......................................Laura T. Fisher	Agamemnon......................................Fred Stone
Pyhrrus..Kyle Hall	Chorus...Amy Warren
Talthybius; Messenger..............Russell Hardin	Hecuba..Caitlin Hart
Helen..Rebecca Jordan	Hecuba (replacement)................Ann Whitney

GEM OF THE OCEAN. By August Wilson. April 28, 2003 (world premiere). Director, Marion McClinton; scenery, David Gallo; lighting, Donald Holder; costumes, Constanza Romero; sound, Rob Milburn and Michael Bodeen; musical direction, Dwight Andrews; dramaturg, Chuck Smith; production stage manager, Joseph Drummond; stage managers, Narda Alcorn, T. Paul Lynch.

Eli...Paul Butler	Solly Two Kings.................Anthony Chisholm
Citizen Barlow..............................Kenny Leon	Aunt Ester...................................Greta Oglesby
Rutherford Selig.....................Raynore Scheine	Caesar...............................Peter Jay Fernandez
Black Mary..................................Yvette Ganier	

Next Theatre, Evanston
Jason Loewith artistic director

ENTERTAINING MR. SLOANE. By Joe Orton. November 11, 2002. Director, Jason Loewith; scenery, Matthew York; costumes, Mark Botelho; lighting, Darin Keesing; stage manager, Lara Maerz.

Kath..Wendy Robie	Dadda...Maury Cooper
Ed...Larry Neumann	Sloane.......................................Brian Hamman

IN THE BLOOD. By Suzan-Lori Parks. February 3, 2003. Director, Lisa Portes; scenery, Richard and Jacqueline Penrod; costumes, Kristine Knanishu; lighting, Jaymi Lee Smith; sound, Andre Pluess and Ben Sussman; dramaturg, Celise Kalke.

Performed by Karen Aldredge, Cassandra Bissell, Steve Haggard, Bill McGough, Phillip Van Lear, Celeste Williams.

Steppenwolf Theatre Company, Chicago
Martha Lavey artistic director, Michael Gennaro executive director

WE ALL WENT DOWN TO AMSTERDAM. By Bruce Norris. June 12, 2002 (world premiere). Director, Amy Morton; scenery, Todd Rosenthal; costumes, Mary Ellen Park; lighting, JR Lederle; sound, Ray Nardelli; stage manager, Michelle Medvin.

Wood..Jim Mohr	Cox...K. Todd Freeman

Dixon	William Dick	The Man	Tom Irwin
Steffie	Stephanie Childers	Old Woman	Joanna Maclay

UNTIL WE FIND EACH OTHER. By Brooke Berman. October 24, 2002 (world premiere). Director, Anna D. Shapiro; scenery, Zane Pihlstrom; costumes, Mary Trumbour; lighting, Phoebe Daurio; sound, Franco DeLeon; stage manager, Michelle Medvin.

Sophy	Stephanie Bernstein	Miriam	McKenna Kerrigan
Justin	Louis Cancelmi	Tangee	Niki Prugh
Rabbie; Steve	Luke Hatton		

I JUST STOPPED BY TO SEE THE MAN. By Stephen Jeffreys. November 14, 2002 (US premiere) Director, Randall Arney; scenery, Thomas Lynch; costumes, Kristine Knanishu; lighting, Chris Binder; sound, Richard Woodbury; stage manager, Malcolm Ewen.

Karl	Jim True-Frost	Della	Yvette Ganier
Jesse	Anthony Chisholm		

NO PLACE LIKE HOME. By Jessica Thebus; adapted from the stories of others. January 9, 2003 (world premiere). Director, Ms. Thebus; scenery, Stephanie Nelson; costumes, Brooke Schaffner; lighting, Jaymi Lee Smith; sound, Dave Pavkovic; dramaturg, Mary Alice Doyle; stage manager, Erin Wenzel.

Performed by Lance Stuart Baker, Alison Halstead, Greta Sidwell Honold, Margaret Kustermann, Monica Payne, Linh Thanh Pham, Jacqueline Williams, Cedric Young, Mary Aldousary, Fabrizio Almeida, Lois Atkins, Virginia Brackett, Kevin Davis, Anne McGravie, Kimberly Senior, Louis Washington, Erin West

WORLD SET FREE. By Bryn Magnus. February 25, 2003 (world premiere). Director, Hallie Gordon; choreography, Ann Boyd; scenery, Stephanie Nelson; costumes, Lynn Koscielniak; lighting, Alison Heryer; sound, Josh Schmidt; dramaturg, Rosie Forrest; stage manager, Michelle Medvin.

Performed by Charin Alvarez, Wayne Brown, Patrick Dollymore, James Elly, Hans Fleischman, Eli Goodman, Katie Johnston, Linara Washington.

TAKING CARE. By Mia McCullough. March 6, 2003 (world premiere). Director, Tim Hopper; scenery, Russell Poole; costumes, Jennifer Roberts; lighting, Adam Friedland; sound, Greg Silva; stage manager, Malcolm Ewen.

Ma	Roslyn Alexander	Benny	Guy Van Swearingen

THE VIOLET HOUR. By Richard Greenberg. April 17, 2003. Director, Terry Kinney; scenery, Robert Brill; costumes, Mara Blumenfeld; lighting, James F. Ingalls; sound, Rob Milburn and Michael Bodeen; stage manager, Laura D. Glenn.

Rosamund Plinth	Kate Arrington	Jessie Brewster	Ora Jones
John Pace Seavering	Josh Hamilton	Denis McCleary	Kevin Stark
Gidger	Tim Hopper		

Victory Gardens Theater, Chicago
Dennis Zacek artistic director, Marcelle McVay managing director

ARIADNE'S THREAD. By Anne Noble. September 13, 2002 (world premiere). Director, Sandy Shinner; scenery, Jack Magaw; costumes, Judith Lundberg; lighting, Jaymi Lee Smith; sound, Andre Pluess and Ben Sussman; production stage manager, Ellyn Costello.

Joan	Tyla Abercrumbie	Connor	Joey Honsa
Anderson	Mary Kathryn Bessinger	Niki	Nambi E. Kelley

Gareth .... Laura Jones Macknin   Lea .... Julia Neary
Wendy .... Jenny McKnight
    Time: The present. Place: Chicago, New York and London. Presented in two parts.

GOD AND COUNTRY. Musical by Douglas Post; based on the story of Antigone. November 15, 2002 (world premiere). Director, Jim Corti; scenery, Mary Griswold; costumes, Judith Lundberg; lighting, Jaymi Lee Smith; sound, Bob Garrett; musical direction and arrangements, Andy Jones; production stage manager, Tina M. Jach.

Antigone; Tiresias;   Ismene; Sentry; Haemon;
  Messenger; Chorus .... Karla L. Beard   Eurydice; Chorus .... Dina DiCostanzo
Creon; Chorus .... Jane Blass
    Time: Forty-eight hours in the life of a city. Place: Thebes. Presented in two parts.

BOURBON AT THE BORDER. By Pearl Cleage. January 17, 2003. Director, Andrea J. Dymond; scenery, Mary Griswold; costumes, Patti Roeder; lighting, Mary Badger; sound, Joe Cerqua; production stage manager, Rita Vreeland.

May Thompson .... Velma Austin   Tyrone Washington .... A.C. Smith
Rosa St. John .... Cheryl Lynn Bruce   Charlie Thompson .... E. Milton Wheeler
    Time: September 1995. Place: Detroit, Michigan. Presented in two parts.

UNSPOKEN PRAYERS. By Claudia Allen. March 21, 2003 (world premiere). Director, Dennis Zacek; scenery, Patrick Kerwin; costumes, Kristine Knanishu; lighting, Jeff Pines; music and sound, William J. Norris; dramaturg, Sara Freeman; production stage manager, Tina M. Jach.

Edna; others .... Velma Austin   Sara .... Karlie Nurse
Frank's Boss; others .... Brad Harbaugh   Frank .... Rob Riley
Big Bob; others .... Kenn E. Head   Becca .... Kim Wade
Billie .... Taylor Miller

CONCERTO CHICAGO. By Lonnie Carter. April 17, 2003 (world premiere). Director, Nic Dimond; scenery, B. Emil Boulas; costumes, Christine E. Pascual; lighting, Todd Hensley; dramaturg, Andrea J. Dymond; production stage manager, John David Flak.

    Performed by John Steven Crowley, DJ Misha Fiksel, Nambi E. Kelley, Lisa Tejero, E. Milton Wheeler.

THE END OF THE TOUR. By Joel Drake Johnson. May 23, 2003 (world premiere). Director, Sandy Shinner; scenery, Jeff Bauer, costumes, Judith Lundberg; lighting, Rita Pietraszek; sound, Andre Pluess and Ben Sussman; production stage manager, Tina M. Jach.

Jan Morris Williamson .... Annabel Armour   Tommy Johns .... Marc Silvia
Andrew Morris .... Timothy Hendrickson   Norma Brown .... Kitty Taber
Chuck Williamson .... Rob Riley   Mae Anne Pierce .... Mary Ann Thebus
David Sabin .... Andrew Rothenberg
    Time: The present. Place: Dixon, Illinois.

INDIANA

Indiana Repertory Theatre, Indianapolis
Janet Allen artistic director, Daniel Baker managing director

HE HELD ME GRAND. By James Still. October 2, 2002. Director, David Bradley; choreography, Cynthia Pratt; scenery, Russell Metheny; costumes, Gail Brassard; lighting,

Dennis Parichy; sound, Andrew Hopson; composers, Tim Grimm and Jason Wilber; musical direction, Terry Woods; dramaturgs, Janet Allen and Richard J. Roberts; stage manager, Joel Grynheim.

The Family		The Ancestors	
April Williams	Priscilla Lindsay	Young Lillian	Kristin Dulaney
Jesse Williams	Ryan Artzberger	Pap-Pap	Mark Goetzinger
Pete	Jonathan Gillard Daly	Mam-Mam	Gigi Jennewein
Grace Turner	Cathy Simpson	Lillian	Wendy Rader
Young Grace	Mariah Britton	Dot	Crystal Roberts
Young April	Emily Robbins	Kay	Catherine M. Smith
May Crawford	Jacqueline Knapp	Buddy Becker	Scott Boulware
Edie Alexander	Milicent Wright	Raymond Williams	Jacob Saylor
June	Jan Lucas	Ted	David Alan Anderson
Mr. Scott	Wiley Moore	John Williams	Bob Motz

Time: July 2000 and the past. Place: An old house in Indianapolis. Presented in three parts.

KENTUCKY

Actors Theatre of Louisville, Louisville
Marc Masterson artistic director, Alexander Speer executive director

JITNEY. By August Wilson. September 21, 2002. Director, Timothy Douglas; scenery, Paul Owen; costumes, Randall E. Klein; lighting, Jane Hall; sound, Vincent Olivieri; fight direction, Brent Langdon; dramaturg, Tanya Palmer; production stage manager, Paul Mills Holmes. Presented in association with Syracuse Stage.

Youngblood	Chuma Hunter-Gault	Philmore	Tyrone Mitchell Henderson
Turnbo	Doug Brown	Becker	Charles Weldon
Fielding	William Charles Mitchell	Booster	Charles Parnell
Doub	Johnny Lee Davenport	Rena	Pascale Armand
Shealy	Ray Anthony Thomas		

Time: Early fall, 1977. Place: A gypsy cab station in Pittsburgh, Pennsylvania

PROOF. By David Auburn. January 9, 2003. Director, Sullivan Canady White; scenery, Paul Owen; costumes, Lorraine Venberg; lighting, Tony Penna; sound, Vincent Olivieri; dramaturg, Steve Moulds; stage manager, Paul Mills Holmes.

Robert	Terry Layman	Hal	Matt Seidman
Catherine	Woodwyn Koons	Claire	Chandler Vinton

Place: Back porch of a house in Chicago. Presented in two parts.

THE PAVILION. By Craig Wright. February 7, 2003. Director, Aaron Posner; scenery, Paul Owen; costumes, Lorraine Venberg; lighting, John Stephen Hoey; sound, Vincent Olivieri; dramaturg, Amy Wegener; production stage manager, Paul Mills Holmes.

Narrator	Lee Sellars	Kari	Susan Riley Stevens
Peter	Greg Wood		

Time: The present. Place: The Pavilion, an old dance hall in Pine City, Minnesota. Presented in two parts.

27th Annual Humana Festival of New American Plays. March 2–April 13, 2003.

OMNIUM GATHERUM. By Alexandra Gersten-Vassilaros and Theresa Rebeck. March 2, 2003. Director, Will Frears; scenery, Paul Owen; costumes, Lorraine Venberg; lighting, Tony Penna; sound, Vincent Olivieri; fight direction, Brent Langdon; dramaturg, Sarah Gubbins, stage manager, Kathy Preher.

2003 Humana Festival of New American Plays

Above: Robert Lee Simmons and Richard Furlong in Omnium Gatherum. *Photo: John Fitzgerald*

Left: Dyron Holmes and Cheryl Freeman in Slide Glide the Slippery Slope. *Photo: John Fitzgerald*

Below: John Catron and Greg McFadden in The Faculty Room. *Photo: Harlan Taylor*

Suzie	Kristine Nielsen	Khalid	Edward A. Hajj
Roger	Phillip Clark	Terence	Dean Nolen
Lydia	Roma Maffia	Jeff	Richard Furlong
Julia	Melanna Gray	Mohammed	Robert Lee Simmons

Time: The present. Place: An elegant dinner party. Presented without intermission.

SLIDE GLIDE THE SLIPPERY SLOPE. March 7, 2003. By Kia Corthron. Director, Valerie Curtis-Newton; scenery, Paul Owen; costumes, Rondi Hillstrom Davis; lighting, Tony Penna; sound, Bray Poor; dramaturg, Tanya Palmer; stage manager, Cat Domiano.

Erm	Tonye Patano	Sear	Dyron Holmes
Elo	Cheryl Freeman	Rosie	Bobbi Lynne Scott
Retta	Shona Tucker	Dell	Lizan Mitchell

Time: The present

THE FACULTY ROOM. By Bridget Carpenter. March 11, 2003. Director, Susan Fenichell; scenery, Paul Owen; costumes, Lorraine Venberg; lighting, Mary Louise Geiger; sound and music, Shane Rettig; fight direction, Brent Langdon; dramaturg, Amy Wegener; stage manager, Leslie K. Oberhausen.

Carver	Greg McFadden	Principal Dennis	Colin McPhillamy
Zoe	Rebecca Wisocky	Bill	William McNulty
Adam	Michael Laurence	Student	John Catron

Time: Present. Place: The faculty lounge of a public school. Presented in two parts.

THE LIVELY LAD. By Quincy Long; music by Michael Silversher. March 18, 2003. Director, Timothy Douglas; scenery, Paul Owen; costumes, Suttirat Larlarb; lighting, Mary Louise Geiger; sound, Colbert S. Davis IV; musical direction, Scott Kasbaum; fight direction, Brent Langdon; dramaturg, Amy Wegener; stage manager, Debra A. Freeman.

Martin; others	Dennis Kelly	Jameson	William McNulty
Jonathan Van Huffle	Marc Vietor	Henderson; others	Fred Major
Little Eva	Holli Hamilton	Shotworthy; others	Colin McPhillamy
Dorothea	Celia Tackaberry	Gideon	Lea Coco
Miss McCracken	Shannon Holt		

Time: Some time ago. Place: A metropolis. Presented in two parts.

THE SECOND DEATH OF PRISCILLA. By Russell Davis. March 22, 2003. Director, Marc Masterson; scenery, Paul Owen; costumes, Lorraine Venberg; lighting, Tony Penna; sound, Vincent Olivieri; dramaturg, Sarah Gubbins; stage manager, Nancy Pittelman.

Priscilla	Barbara Gulan	Armanda	Jen Grigg
Peter	Will Bond	Second Priscilla	Jenna Close
Second Peter	Jon Held	Coquelicot	Katherine Hiler
Jacqueline	Graham Smith		

Time: Present. Place: Priscilla's bedroom, the big blue sky outside and a forest. Presented in two parts.

ORANGE LEMON EGG CANARY. By Rinne Groff. March 29, 2003. Director, Michael Sexton; scenery, Paul Owen; costumes, Suttirat Larlarb; lighting, Tony Penna; sound and music, Shane Rettig; dramaturg, Tanya Palmer; production stage manager, Paul Mills Holmes.

Great	Rene Millan	Trilby	Nell Mooney
Henrietta	Wendy Rich Stetson	Egypt	Roz Davis

TREPIDATION NATION. March 28, 2003. A phobic anthology by Keith Josef Adkins, Stephen Belber, Hilary Bell, Glen Berger, Sheila Callaghan, Bridget Carpenter, Cusi

Cram, Richard Dresser, Erik Ehn, Gina Gionfriddo, Kirsten Greenidge, Michael Hollinger, Warren Leight, Julie Marie Myatt, Victoria Stewart, James Still. Director, Wendy McClellan, scenery, Paul Owen; costumes, John P. White; lighting, Paul Werner; sound, Colbert S. Davis IV; dramaturg, Steve Moulds; stage manager, Justin McDaniel.

Performed by Chris Ashworth, Jamie Askew, Kate Bailey, John Catron, Valerie Chandler, Jenna Close, Beth Collins, Daniel Evans, Richard Furlong, Jen Grigg, Jason Kaminsky, Lori McNally, Dimitri Meskouris, Brian Nemiroff, Megan Ofsowitz, Eleni Papaleonardos, Michael Rosenbaum, Natalie Sander, Bobbi Lynne Scott, Robert Lee Simmons, Brad Smith, Justin Tolley.

RHYMICITY. March 28, 2003. Curated by Mildred Ruiz and Steven Sapp; production supervisor, Frazier Marsh.

Performed by Regie Cabico, Gamal A. Chasten, reg e. gaines, Rha Goddess, Mildred Ruiz, Steven Sapp.

Ten-Minute Plays. April 5–6, 2003.

TRASH ANTHEM. By Dan Dietz. Director, Jennifer Hubbard.

Woman	Rebecca Wisocky	Boots	Michael Laurence

Place: Little house.

THE ROADS THAT LEAD HERE. By Lee Blessing. Director, Joseph Haj.

Jason	Lea Coco	Xander	Jason Kaminsky
Marcus	Justin Tolley		

Time: Here and now. Place: Their father's house.

FIT FOR FEET. By Jordan Harrison. Director, Timothy Douglas; scenery, Paul Owen; costumes, John P. White and Mike Floyd; lighting, Paul Werner; sound, Colbert S. Davis IV; dramaturg, Steve Moulds; stage manager, Leslie K. Oberhausen.

Claire	Holli Hamilton	Jimmy	Greg McFadden
Linda	Celia Tackaberry	A prominent dance critic	Shannon Holt

MARYLAND

Center Stage, Baltimore
Irene Lewis artistic director, Michael Ross managing director

NO FOREIGNERS BEYOND THIS POINT. By Warren Leight. November 27, 2002 (world premiere). Director, Tim Vasen; scenery, Christine Jones; costumes, Tom Broecker; lighting, Matthew Frey; sound, Fitz Patton; dramaturg, Charlotte Stoudt; stage manager, Linda Marvel.

Paula Wheaton	Carrie Preston	Lao Wan; Lao Hu; Peasant	Les J.N. Mau
Andrew Baker	Ean Sheehy	Mr. Wang; Sherman;	
Principal Wang;Ying; Peasant	Ben Wang	Peasant; Customs Official	Andrew Pang
Teacher Chen; Xiao Er	Jane Wong	Xiao Wan; Xiao Da	Nancy Wu
Vice Principal Huang;			
Lincoln; Peasant	John Woo Taak Kwon		

Presented in two parts.

INTIMATE APPAREL. By Lynn Nottage. February 26, 2003 (world premiere). Director, Kate Whoriskey; scenery, Walt Spangler; costumes, Catherine Zuber; lighting, Scott Zielinski; sound, Lindsay Jones, music, Reginald Robinson; dramaturg, Jerry Patch; stage manager, Mike Schleifer. Presented in association with the South Coast Repertory.

2003 Humana
Festival of New
American Plays

Ten-Minute
Plays

Above: Rebecca Wisocky in
Trash Anthem. *Photo: Harlan
Taylor*

*Right: Jason Kaminsky and
Justin Tolley in* The Roads
That Lead Here. *Photo:
Harlan Taylor*

*Below: Celia Tackaberry, Holli
Hamilton, Greg McFadden in*
Fit for Feet. *Photo: Harlan
Taylor*

Mrs. Dickson .... Brenda Pressley   Mrs. Van Buren .... Sue Cremin
Esther .... Shané Williams   Mr. Marks .... Steven Goldstein
George Armstrong .... Kevin Jackson   Mayme .... Erica Gimpel
    Time: 1905. Place: Manhattan. Presented in two parts.

MASSACHUSETTS

American Repertory Theatre, Cambridge
Robert Woodruff artistic director, Robert J. Orchard managing director

UNCLE VANYA. By Anton Chekhov; translated by Paul Schmidt; adapted by János Szász. November 30, 2002. Director, Mr. Szász; scenery, Riccardo Hernández; costumes, Edit Szücs; lighting, Christopher Akerlind; sound, David Remedios; dramaturg, Ryan McKittrick; production stage manager, Chris De Camillis.

Marina .... Karen MacDonald   Sonya .... Phoebe Jonas
Mikhail Lvovich Astrov .... Arliss Howard   Yelena .... Linda Powell
Ivan Patrovich (Vanya) .... Thomas Derrah   Yefim .... Elbert Joseph
Alexander Serebriakov .... Will LeBow   Bartender .... Genna Ravvin
Ilya Ilych Telegin .... Remo Airaldi;   Bar patrons .... Jonathan Mirin, Paul DiMilla,
                                    Benjamin Evett   John Michael Dupuis, Jason Grossman
    Presented in two parts.

THE CHILDREN OF HERAKLES. By Euripides; translated by Ralph Gladstone. January 8, 2003. Director, Peter Sellars; costumes, Brooke Stanton; lighting, James F. Ingalls; sound, Shahrokh Yadegari; production stage manager, Nancy Harrington.

Iolaus .... Jan Triska   Eurystheus .... Cornel Gabara
Copreus .... Elaine Tse   Moderator; Chorus .... Christopher Lydon
Demophon .... Brenda Wehle   Chorus .... Heather Benton
Macaria; Alcmene .... Julyana Soelistyo   Musician .... Ulzhan Baibussynova
Attendant .... Albert S.
    Presented in two parts.

LA DISPUTE. By Pierre Marivaux; translated by Gideon Lester; adapted by Anne Bogart. February 1, 2003. Director, Ms. Bogart; scenery, Neil Patel; costumes, James Schuette; lighting, Christopher Akerlind; sound, Darron L. West; dramaturg, Barbara Whitney; production stage manager, Elizabeth Moreau. Presented in association with the SITI Company.

The Prince .... Frank Raiter   Mesrou .... Remo Airaldi
Hermione .... Lynn Cohen   Adine .... Kelly Maurer
Églé .... Ellen Lauren   Mesrin .... Will Bond
Azor .... Stephen Webber   Meslis .... Barney O'Hanlon
Carise .... Lizzy Cooper Davis   Dina .... Akiko Aizawa
    Ensemble: Curtis August, Ashley Wren Collins, Dan Domingues, Benjamin Evett, Mark Alexandre Fortin, Donei Hall, Georgia Hatzis, Jason Kaufman, Jennifer Mackey, Mindy Woodhead.

HIGHWAY ULYSSES. By Rinde Eckert; based on Homer's *Odyssey*. March 5, 2003 (world premiere). Director, Robert Woodruff; scenery and costumes, David Zinn; lighting, David Weiner; sound, David Remedios; musical direction, Peter Foley; dramaturg, Ryan McKittrick; stage manager, M. Pat Hodge.

Bride .... Nora Cole   Son .... Dana Marks
Ulysses .... Thomas Derrah
    Ensemble: Heather Benton, Rinde Eckert, Will LeBow, Karen MacDonald, Michael Potts.

Berkshire Theatre Festival, Stockbridge
Kate Maguire executive director

QUARTET. By Ronald Harwood. July 10, 2002 (US premiere). Director, Vivian Matalon; scenery, R. Michael Miller; costumes, Tracy Christensen; lighting, Ann G. Wrightson; sound, Phillip Scott Peglow; stage manager, Mona El-Khatib.

Cecily Robson	Kaye Ballard	Jean Horton	Elizabeth Seal
Wilfred Bond	Paul Hecht	Reginald Paget	Robert Vaughn

Place: Living room, outside of which is Kent countryside. Presented in two parts.

DIMETOS. By Athol Fugard. June 17, 2002 (US premiere). Director, Peter Wallace; scenery, Katya DeBear; costumes, Elizabeth Bourgeois; lighting, Deb Sullivan; sound, Phillip Scott Peglow; production stage manager, Peter Durgin.

Dimetos	Eric Hill	Sophia	Anne O'Sullivan
Lydia	Tara Franklin	Danilo	Jeremy Davidson

Huntington Theatre Company, Boston
Nicholas Martin artistic director

MARTY. Musical with book by Rupert Holmes; music by Charles Strouse; lyrics by Lee Adams; based on the screenplay by Paddy Chayefsky and on the United Artists film. October 30, 2002 (world premiere). Director, Mark Brokaw; choreography, Rob Ashford; scenery, Robert Jones; costumes, Jess Goldstein, lighting, Mark McCullough; sound, Kurt Eric Fischer; orchestrations, Don Sebesky and Larry Hochman; production stage manager, James FitzSimmons.

Marty	John C. Reilly	Father DiBlasio	Michael Allosso
Mrs. Fusari	Cheryl McMahon	Bandleader	Alexander Gemignani
Angie	Jim Bracchitta	Mrs. Pilletti	Barbara Andres
Tilio	Alexander Gemignani	Mary Feeney	Kate Middleton
Aunt Catherine	Marilyn Pasekoff	Clara	Anne Torsiglieri
Virginia	Jennifer Frankel	Mr. Ryan	Michael Walker
Thomas	Evan Pappas	Andy	Tim Douglas
Patsy	Frank Aronson	Keegan	Kent French
Joe	Joey Sorge	Rita	Shannon Hammons
Ralph	Robert Montano	Dance Hall Patrons	Jim Augustine,
Leo	Matt Ramsey		Bethany J. Cassidy
Bartender	Tim Douglas		

Musical numbers: "Marty," "Whaddya Feel Like Doin'?," "Saturday Night Girl," "Play the Game," "That Blue Suit," "Why Not You and Me?," "She Sees Who I Am," "Recessional," "My Star," "Niente Da Fare," "What Else Could I Do?," "Almost," "Life Is Sweet," "Wish I Knew a Love Song."

Presented in two parts.

THE BLUE DEMON. By Darko Tresnjak. January 12, 2003 (world premiere). Director, Mr. Tresnjak; scenery, David P. Gordon; costumes, Linda Cho; lighting, Rui Rita; sound, Kurt Kellenberg; music, Michael Friedman; production stage manager, Thomas M. Kauffman.

The Hunchback's Tale		The Sultan	Gregory Derelian
Scheherazade	Roxanna Hope	The Executioner	Paul Cortez
The Jeweler	Darius de Haas	The Three Concubines	Mehera Blum,
The Tailor	Tom Titone		Lauren Hatcher, Mariessa Portelance
The Scrivener	Matt Ramsey	The Three Imperial Guards	Michael Cohen,
The Jester	Kirk McDonald		Sean-Michael Hodge-Bowles, Ben Sands

The Four Musicians .... Gabriel Boyers, Gunnard Dobozé, Kareem Roustom, Mike Wiese

The Tailor's Tale
The Husband .... Brian Sgambati
The Wife .... Anna Belknap
The Wizard .... Tom Flynn
The Servant .... Kirk McDonald
The Three Rabbis .... Mehera Blum, Lauren Hatcher, Mariessa Portelance
The Sultan of Akra .... Dara Fisher

The Scrivener's Tale
The King .... Tom Flynn

The Prince .... Brian Sgambati
The Chancellor .... Matt Ramsey
The Princess .... Anna Belknap
The Puppeteer .... Paul Cortez
The Witch .... Dara Fisher
The Three Mourners .... Mehera Blum, Lauren Hatcher, Mariessa Portelance

The Jeweler's Tale
The Beggar .... Brian Sgambati
The Three Virgins .... Mehera Blum, Lauren Hatcher, Mariessa Portelance
The Peddler .... Kirk McDonald
The Old Sultan .... Tom Flynn
The Vizier .... Dara Fisher
The Last Virgin .... Anna Belknap

BREATH, BOOM. By Kia Corthron. March 7, 2003. Director, Michael John Garcés; scenery, Adam Stockhausen; costumes, Karen Perry; lighting, Kirk Bookman; sound and music, Martin Desjardins; fight direction, Rick Sordelet; production stage manager, Thomas M. Kauffman.

Prix .... Kellee Stewart
Angel .... Zabryna Guevara
Malika; Jo .... Carla J. Hargrove
Comet .... Dwandra Nickole
Jerome .... Edwin Lee Gibson
Mother .... Jacqui Parker

Cat .... Tawanna Benkow
Fuego; Jo's friend .... Katrina Toshiko
Shondra; Pepper .... Chinasa Ogbuagu
Denise .... Jan Leslie Harding
Girl .... Tawanna Benbow
Jupiter .... Ramona Alexander

Shakespeare and Company, Lenox
Tina Packer artistic director

THE VALLEY OF DECISION. By Dennis Krausnick; adapted from the book by Edith Wharton. June 1, 2002 (world premiere). Director, Rebecca Holderness; scenery, Lauren Kurki; costumes, Jennifer Halpern; lighting, Stephen D. Ball; sound, Jason Fitzgerald; stage manager, Rio Maria Doyle.

Innkeeper .... Andrew Borthwick-Leslie
Odo Valsecca .... Ethan Flower
Fulvia Vivaldi .... Elizabeth Aspenlieder
Orazio De Crucis .... Lon Troland Bull

Count LelioTrescorre .... Mel Cobb
Carlo da Gamba .... Michael Burnet
Count Alfieri .... Andrew Borthwick-Leslie
Duchess .... Catherine Taylor-Williams

Time: 1783–89. Place: The ducal chambers in the palace at Pianura, an imaginary duchy in Lombardy. Presented in two parts.

ETHAN FROME. By Dennis Krausnick; adapted from the book by Edith Wharton. July 31, 2002. Director, Mr. Krausnick; costumes, Govane Lohbauer; lighting, Nathan Towne-Smith; sound, Mark Huang; production stage manager, Brenda J. Lillie.

Homer Winterston & Co. .... Dave Demke
Ethan Frome .... Kevin G. Coleman

Zenobia Frome .... Mary Guzzy
Mattie Silver .... Elizabeth Aspenlieder

Time: Winter 1860 and 1884. Place: The Frome family farm and the environs of Starkfield in Berkshire County, Massachusetts. Presented without intermission.

SUMMER. By Dennis Krausnick; adapted from the book by Edith Wharton. August 1, 2002. Director, Tina Packer; costumes, Govane Lohbauer; lighting, Nathan Towne-Smith; sound, Mark Huang; production stage manager, Brenda J. Lillie.

A touch, a kiss: Elizabeth Aspenlieder and Ethan Flower in The Valley of Decision. *Photo: Kevin Sprague*

Lawyer Royall .... Michael Hammond
Chorus; townsperson .... Dave Demke
Chorus; townsperson .... Mary Guzzy
Charity Royall .... Carolyn Roberts
Lucius Harney .... Henry David Clarke
Chorus; townsperson .... Jonathan Croy
Chorus; townsperson .... Jennie Israel
    Time: Summer 1898. Place: North Dormer, Massachusetts. Presented in two parts.

THE FIERY RAIN. By Dennis Krausnick; adapted from Edith Wharton. August 2, 2002. Director, Dan McCleary; costumes, Govane Lohbauer; lighting, Nathan Towne-Smith; sound, Mr. McCleary; stage manager, John Godbout.

Henry James .... Dennis Krausnick
William Morton Fullerton .... Allyn Burrows
Edith Wharton .... Tod Randolph
    Time: 1907–10. Place: Rye, England; London, Paris, Lenox, Massachusetts. Presented without intermission.

THE SCARLET LETTER. By Carol Gilligan; adapted from the novel by Nathaniel Hawthorne. September 7, 2002 (world premiere). Director, Tina Packer; choreography, Susan Dibble; scenery, Judy Gailen; costumes, Harry Johnson; lighting, Karen Perlow; sound, Jason Fitzgerald; production stage manager, Brenda J. Lillie.

Reverend Wilson .... Dave Demke
Reverend Dimmesdale .... Jason Asprey
Governor Bellingham .... Jonathan Croy
Reverend Wilson .... Dave Demke
Mistress Hibbard .... Mary Guzzy
Roger Chillingworth .... Michael Hammond
Pearl .... Kate Holland
Hester Prynne .... Jennie Israel
Townsperson .... Tom Wells
Townsperson .... Catherine Taylor-Williams
    Time: Mid-19th century. Place: In and around Boston. Presented in two parts.

THE FLY-BOTTLE. By David Egan. May 24, 2003 (world premiere). Director, Tina Packer; scenery, Bob Lohbauer; costumes, Govane Lohbauer; lighting, Nathan Towne-Smith; stage manager, Jessica S. Gluck.

Karl Popper .... Dave Demke   Bertrand Russell .... Dennis Krausnick
Ludwig Wittgenstein .... Michael Hammond

MINNESOTA

Guthrie Theater, Minneapolis
Joe Dowling artistic director, Susan Trapnell managing director

RESURRECTION BLUES. By Arthur Miller. August 10, 2002 (world premiere). Director, David Esbjornson; scenery, Christine Jones; costumes, Elizabeth Hope Clancy; lighting, Marcus Dilliard; sound, Scott W. Edwards; dramaturg, Carla Steen; stage manager, Russell W. Johnson. (2003 ATCA/Steinberg New Play Citation)

Gen. Felix Barriaux .... John Bedford Lloyd   Phil .... Peter Thoemke
Henri Schultz ....Jeff Weiss   Sarah .... Laura Esping
Police Captain .... Emil Herrera   Jeanine .... Wendy vanden Heuvel
Emily Shapiro .... Laila Robins   Stanley .... Bruce Bohne
Skip L. Cheeseboro .... David Chandler
    Place: In a Latin American nation. Presented in two parts.

Theatre de la Jeune Lune, Minneapolis
Barbra Berlovitz, Vincent Gracieux, Robert Rosen, Dominique Serrand, Steven Epp
artistic directors
Steve Richardson producing director

HAMLET. By William Shakespeare; adapted by Paddy Hayter and Theatre de la Jeune Lune. October 17, 2002. Director, Mr. Hayter; scenery and masks, Fredericka Hayter; costumes, Sonya Berlovitz; lighting, Marcus Dilliard; music, Eric Jensen; stage manager, Andrea Hendricks.

Claudius .... Vincent Gracieux   Osric .... Nicholas Blumm
Gertrude .... Barbra Berlovitz   Priest ....Henry Allen
Hamlet .... Steven Epp   Marcellus .... Nicholas Blumm
Ghost of Hamlet's father .... Henry Allen   Francisco .... Sarah Agnew
Polonius .... Serge Pesic   Bernardo .... Kristopher Lencowski
Laertes .... Stephen Cartmell   Gravediggers .... Serge Pesic, Henry Allen
Ophelia ....Sarah Agnew   Player King ....Henry Allen
Horatio ....Jason Lambert   Players and Chorus .... The Company

THE MAN WHO LAUGHS. By Victor Hugo; adapted in collaboration with Kevin Kling. March 25, 2003 (world premiere). Director, Robert Rosen; scenery, Vincent Gracieux; costumes, Sonya Berlovitz; lighting, Karin Olson; stage manager, Liz Neerland.

Ursus.. Robert Rosen   Gwynplaine .... Ben Kernan
Homo; Barkilphedro ....Vincent Gracieux   Dea; Josiana .... Christina Baldwin

FIGARO. By Steven Epp; music adapted by Bradley Greenwald; conceived by Dominique Serrand and Mr. Epp; based on works by Beaumarchais, W.A. Mozart and Lorenzo da Ponte. May 23, 2003 (world premiere). Direction and scene design, Mr. Serrand; costumes, Sonya Berlovitz; lighting, Karin Olson; musical direction, Barbara Brooks; video, Mr. Serrand, Elizabeth Huber and Daniel Lori; sound, Katharine Horowitz; stage manager, Ann K. Terlizzi.

Fig...................................... Steven Epp   Suzanne .... Barbra Berlovitz
Figaro .... Charles Schwandt   Susanna .... Momoko Tanno

Count Almaviva	Bradley Greenwald	Basilio	Tom Speckhard
Mr. Almaviva	Dominique Serrand	Bartolo	Chandler Molbert
Countess	Jennifer Baldwin Peden	Marcellina	Loralie Kirkpatrick
Cherubino	Christina Baldwin	Leon	Nathan Keepers; Max Friedman
Bazile	Jason Lambert		

Presented in two parts.

MISSOURI

Missouri Repertory Theatre, Kansas City
Peter Altman producing artistic director

INCOGNITO. By Michael Sidney Fosberg. September 14, 2002. Director, Michael E. Myers; scenery, Ryan McKinty-Trupp; lighting, Jeffrey Cady; production stage manager, Mary R. Honour. Presented in association with Tom Spiroff.

Performed by Mr. Fosberg.

Time: 1997. Place: Various cities in the United States. Presented in two parts.

INDIAN INK. By Tom Stoppard. May 7, 2003. Director, Risa Brainin; scenery, Nayna Ramey; costumes, Devon Painter; lighting, Michael Klaers; sound, Tom Mardikes; composer, Michelle DiBucci; dramaturg, Melissa J.A. Carle; production stage manager, Keri Muir.

Flora Crewe	Mary Beth Fisher	Anish Das	Nikhil Kamkolkar
Coomaraswami	Sanji Jhaveri	Captain David Durance	R. Ward Duffy
Nazrul	Vasudeva Ramaswamy	Resident	Robert Gibby Brand
Eleanor Swan	Pauline Flanagan	Englishwoman	Peggy Friesen
Eldon Pike	Larry Paulsen	Englishman; Eric ....,Joseph Price
Dilip; Questioner	Jeremy Gram Weaver	Rajah; Politician	Krishen Mehta
Nirad Das	Samrat Chakrabarti	Nell	Regan Glover

Ensemble: Jyotirmay Ray Ghatak Chaudhuri, Diane Ouradnik.

Time: 1930; mid-1980s. Place England; India. Presented in two parts.

NEW JERSEY

Centenary Stage Company, Hackettstown
Carl Wallnau producing director

THE TILLIE PROJECT. By Jeanne Murray Walker. October 11, 2002 (world premiere). Director, Carl Wallnau; scenery and lighting, Charles Ard; costumes, Julia Sharp; sound, Joseph Langham.

Performed by Larky Barnes, Steven L. Barron, Dina Ann Comolli, Desiree Fitzgerald, Christopher Kromer, Victoria Mack, Al Mohrmann, Katie Moen, Claire Montgomery, Carolyn Popp, Doug Spaulding.

ALICE IN IRELAND. By Judy Sheehan. February 28, 2003 (world premiere). Director, Barbara Bosch; scenery, Gordon Danielli; costumes, Julia Sharp; lighting, Ed Matthews; sound, Joseph Langham; stage manager, Pat Sheffield.

Alice Hart	Jill Abramovitz	Eamon; Tony;	
Lily Hart	Dana Halsted	Danny; Eddie	Carmine Covello;
Conor	Peter Husovsky		Keith Medash
Bridie Hart	Maybeth Ryan	Michael; Brendon	Sean Patrick

Trevor; Jimmy;
   Dennis; Fr. O'Connell .... Al Mohrmann
Mary Anne .... Carolyn Coulson-Grigsby

Stewardess; Kathleen;
   Nora; Brenda .... Desiree Fitzgerald

2003 Women Playwrights Series: Workshop Presentations.

LAST KISS. By Dominique Cieri. April 9, 2003. Director, Laura Ekstrand.

Crissy	Larissa Auble	Bean	Victoria Mack
Fran	Stephanie Carr	Kevin	Christopher Kromer
Mimi	Melissa Jane Martin	Narrator	Desiree Fitzgerald

SISTER WEEK. By Heather McCutchen. April 16, 2003. Director, Margo Whitcomb.

Sally	Jessica Beltz	June	Dina Ann Comolli
Janie	Mary Ethel Schmidt	May	Maria Brodeur
Mary Martha	Gayle Stahlhuth	Narrator	April Dunlop
Jay Jay	Ryan Defoe		

FINDING THE EYE. By Susan Johnston. Director, Daniella Topol. April 23, 2003. Lights and sound, April Dunlop.

Hannah	Rachel Sledd	Matteo	Caesar Samayoa
Kelly	Dawne Swearingen	Mama	Teo Dorina Bello
Ollie	Piter Fattouche	Narrator; Nurse	Laura Quackenbush

McCarter Theatre, Princeton

Emily Mann artistic director, Jeffrey Woodward managing director

CROWNS. By Regina Taylor; adapted from the book by Michael Cunningham and Craig Marberry. October 15, 2002 (world premiere). Director, Ms. Taylor; choreography, Ronald K. Brown; scenery, Riccardo Hernández; costumes, Emilio Sosa; lighting, Robert Perry; sound, Darron L. West; musical direction, Linda Twine; dramaturg, Janice Paran; production stage manager, Cheryl Mintz.

Man	Lawrence Clayton	Wanda	Janet Hubert
Yolanda	Carmen Ruby Floyd	Mother Shaw	Ebony Jo-Ann
Jeanette	Harriett D. Foy	Velma	Lillias White
Mabel	Lynda Gravátt		

FICTION. By Steven Dietz. March 25, 2003 (world premiere). Director, David Warren; scenery, James M. Youmans; costumes, David C. Woolard; lighting, Donald Holder; music and sound, John Gromada; dramaturg, Liz Engelman; production stage manager, Alison Cote.

Michael	Robert Cuccioli	Linda	Laila Robins
Abby	Marianne Hagan		

UNCLE VANYA. By Anton Chekhov; adapted by Emily Mann. May 2, 2003 (world premiere). Director, Ms. Mann; scenery, Michael Yeargan; costumes, Myung Hee Cho; lighting, Nancy Scertier; music, Baikida Carroll; production stage manager, Cheryl Mintz. Presented in association with La Jolla Playhouse.

Astrov	Michael Siberry	Ilya Telegin	Jonathan Hogan
Martina	Isa Thomas	Yelena	Natacha Roi
Vanya	Steven Skybell	Maria	Georgine Hall
Serebryakov	William Biff McGuire	Watchman	Bill Caleo
Sonya	Amanda Plummer		

Playwrights Theatre of New Jersey, Madison
John Pietrowski artistic director, Elizabeth Murphy producing director

BIG BOYS. By Rich Orloff. January 9, 2003 (world premiere). Director, John Pietrowski; scenery, Yoshinori Tanokura; costumes, Patricia E. Doherty; lighting, Richard Currie; sound, Jeff Knapp; production stage managers, Barbara Dente, Rose Riccardi. Presented in association with New Jersey Repertory Theater.

Victor	Al Mohrmann	Norm	Michael Irvin

GREEK HOLIDAY. By Stephen Hollis. May 1, 2003 (world premiere). Director, Mr. Hollis; scenery, Richard Turick; costumes, Bettina Bierly; lighting, Richard Currie; sound, Jeff Knapp; production stage manager, Barbara Dente.

Debra	Sarah Knapp	Janet	Melissa Gray
Alex	Timothy McCracken		

NEW YORK

Arena Players Repertory Company, East Farmingdale
Frederic DeFeis producer

THE JEW I MET ON KRISTALLNACHT. By Peter Campbell. February 6, 2003 (world premiere). Director, Frederic DeFeis; scenery, Fred Sprauer; costumes, Lois Lockwood; lighting, Al Davis; stage manager, Skeeter Boxberger.

Stefan Reiss	Evan Donnellan	Adam Klein	Carl Nehring
Hugo Reiss	Martin Edmond	Eric Schleicher	Vito Piplione
Sofie Reiss	Lynne Foster	Kurt Roehm	James Duggan
Gehli Reiss	Darcy Donnellan		

Time: Early evening, November 9, 1938. Place: The Reiss home in Berlin; an alley. Presented in two parts.

Geva Theatre, Rochester
Mark Cuddy artistic director

36 VIEWS. By Naomi Iizuka. February 18, 2003. Director, Chay Yew, scenery, Daniel Ostling; costumes, Lydia Tangi; lighting, Mary Louise Geiger; sound, Dan Roach; music, Nathan Wang; stage manager, Kirsten Brannen.

Elizabeth Newman-Orr	Elisabeth Adwin	Setsuko Hearn	Maile Holck
Claire Tsong	Melody Butiu	John Bell	Gregory Patrick Jackson
Darius Wheeler	Harry Carnahan	Owen Matthiassen	Alan Nebelthau

Studio Arena Theatre, Buffalo
Gavin Cameron-Webb artistic director, Ken Neufeld executive director

SHOOTING CRAPS. By Tom Dulack. January 10, 2003 (East Coast premiere). Director, Gavin Cameron-Webb; scenery, Harry A. Feiner; costumes, Donna McCarthy; lighting, Brian Cavanagh; production stage manager, Jessica Berlin.

Lena Caruso	Geraldine Librandi	Charlie Fox	James Dybas
Carmine Caruso	Teddy Coluca	Buffalo Calf	Tony Hoty
Joanna Caruso	Daniella Di Vecchio	Clayton Robinson	Michael Nichols

THE DRAWER BOY. By Michael Healey. February 14, 2003. Director, Gavin Cameron-Webb; scenery, Robert Cothran; costumes, Deborah Shippee; lighting, Stephen Quandt; sound; Chester Popiolkowski; stage manager, Nanci Sochol. Presented in association with Marilyn Abrams and Bruce Jordan.

Angus	J.R. Horne	Miles	Brian Hutchison
Morgan	John Ahlin		

Syracuse Stage, Syracuse
Robert Moss artistic director, Jim Clark producing director

BACKSLIDING IN THE PROMISED LAND. By Michele Lowe. January 15, 2003 (world premiere). Director, Robert Moss; scenery, Adam Stockhausen; costumes, Nanzi Adzima; lighting, Matthew Frey; sound, Jonathan Herter; stage manager, Michelle Ferguson.

Enid	Jacqueline Brookes	Saul; Janitor	Tommy Schrider
Mimi	Suzanne Grodner	Jenny; Nurse	Kelly Trumbell
Herman	Munson Hicks	Leo	Alex Friedman
Naomi	Anne Penner	Leo	Ryan Ferguson
Ludmilla	Judith Roberts		

THE CRUCIBLE. By Arthur Miller. February 19, 2003. Director, Timothy Douglas; scenery, Tony Cisek; costumes, Tracy Dorman; lighting, Michael Gilliam; sound, Jonathan Herter; stage manager, Stuart Plymesser.

Abigail	Cynthia Addai-Robinson	Betty Parris	Emily Agy
Ann Putnam; Sarah Good	Inga Ballard	Tituba	Marsha Stephanie Blake
Cheever	Doug Brown	Thomas Putnam	Johnny Lee Davenport
A girl of Salem	Ariel Elisabeth Dupas	Francis Nurse	Richard Harris
Rev. Parris	Tyrone Mitchell Henderson	Giles Corey	Malcolm Ingram
Mary Warren	Tamara E. Johnson	Elizabeth Proctor	Rachel Leslie
Reverend John Hale	Larry John Meyers	Willard	Markiss Simpson
Danforth	Kim Sullivan	John Proctor	Ray Anthony Thomas
Mercy Lewis	Renee Threatte	Rebecca Nurse	Jane Welch

COPENHAGEN. By Michael Frayn. April 2, 2003. Director, Michael Donald Edwards; scenery, Andrew Lieberman; costumes, Kaye Voyce; lighting, Les Dickert; sound, Jonathan Herter; stage manager, Michelle Ferguson.

Heisenberg	John Leonard Thompson	Bohr	Paul Whitworth
Margrethe	Nancy Snyder		

SUCH SMALL HANDS. By Tina Howe. April 30, 2003 (world premiere). Director, Robert Moss; scenery, Donald Eastman; costumes, Michael Krass; lighting, Chris Dallos; sound, Jonathan Herter; stage manager, Stuart Plymesser.

Performed by Elizabeth Franz

Ohio

Cincinnati Playhouse in the Park, Cincinnati
Edward Stern producing artistic director, Buzz Ward executive director

AN INFINITE ACHE. By David Schulner. February 6, 2003. Director, Greg Leaming; scenery, Marjorie Bradley Kellogg; costumes, Claudia Stephens; lighting, Dan Kotlowitz; composer, Fabian Obispo; stage manager, Suann Pollock.

Hope .... Eunice Wong   Charles .... Mark Alhadeff
    Time: It moves differently here. Place: A bedroom.

THE LOVE SONG OF J. ROBERT OPPENHEIMER. By Carson Kreitzer. March 27, 2003 (world premiere). Director, Mark Wing-Davey; scenery, Douglas Stein; costumes, Catherine Zuber; lighting, David Weiner; sound, Marc Gwinn; dramaturg, Kathleen Tobin; stage manager, Jenifer Morrow.

J. Robert Oppenheimer .... Curzon Dobell
Lilith .... Judith Hawking
Young Scientist;
    British Envoy; Strauss .... Jason Bowcutt
Scientist One; Rabi;
    Security One; General Groves;
    Scientist Voice; J. Edgar Hoover;
    Committee Voice .... Michael Pemberton
    Presented in two parts.

Teller; Voice Over;
    Security Two; Lansdale;
    Scientist Voice .... Steven Rattazzi
Kitty Oppenheimer .... Blaire Chandler
Jean Tatlock; Censor;
    Reporter; Nurse;
    Mother .... Carolyn Baeumler

Cleveland Play House, Cleveland
Peter Hackett artistic director, Dean R. Gladden managing director

BRIGHT IDEAS. By Eric Coble. October 18, 2002 (world premiere). Director, David Colacci; scenery and lighting, Pavel Dobrusky; costumes, Amanda Whidden; sound, Robin Heath; production stage manager, John Godbout.

Genevra Bradley .... Susan Ericksen
Joshua Bradley .... Andrew May
Parent #1; others .... Elizabeth Rainer
    Presented in two parts.

Parent #2; others .... Kate Hodge
Parent #3; others .... Chip DuFord

OREGON

Oregon Shakespeare Festival, Ashland
Libby Appel artistic director, Paul Nicholson executive director

CONTINENTAL DIVIDE: DAUGHTERS OF THE REVOLUTION and MOTHERS AGAINST. By David Edgar. March 1, 2003 (world premiere). Director, Tony Taccone; scenery, William Bloodgood; costumes, Deborah M. Dryden; lighting, Alexander V. Nichols; sound, Jeremy J. Lee; dramaturgs, Lue Morgan Douthit, Douglas Langworthy, Luan Schooler; stage managers, Jill Rendall (*Mothers*), Kimberly Jean Barry (*Daughters*). Presented in association with Berkeley Repertory Theatre.

Mothers Against
Sheldon .... Bill Geisslinger
Mitch .... Tony DeBruno
Connie .... Robynn Rodriguez
Lorianne .... Susannah Schulman
Caryl .... Vilma Silva
Don .... Michael Elich
Vincent .... Derrick Lee Weeden
Deborah .... Christine Williams
Daughters of the Revolution
Michael; ensemble .... Mark Murphey
Abby; ensemble .... Catherine Lynn Davis
Rebecca; ensemble .... Demetra Pittman

Blair; ensemble .... Linda Alper
Lorraine; ensemble .... Susannah Schulman
Mitch; ensemble .... Tony DeBruno
Ira; ensemble .... Richard Elmore
Carmen; ensemble .... Vilma Silva
Kwesi; ensemble .... Derrick Lee Weeden
Juniper; ensemble .... Catherine E. Coulson
Bill; Bud; Jimmy;
    Zee; ensemble .... Michael Elich
Arnie; Eddie;
    Tom; ensemble .... Bill Geisslinger
Amber; ensemble .... Robynn Rodriguez
Smokebomb; ensemble ...... Christine Williams

Oregon Shakespeare
Festival
2002–2003 Season

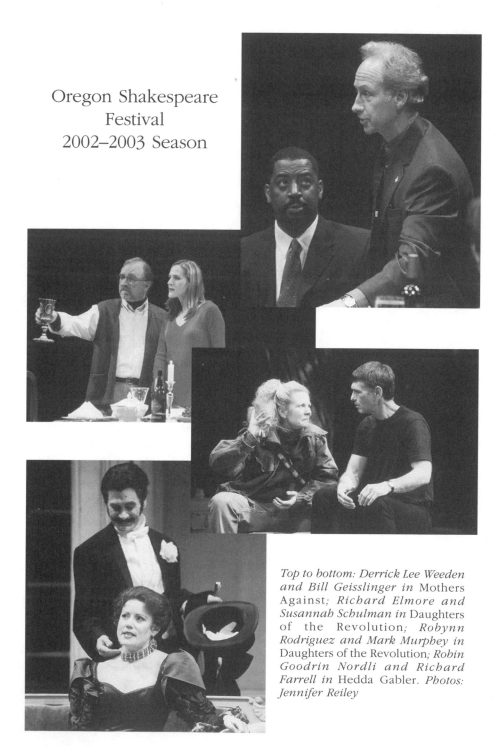

Top to bottom: *Derrick Lee Weeden
and Bill Geisslinger in* Mothers
Against; *Richard Elmore and
Susannah Schulman in* Daughters
of the Revolution; *Robynn
Rodriguez and Mark Murphey in*
Daughters of the Revolution; *Robin
Goodrin Nordli and Richard
Farrell in* Hedda Gabler. *Photos:
Jennifer Reiley*

Poppyseed; ensemble .... Nell Geisslinger   Jools; ensemble .... Mirron E. Willis
Young Jack; ensemble .... James Ingersoll
    Two thematically related plays performed in repertory.

HEDDA GABLER. By Henrik Ibsen; translated by Jerry Turner. April 23, 2003. Director,
Bill Rauch; scenery, Rachel Hauck; costumes, Shigeru Yaji; lighting, Geoff Korf; composer,
Todd Barton; dramaturg, Lue Morgan Douthit; stage manager, Jill Rendall.

George Tesman ....Jeffrey King   Judge Brack .... Richard Farrell
Hedda Gabler .... Robin Goodrin Nordli   Eilert Løvborg .... Jonathan Haugen
Miss Juliana Tesman .... Eileen DeSandre   Berte .... Margaret Schenck
Mrs. Thea Elvsted .... Terri McMahon   General Gabler .... James Edmondson
    Place: The Tesman Villa in the western part of Christiania. Presented in two parts.

Pennsylvania

Arden Theatre Company, Philadelphia
Terrence J. Nolen producing artistic director, Amy L. Murphy managing director

DAEDALUS: A FANTASIA OF LEONARDO DA VINCI. By David Davalos. September 17,
2002 (world premiere). Director, Aaron Posner, scenery, Tony Cisek; costumes, Margaret
K. McCarty; lighting, James Leitner; sound, James Sugg; production stage manager,
Jason Pizzi.

Leonardo da Vinci .... Greg Wood   Cecilia Bergamini;
Gonzalo Napoletano;   Isabella d'Este;
  Vitellozzo Vitelli .... Buck Schirner   Primavera .... Julie Czarnecki
Lodovico Sforza;   Cesare Borgia .... Peter Pryor
  Baldassare Castiglione;   Lucrezia Borgia .... Monica Koskey
  Niccoló Machiavelli .... Scott Greer   Lisa di Tirisio .... Grace Gonglewski

NORTHEAST LOCAL. By Tom Donaghy. January 30, 2003. Director, Terrence J. Nolen;
scenery, Christopher Pickart; costumes, Alison Roberts; lighting, James Leitner; sound,
Jorge Cousineau; production stage manager, Patricia Sabato.

Mickey .... William Zielinski   Mair .... Dale Soules
Gi .... Catharine K. Slusar   Jesse .... Raphael Peacock

InterAct Theatre Company, Philadelphia
Seth Rozin producing artistic director

GOING TO ST. IVES. By Lee Blessing. October 18, 2002. Director, Seth Rozin; scenery,
Nick Embree; costumes, Karen Ann Ledger; lighting, Peter Whinnery; sound, Nick Rye;
dramaturg, Larry Loebell; stage manager, Brady Gonsalves.

May N'Kame .... Claudia Robinson   Dr. Cora Gage .... Catharine K. Slusar
    Presented in two parts.

CRY HAVOC. By Tom Coash. January 10, 2003 (world premiere). Director, Seth Rozin;
scenery, Daniel Boylen; costumes, Karen Ann Ledger; lighting, Peter Whinnery;
dramaturg, Larry Loebell; stage manager, Brady Gonsalves.

Muhammed .... Piter Fattouche   Ms. Nevers .... Maureen Torsney-Weir
Nicholas .... Tom Byrn
    Time: Present. Place: Cairo.

ROSEMARY. By Jim O'Connor. March 28, 2003. Director, Roger Danforth; scenery, Roman Tatarowicz; costumes, Karen Ann Ledger; lighting, Peter Jakubowski; sound, Kevin Francis; dramaturg, Larry Loebell; stage manager, Brady Gonsalves.

Joe .... Dan Kern
Rose; Spokesperson;
Edith .... Cecilia Riddett
Rosemary .... Michelle Courvais
Joe Jr.; Charles;
Doctor 2; Steven .... Patrick Doran

Kathleen; Nun;
Nurse; Dr. Dugan .... Kirsten Quinn
Jack; Doctor 1;
Christopher .... Brian T. Delaney

Time: 1936 to the present. Place: Various locations in the US and Europe.

National Showcase of New Plays. June 20–29, 2002.

FOREIGN EXCHANGE. By Peter Hays. June 20, 2002. Director, John Pietrowski. Playwrights Theatre of New Jersey, Madison.

THE WHY. By Victor Kaufold. June 20, 2002. Director, Seth Rozin. InterAct Theatre Company.

MOURNING DOVE. By Emil Sher. June 21, 2002. Director, Richard Rose. Necessary Angel Theatre Company, Toronto.

A MEMORY OF RESISTANCE. By Lou Lippa. June 21, 2002. Director, Paul Meshejian. The People's Light and Theatre Company, Malvern, Pennsylvania.

DEATH OF THE SUN. By Sonya Aronowitz. June 21, 2002. Director, James Marvel. Passage Theatre Company, Trenton, New Jersey.

THE QUEEN'S 2 BODIES. By Jeanne Murray Walker. June 21, 2002. Director, Drucie McDaniel. InterAct Theatre Company.

MAYHEM. By Kelly Stuart. June 22, 2002. Director, Michael Dixon. The Guthrie Theater, Minneapolis.

A STRONGER FAITH. By Ken Prestininzi. June 22, 2002. Director, Nancy Kiracofe. ShenanArts, Staunton, Virginia.

THE BALLAD OF JOHN WESLEY REED. June 27, 2002. By Larry Loebell. Director, Roger Danforth. InterAct Theatre Company.

EIGHTEEN. By Allison Moore. June 27, 2002. Director, Dan Day. Kitchen Dog Theater, Dallas.

SLIGHT DEFECT—A DESERT HOLIDAY. By Ron Simonian. June 28, 2002. Director, Cynthia Levin. Unicorn Theatre, Kansas City, Missouri.

CENTRAL AVENUE. By Stephen Sachs. June 28, 2002. Director, Shirley Jo Finney. The Fountain Theatre, Los Angeles.

HAPPY NEW CENTURY, DR. FREUD. By Sabina Berman; translated by Kirsten Nigro. June 28, 2002. Director, Michael Johnson-Chase. The Lark Theatre Company, New York City, and Borderlands Theater, Tucson.

PHIDIAS8. By Michael Whistler. June 28, 2002. Director, James Haskins. InterAct Theatre Company.

SPAIN. By Jim Knable. June 28, 2002. Director, Tom Prewitt. Woolly Mammoth Theatre Company, Washington, DC.

ESSANAY. By Paul Peditto. June 28, 2002. Director, Scott Vehill. Prop Thtr Group, Chicago.

ROSEMARY. By Jim O'Connor. June 29, 2002. Director, Jonathan Lavan. Prop Thtr Group, Chicago.

HOW HIS BRIDE CAME TO ABRAHAM. By Karen Sunde. June 29, 2002. Director, Ken Marini. Playwrights Theatre of New Jersey, Madison.

Philadelphia Theatre Company, Philadelphia
Sara Garonzik producing artistic director, Ada G. Coppock general manager

BARBRA'S WEDDING. By Daniel Stern. June 5, 2002 (world premiere). Director, David Warren; scenery, Neil Patel; costumes, David C. Woolard; lighting, Donald Holder and Traci Klainer; sound, Fitz Patton; dramaturg, Michele Volansky.

Molly Schiff .... Julie White   Jerry Schiff .... John Pankow
    Time: July 1, 1998. Place: Malibu, California. Presented without intermission.

FULLY COMMITTED. By Becky Mode. October 16, 2002. Director, Gus Kaikkonen; scenery, Nick Embree; costumes, Margaret K. McCarty; lighting, William Armstrong; sound, Joshua H. Cohen; dramaturg, Michele Volansky; stage manager, Rachel R. Bush.

Sam Peliczowski .... Kraig Swartz
    Time: Early December. Place: Four-star restaurant on Manhattan's Upper East Side. Presented without intermission.

Stages 2002 New Play Readings. October 21–November 11, 2002.

FATHER-JOY. By Sheri Wilner. October 21, 2002. Director, Pam MacKinnon.

UNTITLED. Tom Donaghy. October 28, 2002. Director, Mr. Donaghy.

A SMALL, MELODRAMATIC STORY. By Stephen Belber. November 4, 2002. Director, Bob Hedley.

A PICASSO. By Jeffrey Hatcher. November 11, 2002. Director, John Tillinger.

KING HEDLEY II. By August Wilson. January 29, 2003. Director, Seret Scott; scenery, Yael Pardess; costumes, Janus Stefanowicz; lighting, Michael Gilliam; sound, Eileen Tague; composer, David Fonteno; fight direction, Ian Rose; dramaturg, Michele Volansky; stage manager, Rachel R. Bush.

Stool Pigeon .... Johnnie Hobbs Jr.   Mister .... Bryan Hicks
Ruby .... Lynda Gravátt   Tonya .... Sandra Daley
King .... Brian Anthony Wilson   Elmore .... Al White
    Time: 1985. Place: The Hill District, Pittsburgh, Pennsylvania. Presented in two parts.

THE LAST FIVE YEARS. Song cycle by Jason Robert Brown. March 19, 2003. Director, Joe Calarco; scenery, Michael Fagin; costumes, Anne Kennedy; lighting, Chris Lee; sound, Nick Kourtides; musical director, Ron Melrose; dramaturg Michele Volansky.

Cathy .... Nicole Van Giesen   James .... Wayne Wilcox
    Time: The present. Presented without intermission.

A PICASSO. By Jeffrey Hatcher. May 31, 2003 (world premiere). Director, John Tillinger; scenery, Derek McLane; costumes, Linda Cho; lighting, Duane Schuler; sound, Matthew Callahan; dramaturg, Michele Volansky.

Pablo Picasso .... Jeffrey DeMunn   Miss Fischer .... Lisa Banes
    Time: Late October 1941. Place: A vault below the streets of Paris.

Walnut Street Theatre, Philadelphia

Bernard Havard producing artistic director, Mark D. Sylvester managing director

THE LAKE. By Robert Caisley. March 4, 2003 (world premiere). Director, Richard M. Parison Jr., scenery, Todd Edward Ivins; costumes, Colleen McMillan; lighting, Troy A. Martin-O'Shia; sound, J. Hagenbuckle; production stage manager, Frank Anzalone.

Alec	Seth Reichgott	Nicola	Juliette Dunn
Liam	Jeremy Webb	Martin	Dan Olmstead

Time. The present. Place. A cabin by a lake. Presented in two parts.

SUMMONS TO SHEFFIELD. By Will Stutts. April 1, 2003 (world premiere). Director, Mr. Stutts; scenery, Virginia Jarvis; costumes, Mary Andrea Folino; lighting, Shelley Hicklin; sound, John Mock; production stage manager, Frank Anzalone.

Ben	Will Stutts	Laura-Lucille	Maureen Torsney-Weir
Sarah	Susan Wilder	Wren	Adam Way
Diane	Mollie Hall		

Time. A few years ago. Place. The Cunningham home, near Sheffield, Alabama.

Wilma Theater, Philadelphia

Blanka Zizka and Jiri Zizka producing artistic directors, Naomi Grabel managing director

DIRTY BLONDE. By Claudia Shear. September 18, 2002. Director, Ethan McSweeny; scenery, Andrew Jackness; lighting, John Stephen Hoey; costumes, Michael Sharpe; sound, Eileen Tague; dramaturg, Nakissa Etemad; stage manager, Patreshettarlini Adams.

Charlie	Kevin Carolan	The Man	Albert Macklin
Jo; Mae	Ryan Dunn		

EVERY GOOD BOY DESERVES FAVOR. By Tom Stoppard and André Previn. November 20, 2002. Director, Jiri Zizka; scenery, Anne Patterson; costumes, Janus Stefanowicz; conductor, Rossen Milanov; lighting, John Stephen Hoey; dramaturg, Nakissa Etemad.

Alexander	Richard Easton	Teacher	Polly Holliday
Ivanov	David Strathairn	The Colonel	David Howey
Doctor	Paul Hecht	Sacha	Dennis Michael Hall

THE MAGIC FIRE. By Lillian Groag. December 11, 2002. Director, Blanka Zizka; scenery, David P. Gordon; costumes, Janus Stefanowicz; lighting, Russell H. Champa; dramaturg, Nakissa Etemad; stage manager, Patreshettarlini Adams.

Gianni Guarneri	Charles Antalosky	Lise Berg	Robin Moseley
Elena Guarneri	Janis Dardaris	Paula Guarneri	Angela Pietropinto
Albreto Barcos	James Gale	Otto Berg	Martin Rayner
General Henri Fontannes	Dan Kern	Rosa Arrúa	Jo Twiss
Maddelena Guarneri	Kaye Kingston	Amalia Berg	Susan Wilder
Clara Stepaneck	Mikel Sarah Lambert	Lise 2	Samantha Wischnia

BIG LOVE. By Charles L. Mee. March 26, 2003. Director, Jiri Zizka; choreography, Brian Sanders; scenery, Jerry Rojo; costumes, Janus Stefanowicz; lighting, Jerold Forsyth; sound, Bill Moriarty; dramaturg, Nakissa Etemad; fight direction, J. Alex Cordaro; stage manager, Patreshettarlini Adams.

Lydia	Danielle Langlois	Bella; Eleanor	Carmen Roman
Olympia	Amy Gorbey	Piero; Leo	Robert Ari
Thyona	Danielle Skraastad	Giuliano	Ben Dibble

Constantine .... Steven Rishard   Nikos .... Paola Andino
Oed .... Michael J. Ewing
    Brides: Adrianna Carey, Madi Distefano, Mary McCool, Julianna Zinkel.
    Grooms: David James Bender, J. Alex Cordaro, Benjamin Kanes, David Konyk.

RED. By Chay Yew. May 28, 2003. Director, Blanka Zizka; choreography, Jamie H.J. Guan; scenery, Klara Zieglerova; costumes, Hiroshi Iwasaki; lighting, Russell H. Champa; sound, James Sugg; dramaturg, Nakissa Etemad; stage manager, Patreshettarlini Adams.

Sonja ....Jade Wu   Ling .... Lydia Look
Hua .... Francis Jue

Rhode Island

Trinity Repertory Company, Providence
Oskar Eustis artistic director, Edgar Dobie managing director

THE LONG CHRISTMAS RIDE HOME. By Paula Vogel. May 21, 2003 (world premiere). Director, Oskar Eustis; choreography, Donna Uchizono; scenery, Loy Arcenas; costumes, William Lane; lighting, Pat Collins; sound, Darron L. West; puppets, Basil Twist; stage manager, Jennifer Sturch.

Man .... Timothy Crowe   Claire .... Angela Brazil
Woman .... Anne Scurria   Minister........................... Sean Martin Hingston
Rebecca .... Rachel Warren   Musician .... Sumie Kaneko
Stephen .... Stephen Thorne
    Puppeteers: Joshua Boggioni, Joanna Cole, Virginia Eckert; Andy Gaukel, Maya Parra, Paul Ricciardi.

Texas

Alley Theatre, Houston
Gregory Boyd artistic director, Paul R. Tetreault managing director

THE GENERAL FROM AMERICA. By Richard Nelson. October 16, 2002. Director, Mr. Nelson; scenery, Douglas Stein; costumes, Susan Hilferty; lighting, James F. Ingalls; sound, Scott Lehrer; stage manager, Christa Bean.

The Arnolds
  Benedict Arnold .... Corin Redgrave   Lady Clinton .... Alice Cannon
  Peggy .... Yvonne Woods   The Americans
  Hannah .... Kate Kearney-Patch   George Washington .... Jon DeVries
The British   Alexander Hamilton .... Jesse Pennington
  Sir Henry Clinton .... Nicholas Kepros   Joseph Reed;
  John Andre .... Paul Anthony McGrane   Robinson .... Sean Cullen
Stephen Kemble;   Timothy Matlack;
  Van Wart .... Thomas H. Hammond   Pauling .... Thomas Sadoski
    Time: Midway through the Revolutionary War. Place: America. Presented in two parts.

FRAME 312. By Keith Reddin. October 30, 2002. Director, Peter Masterson; scenery, Kevin Rigdon; costumes, Linda Ross; lighting, Rui Rita; sound, Joe Pino.

Lynette (1960s) .... Elizabeth Bunch   Stephanie .... Jenny Maguire
Lynette (1990s) .... Carlin Glynn   Margie; Marie; Doris .... Stephanie Kurtzuba

Tom; Roy; Agent Barry .... Jeffrey Bean   Graham .... James Black
    Time: The 1960s and 1990s. Presented in two parts.

THE GOAT, OR WHO IS SYLVIA? By Edward Albee. January 22, 2003. Director, Pam
MacKinnon; scenery, Tony Straiges; costumes, Daryl A. Stone; lighting, Kevin Rigdon;
sound, Joe Pino; fight direction, Brian Byrnes; stage manager, Lori Lundquist.

Stevie .... Elizabeth Heflin   Ross .... James Belcher
Martin .... Todd Waite   Billy .... Matt Hune
    Presented without intermission.

Allied Theatre Group, Fort Worth
Jim Covault artistic director, Diane Anglim managing director

FOR LINDBERGH. By Pam Dougherty. September 21, 2002 (world premiere). Director,
Jim Covault; scenery, Mr. Covault, Peggy Kruger-O'Brien and Ms. Dougherty; costumes,
Ms. Kruger-O'Brien and Ms. Dougherty; lighting, Michael O'Brien; sound, Jamie Horn;
stage manager, Ms. Kruger O'Brien.

    Performed by Ms. Dougherty.

Kitchen Dog Theater, Dallas
Dan Day artistic director, Tina Parker administrative director

BARBETTE. By Bill Lengfelder and David Goodwin. June 8, 2002 (world premiere).
Director, Mr. Lengfelder; choreography, Fanny Jerwich, Mr. Lengfelder, Bree Sunshine
Smith, Joey Steakley and Jere Stevens Tulk; scenery and lighting, Eric Cope; costumes,
Christina Vela; sound, Mark Griffin; stage manager, Brian Frederick.

Young Barbette.............................. Mr. Steakley   Jean Cocteau; Cowboy #2 .... Jon Snow
Dr. Boyd; MC; Principal .... John Davies   Old Barbette .... Mr. Lengfelder
Sailor; Preacher; Cowboy #1 ..... Aaron Roberts   Hattie Broadway;
L'Ame... Ms. Smith   Francesca Alfaretta .... Ms. Tulk

Theatre Three, Dallas
Jac Alder executive producer

TRANSATLANTIC LIAISON. By Fabrice Rozié. March 10, 2003 (US premiere). Director,
John McLean; scenery, Harland Wright; costumes, Patty Korbelic Williams; lighting,
Mike Garner; sound, Bear Hamilton; music, Areski Belkacem; musical director, Terry
Dobson; production stage manager, Mr. Wright.

Simone de Beauvoir .... Elizabeth Rothan   Nelson Algren ..... Matthew Stephen Tompkins
    Presented in two parts.

Theatre Under the Stars, Houston
Frank M. Young president

SOME LIKE IT HOT. June 8, 2002. Musical with book by Peter Stone; music by Jule
Styne; lyrics by Bob Merrill; based on the screenplay by Billy Wilder and I.A.L. Diamond;
based on a story by Robert Thoeren. Director and choreographer, Dan Siretta; scenery,
James Leonard Joy; costumes, Suzy Benzinger, lighting, Ken Billington; sound and
production stage manager, Christopher K. Bond.

Osgood .... Tony Curtis	Sweet Sue .... Lenora Nemetz
Sugar .... Jodi Carmeli	Spats .... William Ryall
Jerry .... Timothy Gulan	Beinstock .... Gerry Vichi
Joe .... Arthur Hanket	

Musical numbers: "We Play in the Band," "Penniless Bums," "Tear the Town Apart," "The Beauty That Drives Men Mad," "Runnin' Wild," "We Could Be Close," "Sun on My Face," "November Song," "Doin' It For Sugar," "Sun on My Face" (Reprise), "Shell Oil"/"Hey, Why Not!" "I Fall in Love Too Easily," "Magic Nights," "It's Always Love," "When You Meet A Man in Chicago," "People in In My Life," "Some Like It Hot."

WHATEVER HAPPENED TO BABY JANE? Musical with book by Henry Farrell, music by Lee Pockriss; lyrics by Hal Hackady. October 9, 2002 (world premiere). Director, David Taylor; choreography, Dan Siretta; scenery, Jerome Sirlin; costumes, Eduardo Sicangco; lighting, Richard Winkler; sound, Beth Berkeley; orchestrations, Chris Walker; musical direction, Michael Biagi; production stage manager, Roger Allan Raby.

Jane Hudson .... Millicent Martin	Young Blanche .... Mary Illes
Blanche Hudson .... Leslie Denniston	Young Martin .... A.J. Vincent
Edna .... Bambi Jones	Young Jane;
Edwin .... Jim Blanchette	Flora Hudson .... Joanne Bonasso
Baby Jane .... Lea Marie Golde;	Walter Stone;
Brooke Singer	Mailman .... John Raymond Barker
Daddy .... Jim Weston	Mr. Gault .... Paul Hope
Baby Blanche .... Cara Cochran	Bonnie Dunbar .... Francie Mendenhall

Musical numbers: "Whatever Happened to Baby Jane?," "Where Would I Be Without You There?," "Daddy," "If I Was That Lady," "Four Walls," "You're There, Blanche," "Talent," "Two Who Move as One," "Sisters," "China Doll," "What Do You Think?," "I Still Have Tomorrow," "Whatever Happened to Baby Jane?" (Reprise), "China Doll," "He's Here," "When Am I Going to Be Me?," "If This House Could Talk," "Do I Care?," "Time We Had a Party," "Her."

Place: Hollywood home of the Hudson sisters and in the minds of both Blanche and Jane.

VIRGINIA

Signature Theatre, Arlington
Eric Schaeffer artistic director, Sam Sweet managing director

THE DIARIES. By John Strand. June 4, 2002 (world premiere). Director, P.J. Paparelli; scenery, Ethan Sinnott; costumes, T. Tyler Stumpf; lighting, Jonathan Blandin; sound, Adam Warnick.

Steve Alton .... Edward Gero	Student .... Daniel Frith
Daughter .... Julia Coffey	Doctress .... Sybil Lines
Time: 1978.	

WASHINGTON

ACT Theatre, Seattle
Kurt Beattie artistic director, Jim Loder managing director, Vito Zingarelli producing director,

DIRTY BLONDE. By Claudia Shear; conceived by Ms. Shear and James Lapine. June 6, 2002. Director, Jeff Steitzer; choreography, Steve Tomkins; scenery, Scott Weldin; costumes, Carolyn Keim; lighting, Don Darnutzer; sound, Dominic CodyKramers; musical direction, Mark Anders; stage manager, Amy Gornet.

Jo; Mae .... Julie Briskman
Charlie; others .... Michael Winters
    Presented without intermission.

Various roles .... Mark Anders

WINTERTIME. By Charles L. Mee. August 22, 2002. Director, Brian Kulick; scenery, Walt Spangler; costumes, Deb Trout; lighting, Geoff Korf; sound, Dominic CodyKramers; stage manager, Anne Kearson.

Ariel .... Sarah Grace Wilson
Jonathan .... Michael A. Newcomer
Maria .... Suzanne Grodner
Francois .... Daniel Oreskes
Frank .... Robert Dorfman
    Presented in two parts.

Edmund .... Timothy McCuen Piggee
Bertha .... Beth Andrisevic
Hilda .... Laura Kenny
Bob .... Paul Morgan Stetler
Jacqueline; Attendant .... Liz McCarthy

FUDDY MEERS. By David Lindsay-Abaire. September 19, 2002. Director, Kurt Beattie; scenery, Hugh Landwehr; costumes, Rose Pederson; lighting, Chris Parry; music and sound, Jim Ragland; fight direction, Robert Macdougall; stage manager, Jeffrey K. Hanson.

Claire .... Cindy Basco
Richard .... Stephen Godwin
Kenny .... Tim Gouran
The Limping Man .... R. Hamilton Wright
    Presented in two parts.

Gertie .... Lori Larsen
Millet .... Peter Crook
Heidi, the Lady Cop .... Leslie Law

THE EDUCATION OF RANDY NEWMAN. Musical with music and lyrics by Randy Newman; conceived by Michael Roth, Jerry Patch and Mr. Newman. October 24, 2002. Directors, Gordon Edelstein and Myron Johnson; scenery, Douglas Stein; costumes, Martin Pakledinaz; lighting, David Weiner; projections, Wendall K. Harrington; sound, Beth Berkeley; stage manager, Anne Kearson.

    With: Lovena Fox, Daniel Jenkins, William Katt, Allan Louis, Brooke Sunny Moriber, Cathy Richardson, Jeff Trachta.

    Musical numbers: "Henry Adams," "Dixie Flyer," "New Orleans Wins the War," "If We Didn't Have Jesus," "Four Eyes," "Louisiana 1927," "Kingfish," "Sail Away," "Rednecks," "Lullaby," "Roll With the Punches," "My Country"/"Follow the Flag," "There's a Party at My House," "Mom's Advice," "Days of Heaven," "Shame," Septet: "Bad Boy," "Mama Told Me Not to Come," "New Orleans Wins the War" (Reprise), "I Love LA," "It's Money That I Love," "Vine Street"/"Summer"/"Lucinda;" "I Think It's Going to Rain Today," "Love Story," "Better Off Dead," "I'll Be Home," "Song for the Dead," "Political Science," "Short People," "My Life is Good," "Stupid Little Songs," "Miami," "Real Emotional Girl," "You Can Leave Your Hat On," "When He Loved Me," "Take Me Back," "I Just Want You to Hurt Like I Do," "Sage Advice," "Pants"/"I'm Dead", "No One Dies in Rock and Roll," "Feels Like Home," "Duck With Money," "Laugh and be Happy," "The World Isn't Fair," "Days of Heaven."

Empty Space Theatre, Seattle
Allison Narver artistic director, John Bradshaw managing director

G-D DOESN'T PAY RENT HERE. By Kate Moira Ryan and Judy Gold. June 5, 2002 (world premiere). Director, Allison Narver; scenery, Matthew Smucker; lighting, Gina Scherr; sound, Nathan Anderson; costumes, Heather Shannon Moore; stage manager, Rod Pilloud.

    Performed by Ms. Gold.

RASH. By Lauren Weedman. October 30, 2002 (world premiere). Director, Trip Cullman; scenery, Adam Stockhausen; costumes, Miguel Angel Huidor; lighting, Paul Whitaker;

sound designer, Nathan Anderson, music and lyrics, David Russell, dramaturg, Adam Greenfield.

Performed by Ms. Weedman.

STRANGE ATTRACTORS. By David Adjmi January 15, 2003 (world premiere). Director, Chay Yew; scenery, Matthew Smucker; costumes, Dennis Milam Bensie; lighting, Patti West; sound, Nathan Anderson; fight direction, Kelly Boulware; stage manager, Amy Poisson.

Betsy	Heidi Schreck	Vanna	Shelley Reynolds
Josh	Ian Bell	Alexander	Duke Novak

UNDERNEATH THE LINTEL. By Glen Berger. March 19, 2003. Director, Alan Greenfield; scenery, Peggy McDonald; costumes, Heather Shannon Moore; lighting, Patti West; sound, Nathan Anderson; stage manager, Rod Pilloud.

Librarian .... Todd Jefferson Moore

PROJECT X: BEFORE THE COMET COMES. By Nikki Appino. May 7, 2003 (world premiere). Director, Ms. Appino; scenery and lighting, Meg Fox; costumes, Frances Kenny; sound, Wayne Horvitz; music composed and performed by Robin Holcomb. Presented in association with House of Dames Productions.

Young Man	Nick Garrison	Old Man	Todd Jefferson Moore
Young Woman	Gina Malvestuto	Old Woman	Marianne Owen

Intiman Theatre Company, Seattle
Bartlett Sher artistic director, Laura Penn managing director

LACKAWANNA BLUES. By Ruben Santiago Hudson. June 19, 2002 (West Coast premiere). Director, Loretta Greco; scenery and costumes, Myung Hee Cho; lighting, James Vermeulen; music, Bill Sims Jr.

Performed by Mr. Santiago-Hudson and Mr. Sims Jr.

NICKEL AND DIMED. By Joan Holden. Based on *Nickel and Dimed: On (Not) Getting By in America* by Barbara Ehrenreich. August 2, 2002 (world premiere). Director, Bartlett Sher; scenery, John Arnone; costumes, Rose Pederson; lighting, Mary Louise Geiger; music, Michael McQuilken; dramaturg, Mame Hunt; production stage manager, J.R. Welden. Presented in association with the Mark Taper Forum.

Editor; Ted; Pete;
  Howard; ensemble .... Jason Cottle
Joan;
  Holly; ensemble .... Kristin Flanders
Nita; Carlie;
  Melissa; ensemble .... Cynthia Jones

Barbara .... Sharon Lockwood
Gail;
  Marge; ensemble .... Cristine McMurdo-Wallis
Hector; Maddy;
  Kimberly; ensemble .... Olga Sanchez
Musician .... Michael McQuilken

Time: Present. Place: Florida, Maine and Minnesota. Presented in two parts.

Seattle Repertory Theatre, Seattle
Sharon Ott artistic director, Benjamin Moore managing director

WHEN GRACE COMES IN. By Heather McDonald. October 7, 2002 (world premiere). Director, Sharon Ott; scenery, Daniel Ostling; costumes, Frances Kenny; lighting, Christopher Reay; music and sound, Christopher Walker; dramaturg, Shirley Fishman; stage manager, Bret Torbeck. Presented in association with La Jolla Playhouse.

Margaret Grace Braxton	Jane Beard	Senator Bill Braxton	Mark Chamberlin
Claw Braxton	Tommy R. Fleming	Roz Lapinski;	
Doune Braxton	Miriam Cohen Kiel	Aunt Blossom;	
Halley Braxton	Amber Hughes	Doctor; Aide	Stephanie Berry
Simon; Paleontologist;		Belle;	
Fabrizio Nacarelli	Kevin C. Loomis	Italian Restorer	Anne Gee Byrd

Time: Now and before. Place: In and around Washington, DC; Mabou, a small town in Cape Breton; Nova Scotia; Venice, Italy. Presented in two parts.

THE TRIUMPH OF LOVE. By Pierre Marivaux; adapted by Stephen Wadsworth; based on a translation by Mr. Wadsworth and Nadia Benabid. January 13, 2003. Director, Mr. Wadsworth; scenery, Thomas Lynch; costumes, Martin Pakledinaz; lighting, Russell H. Champa; sound, Christopher Walker. Presented in association with the Missouri Repertory Theatre.

Dimas	Burton Curtis	Agis	Adam Greer
Harlequin	Dan Donohue	Léontine	Sharon Lockwood
Léonide	Jennifer Erin Roberts	Hermocrate	Frank Corrado
Corin	Mary Bacon		

Presented in three parts.

THINGS BEING WHAT THEY ARE. By Wendy MacLeod. April 7, 2003 (world premiere). Director, Kurt Beattie; scenery, Don Yanik; costumes, Carolyn Keim; lighting, Greg Sullivan; sound, Dominic CodyKramers; dramaturg, Mervin P. Antonio; stage manager, J.R. Welden.

Jack	Jeff Steitzer	Bill	R. Hamilton Wright

HOW I LEARNED WHAT I LEARNED. By August Wilson. May 22, 2003 (world premiere). Director, Todd Kreidler; stage manager, Michael B. Paul.

Performed by Mr. Wilson.

Presented without intermission.

Hot Type: Sizzling New Plays. May 26–June 1, 2003.

OVER THE MOON. By Steven Dietz; adapted from *The Small Bachelor* by P.G. Wodehouse. May 26, 2003. Director, David Ira Goldstein; stage directions, Jamie Morgan. Presented in association with Arizona Theatre Company.

George Finch	R. Hamilton Wright	Mrs. Waddington	Suzy Hunt
Hamilton Beamish	Mark Chamberlin	Molly Waddington	Liz McCarthy
Mullett	Peter Crook	Ferris	Sean Griffin
Fanny	Katie Forgette	Madame Eulalie	Kirsten Potter
Sigsbee Waddington	Eddie Levi Lee	Garroway	Jeff Steitzer

Presented in two parts.

BEAUTY OF THE FATHER. By Nilo Cruz. May 27, 2003. Director, Sharon Ott; stage directions, Eva Osusky. Commisioned by South Coast Repertory, Costa Mesa, California.

Federico Garcia Lorca	John Ortiz	Paquita	Suzanne Bouchard
Emiliano	Hector Elizondo	Karim	Dennis Mosley
Marina	Florencia Lozano		

Time: Summer 1998. Place: Salobrena, a small town in Granada, Spain. Presented in two parts.

THE O'CONNOR GIRLS. By Katie Forgette. May 28, 2003. Director, Christine Sumption; stage directions, R. Hamilton Wright.

Sarah O'Connor	Sally Smythe	Elizabeth O'Connor	Cynthia Lauren Tewes

Martha O'Connor .... Kate Purwin   Aunt Margie .... Laura Kenny
Dr. David Stevens .... Mark Chamberlin
    Time: The week after Christmas 1997. Place: A small town in Minnesota. Presented in two parts.

DON CARLOS. By Friedrich von Schiller; translated by Michael Feingold. May 31, 2003. Director, Carey Perloff; stage directions, Christopher Bange; dramaturg, Paul Walsh. Commissioned and developed by American Conservatory Theater, San Francisco.

Philip .... Laurence Ballard   Lerma; others .... Phil Davidson
Domingo .... Dan Kremer   Mondecar; others .... Jamie Morgan
Don Carlos .... Kelly Conway   Alba; others .... Jeff Steitzer
Posa; others .... Bradford Farwell   Olivares; others .... Lori Larsen
Elizabeth; others .... Maren Perry   Eboli; others .... Carol Roscoe
    Presented in two parts.

WISCONSIN

Milwaukee Repertory Theater, Milwaukee
Joseph Hanreddy artistic director, Timothy J. Shields managing director

MOBY DICK. By Eric Simonson; adapted from the novel by Herman Melville. September 4, 2002 (world premiere). Director, Mr. Simonson; choreography, Cate Deicher; scenery, Kent Dorsey; costumes, Kärin Kopischke; lighting, Nancy Schertler; sound, Barry G. Funderburg; fight direction, Lee E. Ernst; musical director, Randal Swiggum; dramaturg, Paul Kosidowski; production stage manager, Judy Berdan.

Ishmael .... Charlie Kimball   Father Mapple; Carpenter .... Peter Silbert
Peter Coffin; Flask .... Scott Wakefield   Elijah; Tashtego .... Joseph Melendez
Stubb; Captain Peleg .... Sean Dougherty   Pip .... Marsha Stephanie Blake
Starbuck .... Lee E. Ernst   Labo .... Rodney To
Queequeg .... Leon Addison Brown   Daggoo .... M. Martin Mapoma
Mary; Andy .... Laura Gordon   Olsson .... Jacques Roy
Captain Bildad; English Captain;   Captain Ahab .... Steve Pickering
    Captain Gardiner .... Torrey Hanson
    Ensemble: Joshua Atkins, Peter S. Case, Rob Howard, Joe Morris, Hunter Stiebel
    Time: Early 1840s. Place: New Bedford, Nantucket; Atlantic, Indian, and Pacific Oceans. Presented in two parts.

A DELICATE BALANCE. By Edward Albee. September 6, 2002. Director, Edward Morgan; scenery, Joseph Varga; costumes, Amela Baksic; lighting, Joseph Appelt; sound, Mikhail Moore, production stage manager, Judy Berdan.

Tobias .... James Pickering   Julia .... Deborah Staples
Agnes .... Elizabeth Norment   Edna .... Rose Pickering
Claire .... Laurie Birmingham   Harry .... John Kishline
    Place: The living room of a large and well-appointed suburban house. Presented in three parts.

ESCAPE FROM HAPPINESS. By George F. Walker. October 18, 2002. Director, Joseph Hanreddy; scenery, Todd Rosenthal; costumes, Martha Hally; lighting, Nancy Schertler; music and sound, Michael Keck; fight direction, Lee E. Ernst; dramaturg, Paul Kosidowski; production stage manager, Judy Berdan.

Gail .... Elizabeth Ledo   Dian Black .... Deborah Staples
Nora .... Judith K. Hart   Mike Dixon .... James Pickering
Junior .... John Hoogenakker   Tom .... Jim Baker

Mary Ann .... Diana LaMar
Elizabeth .... Laura Gordon
  Presented in two parts.

Stevie Moore .... Jeremy Dubin
Rolly Moore .... Lee E. Ernst

INVENTING VAN GOGH. By Steven Dietz. February 21, 2003. Director, Kurt Beattie; scenery, Scott Weldin; costumes, Rachel Anne Healy; lighting, Brian Sidney Bembridge; sound, Barry G. Funderburg; dramaturg, Paul Kosidowski; production stage manager, Judy Berdan.

Patrick Stone .... Brian Vaughn
Vincent van Gogh .... Torrey Hanson
Dr. Jonas Miller;
  Dr. Paul Gachet .... Jonathan Smoots

Hallie Miller;
  Marguerite .... Kirsten Potter
René Bouchard;
  Paul Gaugin .... Mark Corkins

FACTS AND
FIGURES

LONG RUNS ON BROADWAY

○ ○ ○ ○ ○

T HE FOLLOWING SHOWS have run 500 or more continuous performances in a single production, usually the first, not including previews or extra non-profit performances, allowing for vacation layoffs and special one-booking engagements, but not including return engagements after a show has gone on tour. In all cases, the numbers were obtained directly from the show's production offices. Where there are title similarities, the production is identified as follows: (p) straight play version, (m) musical version, (r) revival, (tr) transfer.

THROUGH MAY 31, 2003

PLAYS MARKED WITH ASTERISK WERE STILL PLAYING JUNE 1, 2003

Plays	*Performances*	*Plays*	*Performances*
Cats	7,485	Born Yesterday	1,642
Les Misérables	6,680	The Best Little Whorehouse in Texas	1,639
*The Phantom of the Opera	6,397	Crazy for You	1,622
A Chorus Line	6,137	Ain't Misbehavin'	1,604
Oh! Calcutta! (r)	5,959	Mary, Mary	1,572
Miss Saigon	4,097	Evita	1,567
*Beauty and the Beast	3,719	The Voice of the Turtle	1,557
42nd Street	3,486	Jekyll & Hyde	1,543
Grease	3,388	Barefoot in the Park	1,530
Fiddler on the Roof	3,242	Brighton Beach Memoirs	1,530
Life With Father	3,224	Dreamgirls	1,522
Tobacco Road	3,182	Mame (m)	1,508
*Rent	2,951	Grease (r)	1,503
Hello, Dolly!	2,844	Same Time, Next Year	1,453
*Chicago (m)(r)	2,723	Arsenic and Old Lace	1,444
My Fair Lady	2,717	The Sound of Music	1,443
Annie	2,377	Me and My Girl	1,420
*The Lion King	2,345	How to Succeed in Business	
Man of La Mancha	2,328	Without Really Trying	1,417
Abie's Irish Rose	2,327	Hellzapoppin'	1,404
Oklahoma!	2,212	The Music Man	1,375
*Cabaret (r)	2,125	Funny Girl	1,348
Smokey Joe's Cafe	2,036	Mummenschanz	1,326
Pippin	1,944	*Aida	1,324
South Pacific	1,925	Angel Street	1,295
The Magic Show	1,920	Lightnin'	1,291
Deathtrap	1,793	Promises, Promises	1,281
Gemini	1,788	The King and I	1,246
Harvey	1,775	Cactus Flower	1,234
Dancin'	1,774	Sleuth	1,222
La Cage aux Folles	1,761	Torch Song Trilogy	1,222
Hair	1,750	1776	1,217
The Wiz	1,672	Equus	1,209

Plays	Performances	Plays	Performances
Sugar Babies	1,208	The Bat	867
Guys and Dolls	1,200	My Sister Eileen	864
Amadeus	1,181	*42nd Street (r)	861
Cabaret	1,165	No, No, Nanette (r)	861
Mister Roberts	1,157	Ragtime	861
Annie Get Your Gun	1,147	Song of Norway	860
Guys and Dolls (r)	1,144	Chapter Two	857
The Seven Year Itch	1,141	A Streetcar Named Desire	855
Bring in 'da Noise, Bring in 'da Funk	1,130	Barnum	854
Butterflies Are Free	1,128	Comedy in Music	849
Pins and Needles	1,108	Raisin	847
Plaza Suite	1,097	Blood Brothers	839
Fosse	1,092	You Can't Take It With You	837
They're Playing Our Song	1,082	La Plume de Ma Tante	835
Grand Hotel (m)	1,077	Three Men on a Horse	835
Kiss Me, Kate	1,070	The Subject Was Roses	832
Don't Bother Me, I Can't Cope	1,065	Black and Blue	824
The Pajama Game	1,063	The King and I (r)	807
Shenandoah	1,050	Inherit the Wind	806
Annie Get Your Gun (r)	1,046	Anything Goes (r)	804
The Teahouse of the August Moon	1,027	Titanic	804
Damn Yankees	1,019	No Time for Sergeants	796
Contact	1,010	Fiorello!	795
Never Too Late	1,007	Where's Charley?	792
Big River	1,005	The Ladder	789
The Will Rogers Follies	983	Forty Carats	780
Any Wednesday	982	Lost in Yonkers	780
Sunset Boulevard	977	The Prisoner of Second Avenue	780
A Funny Thing Happened on the Way to the Forum	964	M. Butterfly	777
The Odd Couple	964	The Tale of the Allergist's Wife	777
Anna Lucasta	957	Oliver!	774
Kiss and Tell	956	The Pirates of Penzance (1980 r)	772
Show Boat (r)	949	The Full Monty	770
Dracula (r)	925	Woman of the Year	770
Bells Are Ringing	924	My One and Only	767
The Moon Is Blue	924	Sophisticated Ladies	767
Beatlemania	920	Bubbling Brown Sugar	766
Proof	917	Into the Woods	765
The Elephant Man	916	State of the Union	765
Kiss of the Spider Woman	906	Starlight Express	761
Luv	901	The First Year	760
The Who's Tommy	900	Broadway Bound	756
Chicago (m)	898	You Know I Can't Hear You When the Water's Running	755
Applause	896	Two for the Seesaw	750
Can-Can	892	Joseph and the Amazing Technicolor Dreamcoat (r)	747
Carousel	890	Death of a Salesman	742
I'm Not Rappaport	890	For Colored Girls . . .	742
Hats Off to Ice	889	Sons o' Fun	742
Fanny	888	Candide (m, r)	740
Children of a Lesser God	887	Gentlemen Prefer Blondes	740
Follow the Girls	882	The Man Who Came to Dinner	739
Kiss Me, Kate (m)(r)	881	Nine	739
City of Angels	878	Call Me Mister	734
*The Producers	875	Victor/Victoria	734
Camelot	873	West Side Story	732
I Love My Wife	872		

Plays	Performances
High Button Shoes	727
Finian's Rainbow	725
Claudia	722
The Gold Diggers	720
Jesus Christ Superstar	720
Carnival	719
The Diary of Anne Frank	717
A Funny Thing Happened on the Way to the Forum (r)	715
I Remember Mama	714
Tea and Sympathy	712
Junior Miss	710
Footloose	708
Last of the Red Hot Lovers	706
The Secret Garden	706
Company	705
Seventh Heaven	704
Gypsy (m)	702
The Miracle Worker	700
That Championship Season	700
*Urinetown	700
The Music Man (m)(r)	698
Da	697
Cat on a Hot Tin Roof	694
Li'l Abner	693
The Children's Hour	691
Purlie	688
Dead End	687
The Lion and the Mouse	686
White Cargo	686
Dear Ruth	683
East Is West	680
Come Blow Your Horn	677
The Most Happy Fella	676
Defending the Caveman	671
The Doughgirls	671
The Impossible Years	670
Irene	670
Boy Meets Girl	669
The Tap Dance Kid	669
Beyond the Fringe	667
Who's Afraid of Virginia Woolf?	664
Blithe Spirit	657
A Trip to Chinatown	657
The Women	657
Bloomer Girl	654
The Fifth Season	654
Rain	648
Witness for the Prosecution	645
Call Me Madam	644
Janie	642
The Green Pastures	640
Auntie Mame (p)	639
A Man for All Seasons	637
Jerome Robbins' Broadway	634
The Fourposter	632
The Music Master	627

Plays	Performances
Two Gentlemen of Verona (m)	627
The Tenth Man	623
The Heidi Chronicles	621
Is Zat So?	618
Anniversary Waltz	615
The Happy Time (p)	614
Separate Rooms	613
Affairs of State	610
Oh! Calcutta! (tr)	610
Star and Garter	609
The Mystery of Edwin Drood	608
The Student Prince	608
Sweet Charity	608
Bye Bye Birdie	607
Riverdance on Broadway	605
Irene (r)	604
Sunday in the Park With George	604
Adonis	603
Broadway	603
Peg o' My Heart	603
Master Class	601
Street Scene (p)	601
Flower Drum Song	600
Kiki	600
A Little Night Music	600
Art	600
Agnes of God	599
Don't Drink the Water	598
Wish You Were Here	598
Sarafina!	597
A Society Circus	596
Absurd Person Singular	592
A Day in Hollywood/ A Night in the Ukraine	588
The Me Nobody Knows	586
The Two Mrs. Carrolls	585
Kismet (m)	583
Gypsy (m, r)	582
Brigadoon	581
Detective Story	581
No Strings	580
Brother Rat	577
Blossom Time	576
Pump Boys and Dinettes	573
Show Boat	572
The Show-Off	571
Sally	570
Jelly's Last Jam	569
Golden Boy (m)	568
One Touch of Venus	567
The Real Thing	566
Happy Birthday	564
Look Homeward, Angel	564
Morning's at Seven (r)	564
The Glass Menagerie	561
I Do! I Do!	560
Wonderful Town	559

Plays	Performances	Plays	Performances
The Last Night of Ballyhoo	557	Godspell (tr)	527
Rose Marie	557	Fences	526
Strictly Dishonorable	557	The Solid Gold Cadillac	526
Sweeney Todd	557	Biloxi Blues	524
The Great White Hope	556	Irma La Douce	524
A Majority of One	556	The Boomerang	522
The Sisters Rosensweig	556	Follies	521
Sunrise at Campobello	556	Rosalinda	521
Toys in the Attic	556	The Best Man	520
Jamaica	555	Chauve-Souris	520
Stop the World—I Want to Get Off	555	Blackbirds of 1928	518
Florodora	553	The Gin Game	517
Noises Off	553	Sunny	517
Ziegfeld Follies (1943)	553	Victoria Regina	517
Dial "M" for Murder	552	Fifth of July	511
Good News	551	Half a Sixpence	511
Peter Pan (r)	551	The Vagabond King	511
How to Succeed in Business		The New Moon	509
Without Really Trying (r)	548	The World of Suzie Wong	508
Let's Face It	547	The Rothschilds	507
Milk and Honey	543	On Your Toes (r)	505
Within the Law	541	Sugar	505
Pal Joey (r)	540	Shuffle Along	504
The Sound of Music (r)	540	Up in Central Park	504
What Makes Sammy Run?	540	Carmen Jones	503
The Sunshine Boys	538	Saturday Night Fever	502
What a Life	538	The Member of the Wedding	501
Crimes of the Heart	535	Panama Hattie	501
Damn Yankees (r)	533	Personal Appearance	501
The Unsinkable Molly Brown	532	Bird in Hand	500
The Red Mill (r)	531	Room Service	500
Rumors	531	Sailor, Beware!	500
A Raisin in the Sun	530	Tomorrow the World	500

LONG RUNS OFF BROADWAY

Plays	Performances	Plays	Performances
The Fantasticks	17,162	The Blacks	1,408
*Perfect Crime	6,672	The Vagina Monologues	1,381
*Tubes	5,805	One Mo' Time	1,372
Tony 'n' Tina's Wedding	4,914	Grandma Sylvia's Funeral	1,360
*Stomp	3,883	Let My People Come	1,327
Nunsense	3,672	Late Nite Catechism	1,268
*I Love You, You're Perfect,		Driving Miss Daisy	1,195
Now Change	2,836	The Hot l Baltimore	1,166
The Threepenny Opera	2,611	I'm Getting My Act Together	
Forbidden Broadway 1982–87	2,332	and Taking It on the Road	1,165
Little Shop of Horrors	2,209	Little Mary Sunshine	1,143
Godspell	2,124	Steel Magnolias	1,126
Vampire Lesbians of Sodom	2,024	El Grande de Coca-Cola	1,114
*De La Guarda	1,952	The Proposition	1,109
Jacques Brel	1,847	*The Donkey Show	1,103
Forever Plaid	1,811	Our Sinatra	1,096
Vanities	1,785	Beau Jest	1,069
*Naked Boys Singing!	1,622	Tamara	1,036
You're a Good Man, Charlie Brown	1,597	One Flew Over the Cuckoo's Nest (r)	1,025

Plays	Performances	Plays	Performances
The Boys in the Band	1,000	America Hurrah	634
Fool for Love	1,000	Oil City Symphony	626
Other People's Money	990	The Countess	618
Cloud 9	971	Hogan's Goat	607
Secrets Every Smart Traveler Should Know	953	Beehive	600
		Criss Angel Mindfreak	600
Sister Mary Ignatius Explains It All for You & The Actor's Nightmare	947	The Trojan Women	600
		The Syringa Tree	586
Your Own Thing	933	The Dining Room	583
Curley McDimple	931	Krapp's Last Tape & The Zoo Story	582
Leave It to Jane (r)	928	Three Tall Women	582
Hedwig and the Angry Inch	857	The Dumbwaiter & The Collection	578
Forbidden Broadway Strikes Back	850	Forbidden Broadway 1990	576
When Pigs Fly	840	Dames at Sea	575
The Mad Show	871	The Crucible (r)	571
Scrambled Feet	831	The Iceman Cometh (r)	565
The Effect of Gamma Rays on Man-in-the-Moon Marigolds	819	Forbidden Broadway 2001: A Spoof Odyssey	552
Over the River and Through the Woods	800	The Hostage (r)	545
		Wit	545
A View From the Bridge (r)	780	What's a Nice Country Like You Doing in a State Like This?	543
The Boy Friend (r)	763		
True West	762	Forbidden Broadway 1988	534
Forbidden Broadway Cleans Up Its Act!	754	Gross Indecency: The Three Trials of Oscar Wilde	534
Isn't It Romantic	733	Frankie and Johnny in the Clair de Lune	533
Dime a Dozen	728		
The Pocket Watch	725	Six Characters in Search of an Author (r)	529
The Connection	722	All in the Timing	526
The Passion of Dracula	714	*Forbidden Broadway: 20th Anniversary Celebration	526
Love, Janis	713		
Adaptation & Next	707	Oleanna	513
Oh! Calcutta!	704	*Menopause the Musical	512
Scuba Duba	692	Making Porn	511
The Foreigner	686	The Dirtiest Show in Town	509
The Knack	685	Happy Ending & Day of Absence	504
Fully Committed	675	Greater Tuna	501
The Club	674	A Shayna Maidel	501
The Balcony	672	The Boys From Syracuse (r)	500
Penn & Teller	666		
Dinner With Friends	654		

NEW YORK DRAMA CRITICS' CIRCLE
1935–1936 TO 2002–2003
○ ○ ○ ○ ○

LISTED BELOW ARE the New York Drama Critics' Circle Awards from 1935–1936 through 2002–2003 classified as follows: (1) Best American Play, (2) Best Foreign Play, (3) Best Musical, (4) Best, Regardless of Category (this category was established by new voting rules in 1962–63 and did not exist prior to that year).

1935–36 (1) *Winterset*
1936–37 (1) *High Tor*
1937–38 (1) *Of Mice and Men*, (2) *Shadow and Substance*
1938–39 (1) No award, (2) *The White Steed*
1939–40 (1) *The Time of Your Life*
1940–41 (1) *Watch on the Rhine*, (2) *The Corn Is Green*
1941–42 (1) No award, (2) *Blithe Spirit*
1942–43 (1) *The Patriots*
1943–44 (2) *Jacobowsky and the Colonel*
1944–45 (1) *The Glass Menagerie*
1945–46 (3) *Carousel*
1946–47 (1) *All My Sons*, (2) *No Exit*, (3) *Brigadoon*
1947–48 (1) *A Streetcar Named Desire*, (2) *The Winslow Boy*
1948–49 (1) *Death of a Salesman*, (2) *The Madwoman of Chaillot*, (3) *South Pacific*
1949–50 (1) *The Member of the Wedding*, (2) *The Cocktail Party*, (3) *The Consul*
1950–51 (1) *Darkness at Noon*, (2) *The Lady's Not for Burning*, (3) *Guys and Dolls*
1951–52 (1) *I Am a Camera*, (2) *Venus Observed*, (3) *Pal Joey* (Special citation to *Don Juan in Hell*)
1952–53 (1) *Picnic*, (2) *The Love of Four Colonels*, (3) *Wonderful Town*
1953–54 (1) *The Teahouse of the August Moon*, (2) *Ondine*, (3) *The Golden Apple*
1954–55 (1) *Cat on a Hot Tin Roof*, (2) *Witness for the Prosecution*, (3) *The Saint of Bleecker Street*
1955–56 (1) *The Diary of Anne Frank*, (2) *Tiger at the Gates*, (3) *My Fair Lady*
1956–57 (1) *Long Day's Journey Into Night*, (2) *The Waltz of the Toreadors*, (3) *The Most Happy Fella*
1957–58 (1) *Look Homeward, Angel*, (2) *Look Back in Anger*, (3) *The Music Man*

1958–59 (1) *A Raisin in the Sun*, (2) *The Visit*, (3) *La Plume de Ma Tante*
1959–60 (1) *Toys in the Attic*, (2) *Five Finger Exercise*, (3) *Fiorello!*
1960–61 (1) *All the Way Home*, (2) *A Taste of Honey*, (3) *Carnival*
1961–62 (1) *The Night of the Iguana*, (2) *A Man for All Seasons*, (3) *How to Succeed in Business Without Really Trying*
1962–63 (4) *Who's Afraid of Virginia Woolf?* (Special citation to *Beyond the Fringe*)
1963–64 (4) *Luther*, (3) *Hello, Dolly!* (Special citation to *The Trojan Women*)
1964–65 (4) *The Subject Was Roses*, (3) *Fiddler on the Roof*
1965–66 (4) *The Persecution and Assassination of Marat as Performed by the Inmates of the Asylum of Charenton Under the Direction of the Marquis de Sade*, (3) *Man of La Mancha*
1966–67 (4) *The Homecoming*, (3) *Cabaret*
1967–68 (4) *Rosencrantz and Guildenstern Are Dead*, (3) *Your Own Thing*
1968–69 (4) *The Great White Hope*, (3) *1776*
1969–70 (4) *Borstal Boy*, (1) *The Effect of Gamma Rays on Man-in-the-Moon Marigolds*, (3) *Company*
1970–71 (4) *Home*, (1) *The House of Blue Leaves*, (3) *Follies*
1971–72 (4) *That Championship Season*, (2) *The Screens* (3) *Two Gentlemen of Verona* (Special citations to *Sticks and Bones* and *Old Times*)
1972–73 (4) *The Changing Room*, (1) *The Hot l Baltimore*, (3) *A Little Night Music*
1973–74 (4) *The Contractor*, (1) *Short Eyes*, (3) *Candide*
1974–75 (4) *Equus* (1) *The Taking of Miss Janie*, (3) *A Chorus Line*
1975–76 (4) *Travesties*, (1) *Streamers*, (3) *Pacific Overtures*

1976–77 (4) *Otherwise Engaged*, (1) *American Buffalo*, (3) *Annie*
1977–78 (4) *Da*, (3) *Ain't Misbehavin'*
1978–79 (4) *The Elephant Man*, (3) *Sweeney Todd, the Demon Barber of Fleet Street*
1979–80 (4) *Talley's Folly*, (2) *Betrayal*, (3) *Evita* (Special citation to Peter Brook's Le Centre International de Créations Théâtrales for its repertory)
1980–81 (4) *A Lesson From Aloes*, (1) *Crimes of the Heart* (Special citations to *Lena Horne: The Lady and Her Music* and the New York Shakespeare Festival production of *The Pirates of Penzance*)
1981–82 (4) *The Life & Adventures of Nicholas Nickleby*, (1) *A Soldier's Play*
1982–83 (4) *Brighton Beach Memoirs*, (2) *Plenty*, (3) *Little Shop of Horrors* (Special citation to Young Playwrights Festival)
1983–84 (4) *The Real Thing*, (1) *Glengarry Glen Ross*, (3) *Sunday in the Park With George* (Special citation to Samuel Beckett for the body of his work)
1984–85 (4) *Ma Rainey's Black Bottom*
1985–86 (4) *A Lie of the Mind*, (2) *Benefactors* (Special citation to *The Search for Signs of Intelligent Life in the Universe*)
1986–87 (4) *Fences*, (2) *Les Liaisons Dangereuses*, (3) *Les Misérables*
1987–88 (4) *Joe Turner's Come and Gone*, (2) *The Road to Mecca*, (3) *Into the Woods*
1988–89 (4) *The Heidi Chronicles*, (2) *Aristocrats* (Special citation to Bill Irwin for *Largely New York*)
1989–90 (4) *The Piano Lesson*, (2) *Privates on Parade*, (3) *City of Angels*

1990–91 (4) *Six Degrees of Separation*, (2) *Our Country's Good*, (3) *The Will Rogers Follies* (Special citation to Eileen Atkins for her portrayal of Virginia Woolf in *A Room of One's Own*)
1991–92 (4) *Dancing at Lughnasa*, (1) *Two Trains Running*
1992–93 (4) *Angels in America: Millennium Approaches*, (2) *Someone Who'll Watch Over Me*, (3) *Kiss of the Spider Woman*
1993–94 (4) *Three Tall Women* (Special citation to Anna Deavere Smith for her unique contribution to theatrical form)
1994–95 (4) *Arcadia*, (1) *Love! Valour! Compassion!* (Special citation to Signature Theatre Company for outstanding artistic achievement)
1995–96 (4) *Seven Guitars*, (2) *Molly Sweeney*, (3) *Rent*
1996–97 (4) *How I Learned to Drive*, (2) *Skylight*, (3) *Violet* (Special citation to *Chicago*)
1997–98 (4) *Art*, (1) *Pride's Crossing*, (3) *The Lion King* (Special citation to the revival production of *Cabaret*)
1998–99 (4) *Wit*, (3) *Parade*, (2) *Closer* (Special citation to David Hare for his contributions to the 1998–99 theater season: *Amy's View*, *Via Dolorosa* and *The Blue Room*)
1999–00 (4) *Jitney*, (3) *James Joyce's The Dead*, (2) *Copenhagen*
2000–01 (4) *The Invention of Love*, (1) *Proof*, (3) *The Producers*
2001–02 (4) *Edward Albee's The Goat, or Who is Sylvia?* (Special citation to Elaine Stritch for *Elaine Stritch at Liberty*)
2002–03 (4) *Take Me Out*, (2) *Talking Heads*, (3) *Hairspray*

NEW YORK DRAMA CRITICS' CIRCLE VOTING 2002–2003
Charles Isherwood (*Variety*), President

AT ITS MAY 13, 2003 meeting the New York Drama Critics' Circle elected to honor three productions of the 2002–03 season. The group voted a best-of-bests award to Richard Greenberg's *Take Me Out* with a foreign-play honor going to Alan Bennett's *Talking Heads*. The stage adaptation of the John Waters's film *Hairspray* received the best-musical honor.

Of the 20 members of the Circle, only Elysa Gardner of *USA Today* was absent; there was no proxy voting. The management of *The New York Times* had earlier required that Ben Brantley and Bruce Weber withdraw from the organization. The first ballot voting for best play was divided as follows: *Take*

Me Out 4 (David Cote, *Time Out New York*; Ken Mandelbaum, Broadway.com; Jeremy McCarter, *The New York Sun*; David Sheward, *Back Stage*), *Our Lady of 121st Street* 3 (John Heilpern, *The New York Observer;* Jacques le Sourd, Gannett *Journal News*; Jason Zinoman, *Time Out New York*), *Far Away* 3 (Charles Isherwood, *Variety*; Michael Sommers, *The Star-Ledger*/Newhouse Newspapers; Linda Winer, *Newsday*), *House* and *Garden* 2 (Clive Barnes, *New York Post*; Howard Kissel, *Daily News*), *She Stoops to Comedy* 2 (Michael Feingold, *The Village Voice*; Donald Lyons, *New York Post*), *The Exonerated* 2 (Robert Feldberg, *The Bergen Record*; Frank Scheck, *The Hollywood Reporter*), *Buicks* 1 (John Simon, *New York*), *Fucking A* Richard Zoglin, *Time*), *The Mercy Seat* 1 (Michael Kuchwara, The Associated Press).

No play garnered a majority of votes on the first ballot—9 plays received affirmation in that round—so the group went to a weighted system for the next round, which allowed voters to select first, second and third choices. No winner emerged in the second round—during which 17 plays received some combination of votes. A third ballot matched the top vote-getters of the previous round. With 19 members present, *Take Me Out* received 12 votes to 4 votes for *Our Lady of 121st Street* in the final voting. *Far Away* finished third with 1 vote. Kissel and Simon abstained in the final round.

Hairspray received 12 votes on the first ballot to win the best-musical honor. Its competition included *Avenue Q*, *Hank Williams: Lost Highway* and *Movin' Out*, which each received 2 votes. The short-lived *Amour* received 1 vote.

The best foreign-play honoree, *Talking Heads*, was chosen on a weighted second ballot that included *Bailegangaire*, *Blue/Orange*, *Dublin Carol*, *Far Away*, *House* and *Garden*, *Observe the Sons of Ulster Marching Towards the Somme*, *The Play What I Wrote*, *Scattergood*, *Smelling a Rat* and *Vincent in Brixton*. Honorees received their accolades at a Sardi's cocktail party May 20, 2003.

PULITZER PRIZE WINNERS
1916–1917 TO 2002–2003

1916–17	No award
1917–18	*Why Marry?* by Jesse Lynch Williams
1918–19	No award
1919–20	*Beyond the Horizon* by Eugene O'Neill
1920–21	*Miss Lulu Bett* by Zona Gale
1921–22	*Anna Christie* by Eugene O'Neill
1922–23	*Icebound* by Owen Davis
1923–24	*Hell-Bent fer Heaven* by Hatcher Hughes
1924–25	*They Knew What They Wanted* by Sidney Howard
1925–26	*Craig's Wife* by George Kelly
1926–27	*In Abraham's Bosom* by Paul Green
1927–28	*Strange Interlude* by Eugene O'Neill
1928–29	*Street Scene* by Elmer Rice
1929–30	*The Green Pastures* by Marc Connelly
1930–31	*Alison's House* by Susan Glaspell
1931–32	*Of Thee I Sing* by George S. Kaufman, Morrie Ryskind, Ira and George Gershwin
1932–33	*Both Your Houses* by Maxwell Anderson
1933–34	*Men in White* by Sidney Kingsley
1934–35	*The Old Maid* by Zoe Akins
1935–36	*Idiot's Delight* by Robert E. Sherwood
1936–37	*You Can't Take It With You* by Moss Hart and George S. Kaufman
1937–38	*Our Town* by Thornton Wilder
1938–39	*Abe Lincoln in Illinois* by Robert E. Sherwood
1939–40	*The Time of Your Life* by William Saroyan
1940–41	*There Shall Be No Night* by Robert E. Sherwood
1941–42	No award
1942–43	*The Skin of Our Teeth* by Thornton Wilder
1943–44	No award
1944–45	*Harvey* by Mary Chase
1945–46	*State of the Union* by Howard Lindsay and Russel Crouse
1946–47	No award
1947–48	*A Streetcar Named Desire* by Tennessee Williams
1948–49	*Death of a Salesman* by Arthur Miller
1949–50	*South Pacific* by Richard Rodgers, Oscar Hammerstein II and Joshua Logan
1950–51	No award
1951–52	*The Shrike* by Joseph Kramm
1952–53	*Picnic* by William Inge
1953–54	*The Teahouse of the August Moon* by John Patrick
1954–55	*Cat on a Hot Tin Roof* by Tennessee Williams
1955–56	*The Diary of Anne Frank* by Frances Goodrich and Albert Hackett
1956–57	*Long Day's Journey Into Night* by Eugene O'Neill
1957–58	*Look Homeward, Angel* by Ketti Frings
1958–59	*J.B.* by Archibald MacLeish
1959–60	*Fiorello!* by Jerome Weidman, George Abbott, Sheldon Harnick and Jerry Bock
1960–61	*All the Way Home* by Tad Mosel
1961–62	*How to Succeed in Business Without Really Trying* by Abe Burrows, Willie Gilbert, Jack Weinstock and Frank Loesser
1962–63	No award
1963–64	No award
1964–65	*The Subject Was Roses* by Frank D. Gilroy
1965–66	No award
1966–67	*A Delicate Balance* by Edward Albee
1967–68	No award
1968–69	*The Great White Hope* by Howard Sackler
1969–70	*No Place To Be Somebody* by Charles Gordone
1970–71	*The Effect of Gamma Rays on Man-in-the-Moon Marigolds* by Paul Zindel
1971–72	No award
1972–73	*That Championship Season* by Jason Miller
1973–74	No award
1974–75	*Seascape* by Edward Albee
1975–76	*A Chorus Line* by Michael Bennett, James Kirkwood, Nicholas Dante, Marvin Hamlisch and Edward Kleban
1976–77	*The Shadow Box* by Michael Cristofer
1977–78	*The Gin Game* by D.L. Coburn
1978–79	*Buried Child* by Sam Shepard
1979–80	*Talley's Folly* by Lanford Wilson
1980–81	*Crimes of the Heart* by Beth Henley
1981–82	*A Soldier's Play* by Charles Fuller
1982–83	*'night, Mother* by Marsha Norman
1983–84	*Glengarry Glen Ross* by David Mamet
1984–85	*Sunday in the Park With George* by James Lapine and Stephen Sondheim
1985–86	No award
1986–87	*Fences* by August Wilson

1987–88	*Driving Miss Daisy* by Alfred Uhry
1988–89	*The Heidi Chronicles* by Wendy Wasserstein
1989–90	*The Piano Lesson* by August Wilson
1990–91	*Lost in Yonkers* by Neil Simon
1991–92	*The Kentucky Cycle* by Robert Schenkkan
1992–93	*Angels in America: Millennium Approaches* by Tony Kushner
1993–94	*Three Tall Women* by Edward Albee
1994–95	*The Young Man From Atlanta* by Horton Foote
1995–96	*Rent* by Jonathan Larson
1996–97	No award
1997–98	*How I Learned to Drive* by Paula Vogel
1998–99	*Wit* by Margaret Edson
1999–00	*Dinner With Friends* by Donald Margulies
2000–01	*Proof* by David Auburn
2001–02	*Topdog/Underdog* by Suzan-Lori Parks
2002–03	*Anna in the Tropics* by Nilo Cruz

2003 TONY AWARDS

○○○○○

THE AMERICAN THEATRE WING'S 57th annual Tony Awards, named for Antoinette Perry, are presented in recognition of distinguished achievement in the Broadway theater. The League of American Theatres and Producers and the American Theatre Wing present these awards, founded by the Wing in 1947. Legitimate theater productions opening in 40 eligible Broadway theaters during the present Tony season—May 2, 2002 to May 7, 2003—were considered by the Tony Awards Nominating Committee (appointed by the Tony Awards Administration Committee) for the awards in 22 competitive categories. The 2002–2003 Nominating Committee included Maureen Anderman, actor; Price Berkley, publisher; Ira Bernstein, manager; Robert Callely, administrator; Schulyer G. Chapin, executive; Veronica Claypool, manager; Betty Corwin, archivist; Gretchen Cryer, composer; Merle Debuskey, press; Edgar Dobie, manager; David Marshall Grant, actor; Micki Grant, composer; Julie Hughes, casting; Betty Jacobs, consultant; Robert Kamlot, manager; David Lindsay-Abaire, playwright; Theodore Mann, producer; Gilbert Parker, agent; Shirley Rich, casting; David Richards, journalist; Aubrey Reuben, photographer; Arthur Rubin, producer; Judith Rubin, executive; Bill Schelble, press; Meg Simon, casting; Sister Francesca Thompson, educator; Rosemarie Tichler, casting; Jon Wilner, producer.

The Tony Awards are voted from the list of nominees by members of the theater and journalism professions: the governing boards of the five theater artists' organizations—Actors' Equity Association, the Dramatists Guild, the Society of Stage Directors and Choreographers, the United Scenic Artists and the Casting Society of America—the members of the designated first night theater press, the board of directors of the American Theatre Wing and the membership of the League of American Theatres and Producers. Because of fluctuation in these groups, the size of the Tony electorate varies from year to year. For the 2002–2003 season there were 724 qualified Tony voters.

The 2002–2003 nominees follow, with winners in each category listed in **bold face type**.

BEST PLAY (award goes to both author and producer). *Enchanted April* by Matthew Barber, produced by Jeffrey Richards, Richard Gross/Ellen Berman/Les Goldman, Raymond J. and Pearl Berman Greenwald, Irving Welzer, Tonja Walker Davidson, Libby Adler Mages/Mari Glick, Howard R. Berlin, Jerry Frankel, Terry E. Schnuck, Frederic B. Vogel, Dori Berinstein /Barrie and Jim Loeks/Dramatic Forces. ***Take Me Out* by Richard Greenberg, produced by Carole Shorenstein Hays, Frederick DeMann, the Donmar Warehouse and the Public Theater**. *Say Goodnight, Gracie* by Rupert Holmes, produced by William Franzblau, Jay H. Harris, Louise Westergaard, Larry Spellman, Elsa Daspin Haft, Judith Resnick, Anne Gallagher, Libby Adler Mages/Mari Glick, Martha R. Gasparian, Bruce Lazarus, Lawrence S. Toppall, Jae French. *Vincent in Brixton* by Nicholas Wright, produced by Lincoln Center Theater, André Bishop, Bernard Gersten, The Royal National Theatre, Ambassador Theatre Group Ltd., Maidstone Productions, Robert Fox Ltd., Elliott F. Kulick, Incidental Coleman Tod, the Shubert Organization.

BEST MUSICAL (award goes to the producer). *Amour* produced by the Shubert Organization, Jean Doumanian Productions, Inc., USA Ostar Theatricals. *A Year With Frog and Toad* produced by Bob Boyett, Adrianne Lobel, Michael Gardner, Lawrence Horowitz, Roy Furman, Scott E. Nederlander, the Children's Theatre Company. ***Hairspray* produced by Margo Lion, Adam Epstein, the Baruch-Viertel-Routh-Frankel Group, James D. Stern/Douglas L. Meyer, Rick Steiner/Frederic H. Mayerson, SEL and the Gordon/Frost Organization, New Line Cinema, Clear Channel Entertainment, Allan S. Gordon/Elan V. McAllister, Dede Harris/Morton Swinsky, John and Bonnie Osher**. *Movin' Out* produced by James L. Nederlander, Hal Luftig, Scott E. Nederlander, Terry Allen Kramer, Clear Channel Entertainment, Emanuel Azenberg.

BEST BOOK OF A MUSICAL. Didier van Cauwelaert, with English adaptation by Jeremy Sams, for *Amour*. Willie Reale for *A Year With Frog and Toad*. David Henry Hwang for *Flower Drum Song*. **Mark O'Donnell** and **Thomas Meehan** for ***Hairspray***.

BEST ORIGINAL SCORE (music and lyrics). Robert Reale (music) and Willie Reale (lyrics) for *A Year With Frog and Toad*. Michel Legrand (music) and Didier van Cauwelaert, with English adaptation by Jeremy Sams, (lyrics) for *Amour*. **Marc Shaiman** (music) and **Scott Wittman** and **Marc Shaiman** (lyrics) for ***Hairspray***. Jeff Blumenkrantz, Bob Stillman, Jason Robert Brown, Danny Arena, Sara Light, Lauren Lucas, Jerry Silverstein, Martie Maguire, Wayland D. Holyfield, Bob Lee House, Carl L. Byrd, Pevin Byrd-Munoz, Luke Reed, Roger Brown, Jerry Chestnut, Marcus Hummon, Clint Black, James Hayden Nicholas, Tommy Conners, Skip Ewing, Charles Daniels, Tom Crain, Fred Edwards, Taz DiGregorio, Jim Marshall, Charlie Hayward, Wanda Mallette, Patti Ryan, Ronnie Dunn and Bob Morrison (music and lyrics) for *Urban Cowboy*.

BEST REVIVAL OF A PLAY (award goes to the producer). *A Day in the Death of Joe Egg* produced by Roundabout Theatre Company, Todd Haimes, Ellen Richard, Julia C. Levy, Sonia Friedman Productions. *Dinner at Eight* produced by Lincoln Center Theater, André Bishop, Bernard Gersten. *Frankie and Johnny in the Clair de Lune* produced by the Araca Group, Jean Doumanian Productions, USA Ostar Theatricals, Jam Theatricals, Ray and Kit Sawyer. ***Long Day's Journey Into Night* produced by David Richenthal, Max Cooper, Eric Falkenstein, Anthony and Charlene Marshall, Darren Bagert, Kara Medoff, Lisa Vioni, Gene Korf**.

BEST REVIVAL OF A MUSICAL (award goes to the producer). *Gypsy* produced by Robert Fox, Ron Kastner, Roger Marino, Michael Watt, Harvey Weinstein, WWLC.

La Bohème produced by Jeffrey Seller, Kevin McCollum, Emanuel Azenberg, Bazmark Live, Bob and Harvey Weinstein, Korea Pictures/Doyun Seol, Jeffrey Sine/ Ira Pittelman/Scott E. Nederlander, Fox Searchlight Pictures. *Man of La Mancha* produced by David Stone, Jon B. Platt, Susan Quint Gallin, Sandy Gallin, Seth M. Siegel, USA Ostar Theatricals, Mary Lu Roffe. **Nine produced by Roundabout Theatre Company, Todd Haimes, Ellen Richard, Julia C. Levy**.

BEST SPECIAL THEATRICAL EVENT. *Bill Maher: Victory Begins at Home* produced by Eric Krebs, Jonathan Reinis, CTM Productions, Anne Strickland Squadron, Michael Viner, David and Adam Friedson, Allen Spivak/Larry Magid, M. Kilburg Reedy. *The Play What I Wrote* produced by David Pugh, Joan Cullman, Mike Nichols, Hamilton South, Charles Whitehead, Stuart Thompson. *Prune Danish* produced by Jyll Rosenfeld, Jon Stoll. **Russell Simmons's Def Poetry Jam on Broadway produced by Russell Simmons, Stan Lathan, Jonathan Reinis, Richard Martini, Larry Magid, Allen Spivak, Kimora Lee Simmons, Jeffrey Chartier, Stacy Carter, Island Def Jam Music Group**.

BEST PERFORMANCE BY A LEADING ACTOR IN A PLAY. Brian Bedford in *Tartuffe*, **Brian Dennehy in Long Day's Journey Into Night**, Eddie Izzard in *A Day in the Death of Joe Egg*, Paul Newman in *Our Town*, Stanley Tucci in *Frankie and Johnny in the Clair de Lune*.

BEST PERFORMANCE BY A LEADING ACTRESS IN A PLAY. Jayne Atkinson in *Enchanted April*, Victoria Hamilton in *A Day in the Death of Joe Egg*, Clare Higgins in *Vincent in Brixton*, **Vanessa Redgrave in Long Day's Journey Into Night**, Fiona Shaw in *Medea*.

BEST PERFORMANCE BY A LEADING ACTOR IN A MUSICAL. Antonio Banderas in *Nine*, **Harvey Fierstein in Hairspray**,

Malcolm Gets in *Amour*, Brian Stokes Mitchell in *Man of La Mancha*, John Selya in *Movin' Out*.

BEST PERFORMANCE BY A LEADING ACTRESS IN A MUSICAL. Melissa Errico in *Amour*, Mary Elizabeth Mastrantonio in *Man of La Mancha*, Elizabeth Parkinson in *Movin' Out*, Bernadette Peters in *Gypsy*, **Marissa Jaret Winokur in Hairspray**.

BEST PERFORMANCE BY A FEATURED ACTOR IN A PLAY. Thomas Jefferson Byrd in *Ma Rainey's Black Bottom*, Philip Seymour Hoffman in *Long Day's Journey Into Night*, Robert Sean Leonard in *Long Day's Journey Into Night*, **Denis O'Hare in Take Me Out**, Daniel Sunjata in *Take Me Out*.

BEST PERFORMANCE BY A FEATURED ACTRESS IN A PLAY. Christine Ebersole in *Dinner at Eight*, Linda Emond in *Life (x) 3*, Kathryn Meisle in *Tartuffe*, **Michele Pawk in Hollywood Arms**, Marian Seldes in *Dinner at Eight*.

BEST PERFORMANCE BY A FEATURED ACTOR IN A MUSICAL. Michael Cavanaugh in *Movin' Out*, John Dossett in *Gypsy*, **Dick Latessa in Hairspray**, Corey Reynolds in *Hairspray*, Keith Roberts in *Movin' Out*.

BEST PERFORMANCE BY A FEATURED ACTRESS IN A MUSICAL. Tammy Blanchard in *Gypsy*, **Jane Krakowski in Nine**, Mary Stuart Masterson in *Nine*, Chita Rivera in *Nine*, Ashley Tuttle in *Movin' Out*.

BEST SCENIC DESIGN. John Lee Beatty for *Dinner at Eight*, Santo Loquasto for *Long Day's Journey Into Night*, **Catherine Martin for La Bohème**, David Rockwell for *Hairspray*.

BEST COSTUME DESIGN. Gregg Barnes for *Flower Drum Song*, **William Ivey Long for Hairspray**, Catherine Martin and Angus Strathie for *La Bohème*, Catherine Zuber for *Dinner at Eight*.

BEST LIGHTING DESIGN. Donald Holder for *Movin' Out*, **Nigel Levings** for *La Bohème*, Brian MacDevitt for *Nine*, Kenneth Posner for *Hairspray*.

BEST CHOREOGRAPHY. Robert Longbottom for *Flower Drum Song*, Jerry Mitchell for *Hairspray*, Melinda Roy for *Urban Cowboy*, **Twyla Tharp** for ***Movin' Out***.

BEST DIRECTION OF A PLAY. Laurence Boswell for *A Day in the Death of Joe Egg*, Robert Falls for *Long Day's Journey Into Night*, **Joe Mantello** for ***Take Me Out***, Deborah Warner for *Medea*.

BEST DIRECTION OF A MUSICAL. David Leveaux for *Nine*, Baz Luhrmann for *La Bohème*, **Jack O'Brien** for ***Hairspray***, Twyla Tharp for *Movin' Out*.

BEST ORCHESTRATIONS. **Billy Joel** and **Stuart Malina** for ***Movin' Out***, Nicholas Kitsopoulos for *La Bohème*, Jonathan Tunick for *Nine*, Harold Wheeler for *Hairspray*.

LIFETIME ACHIEVEMENT. **Cy Feuer**.

REGIONAL THEATRE TONY AWARD. **The Children's Theatre Company**, Minneapolis, Minnesota.

TONY AWARD WINNERS, 1947–2003

LISTED BELOW ARE the Antoinette Perry (Tony) Award winners in the catgories of Best Play and Best Musical from the time these awards were established in 1947 until the present.

1947—No play or musical award
1948—*Mister Roberts*; no musical award
1949—*Death of a Salesman*; *Kiss Me, Kate*
1950—*The Cocktail Party*; *South Pacific*
1951—*The Rose Tattoo*; *Guys and Dolls*
1952—*The Fourposter*; *The King and I*
1953—*The Crucible*; *Wonderful Town*
1954—*The Teahouse of the August Moon*; *Kismet*
1955—*The Desperate Hours*; *The Pajama Game*
1956—*The Diary of Anne Frank*; *Damn Yankees*
1957—*Long Day's Journey Into Night*; *My Fair Lady*
1958—*Sunrise at Campobello*; *The Music Man*
1959—*J.B.*; *Redhead*
1960—*The Miracle Worker*; *Fiorello!* and *The Sound of Music* (tie)
1961—*Becket*; *Bye Bye Birdie*
1962—*A Man for All Seasons*; *How to Succeed in Business Without Really Trying*
1963—*Who's Afraid of Virginia Woolf?*; *A Funny Thing Happened on the Way to the Forum*
1964—*Luther*; *Hello, Dolly!*
1965—*The Subject Was Roses*; *Fiddler on the Roof*
1966—*The Persecution and Assassination of Marat as Performed by the Inmates of the Asylum of Charenton Under the Direction of the Marquis de Sade*; *Man of La Mancha*
1967—*The Homecoming*; *Cabaret*

1968—*Rosencrantz and Guildenstern Are Dead*; *Hallelujah, Baby!*
1969—*The Great White Hope*; *1776*
1970—*Borstal Boy*; *Applause*
1971—*Sleuth*; *Company*
1972—*Sticks and Bones*; *Two Gentlemen of Verona*
1973—*That Championship Season*; *A Little Night Music*
1974—*The River Niger*; *Raisin*
1975—*Equus*; *The Wiz*
1976—*Travesties*; *A Chorus Line*
1977—*The Shadow Box*; *Annie*
1978—*Da*; *Ain't Misbehavin'*
1979—*The Elephant Man*; *Sweeney Todd, the Demon Barber of Fleet Street*
1980—*Children of a Lesser God*; *Evita*
1981—*Amadeus*; *42nd Street*
1982—*The Life & Adventures of Nicholas Nickleby*; *Nine*
1983—*Torch Song Trilogy*; *Cats*
1984—*The Real Thing*; *La Cage aux Folles*
1985—*Biloxi Blues*; *Big River*
1986—*I'm Not Rappaport*; *The Mystery of Edwin Drood*
1987—*Fences*; *Les Misérables*
1988—*M. Butterfly*; *The Phantom of the Opera*
1989—*The Heidi Chronicles*; *Jerome Robbins' Broadway*

1990—*The Grapes of Wrath; City of Angels*
1991—*Lost in Yonkers; The Will Rogers Follies*
1992—*Dancing at Lughnasa; Crazy for You*
1993—*Angels in America, Part I: Millennium Approaches; Kiss of the Spider Woman*
1994—*Angels in America, Part II: Perestroika; Passion*
1995—*Love! Valour! Compassion!; Sunset Boulevard*

1996—*Master Class; Rent*
1997—*The Last Night of Ballyhoo; Titanic*
1998—*Art; The Lion King*
1999—*Side Man; Fosse*
2000—*Copenhagen; Contact*
2001—*Proof; The Producers*
2002—*The Goat, or Who is Sylvia; Thoroughly Modern Millie*
2003—*Take Me Out; Hairspray*

2003 LUCILLE LORTEL AWARDS

THE LUCILLE LORTEL AWARDS for outstanding Off Broadway achievement were established in 1985 by a resolution of the League of Off Broadway Theatres and Producers, which administers them and has presented them annually since 1986. Eligible for the 18th annual awards in 2003 were all Off Broadway productions that opened between April 1, 2002 and March 31, 2003. Winners were selected by a committee comprising David Cote, Mark Dickerman, Susan Einhorn, Beverly Emmons, George Forbes, Charles Isherwood, Walt Kiskaddon, Sheila Mathews, Gerald Rabkin, Mark Rossier, Marc Routh, Donald Saddler, Tom Smedes, David Stone, Anna Strasberg, Barbara Wolkoff.

PLAY. *Take Me Out* by Richard Greenberg.

MUSICAL. *Avenue Q* music and lyrics by Robert Lopez and Jeff Marx, book by Jeff Whitty.

REVIVAL. *Fifth of July* by Lanford Wilson, produced by Signature Theatre Company.

ACTOR. **Daniel Sunjata** in *Take Me Out*.

ACTRESS. **Tovah Feldshuh** in *Golda's Balcony*.

FEATURED ACTOR. **Denis O'Hare** in *Take Me Out*.

FEATURED ACTRESS. **Jan Maxwell** in *My Old Lady*.

DIRECTION. **Joe Mantello** for *Take Me Out*.

CHOREOGRAPHY. **Devanand Janki** for *Zanna, Don't!*

SCENERY. **Alexander Dodge** for *Observe the Sons of Ulster Marching Towards the Somme*.

COSTUMES. **Michael Bottari** and **Ronald Case** for *Shanghai Moon*.

LIGHTING. **Donald Holder** for *Observe the Sons of Ulster Marching Towards the Somme*.

SOUND. **Brett Jarvis** for *Avenue Q*.

BODY OF WORK. **Vineyard Theatre**.

LIFETIME ACHIEVEMENT. **Stephen Sondheim**.

EDITH OLIVER AWARD. **Marian Seldes**.

UNIQUE THEATRICAL EXPERIENCE. *The Exonerated*.

LORTEL AWARD WINNERS 1986–2003

LISTED BELOW ARE the Lucille Lortel Award winners in the categories of Outstanding Play and Outstanding Musical from the time these awards were established until the present.

1986—*Woza Africa!*; no musical award
1987—*The Common Pursuit*; no musical award
1988—No play or musical award

1989—*The Cocktail Hour*; no musical award
1990—No play or musical award
1991—*Aristocrats; Falsettoland*

1992—*Lips Together, Teeth Apart; And the World Goes 'Round*
1993—*The Destiny of Me; Forbidden Broadway*
1994—*Three Tall Women; Wings*
1995—*Camping With Henry & Tom; Jelly Roll!*
1996—*Molly Sweeney; Floyd Collins*
1997—*How I Learned to Drive; Violet*
1998—*Gross Indecency*, and *The Beauty Queen of Leenane* (tie); no musical award

1999—*Wit*; no musical award
2000—*Dinner With Friends*; *James Joyce's The Dead*
2001—*Proof*; *Bat Boy: The Musical*
2002—*Metamorphoses*; *Urinetown*
2003—*Take Me Out*; *Avenue Q*

AMERICAN THEATRE CRITICS/STEINBERG NEW PLAY AWARDS AND CITATIONS
○ ○ ○ ○ ○
INCLUDING PRINCIPAL CITATIONS AND NEW PLAY AWARD WINNERS, 1977–2003

BEGINNING WITH THE season of 1976–77, the American Theatre Critics Association (ATCA) has cited one or more outstanding new plays in United States theater. The principal honorees have been included in *Best Plays* since the first year. In 1986 the ATCA New Play Award was given for the first time, along with a $1,000 prize. The award and citations were renamed the **American Theatre Critics/Steinberg New Play Award and Citations** in 2000 (see essays on the 2003 ATCA/Steinberg honorees in the Season Around the United States section of this volume). The award dates were renumbered beginning with the 2000–2001 volume to correctly reflect the year in which ATCA conferred the honor.

New Play Citations (1977–1985)

1977—*And the Soul Shall Dance* by Wakako Yamauchi
1978—*Getting Out* by Marsha Norman
1979—*Loose Ends* by Michael Weller
1980—*Custer* by Robert E. Ingham
1981—*Chekhov in Yalta* by John Driver and Jeffrey Haddow
1982—*Talking With* by Jane Martin
1983—*Closely Related* by Bruce MacDonald
1984—*Wasted* by Fred Gamel
1985—*Scheherazade* by Marisha Chamberlain

New Play Award (1986–1999)

1986—*Fences* by August Wilson
1987—*A Walk in the Woods* by Lee Blessing
1988—*Heathen Valley* by Romulus Linney
1989—*The Piano Lesson* by August Wilson
1990—*2* by Romulus Linney

1991—*Two Trains Running* by August Wilson
1992—*Could I Have This Dance?* by Doug Haverty
1993—*Children of Paradise: Shooting a Dream* by Steven Epp, Felicity Jones, Dominique Serrand and Paul Walsh
1994—*Keely and Du* by Jane Martin
1995—*The Nanjing Race* by Reggie Cheong-Leen
1996—*Amazing Grace* by Michael Cristofer
1997—*Jack and Jill* by Jane Martin
1998—*The Cider House Rules, Part II* by Peter Parnell
1999—*Book of Days* by Lanford Wilson.

ATCA/Steinberg New Play Award and Citations

2000—*Oo-Bla-Dee* by Regina Taylor
Citations: *Compleat Female Stage Beauty* by Jeffrey Hatcher; *Syncopation* by Allan Knee

2001—*Anton in Show Business* by Jane Martin
  Citations: *Big Love* by Charles L. Mee;
  King Hedley II by August Wilson
2002—*The Carpetbagger's Children* by Horton
  Foote
  Citations: *The Action Against Sol
  Schumann* by Jeffrey Sweet; *Joe and Betty*
  by Murray Mednick

2003—*Anna in the Tropics* by Nilo Cruz
  Citations: *Recent Tragic Events* by Craig
  Wright; *Resurrection Blues* by Arthur
  Miller

ADDITIONAL PRIZES AND AWARDS 2002–2003

THE FOLLOWING IS a list of major awards for achievement in the theater this season. The names of honorees appear in **bold type**.

2001–2002 GEORGE JEAN NATHAN AWARD. For dramatic criticism. **Daniel Mendelsohn**.

22ND ANNUAL WILLIAM INGE THEATRE FESTIVAL AWARD. For distinguished achievement in American theater. **Romulus Linney**. New voice: **Theresa Rebeck**.

2003 M. ELIZABETH OSBORN AWARD. Presented by the American Theatre Critics Association to an emerging playwright. **John Walch** for *The Dinosaur Within*.

25TH ANNUAL KENNEDY CENTER HONORS. For distinguished achievement by individuals who have made significant contributions to American culture through the arts. **James Earl Jones, James Levine, Chita Rivera, Paul Simon, Elizabeth Taylor**.

6TH ANNUAL KENNEDY CENTER–MARK TWAIN PRIZE. For American humor. **Lily Tomlin**.

2002 NATIONAL MEDALS OF THE ARTS. For individuals and organizations who have made outstanding contributions to the excellence, growth, support and availability of the arts in the United States, selected by the President from nominees presented by the National Endowment. **Florence Knoll Bassett, Trisha Brown, Uta Hagen, Lawrence Halprin, Al Hirschfeld, George Jones, Ming Cho Lee, Philippe de Montebello, William "Smokey" Robinson Jr**.

2003 DRAMATIST GUILD AWARDS. 2002 Elizabeth Hull–Kate Warriner Award to the playwright whose work deals with social, political or religious mores of the time, selected by the Dramatists Guild Council. **Dael Orlandersmith** for *Yellowman*. Frederick Loewe Award for Dramatic Composition: **Jerry Herman**. Flora Roberts Award: **Jonathan Reynolds**. Lifetime Achievement: **Neil Simon**.

2003 HENRY HEWES DESIGN AWARDS (formerly American Theatre Wing Design Awards). For design originating in the US, selected by a committee comprising Jeffrey Eric Jenkins (chairman), Tish Dace, Glenda Frank, Mario Fratti, Randy Gener, Mel Gussow, Henry Hewes and Joan Ungaro. Scenic design: **John Lee Beatty**, *Book of Days, Dinner at Eight, My Old Lady, Tartuffe*. Costume design: **Jane Greenwood**, *Tartuffe;* **Catherine Zuber**, *Dinner at Eight, Far Away*. Lighting design: **Brian MacDevitt**, *Frankie and Johnny in the Clair de Lune, Long Day's Journey Into Night, Nine*. Noteworthy Effects: **Richard Foreman**, *Panic! (How to Be Happy!)* (production design).

25TH ANNUAL SUSAN SMITH BLACKBURN PRIZE. For women who have written works of outstanding quality for the English-speaking theater. **Dael Orlandersmith** for *Yellowman*. Honorable mention: **Bryony Lavery** for *Frozen*.

2002 GEORGE FREEDLEY MEMORIAL AWARD. For the best book about live theater published in the United States the previous year. *Ridiculous! The Theatrical Life and Times of Charles Ludlam* by **David Kaufman**.

22ND ANNUAL ASTAIRE AWARDS. For excellence in dance and choreography, administered by the Theatre Development Fund and selected by a committee comprising Douglas Watt (chairman), Clive Barnes, Howard Kissel, Michael Kuchwara, Donald McDonagh, Richard Philp, Charles L. Reinhart and Linda Winer. Choreography: **Twyla Tharp** for *Movin' Out*. Female dancer: **Elizabeth Parkinson** in *Movin' Out*. Male dancer: **John Selya** in *Movin' Out*. Lifetime Achievement: **Chita Rivera**.

58TH ANNUAL CLARENCE DERWENT AWARDS. Given to a female and a male performer by Actors Equity Association based on New York work that demonstrates promise. **Kerry Butler** and **Denis O'Hare**.

2003 RICHARD RODGERS AWARDS. For staged readings of musicals in nonprofit theaters, administered by the American Academy of Arts and Letters and selected by a jury including Stephen Sondheim (chairman), Lynn Ahrens, Jack Beeson, William Bolcom, John Guare, Sheldon Harnick, and Richard Maltby Jr. and Robert Ward. Richard Rodgers Development Awards: *The Fabulist* by David Spencer and Stephen Witkin; *The Tutor* by Maryrose Wood and Andrew Gerle.

69TH ANNUAL DRAMA LEAGUE AWARDS. For distinguished achievement in the American theater. Play: *Take Me Out*. Musical: *Hairspray*. Revival of a play or musical: *A Day in the Death of Joe Egg*. Performance: **Harvey Fierstein** in *Hairspray*. Julia Hansen Award for excellence in directing: **Joe Mantello**. Achievement in Musical Theatre: **Twyla Tharp**. Unique contribution to theater: **Roundabout Theatre Company**.

2003 GEORGE OPPENHEIMER AWARD. To the best new American playwright, presented by *Newsday*. **Tom Dowlin** for *Corner Wars*.

2003 NEW DRAMATISTS LIFETIME ACHIEVEMENT AWARD. To an individual who has made an outstanding artistic contribution to the American theater. **August Wilson**.

2003 *THEATRE WORLD* AWARDS. For outstanding debut performers in Broadway or Off Broadway theater during the 2002–2003 season, selected by a committee including Clive Barnes, Peter Filichia, Harry Haun, Frank Scheck, Michael Sommers, Douglas Watt and Linda Winer. **Antonio Banderas** in *Nine*, **Tammy Blanchard** in *Gypsy*, **Thomas Jefferson Byrd** in *Ma Rainey's Black Bottom*, **Jonathan Cake** in *Medea*, **Victoria Hamilton** in *A Day in the Death of Joe Egg*, **Clare Higgins** in *Vincent in Brixton*, **Jackie Hoffman** in *Hairspray*, **Mary Stuart Masterson** in *Nine*, **John Selya** in *Movin' Out*, **Daniel Sunjata** in *Take Me Out*, **Jochum ten Haaf** in *Vincent in Brixton* and **Marissa Jaret Winokur** in *Hairspray*.

48TH ANNUAL DRAMA DESK AWARDS. For outstanding achievement in the 2002–2003 season, voted by an association of New York drama reporters, editors and critics from nominations made by a committee. New play: *Take Me Out*. New musical: *Hairspray*. Revival of a play: *Long Day's Journey Into Night*. Revival of a musical: *Nine*. Book of a musical: **Mark O'Donnell** and **Thomas Meehan** for *Hairspray*. Music: **Marc Shaiman** for *Hairspray*. Lyrics: **Scott Wittman** and **Marc Shaiman** for *Hairspray*. Actor in a play: **Eddie Izzard** in *A Day in the Death of Joe Egg*. Actress in a play: **Vanessa Redgrave** in *Long Day's Journey Into Night*. Featured actor in a play: **Denis O'Hare** in *Take Me Out*. Featured actress in a play: **Lynn Redgrave** in *Talking Heads*. Actor in a musical (tie): **Antonio Banderas** in *Nine* and **Harvey Fierstein** in *Hairspray*. Actress in a musical: **Marissa Jaret Winokur** in *Hairspray*. Featured actor in a musical: **Dick Latessa** in *Hairspray*. Featured actress in a musical: **Jane Krakowski** in *Nine*. Solo performance: **Tovah Feldshuh** in *Golda's Balcony*. Director of a play: **Robert Falls** for *Long Day's Journey Into Night*. Director of a musical: **Jack O'Brien** for *Hairspray*.

Choreography: **Twyla Tharp** for *Movin' Out.* Orchestrations: **Harold Wheeler** for *Hairspray.* Set design of a play: **John Lee Beatty** for *Dinner at Eight.* Set design of a musical: **Catherine Martin** for *La Bohème.* Costume design: **William Ivey Long** for *Hairspray.* Lighting design: **Nigel Levings** for *La Bohème.* Sound design: **Acme Sound Partners** for *La Bohème.* Unique Theatrical Experience: **The Exonerated.**

53RD ANNUAL OUTER CRITICS' CIRCLE AWARDS. For outstanding achievement in the 2002–2003 season, voted by critics on out-of-town periodicals and media. Broadway play: *Take Me Out.* Off Broadway play: *The Exonerated.* Revival of a play. *A Day in the Death of Joe Egg.* Actor in a play: **Eddie Izzard** in *A Day in the Death of Joe Egg.* Actress in a play: **Jayne Atkinson** in *Enchanted April.* Featured actor in a play: **Denis O'Hare** in *Take Me Out.* Featured actress in a play: **Linda Emond** in *Life (x) 3.* Director of a play: **Joe Mantello** for *Take Me Out.* Broadway musical: *Hairspray.* Off-Broadway musical: *A Man of No Importance.* Revival of a musical: *Nine.* Actor in a musical: **Antonio Banderas** in *Nine.* Actress in a musical: **Marissa Jaret Winokur** in *Hairspray.* Featured actor in a musical: **Dick Latessa** in *Hairspray.* Featured actress in a musical: **Jane Krakowski** in *Nine.* Director of a musical: **Jack O'Brien** for *Hairspray.* Choreography: **Twyla Tharp** for *Movin' Out.* Scenic design: **Catherine Martin** for *La Bohème.* Costume design: **William Ivey Long** for *Hairspray.* Lighting design: **Nigel Levings** for *La Bohème.* Solo performance: **Frank Gorshin** in *Say Goodnight, Gracie.* John Gassner Playwriting Award: **Matthew Barber** for *Enchanted April.* Special Achievement Award: **Ensemble performance, the cast of *Talking Heads.***

48TH ANNUAL *VILLAGE VOICE* OBIE AWARDS. For outstanding achievement in Off and Off-Off Broadway theater. Performance: **Kathleen Chalfant, Daniel Davis, Christine Ebersole, Valerie Mahaffey, Lynn Redgrave, Brenda Wehle** in *Talking Heads*; **Mos Def** in *Fucking A*;

Rosemary Harris in *All Over*; **Ty Jones, J. Kyle Manzay** in *The Blacks: A Clown Show*; **Stephen Mellor** in *Bitter Bierce, Or the Friction We Call Grief*; **Edward Norton** in *Burn This*; **Jim Norton** in *Dublin Carol*; **Denis O'Hare** in *Take Me Out*; **Jason Petty** in *Hank Williams: Lost Highway*; **Simon Russell Beale** in *Uncle Vanya*; **Fiona Shaw** in *Medea*; Barry Del Sherman in *The Mystery of Attraction.* Direction: **Emily Mann** for *All Over*; **Deborah Warner** for *Medea.* Sustained excellence in lighting design: **Kenneth Posner.** Set design: **Anthony Ward** for *Uncle Vanya.* Costume design: **Kimberly Glennon** for *The Blacks: A Clown Show.* Mask design: **Anne Lommel** for *The Blacks: A Clown Show.* Lifetime achievement: **Mac Wellman.**

Special Citations: **Art Acuña, Loy Arcenas, Lonnie Carter, Ramon de Ocampo, Ron Domingo, Jojo Gonzalez, Orlando Pabotoy** and **Ralph B. Peña** for *The Romance of Magno Rubio*; **Brooklyn Academy of Music International Programming**; **Lisa D'Amour, Katie Pearl** and **Kathy Randels** for *Nita and Zita*; **David Greenspan** for *She Stoops to Comedy*; **Morgan Jenness** for Longtime Support of Playwrights; **John Kani** and **Winston Ntshona** for *The Island*; **Erika Munk** for editing *Theater*; **Ellen Maddow, Paul Zimet, Diane Beckett, Gary Brownlee, Randolph Curtis Rand, Steven Rattazzi, Tina Shepard, Louise Smith, Nic Ularu, Kiki Smith, Carol Mullins, Karinne Keithley** and **"Blue" Gene Tyranny** for **Talking Band**'s *Painted Snake in a Painted Chair.* Grants: **Collapsable Hole, Galapagos, The Immigrant Theatre Project.** Ross Wetzsteon Award: **Soho Think Tank's Ice Factory Series** at the **Ohio Theater.**

13TH ANNUAL CONNECTICUT CRITICS' CIRCLE AWARDS. For outstanding achievement in Connecticut theater during the 2001–2002 season. Production of a play: **Yale Repertory Theatre** for *Medea/Macbeth/Cinderella.* Production of a musical: **Goodspeed Musicals** for *Me and My Girl.* Actress in a play: **Annalee Jefferies** in *The Night of the Iguana.* Actor in a play (tie):

Leon Addison Brown in *"Master Harold" . . . and the Boys* and **James Colby** in *The Night of the Iguana*. Actress in a musical: **Josie de Guzman** in *The King and I*. Actor in a musical: **Hunter Bell** in *Me and My Girl*. Direction of a play: **Bill Rauch** and **Tracy Young** for *Medea/Macbeth/Cinderella*. Direction of a musical: **Scott Schwartz** for *Me and My Girl*. Choreography: **Lisa and Gary McIntyre** for *Swing!* Set design: **Jeff Cowie** for *The Night of the Iguana*. Lighting design: **Robert Wierzel** for *Wintertime*. Costume design: Christal Weatherly for *Wintertime*. Sound design: Christopher A. Granger for *A Lesson Before Dying*. Ensemble performance: **James Alexander**, Rosena M. Hill, Danette E. Sheppard, Charles E. Wallace and Carla Woods in *Ain't Misbehavin'*.

Roadshow: **Stamford Center for the Arts** for *bobrauschenbergamerica*. Debut award: **Royce Johnson** in *A Lesson Before Dying*. Tom Killen Memorial Award: **John G. Rowland**, Governor of the State of Connecticut.

21ST ANNUAL ELLIOT NORTON AWARDS. For outstanding contribution to the theater in Boston, voted by a Boston Theater Critics Association Selection Committee comprising Terry Byrne, Carolyn Clay, Iris Fanger, Joyce Kulhawik, Jon L. Lehman, Bill Marx, Ed Siegel and Caldwell Titcomb. New play: **Ronan Noone** for *The Blowin of Baile Gall* at Boston Playwrights' Theatre. Norton Prize: **Jeremiah Kissel**. Productions—Large visiting company: *Medea* produced by Broadway in Boston at the Wilbur Theatre; Small visiting company: *A New War* from Wellfleet Harbor Actors Theater; Large resident company: *Highway Ulysses* produced by American Repertory Theatre; Small resident company: *Betrayal* produced by Nora Theatre Company; Local fringe company: *Spinning Into Butter* produced by The Theatre Cooperative. Solo performance: **Annette Miller** in *Golda's Balcony*. Musical production—*Bat Boy: The Musical* produced by SpeakEasy Stage Company. Actor—Large company: **Arliss**

Howard in *Uncle Vanya*; Small company: **Billy Meleady** in *Howie the Rookie, The Lepers of Baile Baiste* and *The Blowin of Baile Gall*. Actress—Large company: **Fiona Shaw** in *Medea*; Small company: **Laura Latreille** in *The Shape of Things*; Fringe company: Naeemah A. White-Peppers for *Bee-Luther-Hatchee* and *Chain*. Director—Large company: **Anne Bogart** for *La Dispute*; Small company: **Paul Daigneault** in *Passion* and *Bat Boy*. Scene design—Large company: **David P. Gordon** for *The Blue Demon*; Small company: **Richard Chambers** for *The Blowin of Baile Gall*. Guest of Honor: **Brian Dennehy**.

19TH ANNUAL HELEN HAYES AWARDS. In recognition of excellence in Washington, D.C., theater, presented by the Washington Theatre Awards Society.

Resident productions—Play: *Hamlet* produced by Synetic Theater. Musical: *Sweeney Todd* produced by the Kennedy Center. Lead actress, musical: **Christine Baranski** in *Sweeney Todd*. Lead actor, musical: **Rick Hammerly** in *Hedwig and the Angry Inch*. Lead actress, play: **Holly Twyford** in *The Shape of Things*. Lead actor, play: **Jon Cohn** in *The Taste of Fire*. Supporting actress, musical: **Lori Tan Chinn** in *South Pacific*. Supporting actor, musical: **Ted L. Levy** in *Hot Mikado*. Supporting actress, play: **Nancy Robinette** in *The Little Foxes*. Supporting actor, play: **Michael Ray Escamilla** in *Recent Tragic Events*. Director, play: **Paata Tsikurishvili** for *Hamlet*. Director, musical (tie): **Christopher Ashley** for *Sweeney Todd*; **Toby Orenstein** for *Jekyll & Hyde: The Musical*. Set design, play or musical (tie): **James Kronzer** for *Shakespeare, Moses and Joe Papp*; and **Hugh Landwehr** for *The Little Foxes*. Costume design, play or musical: **Jelena Vukmirovic** and **Marie Schneggenburger** for *Mississippi Pinocchio*. Lighting design, play or musical: **Howell Binkley** for *Sweeney Todd*. Sound design, play or musical: **Mark K. Anduss** for *Tiny Alice*. Choreography: **Irina Tsikurishvili** for *Hamlet*. Musical direction: **Rob Berman** for *Sunday in the Park With George*.

Non-resident productions—Production: *Lypsinka! The Boxed Set* produced by the Studio Theatre. Lead actress: **Sarah Jones** in *Surface Transit*. Lead actor: **Brian Stokes Mitchell** in *Man of La Mancha*. Supporting performer: **Kelli Fournier** in *Aida*.

Charles MacArthur Award for outstanding new play: *Shakespeare, Moses and Joe Papp* by **Ernie Joselovitz**. Charles MacArthur Award for outstanding new musical: *Polk County* by **Zora Neale Hurston** and **Dorothy Waring**, adapted by **Kyle Donnelly** and **Cathy Madison**, music by **Stephen Wade**.

34TH ANNUAL JOSEPH JEFFERSON AWARDS. For achievement in Chicago theater during the 2001–2002 season, given by the Jefferson Awards Committee in 24 competitive categories. Twenty-eight producing organizations were nominated for various awards, 17 different companies were honored. The Chicago Shakespeare Theater, topped all other companies by winning seven awards. Marriott Theatre in Lincolnshire received four awards again this year, but the Writers Theatre followed closely with three.

Resident productions—New work: *The Liquid Moon* by **John Green**; *Waving Goodbye* by **Jamie Pachino**. New Adaptation: *Rosa Lublin* by Robin Chaplik; *The Visit* **Terrence McNally**, **John Kander** and **Fred Ebb**. Production of a play: **Writers Theatre** for *The Price*. Production of a musical: **Chicago Shakespeare Theater** for *Pacific Overtures*. Director of a play: **David Cromer** for *The Price*. Director of a musical: **Gary Griffin** for *Pacific Overtures*. Director of a revue: **Joshua Funk** for *Holy War, Batman! or The Yellow Cab of Courage*. Actor in a principal role, play: **John Sierros** in *Dylan*. Actress in a principal role, play: **Lusia Strus** in *Go Away–Go Away*. Actor in a supporting role, play: **Guy Adkins** in *Misalliance*. Actress in a supporting role, play: **Peggy Roeder** in *Indian Ink*. Actor in a principal role, musical: **Joseph Anthony Foronda** in

Pacific Overtures; **Kevin Gudahl** in *1776*. Actress in a principal role, musical: **Kate Fry** in *My Fair Lady*. Actor in a supporting role, musical: **Kevin Gudahl** in *Pacific Overtures*. Actress in a supporting role, musical: **Marilynn Bogetich** in *My Fair Lady*. Actor in a revue: **Keegan-Michael Key** in *Holy War, Batman! or The Yellow Cab of Courage*. Ensemble: *The Laramie Project* produced by Next Theatre. Scenic design: **James Schuette** for *The Royal Family*. Costume design: **Mariann Verheyen** for *As You Like It*. Lighting design: **Diane Ferry Williams** for *Miss Saigon*. Sound design: **Duncan Robert Edwards** for *Miss Saigon*. Choreography: **David H. Bell** and **Lainie Sakakura** for *Damn Yankees*. Original music: **Alaric Jans** for *The Tempest*. Musical direction: **Tom Murray** for *Pacific Overtures*.

Non-resident productions—Production: **Fox Searchlight Pictures**, **Lindsay Law** and **Thomas Hall** for *The Full Monty*. Actor in a principal role: **John Leguizamo** in *Sexaholix . . . a Love Story*. Actress in a principal role: **Bob Stillman** in *Dirty Blonde*.

Lifetime Achievement: **Mike Nussbaum** Special Awards: The City of Chicago and **Lois Weisberg**, Cultural Affairs commissioner, "for extraordinary support and service to the theater community in Chicago"; **Maggie Daley**, for "energetic promotion of theater in Chicago."

30TH ANNUAL JOSEPH JEFFERSON CITATIONS WING AWARDS. For outstanding achievement in professional productions during the 2002–2003 season of Chicago area theaters not operating under union contracts. Productions (play): *Awake and Sing* produced by **TimeLine Theatre Company**; *Machinal* produced by **The Hypocrites**. Productions (musical): *The Secret Garden* produced by **Circle Theatre**; *Sunday in the Park With George* produced by **Pegasus Players**. Ensembles: *Awake and Sing*; *Around the World in 80 Days* (Lifeline Theatre); *Machinal*; *Nana* (Trap Door Theatre). Directors (play): **Louis Contey** for *Awake* *and Sing*; **Sean Graney** for *Machinal*; **Dorothy Milne** for *Around the World in 80 Days*. Director (musical): **Gareth Hendee** for *Sunday in the Park With George*. New works: **Stephen Clark** for *Stripped*; **Robert Koon** for *Vintage Red and the Dust of the Road*. New adaptations: **John Hildreth** for *Around the World in 80 Days*; **Jim Lasko** for *Seagull*. Actress in a principal role (play): **Mechelle Moe** in *Machinal*. Actors in a principal role (play): **PJ Powers** in *Hauptmann*; **Jim Slonina** in *Seagull*. Actors in a principal role (musical): **Charlie Clark** in *Company*; **Joel Sutliffe** in *Sunday in the Park With George*. Actresses in a supporting role (play): **Corryn Cummins** in *Hot L Baltimore*; **Liz Fletcher** in *Golden Boy*. Actresses in a supporting role (musical): **Rebecca Finnegan** in *Company*; **Suzanne Genz** in *A New Brain*; **Sarah Swanson** in *The Secret Garden*; **Megan Van De Hey** in *A New Brain*. Actors in a supporting role (play): **Rich Baker** in *Awake and Sing*; **Robert Kauzlaric** in *Around the World in 80 Days*; **Derrick Nelson** in *The Royal Hunt of the Sun*; **George W. Seegebrecht** in *Taking Steps*. Actor in a supporting role (musical): **Henry Michael Odum** in *The Fantasticks*. Scenic designs:**Alan Donahue** for *Around the World in 80 Days*; **Noelle C.K. Hathaway** for *Awake and Sing;* **Stephanie Nelson** for *Salao: the Worst Kind of Unlucky*. Costume designs: **Michael Growler** for *Sunday in the Park With George*; **Thomas K. Kieffer** for *Tartuffe*; **Jeffrey Kelly** for *The Secret Garden*. Lighting design: **Heather Graff** and **Richard Peterson** for *Machinal*. Sound design: **Victoria DeIorio** for *Around the World in 80 Days*; **Joseph Fosco** for *Machinal*. Choreography: **Kevin Bellie** for *A New Brain*; **Katrina Williams Brunner** for *Company*. Original music: **Andre Pluess** for *Knives in Hens*. Musical direction: **Eugene Dizon** for *Company*. Puppet design: **Lisa Barcy** and **Jesse Mooney-Bullock** for *Salao: the Worst Kind of Unlucky*. Special award for "creative

energy and leadership in bringing diverse communities into Chicago theater for the pleasure and edification of its audiences": **David G. Zak**.

THE 28TH ANNUAL CARBONELL AWARDS. For outstanding achievement in South Florida theater during the 2002–2003 season. New Work: *Tin Box Boomerang* by **Ivonne Azurdia**. Ensemble: *Constant Star* produced by **Florida Stage**. Production of a play: *Constant Star*. Director of a play: **Michael Hall** for *Fortune's Fool*. Actor in a play: **John Felix** in *Fortune's Fool*. Actress in a play: **Laura Turnbull** in *Crimes of the Heart*. Supporting actor in a play: **David Kwiat** in *Dirty Blonde*. Supporting actress in a play: **Mayhill Fowler** in *The Last Schwartz*. Production of a musical: *Floyd Collins* produced by **The Actors Playhouse**. Director of a musical: **David Arisco** for *Floyd Collins*. Actor in a musical: **Tally Sessions** in *Floyd Collins*. Actress in a musical: **Laura Turnbull** in *Blood Brothers*. Supporting actor in a musical: **John Paul Almon** in *Romeo and Bernadette*. Supporting actress in a musical: **Irene Adjan** in *Blood Brothers*. Musical direction: **Eric Alsford** for *Floyd Collins*. Choreography: **Reggie Whitehead** for *Zombie Prom*. Scenic design: **Gene Seyffer** for *Floyd Collins*. Lighting: **Stuart Reiter** for *Floyd Collins*. Costumes: **Mary Lynne Izzo** for *Big Bang*. Sound: **Nate Rausch** for *Floyd Collins*.

Non-resident productions—Production: **The Lion King**. Actress: **Paulette Ivory** in *Aida*. Actor: Jeremy Kushnier in *Aida*. Director: **Julie Taymor** for **The Lion King**.

Special achievement award: **Nilo Cruz** and the **New Theatre** for *Anna in the Tropics*. George Abbott Award: **Alex W. Dreyfoos**, **Carl L. Mayhue** and **Robert B. Lochie Jr.** Howard Kleinberg Award: **Elizabeth Boone**. Ruth Foreman Award: **Dorothy Willis**. Bill Hindman Award: **David Kwiat**.

THE THEATER HALL OF FAME

○ ○ ○ ○ ○

THE THEATER HALL OF FAME was created in 1971 to honor those who have made outstanding contributions to the American theater in a career spanning at least 25 years, with at least five major credits. Honorees are elected annually by members of the American Theatre Critics Association, members of the Theater Hall of Fame and theater historians. Names of those elected in 2002 and inducted January 27, 2003 appear in ***bold italics***.

GEORGE ABBOTT	JOHN BARRYMORE	ABE BURROWS
MAUDE ADAMS	LIONEL BARRYMORE	RICHARD BURTON
VIOLA ADAMS	HOWARD BAY	MRS. PATRICK CAMPBELL
STELLA ADLER	NORA BAYES	ZOE CALDWELL
EDWARD ALBEE	***JOHN LEE BEATTY***	EDDIE CANTOR
THEONI V. ALDREDGE	SAMUEL BECKETT	MORRIS CARNOVSKY
IRA ALDRIDGE	BRIAN BEDFORD	MRS. LESLIE CARTER
JANE ALEXANDER	S.N. BEHRMAN	GOWER CHAMPION
MARY ALICE	NORMAN BEL GEDDES	FRANK CHANFRAU
WINTHROP AMES	DAVID BELASCO	CAROL CHANNING
JUDITH ANDERSON	MICHAEL BENNETT	***STOCKARD CHANNING***
MAXWELL ANDERSON	RICHARD BENNETT	RUTH CHATTERTON
ROBERT ANDERSON	ROBERT RUSSELL BENNETT	PADDY CHAYEFSKY
JULIE ANDREWS	ERIC BENTLEY	ANTON CHEKHOV
MARGARET ANGLIN	IRVING BERLIN	INA CLAIRE
JEAN ANOUILH	SARAH BERNHARDT	BOBBY CLARK
HAROLD ARLEN	LEONARD BERNSTEIN	HAROLD CLURMAN
GEORGE ARLISS	EARL BLACKWELL	LEE J. COBB
BORIS ARONSON	KERMIT BLOOMGARDEN	RICHARD L. COE
ADELE ASTAIRE	JERRY BOCK	GEORGE M. COHAN
FRED ASTAIRE	RAY BOLGER	ALEXANDER H. COHEN
EILEEN ATKINS	EDWIN BOOTH	JACK COLE
BROOKS ATKINSON	JUNIUS BRUTUS BOOTH	CY COLEMAN
LAUREN BACALL	SHIRLEY BOOTH	CONSTANCE COLLIER
PEARL BAILEY	PHILIP BOSCO	ALVIN COLT
GEORGE BALANCHINE	ALICE BRADY	BETTY COMDEN
WILLIAM BALL	BERTOLT BRECHT	MARC CONNELLY
ANNE BANCROFT	FANNIE BRICE	BARBARA COOK
TALLULAH BANKHEAD	PETER BROOK	KATHARINE CORNELL
RICHARD BARR	JOHN MASON BROWN	NOEL COWARD
PHILIP BARRY	ROBERT BRUSTEIN	JANE COWL
ETHEL BARRYMORE	BILLIE BURKE	LOTTA CRABTREE

CHERYL CRAWFORD

HUME CRONYN

RUSSEL CROUSE

CHARLOTTE CUSHMAN

JEAN DALRYMPLE

AUGUSTIN DALY

E.L. DAVENPORT

GORDON DAVIDSON

OSSIE DAVIS

RUBY DEE

ALFRED DE LIAGRE JR.

AGNES DEMILLE

COLLEEN DEWHURST

HOWARD DIETZ

DUDLEY DIGGES

MELVYN DOUGLAS

EDDIE DOWLING

ALFRED DRAKE

MARIE DRESSLER

JOHN DREW

MRS. JOHN DREW

WILLIAM DUNLAP

MILDRED DUNNOCK

CHARLES DURNING

ELEANORA DUSE

JEANNE EAGELS

FRED EBB

FLORENCE ELDRIDGE

LEHMAN ENGEL

MAURICE EVANS

ABE FEDER

JOSE FERRER

CY FEUER

ZELDA FICHANDLER

DOROTHY FIELDS

HERBERT FIELDS

LEWIS FIELDS

W.C. FIELDS

JULES FISHER

MINNIE MADDERN FISKE

CLYDE FITCH

GERALDINE FITZGERALD

HENRY FONDA

LYNN FONTANNE

HORTON FOOTE

EDWIN FORREST

BOB FOSSE

RUDOLF FRIML

CHARLES FROHMAN

ROBERT FRYER

ATHOL FUGARD

JOHN GASSNER

LARRY GELBART

PETER GENNARO

GRACE GEORGE

GEORGE GERSHWIN

IRA GERSHWIN

BERNARD GERSTEN

JOHN GIELGUD

W.S. GILBERT

JACK GILFORD

WILLIAM GILLETTE

CHARLES GILPIN

LILLIAN GISH

JOHN GOLDEN

MAX GORDON

RUTH GORDON

ADOLPH GREEN

PAUL GREEN

CHARLOTTE GREENWOOD

JOEL GREY

TAMMY GRIMES

GEORGE GRIZZARD

JOHN GUARE

OTIS L. GUERNSEY JR.

TYRONE GUTHRIE

UTA HAGEN

LEWIS HALLAM

T. EDWARD HAMBLETON

OSCAR HAMMERSTEIN II

WALTER HAMPDEN

OTTO HARBACH

E.Y. HARBURG

SHELDON HARNICK

EDWARD HARRIGAN

JED HARRIS

JULIE HARRIS

ROSEMARY HARRIS

SAM H. HARRIS

REX HARRISON

KITTY CARLISLE HART

LORENZ HART

MOSS HART

TONY HART

JUNE HAVOC

HELEN HAYES

LELAND HAYWARD

BEN HECHT

EILEEN HECKART

THERESA HELBURN

LILLIAN HELLMAN

KATHARINE HEPBURN

VICTOR HERBERT

JERRY HERMAN

JAMES A. HERNE

HENRY HEWES

AL HIRSCHFELD

RAYMOND HITCHCOCK

HAL HOLBROOK

CELESTE HOLM

HANYA HOLM

ARTHUR HOPKINS

DE WOLF HOPPER

JOHN HOUSEMAN

EUGENE HOWARD

LESLIE HOWARD

SIDNEY HOWARD

WILLIE HOWARD

BARNARD HUGHES

HENRY HULL

JOSEPHINE HULL

WALTER HUSTON

EARLE HYMAN

HENRIK IBSEN
WILLIAM INGE
BERNARD B. JACOBS
ELSIE JANIS
JOSEPH JEFFERSON
AL JOLSON
JAMES EARL JONES
MARGO JONES
ROBERT EDMOND JONES
TOM JONES
JON JORY
RAUL JULIA
JOHN KANDER
GARSON KANIN
GEORGE S. KAUFMAN
DANNY KAYE
ELIA KAZAN
GENE KELLY
GEORGE KELLY
FANNY KEMBLE
JEROME KERN
WALTER KERR
MICHAEL KIDD
RICHARD KILEY
SIDNEY KINGSLEY
FLORENCE KLOTZ
JOSEPH WOOD KRUTCH
BERT LAHR
BURTON LANE
FRANK LANGELLA
LAWRENCE LANGNER
LILLIE LANGTRY
ANGELA LANSBURY
CHARLES LAUGHTON
ARTHUR LAURENTS
GERTRUDE LAWRENCE
JEROME LAWRENCE
EVA LE GALLIENNE
MING CHO LEE
ROBERT E. LEE
LOTTE LENYA

ALAN JAY LERNER
SAM LEVENE
ROBERT LEWIS
BEATRICE LILLIE
HOWARD LINDSAY
FRANK LOESSER
FREDERICK LOEWE
JOSHUA LOGAN
PAULINE LORD
LUCILLE LORTEL
ALFRED LUNT
CHARLES MACARTHUR
STEELE MACKAYE
DAVID MAMET
ROUBEN MAMOULIAN
RICHARD MANSFIELD
ROBERT B. MANTELL
FREDRIC MARCH
NANCY MARCHAND
JULIA MARLOWE
ERNEST H. MARTIN
MARY MARTIN
RAYMOND MASSEY
SIOBHAN MCKENNA
TERRENCE MCNALLY
HELEN MENKEN
BURGESS MEREDITH
ETHEL MERMAN
DAVID MERRICK
JO MIELZINER
ARTHUR MILLER
MARILYN MILLER
LIZA MINNELLI
HELENA MODJESKA
FERENC MOLNAR
LOLA MONTEZ
VICTOR MOORE
ROBERT MORSE
ZERO MOSTEL
ANNA CORA MOWATT
PAUL MUNI

THARON MUSSER
GEORGE JEAN NATHAN
MILDRED NATWICK
NAZIMOVA
JAMES M. NEDERLANDER
MIKE NICHOLS
ELLIOT NORTON
SEAN O'CASEY
CLIFFORD ODETS
DONALD OENSLAGER
LAURENCE OLIVIER
EUGENE O'NEILL
JERRY ORBACH
GERALDINE PAGE
JOSEPH PAPP
OSGOOD PERKINS
BERNADETTE PETERS
MOLLY PICON
HAROLD PINTER
LUIGI PIRANDELLO
CHRISTOPHER PLUMMER
COLE PORTER
ROBERT PRESTON
HAROLD PRINCE
JOSE QUINTERO
ELLIS RABB
JOHN RAITT
TONY RANDALL
MICHAEL REDGRAVE
ADA REHAN
ELMER RICE
LLOYD RICHARDS
RALPH RICHARDSON
CHITA RIVERA
JASON ROBARDS
JEROME ROBBINS
PAUL ROBESON
RICHARD RODGERS
WILL ROGERS
SIGMUND ROMBERG
HAROLD ROME

LILLIAN RUSSELL	KIM STANLEY	TONY WALTON
DONALD SADDLER	*JEAN STAPLETON*	DOUGLAS TURNER WARD
GENE SAKS	MAUREEN STAPLETON	DAVID WARFIELD
WILLIAM SAROYAN	FRANCES STERNHAGEN	ETHEL WATERS
JOSEPH SCHILDKRAUT	ROGER L. STEVENS	CLIFTON WEBB
HARVEY SCHMIDT	ISABELLE STEVENSON	JOSEPH WEBER
ALAN SCHNEIDER	ELLEN STEWART	MARGARET WEBSTER
GERALD SCHOENFELD	DOROTHY STICKNEY	KURT WEILL
ARTHUR SCHWARTZ	FRED STONE	ORSON WELLES
MAURICE SCHWARTZ	TOM STOPPARD	MAE WEST
GEORGE C. SCOTT	LEE STRASBERG	ROBERT WHITEHEAD
MARIAN SELDES	AUGUST STRINDBERG	OSCAR WILDE
IRENE SHARAFF	ELAINE STRITCH	THORNTON WILDER
GEORGE BERNARD SHAW	CHARLES STROUSE	BERT WILLIAMS
SAM SHEPARD	JULE STYNE	TENNESSEE WILLIAMS
ROBERT E. SHERWOOD	MARGARET SULLAVAN	LANFORD WILSON
J.J. SHUBERT	ARTHUR SULLIVAN	P.G. WODEHOUSE
LEE SHUBERT	JESSICA TANDY	PEGGY WOOD
HERMAN SHUMLIN	LAURETTE TAYLOR	ALEXANDER WOOLLCOTT
NEIL SIMON	ELLEN TERRY	IRENE WORTH
LEE SIMONSON	TOMMY TUNE	TERESA WRIGHT
EDMUND SIMPSON	GWEN VERDON	ED WYNN
OTIS SKINNER	ROBIN WAGNER	VINCENT YOUMANS
MAGGIE SMITH	NANCY WALKER	STARK YOUNG
OLIVER SMITH	ELI WALLACH	FLORENZ ZIEGFELD
STEPHEN SONDHEIM	JAMES WALLACK	PATRICIA ZIPPRODT
E.H. SOTHERN	LESTER WALLACK	

THE THEATER HALL OF FAME
FOUNDERS AWARD

ESTABLISHED IN 1993 in honor of Earl Blackwell, James M. Nederlander, Gerard Oestreicher and Arnold Weissberger, The Theater Hall of Fame Founders Award is voted by the Hall's board of directors to an individual for his or her outstanding contribution to the theater.

1993 JAMES M. NEDERLANDER	1997 OTIS L. GUERNSEY JR.	2000 GERARD OESTREICHER
1994 KITTY CARLISLE HART	1998 EDWARD COLTON	ARNOLD WEISSBERGER
1995 HARVEY SABINSON	1999 NO AWARD	2001 TOM DILLON
1996 HENRY HEWES		2002 NO AWARD

MARGO JONES
CITIZEN OF THE THEATER MEDAL

PRESENTED ANNUALLY TO a citizen of the theater who has made a lifetime commitment to theater in the United States and has demonstrated an understanding and affirmation of the craft of playwriting.

1961 LUCILLE LORTEL
1962 MICHAEL ELLIS
1963 JUDITH RUTHERFORD MARECHAL GEORGE SAVAGE (University Award)
1964 RICHARD BARR, EDWARD ALBEE & CLINTON WILDER RICHARD A. DUPREY (University Award)
1965 WYNN HANDMAN MARSTON BALCH (University Award)
1966 JON JORY ARTHUR BALLET (University Award)
1967 PAUL BAKER GEORGE C. WHITE (Workshop Award)
1968 DAVEY MARLIN-JONES

1968 ELLEN STEWART (Workshop Award)
1969 ADRIAN HALL EDWARD PARONE & GORDON DAVIDSON (Workshop Award)
1970 JOSEPH PAPP
1971 ZELDA FICHANDLER
1972 JULES IRVING
1973 DOUGLAS TURNER WARD
1974 PAUL WEIDNER
1975 ROBERT KALFIN
1976 GORDON DAVIDSON
1977 MARSHALL W. MASON
1978 JON JORY
1979 ELLEN STEWART
1980 JOHN CLARK DONAHUE
1981 LYNNE MEADOW
1982 ANDRE BISHOP
1983 BILL BUSHNELL

1984 GREGORY MOSHER
1985 JOHN LION
1986 LLOYD RICHARDS
1987 GERALD CHAPMAN
1988 NO AWARD
1989 MARGARET GOHEEN
1990 RICHARD COE
1991 OTIS L. GUERNSEY JR.
1992 ABBOT VAN NOSTRAND
1993 HENRY HEWES
1994 JANE ALEXANDER
1995 ROBERT WHITEHEAD
1996 AL HIRSCHFELD
1997 GEORGE C. WHITE
1998 JAMES HOUGHTON
1999 GEORGE KEATHLEY
2000 EILEEN HECKART
2001 MEL GUSSOW
2002 EMILIE S. KILGORE

MUSICAL THEATRE HALL OF FAME

THIS ORGANIZATION WAS established at New York University on November 10, 1993.

HAROLD ARLEN
IRVING BERLIN
LEONARD BERNSTEIN
EUBIE BLAKE
ABE BURROWS
GEORGE M. COHAN
DOROTHY FIELDS
GEORGE GERSHWIN
IRA GERSHWIN
OSCAR HAMMERSTEIN II
E.Y. HARBURG
LARRY HART
JEROME KERN
BURTON LANE
ALAN JAY LERNER
FRANK LOESSER
FREDERICK LOEWE
COLE PORTER
ETHEL MERMAN
JEROME ROBBINS
RICHARD RODGERS
HAROLD ROME

2002–2003 NEW PUBLICATION OF PLAYS, ADAPTATIONS, TRANSLATIONS, COLLECTIONS AND ANTHOLOGIES

○ ○ ○ ○ ○

Compiled by Rue E. Canvin

PLAYS

The Abdication. Ruth Wolff. Dramatic Publishing Co. (acting ed.) $5.95

An Adult Evening of Shel Silverstein. Shel Silverstein. Dramatists Play Service. (acting ed.) $5.95

Bat Boy: The Musical. Keythe Farley, Brian Flemming, Laurence O'Keefe. Dramatists Play Service. (acting ed.) $7

Be Aggressive. Annie Weisman. Dramatists Play Service. (acting ed.) $5.95.

Bell in Campo and The Sociable Companions. Margaret Cavendish. Broadview Press. (paper) $12.95

Bernard Kops: Plays Three. Bernard Kops. Oberon Books. (paper) $25.95

Blithe Spirit. Noël Coward. Methuen. (paper) $13.95

Blasted. Sarah Kane. Methuen. (paper) $13.95

Bones. Peter Straughan. Methuen. (paper) $13.95

Boston Marriage. David Mamet. Random House. (paper) $12

Buffalo Gal. A.R. Gurney. Broadway Play Publishing. (paper) $7.95

Carl the Second. Marc Palmieri. Dramatists Play Service. (acting ed.) $5.95

Damsels in Distress: An Ayckbourn Trilogy. Alan Ayckbourn. Faber and Faber. (paper) $21

The Dazzle and Everett Beekin: Two Plays. Richard Greenberg. Faber and Faber. (paper) $16

The Designated Mourner. Wallace Shawn. Dramatists Play Service. (acting ed.) $5.95

The Dreaming of Aloysius. Louis Lippa. Dramatists Play Service. (acting ed.) $5.95

The Duel and Other Stories. Anton Chekhov. Dover Thrift Editions. (paper) $2

Emma. Howard Zinn. South End Press. (paper) $9

En Suite. Joe O'Byrne. Methuen. (paper) $13.95

Endpapers. Thomas McCormack. Dramatists Play Service.(acting ed.)$.95

Enigma Variations. Eric-Emmanuel Schmitt. Dramatists Play Service. (acting ed.) $5.95

Face to the Wall and Fever Emergencies. Martin Crimp. Faber and Faber. (paper) $16

A Few Stout Individuals. John Guare. Grove Press. (paper) $13

Flower Drum Song (revised). David Henry Hwang with Richard Rodgers & Oscar Hammerstein II. Theatre Communications Group. (paper) $12.95

Force of Nature. Steven Dietz. Dramatists Play Service. (acting ed.) $5.95

The Full Monty. Terrence McNally and David Yazbek. Applause. (paper) $14.95

Glimmer, Glimmer and Shine. Warren Leight. Grove. (paper) $13

The Glory of Living. Rebecca Gilman. Dramatic Publishing. (acting ed.) $5.95

The Goat, or Who Is Sylvia? Edward Albee. Overlook Press. (paper) $22.95

Good Thing. Jessica Goldberg. Dramatists Play Service. (acting ed.) $5.95

Gum and The Mother of Modern Censorship. Karen Hartman. Theatre Communications Group. (paper) $12.95

Hairspray: The Roots. Mark O'Donnell, Thomas Meehan, Marc Shaiman and Scott Wittman. Faber and Faber. (cloth) $35

Hairspray: The Complete Book & Lyrics. Mark O'Donnell, Thomas Meehan and Marc Shaiman. Applause. $14.95

Hand in Hand. Simon Block. Nick Hern Books. (paper) $16.95

The House of Blue Leaves and Chaucer in Rome. John Guare. Penguin/Overlook Press. (paper) $16.95

Imaginary Friends. Nora Ephron. Random House. (paper) $12

Judgment at Nuremberg. Abby Mann. New Directions. (paper) $14

Major Barbara. George Bernard Shaw. Dover Thrift Edition. (paper) $2

The Man Who. Peter Brook and Marie-Helene Estienne. Methuen. (paper) 13.95

The Mercy Seat. Neil LaBute. Faber and Faber. (paper) $13

The Miracle Worker. William Gibson. Simon and Schuster Adult Publishing Group. (paper) $5.99

No Niggers, No Jews, No Dogs. John Henry Redwood. Dramatists Play Service. (acting ed.) $5.95

A Number. Caryl Churchill. Theatre Communications Group. (paper) $11.95

The Play About the Baby. Edward Albee. Dramatists Play Service. (acting ed.) $5.95

Port Authority. Conor McPherson. Theatre Communications Group. (paper) $11.95

Prelude to a Kiss and Other Plays. Craig Lucas. Theatre Communications Group. (paper) $16.95

The Prince of Homburg. Heinrich von Kleist. Oberon. (paper) $16.95

QED. Peter Parnell. Applause. (paper) $8.95

Revelers. Beth Henley. Dramatists Play Service. (paper) $5.95

Salvage: The Coast of Utopia, Part III. Tom Stoppard. (paper) $16

Serious Money. Caryl Churchill. Methuen Student Edition. (paper) $12.95

The Shape of the River. Horton Foote. Applause. (paper) $16.95

Shel's Shorts. Shel Silverstein. Dramatists Play Service. (acting ed.) $5.95

Shipwreck: The Coast of Utopia, Part II. Tom Stoppard. Faber and Faber. (paper) $16

[sic]. Melissa James Gibson. Faber and Faber. (paper) $15

The Skin of Our Teeth. Thornton Wilder. HarperCollins. (paper) $10.95

Something in the Air. Richard Dresser. Dramatic Publishing. (acting ed.) $5.95

The Theory of Everything. Prince Gomolvilas. Dramatic Publishing. (acting ed.) $5.95

Timberlake Wertenbaker: Plays 2. Timberlake Wertenbaker. Faber and Faber. (paper) $15

Urinetown the Musical. Greg Kotis and Mark Hollmann. Faber and Faber. (paper) $14

Vincent in Brixton. Nicholas Wright. Theatre Communications Group/Nick Hern. (paper) $16.95

Voyage: The Coast of Utopia, Part I. Tom Stoppard. Faber and Faber. (paper) $18

Walker and The Ghost Dance. Derek Walcott. Farrar Straus Giroux. (paper) $17

Wonder of the World. David Lindsay-Abaire. Overlook Press. (paper) $14.95

Yellowman. Dael Orlandersmith. Random House. (paper) $10

ADAPTATIONS

Enrico IV. Luigi Pirandello. Adapt. Robert Brustein. Ivan R. Dee. (paper) $7.95

God of Vengeance. Sholom Asch. Adapt. Donald Margulies. Dramatists Play Service. (acting ed.) $5.95

Midnight's Children. Salman Rushdie. Adapt. Mr. Rushdie with Simon Reade and Tim Supple. Random House. (paper) $12.95

The Underpants. Carl Sternheim. Adapt. Steve Martin. Hyperion. (paper) $10.95

TRANSLATIONS

Anton Chekhov Plays. Anton Chekhov. Trans. Peter Carson. Penguin. (paper) $9

Ghosts. Henrik Gibson. Trans. Stephen Mulrine. Nick Hern. (paper) $9.95

Heracles and Other Plays. Euripides. Trans. John Davie. Penguin. (paper) $11

Life Is a Dream. Pedro Calderon de la Barca. Ed. and trans. Stanley Appelbaum. Dover. (paper) $9.95

Lysistrata and Other Plays. Aristophanes. Trans. Alan Sommerstein. Penguin USA. (paper) $11

Medea and Other Plays. Euripides. Trans. John Davie. Penguin USA. (paper) $11

Nightsongs. Jon Fosse. Trans. Gregory Morton. Oberon Books. (paper) $16.95

Pixerecourt: Four Melodramas. Rene-Charles Guilbert de Pixerecourt. Ed. and tran. Daniel Gerould and Marvin Carlson. Center for Advanced Study in Theatre Arts. (paper) $20

Push Up. Roland Schimmelpfennig. Trans. Maja Zade. Nick Hern. (paper) $16.95

The Seagull. Anton Chekhov. Trans. Michael Frayn. Methuen. (paper) $12.95

Six Greek Tragedies. Aeschylus, Euripides, Sophocles. Trans. Marianne McDonald, Kenneth McLeish and Frederic Raphael. Methuen. (paper) $19.95

Tales From the Vienna Woods and Other Plays. Odon Von Horvath. Trans. Michael Mitchell. Ariadne Press. (paper) $25.50

The Tempest. Shakespeare. Adapt. Aime Cesaire. Trans. Richard Miller. Theatre Communications Group. (paper) $11.95

The Theatre of Sabina Berman: The Agony of Ecstasy and Other Plays. Sabina Berman. Trans. Adam Versenyi. Southern Illinois U.P. (paper) $21

The Trojan Women and Hippolytus. Euripides. Trans. Edward P. Coleridge. Dover Thrift Edition. (paper) $1.50

Ubu Roi. Alfred Jarry. Trans. Beverley Keith and G. Legman. Dover Thrift Editions. (paper) $2

Woyzeck. Georg Buchner. Adapt. and trans. Nicholas Rudall. Ivan R. Dee. (paper) $7.95

COLLECTIONS

American Gypsy: Six Native American Plays. Ed. Diane Glancy and Gerald Vizenor. U. Oklahoma P. (cloth) $34.95

Collected Novels and Plays of James Merrill. James Merrill. Ed. J.D. McClatchy and Stephen Yenser. Random House. (cloth) $40

My Friend Hitler and Other Plays. Yukio Mishima. Tran. Hiroaki Sato. Columbia U.P. (paper) $18.95

Plays by Jonathan Reynolds. Jonathan Reynolds. Broadway Play Publishing. (paper $14.95

Plays From the Vineyard Theatre. Douglas Aibel. Broadway Play Publishing. (paper) $17.95

Positive Negative: Women of Color and HIV/AIDS. Ed. Imani Harrington and Chyrell D. Bellamy. Aunt Lute Books. (paper) $18.95

Unwrap Your Candy. Doug Wright. Dramatists Play Service. (acting ed) $5.95

ANTHOLOGIES

The Gertrude Stein Reader. Gertrude Stein. Ed. Richard Kostelanetz. Cooper Square. (paper) 19.95

Heaven and Hell (On Earth): A Divine Comedy. Ed. Jon Jory. Dramatists Play Service. (paper) $5.95

Leading Women: Plays for Actresses, Vol. 1. Ed. Eric Lane and Nina Shengold. Random House. (paper) $17

The Methuen Book of Modern Drama: Plays of the '80s and '90s. Ed. Graham Whybrow. Methuen. (paper) $19.95

New Plays From the Abbey Theatre. Ed. Judy Friel and Sanford Sternlicht. Syracuse U.P. (paper) $19.95

Plays and Playwrights 2003. Ed. Martin Denton. New York Theatre Experience. (paper) $15

The Routledge Anthology of Renaissance Drama. Ed. Simon Barker and Hilary Hinds. (paper) $27.95

Six Greek Comedies: Aristophanes, Euripides, Menander. Ed. J. Michael Walton. Trans. Kenneth McLeish. Methuen. (paper) 19.95

Worthy But Neglected. Ed. Jonathan Bank. Granville Press. Ed. Jonathan Bank. (paper) $15.95

IN MEMORIAM
MAY 2002–MAY 2003
○ ○ ○ ○ ○

PERFORMERS

Andrews, Mary Todd (86) – January 17, 2003

Anholt, Tony (61) – July 26, 2002

Baer, Parley (88) – November 22, 2002

Barrie, Elaine (87) – March 3, 2003

Barry, Betty (79) – January 31, 2003

Bracken, Eddie (87) – November 13, 2002

Bracken, Constance Nickerson (88) – August 19, 2002

Brooks, Hadda (86) – November 21, 2002

Buchholz, Horst (69) March 3, 2003

Burr, Anne (84) – February 1, 2003

Burr, Fritzi (78) – January 17, 2003

Calvert, Phyllis (87) – October 8, 2002

Carter, Nell (54) – January 23, 2003

Cartlidge, Katrin (41) – September 7, 2002

Cash, June Carter (73) – May 15, 2003

Chastain, Don (66) – August 9, 2002

Clark, Norma Lee (75) – November 8, 2002

Clooney, Rosemary (74) – June 29, 2002

Coburn, James (74) – November 18, 2002

Conklin, Peggy (96) – March 19, 2003

Corey, Jeff (88) – August 16, 2002

Crenna, Richard (76) – January 17, 2003

Curtis, Keene (79) – October 13, 2002

Davidson Adamson, Gretchen (77) – August 2, 2002

Dawn, Dolly (86) – December 11, 2002

Denham, Maurice (92) – July 24, 2002

Dobkin, Larry (83) – October 28, 2002

Draper, Rusty (80) – March 28, 2003

Eisley, Anthony (78) – January 29, 2003

Ellis, Mary (105) – January 30, 2003

Evans, Joshua Ryan (20) – August 6, 2002

Evans, Wyn Ritchie (102) – April 11, 2003

Fimple, Dennis (61) – August 23, 2002

Fong, Kam (84) – October 18, 2002

Foy, Irving (94) – April 20, 2003

Friday, Betsy (44) – July 16, 2002

Ganzel, Mark (51) – October 24, 2002

Gardner, Kenny (89) – July 26, 2002

Gayle, Jackie (76) – November 23, 2002

Gibb, Maurice (53) – January 12, 2003

Glazer, Tom (88) – February 21, 2003

Gordon, Rosco (74) – July 11, 2002

Gorman, Cliff (65) – (September 5, 2002)

Graves, Teresa (53) – October 10, 2002

Gray, Delores (78) – June 26, 2002

Gregory, James (90) – September 16, 2002

Guy, Billy (66) – November 12, 2002

Hall, George (85) – October 21, 2002

Harris, Jonathan (87) – October 27, 2002

Harris, Richard (72) – October 25, 2002

Hasso, Signe (91) – June 7, 2002

Hiller, Wendy (90) – May 14, 2003

Hird, Thora (91) – March 15, 2003

Hodges, Joy (88) –January 19, 2003

Hood, Morag (59) – October 5, 2002

Hoppe, Marianne (93) – October 23, 2003

Hoskins, Eric (38) – October 3, 2002

Hull, Bryan (65) – May 11, 2003

Hunter, Kim (79) – September 11, 2002

Jeter, Michael (50) – April 7, 2003

Johnson, Susan (75) – February 24, 2003

Jurado, Katy (78) – July 5, 2002

Kempson, Rachel (92) – May 24, 2003

Kobart, Ruth (78) – December 13, 2002

Kral, Roy (80) – August 2, 2002

Langton, Basil (91) – May 29, 2003

Lee, James (79) – July 16, 2002

Lessing, Florence (86) – September 5, 2002

Lester, Buddy (86) – October 4, 2002

Lieb, Robert P. (88) – September 28, 2002

Luisi, James (73) – June 7, 2002

Manley, Beatrice (81) – September 13, 2002

Marrié, William (33) – November 16, 2002

Martinez, Tony (82) – September 9, 2002

McCarthy, Lin (84) – November 23, 2002

McKern, Leo (82) – July 23, 2002

Mitchell, Billy (71) – November 5, 2002

Montgomery, Marion (67) – July 22, 2002

Montañez, Polo (47) – November 26, 2002

North, Sherle (85) – August 14, 2002

Norton, Cliff (84) – January 25, 2003

O'Connor, Vera Dunn (89) – July 12, 2002

Orlandi, Felice (78) – May 21, 2003
Page, LaWanda (81) – September 14, 2002
Patrick, Dennis (84) – October 13, 2002
Paycheck, Johnny (64) – February 19, 2003
Phillips, Peg (84) – November 7, 2002
Ralston, Vera Hruba (79) – February 9, 2003
Raven, Jackie (51) – August 19, 2002
Rexite, Seymour (91) – October 14, 2002
Rockwell, Robert (82) – January 25, 2003
Ross, Bertram (82) – April 20, 2003
Ross, Ted (68) – September 3, 2002
Scott, Martha (90) – May 28, 2003
Silver, Johnny (84) – February 1, 2003
Simone, Nina (70) – April 21, 2003
Sims, Howard "Sandman" (86) – May 20, 2003
Slavenska, Mia (86) – October 5, 2002
Stack, Robert (84) – May 14, 2003
Steiger, Rod (77) – July 9, 2002
Stewart, Jeanne (94) – February 12, 2003
Strummer, Joe (50) – December 22, 2002
Styler, Adele (78) August 3, 2002
Sullivan, Jean (79) February 27, 2003
Thigpen, Lynne (54) – March 12, 2003
Vallone, Raf (86) – October 31, 2002
Warfield, William (82) – August 27, 2002
Williams, David Wayne (30) – August 14, 2002
Wilson, Lionel (79) – April 30, 2003
Zorina, Vera (86) – April 9, 2003

PRODUCERS, DIRECTORS,
CHOREOGRAPHERS

Atkins, Cholly (89) – April 17, 2003
Carroll, Vinnette (80) – November 5, 2002
Clark, Russell (53) – November 12, 2002
Frankenheimer, John (72) – July 6, 2002
Hill, George Roy (81) – December 27, 2002
Hilton, Wendy (71) – September 21, 2002
Keach, Stacy Sr. (88) – February 13, 2003
Littlewood, Joan (87) – September 20, 2002
Mallow, Tom (71) – June 6, 2002
Noto, Lore (79) – July 8, 2002
Oesterman, Phillip (64) – July 30, 2002
Osterman, Lester (88) –January 28, 2003
Paltrow, Bruce (58) – October 3, 2002
Reinhart, Stephanie (58) – September 23, 2002
Reisz, Karel (76) – November 25, 2002

Rosen, Amy Sue (47) – February 19, 2003
Rosenfield, Lois (78) – May 25, 2003
Schumer, Yvette (86) – September 21, 2002
Selch, Frederick (72) – August 22, 2002
Whitehead, Robert (86) – June 15, 2002

COMPOSERS, LYRICISTS,
SONGWRITERS

Barrie, George (90) – November 16, 2002
Brandt, Alan (78) – September 6, 2002
Bryant, Felice (77) – April 22, 2003
Bucci, Mark (78) – August 22, 2002
Conniff, Ray (85) – October 12, 2002
Dennis, Matt (88) – June 21, 2002
Fisher, Doris (87) – January 22, 2003
Gesner, Clark (64) – July 23, 2002
Gibb, Maurice (53) – January 12, 2003
Green, Adolph (87) – October 24, 2002
Haimsohn, George (77) – January 17, 2003
Kaye, Buddy (84) – November 21, 2002
Lippman, Sidney (89) – March 11, 2003
Magee, Rusty (47) – February 16, 2003
Marnay, Eddy (82) – January 3, 2003
Matz, Peter (73) – August 9, 2002
Naylor, Wesley (44) – August 25, 2002
Newbury, Mickey (62) – September 29, 2002
Regney, Noel (80) – November 24, 2002
Scharf, Walter (92) – February 24, 2003
Worth, Bobby (89) – July 17, 2002
Wyle, George (87) – May 4, 2003

PLAYWRIGHTS

Behan, Brian (75) – November 2, 2002
de Hartog, Jan (88) – September 22, 2002
Ellstein, Sylvia (94) – January 18, 2003
Gelber, Jack (71) – May 9, 2003
Kerr, Jean (80) – January 5, 2003
Knott, Frederick (86) – December 17, 2002
Panama, Norman (88) – January 13, 2003
Phipps, Thomas W. (89) – February 20, 2003
Robinson, Matt (65) – August 5, 2002
Sandford, Jeremy (72) – May 12, 2003
Tinniswood, Peter (66) – January 9, 2003
Yordan, Philip (88) – March 24, 2003
Zindel, Paul (66) – March 27, 2003

DESIGNERS

Bel Geddes, Edith Lutyens (95) – August 16, 2002

Berman, Monty (90) – July 15, 2002

Bjornson, Maria (53) – December 13, 2002

Bourne, Mel (79) January 14, 2002

Herbert, Jocelyn (86) – May 6, 2003

Moiseiwitsch, Tanya (88) – February 18, 2003

Randolph, Robert (76) – March 2, 2003

Slaiman, Marjorie (77) – September 13, 2003

Tagg, Alan (74) – November 4, 2002

MUSICIANS

Bell, Derek (66) – October 15, 2002

Berg, Bob (51) – December 5, 2002

Berry, Bill (72) – November 13, 2002

Braff, Ruby (75) – February 9, 2003

Brown, Ray (75) – July 2, 2002

Browning, John (69) – January 26, 2003

Crosby, Robbin (42) – June 6, 2002

Davenny, Ward (86) – December 10, 2002

Dejan, Duke (93) – July 5, 2002

Donegan, Lonnie (71) – November 3, 2002

Druian, Rafael (80) – September 6, 2002

Eager, Allen (76) – April 13, 2003

Edwards, Teddy (78) – April 20, 2003

Fuller, Walter (93) – April 20, 2003

Greitzer, Shirley (76) – May 29, 2002

Griffith, Johnny (66) – November 10, 2002

Hampton, Lionel (94) – August 30, 2002

Hanna, Roland (70) – November 13, 2002

Hansen, Mary (36) – December 9, 2002

Hellman, Daphne Bayne (86) – August 4, 2002

Houser, Michael (40) – August 10, 2002

Kates, Stephen (59) – January 18, 2003

Kelly, Daniel (71) – August 5, 2002

King, Earl (69) – April 17, 2003

Kral, Roy (80) – August 2, 2002

Marmarosa, Dodo (76) – September 17, 2002

Maxwell, Jimmy (85) – July 20, 2002

McReynolds, Jim (75) – December 31, 2002

Nelsova, Zara (84) – October 10, 2002

Parham, Truck (91) – June 5, 2003

Perlemuter, Vlado (98) – September 4, 2002

Redding, Noel (57) – May 12, 2003

Santamaria, Mongo (85) – February 1, 2003

Shaw, Arvell (79) – December 5, 2002

Van Lake, Turk (84) – September 1, 2002

Williams. Paul (87) – September 14, 2002

Yanovsky, Zal (57) – December 13, 2002

OTHERS OF NOTE

Arledge, Roone (71) – December 5, 2002
Pioneering television executive

Borod, Bob (70) – August 27, 2002
Broadway stage manager

Colton, Edward E. (97) – February 27, 2003
Theatrical lawyer

Eaker, Ira (80) – June 26, 2002
Editor and co founder of *Back Stage*

Fjelde, Rolf (76) – September 10, 2002
Translator of Henrik Ibsen

Glover, William (91) – December 20, 2002
Retired theater critic for the Associated Press

Hewitt, Frankie (71) – February 28, 2003
Led rejuvenation of Ford's Theater

Hirschfeld, Al (99) – January 20, 2003
Theater caricaturist and *Best Plays* contributor for 50 years

Hudson, Fred (74) – February 13, 2003
Artistic director of the Frederick Douglass Creative Arts Center

Jaffe, Eddie (89) – February 25, 2003
Noted Broadway press agent

Liff, Vincent (52) – February 25, 2003
Noted Broadway casting agent

Quo, Beulah (79) – October 23, 2002
Film actress and co-founder of East West Players

Rogers, Fred (74) – February 27, 2003
Beloved host of *Mister Rogers' Neighborhood* on public television

Scharf, Walter (92) – February 24, 2003
Noted composer of popular music for film and television

Watson, Graham (89) – November 14, 2002
Literary agent for Gore Vidal, John Steinbeck and others

Willett, John (85) – August 20, 2002
Translator of Bertolt Brecht

Williams, Tony (65) – October 15, 2002
Literary agent

THE BEST PLAYS AND MAJOR PRIZEWINNERS 1894–2003

○ ○ ○ ○ ○

LISTED IN ALPHABETICAL order below are all works selected as Best Plays in previous volumes of the *Best Plays* series, except for the seasons of 1996–97 through 1999–2000. During those excluded seasons, *Best Plays* honored only major prizewinners and those who received special *Best Plays* citations. Opposite each title is given the volume in which the play is honored, its opening date and its total number of performances. Two separate opening-date and performance-number entries signify two separate engagements when the original production transferred. Plays marked with an asterisk (*) were still playing June 1, 2003 and their number of performances was figured through May 31, 2003. Adaptors and translators are indicated by (ad) and (tr), the symbols (b), (m) and (l) stand for the author of the book, music and lyrics in the case of musicals and (c) signifies the credit for the show's conception, (i) for its inspiration. Entries identified as 94–99 and 99–09 are late-19th and early-20th century plays from one of the retrospective volumes. 94–95, 95–96, 96–97, 97–98, 98–99 and 99–00 are late-20th century plays.

PLAY	VOLUME	OPENED	PERFS
ABE LINCOLN IN ILLINOIS—Robert E. Sherwood	38–39	Oct. 15, 1938	472
ABRAHAM LINCOLN—John Drinkwater	19–20	Dec. 15, 1919	193
ACCENT ON YOUTH—Samson Raphaelson	34–35	Dec. 25, 1934	229
ADAM AND EVA—Guy Bolton, George Middleton	19–20	Sept. 13, 1919	312
ADAPTATION—Elaine May; and			
NEXT—Terrence McNally	68–69	Feb. 10, 1969	707
AFFAIRS OF STATE—Louis Verneuil	50–51	Sept. 25, 1950	610
AFTER THE FALL—Arthur Miller	63–64	Jan. 23, 1964	208
AFTER THE RAIN—John Bowen	67–68	Oct. 9, 1967	64
AFTER-PLAY—Anne Meara	94–95	Jan. 31, 1995	400
AGNES OF GOD—John Pielmeier	81–82	Mar. 30, 1982	599
AH, WILDERNESS!—Eugene O'Neill	33–34	Oct. 2, 1933	289
AIN'T SUPPOSED TO DIE A NATURAL DEATH—(b, m, l)			
Melvin Van Peebles	71–72	Oct. 20, 1971	325
ALIEN CORN—Sidney Howard	32–33	Feb. 20, 1933	98
Alison's House—Susan Glaspell	30–31	Dec. 1, 1930	41
ALL MY SONS—Arthur Miller	46–47	Jan. 29, 1947	328
ALL IN THE TIMING—David Ives	93–94	Feb. 17, 1994	526
ALL OVER TOWN—Murray Schisgal	74–75	Dec. 29, 1974	233
ALL THE WAY HOME—Tad Mosel, based on			
James Agee's novel *A Death in the Family*	60–61	Nov. 30, 1960	333
ALLEGRO—(b, l) Oscar Hammerstein II,			
(m) Richard Rodgers	47–48	Oct. 10, 1947	315
AMADEUS—Peter Shaffer	80–81	Dec. 17, 1980	1,181

AMBUSH—Arthur Richman .... 21–22 ..... Oct. 10, 1921 98
AMERICA HURRAH—Jean-Claude van Itallie .... 66–67 ..... Nov. 6, 1966 634
AMERICAN BUFFALO—David Mamet .... 76–77 ..... Feb. 16, 1977 135
AMERICAN ENTERPRISE—Jeffrey Sweet (special citation) .... 93–94 ..... Apr. 13, 1994 15
AMERICAN PLAN, THE—Richard Greenberg .... 90–91 ..... Dec. 16, 1990 37
AMERICAN WAY, THE—George S. Kaufman, Moss Hart .... 38–39 ..... Jan. 21, 1939 164
AMPHITRYON 38—Jean Giraudoux, (ad) S.N. Behrman .... 37–38 ..... Nov. 1, 1937 153
AND A NIGHTINGALE SANG—C.P. Taylor .... 83–84 ..... Nov. 27, 1983 177
ANDERSONVILLE TRIAL, THE—Saul Levitt .... 59–60 ..... Dec. 29, 1959 179
ANDORRA—Max Frisch, (ad) George Tabori .... 62–63 ..... Feb. 9, 1963 9
ANGEL STREET—Patrick Hamilton .... 41–42 ..... Dec. 5, 1941 1,295
ANGELS FALL—Lanford Wilson .... 82–83 ..... Oct. 17, 1982 65
                                                                    82–83 ..... Jan. 22, 1983 64
ANGELS IN AMERICA, PART I: MILLENNIUM APPROACHES—
    Tony Kushner .... 92–93 ..... May 4, 1993 367
ANGELS IN AMERICA, PART II: PERESTROIKA—
    Tony Kushner .... 93–94 ..... Nov. 23, 1994 216
ANIMAL KINGDOM, THE—Philip Barry .... 31–32 ..... Jan. 12, 1932 183
ANNA CHRISTIE—Eugene O'Neill .... 21–22 ..... Nov. 2, 1921 177
ANNA LUCASTA—Philip Yordan .... 44–45 ..... Aug. 30, 1944 957
ANNE OF THE THOUSAND DAYS—Maxwell Anderson .... 48–49 ..... Dec. 8, 1948 286
ANNIE—(b) Thomas Meehan, (m) Charles Strouse,
    (l) Martin Charnin, based on Harold Gray's
    comic strip Little Orphan Annie .... 76–77 ..... Apr. 21, 1977 2,377
ANOTHER LANGUAGE—Rose Franken .... 31–32 ..... Apr. 25, 1932 344
ANOTHER PART OF THE FOREST—Lillian Hellman .... 46–47 ..... Nov. 20, 1946 182
ANTIGONE—Jean Anouilh, (ad) Lewis Galantiere .... 45–46 ..... Feb. 18, 1946 64
APPLAUSE—(b) Betty Comden and Adolph Green,
    (m) Charles Strouse, (l) Lee Adams,
    based on the film All About Eve
    and the original story by Mary Orr .... 69–70 ..... Mar. 30, 1970 896
APPLE TREE, THE—(b, l) Sheldon Harnick, (b, m) Jerry
    Bock, (add'l b) Jerome Coopersmith,
    based on stories by Mark Twain,
    Frank R. Stockton and Jules Feiffer .... 66–67 ..... Oct. 18, 1966 463
ARCADIA—Tom Stoppard .... 94–95 ..... Mar. 30, 1995 173
ARISTOCRATS—Brian Friel .... 88–89 ..... Apr. 25, 1989 186
ARSENIC AND OLD LACE—Joseph Kesselring .... 40–41 ..... Jan. 10, 1941 1,444
ART—Yasmina Reza .... 97–98 ..... Mar. 1, 1998 600
AS HUSBANDS GO—Rachel Crothers .... 30–31 ..... Mar. 5, 1931 148
AS IS—WILLIAM M. HOFFMAN .... 84–85 ..... MAR. 10, 1985 49
                                                                    84–85 ..... May 1, 1985 285
ASHES—David Rudkin .... 76–77 ..... Jan. 25, 1977 167
AUNT DAN AND LEMON—Wallace Shawn .... 85–86 ..... Oct. 1, 1985 191
AUTUMN GARDEN, THE—Lillian Hellman .... 50–51 ..... Mar. 7, 1951 101
AWAKE AND SING—Clifford Odets .... 34–35 ..... Feb. 19, 1935 209

BAD MAN, THE—Porter Emerson Browne .... 20–21 ..... Aug. 30, 1920 350
BAD HABITS—Terrence McNally .... 73–74 ..... Feb. 4, 1974 273
BAD SEED—Maxwell Anderson,
    based on William March's novel .... 54–55 ..... Dec. 8, 1954 332
BARBARA FRIETCHIE—Clyde Fitch .... 99–09 ..... Oct. 23, 1899 83
BAREFOOT IN ATHENS—Maxwell Anderson .... 51–52 ..... Oct. 31, 1951 30
BAREFOOT IN THE PARK—Neil Simon .... 63–64 ..... Oct. 23, 1963 1,530
BARRETTS OF WIMPOLE STREET, THE—Rudolf Besier .... 30–31 ..... Feb. 9, 1931 370
BEAUTY QUEEN OF LEENANE, THE—Martin McDonagh .... 97–98 ..... Feb. 26, 1998 46
    97–98 ..... Apr. 23, 1998 372
BECKET—Jean Anouilh, (tr) Lucienne Hill .... 60–61 ..... Oct. 5, 1960 193
BEDROOM FARCE—Alan Ayckbourn .... 78–79 ..... Mar. 29, 1979 278
BEGGAR ON HORSEBACK—George S. Kaufman,
    Marc Connelly .... 23–24 .... Feb. 12, 1924 224
BEHOLD THE BRIDEGROOM—George Kelly .... 27–28 ..... Dec. 26, 1927 88
BELL, BOOK AND CANDLE—John van Druten .... 50–51 ..... Nov. 14, 1950 233
BELL FOR ADANO, A—Paul Osborn,
    based on John Hersey's novel .... 44–45 ..... Dec. 6, 1944 304
BENEFACTORS—Michael Frayn .... 85–86 ..... Dec. 22, 1985 217
BENT—Martin Sherman .... 79–80 ..... Dec. 2, 1979 240
BERKELEY SQUARE—John L. Balderston .... 29–30 ..... Nov. 4, 1929 229
BERNARDINE—Mary Chase .... 52–53 ..... Oct. 16, 1952 157
BEST LITTLE WHOREHOUSE IN TEXAS, THE—(b) Larry L.
    King, Peter Masterson, (m, l) Carol Hall .... 77–78 ..... Apr. 17, 1978 64
    78–79 ..... June 19, 1978 1,639
BEST MAN, THE—Gore Vidal .... 59–60 ..... Mar. 31, 1960 520
BETRAYAL—Harold Pinter .... 79–80 ..... Jan. 5, 1980 170
BEYOND THE HORIZON—Eugene O'Neill .... 19–20 ..... Feb. 2, 1920 160
BIG FISH, LITTLE FISH—Hugh Wheeler .... 60–61 ..... Mar. 15, 1961 101
BIG LOVE—Charles L. Mee .... 01–02 ..... Nov. 30, 2001 10
BILL OF DIVORCEMENT, A—Clemence Dane .... 21–22 ..... Oct. 10, 1921 173
BILLY BUDD—Louis O. Coxe, Robert Chapman,
    based on Herman Melville's novel .... 50–51 ..... Feb. 10, 1951 105
BILOXI BLUES—Neil Simon .... 84–85 ..... Mar. 28, 1985 524
BIOGRAPHY—S.N. Behrman .... 32–33 ..... Dec. 12, 1932 267
BLACK COMEDY—Peter Shaffer .... 66–67 ..... Feb. 12, 1967 337
BLITHE SPIRIT—Noël Coward .... 41–42 ..... Nov. 5, 1941 657
BOESMAN AND LENA—Athol Fugard .... 70–71 ..... June 22, 1970 205
BOOK OF DAYS—Lanford Wilson .... 02–03 ..... Nov. 3, 2002 36
BORN IN THE R.S.A.—Barney Simon,
    in collaboration with the cast .... 86–87 ..... Oct. 1, 1986 8
BORN YESTERDAY—Garson Kanin .... 45–46 ..... Feb. 4, 1946 1,642
BOTH YOUR HOUSES—Maxwell Anderson .... 32–33 ..... Mar. 6, 1933 72
BOY GETS GIRL—Rebecca Gilman .... 00–01 ..... Feb. 20, 2001 55
BOY MEETS GIRL—Bella and Samuel Spewack .... 35–36 ..... Nov. 27, 1935 669
BOY FRIEND, THE—(b, m, l) Sandy Wilson .... 54–55 ..... Sept. 30, 1954 485
BOYS IN THE BAND, THE—Mart Crowley .... 67–68 ..... Apr. 15, 1968 1,000

BREATH, BOOM—Kia Corthron .... 01–02 ..... JUNE 10, 2001 17
BRIDE OF THE LAMB, THE—William Hurlbut .... 25–26 ..... Mar. 30, 1926 109
BRIEF MOMENT—S.N. Behrman .... 31–32 ..... Nov. 9, 1931 129
BRIGADOON—(b, l) Alan Jay Lerner,
   (m) Frederick Loewe .... 46–47 ..... Mar. 13, 1947 581
BROADWAY—Philip Dunning, George Abbott .... 26–27 ..... Sept. 16, 1926 603
BROADWAY BOUND—Neil Simon .... 86–87 ..... Dec. 4, 1986 756
BURLESQUE—George Manker Watters, Arthur Hopkins .... 27–28 ..... Sept. 1, 1927 372
BUS STOP—William Inge .... 54–55 ..... Mar. 2, 1955 478
BUTLEY—Simon Gray .... 72–73 ..... Oct. 31, 1972 135
BUTTER AND EGG MAN, THE—George S. Kaufman .... 25–26 ..... Sept. 23, 1925 243
BUTTERFLIES ARE FREE—Leonard Gershe .... 69–70 ..... Oct. 21, 1969 1,128

CABARET—(b) Joe Masteroff, (m) John Kander, (l) Fred
   Ebb, based on John van Druten's play *I Am a
   Camera* and stories by Christopher Isherwood .... 66–67 ..... Nov. 20, 1966 1,165
CACTUS FLOWER—Abe Burrows, based on a play
   by Pierre Barillet and Jean-Pierre Gredy .... 65–66 ..... Dec. 8, 1965 1,234
CAINE MUTINY COURT-MARTIAL, THE—Herman Wouk,
   based on his novel .... 53–54 ..... Jan. 20, 1954 415
CALIFORNIA SUITE—Neil Simon .... 76–77 ..... June 10, 1976 445
CALIGULA—Albert Camus, (ad) Justin O'Brien .... 59–60 ..... Feb. 16, 1960 38
CALL IT A DAY—Dodie Smith .... 35–36 ..... Jan. 28, 1936 194
CAMPING WITH HENRY & TOM—Mark St. Germain .... 94–95 ..... Feb. 20, 1995 88
CANDIDE—(b) Lillian Hellman, based on Voltaire's satire,
   (l) Richard Wilbur, John Latouche, Dorothy Parker,
   (m) Leonard Bernstein .... 56–57 ..... Dec. 1, 1956 73
CANDLE IN THE WIND—Maxwell Anderson .... 41–42 ..... Oct. 22, 1941 95
CARETAKER, THE—Harold Pinter .... 61–62 ..... Oct. 4, 1961 165
CASE OF REBELLIOUS SUSAN, THE—Henry Arthur Jones .... 94–99 ..... Dec. 20, 1894 80
CAT ON A HOT TIN ROOF—Tennessee Williams .... 54–55 ..... Mar. 24, 1955 694
CATS—(m) Andrew Lloyd Webber, based on T.S. Eliot's
   Old Possum's Book of Practical Cats, (add'l l)
   Trevor Nunn, Richard Stilgoe .... 82–83 ..... Oct. 7, 1982 7,485
CELEBRATION—(b, l) Tom Jones, (m) Harvey Schmidt .... 68–69 ..... Jan. 22, 1969 109
CHALK GARDEN, THE—Enid Bagnold .... 55–56 ..... Oct. 26, 1955 182
CHANGELINGS, THE—Lee Wilson Dodd .... 23–24 ..... Sept. 17, 1923 128
CHANGING ROOM, THE—David Storey .... 72–73 ..... Mar. 6, 1973 192
CHAPTER TWO—Neil Simon .... 77–78 ..... Dec. 4, 1977 857
CHICAGO—Maurine Dallas Watkins .... 26–27 ..... Dec. 30, 1926 172
CHICAGO—(b) Fred Ebb, Bob Fosse, (m) John Kander,
   (l) Fred Ebb,based on the play by Maurine Dallas
   Watkins .... 75–76 ..... June 3, 1975 898
CHICKEN FEED—Guy Bolton .... 23–24 ..... Sept. 24, 1923 144
CHILDREN OF A LESSER GOD—Mark Medoff .... 79–80 ..... Mar. 30, 1980 887
CHILDREN'S HOUR, THE—Lillian Hellman .... 34–35 ..... Nov. 20, 1934 691

CHILD'S PLAY—Robert Marasco .... 69–70 ..... Feb. 17, 1970 342
CHIPS WITH EVERYTHING—Arnold Wesker .... 63–64 ..... Oct. 1, 1963 149
CHORUS LINE, A—(c) Michael Bennett, (b) James
   Kirkwood, Nicholas Dante, (m) Marvin Hamlisch,
   (l) Edward Kleban .... 74–75 ..... Apr. 15, 1975 101
                                          75–76 .....July 25, 1975 6,137
CHRISTOPHER BLAKE—Moss Hart .... 46–47 ..... Nov. 30, 1946 114
CIRCLE, THE—W. Somerset Maugham .... 21–22 ..... Sept. 12, 1921 175
CITY OF ANGELS—(b) Larry Gelbart, (m) Cy Coleman,
   (l) David Zippel .... 89–90 ..... Dec. 11, 1989 878
CLARENCE—Booth Tarkington .... 19–20 ..... Sept. 20, 1919 306
CLAUDIA—Rose Franken .... 40–41 ..... Feb. 12, 1941 722
CLEARING IN THE WOODS, A—Arthur Laurents .... 56–57 ..... Jan. 10, 1957 36
CLIMATE OF EDEN, THE—Moss Hart, based on Edgar
   Mittleholzer's novel *Shadows Move Among Them* ...... 52–53 ..... Nov. 13, 1952 20
CLIMBERS, THE—Clyde Fitch .... 99–09 ..... Jan. 21, 1901 163
CLOSER—Patrick Marber .... 98–99 ..... Aug. 22, 1999 172
CLOUD 9—Caryl Churchill .... 80–81 ..... May 18, 1981 971
CLUTTERBUCK—Benn W. Levy .... 49–50 ..... Dec. 3, 1949 218
COCKTAIL HOUR, THE—A.R. Gurney .... 88–89 ..... Oct. 20, 1988 351
COCKTAIL PARTY, THE—T.S. Eliot .... 49–50 ..... Jan. 21, 1950 409
COLD WIND AND THE WARM, THE—S.N. Behrman .... 58–59 ..... Dec. 8, 1958 120
COLLECTION, THE—Harold Pinter .... 62–63 ..... Nov. 26, 1962 578
COME BACK, LITTLE SHEBA—William Inge .... 49–50 ..... Feb. 15, 1950 191
COMEDIANS—Trevor Griffiths... 76–77 ..... Nov. 28, 1976 145
COMMAND DECISION—William Wister Haines .... 47–48 ..... Oct. 1, 1947 408
COMPANY—(b) George Furth, (m, l) Stephen Sondheim .... 69–70 ..... Apr. 26, 1970 705
COMPLAISANT LOVER, THE—Graham Greene .... 61–62 ..... Nov. 1, 1961 101
CONDUCT UNBECOMING—Barry England .... 70–71 ..... Oct. 12, 1970 144
CONFIDENTIAL CLERK, THE—T.S. Eliot .... 53–54 ..... Feb. 11, 1954 117
CONNECTION, THE—Jack Gelber (supplement) .... 60–61 ..... Feb. 22, 1961 722
CONSTANT WIFE, THE—W. Somerset Maugham .... 26–27 ..... Nov. 29, 1926 295
CONTACT—Susan Stroman, John Weidman .... 99–00 ..... Oct. 7, 1999 101
                                          99–00 ..... Mar. 30, 2000 72
CONTRACTOR, THE—David Storey .... 73–74 ..... Oct. 17, 1973 72
CONVERSATIONS WITH MY FATHER—Herb Gardner .... 91–92 ..... Mar. 29, 1992 402
COPENHAGEN—Michael Frayn .... 99–00 ..... Apr. 11, 2000 59
COQUETTE—George Abbott, Ann Preston Bridgers .... 27–28 ..... Nov. 8, 1927 366
CORN IS GREEN, THE—Emlyn Williams .... 40–41 ..... Nov. 26, 1940 477
COUNTRY GIRL, THE—Clifford Odets................................... 50–51 ..... Nov. 10, 1950 235
COUNTY CHAIRMAN, THE—George Ade .... 99–09 ..... Nov. 24, 1903 222
CRADLE SONG, THE—Gregorio and Maria Martinez Sierra,
   (tr) John Garrett Underhill .... 26–27 ..... Jan. 24, 1927 57
CRAIG'S WIFE—George Kelly .... 25–26 ..... Oct. 12, 1925 360
CRAZY FOR YOU—(b) Ken Ludwig, (m) George Gershwin,
   (l) Ira Gershwin, (c) Ken Ludwig, Mike Ockrent,
   (i) Guy Bolton, John McGowan .... 91–92 ..... Feb. 19, 1992 1,622

CREATION OF THE WORLD AND OTHER BUSINESS, THE—
Arthur Miller .... 72–73 ..... Nov. 30, 1972 20
CREEPS—David E. Freeman .... 73–74 ..... Dec. 4, 1973 15
CRIMES OF THE HEART—Beth Henley .... 80–81 ..... Dec. 9, 1980 35
                                                    81–82 ..... Nov. 4, 1981 535
CRIMINAL CODE, THE—Martin Flavin .... 29–30 ..... Oct. 2, 1929 173
CRUCIBLE, THE—Arthur Miller .... 52–53 .... Jan. 22, 1953 197
CRYPTOGRAM, THE—David Mamet .... 94–95 ..... Apr. 13, 1995 62
CURTAINS—Stephen Bill .... 95–96 ..... May 21, 1996 64
CYNARA—H.M. Harwood, R.F. Gore-Browne ..... 31–32 ..... Nov. 2, 1931 210

DA—Hugh Leonard .... 77–78 ..... May 1, 1978 697
DAISY MAYME—George Kelly .... 26–27 ..... Oct. 25, 1926 112
DAMASK CHEEK, THE—John van Druten, Lloyd Morris .... 42–43 ..... Oct 22, 1942 93
DANCE AND THE RAILROAD, THE—David Henry Hwang .... 81–82 ..... July 16, 1981 181
DANCING AT LUGHNASA—Brian Friel .... 91–92 ..... Oct. 24, 1991 421
DANCING MOTHERS—Edgar Selwyn, Edmund Goulding ...... 24–25 ..... Aug. 11, 1924 312
DARK AT THE TOP OF THE STAIRS, THE—William Inge .... 57–58 ..... Dec. 5, 1957 468
DARK IS LIGHT ENOUGH, THE—Christopher Fry .... 54–55 ..... Feb. 23, 1955 69
DARKNESS AT NOON—Sidney Kingsley,
based on Arthur Koestler's novel .... 50–51 ..... Jan. 13, 1951 186
DARLING OF THE GODS, THE—David Belasco,
John Luther Long .... 99–09 ..... Dec. 3, 1902 182
DAUGHTERS OF ATREUS—Robert Turney .... 36–37 ..... Oct. 14, 1936 13
DAY IN THE DEATH OF JOE EGG, A—Peter Nichols .... 67–68 ..... Feb. 1, 1968 154
DAZZLE, THE—RICHARD GREENBERG .... 01–02 ..... MAR. 5, 2002 80
DEAD END—Sidney Kingsley .... 35–36 ..... Oct. 28, 1935 687
DEADLY GAME, THE—James Yaffe,
based on Friedrich Duerrenmatt's novel ...... 59–60 ..... Feb. 2, 1960 39
DEAR RUTH—Norman Krasna .... 44–45 ..... Dec. 13, 1944 683
DEATH OF A SALESMAN—Arthur Miller .... 48–49 ..... Feb. 10, 1949 742
DEATH TAKES A HOLIDAY—Alberto Casella,
(ad) Walter Ferris .... 29–30 ..... Dec. 26, 1929 180
DEATHTRAP—Ira Levin .... 77–78 ..... Feb. 26, 1978 1,793
DEBURAU—Sacha Guitry, (ad) Harley Granville Barker ...... 20–21 ..... Dec. 23, 1920 189
DECISION—Edward Chodorov .... 43–44 ..... Feb. 2, 1944 160
DÉCLASSÉE—Zoë Akins .... 19–20 ..... Oct. 6, 1919 257
DEEP ARE THE ROOTS—Arnaud d'Usseau, James Gow .... 45–46 ..... Sept. 26, 1945 477
DELICATE BALANCE, A—Edward Albee .... 66–67 ..... Sept. 22, 1966 132
DEPUTY, THE—Rolf Hochhuth, (ad) Jerome Rothenberg .... 63–64 ..... Feb. 26, 1964 109
DESIGN FOR LIVING—Noël Coward .... 32–33 ..... Jan. 24, 1933 135
DESIGNATED MOURNER, THE—Wallace Shawn (special
citation) .... 99–00 ..... May 13, 2000 .... 30+
DESIRE UNDER THE ELMS—Eugene O'Neill .... 24–25 ..... Nov. 11, 1924 208
DESPERATE HOURS, THE—Joseph Hayes,
based on his novel .... 54–55 ..... Feb. 10, 1955 212
DESTINY OF ME, THE—Larry Kramer .... 92–93 ..... Oct. 20, 1992 175

DETECTIVE STORY—Sidney Kingsley .... 48–49 ..... Mar. 23, 1949 581
DEVIL PASSES, THE—Benn W. Levy .... 31–32 ..... Jan. 4, 1932 96
DEVIL'S ADVOCATE, THE—Dore Schary,
    based on Morris L. West's novel .... 60–61 ..... Mar. 9, 1961 116
DIAL "M" FOR MURDER—Frederick Knott .... 52–53 ..... Oct. 29, 1952 552
DIARY OF ANNE FRANK, THE—Frances Goodrich, Albert
    Hackett, based on Anne Frank's *The Diary of a*
    Young Girl .... 55–56 ..... Oct. 5, 1955 717
DINING ROOM, THE—A.R. Gurney .... 81–82 ..... Feb. 24, 1982 583
DINNER AT EIGHT—George S. Kaufman, Edna Ferber .... 32–33 ..... Oct. 22, 1932 232
DINNER WITH FRIENDS—Donald Margulies .... 99–00 ..... Nov. 4, 1999 240
DISENCHANTED, THE—Budd Schulberg, Harvey Breit,
    based on Mr. Schulberg's novel .... 58–59 ..... Dec. 3, 1958 189
DISRAELI—Louis N. Parker .... 09–19 ..... Sept. 18, 1911 280
DISTAFF SIDE, THE—John van Druten .... 34–35 ..... Sept. 25, 1934 177
DODSWORTH—Sidney Howard, based on Sinclair Lewis's
    novel .... 33–34 ..... Feb. 24, 1934 315
DOUBLES—David Wiltse .... 84–85 ..... May 8, 1985 277
DOUGHGIRLS, THE—Joseph Fields .... 42–43 ..... Dec. 30, 1942 671
DOVER ROAD, THE—A.A. Milne .... 21–22 ..... Dec. 23, 1921 324
DREAM GIRL—Elmer Rice .... 45–46 ..... Dec. 14, 1945 348
DRESSER, THE—Ronald Harwood .... 81–82 ..... Nov. 9, 1981 200
DRINKING IN AMERICA—Eric Bogosian .... 85–86 ..... Jan. 19, 1986 94
DRIVING MISS DAISY—Alfred Uhry .... 86–87 ..... Apr. 15, 1987 1,195
DUBLIN CAROL—Conor McPherson .... 02–03 ..... Feb. 20, 2003 54
DUEL OF ANGELS—Jean Giraudoux's *Pour Lucrèce*, (ad)
    Christopher Fry .... 59–60 ..... Apr. 19, 1960 51
DULCY—George S. Kaufman, Marc Connelly .... 21–22 ..... Aug. 13, 1921 246
DYBBUK, THE—S. Ansky, (ad) Henry G. Alsberg .... 25–26 ..... Dec. 15, 1925 120
DYLAN—Sidney Michaels .... 63–64 ..... Jan. 18, 1964 153

EASIEST WAY, THE—Eugene Walter .... 09–19 ..... Jan. 19, 1909 157
EASTERN STANDARD—Richard Greenberg .... 88–89 ..... Oct. 27, 1988 46
                                                                      88–89 ..... Mar. 25, 1989 92
EASTWARD IN EDEN—Dorothy Gardner .... 47–48 ..... Nov. 18, 1947 15
EDWARD, MY SON—Robert Morley, Noel Langley .... 48–49 ..... Sept. 30, 1948 260
EFFECT OF GAMMA RAYS ON MAN-IN-THE-MOON
    MARIGOLDS, THE—Paul Zindel .... 69–70 ..... Apr. 7, 1970 819
EGG, THE—Felicien Marceau, (ad) Robert Schlitt .... 61–62 ..... Jan. 8, 1962 8
ELAINE STRITCH AT LIBERTY—Elaine Stritch, John Lahr .... 01–02 ..... Nov. 6, 2001 50
                                                                      01–02 ..... Feb. 21, 2002 69
ELEPHANT MAN, THE—Bernard Pomerance .... 78–79 ..... Jan. 14, 1979 73
                                                                      78–79 ..... Apr. 19, 1979 916
ELIZABETH THE QUEEN—Maxwell Anderson .... 30–31 ..... Nov. 3, 1930 147
EMERALD CITY—David Williamson .... 88–89 ..... Nov. 30, 1988 17
EMPEROR JONES, THE—Eugene O'Neill .... 20–21 ..... Nov. 1, 1920 204

EMPEROR'S CLOTHES, THE—George Tabori .... 52–53 ..... Feb. 9, 1953 16
ENCHANTED, THE—Maurice Valency, based on Jean
    Giraudoux's play *Intermezzo* .... 49–50 ..... Jan. 18, 1950 45
END OF SUMMER—S.N. Behrman .... 35–36 ..... Feb. 17, 1936 153
ENEMY, THE—Channing Pollock .... 25–26 ..... Oct. 20, 1925 203
ENOUGH, FOOTFALLS AND ROCKABY—Samuel Beckett .... 83–84 ..... Feb. 16, 1984 78
ENTER MADAME—Gilda Varesi, Dolly Byrne .... 20–21 ..... Aug. 16, 1920 350
ENTERTAINER, THE—John Osborne .... 57–58 ..... Feb. 12, 1958 97
EPITAPH FOR GEORGE DILLON—John Osborne, Anthony
    Creighton .... 58–59 ..... Nov. 4, 1958 23
EQUUS—Peter Shaffer .... 74–75 ..... Oct. 24, 1974 1,209
ESCAPE—John Galsworthy .... 27–28 ..... Oct. 26, 1927 173
ETHAN FROME—Owen and Donald Davis, based on
    Edith Wharton's novel .... 35–36 ..... Jan. 21, 1936 120
EVE OF ST. MARK, THE—Maxwell Anderson .... 42–43 ..... Oct. 7, 1942 307
EXCURSION—Victor Wolfson .... 36–37 ..... Apr. 9, 1937 116
EXECUTION OF JUSTICE—Emily Mann .... 85–86 ..... Mar. 13, 1986 12
EXTRA MAN, THE—Richard Greenberg .... 91–92 ..... May 19, 1992 39
EXTREMITIES—William Mastrosimone .... 82–83 ..... Dec. 22, 1982 325

FAIR COUNTRY, A—Jon Robin Baitz .... 95–96 ..... Oct. 29, 1995 153
FALL GUY, THE—James Gleason, George Abbott .... 24–25 ..... Mar. 10, 1925 176
FALSETTOLAND—William Finn, James Lapine .... 90–91 ..... June 28, 1990 215
FAMILY BUSINESS—Dick Goldberg .... 77–78 ..... Apr. 12, 1978 438
FAMILY PORTRAIT—Lenore Coffee, William Joyce Cowen .... 38–39 ..... May 8, 1939 111
FAMOUS MRS. FAIR, THE—James Forbes .... 19–20 ..... Dec. 22, 1919 344
FAR COUNTRY, A—Henry Denker .... 60–61 ..... Apr. 4, 1961 271
FARMER TAKES A WIFE, THE—Frank B. Elser, Marc Connelly,
    based on Walter D. Edmonds's novel *Rome Haul* ...... 34–35 ..... Oct. 30, 1934 104
FATAL WEAKNESS, THE—George Kelly .... 46–47 ..... Nov. 19, 1946 119
FENCES—August Wilson .... 86–87 ..... Mar. 26, 1987 526
FIDDLER ON THE ROOF—(b) Joseph Stein, (l) Sheldon
    Harnick, (m) Jerry Bock, based on Sholom
    Aleichem's stories .... 64–65 ..... Sept. 22, 1964 3,242
5TH OF JULY, THE—Lanford Wilson .... 77–78 ..... Apr. 27, 1978 159
FIND YOUR WAY HOME—John Hopkins .... 73–74 ..... Jan. 2, 1974 135
FINISHING TOUCHES—Jean Kerr .... 72–73 ..... Feb. 8, 1973 164
FIORELLO!—(b) Jerome Weidman, George Abbott, (l)
    Sheldon Harnick, (m) Jerry Bock .... 59–60 ..... Nov. 23, 1959 795
FIREBRAND, THE—Edwin Justus Mayer .... 24–25 ..... Oct. 15, 1924 269
FIRES IN THE MIRROR—Anna Deavere Smith .... 91–92 ..... May 12, 1992 109
FIRST LADY—Katherine Dayton, George S. Kaufman .... 35–36 ..... Nov. 26, 1935 246
FIRST MONDAY IN OCTOBER—Jerome Lawrence,
    Robert E. Lee .... 78–79 ..... Oct. 3, 1978 79
FIRST MRS. FRASER, THE—St. John Ervine .... 29–30 ..... Dec. 28, 1929 352
FIRST YEAR, THE—Frank Craven .... 20–21 ..... Oct. 20, 1920 760
FIVE FINGER EXERCISE—Peter Shaffer .... 59–60 ..... Dec. 2, 1959 337

FIVE-STAR FINAL—Louis Weitzenkorn .... 30–31 ..... Dec. 30, 1930 175

FLIGHT TO THE WEST—Elmer Rice .... 40–41 ..... Dec. 30, 1940 136

FLOATING LIGHT BULB, THE—Woody Allen .... 80–81 ..... Apr. 27, 1981 65

FLOWERING PEACH, THE—Clifford Odets .... 54–55 ..... Dec. 28, 1954 135

FOLLIES—(b) James Goldman,
    (m, l) Stephen Sondheim .... 70–71 ..... Apr. 4, 1971 521

FOOL, THE—Channing Pollock .... 22–23 ..... Oct. 23, 1922 373

FOOL FOR LOVE—Sam Shepard .... 83–84 ..... May 26, 1983 1,000

FOOLISH NOTION—Philip Barry .... 44–45 ..... Mar. 3, 1945 104

FOREIGNER, THE—Larry Shue .... 84–85 ..... Nov. 1, 1984 686

FORTY CARATS—Pierre Barillet, Jean-Pierre Gredy,
    (ad) Jay Allen .... 68–69 ..... Dec. 26, 1968 780

42ND STREET—(b) Michael Stewart, Mark Bramble,
    (m, l) Harry Warren, Al Dubin, (add'l l) Johnny
    Mercer, Mort Dixon, based on the novel
    by Bradford Ropes .... 80–81 ..... Aug. 25, 1980 3,486

FOSSE—(choreography) Robert Fosse, (c) Richard
    Maltby Jr., Chet Walker, Ann Reinking .... 98–99 ..... Jan. 14, 1999 1,092

FOURPOSTER, THE—Jan de Hartog .... 51–52 ..... Oct. 24, 1951 632

FOXFIRE—Susan Cooper, Hume Cronyn, (m) Jonathan
    Holtzman; based on materials
    from the *Foxfire* books .... 82–83 ..... Nov. 11, 1982 213

FRANNY'S WAY—RICHARD NELSON .... 01–02 ..... MAR. 26, 2002 32

FRONT PAGE, THE—Ben Hecht, Charles MacArthur .... 28–29 ..... Aug. 14, 1928 276

GENERATION—William Goodhart .... 65–66 ..... Oct. 6, 1965 299

GEORGE WASHINGTON SLEPT HERE—George S. Kaufman,
    Moss Hart .... 40–41 ..... Oct. 18, 1940 173

GETTING OUT—Marsha Norman .... 78–79 ..... Oct. 19, 1978 259

GIDEON—Paddy Chayefsky .... 61–62 ..... Nov. 9, 1961 236

GIGI—Anita Loos, based on Colette's novel .... 51–52 ..... Nov. 24, 1951 219

GIMME SHELTER—Barrie Keefe
    (*Gem, Gotcha* and *Getaway*) .... 78–79 ..... Dec. 10, 1978 17

GIN GAME, THE—D.L. Coburn .... 77–78 ..... Oct. 6, 1977 517

GINGERBREAD LADY, THE—Neil Simon .... 70–71 ..... Dec. 13, 1970 193

GIRL ON THE VIA FLAMINIA, THE—Alfred Hayes,
    based on his novel .... 53–54 ..... Feb. 9, 1954 111

GLASS MENAGERIE, THE—Tennessee Williams .... 44–45 ..... Mar. 31, 1945 561

GLENGARRY GLEN ROSS—David Mamet .... 83–84 ..... Mar. 25, 1984 378

GLORY OF LIVING, THE—Rebecca Gilman .... 01–02 ..... Nov. 15, 2001 17

GOAT, OR WHO IS SYLVIA?, THE—Edward Albee .... 01–02 ..... MAR. 10, 2002 309

GOBLIN MARKET—(ad) Peggy Harmon, Polly Pen
    from the poem by Christina Rosetti, (m) Polly Pen
    (special citation) .... 85–86 ..... Apr. 13, 1986 89

GOLDEN APPLE, THE—(b, l), John Latouche, (m) Jerome
    Moross .... 53–54 ..... Apr. 20, 1954 125

GOLDEN BOY—Clifford Odets .... 37–38 ..... Nov. 4, 1937 250

Good—C.P. Taylor .... 82–83 ..... Oct. 13, 1982 125
Good Doctor, The—(ad) Neil Simon, suggested by
    stories by Anton Chekhov .... 73–74 ..... Nov. 27, 1973 208
Good Gracious Annabelle—Clare Kummer .... 09–19 ..... Oct. 31, 1916 111
Good Times Are Killing Me, The—Lynda Barry .... 90–91 ..... May 21, 1991 207
Goodbye, My Fancy—Fay Kanin .... 48–49 ..... Nov. 17, 1948 446
Goose Hangs High, The—Lewis Beach .... 23–24 .... Jan. 29, 1924 183
Grand Hotel—Vicki Baum, (ad) W. A. Drake .... 30–31 ..... Nov. 13, 1930 459
Grand Hotel: The Musical—(b) Luther Davis, (m, l)
    Robert Wright, George Forrest, (add'l m, l) Maury
    Yeston, based on Vicki Baum's *Grand Hotel* .... 89–90 ..... Nov. 12, 1989 1,077
Grapes of Wrath, The—(ad) Frank Galati
    from the novel by John Steinbeck .... 89–90 ..... Mar. 22, 1990 188
Great Divide, The—William Vaughn Moody .... 99–09 ..... Oct. 3, 1906 238
Great God Brown, The—Eugene O'Neill .... 25–26 ..... Jan. 23, 1926 271
Great White Hope, The—Howard Sackler .... 68–69 ..... Oct. 3, 1968 556
Green Bay Tree, The—Mordaunt Shairp .... 33–34 ..... Oct. 20, 1933 ... 166
Green Goddess, The—William Archer .... 20–21 .... Jan. 18, 1921 440
Green Grow the Lilacs—Lynn Riggs .... 30–31 .... Jan. 26, 1931 64
Green Hat, The—Michael Arlen .... 25–26 ..... Sept. 15, 1925 231
Green Julia—Paul Abelman .... 72–73 ..... Nov. 16, 1972 147
Green Pastures, The—Marc Connelly, based on Roark
    Bradford's *Ol' Man Adam and His Chillun* .... 29–30 ..... Feb. 26, 1930 640
Gross Indecency: The Three Trials of Oscar Wilde—
    Moisés Kaufman .... 97–98 .... June 5, 1997 534
Gus and Al—Albert Innaurato .... 88–89 ..... Feb. 27, 1989 25
Guys and Dolls—(b) Jo Swerling, Abe Burrows, based
    on a story and characters by Damon Runyon,
    (m, l) Frank Loesser .... 50–51 ..... Nov. 24, 1950 1,200
Gypsy—Maxwell Anderson .... 28–29 .... Jan. 14, 1929 64

Hadrian VII—Peter Luke, based on works by Fr. Rolfe .... 68–69 ..... Jan. 8, 1969 359
Hamp—John Wilson, based on an episode from
    a novel by J.L. Hodson .... 66–67 ..... Mar. 9, 1967 101
Hapgood—Tom Stoppard .... 94–95 ..... Dec. 4, 1994 129
Happy Time, The—Samuel Taylor, based on Robert
    Fontaine's book .... 49–50 ..... Jan. 24, 1950 614
Harriet—Florence Ryerson, Colin Clements .... 42–43 ..... Mar. 3, 1943 377
Harvey—Mary Chase .... 44–45 ..... Nov. 1, 1944 1,775
Hasty Heart, The—John Patrick .... 44–45 ..... Jan. 3, 1945 207
He Who Gets Slapped—Leonid Andreyev, (ad) Gregory
    Zilboorg .... 21–22 ..... Jan. 9, 1922 308
Heart of Maryland, The—David Belasco .... 94–99 ..... Oct. 22, 1895 240
Heidi Chronicles, The—Wendy Wasserstein .... 88–89 ..... Dec. 11, 1988 81
                                                                 88–89 ..... Mar. 9, 1989 621
Heiress, The—Ruth and Augustus Goetz, suggested by
    Henry James's novel *Washington Square* .... 47–48 ..... Sept. 29, 1947 410
Hell-Bent fer Heaven—Hatcher Hughes .... 23–24 ..... Jan. 4, 1924 122

HELLO, DOLLY!—(b) Michael Stewart, (m, l) Jerry
Herman, based on Thornton Wilder's *The
Matchmaker* .... 63–64 ..... Jan. 16, 1964 2,844
HER MASTER'S VOICE—Clare Kummer .... 33–34 ..... Oct. 23, 1933 224
HERE COME THE CLOWNS—Philip Barry .... 38–39 ..... Dec. 7, 1938 88
HERO, THE—Gilbert Emery .... 21–22 ..... Sept. 5, 1921 80
HIGH TOR—Maxwell Anderson .... 36–37 ..... Jan. 9, 1937 171
HOGAN'S GOAT—William Alfred .... 65–66 ..... Nov. 11, 1965 607
HOLIDAY—Philip Barry .... 28–29 ..... Nov. 26, 1928 229
HOME—David Storey .... 70–71 ..... Nov. 17, 1970 110
HOME—Samm-Art Williams .... 79–80 ..... Dec. 14, 1979 82
                                                                              79–80 ..... May 7, 1980 279
HOMEBODY/KABUL—Tony Kushner .... 01–02 ..... Dec. 19, 2001 62
HOMECOMING, THE—Harold Pinter .... 66–67 ..... Jan. 5, 1967 324
HOME OF THE BRAVE—Arthur Laurents .... 45–46 ..... Dec. 27, 1945 69
HOPE FOR A HARVEST—Sophie Treadwell .... 41–42 ..... Nov. 26, 1941 38
HOSTAGE, THE—Brendan Behan .... 60–61 ..... Sept. 20, 1960 127
HOT L BALTIMORE, THE—Lanford Wilson .... 72–73 ..... Mar. 22, 1973 1,166
HOUSE OF BLUE LEAVES, THE—John Guare .... 70–71 ..... Feb. 10, 1971 337
HOUSE OF CONNELLY, THE—Paul Green .... 31–32 ..... Sept. 28, 1931 91
HOW I LEARNED TO DRIVE—Paula Vogel .... 96–97 ..... May 4, 1997 400
HOW TO SUCCEED IN BUSINESS WITHOUT REALLY TRYING—
(b) Abe Burrows, Jack Weinstock, Willie Gilbert,
based on Shepherd Mead's novel,
(m, l) Frank Loesser .... 61–62 ..... Oct. 14, 1961 1,417
HURLYBURLY—David Rabe .... 84–85 ..... June 21, 1984 45
                                                                              84–85 ..... Aug. 7, 1984 343

I AM A CAMERA John van Druten, based on
Christopher Isherwood's Berlin stories .... 51–52 ..... Nov. 28, 1951 214
I AM MY OWN WIFE—Doug Wright .... 02–03 ..... May 27, 2003 6
I KNOW MY LOVE—S.N. Behrman, based on Marcel
Achard's *Auprès de Ma Blonde* .... 49–50 ..... Nov. 2, 1949 246
I NEVER SANG FOR MY FATHER—Robert Anderson .... 67–68 ..... Jan. 25, 1968 124
I OUGHT TO BE IN PICTURES—Neil Simon .... 79–80 ..... Apr. 3, 1980 324
I REMEMBER MAMA—John van Druten, based on
Kathryn Forbes's book *Mama's Bank Account* .... 44–45 ..... Oct. 19, 1944 714
ICEBOUND—Owen Davis .... 22–23 ..... Feb. 10, 1923 171
ICEMAN COMETH, THE—Eugene O'Neill .... 46–47 ..... Oct. 9, 1946 136
IDIOT'S DELIGHT—Robert E. Sherwood .... 35–36 ..... Mar. 24, 1936 300
IF I WERE KING—Justin Huntly McCarthy .... 99–09 ..... Oct. 14, 1901 56
I'M NOT RAPPAPORT—Herb Gardner .... 85–86 ..... June 6, 1985 181
                                                                              85–86 ..... Nov. 19, 1985 890
IMAGINARY FRIENDS—Nora Ephron .... 02–03 ..... Dec. 12, 2002 76
IMMORALIST, THE—Ruth and Augustus Goetz,
based on André Gide's novel .... 53–54 ..... Feb. 8, 1954 96
IN ABRAHAM'S BOSOM—Paul Green .... 26–27 ..... Dec. 30, 1926 116

IN THE MATTER OF J. ROBERT OPPENHEIMER—
  Heinar Kipphardt, (tr) Ruth Speirs .... 68–69 ..... Mar. 6, 1969 64
IN THE SUMMER HOUSE—Jane Bowles .... 53–54 ..... Dec. 29, 1953 55
IN TIME TO COME—Howard Koch, John Huston .... 41–42 ..... Dec. 28, 1941 40
INADMISSABLE EVIDENCE—John Osborne .... 65–66 ..... Nov. 30, 1965 166
INCIDENT AT VICHY—Arthur Miller .... 64–65 ..... Dec. 3, 1964 99
INDIANS—Arthur L. Kopit .... 69–70 ..... Oct. 13, 1969 96
INHERIT THE WIND—Jerome Lawrence, Robert E. Lee .... 54–55 ..... Apr. 21, 1955 806
INNOCENTS, THE—William Archibald, based on Henry
  James's *The Turn of the Screw* .... 49–50 ..... Feb. 1, 1950 141
INNOCENT VOYAGE, THE—Paul Osborn, based on
  Richard Hughes's novel *A High Wind in Jamaica* ...... 43–44 ..... Nov. 15, 1943 40
INSPECTOR CALLS, AN—J.B. Priestley .... 47–48 ..... Oct. 21, 1947 95
INTO THE WOODS—(b) James Lapine, (m, l) Stephen
  Sondheim .... 87–88 ..... Nov. 5, 1987 765
INVENTION OF LOVE, THE—Tom Stoppard .... 00–01 ..... Mar. 29, 2001 108
ISLAND, THE—Athol Fugard, John Kani, Winston
  Ntshona .... 74–75 ..... Nov. 24, 1974 52
"IT'S A BIRD IT'S A PLANE IT'S SUPERMAN"—(b) David
  Newman and Robert Benton, (m) Charles Strouse,
  (l) Lee Adams, based on the comic strip
  Superman .... 65–66 ..... Mar. 29, 1966 129
IT'S ONLY A PLAY—Terrence McNally .... 85–86 ..... Jan. 12, 1986 17

J.B.—Archibald MacLeish .... 58–59 ..... Dec. 11, 1958 364
JACOBOWSKY AND THE COLONEL—S.N. Behrman, based on
  Franz Werfel's play .... 43–44 ..... Mar. 14, 1944 417
JAMES JOYCE'S THE DEAD—(b) Richard Nelson, (m) Shaun
  Davey, (l) Richard Nelson, Shaun Davey .... 99–00 ..... Oct. 28 1999 38
                                                                              99–00 ..... Jan. 11, 2000 112
JANE—S.N. Behrman, suggested by W. Somerset
  Maugham's story .... 51–52 ..... Feb. 1, 1952 100
JANE CLEGG—St. John Ervine .... 19–20 ..... Feb. 23, 1920 158
JEFFREY—Paul Rudnick .... 92–93 ..... Mar. 6, 1993 365
JASON—Samson Raphaelson .... 41–42 ..... Jan. 21, 1942 125
JEROME ROBBINS' BROADWAY—(c) Jerome Robbins
  (special citation) .... 88–89 ..... Feb. 26, 1989 634
JESSE AND THE BANDIT QUEEN—David Freeman .... 75–76 ..... Oct. 17, 1975 155
JEST, THE—Sem Benelli, (ad) Edward Sheldon .... 19–20 ..... Sept. 19, 1919 197
JITNEY—August Wilson .... 99–00 ..... Apr. 25, 2000 43
JOAN OF LORRAINE—Maxwell Anderson .... 46–47 ..... Nov. 18, 1946 199
JOE TURNER'S COME AND GONE—August Wilson .... 87–88 ..... Mar. 27, 1988 105
JOHN FERGUSON—St. John Ervine .... 09–19 ..... May 13, 1919 177
JOHN LOVES MARY—Norman Krasna .... 46–47 ..... Feb. 4, 1947 423
JOHNNY JOHNSON—(b, l) Paul Green, (m) Kurt Weill .... 36–37 ..... Nov. 19, 1936 68
JOINED AT THE HEAD—Catherine Butterfield .... 92–93 ..... Nov. 15, 1992 41
JOURNEY'S END—R.C. Sherriff .... 28–29 ..... Mar. 22, 1929 485

JUMPERS—Tom Stoppard .... 73–74 ..... Apr. 22, 1974 48
JUNE MOON—Ring W. Lardner, George S. Kaufman .... 29–30 ..... Oct. 9, 1929 273
JUNIOR MISS—Jerome Chodorov, Joseph Fields .... 41–42 ..... Nov. 18, 1941 710

K2—Patrick Meyers .... 82–83 ..... Mar. 30, 1983 85
KATAKI—Shimon Wincelberg .... 58–59 ..... Apr. 9, 1959 20
KENTUCKY CYCLE, THE—Robert Schenkkan .... 93–94 ..... Nov. 14, 1993 34
KEY LARGO—Maxwell Anderson .... 39–40 ..... Nov. 27, 1939 105
KILLING OF SISTER GEORGE, THE—Frank Marcus .... 66–67 ..... Oct. 5, 1966 205
KINGDOM OF GOD, THE—G. Martinez Sierra,
    (ad) Helen and Harley Granville Barker .... 28–29 ..... Dec. 20, 1928 92
KING HEDLEY II—August Wilson .... 00–01 ..... May 1, 2001 72
KISS AND TELL—F. Hugh Herbert .... 42–43 ..... Mar. 17, 1943 956
KISS OF THE SPIDER WOMAN—(b) Terrence McNally,
    (m) John Kander, (l) Fred Ebb, based on the novel
    by Manuel Puig .... 92–93 ..... May 3, 1993 906
KISS THE BOYS GOODBYE—Clare Boothe .... 38–39 ..... Sept. 28, 1938 286
KNOCK KNOCK—Jules Feiffer .... 75–76 ..... Jan. 18, 1976 41
                                                               75–76 ..... Feb. 24, 1976 152
KVETCH—Steven Berkoff .... 86–87 ..... Feb. 18, 1987 31

LA BÊTE—David Hirson (special citation) .... 90–91 ..... Feb. 10, 1991 25
LA CAGE AUX FOLLES—(b) Harvey Fierstein, (m, l) Jerry
    Herman, based on the play by Jean Poiret .... 83–84 ..... Aug. 21, 1983 1,761
LA TRAGÉDIE DE CARMEN—(ad) Peter Brook, Jean-Claude
    Carrière, Marius Constant from Georges Bizet's
    opera Carmen (special citation) .... 83–84 ..... Nov. 17, 1983 187
LADY FROM DUBUQUE, THE—Edward Albee .... 79–80 ..... Jan. 31, 1980 12
LADY IN THE DARK—(b) Moss Hart, (l) Ira Gershwin,
    (m) Kurt Weill .... 40–41 ..... Jan. 23, 1941 162
LARGO DESOLATO—Vaclav Havel, (tr) Marie Winn .... 85–86 ..... Mar. 25, 1986 40
LARK, THE—Jean Anouilh, (ad) Lillian Hellman .... 55–56 ..... Nov. 17, 1955 229
LAST MEETING OF THE KNIGHTS OF THE WHITE MAGNOLIA,
    THE—Preston Jones .... 76–77 ..... Sept. 22, 1976 22
LAST MILE, THE—John Wexley .... 29–30 ..... Feb. 13, 1930 289
LAST NIGHT OF BALLYHOO, THE—Alfred Uhry .... 96–97 ..... Feb. 27, 1997 557
LAST OF MRS. CHEYNEY, THE—Frederick Lonsdale .... 25–26 ..... Nov. 9, 1925 385
LAST OF THE RED HOT LOVERS—Neil Simon .... 69–70 ..... Dec. 28, 1969 706
LATE CHRISTOPHER BEAN, THE—(ad) Sidney Howard from
    the French of Rene Fauchois .... 32–33 ..... Oct. 31, 1932 224
LATE GEORGE APLEY, THE—John P. Marquand, George
    S. Kaufman, based on John P. Marquand's novel .... 44–45 ..... Nov. 23, 1944 385
LATER LIFE—A.R. Gurney .... 92–93 ..... May 23, 1993 126
LAUGHTER ON THE 23RD FLOOR—Neil Simon .... 93–94 ..... Nov. 22, 1993 320
LEAH KLESCHNA—C.M.S. McLellan .... 99–09 ..... Dec. 12, 1904 131
LEFT BANK, THE—Elmer Rice .... 31–32 ..... Oct. 5, 1931 242
LEND ME A TENOR—Ken Ludwig .... 88–89 ..... Mar. 2, 1989 481

LES LIAISONS DANGEREUSES—Christopher Hampton,
    based on Choderlos de Laclos's novel .... 86–87 ..... Apr. 30, 1987 148
LES MISÉRABLES—(b) Alain Boublil, Claude-Michel
    Schönberg, (m) Claude-Michel Schönberg,
    (l) Herbert Kretzmer, add'l material James Fenton,
    based on Victor Hugo's novel .... 86–87 ..... Mar. 12, 1987 6,680
LESSON FROM ALOES, A—Athol Fugard .... 80–81 ..... Nov. 17, 1980 96
LET US BE GAY—Rachel Crothers .... 28–29 ..... Feb. 19, 1929 353
LETTERS TO LUCERNE—Fritz Rotter, Allen Vincent .... 41–42 ..... Dec. 23, 1941 23
LIFE, A—Hugh Leonard .... 80–81 ..... Nov. 2, 1980 72
LIFE & ADVENTURES OF NICHOLAS NICKLEBY, THE—
    (ad) David Edgar from Charles Dickens's novel .... 81–82 ..... Oct. 4, 1981 49
LIFE IN THE THEATRE, A—David Mamet .... 77–78 ..... Oct. 20, 1977 288
LIFE WITH FATHER—Howard Lindsay, Russel Crouse,
    based on Clarence Day's book .... 39–40 ..... Nov. 8, 1939 3,224
LIFE WITH MOTHER—Howard Lindsay, Russel Crouse,
    based on Clarence Day's book .... 48–49 ..... Oct. 20, 1948 265
LIGHT UP THE SKY—Moss Hart .... 48–49 ..... Nov. 18, 1948 216
LILIOM—Ferenc Molnar, (ad) Benjamin Glazer .... 20–21 ..... Apr. 20, 1921 300
LION IN WINTER, THE—James Goldman .... 65–66 ..... Mar. 3, 1966 92
*LION KING, THE—(b) Roger Allers, Irene Mecchi,
    (m, l) Elton John, Tim Rice, (add'l m, l) Lebo M,
    Mark Mancina, Jay Rifkin, Julie Taymor, Hans
    Zimmer .... 97–98 ..... Nov. 13, 1997 2,345
LIPS TOGETHER, TEETH APART—Terrence McNally .... 91–92 ..... June 25, 1991 406
LITTLE ACCIDENT—Floyd Dell, Thomas Mitchell .... 28–29 ..... Oct. 9, 1928 303
LITTLE FOXES, THE—Lillian Hellman .... 38–39 ..... Feb. 15, 1939 410
LITTLE MINISTER, THE—James M. Barrie .... 94–99 ..... Sept. 27, 1897 300
LITTLE NIGHT MUSIC, A—(b) Hugh Wheeler,
    (m, l) Stephen Sondheim, suggested by Ingmar
    Bergman's film Smiles of a Summer Night .... 72–73 ..... Feb. 25, 1973 600
LIVING ROOM, THE—Graham Greene .... 54–55 ..... Nov. 17, 1954 22
LIVING TOGETHER—Alan Ayckbourn .... 75–76 ..... Dec. 7, 1975 76
LOBBY HERO—Kenneth Lonergan .... 00–01 ..... Mar. 13, 2001 40
                                                                   00–01 ..... May 8, 2001 136
LOMAN FAMILY PICNIC, THE—Donald Margulies .... 89–90 ..... June 20, 1989 16
LONG DAY'S JOURNEY INTO NIGHT—Eugene O'Neill .... 56–57 ..... Nov. 7, 1956 390
LOOK BACK IN ANGER—John Osborne .... 57–58 ..... Oct. 1, 1957 407
LOOK HOMEWARD, ANGEL—Ketti Frings, based on
    Thomas Wolfe's novel .... 57–58 ..... Nov. 28, 1957 564
LOOSE ENDS—Michael Weller .... 79–80 ..... June 6, 1979 284
LOST HORIZONS—Harry Segall, revised by John Hayden .... 34–35 ..... Oct. 15, 1934 56
LOST IN THE STARS—(b, l) Maxwell Anderson, based on
    Alan Paton's novel Cry, the Beloved Country,
    (m) Kurt Weill .... 49–50 ..... Oct. 30, 1949 273
LOST IN YONKERS—Neil Simon .... 90–91 ..... Feb. 21, 1991 780
LOVE LETTERS—A.R. Gurney .... 89–90 ..... Aug. 22, 1989 64
                                                                   89–90 ..... Oct. 31, 1989 96

Love of Four Colonels, The—Peter Ustinov .... 52–53 ..... Jan. 15, 1953 141
Love! Valour! Compassion!—Terrence McNally .... 94–95 ..... Nov. 1, 1994 72
                                                              94–95 ..... Feb. 14, 1995 249
Lovers—Brian Friel .... 68–69 ..... July 25, 1968 148
Loyalties—John Galsworthy .... 22–23 ..... Sept. 27, 1922 220
Lunch Hour—Jean Kerr .... 80–81 ..... Nov. 12, 1980 262
Lute Song—(b) Sidney Howard, Will Irwin from
   the Chinese classic *Pi-Pa-Ki,* (l) Bernard
   Hanighen, (m) Raymond Scott .... 45–46 ..... Feb. 6, 1946 385
Luther—John Osborne .... 63–64 ..... Sept. 25, 1963 211
Luv—Murray Schisgal .... 64–65 ..... Nov. 11, 1964 901
M. Butterfly—David Henry Hwang .... 87–88 ..... Mar. 20, 1988 777
Ma Rainey's Black Bottom—August Wilson .... 84–85 ..... Oct. 11, 1984 275
Machinal—Sophie Treadwell .... 28–29 ..... Sept. 7, 1928 91
Mad Forest—Caryl Churchill .... 91–92 ..... Dec. 4, 1991 54
Madness of George III, The—Alan Bennett .... 93–94 ..... Sept. 28, 1993 17
Madwoman of Chaillot, The—Jean Giraudoux,
   (ad) Maurice Valency .... 48–49 ..... Dec. 27, 1948 368
Magic and the Loss, The—Julian Funt .... 53–54 ..... Apr. 9, 1954 27
Magnificent Yankee, The—Emmet Lavery .... 45–46 ..... Jan. 22, 1946 160
Mahabharata, The—Jean-Claude Carrière,
   (ad) Peter Brook .... 87–88 ..... Oct. 13, 1987 25
Male Animal, The—James Thurber, Elliott Nugent .... 39–40 ..... Jan. 9, 1940 243
Mamma's Affair—Rachel Barton Butler .... 19–20 ..... Jan. 29, 1920 98
Man for All Seasons, A—Robert Bolt .... 61–62 ..... Nov. 22, 1961 637
Man from Home, The—Booth Tarkington, Harry Leon
   Wilson .... 99–09 ..... Aug. 17, 1908 406
Man in the Glass Booth, The—Robert Shaw .... 68–69 ..... Sept. 26, 1968 268
Man of La Mancha—(b) Dale Wasserman, suggested
   by the life and works of Miguel de Cervantes y
   Saavedra, (l) Joe Darion, (m) Mitch Leigh .... 65–66 ..... Nov. 22, 1965 2,328
Man Who Came to Dinner, The—George S. Kaufman,
   Moss Hart .... 39–40 ..... Oct. 16, 1939 739
Margin for Error—Clare Boothe .... 39–40 ..... Nov. 3, 1939 264
Marriage of Bette and Boo, The—Christopher Durang ..... 84–85 ..... May 16, 1985 86
Marvin's Room—Scott McPherson .... 91–92 ..... Dec. 5, 1991 214
Mary, Mary—Jean Kerr .... 60–61 ..... Mar. 8, 1961 1,572
Mary of Scotland—Maxwell Anderson .... 33–34 ..... Nov. 27, 1933 248
Mary Rose—James M. Barrie .... 20–21 ..... Dec. 22, 1920 127
Mary the 3rd—Rachel Crothers .... 22–23 ..... Feb. 5, 1923 162
Mass Appeal—Bill C. Davis .... 81–82 ..... Nov. 12, 1981 214
Master Class—Terrence McNally .... 95–96 ..... Nov. 5, 1995 601
Master Harold . . . and the Boys—Athol Fugard .... 81–82 ..... May 4, 1982 344
Matchmaker, The—Thornton Wilder, based on Johann
   Nestroy's *Einen Jux Will Er Sich Machen,* based on
   John Oxenford's *A Day Well Spent* .... 55–56 ..... Dec. 5, 1955 486
Me and Molly—Gertrude Berg .... 47–48 ..... Feb. 26, 1948 156
Member of the Wedding, The—Carson McCullers .... 49–50 ..... Jan. 5, 1950 501

MEN IN WHITE—Sidney Kingsley .... 33–34 ..... Sept. 26, 1933 351

MERCY SEAT, THE—Neil LaBute .... 02–03 ..... Dec. 18, 2002 29

MERRILY WE ROLL ALONG—George S. Kaufman,
    Moss Hart .... 34–35 ..... Sept. 29, 1934 155

MERTON OF THE MOVIES—George S. Kaufman, Marc
    Connelly, based on Harry Leon Wilson's novel .... 22–23 ..... Nov. 13, 1922 381

METAMORPHOSES—Mary Zimmerman .... 01–02 ..... Oct. 9, 2001 96
                                                                                                01–02 ..... Mar. 4, 2002 400

MICHAEL AND MARY—A.A. Milne .... 29–30 ..... Dec. 13, 1929 246

MILK TRAIN DOESN'T STOP HERE ANYMORE, THE—
    Tennessee Williams .... 62–63 ..... Jan. 16, 1963 69

MINICK—George S. Kaufman, Edna Ferber .... 24–25 ..... Sept. 24, 1924 141

MISS FIRECRACKER CONTEST, THE—Beth Henley .... 83–84 ..... May 1, 1984 131

MISS SAIGON—(b) Alain Boublil, Claude-Michel
    Schönberg (m) Claude-Michel Schönberg, (l)
    Richard Maltby Jr., Alain Boublil, (add'l material)
    Richard Maltby Jr. .... 90–91 ..... Apr. 11, 1991 4,097

MISTER ROBERTS—Thomas Heggen, Joshua Logan,
    based on Thomas Heggen's novel .... 47–48 ..... Feb. 18, 1948 1,157

MNEMONIC—Complicite .... 00–01 ..... Mar. 28, 2001 67

MOLLY SWEENEY—Brian Friel .... 95–96 ..... Jan. 7, 1996 145

MOON FOR THE MISBEGOTTEN, A—Eugene O'Neill .... 56–57 ..... May 2, 1957 68

MOON IS DOWN, THE—John Steinbeck .... 41–42 ..... Apr. 7, 1942 71

MOONCHILDREN—Michael Weller .... 71–72 ..... Feb. 21, 1972 16

MORNING'S AT SEVEN—Paul Osborn .... 39–40 ..... Nov. 30, 1939 44

MOTHER COURAGE AND HER CHILDREN—Bertolt Brecht,
    (ad) Eric Bentley .... 62–63 ..... Mar. 28, 1963 52

MOURNING BECOMES ELECTRA—Eugene O'Neill .... 31–32 ..... Oct. 26, 1931 150

MR. AND MRS. NORTH—Owen Davis, based on Frances
    and Richard Lockridge's stories .... 40–41 ..... Jan. 12, 1941 163

MRS. BUMSTEAD-LEIGH—Harry James Smith .... 09–19 ..... Apr. 3, 1911 64

MRS. KLEIN—Nicholas Wright .... 95–96 ..... Oct. 24, 1995 280

MRS. MCTHING—Mary Chase .... 51–52 ..... Feb. 20, 1952 350

MRS. PARTRIDGE PRESENTS—Mary Kennedy, Ruth
    Hawthorne .... 24–25 ..... Jan. 5, 1925 144

MY CHILDREN! MY AFRICA!—Athol Fugard .... 89–90 ..... Dec. 18, 1989 28

MY FAIR LADY—(b, l) Alan Jay Lerner, based on
    George Bernard Shaw's *Pygmalion,* (m) Frederick
    Loewe .... 55–56 ..... Mar. 15, 1956 2,717

MY ONE AND ONLY—(b) Peter Stone, Timothy S.
    Mayer, (m) George Gershwin from *Funny Face*
    and other shows, (l) Ira Gershwin .... 82–83 ..... May 1, 1983 767

MY SISTER EILEEN—Joseph Fields, Jerome Chodorov,
    based on Ruth McKenney's stories .... 40–41 ..... Dec. 26, 1940 864

MY 3 ANGELS—Samuel and Bella Spewack, based on
    Albert Husson's play *La Cuisine des Anges* .... 52–53 ..... Mar. 11, 1953 344

MYSTERY OF EDWIN DROOD, THE—Rupert Holmes .... 85–86 ..... Aug. 4, 1985 24
                                                                                                85–86 ..... Dec. 12, 1985 608

NATIONAL HEALTH, THE—Peter Nichols .... 74–75 ..... Oct. 10, 1974 53
NATIVE SON—Paul Green, Richard Wright, based on
  Mr. Wright's novel .... 40–41 ..... Mar. 24, 1941 114
NEST, THE—(ad) Grace George, from Paul Geraldy's
  Les Noces d'Argent .... 21–22 ..... Jan. 28, 1922 152
NEVIS MOUNTAIN DEW—Steve Carter .... 78–79 ..... Dec. 7, 1978 61
NEW ENGLAND—Richard Nelson .... 95–96 ..... Nov. 7, 1995 54
NEXT (see Adaptation)
NEXT TIME I'LL SING TO YOU—James Saunders .... 63–64 ..... Nov. 27, 1963 23
NICE PEOPLE—Rachel Crothers .... 20–21 ..... Mar. 2, 1921 247
NICHOLAS NICKLEBY—(see The Life & Adventures of
  Nicholas Nickleby)
NIGHT AND HER STARS—Richard Greenberg .... 94–95 ..... Apr. 26, 1995 39
NIGHT OF THE IGUANA, THE—Tennessee Williams .... 61–62 ..... Dec. 28, 1961 316
'NIGHT, MOTHER—Marsha Norman .... 82–83 ..... Mar. 31, 1983 380
                                                                         83–84 ..... Apr. 14, 1984 54
NINE—(b) Arthur L. Kopit, (m, l) Maury Yeston,
  (ad) Mario Fratti from the Italian .... 81–82 ..... May 9, 1982 739
NO MORE LADIES—A.E. Thomas .... 33–34 ..... Jan. 23, 1934 162
NO PLACE TO BE SOMEBODY—Charles Gordone .... 68–69 ..... May 4, 1969 250
NO TIME FOR COMEDY—S.N. Behrman .... 38–39 ..... Apr. 17, 1939 185
NO TIME FOR SERGEANTS—Ira Levin, based on Mac
  Hyman's novel .... 55–56 ..... Oct. 20, 1955 796
NOCTURNE—Adam Rapp .... 00–01 ..... May 16, 2001 38
NOËL COWARD IN TWO KEYS—Noël Coward (Come Into
  the Garden Maud and A Song at Twilight) .... 73–74 ..... Feb. 28, 1974 140
NOISES OFF—Michael Frayn .... 83–84 ..... Dec. 11, 1983 553
NORMAN CONQUESTS, THE—(see Living Together, Round
  and Round the Garden and Table Manners)
NOT ABOUT NIGHTINGALES—Tennessee Williams .... 98–99 ..... Feb. 25, 1999 125
NUTS—Tom Topor .... 79–80 ..... Apr. 28, 1980 96

O MISTRESS MINE—Terence Rattigan .... 45–46 ..... Jan. 23, 1946 452
ODD COUPLE, THE—Neil Simon .... 64–65 ..... Mar. 10, 1965 964
OF MICE AND MEN—John Steinbeck .... 37–38 ..... Nov. 23, 1937 207
OF THEE I SING—(b) George S. Kaufman, (m) George
  Gershwin, Morrie Ryskind, (l) Ira Gershwin .... 31–32 ..... Dec. 26, 1931 441
OH DAD, POOR DAD, MAMA'S HUNG YOU IN THE CLOSET
  AND I'M FEELIN' SO SAD—Arthur L. Kopit .... 61–62 ..... Feb. 26, 1962 454
OHIO IMPROMPTU, CATASTROPHE AND WHAT WHERE—
  Samuel Beckett .... 83–84 ..... June 15, 1983 350
OKLAHOMA!—(b, l) Oscar Hammerstein II, based on
  Lynn Riggs's play Green Grow the Lilacs,
  (m) Richard Rodgers .... 42–43 ..... Mar. 31, 1943 2,212
OLD MAID, THE—Zoë Akins, based on Edith
  Wharton's novel .... 34–35 ..... Jan. 7, 1935 305
OLD SOAK, THE—Don Marquis .... 22–23 ..... Aug. 22, 1922 423

OLD TIMES—Harold Pinter .... 71–72 ..... Nov. 16, 1971 119
OLD WICKED SONGS—Jon Marans .... 96–97 ..... Sept. 5, 1996 210
OLDEST LIVING GRADUATE, THE—Preston Jones .... 76–77 ..... Sept. 23, 1976 20
OLEANNA—David Mamet .... 92–93 ..... Oct. 25, 1992 513
ON BORROWED TIME—Paul Osborn, based on
   Lawrence Edward Watkin's novel .... 37–38 ..... Feb. 3, 1938 321
ON GOLDEN POND—Ernest Thompson .... 78–79 ..... Sept. 13, 1978 30
                                                                    78–79 ..... Feb. 28, 1979 126
ON TRIAL—Elmer Rice .... 09–19 ..... Aug. 19, 1914 365
ONCE IN A LIFETIME—Moss Hart, George S. Kaufman .... 30–31 ..... Sept. 24, 1930 406
ONCE ON THIS ISLAND—(b, l) Lynn Ahrens, (m) Stephen
   Flaherty, based on the novel *My Love My Love*
   by Rosa Guy .... 89–90 ..... May 6, 1990 24
                                                                    90–91 ..... Oct. 18, 1990 469
ONE SUNDAY AFTERNOON—James Hagan .... 32–33 ..... Feb. 15, 1933 322
ORPHEUS DESCENDING—Tennessee Williams .... 56–57 ..... Mar. 21, 1957 68
OTHER PEOPLE'S MONEY—Jerry Sterner .... 88–89 ..... Feb. 16, 1989 990
OTHERWISE ENGAGED—Simon Gray .... 76–77 ..... Feb. 2, 1977 309
OUR COUNTRY'S GOOD—Timberlake Wertenbaker .... 90–91 ..... Apr. 29, 1991 48
*OUR LADY OF 121ST STREET—Stephen Adly Guirgis .... 02–03 ..... Sept. 29, 2002 15
                                                                    02–03 ..... Mar. 6, 2003 100
OUTRAGEOUS FORTUNE—Rose Franken .... 43–44 ..... Nov. 3, 1943 77
OUR TOWN—Thornton Wilder .... 37–38 ..... Feb. 4, 1938 336
OUTWARD BOUND—Sutton Vane .... 23–24 ..... Jan. 7, 1924 144
OVER 21—Ruth Gordon .... 43–44 ..... Jan. 3, 1944 221
OVERTURE—William Bolitho .... 30–31 ..... Dec. 5, 1930 41

P.S. 193—David Rayfiel .... 62–63 ..... Oct. 30, 1962 48
PACIFIC OVERTURES—(b) John Weidman, (m, l) Stephen
   Sondheim, (add'l material) Hugh Wheeler .... 75–76 ..... Jan. 11, 1976 193
PACK OF LIES—Hugh Whitemore .... 84–85 ..... Feb. 11, 1985 120
PAINTING CHURCHES—Tina Howe .... 83–84 ..... Nov. 22, 1983 206
PARADE—(b) Alfred Uhry, (m,l) Jason Robert Brown .... 98–99 ..... Dec. 17, 1998 85
PARIS BOUND—Philip Barry .... 27–28 ..... Dec. 27, 1927 234
PASSION—(b) James Lapine, (m) Stephen Sondheim,
   based on the film *Passione D'Amore* .... 93–94 ..... May 9, 1994 280
PASSION OF JOSEPH D., THE—Paddy Chayevsky .... 63–64 ..... Feb. 11, 1964 15
PATRIOTS, THE—Sidney Kingsley .... 42–43 ..... Jan. 29, 1943 173
PERFECT GANESH, A—Terrence McNally .... 93–94 ..... June 27, 1993 124
PERFECT PARTY, THE—A.R. Gurney .... 85–86 ..... Apr. 2, 1986 238
PERIOD OF ADJUSTMENT—Tennessee Williams .... 60–61 ..... Nov. 10, 1960 132
PERSECUTION AND ASSASSINATION OF MARAT AS PERFORMED
   BY THE INMATES OF THE ASYLUM OF CHARENTON UNDER
   THE DIRECTION OF THE MARQUIS DE SADE, THE—Peter
   Weiss, English version by Geoffrey Skelton,
   verse (ad) Adrian Mitchell .... 65–66 ..... Dec. 27, 1965 144
PETRIFIED FOREST, THE—Robert E. Sherwood .... 34–35 ..... Jan. 7, 1935 197

*Phantom of the Opera, The—(b) Richard Stilgoe,
  Andrew Lloyd Webber, (m) Andrew Lloyd
  Webber, (l) Charles Hart, (add'l l) Richard Stilgoe,
  adapted from the novel by Gaston Leroux
  (special citation) .... 87–88 ..... Jan. 26, 1988 6,397
Philadelphia, Here I Come!—Brian Friel .... 65–66 ..... Feb. 16, 1966 326
Philadelphia Story, The—Philip Barry .... 38–39 ..... Mar. 28, 1939 417
Philanthropist, The—Christopher Hampton .... 70–71 ..... Mar. 15, 1971 72
Physicists, The—Friedrich Dürrenmatt,
  (ad) James Kirkup .... 64–65 ..... Oct. 13, 1964 55
Piano Lesson, The—August Wilson .... 89–90 ..... Apr. 16, 1990 329
Pick Up Girl—Elsa Shelley .... 43–44 ..... May 3, 1944 198
Picnic—William Inge .... 52–53 ..... Feb. 19, 1953 477
Play About the Baby, The—Edward Albee .... 00–01 ..... Feb. 2, 2001 245
Play's the Thing, The—Ferenc Molnar,
  (ad) P.G. Wodehouse .... 26–27 ..... Nov. 3, 1926 260
Plaza Suite—Neil Simon .... 67–68 ..... Feb. 14, 1968 1,097
Pigeons and People—George M. Cohan .... 32–33 ..... Jan. 16, 1933 70
Pleasure of His Company, The—Samuel Taylor, Cornelia
  Otis Skinner .... 58–59 ..... Oct. 22, 1958 474
Plenty—David Hare .... 82–83 ..... Oct. 21, 1982 45
                                                                     82–83 ..... Jan. 6, 1983 92
Plough and the Stars, The—Sean O'Casey .... 27–28 ..... Nov. 28, 1927 32
Point of No Return—Paul Osborn, based on John P.
  Marquand's novel .... 51–52 ..... Dec. 13, 1951 364
Ponder Heart, The—Joseph Fields, Jerome Chodorov,
  based on Eudora Welty's story .... 55–56 ..... Feb. 16, 1956 149
Poor Bitos—Jean Anouilh, (tr) Lucienne Hill .... 64–65 ..... Nov. 14, 1964 17
Porgy—Dorothy and DuBose Heyward .... 27–28 ..... Oct. 10, 1927 367
Potting Shed, The—Graham Greene .... 56–57 ..... Jan. 29, 1957 143
Prayer for My Daughter, A—Thomas Babe .... 77–78 ..... Dec. 27, 1977 127
Prelude to a Kiss—Craig Lucas .... 89–90 ..... Mar. 14, 1990 33
                                                                     89–90 ..... May 1, 1990 440
Price, The—Arthur Miller .... 67–68 ..... Feb. 7, 1968 429
Pride and Prejudice—Helen Jerome, based on Jane
  Austen's novel .... 35–36 ..... Nov. 5, 1935 219
Pride's Crossing—Tina Howe .... 97–98 ..... Dec. 7, 1997 137
Prisoner of Second Avenue, The—Neil Simon .... 71–72 ..... Nov. 11, 1971 780
*Producers, The—(b) Mel Brooks and Thomas
  Meehan, (m, l) Mel Brooks .... 00–01 ..... Apr. 19, 2001 875
Prologue to Glory—E.P. Conkle .... 37–38 ..... Mar. 17, 1938 70
Proof—David Auburn .... 00–01 ..... May 23, 2000 79
                                                                     00–01 ..... Oct. 24, 2000 917
Quartermaine's Terms—Simon Gray .... 82–83 ..... Feb. 24, 1983 375

R.U.R.—Karel Capek .... 22–23 ..... Oct. 9, 1922 184
Racket, The—Bartlett Cormack .... 27–28 ..... Nov. 22, 1927 119

RAGTIME—(b) Terrence McNally, (m) Stephen Flaherty,
(l) Lynn Ahrens, based on E.L. Doctorow's novel .... 97–98 ..... Jan. 18, 1998 861
RAIN—John Colton, Clemence Randolph, based on
the story by W. Somerset Maugham .... 22–23 ..... Nov. 7, 1922 648
RAISIN IN THE SUN, A—Lorraine Hansberry .... 58–59 ..... Mar. 11, 1959 530
RATTLE OF A SIMPLE MAN—Charles Dyer .... 62–63 ..... Apr. 17, 1963 94
REAL ESTATE—Louise Page .... 87–88 ..... Dec. 1, 1987 55
REAL THING, THE—Tom Stoppard .... 83–84 ..... Jan. 5, 1984 566
REBEL WOMEN—Thomas Babe .... 75–76 ..... May 6, 1976 40
REBOUND—Donald Ogden Stewart .... 29–30 ..... Feb. 3, 1930 114
RED DIAPER BABY—Josh Kornbluth .... 92–93 ..... June 12, 1992 59
REHEARSAL, THE—Jean Anouilh, (ad) Pamela Hansford
Johnson, Kitty Black .... 63–64 ..... Sept. 23, 1963 110
REMAINS TO BE SEEN—Howard Lindsay, Russel Crouse ...... 51–52 ..... Oct. 3, 1951 199
*RENT—(b,m,l) Jonathan Larson .... 95–96 ..... Feb. 13, 1996 56
95–96 ..... Apr. 29, 1996 2,951
REQUIEM FOR A NUN—Ruth Ford, William Faulkner,
adapted from William Faulkner's novel .... 58–59 ..... Jan. 30, 1959 43
REUNION IN VIENNA—Robert E. Sherwood .... 31–32 ..... Nov. 16, 1931 264
RHINOCEROS—Eugene Ionesco, (tr) Derek Prouse .... 60–61 ..... Jan. 9, 1961 240
RITZ, THE—Terrence McNally .... 74–75 ..... Jan. 20, 1975 400
RIVER NIGER, THE—Joseph A. Walker .... 72–73 ..... Dec. 5, 1972 120
72–73 ..... Mar. 27, 1973 280
ROAD—Jim Cartwright .... 88–89 ..... July 28, 1988 62
ROAD TO MECCA, THE—Athol Fugard .... 87–88 ..... Apr. 12, 1988 172
ROAD TO ROME, THE—Robert E. Sherwood .... 26–27 ..... Jan. 31, 1927 392
ROCKABY—(see *Enough, Footfalls* and *Rockaby*)
ROCKET TO THE MOON—Clifford Odets .... 38–39 ..... Nov. 24, 1938 131
ROMANCE—Edward Sheldon .... 09–19 ..... Feb. 10, 1913 160
ROPE DANCERS, THE—Morton Wishengrad .... 57–58 ..... Nov. 20, 1957 189
ROSE TATTOO, THE—Tennessee Williams .... 50–51 ..... Feb. 3, 1951 306
ROSENCRANTZ AND GUILDENSTERN ARE DEAD—Tom Stoppard .. 67–68 ..... Oct. 16, 1967 420
ROUND AND ROUND THE GARDEN—Alan Ayckbourn .... 75–76 ..... Dec. 7, 1975 76
ROYAL FAMILY, THE—George S. Kaufman, Edna Ferber .... 27–28 ..... Dec. 28, 1927 345
ROYAL HUNT OF THE SUN—Peter Shaffer .... 65–66 ..... Oct. 26, 1965 261
RUGGED PATH, THE—Robert E. Sherwood .... 45–46 ..... Nov. 10, 1945 81
RUNNER STUMBLES, THE—Milan Stitt .... 75–76 ..... May 18, 1976 191

ST. HELENA—R.C. Sheriff, Jeanne de Casalis .... 36–37 ..... Oct. 6, 1936 63
SAME TIME, NEXT YEAR—Bernard Slade .... 74–75 ..... Mar. 13, 1975 1,453
SATURDAY'S CHILDREN—Maxwell Anderson .... 26–27 ..... Jan. 26, 1927 310
SCREENS, THE—Jean Genet, (tr) Minos Volanakis .... 71–72 ..... Nov. 30, 1971 28
SCUBA DUBA—Bruce Jay Friedman .... 67–68 ..... Oct. 10, 1967 692
SEA HORSE, THE—Edward J. Moore (James Irwin) .... 73–74 ..... Apr. 15, 1974 128
SEARCHING WIND, THE—Lillian Hellman .... 43–44 ..... Apr. 12, 1944 318
SEASCAPE—Edward Albee .... 74–75 ..... Jan. 26, 1975 65

SEASON IN THE SUN—Wolcott Gibbs .... 50–51 ..... Sept. 28, 1950 367
SEASON'S GREETINGS—Alan Ayckbourn .... 85–86 ..... July 11, 1985 20
SECOND THRESHOLD—Philip Barry,
    revisions by Robert E. Sherwood .... 50–51 ..... Jan. 2, 1951 126
SECRET SERVICE—William Gillette .... 94–99 ..... Oct. 5, 1896 176
SEPARATE TABLES—Terence Rattigan .... 56–57 ..... Oct. 25, 1956 332
SERENADING LOUIE—Lanford Wilson .... 75–76 ..... May 2, 1976 33
SERPENT: A CEREMONY, THE—Jean-Claude van Itallie .... 69–70 ..... May 29, 1973 3
SEVEN GUITARS—August Wilson .... 95–96 ..... Mar. 28, 1996 187
SEVEN KEYS TO BALDPATE—(ad) George M. Cohan, from
    the novel by Earl Derr Biggers .... 09–19 ..... Sept. 22, 1913 320
1776—(b) Peter Stone, (m, l) Sherman Edwards,
    based on a conception by Sherman Edwards .... 68–69 ..... Mar. 16, 1969 1,217
SEX, DRUGS, ROCK & ROLL—Eric Bogosian .... 89–90 ..... Feb. 8, 1990 103
SHADOW AND SUBSTANCE—Paul Vincent Carroll .... 37–38 ..... Jan. 26, 1938 274
SHADOW BOX, THE—Michael Cristofer .... 76–77 ..... Mar. 31, 1977 315
SHADOW OF HEROES—(see Stone and Star)
SHADOWLANDS—William Nicholson .... 90–91 ..... Nov. 11, 1990 169
SHE LOVES ME—(b) Joe Masteroff, based on Miklos
    Laszlo's play Parfumerie, (l) Sheldon Harnick,
    (m) Jerry Bock .... 62–63 ..... Apr. 23, 1963 301
SHINING HOUR, THE—Keith Winter .... 33–34 ..... Feb. 13, 1934 121
SHIRLEY VALENTINE—Willy Russell .... 88–89 ..... Feb. 16, 1989 324
SHORT EYES—Miguel Piñero .... 73–74 ..... Feb. 28, 1974 54
                                                                                 73–74 ..... May 23, 1974 102
SHOW-OFF, THE—George Kelly .... 23–24 ..... Feb. 5, 1924 571
SHRIKE, THE—Joseph Kramm .... 51–52 ..... Jan. 15, 1952 161
[SIC]—Melissa James Gibson .... 01–02 ..... Nov. 19, 2001 38
SIDE MAN—Warren Leight .... 98–99 ..... June 25, 1998 458
SIGHT UNSEEN—Donald Margulies .... 91–92 ..... Jan. 20, 1992 263
SILVER CORD, THE—Sidney Howard .... 26–27 ..... Dec. 20, 1926 112
SILVER WHISTLE, THE—Robert E. McEnroe .... 48–49 ..... Nov. 24, 1948 219
SISTERS ROSENSWEIG, THE—Wendy Wasserstein .... 92–93 ..... Oct. 22, 1992 149
                                                                                 92–93 ..... Mar. 18, 1993 556
SIX CYLINDER LOVE—William Anthony McGuire .... 21–22 ..... Aug. 25, 1921 430
SIX DEGREES OF SEPARATION—John Guare .... 90–91 ..... June 14, 1990 155
                                                                                 90–91 ..... Nov. 8, 1990 485
6 RMS RIV VU—Bob Randall .... 72–73 ..... Oct. 17, 1972 247
SKIN GAME, THE—John Galsworthy .... 20–21 ..... Oct. 20, 1920 176
SKIN OF OUR TEETH, THE—Thornton Wilder .... 42–43 ..... Nov. 18, 1942 359
SKIPPER NEXT TO GOD—Jan de Hartog .... 47–48 ..... Jan. 4, 1948 93
SKRIKER, THE—Caryl Churchill .... 95–96 ..... May 12, 1996 17
SKYLARK—Samson Raphaelson .... 39–40 ..... Oct. 11, 1939 256
SKYLIGHT—David Hare .... 96–97 ..... Sept. 19, 1996 116
SLEUTH—Anthony Shaffer .... 70–71 ..... Nov. 12, 1970 1,222
SLOW DANCE ON THE KILLING GROUND—William Hanley .... 64–65 ..... Nov. 30, 1964 88

SLY FOX—Larry Gelbart, based on *Volpone* by Ben
    Jonson .... 76–77 ..... Dec. 14, 1976 495
SMALL CRAFT WARNINGS—Tennessee Williams .... 71–72 ..... Apr. 2, 1972 192
SOLDIER'S PLAY, A—Charles Fuller .... 81–82 ..... Nov. 20, 1981 468
SOLDIER'S WIFE—Rose Franken .... 44–45 ..... Oct. 4, 1944 253
SPEED-THE-PLOW—David Mamet .... 87–88 ..... May 3, 1988 278
SPIC-O-RAMA—John Leguizamo .... 92–93 ..... Oct. 27, 1992 86
SPLIT SECOND—Dennis McIntyre .... 84–85 ..... June 7, 1984 147
SQUAW MAN, THE—Edward Milton Royle .... 99–09 ..... Oct. 23, 1905 222
STAGE DOOR—George S. Kaufman, Edna Ferber .... 36–37 ..... Oct. 22, 1936 169
STAIRCASE—Charles Dyer .... 67–68 ..... Jan. 10, 1968 61
STAR-WAGON, THE—Maxwell Anderson .... 37–38 ..... Sept. 29, 1937 223
STATE OF THE UNION—Howard Lindsay, Russel Crouse .... 45–46 ..... Nov. 14, 1945 765
STEAMBATH—Bruce Jay Friedman .... 70–71 ..... June 30, 1970 128
STEEL MAGNOLIAS—Robert Harling .... 87–88 ..... June 19, 1987 1,126
STICKS AND BONES—David Rabe .... 71–72 ..... Nov. 7, 1971 121
                                                                         71–72 ..... Mar. 1, 1972 245
STONE AND STAR—Robert Ardrey .... 61–62 ..... Dec. 5, 1961 20
STONE COLD DEAD SERIOUS—Adam Rapp .... 02–03 ..... Apr. 7, 2003 35
STOP THE WORLD–I WANT TO GET OFF—(b, m, l) Leslie
    Bricusse, Anthony Newley .... 62–63 ..... Oct. 3, 1962 555
STORM OPERATION—Maxwell Anderson .... 43–44 ..... Jan. 11, 1944 23
STORY OF MARY SURRATT, THE—John Patrick .... 46–47 ..... Feb. 8, 1947 11
Strange Interlude—Eugene O'Neill .... 27–28 ..... Jan. 30, 1928 426
STREAMERS—David Rabe .... 75–76 ..... Apr. 21, 1976 478
STREET SCENE—Elmer Rice .... 28–29 ..... Jan. 10, 1929 601
STREETCAR NAMED DESIRE, A—Tennessee Williams .... 47–48 ..... Dec. 3, 1947 855
STRICTLY DISHONORABLE—Preston Sturges .... 29–30 ..... Sept. 18, 1929 557
SUBJECT WAS ROSES, THE—Frank D. Gilroy .... 64–65 ..... May 25, 1964 832
SUBSTANCE OF FIRE, THE—Jon Robin Baitz .... 90–91 ..... Mar. 17, 1991 120
SUBURBIA—Eric Bogosian .... 93–94 ..... May 22, 1994 113
SUGAR BABIES—(ad) Ralph G. Allen (special citation) .... 79–80 ..... Oct. 8, 1979 1,208
SUM OF US, THE—David Stevens .... 90–91 ..... Oct. 16, 1990 335
SUMMER OF THE 17TH DOLL—Ray Lawler .... 57–58 ..... Jan. 22, 1958 29
SUNDAY IN THE PARK WITH GEORGE—(b) James Lapine,
    (m, l) Stephen Sondheim .... 83–84 ..... May 2, 1984 604
SUNRISE AT CAMPOBELLO—Dore Schary .... 57–58 ..... Jan. 30, 1958 556
SUNSET BOULEVARD—(b, l) Don Black, Christopher
    Hampton, (m) Andrew Lloyd Webber, based
    on the film by Billy Wilder .... 94–95 ..... Nov. 17, 1994 977
SUNSHINE BOYS, THE—Neil Simon .... 72–73 ..... Dec. 20, 1972 538
SUN-UP—Lula Vollmer .... 22–23 ..... May 25, 1923 356
SUSAN AND GOD—Rachel Crothers .... 37–38 ..... Oct. 7, 1937 288
SWAN, THE—Ferenc Molnar, (tr) Melville Baker .... 23–24 ..... Oct. 23, 1923 255
SWEENEY TODD, THE DEMON BARBER OF FLEET STREET—
    (b) Hugh Wheeler, (m, l) Stephen Sondheim,
    based on a version of *Sweeney Todd*
    by Christopher Bond .... 78–79 ..... Mar. 1, 1979 557

Sweet Bird of Youth—Tennessee Williams .... 58–59 ..... Mar. 10, 1959 375

Table Manners—Alan Ayckbourn .... 75–76 ..... Dec. 7, 1975 76
Table Settings—James Lapine .... 79–80 ..... Jan. 14, 1980 264
Take a Giant Step—Louis Peterson .... 53–54 ..... Sept. 24, 1953 76
*Take Me Out—Richard Greenberg .... 02–03 ..... Sept. 5, 2002 94
                                                              02–03 ..... Feb. 27, 2003 108
Taking of Miss Janie, The—Ed Bullins .... 74–75 ..... May 4, 1975 42
*Talking Heads—Alan Bennett..................................... 02–03 ..... Apr. 6, 2003 63
Talley's Folly—Lanford Wilson .... 78–79 ..... May 1, 1979 44
                                                              79–80 ..... Feb. 20, 1980 277
Tarnish—Gilbert Emery .... 23–24 ..... Oct. 1, 1923 248
Taste of Honey, A—Shelagh Delaney .... 60–61 ..... Oct. 4, 1960 376
Tchin-Tchin—Sidney Michaels, based on François
     Billetdoux's play... 62–63 ..... Oct. 25, 1962 222
Tea and Sympathy—Robert Anderson .... 53–54 ..... Sept. 30, 1953 712
Teahouse of the August Moon, The—John Patrick,
     based on Vern Sneider's novel .... 53–54 ..... Oct. 15, 1953 1,027
Tenth Man, The—Paddy Chayefsky .... 59–60 ..... Nov. 5, 1959 623
That Championship Season—Jason Miller .... 71–72 ..... May 2, 1972 144
                                                              72–73 ..... Sept. 14, 1972 700
There Shall Be No Night—Robert E. Sherwood .... 39–40 ..... Apr. 29, 1940 181
They Knew What They Wanted—Sidney Howard .... 24–25 ..... Nov. 24, 1924 414
They Shall Not Die—John Wexley .... 33–34 ..... Feb. 21, 1934 62
Thousand Clowns, A—Herb Gardner .... 61–62 ..... Apr. 5, 1962 428
Three Postcards—(b) Craig Lucas,
     (m, l) Craig Carnelia .... 86–87 ..... May 14, 1987 22
Three Tall Women—Edward Albee .... 93–94 ..... Apr. 5, 1994 582
Threepenny Opera—(b, l) Bertolt Brecht, (m) Kurt
     Weill, (tr) Ralph Manheim, John Willett .... 75–76 ..... Mar. 1, 1976 307
Thurber Carnival, A—James Thurber .... 59–60 ..... Feb. 26, 1960 127
Tiger at the Gates—Jean Giraudoux's La Guerre de
     Troie n'Aura Pas Lieu, (tr) Christopher Fry .... 55–56 ..... Oct. 3, 1955 217
Time of the Cuckoo, The—Arthur Laurents .... 52–53 ..... Oct. 15, 1952 263
Time of Your Life, The—William Saroyan .... 39–40 ..... Oct. 25, 1939 185
Time Remembered—Jean Anouilh's Léocadia,
     (ad) Patricia Moyes .... 57–58 ..... Nov. 12, 1957 248
Tiny Alice—Edward Albee .... 64–65 ..... Dec. 29, 1964 167
Titanic—(b) Peter Stone, (m, l) Maury Yeston .... 96–97 ..... Apr. 23, 1997 804
Toilet, The—LeRoi Jones (a.k.a. Amiri Baraka) .... 64–65 ..... Dec. 16, 1964 151
Tomorrow and Tomorrow—Philip Barry .... 30–31 ..... Jan. 13, 1931 206
Tomorrow the World—James Gow, Arnaud d'Usseau ..... 42–43 ..... Apr. 14, 1943 500
Topdog/Underdog—Suzan-Lori Parks .... 01–02 ..... Jul. 26, 2001 45
                                                              01–02 ..... Apr. 7, 2002 144
Torch Song Trilogy—Harvey Fierstein (The
     International Stud, Fugue in a Nursery, Widows
     and Children First) .... 81–82 ..... Jan. 15, 1982 117
                                                              82–83 ..... June 10, 1982 1,222
Touch of the Poet, A—Eugene O'Neill .... 58–59 ..... Oct. 2, 1958 284

Tovarich—Jacques Deval, (tr) Robert E. Sherwood .... 36–37 ..... Oct. 15, 1936 356
Toys in the Attic—Lillian Hellman .... 59–60 ..... Feb. 25, 1960 556
Tracers—John DiFusco (c); Vincent Caristi, Richard
    Chaves, John DiFusco, Eric E. Emerson, Rick
    Gallavan, Merlin Marston, Harry Stephens with
    Sheldon Lettich .... 84–85 ..... Jan. 21, 1985 186
Tragedie de Carmen, La—(see La Tragédie de Carmen)
Translations—Brian Friel .... 80–81 ..... Apr. 7, 1981 48
Travesties—Tom Stoppard .... 75–76 ..... Oct. 30, 1975 155
Trelawny of the Wells—Arthur Wing Pinero .... 94–99 ..... Nov. 22, 1898 131
Trial of the Catonsville Nine, The—Daniel Berrigan,
    Saul Levitt .... 70–71 ..... Feb. 7, 1971 159
Tribute—Bernard Slade .... 77–78 ..... June 1, 1978 212
Tuna Christmas, A—Jaston Williams, Joe Sears,
    Ed Howard .... 94–95 ..... Dec. 15, 1994 20
Twilight: Los Angeles, 1992—Anna Deavere Smith .... 93–94 ..... Mar. 23, 1994 13
                                                                                                93–94 ..... Apr. 17, 1994 72
Two Blind Mice—Samuel Spewack .... 48–49 ..... Mar. 2, 1949 157
Two Trains Running—August Wilson .... 91–92 ..... Apr. 13, 1992 160

Unchastened Woman, The—Louis Kaufman Anspacher ..... 09–19 ..... Oct. 9, 1915 193
Uncle Harry—Thomas Job .... 41–42 ..... May 20, 1942 430
Under Milk Wood—Dylan Thomas .... 57–58 ..... Oct. 15, 1957 39
*Urinetown—(b) Greg Kotis, (m) Mark Hollmann,
    (l) Greg Kotis, Mark Hollmann .... 00–01 ..... May 6, 2001 58
                                                                                                01–02 ..... Sept. 20, 2001 700

Valley Forge—Maxwell Anderson .... 34–35 ..... Dec. 10, 1934 58
Valley Song—Athol Fugard .... 95–96 ..... Dec. 12, 1995 96
Venus Observed—Christopher Fry .... 51–52 ..... Feb. 13, 1952 86
Very Special Baby, A—Robert Alan Aurthur .... 56–57 ..... Nov. 14, 1956 5
Victoria Regina—Laurence Housman .... 35–36 ..... Dec. 26, 1935 517
View From the Bridge, A—Arthur Miller .... 55–56 ..... Sept. 29, 1955 149
Violet—(b,l) Brian Crawley, (m) Jeanine Tesori,
    based on The Ugliest Pilgrim by Doris Betts .... 96–97 ..... Mar. 11, 1997 32
Visit, The—Friedrich Dürrenmatt, (ad) Maurice
    Valency .... 57–58 ..... May 5, 1958 189
Visit to a Small Planet—Gore Vidal .... 56–57 ..... Feb. 7, 1957 388
Vivat! Vivat Regina!—Robert Bolt .... 71–72 ..... Jan. 20, 1972 116
Voice of the Turtle, The—John van Druten .... 43–44 ..... Dec. 8, 1943 1,557

Wager, The—Mark Medoff .... 74–75 ..... Oct. 21, 1974 104
Waiting for Godot—Samuel Beckett .... 55–56 ..... Apr. 19, 1956 59
Walk in the Woods, A—Lee Blessing .... 87–88 ..... Feb. 28, 1988 136
Waltz of the Toreadors, The—Jean Anouilh,
    (tr) Lucienne Hill .... 56–57 ..... Jan. 17, 1957 132
Watch on the Rhine—Lillian Hellman .... 40–41 ..... Apr. 1, 1941 378
We, the People—Elmer Rice .... 32–33 ..... Jan. 21, 1933 49

WEDDING BELLS—Salisbury Field .... 19–20 ..... Nov. 12, 1919 168
WEDNESDAY'S CHILD—Leopold Atlas .... 33–34 ..... Jan. 16, 1934 56
WENCESLAS SQUARE—Larry Shue .... 87–88 ..... Mar. 2, 1988 55
WHAT A LIFE—Clifford Goldsmith .... 37–38 ..... Apr. 13, 1938 538
WHAT PRICE GLORY—Maxwell Anderson,
   Laurence Stallings .... 24–25 ..... Sept. 3, 1924 433
WHAT THE BUTLER SAW—Joe Orton .... 69–70 ..... May 4, 1970 224
WHEN LADIES MEET—Rachel Crothers .... 32–33 ..... Oct. 6, 1932 191
WHEN YOU COMIN' BACK, RED RYDER?—Mark Medoff .... 73–74 ..... Dec. 6, 1973 302
WHERE HAS TOMMY FLOWERS GONE?—Terrence McNally .... 71–72 ..... Oct. 7, 1971 78
WHITE HOUSE MURDER CASE, THE—Jules Feiffer .... 69–70 ..... Feb. 18, 1970 119
WHITE STEED, THE—Paul Vincent Carroll .... 38–39 ..... Jan. 10, 1939 136
WHO'S AFRAID OF VIRGINIA WOOLF?—Edward Albee .... 62–63 ..... Oct. 13, 1962 664
WHO'S TOMMY, THE—(b) Pete Townshend, Des
   McAnuff, (m, l) Pete Townshend, (add'l m, l)
   John Entwistle, Keith Moon (special citation) .... 92–93 ..... Apr. 22, 1993 900
WHOSE LIFE IS IT ANYWAY?—Brian Clark .... 78–79 ..... Apr. 17, 1979 223
WHY MARRY?—Jesse Lynch Williams .... 09–19 ..... Dec. 25, 1917 120
WHY NOT?—Jesse Lynch Williams .... 22–23 ..... Dec. 25, 1922 120
WIDOW CLAIRE, THE—Horton Foote .... 86–87 ..... Dec. 17, 1986 150
WILD BIRDS—Dan Totheroh .... 24–25 ..... Apr. 9, 1925 44
WILD HONEY—Michael Frayn, from an untitled play
   by Anton Chekhov .... 86–87 ..... Dec. 18, 1986 28
WINGED VICTORY—Moss Hart, (m) David Rose .... 43–44 ..... Nov. 20, 1943 212
WINGS—Arthur L. Kopit .... 78–79 ..... June 21, 1978 15
                                                                          78–79 ..... Jan. 28, 1979 113
WINGS—(b, l) Arthur Perlman, (m) Jeffrey Lunden,
   based on the play by Arthur L. Kopit .... 92–93 ..... Mar. 9, 1993 47
WINGS OVER EUROPE—Robert Nichols, Maurice Browne .... 28–29 ..... Dec. 10, 1928 90
WINSLOW BOY, THE—Terence Rattigan .... 47–48 ..... Oct. 29, 1947 215
WINTER SOLDIERS—Daniel Lewis James .... 42–43 ..... Nov. 29, 1942 25
WINTERSET—Maxwell Anderson .... 35–36 ..... Sept. 25, 1935 195
WISDOM TOOTH, THE—Marc Connelly .... 25–26 ..... Feb. 15, 1926 160
WISTERIA TREES, THE—Joshua Logan, based on Anton
   Chekhov's The Cherry Orchard .... 49–50 ..... Mar. 29, 1950 165
WIT—Margaret Edson .... 98–99 ..... Oct. 6, 1998 545
WITCHING HOUR, THE—Augustus Thomas .... 99–09 ..... Nov. 18, 1907 212
WITNESS FOR THE PROSECUTION—Agatha Christie .... 54–55 ..... Dec. 16, 1954 645
WOMEN, THE—Clare Boothe .... 36–37 ..... Dec. 26, 1936 657
WONDERFUL TOWN—(b) Joseph Fields, Jerome
   Chodorov, based on their play My Sister Eileen
   and Ruth McKenney's stories, (l) Betty Comden,
   Adolph Green, (m) Leonard Bernstein .... 52–53 ..... Feb. 25, 1953 559
WORLD WE MAKE, THE—Sidney Kingsley, based on
   Millen Brand's novel The Outward Room .... 39–40 ..... Nov. 20, 1939 80

YEARS AGO—Ruth Gordon .... 46–47 ..... Dec. 3, 1946 206

YELLOWMAN—Dael Orlandersmith .... 02–03 ..... Oct. 22, 2002 64

YES, MY DARLING DAUGHTER—Mark Reed .... 36–37 ..... Feb. 9, 1937 405

YOU AND I—Philip Barry .... 22–23 ..... Feb. 19, 1923 178

YOU CAN'T TAKE IT WITH YOU—Moss Hart,
    George S. Kaufman .... 36–37 ..... Dec. 14, 1936 837

YOU KNOW I CAN'T HEAR YOU WHEN THE WATER'S
    RUNNING—Robert Anderson .... 66–67 ..... Mar. 13, 1967 755

YOUNG MAN FROM ATLANTA, THE—Horton Foote .... 94–95 ..... Jan. 27, 1995 24

YOUNG WOODLEY—John van Druten .... 25–26 ..... Nov. 2, 1925 260

YOUNGEST, THE—Philip Barry .... 24–25 ..... Dec. 22, 1924 104

YOUR OWN THING—(b) Donald Driver, (m, l) Hal
    Hester and Danny Apolinar, suggested by William
    Shakespeare's *Twelfth Night* .... 67–68 ..... Jan. 13, 1968 933

YOU'RE A GOOD MAN CHARLIE BROWN—(b, m, l) Clark
    Gesner, based on the comic strip *Peanuts*
    by Charles M. Schulz .... 66–67 ..... Mar. 7, 1967 1,597

ZOOMAN AND THE SIGN—Charles Fuller .... 80–81 ..... Dec. 7, 1980 33

CONTRIBUTORS TO *BEST PLAYS*

○ ○ ○ ○ ○

Rue E. Canvin worked at the *New York Herald Tribune,* first as a secretary in the advertising department and then as an editorial assistant in the drama department for 15 years where she worked with the editors and the arts critics until the demise of the newspaper in 1966. She also worked at the *World Journal Tribune* until it closed the following year. Canvin has served as an assistant editor of the *Best Plays* series since 1963. She has also transcribed taped interviews for the Dramatists Guild and Authors League.

Tish Dace, Chancellor Professor Emerita at the University of Massachusetts Dartmouth and winner of its 1997 Scholar of the Year Award, has published several books, thousands of play reviews, and more than 200 essays, articles and book chapters. She chaired the American Theatre Wing's Henry Hewes Design Awards—earlier known as the Maharam Awards and as the American Theatre Wing Design Awards—for nearly 20 years. Dace served six years as a member of the executive committee of the American Theatre Critics Association, and still serves on the executive committee of the International Association of Theatre Critics. She has been a theater critic for nearly 30 years and the New York critic for *Plays International* since 1986. She has published in such periodicals as the *New York Times,* the *Times* of London, *New York,* the *Village Voice* and *American Theatre.*

Jennifer de Poyen is a theater critic for the *San Diego Union-Tribune.* She also serves as vice president of the San Diego Theatre Critics' Circle, which in 2002 established the Craig Noel Awards for Excellence in the Theatre in honor of the founding father of San Diego theater and to honor the work of San Diego's diverse theatrical community. A former fellow in the National Arts Journalism Program at Columbia University, she is a regular contributor to *Full Focus,* a public television program on the arts.

Christine Dolen has been the *Miami Herald's* theater critic since 1979. She holds bachelor's and master's degrees in journalism from Ohio State University and was a John S. Knight Journalism Fellow at Stanford University in 1984–85. In 1997, she was a member of the Pulitzer Prize drama jury; in 1999, she was a senior fellow in the National Arts Journalism Program at Columbia University. Currently, she is on the advisory council of the American Theatre Critics Association. Before becoming the *Herald's* theater critic, she was arts editor and pop music critic. Her awards include the Green Eyeshade in criticism from the Atlanta Chapter of the Society of Professional Journalists and first place in arts writing in the Missouri Lifestyle Journalism Awards. Dolen received the George Abbott Award for Outstanding Achievement in the Arts at the 2001 Carbonell Awards.

Mel Gussow, a cultural writer for the *New York Times,* is the author of the biography, *Edward Albee: A Singular Journey,* and of *Conversations with Miller,* as well as books about Harold Pinter, Tom Stoppard and Samuel Beckett. He has also written *Theater on the Edge: New Visions, New Voices,* a collection of theater reviews and essays, and was co-editor of the Library of America's two volume edition of the plays of Tennessee Williams. In 2002, he was awarded the Margo Jones Medal and, in previous years, the George Jean Nathan Award for Dramatic Criticism and a Guggenheim Fellowship.

Paul Hardt of Stuart Howard Associates works in casting for theatre, television and film. His casting credits include the national tours of *The Who's Tommy*, *Leader of the Pack* and *Game Show*. Stuart Howard Associates currently works with *Fame on 42nd Street*, *Sly Fox* and the upcoming 50th anniversary production of *West Side Story*.

Claudia W. Harris received her PhD in Irish Studies and Dramatic Literature from Emory University in Atlanta, Georgia, and has been a member of English faculty at Brigham Young University since 1990. Her undergraduate degree in English and Theatre is from the University of Minnesota; her Master's degrees in English, and in Counseling and Psychological Services are from Georgia State University. As an academic, freelance journalist and theater critic, she has developed over the years an abiding interest in Ireland, which takes her there several times every year. As co-chair of the International Committee of the American Theatre Critics Association, she is able to see and write about theater from around the world. She is a correspondent and theater critic for the *Salt Lake Tribune*, and is Utah correspondent for *Back Stage*.

Alec Harvey is features editor and theater critic for the *Birmingham News* in Alabama, as well as editor of *Critics Quarterly*, the American Theatre Critics Association's quarterly newsletter. For the past three years, he served as chair of ATCA's New Play Awards committee, which administers the ATCA/Steinberg New Play Award, given to the best new American play presented outside of New York, and the M. Elizabeth Osborn Award, given to an emerging playwright. He is also active with the American Association of Sunday and Feature Editors. He lives in Birmingham.

Charles Isherwood is the chief theater critic of *Variety*. He has been with the publication for 10 years, working as an editor and critic in both the Los Angeles and New York offices. He also writes regularly about theater for the *Times* of London and serves as president of the New York Drama Critics' Circle.

John Istel has been an arts journalist for the last 15 years, contributing to such publications as *The Atlantic, Elle, American Theatre,* and the *Village Voice*. He has worked as an editor for *Stagebill*, Billboard/Back Stage Books, and *American Theatre*. He has taught at City University of New York and New York University, and has contributed to many reference works, including *Contemporary Playwrights*, the *Reference Guide to American Literature*, and the last two volumes of *Best Plays*. In 2002, he founded ICAP (Istel Creative Arts Publishing), which provides consulting, editorial and writing services to such arts institutions as Carnegie Hall, Lincoln Center, and Roundabout Theatre Company.

Jeffrey Eric Jenkins is the sixth editor of the *Best Plays* series founded by drama critic Burns Mantle in 1920. He has served as theater critic, contributor and editor for a variety of newspapers, magazines and journals. Since 1998, he has been a faculty member in the Drama Department at New York University's Tisch School of the Arts, where he has taught theater studies—with an emphasis in United States drama and theater. Jenkins has also taught at Carnegie Mellon University, the University of Washington, and SUNY–Stony Brook. He received degrees in drama and theater arts from Carnegie Mellon University and San Francisco State University, and he has directed more than two dozen productions in professional and educational theaters across the United States. Jenkins is a former board member of the American Theatre Critics Association (1995–2001) and served as the association's chairman from 1999 to 2001. He chairs the American Theatre Wing's Henry Hewes Design Awards, and is a board member of the American Theatre and Drama Society and the Theater Hall of Fame. Jenkins serves on the advisory committees of the American Theatre Wing and the William Inge Theatre Festival.

Vivian Cary Jenkins spent more than twenty years as a healthcare administrator and now teaches aspiring administrators at the graduate and undergraduate levels.

Prior to her work in healthcare, she was a dancer and a Peace Corps volunteer in Honduras.

Robert Kamp is the owner I Can Do That Productions, Inc., a graphic design company in New York City. Prior to starting his own business, Bob worked for several arts and entertainment publications including *Stagebill* and *City Guide Magazine*. Bob designed the *Best Plays* logo, and has worked on the book's photos and graphic images since the 2000–2001 edition.

Julius Novick served for several decades as a theater critic at the *Village Voice*. He has also written for the *New York Times*, the *Los Angeles Times*, the *New York Observer*, *The Nation*, *American Theatre* and many other publications. He is the author of *Beyond Broadway: The Quest for Permanent Theatres*. A winner of the George Jean Nathan Award for Dramatic Criticism, he has served twice on the drama jury for the Pulitzer Prize. Now Emeritus Professor of Drama Studies at Purchase College, SUNY, he is working on a book-length study of how Jewish life in America has been reflected in mainstream American theater.

Christopher Rawson has been since 1983 drama critic and (more recently) drama editor of the *Pittsburgh Post-Gazette*. Along with local reviews, features, news and columns, he also reviews regularly in New York and London. His love of theater is partly inherited from his father, actor Richard Hart, but he started professional life in 1968 in the English Department at the University of Pittsburgh, where he still teaches Shakespeare, critical writing and satire. His BA is from Harvard and his MA and PhD from the University of Washington. A former chairman of the American Theatre Critics Association, he is a member of the executive committee of the Theater Hall of Fame, managing the selection process with Henry Hewes.

Jeffrey Sweet's books include *Something Wonderful Right Away* (about Second City), *The Dramatist's Toolkit* and *Solving Your Script*. A resident writer of Chicago's Tony Award-winning Victory Gardens Theater, his plays include two that have been honored by the American Theatre Critics Association with New Play Citations: *American Enterprise* and *The Action Against Sol Schumann*. Other plays include *Porch*, *The Value of Names*, *Flyovers*, *Bluff* and the musical *I Sent a Letter to My Love* (written with composer Melissa Manchester). He currently teaches playwriting at Purchase College, SUNY and serves on the council of the Dramatists Guild.

Michele Volansky is in her fourth season as dramaturg for Philadelphia Theatre Company. She has guest dramaturged at South Coast Repertory, the Atlantic Theater Company, Victory Gardens Theater and Next Theatre, in addition to her work as a staff dramaturg at Actors Theatre of Louisville (1992–95) and Steppenwolf Theatre Company (1995–2000). She is the 1999 inaugural recipient of the Elliot Hayes Award for Dramaturgy and is the president of LMDA, the Literary Managers and Dramaturgs of the Americas. Volansky is a member of the advisory board for *Theatre Forum* magazine, has served as an artistic consultant for the TCG playwright residency program and as a reader for the Eugene O'Neill Theater Center's National Playwrights Conference. She is a Lecturer in Drama at Washington College, in Maryland, where she earned a BA in English. She also holds an MA in theater from Villanova University.

Charles Wright lives in New York City and writes about books and theater for a variety of publications. A native of East Tennessee, he holds degrees from Vanderbilt University, Oxford University and the University of Pennsylvania. During the past nine years, as a business affairs executive at A&E Television Networks, he has been involved in commissioning and production of hundreds of hours of documentary programming including *The Farm: Angola, USA*, which received the 1998 Grand Jury Prize at Sundance and was nominated for an Academy Award as best documentary feature the following year.

Index

Titles in bold are play titles.
Page numbers in italic indicate essay citations.
Page numbers in bold italic indicate Broadway and Off Broadway listings.
Nouns or numbers in parentheses delineate different persons.

A&E Television Networks 423
Aaron, Joyce 261
Aaron, Randy 260
Aarone, Donnell 179
Aaronville Dawning 299
Abadie, William 270
Abbamonte, Antoinette
 324, 325
Abbey Theatre 22, 149
Abbott, George
 9, 134, 135, 380, 421
ABC Television 25
Abdala, Enrique 145
Abercrumbie, Tyla 327
Abingdon Theatre Company
 258
Abortion 102
Abraham, F. Murray 206
Abraham, Jolly 314
Abramovitz, Jill 339
Abrams, Arthur 256
Abrams, Marilyn 342
Abrams, Richarda 263
Abrons, Richard 254
Abston, Melvin 224
Abtahi, Omid 302
Acadine, Sophie 273
Access Theater 258
Accidental Activist, The 262
Accidental Nostalgia 248
Acebo, Christopher 307
Acevedo, Dacyl 265
Acheson, Dana Powers 266
Acheson, Matthew 264
Acito, Tim 30, 202, 243, 316
Ackerman, Joan 260
Ackroyd, David 261
Acme Sound Partners
 136, 146, 164, 173,
 175, 176, 377
Across the Way 278
Act of Contrition 259
ACT Theatre 189, 203, 351
Acting Company, The 258
**Action Against Sol
 Schumann, The**
 375, 423
Actors Company Theatre
 (TACT), The 259

Actors' Equity 5, 6, 299
Actors Equity Association 376
Actor's Playground Theatre,
 The 259
Actors Playhouse (NYC) 259
Actors Playhouse, The
 (Florida) 380
Actors Studio 23, 163, 241
Actors Theatre of Louisville
 277, 329, 423
Acuña, Art 266, 377
Adair, Arthur Maximillian
 249, 250
Adams, Candi
 144, 150, 178, 192, 214
Adams, D 307, 308
Adams, J. Todd 311
Adams, J.B. 216
Adams, Kevin
 154, 177, 200, 258
Adams, Lee 335
Adams, Patreshettarlini
 348, 349
Adams, Paul 261
Adams, Randy 311
Adams, Richard Todd
 227, 269
Adams, Sarah 145
Adams, Ty 261
Adamson, Eve 264
Addai-Robinson, Cynthia
 342
Adderley, Konrad 198
Addictions 262
Adelson, Matthew E. 315
Aderer, Konrad 264
Adilifu, Kamau 212
Adilman, Marci 175
Adjan, Irene 380
Adjmi, David 353
Adkins, David 301, 314
Adkins, Guy 323, 324, 379
Adkins, Keith Josef 300, 331
Adler, Jay 159, 174
Adler, Jerry 314
Adler, Joanna P. 253, 314
Adler, Steven 303
Adler, Sue 145
Adopt a Sailor 271, 272

Adult Entertainment
 14, 28, **192**
**Adventures While
 Preaching the Gospel
 of Beauty** 318
Adwin, Elisabeth 341
Adyanthaya, Aravind Enrique
 248
Adzima, Nanzi 342
Aeschylus 270
Affannato, Rich 223
Afro-Bradley, Henry 266
After 271
After Marseilles/Ikamva
 313
Agee, Martin 160
Agnes, M. 220
Agnew, Sarah 338
Aguilar, Ruth 268
Agy, Emily 342
Aharanwa, Maechi 261
Ahearn, Dan 273
Ahlin, John 342
Ahlstedt, Borje 171
Ahnquist, Jordan 263
Ahrens, Lynn
 36, 183, 270, 376
Ai, Angela 263
Aibel, Douglas 256
Aida 7, **128**, 215, 379, 380
Aidem, Betsy 98, 99, 261
Aiello, Danny 192
Ain't Misbehavin' 35, 378
Air Raid 267
Airaldi, Remo 334
Aizawa, Akiko 334
Akalaitis, JoAnne
 234, 236, 237, 323
Akashi, Yoko 264
Akerlind, Christopher
 256, 305, 334
Akesson, Hans 171
Alabama Shakespeare Festival
 173, 299
Alagic, Tea 268
Alai, Dean 262
Albach, Carl 145
Albee, Edward 36, 128, 173,
 237, 241, 312, 350, 355

Alberto, Henry 260
Albom, Mitch 28, 189
Albrecht, Timothy 185
Alcaraz, Robert 307
Alchemists, The 269
Alcorn, Narda 326
Alder, Jac 350
Aldousary, Mary 327
Aldredge, Karen 326
Aldridge, Heather 259
Aldridge, Tamela 261
Alers, Karmine 228
Alex, Timothy J. 143, 144
Alexander, Adinah 156
Alexander, Cheryl 179
Alexander, James 378
Alexander, Jane 303
Alexander, Jason 227
Alexander, Jessica 264
Alexander, Jill 163
Alexander, Julie 250
Alexander, Kevin 265
Alexander, Khandi 219
Alexander, Musashi 154
Alexander, Neil 155
Alexander, Ramona 336
Alexander, Roslyn 327
Alexander, Zakiyyah 253
Alexandra's Web 269
Alfieri, Richard 321
Alhadeff, Mark 267, 343
Ali, Hisham 300
Ali, Muhammad 95
Alice in Ireland 339
Alice in Wonderland 240
Alifante, Nicole 262
Alioto, Alexander 259
Alkalae, Nina 188
All Over 14, 36, *173–174*, 174, 377
All the World's a Stage 266
Alladin, Opal 317
Allaf, Annas 305
Allagree, Andrew 139
Allen, Billie 322
Allen, Chad 188
Allen, Claudia 328
Allen, Debbie 303
Allen, Douglas 250
Allen, Gracie 24
Allen, Henry 338
Allen, Janet 328, 329
Allen, Joe 185
Allen, Lewis 129
Allen, Morgan 253
Allen, Peter 193
Allen, Philip G. 321
Allen, Richard 299

Allen, Sandra 16, 136
Allen, Scott 198
Allen, Thomas Michael 185
Allen, Woody 35, 213
Allers, Roger 127
Alley, Lindsey 141
Alley Theatre 170, 349
Allgood, Anne 75, 149, 150, 206, 308
Alliance Theatre Company 322
Allied Theatre Group 350
Allin, Jeff 311
Allison, Dorothy 32, 211
Allosso, Michael 335
Alltop, Michael 245, 266
Allyn, David 268
Allyn, Wendy 261
Alma and Mrs. Woolf 260
Almedilla, Joan 223
Almeida, Fabrizio 327
Almon, John Paul 321, 380
Almos, Carolyn 267
Almos, Matt 267
Almost Blue 259
Almost Full Circle at the Guggenheim 260
Almost Grown Up 264
Almost Live From the Betty Ford Clinic 263
Aloha Flight 243 264
Alper, Linda 343
Alpert, Herb 176
Alsford, Eric 380
Alter, Eric 261
Altered Stages 259
Alterman, Glenn 260
Altman, Chelsea 192
Altman, Jane 261, 267
Altman, Jason 268
Altman, Peter 339
Altman, Sean 256
Altmeyer, Timothy 163
Altomare, Lisa 263
Alvarez, Charin 327
Alvarez, Gabriel Enrique 198
Alvarez, Lynne 255
Alvin, Farah 166
Amaral, Bob 224
Amas Musical Theatre 30, 179, 180, 202, 243
Ambassador Theatre Group Ltd. 154, 370
Ambrose, Lauren 311
Ambrosone, John 319
American Association of Sunday and Feature Editors 422

American Conservatory Theater 300, 355
American Daughter, An 319
American Dreams: Lost and Found 258
American Enterprise 423
American Federation of Musicians 5
American Globe Theatre 259
American Ma(u)l 263
American Magic 259
American Menu 254
American Place Theatre 119, 130
American Repertory Theatre 190, 334, 378
American Theatre 106, 421, 422, 423
American Theatre and Drama Society 422
American Theatre Critics Association x, xii, 41, 173, 277, 278, 421, 422, 423
American Theatre Critics/ Steinberg New Play Award xii, xiii, xvi, 277
American Theatre Critics/ Steinberg New Play Citation xii
American Theatre of Actors, The 259
American Theatre Wing 421, 422
Ames, Jonathan 255
Ami, Shoshana 273
Amieva, Sophie 249
Amkpa, Awam xiv
Amory, Kate Kohler 263
Amour 4, 16, 137, *138*, 367, 370, 371
Amphitryon 135
Amram, Adira 260
Anania, Michael 320
Anastassakis, Yiannis 188
Ancheta, Susan 136
Anderman, Maureen 369
Anders, Andrea 221
Anders, Mark 351, 352
Anders, Wynne 261, 267
Anderson, Arwen 301
Anderson, Carl 229
Anderson, Christian 230
Anderson, David Alan 329
Anderson, Dennis 146, 164
Anderson, Dion 308

Anderson, Frank 263
Anderson, Lawrence 227
Anderson, Maxwell
    (playwright) 171
Anderson, Maxwell L. (actor)
    265
Anderson, Michael 264
Anderson, Nancy 180, 317
Anderson, Nathan 352, 353
Anderson, Paul 186
Anderson, Russ 268
Anderson, Stephen Lee 158
Anderson, Stig 128
Andersson, Benny 128
Andino, Paola 349
Andos, Randy 149, 160
Andreano, Liliana 263
Andres, Barbara
    218, 265, 335
Andres, Ryan 145
Andress, Carl 245
Andress, Rosemary K. 269
Andrews, Dwight 153, 326
Andrews, Marnie 261
Andric, Ivo 249
Andrisevic, Beth 352
Anduss, Mark K. 378
Angel, Criss 170
Angela, Sharon 265
Angels in America 77, 105
Anglim, Diane 350
Anna Christie 270
Anna in the Tropics xii,
    xvi, 248, 277, *279–286*,
    280, 283, 311, 320,
    375, 380
Anna Karenina
    280, 282, 283, 285
Annals of the New York Stage
    ix
Annie Wright Seminary 71
Anonymous Remailers 272
Anouilh, Jean 259
Anschutz, Sue 166
Antalosky, Charles 348
**Anthems: Culture Clash in
    the District** 317
Anthony, Eric 132, 133
Anthony, Stephen G.
    205, 266
Antigone
    14, 36, *188*, 262, 328
Antigone's Red 271
Antonia, Kathleen 301
Antonio, Jose 269
Antonio, Mervin P. 354
Antunovich, Lynn 269
Anything's Dream 263

Anzalone, Frank 348
Apfel, Wesley 260
Apollo Theater 30, 31, 37,
    176
Aponte, Justin 256
Appel, Libby 343
Appel, Peter 262
Appelt, Joseph 355
Appino, Nikki 353
Apple 266
Applegate, Fred 227
Appleyard, Russ 302
Aquila Theatre Company
    36, 174
Aquino, Amy 306, 307, 311
Aquino, Jessica 260
Arabian, Michael 315
Araca Group, The
    131, 187, 370
Aranas, Raul 136
Arand, Christine 145, 146
Arber, Gyda 260
Arbuckle, Sean 222, 259
Arcelus, Sebastian 228
Arcenas, Loy
    183, 203, 266, 349, 377
Archer, Julie 233, 251
Archer, Nicholas 319
Arclight Theatre 259
Ard, Charles 339
Arden Theatre Company 345
Arditti, Paul 188, 193, 195
Arena, Danny 157, 370
Arena Players Repertory
    Company 341
Arena Stage 41, 317
Argila, Steven 316
Argument, The 248, 252
Arhelger, Joan 302
Ari, Robert 180, 348
Ariadne's Thread 327
Arias, Joey 269
Arisco, David 380
Arizona Theatre Company
    354
Arkansas Repertory Theatre
    300
Arkin, Adam 311
Arkin, Anthony 130
Arko, Brenda 180
Arlen, Harold 196
Armand, Pascale 314, 329
Armit, Jason 322
Armoroso, Amorika M. 269
Armour, Annabel 328
Armstrong, Karen 151
Armstrong, Mark 264
Armstrong, William 252, 347

Arnaz, Lucie 321
Arney, Randall 302, 303, 327
Arnold, David A. 188
Arnold, Joseph 261
Arnone, John 303, 353
Arnov, Michael 270
Aronow, Scott 196
Aronowitz, Sonya 346
Aronson, Billie 246
Aronson, Frances 258
Aronson, Frank 335
Aronson, Letty 213
**Around the World in 80
    Days** 379, 380
Arrangements 318
Arredondo, Rosa Evangelina
    176
Arrington, Amy Jo 226
Arrington, Kate 309, 327
Arrow, David 301
Arruda, Chris 263
Ars Nova Theater 259
Art 12
**Art, Life and Show Biz: A
    Non-Fiction Play** 235
Art Versus Life 300
Artaud, Antonin 240
Artificial Intelligence 169
Arturo Ui 187
Artzberger, Ryan 329
Arvanitis, Nikos 188
Arvin, Mark 138
**As Long As We Both Shall
    Laugh** 4, 25, *159*
As You Like It
    14, 34, *210*, 273, 379
Asbury, Donna Marie 219
Ascending Lulu 254
Aschenbrenner, Eric 265
Ascher, James 271
Ash, Kathryn 252
Ashcroft, John 49
Ashford, Rob 135, 335
Ashkenasi, Danny 250
Ashley, Christopher 319, 378
Ashley, Elizabeth 12, 163
Ashley, Freddie 322
Ashley, Ryan 229
Ashman, Howard 127
Ashmanskas, Brooks 164
Ashworth, Chris 332
Askew, Jamie 332
Askin, Peter 272
Aspel, Brad 216
Aspen Group 133
Aspenlieder, Elizabeth
    336, 337
Asprey, Jason 263, 337

Assadourian, Joseph 248
Associated Press, The
    11, 20, 21, 367
Astaire Award 376
Astaire, Fred 193
Astronaut, The 315
At a Plank Bridge 256
ATCA/Steinberg New Play
    Award 277,
    279, 287, 320, 374, 422
ATCA/Steinberg New Play
    Citation
    277, 279, 293, 319, 338
Atherlay, John M. 182
Atkins, Joshua 355
Atkins, Lois 327
Atkinson, Jayne 12, 21, 141,
    163, 371, 377
Atkinson, Kristin 250
Atlantic, Dena 314
Atlantic, The 422
Atlantic Theater Company
    27, 35, 52, 190,
    196, 213, 244, 423
Atlas, Ravil 206
Attias, Michaël 268
**Attractive Women on the
    Train, The** 273
ATV Music Publishing LLC
    205
Auberjonois, René 146
Auble, Larissa 340
Auburn, David 128, 329
AuCoin, Kelly 260, 263
August, Bille 267
August, Curtis 334
August, Ian 250
August, Pernilla 171
Augustin, Julio 270
Augustine, Jim 335
Aujla, Ravi 204
Aukin, Daniel 255, 256
Aulino, Tom 216
Aunt Pitti-Pat in the Tower
    271
Auntie Mayhem 260
Aural Fixation 151
Aurora Theatre Company 301
Auster, Paul 238
Austin, Gary 266
Austin, Jennifer 304
Austin, Velma 328
Austin-Williams, Jaye 272
**Autobiography of God as
    Told by Mel
    Schneider, The** 268
Autograph 157

Avenue Q viii, 237, 258,
    314, 367, 373
Avery, Alicia 262
Avey, Adrianne 305
Avila, Christine 305
Avila, John 307
Awake and Sing 379, 380
Awata, Urara 250
Axelrod, Janet A. 136
Axen, Eric 269
Ayckbourn, Alan 171
Ayles, Chris 301
Aymé, Marcel 138
Azenberg, Emanuel
    138, 144, 370, 371
Azurdia, Ivonne 380
Azurdia, Richard 307

Babad, Herman 266
Babak, Cynthia 258
Babatunde, Obba 219
Babb, Zakia 250
Babe, Thomas 255
Babson, Leila 196
Bacalzo, Dan 259
Bach, Sebastian 229
Bacharach, Burt 27, 166
Back, Maribeth 304
Back Stage
    239, 278, 367, 422
**Backsliding in the
    Promised Land** 342
Bacon, Jenny 317, 323
Bacon, Mary
    252, 259, 262, 354
Bacon, Roy 266
Bad Bugs Bite 249
Bad Women 264
Baden, Leslie 176, 205, 207
Bader, Jenny Lyn 267
Badgen, Ron 260
Badger, Mary 328
Badgett, Will 249, 264
Bae, Terrence 268
Baeta, Virginia 262
Baeumler, Carolyn
    254, 271, 272, 314, 343
Bag of Marbles 252
Bagden, Ron 216
Bageot, Karine 138, 139
Bagert, Darren 167, 370
Baibussynova, Ulzhan 334
Baik, Young Ju 317
Bailegangaire 247, 367

Bailey, Bill 31, 188
Bailey, Christopher Eaton 206
Bailey, Christopher J. 255
Bailey, D'Vorah 307
Bailey, Erika 266
Bailey, Kate 332
Bain, Regina Hilliard 308
Baiocchi, Frank 222
Baird, Mary 302
Baisch, Maggie 154
Baity, Linda Sullivan 311
Baitz, Jon Robin 307
Baker, Ali 301
Baker, Becky Ann 245
Baker, Daniel 328
Baker, Darrin 222
Baker, David Aaron 303
Baker, Edward Allan
    264, 269
Baker, Elna 250
Baker, Jim 355
Baker, Lance Stuart
    323, 324, 327
Baker, Max 254
Baker, Rich 380
Baker, Sarah 258
Baker, Simon 157
Baker, Travis 267
Baksic, Amela 173, 355
Bakunas, Steve 140, 141
Balaban, Bob 38, 184, 185
Baldassari, Mike 159
Baldauff, Julie 157
Balderrama, Michael
    155, 320
Baldini, Gabriella 170
Baldinu, Pichon 170
Baldoni, Gail 180
Baldwin, Alec 271
Baldwin, Christina 338, 339
Baldwin, Craig 175
Ball, Erica 262
Ball Four 106
Ball, Jessica 263
Ball, Stephen D. 336
Ballad of Billy K., The 314
**Ballad of John Wesley Reed,
    The** 346
Ballard, Inga 342
Ballard, Kaye 335
Ballard, Laurence 355
Ballard, Patrick 316
Balm in Gilead 44
Balugay, Myla 302
Balzer, Julie Fei-Fan 269
Bamman, Gerry 254
Banda, A. Raymond 263

Banderas, Antonio
    19, 160, 371, 376, 377
Bandhu, Pun 264
Banes, Lisa 347
Bang! 268
Bange, Christopher 355
Bank, Jonathan 251, 252
Bank Street Theatre 259
Bankerd, Lance 263
Banks, Ronald M. 323
Bannister-Colón, Laurie 265
Baptizing Adam 268
Baquerot, Aliane 139
Bar, Hadas Gil 250
Barall, Michi 267, 271, 303
Baranski, Christine 378
Baratta, Maria 262
Barbanell, Ari 265
Barber, Matthew
    12, 163, 370, 377
Barber, Tatianna 303
Barberry, Jess 263
Barbette 350
Barbour, James 216
Barbour, Thomas 270
Barboussi, Vasso 188
Barbra's Wedding
    14, 28, *198*, 199, 347
Barchiesi, Franca 262
Barcy, Lisa 380
Barden, Alice 258
Bardwell, Gina 271
Barfield, Tanya 318
Barkan, Elizabeth 256
Barke, Tim 261
Barker, Amy 263
Barker, Gary 222
Barker, John Raymond 351
Barker, Rochelle 322
Barlow, David 255
Barlow, John
    139, 141, 147, 149,
    153, 162, 163, 182,
    185, 189, 200, 208
Barlow-Hartman
    139, 141, 147, 149,
    153, 162, 163, 173,
    182, 185, 188, 189,
    195, 200, 202, 208
Barnes, Clive 367, 376
Barnes, Ezra 252
Barnes, Geoffrey 259
Barnes, Gregg 136, 371
Barnes, Larky 339
Barnes, Lisa 263, 266
Barnes, William Joseph 154
Barnett, Bill 269

Barnett, Brigitte 249
Barnett, Regina 300
Barnhart, Jen 258
Baron, Art 161
Baron, Jeff 270
Barouh, Stan 288, 291
Barr, David III 324
Barr, Drew 262
Barranca, Victor 256
Barrault, Jean-Louis 236
Barreca, Christopher 309
Barrera, David 311
Barrett, Brent 219, 220
Barrett, Joy 272
Barrett, Laurinda 259
Barrie-Wilson, Wendy
    141, 142
Barrier, Randee 268
Barrish, Seth 260
Barron, Amanda 263
Barron, Mia 181, 210, 253
Barron, Steven L. 263, 339
Barros, Spencer Scott 299
Barrow Group, The 260
Barrueto-Cabello, Felipe 304
Barry, B.H. 256
Barry, Kimberly Jean 343
Barry, Paul 267
Barsha, Debra 33, 198
Barsky, Neil 268
Bart, Roger 227
Bartenders 14, 31, *190*
Bartenieff, Alexander 256
Bartholomai, Linda 317
Bartlett, Peter 216
Bartlett, Rob 220
Bartlett, Tom 139
Bartner, Robert G.
    136, 152, 172
Barton, Bruce 261
Barton, Caitlin 259
Barton, Fred 269
Barton, Steve 226
Barton, Todd 345
Bartosik, Steve 143
Baruch, Steven 182, 185
Baruch-Viertel-Routh-Frankel
    Group, The 132, 370
Barzee, Anastasia 229, 319
Basarab, Heather 304
Basche, David Alan 262
Basco, Cindy 352
Baseball Hall of Fame 103
bash: the latterday plays 79
Bashey, Ismail 254
Basil, John 259
Basset Table, The 264

Bassett, Florence Knoll 375
Bassett, J. Philip 133
Bast, Stephanie 161
Bastock, Michael 270
Bat Boy 378
Bat Boy: The Musical
    322, 378
Bateman, Jeffrey 260
Bates, Alan 9
Bates, Jerome Preston
    258, 269
Bates, Jessica 259
Batistick, Mike 248
Batman, Jack W. 163
Batnagar, Krish 269
Batt, Bryan 217
Battaglia, Eve 185
Battaglia, Lynn 259
Battat, Jacob 270
Battersby, Charles 266
Battle, Hinton 219
Battle of Black and Dogs
    268
Battle of Stalingrad 237
Batwin and Robin
    Productions
    176, 198, 204
Bauer, Beaver 301
Bauer, C. Andrew 272
Bauer, Jeff 328
Bauer, Jim 264
Bauer, Laura
    131, 190, 193, 213
Bauer, Matt 164
Bauer, P. Seth 273
Bauer, Ruth 264
Baum, L. Frank 100
Bauman, Jessica 270
Baura, Gary 249
Baxter, Kalimi 272
Baxter, Robin 225
Bayes, Christopher 323
Bayles, Dallyn Vail 223
Bayron, Harry 212
Bazmark Live 144, 371
Bazzle, Bradley 264
Bazzone, Mark 253
BBC America Comedy Live
    188
Beach, Gary 216, 217, 227
Beach Radio 260
Beacon Hill Book Club, The
    315
Beal, Harrison 216
Beal, John 206, 212
Beale, Simon Russell
    37, 193, 194, 195, 377

Beam, Fred Michael 324, 325
Bean, Christa 349
Bean, Jeffrey 350
Bean, Noah 314
Bean, R. 220
Bean, Reathel 141, 142
Bean, Shoshana 132, 133
Beane, Douglas Carter 245
Beard, Alec 152
Beard, Jane 354
Beard, Karla L. 328
Beard of Avon, The 324
Beat 267
Beattie, Kurt
    311, 351, 352, 354, 356
Beatty, John Lee
    22, 44, 131, 135,
    151, 152, 182, 196,
    206, 212, 255, 312,
    371, 375, 377, 381
Beaumarchais 338
Beauregard, Jon 267
Beauty and the Beast
    127, 216
Beauty of the Father 354
Beauty's Daughter 119
Beaver, Jerry 178, 189
Beazer, Tracee 198
Beber, Neena 252, 319
**Bebop Heard in Okinawa,
    The** 314
Bechert, Andrea 311
Bechtel, Erich 163
Beck, Emily 255
Beck, Julian 240
Becker, Carson Grace 324
Beckett, Diane 249, 377
Beckett, Samuel
    51, 88, 233, 234,
    237, 261, 269, 421
Beckim, Chad 263
Beckler, Steven 133
Beckwith, Eliza 245
Becnel, Carmelita 313
Becoming Bernarda 255
Bed Among the Lentils
    xii, 116, *208*
bedbound 239, 248
Bedford, Brian
    22, 151, 152, 371
Bedi, Purva 264
Bee-Luther-Hatchee 378
Beecher, James 254
Beep 269
Beeson, Jack 376
Befeler, Roger 216
**Before Death Comes for the
    Archbishop** 258

Beginning, The 259
Begleiter, Marcie 258
Behn, Aphra 262
Beitzel, Robert 253, 269, 314
Bek, Jef 303
Bekins, Richard 268, 273
Belasco, Mark 269
Belber, Stephen
    37, 197, 267,
    270, 331, 347
Belcher, James 350
Belcon, Natalie Venetia
    228, 258
Belgrader, Andrei 323
Belkacem, Areski 350
Belknap, Anna 307, 336
Bell, David (actor) 267
Bell, David H.
    (choreographer) 379
Bell, Gail Kay 265
Bell, Glynis 254, 270
Bell, Hilary 331
Bell, Hunter 378
Bell, Ian 353
Bell, Kristen 319
Bell, Nancy 203, 311
Bell, Neal 271
Bellamy, Brad 246
Bellazzin, Richard 265
Belles of the Mill 266
Bellie, Kevin 380
Bellingham, Rebecca 247
Bello, Teo Dorina 340
Belluso, John 253
Belton, Ian 267
Belton, Nicholas 201
Beltz, Jessica 340
Bembridge, Brian Sidney 356
Ben-David, Adam 146
Benabid, Nadia 354
Benanti, Laura 19, 160
Benari, Neal 216
Benator, Andrew 260
Benbow, Tawanna 336
Bench, The 322
Bender, David James 349
Bendul, Kristine 212
Benesch, Vivienne 254
Benja K. 254
Benjamin, Ari 249
Benjamin, Maggie 228
Benjamin, P.J. 220, 315
Benko, Tina 158, 265
Benkow, Tawanna 336
Bennett, Alan
    xii, xiii, xv, 29, *111–
    118*, 208, 366
Bennett, Andrew 37, 201

Bennett, Craig 225
Bennett, David 254, 271
Bennett, Jamie 259
Bennett, Jordan 321
Bennett, Keith 224
Bennett, Mark
    152, 204, 256, 305
Bennett, Matthew 138
Bennett, William 81
Benning, Clay 322, 323
Bennion, Chris 183
Benoit, David 146
Benoit, John 250
Bensie, Dennis Milam 353
Bensinger, Mimi 315
Benson, Martin 309, 311
Benson, Peter 206, 207, 218
Benson, Stephen 166
Bensussen, Melia 313, 314
Bentley, Kenajuan 271, 272
Benton, Heather 334
Benz, Deena 180
Benzinger, Suzy
    139, 192, 350
Berc, Shelley 323
Berdan, Judy 355, 356
Berfelde, Lothar 59–67
Berg, Neil 171
Bergasse, Joshua 133
Bergelson, Ilene 267
Bergen, Polly 218, 271
Bergen Record, The 367
Berger, Glen 170, 331, 353
Berger, Jesse 263
Berger, Stephanie 194
Bergl, Emily 311
Bergman, Evan 259
Bergman, Ingmar 36, 171
Berinstein, Dori 370
Berkeley, Beth 351, 352
Berkeley Repertory Theatre
    301, 343
Berkley, Price 369
Berkow, Jay 180
Berkowitz, D. Michael 245
Berkowitz, Roy 261
Berkshire, Devon 270
Berkshire Theatre Festival
    315, 335
Berlin, Howard R. 163, 370
Berlin, Irving 193
Berlin, Jeannie 192
Berlin, Jessica 341
Berlin, Pamela 173, 262
Berlind, Roger 148
Berliner, Jay 212
Berlinsky, Harris 264
Berlovitz, Barbra 338

Berlovitz, Sonya 301, 338
Berman, Brooke 252, 253, 314, 327
Berman, Ellen 163, 370
Berman, Heather 269
Berman, Rob 183, 378
Berman, Sabina 346
Bermowitz, Amie 272
Bermudez, Kina 256
Bernard Telsey Casting 133, 138, 144, 146, 147, 163, 168, 174, 190, 200, 213
Berneche, Alicia 244, 324
Bernice/Butterfly: A Two Part Invention 312
Bernstein, Ira 369
Bernstein, Leonard 271
Bernstein, Stephanie 327
Bernstine, Quincy Taylor 299
Bernstone, Jennifer 263
Bernzweig, Jay 264
Berresse, Michael 219, 220
Berry, Gabriel 201, 245, 319
Berry, Sarah Uriarte 223, 319
Berry, Stephanie 354
Berson, Misha 278
Bertolacci, Kevin 152
Bertran, Moe 259, 260
Bess, Abigail Zealey 246
Bessinger, Mary Kathryn 327
Besterman, Brian 144
Betley, Marge 318
Betrayal 378
Bettenbender, Ben 269
Bewilderness 14, 31, ***188***
Bewley, Sarah 272
Bexley, Oh(!) Or, Two Tales of One City 14, 31, ***201***
Beyond Broadway: The Quest for Permanent Theatres 423
Beyond the Fringe 111
Beyond the Veil 266
Bhatt, Sujata G. 302
Biagi, Michael 193, 351
Biagi, Randall 193
Bianchi, Ed 264
Biancomano, Frank 256
Bibb, Teri 226
Biberi, James 259
Bielefeldt, Fumiko 304
Bierce, Ambrose 236
Bierly, Bettina 341
Big Al 259
Big Bang 380
Big Boys 300, 341
Big Love 348
Biggers, Barbara 160
Biggs, Casey 212, 316
Biggs, Jason 221
Bilecky, Scott 262
Bill Evans and Associates 130, 138, 142, 167
Bill Hindman Award 380
Bill Maher: Victory Begins at Home 4, ***167***, 371
Billboard/Back Stage Books 422
Billie 249
Billig, Robert 143
Billington, Ken 147, 206, 212, 312, 350
Billman, Sekiya 245
Billy Budd 109
Bilton, Wendy 270
Binder, Chris 327
Binder, Jay 139, 156, 182, 196, 198, 206, 212
Binder, Jeffrey 224
Binion, Sandy 198
Binkley, Howell 141, 166, 191, 198, 204, 319, 378
Binsley, Richard 225
Birdsong, Mary 192
Birdy 258
Birdy's Bachelorette Party 262
Birkelund, Olivia 266
Birmingham, Laurie 355
Birmingham News 277, 278
Birmingham News, The 422
Biro 248
Bish, David 263
Bishop, André 128, 150, 154, 183, 196, 204, 370
Bishop, Barton 258
Bishop, Stephen 223
Bishop, Tom 238
Bishop-Stone, Sarah 314
Bisno, Debbie 153
Bissell, Cassandra 326
Bitetti, Bronwen 264
Bitter Bierce, Or the Friction We Call Grief 236, 255, 377
Bizarro Bologna Show, The 267
Bizjak, Amy 261
Black 47 247
Black Alert in Sarajevo 271
Black, Christopher 264, 265
Black, Clint 157, 370
Black Ensemble Theater, The 31, 207
Black Ice 141
Black, James 350
Black, Jeremy 260
Black, Lisa 249
Black Monk, The 317
Black, Paul Vincent 301
Blackballin' 318
Blacker, Robert 61
Blackman, Robert 205
Blacks: A Clown Show, The 239, 261, 377
Blackwell, David 303
Blackwell, Susan 265
Blair, Jayson 78
Blake, Marsha Stephanie 342, 355
Blake, Patrick 184
Blake, Richard H. 215, 228
Blake, Stephanie 175
Blakesley, Darcy 261
Blanchard, Steve 216
Blanchard, Tammy 164, 165, 371, 376
Blanchette, Jim 351
Blanco, Arian 269
Blanco, Michael 185
Blandin, Jonathan 351
Blank, Jessica 38, 184
Blank, Larry 193
Blankenbuehler, Andy 143
Blankenship, Hal 260, 261
Blankfort, Jase 258
Blasé, Linda 213
Blasius, Chuck 260
Blass, Jane 328
Bleckmann, Theo 245
Bless Me, Father 269
Blessing in Disguise 270
Blessing, Lee 253, 272, 314, 332, 345
Blind Mouth Singing 248
Blinkoff, Daniel 309
Blinn, David 206
bliss 269
Block, Dan 161
Block, Larry 252, 263
Blocker, Liz 314
Blommaert, Susan 202
Blood Brothers 380
Blood Wedding 252
Bloodgood, William 343
Bloom, Michael 311, 314
Bloom, Tom 245
Bloomberg, Mayor Michael 6
Blooming of Ivy, A 246

Blount, William 206
Blowin of Baile Gall, The 378
Blue Demon, The 335, 378
Blue Flower 264
Blue Heaven 262
Blue Heron Arts Center 260
Blue Man Group *169–170*
Blue Sky Transmission: A Tibetan Book of the Dead 249
Blue Surge 304
Blue Velvet 43
Blue/Orange 14, 35, *190*, 191, 367
Bluff 423
Bluhm, Anni 264
Blum, Gerald 268
Blum, Joel 315
Blum, Mark 221, 314
Blum, Mehera 335, 336
Blumberg, Kate 36, 213
Blume, Kathryn 262
Blumenfeld, Mara 244, 324, 327
Blumenkrantz, Jeff 156, 370
Blumm, Nicholas 338
Blunt, Ed 185
Bluteau, Lothaire 186
Bly, Mark 316
Bobbie, Walter 203, 271, 272, 312
Bobby, Anne 222
Bobgan, Raymond 249
bobrauschenbergamerica 378
Boccato, Richard 268
Bocchetti, Mike 268
Bochenski's Brain 264
Bock, Adam 262
Bodd, Patrick 266
Bode, Raine 250
Bodeen, Michael 141, 153, 162, 244, 324, 326, 327
Bodega Lung Fat 248
Bodle, Jane 223
Bodner, Amy 226
Body Familiar 304
Boe, Alfred 145
Boesche, John 244
Boevers, Jessica 224
Bofill, Maggie 247, 255
Bogardus, Janet 245
Bogardus, Stephen 143
Bogart, Anne 334, 378
Bogart, Dominic 256
Bogetich, Marilynn 379

Boggioni, Joshua 349
Bogner, Dunia 263
Bogosian, Eric 236, 255, 309
Bohème, La 4, 18, *144*, 145, 371, 372, 377
Bohle, Ruppert 186
Bohmer, Ron 226
Bohne, Bruce 338
Boitel, Raphaëlle 267
Bokhour, Ray 220
Bolan, Chris 225
Bolcom, William 376
Bolinger, Don 300
Böll, Heinrich 250
Boll, Patrick 256, 261
Bollinger, Lee C. 204
Bolman, Scott 317
Bolton, Guy 263
Bonasso, Joanne 351
Bond, Christopher K. 350
Bond, Clint Jr. 131, 188
Bond, Jeff 253
Bond, Justin 253, 261
Bond, Will 331, 334
Bondoc, Eric 323
Bonds, Rufus Jr. 224, 228
Boneau, Chris xiii, 146, 154, 182, 187, 190, 193, 195, 196, 203, 209, 213, 214
Boneau/Bryan-Brown xiii, 131, 135, 137, 146, 152, 154, 157, 158, 159, 161, 164, 166, 174, 182, 187, 188, 190, 193, 195, 196, 198, 203, 204, 209, 213, 214
Bongiorno, Joe 145
Bonitto, Sondra M. 196
Bonner, Ann 250
Bonney, Jo 248, 252, 255
Boobs! The Musical 14, 31, *214*
Book of Days x, xv, *41–49*, 42, 45, 48, 235, 255, 318, 375
Book of Job, The 250
Bookman, Kirk 245, 247, 248, 336
Boone, Elizabeth 380
Booth, Susan V. 322
Boothe, Cherise 252, 261
Bopp, Willi 204
Borba, Andrew 307
Borchard, Thomas 195
Borden, Walter 260

Borderlands Theater 346
Borg, Christopher 261
Boritt, Beowulf 205, 322
Borle, Christian 138, 204, 229
Borowka, Steve 263
Borowski, Michael S. 144, 150, 181, 191, 192, 201, 210, 214
Borrero, Camila 301
Borthwick-Leslie, Andrew 336
Börtz, Daniel 171
Bos, Hannah 270
Bosch, Barbara 261, 268, 339
Bosch, Michelle 162
Bosco, Nick 268
Bosley, James 267
Bosley, Tom 216, 218
Bossardet, Danyelle 216
Bostnar, Lisa 252
Boston Marriage 14, 33, *189–190*
Boston, Matthew 258, 266
Boston Playwrights' Theatre 378
Boswell, Laurence 159, 372
Botchan, Rachel 268
Botelho, Mark 326
Botello, Kate 269
Bottari, Michael 245, 373
Bottle, Caroline 265
Bottle Factory Theater Company, The 260
Boublil, Alain 127
Bouchard, Suzanne 354
Bougere, Teagle F. 245
Boulas, B. Emil 328
Boulevard of Broken Dreams 321
Boulevard X 266
Boulware, Kelly 353
Boulware, Scott 329
Bourbon at the Border 328
Bourgeois, Elizabeth 335
Bouton, Jim 106, 108
Boutrup, Jens Svane 270
Boutte, Duane 252
Bove, Mark 155, 156, 320
Bovshow, Buzz 253
Bowcutt, Jason 343
Bowdan, Jack 156, 182
Bowditch, Rachel 250
Bowen, Ann 266
Bowen, Graham 164
Bower, Sharron 245
Bowers, Bill 224
Bowers, Emma 260, 317

Bowersock, Karin 259
Bowery Poetry Club 260
Bowman, Benjamin G. 138
Bowman, Margaret 205, 266
Bowyer, Clodagh 247
Box of Pearls 258
Boxberger, Skeeter 341
Boy Gets Girl 303
Boyce, Rolando 324
Boyd, Ann 327
Boyd, D'Ambrose 179
Boyd, Gerald 78
Boyd, Gregory 349
Boyd, Guy 94, 95, 99, 261
Boyd, Julie 246, 252, 314
Boyd, Kate 301, 304
Boyd, Ken 265
Boyd, Patrick 260
Boyer, Andrew 216, 300
Boyer, Katherine Lee
    142, 163
Boyer, Steven 130, 254
Boyers, Gabriel 336
Boyett, Bob
    146, 161, 303, 370
Boyle, Seamus 269
Boylen, Daniel 345
Boys and Girls *171*
Boys From Syracuse, The
    4, 9, 134, *134–135*
Bozell, Tom 263
Braben, Eddie 157
Bracchitta, Jim 335
Bracco, Lorraine 221, 271
Brack, Ryan 267
Brackett, Virginia 327
Braden, John 141
Bradford, Josh 252, 256
Bradley, David 193, 195, 328
Bradley, Everett 196
Bradley, Henry 261
Bradley, Neil 269
Bradley, Scott 313
Bradshaw, John 352
Brady, Alexander 138, 139
Brady, John E. 224
Brady, Jonathan 266
Brady, Kathleen M. 312
Brady, Steve 264
Braff, Zach 175
Brainin, Risa 339
Brake, Brian 156
Bramble, Mark 128
Branagh, Kenneth 157
Brancoveanu, Eugene 145
Brand, Robert Gibby
    216, 339
Brandt, Kirsten 254

Brannen, Kirsten 341
Brantley, Ben
    8, 9, 11, 29, 366
Brantman, Jason 185
Brassard, Gail 328
Brathwaite, Charlotte 249
Brathwaite, Jonathan 268
Braude, Oleg 250
Braunsberg, Andrew 146
Brave New World 270
Brawley, Lucia 253, 266
Braxton, Brenda
    179, 196, 219
Braxton, Toni 215, 216
Brazda, Kati 324
Brazil, Angela 349
Bread and Circus 3099 250
Breaker, Daniel 263
Breath, Boom 317, 336
Brecht, Bertolt
    33, 36, 186, 237, 241
Breckenridge, Rob 252, 259
Breckfield, Jeff 272
Breedlove, Gina 224
Breen, Patrick 307
Brehm, Justin 263
Breithaupt, Stephen 229
Breland, Jefferson 318
Brennan, Ian 324
Brennan, Kathleen 237, 245
Brennan, Tom 141
Brescia, Lisa 215
Breuer, Lee 234, 236, 251
Breving, Andrew 264
Brevoort, Deborah 238, 254
Brewczynski, Amy 309
Brice, Richard 164
Brick, Jeffrey 307
Bridgett, Darren 305
Briel, Joel 250
Brier, Kathy 172
Brigden, Tracy 313, 314
Briggs, David 245
Brigham Young University
    422
Bright Ideas 343
Brightman, Sarah 226
Briguccia, Vincent 261
Brill, Robert
    189, 190, 195, 327
Briner, Allison 315
Brink-Washington, Daniel
    263
Briskman, Julie 352
Brito, Silvia 255
Britton, Mariah 329
Broad Channel 14, 31, *209*
Broadbent, Jim 13

Broadhurst, Jeffrey 134
Broadway Council 6
Broadway in Boston
    197, 378
Broadway.com 367
Brock, Lee 260
Brocone, Genna 268
Brod, Broke 264
Broderick, Deirdre 249
Broderick, Matthew 227
Brodeur, Maria 340
Broecker, Tom 332
Brogan, Meg 317
Brohm, Elizabeth A. 303
Brohn, William David 183
Brokaw, Mark
    259, 271, 272, 319, 335
Broken Head, A 271
Brolly, Brian 137, 152
Bronx Casket Company
    264
Bronx Witch Project, The
    248
Brook, Peter 24
Brook-Kothlow, Marit 304
Brooker, Meg 260, 268
Brookes, Jacqueline 342
Brooking, Fallon McDevitt
    269
Brooklyn Academy of Music
    22, 33, 36, 37,
    149, 171, 193, 194,
    204, 207, 237, 244, 377
Brooklyn Boy 311
Brooks, Barbara 338
Brooks, De Anna N.J. 323
Brooks, Donald L. 256
Brooks, Hal 259, 260
Brooks, Jeff 216
Brooks, Mel 128
Brooks, Taylor 258
Broom, Louis 265
Brophy, John 202
Brosilow, Michael 325
Brothers Grimm 303
Brothers Karamazov, The
    263
Brouk, Tricia 262
Brouwer, Peter 258
Broward Center for the
    Performing Arts 135
Brown, Benjamin Franklin
    166, 176
Brown, Blair 214, 218, 319
Brown, Brennan
    253, 265, 271, 313
Brown, Carlyle 299
Brown, Charles 38, 184

Brown, Chuck 262
Brown, Cynthia 267
Brown, Danielle Melanie 269
Brown, David (producer) 197
Brown, David Jr. (actor)
    184, 273
Brown, Deborah 142
Brown, Doug 329, 342
Brown, Irina 261
Brown, Jason Robert
    6, 19, 156, 157,
    195, 272, 320, 347, 370
Brown, Jeb 130
Brown, Jessica Leigh 161
Brown, Judy 258
Brown, Keirin 262
Brown, Laura Grace 187, 245
Brown, Leon Addison
    355, 378
Brown, Lew 180
Brown, Luqman 248
Brown, Michael (designer)
    185, 210, 318
Brown, Michael Henry
    (playwright) 253
Brown, P.J. 269
Brown, Paul 144
Brown, Peter 185
Brown, Renee Monique 176
Brown, Robert Curtis 311
Brown, Robin Leslie 268
Brown, Roger 157, 370
Brown, Ronald K. 191, 340
Brown, Siobhan Juanita 259
Brown, Sterling K. 175, 186
Brown, Tim 264
Brown, Trisha 375
Brown, Wayne 327
Brown-Orleans, James 224
Browne, Christopher 264
Browne, Roscoe Lee
    196, 239
Brownlee, Addie 263
Brownlee, Gary 249, 377
Brownson, Karmenlara
    xiv, 262
Brownstein, Norman 147
Broyles, Tracy 249
Bruce, Cheryl Lynn 326, 328
Bruce, Claudia 249
Bruel, Kaya 245
Brumble, Stephen Jr. 265
Brummel, David 244, 321
Brunell, Catherine 224
Brunner, Katrina Williams
    380
Brunner, Michael 155, 183
Bruno, Lou 136

Brustein, Robert i, xiii
Brustofski, Larry 269
Bruton, Amanda 270
Bryan-Brown, Adrian
    xiii, 131, 135, 137,
    152, 157, 158, 159,
    161, 164, 166, 174,
    188, 198, 204
Bryant, Brienan 261
Bryant, David 223
Bryant, Kimilee 226
Bryant, Lee 252
Bryant, Shannon 256
Bryant, Tom 309
Bryggman, Larry 227
Bryne, Barbara 319
Buccaneer, The 269
Bucciarelli, Renee 265
Buchanan, Georgia 258
Buchanan, Linda 324
Buchman, Allan 184
Büchner, Georg 245, 262
Buckley, Betty 204
Buckley, Candy 218
Buckley, Mike 304
Buckley, Patrick Michael 265
Buddeke, Kate 164
Buderwitz, Tom 302
Budries, David 309, 312, 316
Buell, Bill 175, 258, 266
Buffini, Moira 270
Buggeln, Samuel 267
Buicks 266, 367
Bull, Ginevra 270
Bull, Lon Troland 336
Bullins, Ed 261
Bulos, Yusef 189
Bulosan, Carlos 266
Bunch, Elizabeth 265, 349
Bundy, James 316, 317
Bundy, Laura Bell 132, 221
Bunin, Keith 34, 181
Bunn, David Alan 179
Bunsee, Antony 204
Bunting, Pearce 225
Buntrock, Stephen R.
    223, 226
Buñuel, Agustin 326
Buol, John Jay 259
Buon Natale, Bruno 266
Buonopane, Todd 244, 263
Burdette, Nicole 271
Burgi, Chuck 139
Burgoyne, Marissa 222
Burich, George 272
Buried Child 100, 101
Burke, Brenda 304
Burke, Christopher 272, 273

Burke, Mary Catherine
    256, 270
Burke, Marylouise 195
Burke, Richard 272
Burke-Kaiser, Tom 315
Burkell, Scott 260
Burkett, Shannon 173, 211
Burkholder, Page 272
Burmester, Leo 155, 320
Burn This
    14, 36, *178*, 217, 235, 377
Burnet, Michael 336
Burnett, Carol 10, 140, 141
Burnett, Janinah 145, 146
Burnett, Matthew 318
Burnett, McCaleb 303
Burning Blue 269
Burns, George 24, 135
Burns, Heather 213
Burns, Nica 148
Burns, Ralph 212
Burns, Trad A. 249
Burrell, Fred 174
Burrell, Ty 178, 217, 254
Burridge, Hollis 149, 164
Burritt, Elizabeth 304
Burrow, Timm 303
Burrows, Allyn 301, 337
Burrows, Sidney Jr. 301
Burson, Linda 266
Burstein, Danny 222
Burstyn, Ellen 308
Burtka, David 164
Burton, Arnie 209, 269
Burton, DyShaun 263
Burton, Kate 33, 189
Burton, Matthew 182
Burton, Suellen 326
Burward-Hoy, Ken 206
Burwell, Carter 251
Buscemi, Steve 36, 186
Busch, Charles 128, 238, 245
Bush, Bob 145
Bush, Rachel R. 347
**Business Lunch in the
    Russian Tea Room**
    266
Buster, Diane Michelle 265
Butelli, Louis 175
Buterbaugh, Keith 227
Butiu, Melody 309, 310, 341
Butkus, Denis 259, 265
Butler, Helen 321
Butler, Isaac 270
Butler, Kerry
    132, 216, 223, 376
Butler, Paul 261, 326
Butler, Shelley 313

Butler, Tom 270
Butter and Egg Man, The
    35, 244
Butterell, Jonathan 161, 183
Butz, Norbert Leo
    217, 228, 266
Buurman, Jasper 249
By Her Side 259
By the Music of the Spheres
    324, 325
Bye, Bye 252
Byers, Joe 258
Byk, Jim 137, 164, 182, 187,
    193, 195, 203, 214
Bynner, Witter 264
Byrd, Anne Gee 354
Byrd, Carl L. 157, 370
Byrd, Thomas Jefferson
    152, 153, 371, 376
Byrd-Munoz, Pevin 157, 370
Byrn, Tom 345
Byrne, Pete 272
Byrne, Terry 378
Byrnes, Brian 256, 350
Byrnes, Michael 255
Byrnes, Tommy 139

Cabaret 20, *128*, 217
Cabico, Regie 332
Cacioppo, P.J. 269
Cadell, Selina 193, 195
Cady, Jeffrey 339
Caesar, Irving 180
Café a Go Go 260
Café a Go Go Theatre 260
Caffey, Marion J. 266, 315
Cahill, Cynthia 309
Cahn, Danny 133
Cahn, Victor L. 272
Cahoon, Kevin 224
Cain, Candice 307, 309
Cain, William 173
Caine, Michael 60
Caird, John 214
Caisley, Robert 348
Cake, Jonathan
    148, 149, 244, 376
Calarco, Joe 347
Calaway, Belle 218, 219
Caldwell, George 172, 173
Caldwell, Jeff 323
Caldwell, Lauren 321
Cale, David 268

Caleo, Bill 340
Calhoun, Matthew 263
Caliban, Richard 261
Calin, Angela Balogh 311
Call the Children Home
    255
Callaghan, Sheila 264, 331
Callahan, Matthew 347
Callas, Maria 76
Callaway, Liz 166, 167
Callely, Robert 369
Calleri, James 181, 214
Callicutt, Jonathan 187
Calo, Peter 133
Calpito, Isaac 260
Calvello, Jessica 261, 269
Calveri, Joey 229
Calzolari, Laura 320
Camacho, Blanca 255
Camera, John 268
Cameron, Bruce 196
Cameron, Jibz 305
Cameron, Rob 272
Cameron Webb, Gavin
    341, 342
Camp, Joanne 151, 268
Camp, Joshua 250
Camp, Karma 319
Campbell, Alan
    42, 44, 45, 48, 255
Campbell, Alexi Kaye 204
Campbell, Almeria 262
Campbell, Annie 246
Campbell, Bill Ford 300
Campbell, Christian 230
Campbell, Christopher 262
Campbell, Cori Lynn 263
Campbell, Drae 262
Campbell, Greg 304
Campbell, Justin 256
Campbell, Kane 12, 163
Campbell, Kirsten 148
Campbell, Mary-Mitchell 314
Campbell, Nell 160
Campbell, Peter 341
Campbell, Rob 192, 324
Campion, Kieran 141, 142
Campo, Helen 146
Campo, John 212
Canavan, Elizabeth
    88, 89, 200, 265
Cancelmi, Louis 154, 327
Cangelosi, Margaret 314
Cannavale, Bobby 202
Cannistraro, Mark 261, 270
Cannon, Alice 256, 349
Cannon, Jessica 260
Canonico, Gerard 171

Canonigo, Rosanna 260
Cantler, William
    190, 213, 251
Cantone, Mario
    271, 309, 310
Cantor, Carolyn 98, 261
Cantor, Daniel 189
Canvin, Rue E.
    i, xiii, 299, 387, 421
CAP 21 Theater 260
Caparelliotis, David
    187, 193, 195
**Capitol Steps: When Bush
    Comes to Shove** *171*
Caplan, Henry 264
Caplan, Matt 228
Capone, Joseph 265
Capone, Tony 206
Capote, Truman 196
Capozzi, Joe 269
Capps, Lisa 223
Cara Lucia 233, 251
Carbonell Awards 380
Carden, Stuart 269
Cardinalli, Valentina 266
Carey, Adrianna 349
Carey, Helen 314
Carey, Jared T. 181
Carey, Jess 259
Carino, Joel 263, 264
Cariou, Len
    212, 227, 271, 303
Carl, Christopher 226
Carle, Melissa J.A. 339
Carlebach, Joshua 256
Carlin, Aviva Jane 264
Carlin, Joy 309
Carlin, Tony 158
Carlisle, Craig 250, 271
Carlson, Jeffrey 151, 221
Carmeli, Jodi 230, 351
Carmello, Carolee 204, 229
Carnahan, Harry 341
Carnahan, Jim
    135, 152, 158, 159,
    161, 164, 166, 208
Carnegie Hall 422
Carnegie Mellon University
    422
Carnelia, Craig
    10, 70, 129, 149, 308
Carolan, Kevin 348
Caron, David 175
Carousel 44
Carpenter, Barnaby 197
Carpenter, Bridget 253, 331
Carpenter, Cassandra 300
Carpenter, Jack 304

Carpenter, Karen 308
**Carpetbagger's Children,
    The 170**, 375
Carr, Ann 270
Carr, Geneva 246
Carr, Stephanie 340
Carrafa, John 147, 319
Carrasco, Roxane 219
Carrasquillo, Julien A. 245
Carrick, William 147
Carrico, Stewart 268
Carrillo, Juliette 311
Carroll, Baikida 340
Carroll, Barbara
    151, 155, 197
Carroll, John 212
Carroll, Kevin 153, 177
Carroll, Kristina 260
Carroll, Melissa 261
Carroll, Ronn 183
Carroll, Teige 240
Carrubba, Philip 202
Carter, Brian 271, 272
Carter, Caitlin 212
Carter, Eric 263
Carter, Gerrard 155, 320
Carter, Jeanine 272
Carter, John 173
Carter, Lisa 175
Carter, Lonnie 266, 328, 377
Carter, McKinley 324
Carter, Michelle 304
Carter, Myra 173
Carter, Nell 35
Carter, Sage Marie 308
Carter, Sam 264
Carter, Stacy 371
Cartmell, Stephen 338
Caruthers, Cliff 311
Carvajal, Celina 198
Carver, Brent 201
Cascio, Anna Theresa 209
Case, Andrew 269
Case, Peter S. 355
Case, Ronald 245, 373
Casella, Max 224
Casey, Chan 270
Casey, Shawna 265
Casper, Christian 307
Cassel, John 269
Cassidy, Bethany J. 335
Cassidy, Orlagh 262
Cassidy, Patrick 215
Cassier, Brian 134, 160
Castay, Leslie 217
Castellano, Anthony 264
Castellanos, Teo 247

Castillo, Raul 247
Castillo, Sol 311
Castillo Theatre 260
Castle, Elowyn 254
Castle, Robert 270
Catanese, Ivana 245
Cataract 253
Catcall 262
Cates, Gilbert 302
Cates, Kristy 214, 316
Cathey, Reg E. 271
Catron, John 330, 331, 332
Catti, Christine 186, 200
Cavanagh, Brian 341
Cavanagh, Tom 229
Cavanaugh, Michael
    138, 139, 371
Cave, Jim 301, 304
Cave, Lisa Dawn 141
Cave, Suzanne 202
Cavedweller 14, 31, *211*
Cavenaugh, Matt
    155, 156, 320
Ceballo, Kevin 166, 167
Cedano, Johnathan 260
Celebrating Sondheim
    4, 25, **141**
Çelik, Aysan 253, 263, 270
Cellario, Maria 272
Celtic Christmas, A 247
Centenary Stage Company
    37, 211, 339
Centeno, Francisco 133
Center Stage 260, 309, 332
Center Theatre Group
    136, 182
Centlivre, Susannah 264
Central Avenue 346
Ceraulo, Rich 136
Cerezo, Antonio 250
Cerqua, Joe 328
Cerveris, Michael 319
Cerveris, Todd 262
Chae, Esther K. 302
Chaikin, Joseph 240, 261
Chain 378
Chaisson, Gilles 271
Chait, Marcus 155, 320
Chakrabarti, Samrat 339
Chalfant, Kathleen
    116, 118, 208, 377
Chamberlain, Andrea 222
Chamberlain, Travis 263
Chamberlin, Aubrey 268
Chamberlin, Mark 354, 355
Chambers, David 309
Chambers, Lindsey 263

Chambers, Richard 378
Champa, Russell H.
    119, 187, 348, 349, 354
Champagne, Lenora 268
Champlin, Donna Lynne
    10, 140, 201
Chan, Claire 136
Chan, Eric 136
Chan, Joanna 268
Chan, Jovinna 265
Chandler, Blaire 343
Chandler, David
    250, 252, 253, 294, 338
Chandler, Valerie 332
Chang, Christina 271
Chang, Jennifer 267
Chani, Pushpinder 204
Channing, Stockard 381
Chapadjiev, Sophia 264
Chapin, Schulyer G. 369
Chaplik, Robin 379
Chapman, Clay McLeod 270
Chapman, John i
Chapman, Mo 189
Chapman, Tracy Nicole 224
Chappell, Kandis 311
**Charity That Began at
    Home, The** 252
Charles, Walter 134
Charlston, Erik 212
Charney, Jordan 258
Chartier, Jeffrey 371
Chase, David 136, 196
Chase, Eric 261
Chase, Jennifer 206
Chase, Kristin Stewart
    264, 269
Chase, Will 215, 230
Chashama 93, 261
Chastain, Sheffield 308
Chasten, Gamal A. 332
Chatterton, John 266
Chaudhuri, Jyotirmay Ray
    Ghatak 339
Chaudhuri, Una xiv
Chavez Ravine 307
Chayefsky, Paddy 335
Cheat 258
Chekhov, Anton
    193, 264, 317, 334, 340
Chen, Tina 256
Cheng, Kipp Erante 263
Chepulis, Kyle 255
Chernov, Hope 255, 256
Cherns, Penelope 271
Chernus, Michael
    252, 253, 314, 319

Cherry, Ben 270
Cherry, Erin 261
Cherry Lane Theatre 261
Cherry Orchard, The 24
Chesnut, Jerry 157
Chester, Nora 259
Chestnut, Jerry 370
Cheung, Cindy 246, 252
Chewning, Frances 240
Chianese, Dominic 186
Chiang, Dawn 312
Chiasson, Gilles 145
Chibas, Marissa 305
Chicago *127*, 218
Chicago Shakespeare Theater 379
Chicago Tribune 17
Chicoine, Susan 186
Childers, Stephanie 327
Children of Herakles, The 334
Children of Paradise 236
Children's Theatre Company 19
Children's Theatre Company, The 162, 370, 372
Childs, Casey 197, 255
Child's Christmas in Wales, A 247
Childs, Kirsten 196
Chin, Staceyann 141
Chin, Tsai 305
Chin, Wilson 317
Chinese Art of Placement, The 270
Chinese Tale, A 248
Chinn, Lori Tan 378
Chiodo, Louis 258
Chiodo, Thomas 180
Chip in the Sugar, A 112, 114, *208*
Chipman, Kerry 254
Chisholm, Anthony 326, 327
Chisholm, Lloyd 314
Cho, Linda 307, 335, 347
Cho, Myung Hee 340, 353
Choi, Marcus 136
Cholet, Blanche 261
Chong, Ping 248, 249
Chris, Marilyn 308
Christen, Robert 324
Christensen, Tracy 198, 335
Christian, Angela 229
Christian, Eric L. 216
Christianity Today 43
Christmas with the Crawfords 269

Christopher, Amy 197
Christopher, Roy 321
Christopher T. Washington Learns to Fight 259
Chu, Lap-Chi 255, 307, 308, 309
Chu, Nancy S. 262, 267
Chu, Robert Lee 268
Chun, Marc 269
Church, Vernon 256
Churchill, Caryl 31, 188
Chybowski, Michael 175, 181
Cibula-Jenkins, Nan 322, 326
Cicci, Jason 268
Ciccone, Christine 249
Cieri, Dominique 340
Cimmet, Alison 269
Cincinnati Enquirer 278
Cincinnati Playhouse in the Park 342
Cinderella 316
Cino, Maggie 264
Circle Repertory Company 178
Circle Theatre 379
Cirque Jacqueline 269
Cirrius, Nebraska 266
Cisek, Tony 342, 345
City Center Encores! 9, 37, 196, 205, 212
City Guide Magazine 423
City Newspaper 278
City of Dreams 245, 266
City University of New York 422
Citygirl, Geeta 267
Ciulla, Celeste 268
Claar, E. Alyssa 146
Claire, Jessica 270
Clancy, Dan 259
Clancy, Elizabeth Hope 182, 303, 338
Clancy, John 198
Clandestine Crossing 254
Clarence Derwent Awards 376
Clark, C.A. 154, 178
Clark, Charlie 380
Clark, H. 263
Clark, Jim 342
Clark, Kelly Anne 222
Clark, Michael 319
Clark, Phillip 331
Clark, Stephen 380
Clark, Victoria 218, 229
Clark-Price, Stafford 264
Clarke, Henry David 337

Clarke, Hope 299
Clarke, Martha 170
Clarke, Peter Philip 260
Clarke, Tanya 130
Clarkson, Scott 261
Class Mothers '68 263
Classic Stage Company 239, 245
Classical Theatre of Harlem 239, 261
Clausen, Diane 323
Clay, Caroline 261
Clay, Caroline Stephanie 316
Clay, Carolyn 378
Clayburgh, Jill 38, 184, 271
Clayburgh, Jim 233, 251
Claypool, Veronica 369
Clayton, Lawrence 191, 229, 340
Cleage, Pearl 328
Cleale, Lewis 138
Clear Channel Entertainment 132, 138, 147, 370
Clear, Patrick 140
Cleary, Malachy 142
Cleevely, Gretchen 96, 98, 261, 262
Clement, Ken 320
Clemente, Aixa 305
Clemente Soto Velez Cultural Center (CSV) 262
Cleveland Play House 343
Cleveland Raining 253
Clifford, Christen 271
Climate 261, 271
Cline, Gina E. 250
Cline, Nathan 270
Cline, Perry 137
Close, Jenna 331, 332
Clost, Benjamin 224
Clow, James 229
Clubbed Thumb 262
Clubland 252
Clurman, Harold 263
Coalition of Broadway Unions and Guilds 6
Coash, Tom 345
Cobb, Mel 336
Coble, Eric 343
Cochran, Cara 351
Cochrane, Anthony 175
Cochrane, Brendan 248
Cochren, Felix E. 324
Coco 164
Coco, Lea 331, 332
Coconut Grove Playhouse 156, 320

Cocooning 270
Cocteau, Jean 264
Coda 246, 269
Cody, Jennifer 187
CodyKramers, Dominic
    351, 352, 354
Coffey, Julia 351
Coffin, Gregg 318
Coffman, David 243
Cohen, Benjamin Brooks 164
Cohen, Buzz 210
Cohen, Jeff 273
Cohen, Jeri Lynn 301
Cohen, Joshua H. 347
Cohen, Lynn 252, 334
Cohen, Lynne 145
Cohen, Michael 335
Cohen, Scott 272
Cohen-Cruz, Jan xiv
Cohn, Charlotte 145
Cohn Davis Associates 173
Cohn, Jon 378
Coiro, Rhys 151
Cokas, Nick 225
Colacci, David 343
Colangelo, Anthony 160
Colby, James 378
Cole, Jimmon 265
Cole, Joanna 349
Cole, Kay 321
Cole, Nora 334
Cole, Robert 23, 152
Colella, Jenn 155, 156, 320
Coleman, Chad L. 273
Coleman, Dara 246, 247
Coleman, David 175
Coleman, Kevin G. 336
Coleman, Rosalyn 254
Colin, Margaret 37, 158, 188
Collapsable Hole 377
Collier, Casey 311
Collins, Ashley Wren 334
Collins, Beth 332
Collins, Christine 317
Collins, David 267
Collins, Elsbeth M. 303
Collins, Floyd 380
Collins, Owen 175
Collins, Pat 130, 178, 349
Collins, Rufus 158, 301
Colman, Steve 141
Colón, Oscar A. 247, 255
Colón-Zayas, Liza
    90, 199, 200, 265
Color Mad Inc. 176
Colossus of Rhodes, The
    300, 314
Colston, Robert 256

Colton, John 268
Coluca, Teddy 265, 341
Columbia University
    37, 204, 421
Columbinus 318
Come a Little Closer 316
Come Light the Menorah
    259
Comeau, Jessica 145
Comedians 238, 254
Comedy of Errors, The 14,
    36, 135, **174–175**
Comfort, Jane 138
Comolli, Dina Ann 339, 340
Company 380
Complicite 36, 186
Compton, J.C. 261
Comstock, Eric 170
Conarro, Ryan 267
Concerto Chicago 328
Condren, Conal 266
Cone, Michael 145
Congdon, Constance
    272, 313
Conlee, John Ellison 244
Conley, Alexandra 255
Conley, Matt 273
Conlin, Vanessa 145
Conn, Didi 24, 135
Connecticut Critics' Circle
    Awards xiii, 377
Connection, The 240, 241
Connections 256
Connell, Gordon 254
Connell, Jane 230
Connelly, Brendan 250, 255
Connelly, John 145
Connelly Theatre 262
Conners, Tommy 370
Connington, Bill 249
Connolly, Ryan 250
Connors, Michael 260, 263
Connors, Tommy 157
Conolly, Patricia 163
Conroy, Jarlath 183
Conroy, Jim 269
Constant Star 380
Contact 9, 17, *128*
Contemporary Playwrights
    422
Contey, Louis 379
Conti, Eva 143
Continental Divide 343
Conversations with Miller 421
Converse, Frank 21, 141
Conway, Dan 319
Conway, Kathryn 147
Conway, Kelly 355

Conway, Kevin 22, 150, 151
Coogan, Tracy 264
Cook, Barbara 9, 25
Cook, Julia 259
Cookin' at the Cookery
    266, 315
Coonrod, Karin 256
Cooper, Cara 156
Cooper, Chuck
    29, 172, 219, 252
Cooper, Elisabeth 322
Cooper, Helmar Augustus
    153
Cooper, Maury 326
Cooper, Max 167, 370
Cooper, Pamela 182
Cooper, Sean 145, 146
Cooper-Hecht, Gail 254, 258
Cope, Eric 350
Copeland, Carolyn Rossi 171
Copeland, Dawn 260
Copeland, Marissa 210
Copenhagen 105, 342
Copenhaver, Kevin 312
Copozzi, Darren 263
Copp, Aaron M. 308
Coppinger, Nicole 315
Coppock, Ada G. 347
Corbett, Patricia 145
Corbiere, Walter 313
Corcoran, Tim 272
Cordaro, J. Alex 348, 349
Cordileone, Nick 304
Cordon, Susie 191
Corduner, Allen 254
Coriaty, Peter J. 265
Corkins, Mark 356
Corky Productions, LLC 321
Corman, Maddie 262
Cormican, Peter 247
Corn 269
Corn Exchange, The
    37, 201, 202
Cornelia, Craig 271
Cornelisse, Tonya 269
Cornell, Heather 157
Cornell, Sarah 227
Corner Wars 263, 376
Cornholed! 264
Cornwell, Eric 141
Cornwell, Jason 261
Corrado, Frank 354
Corre, Bo 256
Correa, AnaMaria 247
Corren, Donald 209, 269
Corrigan, Kevin 262
Cort, Bud 271
Cortese, Drew 34, 210

Cortez, Paul 335, 336
Corthron, Kia
    271, 299, 317, 331, 336
Corti, Jim 328
Cortiñas, Jorge Ignacio 248
Corwin, Betty 369
Corwin, John 34, 192
Coseglia, Jared 263
Cosentino, Paul 258
Cosson, Steve 248
Costabile, David 245
Costabile, Richard 174
Costantakos, Evangelia 145
Costello, Ellyn 327
Costelloe, David 247
Coster, Ritchie 314
Cote, Alison 191, 340
Cote, David 367, 373
Cote, Doug 265
Cothran, Robert 342
Cotter, Margaret 208
Cottle, Jason 353
Cotton, Keith 133
Cotton, Shamika 273
Cottrell, Richard
    173, 174, 261
Coudert, Sandra 209
Coughlan, John Alban 216
Coughlin, Bruce 164, 201
Coughlin, Ruth 254
Coulson, Catherine E. 343
Coulson-Grigsby, Carolyn
    340
Coulter, Steve 322
Counter Girls 261
Countryman, Michael 312
Court Theatre 323
Courtade, Jennifer 322
Courtney, Erin 248
Courtney, Philip 269
Courvais, Michelle 346
Cousens, Heather 203
Cousineau, Jorge 345
Covault, Jim 350
Covello, Carmine 339
Coward, Noël 129
Cowell, Matt 191
Cowie, Jeff 191, 378
Cowles, Peggy 260
Cowley, Hannah 253
Cox, Jane 197, 245, 254
Cox, Julie 206
Cox, Tim 269
Coxe, Helen 246
Coyle, Bill 139, 208
Coyle, Bruce W. 320
Coyne, Sterling 272
Cozior, Jimmy 176

Crace, Jim 239, 256
Craig, Deborah S.
    253, 259, 264
Craig, Lawrence 145
Craig, Liam 256, 307
Craig Noel Awards 421
Crain, Tom 157, 370
Cram, Cusi 331
Cramer, David 304
Crane, Holly Jo 223
Crane, Warren 130
Crawford, Kim 265
Crawford, Michael
    17, 146, 147, 226
Crawford, Richard 256
Crayton, Mark 324
Crazy Girl, The 271
Crazy Locomotive, The
    239, 261
Creamer, Tom 324
Creasey, Maria Teresa 314
Creative Artists Laboratory
    Theatre 262
Creative Theatrics'
    Performance Team 272
Creek, Luther 184
Creel, Gavin 229
Cremin, Sue 309, 334
Cressman, Michael Todd 223
Cresswell, Luke 169
Creswell, Bashirrah 224
Crimes of the Heart 380
Crimson Productions 180
Criss Angel Mindfreak 170
Critics Quarterly 422
Croft, Paddy 259
Croiter, Jeff 193, 198, 255
Croman, Dylis 212
Cromarty, Alice 135
Cromarty and Company
    135, 172
Cromarty, Peter 135, 172
Cromelin, Caroline 270
Cromer, David 379
Cromwell, David 244
Cronin, Christopher T.
    138, 158
Crook, Peter 352, 354
Crooks, David 146
Croom, Gabriel A. 176
Croot, Cynthia 272
Crosby, B.J. 176, 177, 220
Cross, Chaon 323, 324
Cross, Tim 270
Crow, Laura 255
Crow, Wayne 313
Crowe, Timothy 349
Crowl, Jason 264

Crowley, Dennis
    159, 166, 204
Crowley, John Steven 328
Crowns 14, 33, 191, 340
Croy, Jonathan 337
Crucible, The 9, 128, 342
Crudup, Billy 36, 186
Cruikshank, Holly 138, 139
Cruise, Julee 198
Crumb, Ann 261
Cruse, Andrew 267
Cruse, Kimothy 316
Cruz, Gilbert 321
Cruz, Michael 266
Cruz, Nilo xii, xvi, 248, 277,
    279–286, 311, 320,
    354, 375, 380
Crun, Wilson 228, 230
Cry Havoc 345
Cryer, Gretchen 369
Cryer, Suzanne 191
CTM Productions 167, 371
Cu Leong, Philippe 261
Cuban Operator Please 269
Cucci, Tony 153
Cuccioli, Robert
    37, 188, 262, 340
Cucuzza, Robert 268
Cuddy, Mark 318, 341
Cudia, John 227
Cuervo, Alma 218, 253
Culbert, John 323, 326
Culbreath, Lloyd
    196, 212, 219
Culek, Robert 255
Cullen, Sean 256, 349
Cullinan, Ivanna 265
Culliver, Karen 226
Cullman, Joan 157, 371
Cullman, Trip
    154, 177, 209, 248,
    269, 352
Cullum, JD 309, 311
Cullum, John 229
Culpepper, Dan 206
Culture Clash 304, 307, 309
Culture Clash in Americca
    309
Culture Club 262
Culture Project, The 184
Cumming, Alan
    217, 238, 273
Cumming, Michelle 320
Cummings, Jack III 262
Cummings, Krysten 228
Cummings, Tim 131
Cummins, Corryn 380
Cummins, Scott 324

Cumpsty, Michael
    12, 163, 221
Cunningham, Christina 186
Cunningham, Jo Ann 260
Cunningham, John 138
Cunningham, John C. 269
Cunningham, Michael
    191, 340
Cunningham, Sean 267
Cunningham, T. Scott 270
Curcio, Vincent 315
Curley, Geoffrey M. 326
Curran, Sean 201
Curran, Shawn 268
Currie, Richard 341
Curry, Beth 321
Curry, Rosa 176, 177
Curtin, Catherine 271, 272
Curtin, Jane 21, 141, 225
Curtis, Burton 354
Curtis, Tony 230, 351
Curtis-Newton, Valerie
    299, 331
Curve 249
Cushing, James 129
Cushman, Charlotte 171
Cusick, Melissa
    171, 193, 195, 204, 207
Cuskern, Dominic 268
Cusson, Ann-Marie 252
Cutler, Joe 214
Cvijetic, Stefani 316
Cvitanov, Kevin 263
Cwikowski, Bill 246
Cymbeline 323
Czarnecki, Julie 345

D., Eva 207
da Ponte, Lorenzo 338
D'Abruzzo, Stephanie
    258, 314
Dace, Tish
    i, x, xv, 41, 375, 421
Dadiani, Marika 250
**Daedalus: A Fantasia of
    Leonardo da Vinci**
    345
D'Agostini, David Raphael
    307
D'Agrossa, Anna 264
Dahlquist, Gordon 252, 253
Daignault, Leo 230
Daigneault, Paul 378
Daily, Dan 268
Daily News 367

Daily, Paul 260
Daisey, Mike 171
Daisy in the Dreamtime
    258
Daisy Mayme 268
Dakota Project, The 264
Daldry, Stephen 31, 188
Dale, Jim 238, 254
D'Alessandro, Franco 262
Daley, Maggie 379
Daley, Norman 314
Daley, Sandra 252, 347
Dalgleish, Jack M. 202
Dalí, Salvador 60
Dalio, Marc G. 216
Dallas Summer Musicals, Inc.
    137
Dallimore, Stevie Ray 211
Dallos, Chris 188, 342
Dalton, Jill 266
Dalton, Nicholas 266
Daly, Jonathan Gillard 329
Daly, Tyne 20
d'Amboise, Charlotte
    218, 219
D'Ambrosio, Franc 226
D'Ambrosio, Tom
    133, 168, 191, 195
Damn Yankees 6, 110, 379
D'Amour, Lisa 253, 377
Dana, F. Mitchell 320
Dance of the Vampires
    4, 17, *146*, 147
Dance Theater Workshop 262
Dancing on Moonlight 252
Dancing Princesses, The
    272
d'Ancona, Miranda 270
Dandridge, Merle 228
Dandridge, Sarah 266
Danforth, Roger 346
Dang, Tim 302
Danger of Strangers 260
Daniele, Graciela 195, 204
Danielian, Barry 139
Danielli, Gordon 211, 339
Daniels, Charles 157, 370
Daniels, Jeff 278
Daniels, Matt 266
Daniels, Nikki Renée 166
Daniels, Sean 322
Danis, Amy 182
Dann, Eveleena 250
Danson, Randy 303
Dantuono, Michael 221
Danvers, Marie 206, 226
D'Aquila, Fabio 170
Darby, Brigit 267

Dardaris, Janis 348
Darion, Joe 142
Darlow, Cynthia 259, 312
Darnutzer, Don 205, 351
Darragh, Anne 304
Darragh, Patch 141, 142
Darrow, Nathan 261
Darweish, Kammy 204
Darwin, Charles 237
Daryl Roth Theatre 262
Das, Meneka 204
Dashiell, Anita 305
**Daughters of the
    Revolution** 343, 344
Daurio, Phoebe 327
Davalos, David 345
D'Avanzo, Sylvia 145
Davenport, Johnny Lee
    329, 342
Davenport, Robert 262
Daves, Evan 141
Davey, Patrick 260
Davey, Shaun 197
David, Angel 247
David, Hal 27, 166
David, James 166
David, Keith 253
Davidson, Gordon
    136, 182, 305
Davidson, Jack 152
Davidson, Jeremy 314, 335
Davidson, Phil 355
Davidson, Tonja Walker
    163, 370
Davies, Amanda 244
Davies, Irving 157
Davies, John 350
Davies, Stephen Bel 245
Davila, Ivan
    259, 260, 271, 272
Davis, Al 341
Davis, Ben 145, 223
Davis, Briana 268
Davis, Catherine Lynn 343
Davis, Colbert S. IV 331, 332
Davis, Daniel
    112, 114, 118, 208, 377
Davis, Eisa 252, 253
Davis, Helene 173
Davis, Jen Cooper 192
Davis, K.C. 252
Davis, Keith 261, 270, 273
Davis, Kevin 327
Davis, Kristin 271, 272
Davis, Lizzy Cooper 252, 334
Davis, Mary Bond 132, 221
Davis, Mylika 272
Davis, Nathan 326

Davis, Randy A. 176
Davis, Raquel 256
Davis, Rondi Hillstrom 331
Davis, Roz 261, 331
Davis, Russell 331
Davis, Todd 249
Davis, Vicki R. 252
Davis, Will 270
Davis-Green, Marie 317
Davison, Bruce 311
Davolos, Sydney 161
Dawes, Bill 269
Dawson, Deanne 269
Dawson, Margaret 272
Dawson, Michelle 254
Dawson, Neil 261
Dawson, Trent 254, 259
Day, Dan 346, 350
**Day in the Death of Joe
    Egg, A** 4, 23, *158–159*,
    159, 370, 371, 372,
    376, 377
Day, Jamie 312
Day, Johanna
    227, 269, 318, 319
Day, Tarissa 263
Day, Tom 268
Daye, Bobby Scott 314
Daykin, Judith E.
    196, 205, 212
Dayne, Taylor 215
Days, Maya 212, 215, 228
de Acha, Rafael 320
De Camillis, Chris 334
De Candia, Rosie 321
de Cervantes y Saavedra,
    Miguel 144
de Ganon, Clint 133
de Guzman, Donna Sue 267
de Guzman, Josie 313, 378
de Haas, Darius 335
de la Fuente, Joel 264, 267
De La Guarda *170*
De Laurentis, Semina 315
De Leon Escaler, Ernest 137
de Michele, Heather 264
de Montebello, Philippe 375
de Ocampo, Ramon
    253, 266, 314, 377
de Poyen, Jennifer
    xi, xv, 85, 200, 421
de Sade, Marquis 60
de Suze, Alexandra 206
de Vega, Lope 264
Dead Man's Socks 266
Deakins, Lucy 258
Deakins, Mark 303
Dealy, Bill 256, 270

Dean, Bradley 143, 144
Dean, Charles 301
Dear Prudence 269
DeArmon, Eric 200
Death in Venice 266
Death of a Salesman 95
Death of Frank 267
Death of the Sun 346
Death of Tintagiles, The
    264
Debbie Does Dallas
    14, 30, *187–188*
DeBear, Katya 335
deBenedet, Rachel 160
Deblinger, David 252, 265
DeBord, Jason 185
DeBruno, Tony 343
Debuskey, Merle 369
DeCarlo, Kenny 145
DeChristopher, Dave 260
Deck, Deanna 213
DeCorleto, Drew 265
DeCoux, Nathan 260
Dee, Ruby 322
Deep River 304
Def, Mos 202, 377
DeFeis, Frederic 341
Defoe, Ryan 340
DeGioia, Eric 206
Deicher, Cate 355
DeIorio, Victoria 380
DeJesus, Ron 138, 139
Del Guidice, Judy 269
Del Negro, Matthew 269
Del Sherman, Barry 273
Del Valle, Mayda 141
Del Valle, Melissa Delaney
    247
DelaCruz, Scott 180, 258
Delaney, Brian T. 346
Delaney, Vincent 300
Delany, Colleen 319
DeLaria, Lea 195, 220
Delate, Brian 163
deLeeuw, Meyer 260
DeLeon, Aya 268
DeLeon, Franco 327
Delgado, Emilio 269
Delgado, Judith 253
DelGaudio, Dennis 139
Delicate Balance, A 355
DeLillo, Don 260
Delisco 216
Delventhal, Thom 313
DeMaio, Tommy 129
Demaline, Jackie 278
DeMann, Frederick 153, 370
DeMann, Pilar 154

Demar, Jonathan 269
DeMarse, James 259
Demery, Brandon 192
Demke, Dave 336, 337, 338
Demon Baby 248
Demont, Lisa 245
Dempsey, Joe 326
Dempsey, Michael 168
Dempster, Curt 245
DeMunn, Jeffrey
    21, 141, 347
Denithorne, Peg 261
Denman, Jeffry 263
Dennehy, Brian
    24, 168, 371, 378
Dennen, Barry 229
Denniston, Leslie 351
Dent, John 143
Dent, Kelly 146
Dente, Barbara 341
Denton, Dylan 148, 244
D'Entrone, Eric 270
Denuszek, Jason 323
Denver Center Theatre
    Company 205, 312
Denver, John 30
Denzer, Chris 265
DeOni, Chris 253
DePoy, Philip 322
Derasse, Domenic 206
Derelian, Gregory 335
Derrah, Thomas 334
Derrick, Cleavant 230
Desai, Angel 245, 314
DeSandre, Eileen 345
Desch, Brad 262
Design Your Kitchen 262
Desjardins, Martin
    317, 319, 336
deSpain, Brandon 265
DesRochers, Rick 324
DeSylva, B.G. 180
Details 267
Devils of Loudun, The 249
Devine, Nicholas 249
Devine, Sean 256
Devlin, Es 159
DeVries, David 217
DeVries, Jon 256, 349
DeVries, Michael 225
Dewar, Jenny 142
Dewhurst, Jeffrey 249
DeWitt, David 260, 261
DeWitt, Rosemarie 244
deWolf, Cecilia 246
DeWolf, Nat 154
Dey, Naleah 212
Di Donna, Suzanne 264

Di Martino, Annie 261
Di Novelli, Donna 248
Di Stasi, Laurence 324
Di Vecchio, Daniella 341
Diamond, I.A.L. 350
Diamond, Liz 314, 317
Diana, Rachel 250
Diaries, The 351
Dias, John 178
Dias, Romi 260
Diaz, Carlos 250
Diaz, Fiora 321
Diaz, Natascia 143, 144, 319
Dibble, Ben 348
Dibble, Sean 249
Dibble, Susan 337
Dibiasio, Matt 263
DiBucci, Michelle 339
DiBuono, Toni 134, 262
DiCanzio, William 313
DiCaprio, Leonardo 18
Dick, Adam 265
Dick Cavett Show, The 70
Dick, Paul 266
Dick, William 327
Dickens, Matthew 303
Dickerman, Mark 373
Dickerson, Brian 265
Dickerson, Nicole 300
Dickerson, Will 324
Dickert, Les 342
Dickinson, Emily 62
Dickstein, Rachel 254
DiCostanzo, Dina 328
Dido (and Aeneas) 269
Diehl, John 265
Dietz, Dan 332
Dietz, Ryan 249
Dietz, Steven 340, 354, 356
Dietz, Susan 152
Diflo, Mick 254
Diggs, Taye 220, 228
Digiancinto, Dena 229
Dignan, Pat 250
DiGregorio, Taz 157, 370
Dill, Sean 266
Dilliard, Marcus 301, 338
Dillingham, Charles 136, 305
Dillman, Laura 266
Dillon, Mia 21, 141, 252
Dilly, Erin 134
DiMaggio, Stephanie 254
Dimetos 335
DiMilla, Paul 334
Dimino, Donna 263
Dimond, Nic 328
DiMonda, Vic 249
Dimson Theatre 262

DiMurro, Tony 260, 262
Dinelaris, Alexander 202, 243
Dini, Gary 248
Dinklage, Jonathan 166
Dinklage, Peter 263
Dinner at Eight
    4, 22, *150–151*,
    151, 370, 371, 375, 377
Dinner With Friends 326
Dinnerman, Amy
    135, 152, 161, 174
Dinosaur Within, The
    277, 278, 375
Dionisio, Ma-Anne 136, 223
Diosa 313
DiPietro, Jay 268
DiPietro, Joe 169
**Dipteracon, or Short Lived
    S*%t Eaters** 250
Directors Company, The 262
DiRocco, Henry 310
Dirty Blonde
    72, 348, 351, 379, 380
Dirty Laundry 266
Dirty Story 238, 265
Disorderly Conduct 272
Dispute, La 334
Distefano, Madi 349
Divine Comedy, A 304
DiVita, Diane 153, 173
Dixon, Beth 173
Dixon, Brandon Victor
    196, 224
Dixon, Keith 173
Dixon, MacIntyre 164, 216
Dixon, Michael 346
Dixon, Tami 261
Dixon, Tonya 223
Dizon, Eugene 380
Dlamini, Nomvula 224
Dlugos, Gregory J. 160
Dmitriev, Alex 258
DMV Tyrant 266
Dobbins, Adia Ginneh 224
Dobell, Curzon 256, 343
Dobie, Edgar 349, 369
Dobozé, Gunnard 336
Dobrish, Jeremy 261, 263
Dobrusky, Pavel 343
Dobson, Terry 350
Dockery, Leslie 179, 265
Doctor, Bruce 134
**Doctor Will See You Now,
    The** 266
Dodd, Jonathan xiii
Dodge, Alexander 197, 373
Dodger Management Group
    198

Dodger Stage Holding
    141, 198
Doers, Matthew 248
Doherty, Denny 272
Doherty, Jeffrey Johnson 185
Doherty, Patricia E. 341
Doherty, Vincent 202
Dokuchitz, Jonathan
    134, 166, 167
Dolan, Donovan 268
Dolan, Judith 141, 262
Dold, Mark H. 245
Dolen, Christine
    i, xii, xvi, 277, 279, 421
Dolenz, Micky 216
Dollymore, Patrick 327
Domiano, Cat 331
Dominczyk, Dagmara
    12, 163
Domingo, Colman 263, 302
Domingo, Ron 252, 266, 377
Domingues, Dan 334
Domoney, Kurt 263
Domski, Jude 270
Don Carlos 355
Don Juan 256, 257
Donaghy, Tom 171, 345, 347
Donahoe, Emily 303
Donahue, Alan 380
Donaldson, Martha 188, 208
Donaldson, Walter 180
Dondlinger, Mary Jo 248, 258
Donen, Stanley 192
Donkey Show, The *170*
Donmar Warehouse
    10, 36, 104, 154,
    177, 178, 193, 194,
    195, 370
Donna Paradise 269
Donnellan, Darcy 341
Donnellan, Evan 341
Donnelly, Candice 208, 212
Donnelly, Kyle 379
Donnelly, Terry 247
Donohue, Dan 354
Donovan, Conor 141
Donovan, Maripat 169
Donovan, Sean 268
Donowaki, Kyoko 250
Door Wide Open 260
DoPico, Madeleine Jane 262
Doran, Bathsheba 261
Doran, Jesse 258
Doran, Patrick 346
Dorfman, Robert 224, 352
Dorian, Stephanie 266
Dorman, Tracy 342
Dornfeld, Autumn 252

Dorsen, Annie 262
Dorsey, Court 249
Dorsey, Kena Tangi 312
Dorsey, Kent 309, 355
Dos Passos, John 74, 259
Doshi, Marcus 256
Dossett, John
    150, 164, 165, 319, 371
Dostoevsky, Fyodor 263
Dotson, Bernard 149, 308
Doty, Johnna 255
Dougherty, Doc 31, 209
Dougherty, Pam 350
Dougherty, Sean 355
Douglas Fairbanks Theatre
    263
Douglas, Tim 335
Douglas, Timothy
    329, 331, 332, 342
Doumanian, Jean
    131, 138, 370
Douthit, Lue Morgan
    343, 345
Douzos, Adriana
    157, 190, 196, 198
Dove, Lilith 269
Dower, David 304
Dowlin, Tim 263
Dowlin, Tom 376
Dowling, Jocelyn 146
Dowling, Joe (director) 22,
    152, 338
Dowling, Joey (actor) 212
Down a Long Road
    14, 31, *213*
Down in the Depths 273
Down, Katie 254
Downey, Gerald 267
Downey, Melissa 138
Doyle, Jim 269
Doyle, Kathleen 254
Doyle, Lori M. 166
Doyle, Mary Alice 327
Doyle, Mike 269
Doyle, Richard 311
Doyle, Rio Maria 336
Doyle, Timothy 163
Doyun Seol 144, 371
DR2 Theatre 263
Dragotta, Robert 136
Drake, David 262
Drake, Donna 214, 269
Drake, Larry 311
Drama Book Shop xiii
Drama Dept. 238, 245
Drama Desk Award 376
Drama League Award 376
Dramatic Forces 136, 370

Dramatists Guild 423
Dramatists Play Service 41
Dramatist's Toolkit, The 423
Drance, George 250
Draper, Alex 173
Drapkin, Russel 196
Draud, Rocky 321
Draves, J. Kevin 214
Drawer Boy, The
    308, 310, 311, 342
Drawn and Quartered 247
Dream a Little Dream 272
Dream of No Words 313
Dreams of Sarah
    Breedlove, The 300
Dressed Like an Egg 234
Dressel, Michael 163
Dresser, Richard 332
Drew, Jeffrey 270
Drew, Sarah 154
Drewes, Glenn 212
Dreyblatt, Arnold 250
Dreyfoos, Alex W. 380
Dreyfuss, Richard 38, 184
Driffield, Joseph 245
Driscoll, Kermit 156
Driver, Kip 270
Drukman, Steven 314
Drummer, Lindsay 304
Drummond, Joseph 324, 326
Dryden, Deborah M. 343
D'Souza, Laine 262
D'Souza, Neil 204
Duarte, Myrna 256
Dubin, Al 128
Dubin, Jeremy 356
Dublin Carol xi, xv, 14, 35,
    51–57, 52, 54,
    56, *196*, 367, 377
DuBoff, Jill B.C.
    167, 258, 319
DuBois, Peter 253
Dubreuil, Alexa 267
Dubrowsky, Kristin 260
Duchamp, Marcel 60
Dudding, Joey 164
Dudley, Anton 261
Dudu Fisher: Something
    Old, Something New
    14, 31, *185*
Duell, William 254
Duffield, Marjorie 272
Duffy, R. Ward 339
Duffy, Scott 259
DuFord, Chip 343
Dug Out 264
Duggan, Annmarie 180
Duggan, James 341

Duguay, Brian 273
Duke, Cherry 206
Duke, Patty 226
Dulack, Tom 300, 341
Dulaney, Kristin 329
DuMaine, Rebecca 263
duMaine, Wayne 143
Dumakude, Thuli 224
Duncan, Laura Marie 265
Duncan, Sandy 218, 255
Duncan-Gibbs, Mamie 219
Dundas, Shane 267
Dundon, Marie Bridget 265
Dunlop, April 340
Dunn, Jennifer 263
Dunn, Juliette 348
Dunn, Lindsay 146
Dunn, Ronnie 157, 370
Dunn, Ryan 348
Dunn, Wally 164
Dunn-Rankin, Jonathan 304
Dupas, Ariel Elisabeth 342
Duplantier, Donna 317
DuPont, Anne 258
Duprey, Leslie 264
Dupuis, John Michael 334
Duquesnay, Ann 266
Duran, Sherrita 206
Durang, Christopher
    266, 271, 272, 310
Duras, Marguerite 262
Durgin, Peter 335
Durham, Nathan 202
Duricko, Erma 261
Durkee, Savitri 268
Durkin, Dave 268
Durkin, Todd Allen 267
Durning, Charles 36, 186
Durran, Jacqueline 149
Dusenbury, Tom 267
d'Usseau, Arnaud 260
Dutton, Charles S. 22, 153
Duva, Christopher
    252, 253, 264, 265
Duvert, Michael 154
Duwon, Tony 207
Duykers, John 244, 324
Dwyer, Terrence 303
Dybas, James 341
Dybisz, Kenneth 166
Dyck, Jordan 272
Dygert, Tammy 321
Dykstra, Brian 258
Dylan 379
Dymond, Andrea J. 328
Dysart, Eric 132, 133
Dyszel, Bill 261

Eagan, Jason Scott 195
Eagar, Erin 264
Eakeley, Benjamin 269
Eakes, Jenny 260
Earl, Shaun 228
Earley, Kevin 223
Early, Kathleen 247, 248
Earth's Sharp Edge, The
    250
Easley, Bill 176
East West Players 302
Easter, Allison 250
Easterbrook, Leslie 316
Eastman, Donald 342
Easton, Richard
    36, 196, 225, 348
Eaton, Mark 171
Eaves, Dashiell 197
Eaves, Obadiah 202
Ebb, Fred 127, 128, 379
Ebersold, Scott 253, 266
Ebersole, Christine
    22, 115, 117, 118,
    150, 151, 208, 221,
    371, 377
Echoles, Rueben D. 207
Eckert, Rinde 271, 334
Eckert, Virginia 349
Edel, Carrie 273
Edelman, Gregg 223
Edelstein, Barry
    239, 245, 271
Edelstein, Gordon
    253, 314, 352
Edgar, David 343
Edgardo Mine 312
Edge Theater Company 93
Edgerly, Corinne 262, 272
Edgerton, Annie 267
Edgerton, Jeff 312
Edgerton, Nina 265
Edgewood Productions 190
Edinburgh Festival 37, 202
Edington, Pamela 173
Edmond, Martin 341
Edmondson, James 345
Education of Randy
    Newman, The 352
Edward Albee: A Singular
    Journey 421
Edwards, Alison 174
Edwards, Anderson 172
Edwards, Bill 266
Edwards, Duncan Robert 379
Edwards, Fred 157, 370

Edwards, Jason 267
Edwards, Luanne 249
Edwards, Michael Donald
    342
Edwards, Scott W. 338
Effect of Gamma Rays on
    Man-in-the-Moon
    Marigolds, The 264
Egan, David 337
Egan, John Treacy 227
Egan, Rich 256
Egan, Robert 305, 307
Egan, Susan 216, 217
Egg 311
Eggington, Paul 304
Egi, Stan 309
Egolf, Gretchen 311
Ehlers, Heather 311
Ehn, Erik 332
Ehrenreich, Barbara 307, 353
Eich, Stephen 302
Eidem, Bruce 164
Eigenberg, David 153
8½ 19
8 Bob Off 304
Eighteen 264, 346
Eilenberg, Larry 304
Einhorn, Susan 373
Einstein, Albert 240
Einstein's Dreams 263
Eisenbach, Dave 239
Eisenberg, Deborah 195
Eisenberg, Ned 265, 272
Eisenhauer, Peggy
    138, 164, 176, 195
Eisenman, Andrew 264
Eisenstein, Alexa 188, 189
Eisner, Morten 245
Ekeh, Onome 272
Ekstrand, Laura 340
Ekulona, Saidah Arrika
    271, 272, 317
El Samahy, Nora 302
El-Khatib, Mona 335
Elaine Stritch: At Liberty 3
Elder, David 221
Eldridge, David 302
Eleanore and Isadora: A
    Duet of Sorrows 258
Electra 313
Elegies 14, 36, 204
Elegy 264
Elephant Man, The 9, *129*
Elevator 271
Elg, Taina 262
Elias, Doren 304
Elice, Eric 192
Elich, Michael 343

Elizabeth Hull–Kate Warriner
    Award 375
Elizondo, Hector 354
Elle 238, 273
Ellett, Trey 228
Elliard, Leslie 252, 253
Elliot Hayes Award 423
Elliot Norton Award xiii, 378
Elliott, David 184
Elliott, Paul 321
Elliott, Scott 254, 261
Elliott, Shawn 253, 254, 314
Ellipsis 269
Ellis, Michael Shane 266
Ellis, Scott 9, 135, 166
Ellison, Bill 164
Ellison, Nancy 192
Ellison, Todd 138
Ellman, Bruce 195, 203
Ellmore, Mark 322
Ellsmore, Siho 264, 267
Elly, James 323, 327
Elmore, Richard 343, 344
Elmore, Steve 316
Elrod, Carson 211, 225
Elson, Elizabeth 268
Elsperger, Bruce 309
Ely, Christian 266
Embarrassments 314
Embree, Nick 345, 347
Emelson, Beth
    190, 196, 213, 244
Emerick, Shannon 261
Emerson, Michael 270
Emery, Esther 304
Emery, Julie Ann 303
Emery, Lisa 261
Emmes, David 309, 311
Emmons, Beverly 373
Emond, Linda
    12, 158, 186, 371, 377
Emory University 422
Empty Space Theatre 352
Enchanted April
    4, 11, 12, *163*,
    370, 371, 377
Enchanted April, The 163
End of the Tour, The 328
Enders, Camilla 268
Endpapers 14, 28, *173*
Endre, Lena 171
Endy, Alex 264
Eng, Randall 314
Eng, Steven 323
Engel, David 253
Engelkes, Charlotte 204
Engelman, Liz 340
England, Mel 270

Engle, Tod 267
Engler, Michael 118, 208
Engquist, Richard 179
Ensemble Studio Theatre
      238, 245
Ensign, Evan 150, 308
Ensler, Eve 170, 271, 272
Entertaining Mr. Sloane
      326
Entitled Entertainment
      168, 179
Entriken, Dan 145, 146
Ephron, Henry 69
Ephron, Nora x, xiii, xv, 10,
      69–78, 149, 308
Ephron, Phoebe 69
Epp, Steven 338
Epstein, Adam 192, 370
Epstein, Alvin 189, 190
Epstein, Donny 185
Erba, Edoardo 269
Erdman, Ernie 180
Erdossy, Adam 314
Erendira 264
Ergo Entertainment 168, 185
Erickson, Susan 343
Erickson, Nick 302
Erickson, T. Charles 257
Ernst, Lee F. 355, 356
Errico, Melissa
      16, 138, 271, 371
Esbjornson, David
      182, 189, 298, 303, 338
Escamilla, Michael Ray
      252, 256, 291, 319, 378
Escape From Happiness
      355
Esler, David 249
Esparza, Raúl 217, 254, 319
Esper, Michael 245
Esping, Laura 338
Espinosa, Al 175
Espinoza, Brandon 164
Essanay 346
Essman, Nina 144
Esterman, Laura 260
Estévez, Abilio 247
Esther, Queen 176, 177
Estrera, Philip 260
Etemad, Nakissa 348, 349
Ethan Frome 336
Etta Jenks 268
Ettinger, Daniel 319
Eugene O'Neill Theater Center
      313, 423
Euripides 148, 236, 244, 264,
      270, 273, 316, 334
Eurydice 259, 318

Eustis, Oskar 173, 349
Evan, Rob 146, 171
Evangelisto, Christie 316
Evans, Bill
      130, 138, 142, 167
Evans, Christine 264
Evans, Daniel 332
Evans, David 136
Evans, Dawn 260
Evans, Jef 301
Evans, Jessma 263, 268
Evans, Joan 260
Evans, Leo Ash 263
Evans, Omar 263
Evans, Scott Alan 259
Evans, Venida 179
Evered, Charles 271, 272
Everhart, Kurt 252, 259
**Every Good Boy Deserves
      Favor** 348
Evett, Benjamin 334
Evett, Marianne 278
Evolution 263
Ewell, Dwight 273
Ewen, Malcolm 327
Ewin, Paula 272
Ewing, Michael J. 349
Ewing, Skip 157, 370
Excelsior 264
Exit, Eric Y. 325
Exodus 271
Exonerated, The 14, 38,
      184–185, 367, 377
Expat/Inferno 248, 253
Exposed 318
Eyre, Richard 155
Ezell, Wayman 314

Fabel, Kyle 259
Faber, Ron 261
Fabulist, The 376
Facer, Susan 226
Faculty Room, The 330, 331
Fadale, Cristina 228
Fagin, Michael 347
Faiella, Lori 272
Fair Game 254
Fairbairn, Bill 265
Fairbanks, Douglas 263
Fairchild, Diane D. 323
Falco, Edie 8, 131, 221, 272
Falcone, Terianne 266
Falkenstein, Eric 167, 370
Fallon, Sharon 130

Falls, Robert
      24, 128, 168, 324,
      372, 376
Fame on 42nd Street 422
Fandrei, Graham 145, 146
Fanger, Iris 378
Fann, Ashalee 303
Fanning, Gene 263
Fanning, Tony 308
Fantaci, Jim 192
Fantasticks, The 380
Far and Wide 239, 252
Far Away 14, 31, *188*, 189,
      367, 375
Farazis, Takis 188
Farber, Gene 245
Farber, Seth 133
Farentino, James 303
Faridany, Francesca 302
Farkas, Michael 264
Farley, Keythe 322
Farley, Leo 272
Farm: Angola, USA, The 423
Farnsworth, Matt 314
Farrar, Ann 270
Farrar, Thursday 223
Farrell, Erin 256
Farrell, Henry 351
Farrell, I. Thecla 260
Farrell, Richard 344, 345
Farrell, Sean 195, 247
Farrell, Tim 253
Farrell, Tom Riis 186
Farwell, Bradford 355
Fasbender, Bart 176
Fascination 313
Fashion 266
Fashion Institute of
      Technology 290
Faster 269
Father-Joy 347
Fatone, Joey 228
Fattouche, Piter 340, 345
Faulkner, Todd 270
Fauss, M. Michael 323
Faust, Bobby 145
Faustus 266
Faye, Pascale 138
Fazio, Santo 265
Feagan, Leslie 269
Fear and Friday Nights 268
Fearless Vampire Killers, The
      17
Fechter, Steven 269
Federle, Tim 164
Fegley, Michael 250
Feichtner, Vadim 204
Feiffer, Halley 261

Feil, Simon 263
Feinberg, Amy 264
Feiner, Harry A. 341
Feingold, Michael
    171, 355, 367
Feldberg, Robert 367
Feldman, Aaron 266
Feldman, Lawrence 212
Feldman, Melissa
    90, 199, 200, 265
Feldman, Rachel 263
Feldman, Tibor 266
Feldshuh, Tovah
    37, 204, 373, 376
Felix, John 380
Fellini, Federico 19
Feltch, John 163, 314
Fendig, David 318, 319
Feng, Han 248
Fenichell, Susan 331
Fenkart, Bryan 262
Fennell, Bob
    144, 150, 178, 181,
    191, 192, 201, 210, 214
Fennell, Denise 262
Fenton, James 127
Ferber, Edna 22, 150
Ferencz, George 250
Ferguson, Jesse Tyler
    195, 314
Ferguson, Michelle 342
Ferguson, Ryan 342
Ferland, Danielle
    19, 161, 267
Ferm, Shayna 258
Fernandez, Peter Jay
    172, 269, 326
Fernandez-Coffey, Gabriela
    267
Ferrá, Max 246, 247
Ferrara, Susan 265
Ferrone, Richard 259
Ferver, Jack 253
Feser, Craig 253
Fetherolf, Andrew 269
Feuchtwanger, Peter R. 167
Feuer, Cy 372
Feuer, Donya 171
Feyer, Daniel 269
Feynman, Richard 128
Fiction 340
Field, Crystal 256
Field of Fireflies 264
Field, Sally 9, 221
Fielding, Jonathan 262
Fields, Edith 265
Fields, Heather 156
Fields, Joseph 16, 136

Fierstein, Harvey
    ix, 3, 5, 132, 221, 371, 376
Fiery Rain, The 337
Fife, Michael 262
5th Avenue Theatre 3, 133
Fifth of July 235, 255, 373
Figaro 338
Fighting Words 317
Figueroa, Rona 160, 223
Fiksel, DJ Misha 328
Filerman, Michael 200
Filichia, Peter 376
Filijan, Karin 304
Filloux, Catherine 253
Finding the Eye 340
Findlay, Diane J. 315, 316
Fine, Rosemary 233, 251
Fineman, Carol R.
    175, 176, 178, 189,
    198, 202, 205, 207, 210
Finer Noble Gases 102
Finley, Felicia 215
Finn, Rob 141, 147, 162, 200
Finn, William 36, 204
Finnegan, Rebecca 380
Finnegans Wake 233
Finneran, Katie 218, 225
Finney, Albert 36, 183
Finney, Shirley Jo 346
Finnie, Leo V. III 299
Firman, Linsay 252, 253, 254
First Day of School 271
First Love 304
Firth, Katie 265, 270
Fisch, Irwin 162
Fischer, Allison 172
Fischer, Kurt Eric 335
Fischer, Takayo 302
Fish, Daniel 245, 317
Fishelson, David 204
Fisher, Dara 307, 314, 336
Fisher, Dudu 31, 185
Fisher, Ellen 245
Fisher, Joe 252
Fisher, Joely 217
Fisher, Jules 138, 164, 176
Fisher, Kate 223
Fisher, Laura T. 326
Fisher, Linda 247, 251
Fisher, Mary Beth 326, 339
Fisher, Rick 188
Fisher, Rob
    196, 205, 206, 212
Fisher, Wade 260
Fishman, Alan H.
    171, 193, 204, 207, 244
Fishman, Carol 176, 191, 195
Fishman, Shirley 353

Fit for Feet 332, 333
Fitzgerald, Christopher
    138, 197
Fitzgerald, David 260
Fitzgerald, Desiree 339, 340
Fitzgerald, Glenn
    35, 190, 191
Fitzgerald, Jason 336, 337
Fitzgerald, John 330
Fitzgerald, Paul 187, 225
Fitzgerald, Peter
    130, 139, 156, 193,
    198, 308, 320
Fitzgerald, Shannon 256
Fitzgerald, T. Richard
    185, 192
Fitzgibbons, Mark 245
Fitzmaurice, Colm 206
Fitzpatrick, Allen 255
Fitzpatrick, Julie 260
Fitzsimmons, Andrew 269
FitzSimmons, James 335
Fitzsimmons, Kelly Jean 266
Fitzwater, Anna 264
Five Frozen Embryos 267
Flack 266
Flaherty, Stephen
    36, 183, 270
Flak, John David 328
Flanagan, John 304
Flanagan, Laura 271
Flanagan, Margiann 258
Flanagan, Pauline 247, 339
Flanders, Kristin
    256, 257, 353
Flanery, Bridget 269, 308
Flaningam, Louisa 258
Flashing Stream, The 270
Flateman, Charles 176
Flea Theater, The 238, 263
Fleischman, Hans 327
Fleischmann, Stephanie 252
Fleming, Adam 132, 133
Fleming, Eugene
    166, 167, 255
Fleming, Sam 172
Fleming, Tommy R. 354
Flemming, Brian 322
Fletcher, Gregory 261, 267
Fletcher, Jim 250
Fletcher, Liz 380
Flintstone, Trauma 269
Floating Home 269
Floating World 269
Flood, Karen 255
Flora, Pat A. 318, 323
Flora Roberts Award 375
Florax, Peter 268

Florida Stage 380
Flower Drum Song
    4, 16, 136, *136–*
    137, 370, 371, 372
Flower, Ethan 336, 337
Floyd, Carmen Ruby
    191, 340
Floyd Collins 380
Floyd, Mike 332
Floyd, Patricia R. 254
Fly-Bottle, The 337
Flying Machine, The 256
Flynn, Laura James 247
Flynn, Tom 336
Flyovers 423
Foard, Merwin 226
Fodor, Barbara and Peter 155
Fogarty, Brud 301
Fogarty, Sharon 255, 251
Fogel, Donna Jean 259, 260
Fois, Laura 266
Foley 14, 37, *201–202*
Foley, Eamon 164
Foley, Peter 271, 334
Foley, Sean 157, 158
Folino, Mary Andrea 348
Followell, James 198
Folson, Eileen 146, 164
Fondoukis, Kosmas 188
Font, Vivia 253, 272
Fonteno, David 347
Foote, Horton 170, 375
For Lindbergh 350
Forbes, George 373
Ford, Bethany 312
Ford, Jennie 156
Ford, Mark Richard 228
Ford, Paul 25, 141
Ford, Rachel 264
Foreign Exchange 346
Foreman, Karole 225
Foreman, Richard
    233, 234, 236, 237,
    268, 375
Foreman, Ruth 380
Foret, Nicole 155, 156, 320
Forgette, Katie 354
Forman, Ken 268
Fornes, Maria Irene 256
Fornes, María Irene 239, 285
Foronda, Joseph Anthony
    379
Forrest, Rosie 327
Forrester, Sean 254
Forsman, Carl 265
Forsyth, Jerold 348
Fortenberry, Philip 166
Fortin, Mark Alexandre 334

Fortunato, Sean 323
Fortune's Fool 9, *129*, 380
45th Street Theatre 263
45 Bleecker 263
42nd Street *128*, 220
47th Street Theatre 263
Fosberg, Michael Sidney 339
Fosco, Joseph 380
Fosse, Bob 127
Foster, Benim 254
Foster, Charles 249
Foster, Duane Martin 196
Foster, Flannery 268
Foster, Hunter 229
Foster, Janet 153
Foster, Lynne 341
Foster, Sutton 223, 229
Foster, Tobi 223
Foucard, Alexandra 196
Fountain Theatre 346
4/19(/95) 271
Fournier, Kelli 215, 379
Fournier, Todd 229
14th Street Y 263
Fourth Sister, The 258
Fourth Wall, The 238, 255
Foust, Joe 324
Fowler, Beth 217
Fowler, Mayhill 380
Fowler, Molly 209
Fowler, Monique 308
Fowler, Rachel 259
Fowler, Scott 138, 139
Fox, Alan 163
Fox, Ben 21, 141
Fox, Eamon 202
Fox, Josh 249
Fox, Lovena 352
Fox, Meg 353
Fox, Robert
    154, 163, 164, 370
Fox Searchlight Pictures
    144, 371, 379
Foy, Conor 307
Foy, Harriett D.
    191, 253, 340
Fragalid, Helle 267
Fraioli, David 263
Frame 312 322, 349
Franciosa, Christopher 252
Francis, Cameron 270
Francis, David Paul 316
Francis, Juliana 253
Francis, Kevin 346
Francis, Stacy 196
Franck, Alison 130
Frank, Glenda 375
Frankel, Jennifer 335

Frankel, Jerry 163, 370
Frankel, Richard 182, 185
**Frankie and Johnny in the
    Clair de Lune**
    4, 8, 20, *131*,
    221, 370, 371, 375
Franklin, Tara 335
Franklin Thesis, The 264
Frantz, Marisa 256
Franz, Elizabeth 342
Franzblau, William 135, 370
Franzman, Jared 263
Fraser, Alison 245
Fraser, Jon 261
Fratti, Mario 19, 160, 375
Fratti, Valentina 261
Fräulein Else 302
Frayn, Michael 128, 342
Frears, Will 329
Frederick, Brian 350
Frederick Loewe Award 375
Frederick, Patrick 258
Fredrik, Burry 316
Freeburg, Christine D. 323
Freed, Amy 311, 317, 324
Freedman, Glenna
    141, 156, 193
Freedman, Katherine 273
Freeman, Cheryl 330, 331
Freeman, Debra A. 331
Freeman, K. Todd 326
Freeman, Ryan 262
Freeman, Sara 328
Freeman, Steven 96, 99
Freeman, Tony 198, 224
Freer, Karen 262
Freitag, Barbara 156
French, Arthur 261
French Company of the New
    Orleans Theatre 152
French, Jae 135, 370
French, Kent 335
Freud, Sigmund 100
Freundlich, Ursula 320
Frey, Matthew 210, 332, 342
Fri, Sean 265
Fried, Joshua 264
Friedland, Adam 327
Friedman, Alex 342
Friedman, Carrie 133, 168
Friedman, Dee Dee 273
Friedman, Max 339
Friedman, Melissa 270
Friedman, Michael
    248, 256, 335
Friedman, Neil 324
Friedman, Peter 182
Friedman, Renata 267

Friedman, Sonia 370
Friedson, David and Adam
    167, 371
Friel, Brian 193
Friend, David 170
Friend, Jenny R. 308, 309
Friends Like These 300
Friesen, Peggy 339
Frink, Arlene 265
Frisch, Peter 258
Frith, Daniel 351
From the Top 272
Fromm, Richard 259
Frosk, John 212
Frost, Sue 312
Frozen 375
Fry, Kate 324, 379
Fuchs, Ken 263
Fuchs, Michael 146, 147
Fucking A
    14, 33, *202*, 367, 377
Fuddy Meers 352
Fuenteovejuna 264
Fugard, Athol 37, 207, 335
Fujiyabu, Kaori 250
Fula From America, The
    299
Fulcomer, Alden 316
Fulham, Mary 249
Full Focus 421
Full Monty, The
    9, *128*, 230, 379
**Full Spectrum: A Techno-
    Theatre Experiment**
    246
Fuller, Dale 270
Fuller, David 264, 265
Fuller, Larry 260
Fuller, Penny 212
Fully Committed 347
Fumusa, Dominic 177
Funaro, Robert 268
Fundamental 264
Funderburg, Barry G.
    355, 356
Funeral Parlor 266
Funicello, Ralph 307
Funk, Andrew 244, 324
Funk, Joshua 379
**Fuqua Slone Reisenglass
    Appraisal, The** 261
Furlong, Richard
    330, 331, 332
Furman, Jay 176
Furman, Jill 192
Furman, Roy
    146, 161, 192, 193, 370
Furth, George 319

Furukawa, Irene Sanaye 302
Future?, The 262
Fyfe, Jim 246

G-d Doesn't Pay Rent Here
    352
Gabara, Cornel 334
Gabriadze, Rezo 237
Gabriel, Gene 153, 177
Gabrielle, Josefina 226
Gabrielle, Maya 271
Gaffin, Arthur 161
Gagnon, David 206
Gailen, Judy 337
Gaines, Boyd 218
Gaines, Davis 226
gaines, reg e. 332
Gajda, Lisa 155
Gajdusek, Karl 254
Gajic, Olivera 197
Galantich, Tom 134
Galapagos 377
Galassini, Sara 250
Gale, Bill 278
Gale, Jack 206, 212
Gale, James 247, 348
Galilee, Clove 233, 251
Galileo Galilei 244, 324
Galindo, Eileen
    304, 305, 307
Galindo, Louis 253
Gallagher, Anne 135, 370
Gallagher, Fiona 317
Gallagher, Helen 235
Gallagher, Jerry 179
Gallagher, John Jr. 195
Gallagher, Peter 225, 271
Gallagher, Robert 223
Gallant John-Joe, The 264
Galligan, Carol 260
Gallin, Sandy 142, 371
Gallin, Susan Quint 142, 371
Gallo, David 147, 153, 326
Gallo, Glory 261
Gallo, Paul 144
Gallop, Mark 250
Gambatese, Jennifer
    19, 132, 133, 161
Gamble, Julian 151, 255
Gambrel, TJ 267
Game Show 422
Gandhi, Mahatma 95
Gandy, Irene 163
Ganeles, Robyn 317

Ganier, Yvette
    252, 325, 326, 327
Ganser, L.J. 270
Gant, Mtume 269
Gantt, Leland 153, 252
Garayva, Gloria 253
Garcés, Michael John
    246, 247, 252, 271,
    317, 319, 321, 336
Garcia, Alejandro 170
Garcia, Jesús 145
García Márquez, Gabriel 264
Garcia, Minerva 307
Garcia, Perry 247
Garcia, Roland 262
Garcia-Gelpe, Marina 268
Garden *171*, 367
Gardiner, Leah 252
Gardiner, Muriel 72, 75
Gardner, Angel 249
Gardner, Cecilia Hobbs 145
Gardner, Elysa 366
Gardner, Herb 129
Gardner, Kim 256
Gardner, Lisa 267
Gardner, Lori 258
Gardner, Michael
    146, 161, 370
Garello, Lawrence 263
Gargani, Michael 262
Garman, Andrew 163
Garmen, Andrew 271
Garner, André 179
Garner, Crystal 206
Garner, Mike 350
Garner, Patrick 173
Garner, Sandra 204
Garnier, François 65
Garonzik, Sara 347
Garrett, Bob 328
Garrett, Jack 267
Garrick, Barbara 245
Garrison, Gary 259
Garrison, Mary Catherine 187
Garrison, Nick 353
Garrity, Jack 267
Garson, Willie 303
Garvey-Blackwell, Jennifer
    258
Garzia, Bernie 171
Gash, Kent 255, 323
Gasman, Ira 33, 198
Gasparian, Martha R.
    135, 370
Gasteyer, Ana 195
Gaston, Lydia 264
Gaston, Michael 158
Gate Theatre 52

Gates, Thomas J. 185
Gathe, Victoria A. 302
Gatton, Vince 268
Gaukel, Andy 349
Gavigan, Jenna 164
Gaviria, Adriana 261
Gawlik, Jennifer 313
Gay, Jackson 269
Gaylor, Angela 272
Geeson, Judy 303
Geffen Playhouse 302
Gehringer, Linda 309
Geiger, Mary Louise
    331, 341, 353
Geis, Alexandra 260
Geissinger, Katie 145, 245
Geisslinger, Bill 343, 344
Geisslinger, Nell 345
Geither, Mike 249
Gelbart, Larry 382
Gelber, Jack 240
Gelber, Jordan 258, 314
Geller, Marc 263
Gelormini, Bruno 270
Gelpe, Leah 317
Gem of the Ocean
    313, 325, 326
Gemignani, Alexander 335
Gener, Randy 375
General From America, The
    256, 257, 349
Generalovich, Tracy 217
Genest, Edmond 313
Genet, Jean
    238, 239, 261, 273
Geneva 249
Gennaro, Michael 326
Gentry, Ken 185
Genz, Suzanne 380
Genzlinger, Neil 267
George Abbott Award
    380, 421
George, Emmitt C. 268
George Freedley Memorial
    Award 375
George Jean Nathan Award
    375, 421, 423
George, Libby 260
George, Lovette 262, 315
George, Madeleine 253, 314
George Oppenheimer Award
    376
George, Phill 314
George, Rhett G. 198
George Street Playhouse 180
Georgia State University 422
Geralis, Antony 138
Gerckens, T.J. 244, 324

Gereghty, Ruthanne 266
Gerety, Peter 202, 262
Gerle, Andrew 376
Gero, Edward 351
Gerroll, Daniel
    12, 163, 238, 239, 245
Gershon, Gina 218
Gershwin, George
    180, 193, 263
Gershwin, Ira 263
Gersten, Bernard
    128, 150, 154, 183,
    196, 204, 370, 382
Gersten, David 200
Gersten-Vassilaros, Alexandra
    329
Gerstenberger, Emil 206
Gets, Malcolm
    16, 137, 138, 203, 371
Gettelfinger, Sara 134, 160
Getto, Erica 158
Geva Theatre 318, 341
GFO 132
Ghaffari, Mohammad 251
Ghassemi, Deligani Alaeaddin
    251
Ghassemi, Mohammadreza
    251
Ghedia, Mala 204
Ghir, Kulvinder 204
Ghosts 239, 245
Giacalone, Johnny
    34, 210, 313
Giacosa, Giuseppe 144
Giamatti, Paul 186
Gianfrancesco, Edward T.
    179
Gianino, Antonia 174, 205
Giannini, Maura 146, 164
Giardina, Anthony 313
Giarrizzo, Guy 261
Gibbons, Tessa 267
Gibbs, Jennifer 263, 265
Gibbs, Kathi 304
Gibbs, Nancy Nagel 144
Gibbs, Sheila 224
Gibson, Darren 196, 212
Gibson, Deborah 216, 218
Gibson, Edwin Lee 336
Gibson, Julia 269, 270
Gibson, Meg 317
Gibson, William 37, 204
Gibson-Clark, Tanya 255
Giddish, Kelli 314
Gien, Pamela 170
Gifford, Sarah 270
Gigl, Aloysius 172
Gilbert, James 263

Gilbert, Sara 38, 184
Gilburne, Jessica 179
Gilfry, Rodney 206, 207
Gilger, Paul 197
Gill, Michel 245
Gill, Temple 136
Gilliam, Michael
    307, 342, 347
Gilligan, Carol 337
Gillis, Graeme 245
Gillman, Jason 315
Gilman, Rebecca 303, 304
Gilman, Zachary 260
Gilmore, Allen 323
Gilmour, Susan 223
Gilpin Players 180
Gilsig, Jessalyn 255
Gimmick, The 119
Gimpel, Erica 309, 334
Gines, Christopher 170
Gines, Shay 263
Ginsberg, Allen 267
Ginzler, Robert 164
Gionfriddo, Gina 332
Gionson, Mel 264, 267
Girard, Stephanie 266
Girl of 16, A 262
Giroday, Francois 303
Giron, Arthur 247
Girvin, Terri 260
Gittings, Jennifer Brawn 308
Given, Tess 324
Gizmo Love 313
Gladden, Dean R. 343
Gladis, Michael J.X. 252, 255
Gladstone, Ralph 334
Glascock, Scott 270
Glass, Philip 244, 324, 326
Glassberg, Marcalan 265
Glaszek, Andrew 268
Glatman, Ellen 311
Glaudini, John 172
Glazer, Amy 304
Gleason, Tim Martin 227
Glenn, Don Wilson 254
Glenn, Eileen 264, 265
Glenn, Laura D. 327
Glennon, Kimberly 377
Glick, Mari 135, 163, 370
Glikas, Bruce 167
Glimmer of Hope 261
Globe Theatres 150
Glore, John 307
Gloria Maddox Theatre 263
Glorioso, Bess Marie 131
Glover, Brian P. 249
Glover, Keith
    29, 172, 252, 254

Glover, Regan 339
Glovinsky, Henry 268
Glowacki, Janusz 258
Gluck, David 304
Gluck, Jessica S. 337
Glushak, Joanna 308
Glynn, Carlin 349
Go Away–Go Away 379
**Goat, or Who Is Sylvia?,
    The** 9, *128*, 221, 350
God and Country 328
God and Mr. Smith 267
Godbout, John 337, 343
Goddess, Rha 332
Godfadda Workout, The
    170
Godfrey, Joe 270
Godineaux, Edgar 146
Goding, Teresa L. 265
God's Comic 250
God's Daughter 258
Godwin, Stephen 352
Goebbels, Heiner 37, 204
Goede, Jay
    19, 161, 162, 218, 267
Goekjian, Samuel V. 163
Goctzinger, Mark 329
Going Native 314
Going to St. Ives 345
Golay, Seth 266
Gold, Alice 270
Gold, Judy 352
Gold, Michael 256
Gold, Natalie 272
Golda's Balcony
    14, 37, *204–205*,
    373, 376, 378
Goldberg, Janice 261
Goldberg, Marc 160
Goldberg, Max 256
Goldberg, Wendy C. 41, 318
Goldberg, Whoopi
    22, 152, 153, 176
Golde, Lea Marie 351
Golden Bear, The 256
Golden Boy 380
Golden, Peg McFeeley 152
Goldenhersh, Heather 253
Goldfarb, Abe 264, 270
Goldfarb, Sidney 264
Goldfeder, Laurie 149, 161
Goldfinger, Michael 186
Goldfrank, Lionel III 163
Goldin, Igor 266
Goldman, Les 370
Goldoni, Carlo 255
Goldsberry, Rene Elise 224
Goldsmith, Oliver 239, 268

Goldstein, Daniel 252, 314
Goldstein, David Ira 354
Goldstein, Jess
    154, 163, 177, 200,
    204, 335
Goldstein, Steven 309, 334
Golub, Peter 182
Goluboff, Bryan 259
Gomex, Lino 206
Gomez, Carlos 307
Gomez, David 138, 139
Gomez, Lino 143
Gomez, Marga 249
Gone Home 14, 34, 192
Gonglewski, Grace 345
Gonsalves, Brady 345, 346
Gonzales, Aldrin 216
Gonzales, Mandy 215
Gonzalez, Amy 311
Gonzalez, Charlene 261
Gonzalez, Ching 245
Gonzalez, Jojo 202, 266, 377
Gonzalez, Mandy
    17, 146, 147
Gooch, Katherine 249
Good Boys 278
Good, John 260, 268
Good, Tara 254
Good Thief, The 51
Goode, Jennifer 145, 146
Goode, Joe 304
Gooding, Calvin 270
Goodman, Alfred 206
Goodman, Eli 327
Goodman, Grant 263
Goodman, Henry
    22, 152, 227
Goodman, John 36, 186
Goodman, Paul Scott 267
Goodman, Robyn 200, 265
Goodman Theatre
    10, 141, 324, 325
Goodrich, Joseph 252, 264
Goodspeed Musicals
    312, 377
Goodstein, Gerry 257
Goodun, Elfeigo N. III 207
Goodwin, David 350
Goodwin, Deidre
    134, 160, 219
Goodwin, Philip 152, 319
Goodwin-Groen, Paul
    145, 253
Goranson, Alicia
    245, 253, 258
Gorbey, Amy 348
Gordon, Aaron 261
Gordon, Ain 235, 236

Gordon, Allan S. 132, 370
Gordon, Carl 152, 153
Gordon, Charles 134
Gordon, David (director) 236
Gordon, David P. (designer)
    246, 258, 335, 348, 378
Gordon, Hallie 327
Gordon, Lana 224
Gordon, Laura 355, 356
Gordon, Miriam 267
Gordon, Ricky Ian 34, 201
Gordon, Terri 273
Gordon/Frost Organization,
    The 370
Gornet, Amy 351
Gorrek, Matt 259, 260
Gorshin, Frank 24, 135, 377
Gospel at Colonus, The 234
Goss, Bick 262
Gossett, Louis Jr. 239
Gotanda, Philip Kan 309
Gottesman, Yetta
    247, 254, 265
Gottlieb, Jon 182, 303, 307
Gottlieb, Lizzie 263
Gottschalk, Christopher 307
Gough, Shawn 183
Gould, Erica 271, 272
Gould, Rob 246
Gould, Robert 246, 316
Gouran, Tim 352
Govich, Milena 134
Goyette, Marie 204
Grabel, Naomi 348
Gracieux, Vincent 338
Graduate, The *129*, 221
Graff, Heather 380
Graff, Randy 223, 312, 319
Graffeo, Marylee 222
Graham, Dion 252
Graham, Enid 150
Graham, Greg 133
Graham, Nathan Lee 314
Graham-Adriani, Suzy 314
Graham-Handley, Emily 140
Gramm, Joseph Lee 268
Granata, Dona 138
Granata, Julie 324
Grand Design, The 272
Grande-Marchione, Frank
    263
Grandy, Marya 185
Graney, Sean 380
Granger, Christopher A. 378
Grant, David Marshall 369
Grant, Joan 260
Grant, Kate Jennings
    198, 227

Grant, Micki 369
Grant, William H. III 255, 303
Grappo, Connie 260
Grappone, Raymond 136
Grasmere 261
Grate, Gail 319
Gravátt, Lynda 191, 340, 347
Gravellese, Gerard 259
Gravens, David 254
Graves, Christopher 269
Graves, Michael 267
Grawemeyer, J. 260
Gray, Damian 271
Gray, David Barry 197
Gray, Douglas 207
Gray, John 315
Gray, Linda 221
Gray, Matthew 256
Gray, Melanna 331
Gray, Melissa 341
Gray, Natalie 323
Gray, Nicholas 264
Gray, Pamela 253
Gray, Spalding 62
Gray, Zach 324
Graynor, Ari 176
Great Scott Productions 196
Greaves, Danielle Lee
      132, 133, 228
Greber, Denise 250
Greco, Loretta 265, 353
Greco, Nick 262
Greek Holiday 341
Green, Adolph 271
Green, Amanda 314
Green, Ashley 260
Green, Chris 264
Green, Colton 259
Green, David 264
Green Grow the Lilacs 129
Green, Jackie
      131, 157, 164, 182,
      187, 188, 193, 195
Green, Jessica 256
Green, John 379
Green, William 267
Greenberg, Julia 211
Greenberg, Richard
      xi, xiii, xv, 10,
      11, 103–110, 153,
      177, 309, 327, 366,
      370, 373
Greene, Graham 259
Greenfeld, Josh 250
Greenfield, Adam 353
Greenfield, Alan 353
Greenfield-Sanders, Timothy
      248

Greenhill, Susan 263
Greenidge, Kirsten 252, 332
Greenspan, David
      34, 133, 209, 210,
      248, 249, 252, 267, 377
Greenwald, Bradley 338, 339
Greenwald, Raymond J. and
      Pearl Berman 163
Greenwood, Jane
      22, 152, 163, 178,
      183, 308, 317, 324, 375
Greer, Adam 354
Greer, D.M.W. 269
Greer, Justin 155, 320
Greer, Keith 261
Greer, Matthew 218
Greer, Scott 345
Gregory, Andre 240
Gregory, Chester 323
Gregory, Chester II 207, 222
Greif, Michael
      32, 33, 202, 211
Grenfell, Katy 133
Grenier, Bernard 179
Grey, Jane 168, 192
Grey, Joel 220, 271
Grice, Brian O. 176
Gridley, Steven 269
Grier, Jean Michelle 224
Gilfasi, Joe 151
Griffin, Edward 264, 265
Griffin, Gary 206, 379
Griffin, Jennifer 316
Griffin, Mark 350
Griffin Productions 173
Griffin, S.A. 311
Griffin, Sean 270, 354
Griffith, Katherine 314
Griffith, Kristin 245, 252
Griffith, Laura 312
Griffith, Natalie 151
Griffith, P.J. 225
Griffith, Sheila 167
Griffiths, Heidi
      154, 178, 202, 210
Griffiths, Trevor 238, 254
Grigg, Jen 331, 332
Griggs, George 265
Grigolia-Rosenbaum, Jacob
      269
Grigsby, Kimberly 198
Grimaldi, James 270
Grimberg, Deborah 239, 246
Grimes, Kenny 213
Grimes, Tammy 382
Grimm, David 252, 253, 313
Grimm, Tim 329
Grimmette, Bill 318

Grimsley, Jim 313
Grinwis, Emmy 317
Griswold, Mary 328
Grizzard, George 312
Groag, Lillian 301, 348
Grodner, Suzanne 342, 352
Groener, Harry 76, 149, 308
Groeschel, Amy 272
Groff, Rinne 271, 331
Groff, Steve 270
Gromada, John
      163, 191, 200, 255, 340
Gross, Barbara 278
**Gross Indecency: The
      Three Trials of Oscar
      Wilde** 61, 72
Gross, Monika 272
Gross, Richard 163, 370
Gross, Yeeshas 185
Grossman, Jason 334
Ground Floor Theater 263
Grove, Barry
      182, 187, 192, 195,
      203, 214
Grove Press 41
Groves, Kelly 267
Growler, Michael 380
Gruen, John 198
Grünberg, Klaus 204
Grunwald, Roger 260
Gruppei, Adam
      145, 146, 222
Gruss, Amanda 260
Grutza, Jennifer 313
Grynhcim, Joel 329
Guan, Jamie H.J. 349
Guare, John
      129, 271, 272, 376
Gubbins, Sarah 329, 331
Gudahl, Kevin 379
Guenthner, Patty 322
Guernsey, Otis L. Jr. i
Guevara, Zabryna 336
Guice, J. Jeffrey 321
Guilarte, Andrew 245
Guilbert, Ann 32, 174, 175
Guiles, Coats 146
Guillory, Letitia 313, 314
Guirgis, Stephen Adly
      xi, xiii, xv, 28,
      85–92, 200, 265
Guisinger, Nathan 265, 270
Gulan, Barbara 331
Gulan, Timothy
      224, 230, 351
Gularte, Stephanie 301
Gulla, Joe 259
Guncler, Sam 182, 272

Gundersheimer, Lee 267
Gunderson, Lauren 261
Gunn, Anna 311
Gunn, Suzette 263
Gunning, Michael 149
Gupta, Rahul 301
Gupton, Damon 319
Gurganus, Allan 308
Gurian, Daniel 261
Gurner, Jeff 224
Gurney, A.R. 238, 255, 263
Gurwin, Danny 319
Gurwitch, Annabelle 265
Gusman, Matthew 142
Gussow, Mel i, xiii, xvi, 233, 375, 385, 421
Guterman, Clifton 322
Guthrie Theater 170, 278, 293, 297, 338, 346
Gutierrez, Gerald 22, 151
Gutterman, Cindy and Jay 205
Guttman, Eddie 247, 248
Guy, Jasmine 219
Guy, Larry 145
Guy, Rebecca 258
Guyer, Murphy 221
Guys, The 287
Guzzi, Ann 186
Guzzy, Mary 336, 337
Gwinn, Marc 343
Gyllenhaal, Maggie 254
Gypsy 4, 19, *164–166*, 165, 370, 371, 376

H.A.M.L.E.T. 249
Haase, Ashley Amber 146
Haasova, Monika 249
Habeck, Michelle 323, 324
Habitat 270
Hackady, Hal 351
Hackett, Peter 343
Hackler, Blake 269
Hadden, John 260
Hadley, Jonathan 248, 270
Haft, Elsa Daspin 135, 370
Hagan, Marianne 340
Hagen, Uta 375
Hagenbuckle, J. 348
Haggard, Steve 326
Hahn, Kristen 141
Haidle, Noah 264

Haimes, Todd 134, 151, 158, 159, 160, 166, 173, 370, 371
Haims, Nolan 267
Hairspray vii, viii, ix, 3, 4, 5, 7, 9, 16, 76, 77, 132, *132–134*, 221, 366, 367, 370, 371, 372, 376, 377
Hairston, Jerome 318
Haiti 271
Haj, Joseph 332
Hajj, Edward A. 331
Halaska, Linda 192
Halbach, John 152
Hale, Tony 265
Hall, Alaina Reed 316
Hall, Amy 196
Hall, Carlyle W. Sr. 144
Hall, Connie 249
Hall, Davis 270
Hall, Dennis Michael 171, 348
Hall, Donei 334
Hall, George 134
Hall, Georgine 340
Hall, Gretchen S. 262
Hall, Jake 256
Hall, Jane 329
Hall, Kyle 326
Hall, Michael (Florida) 380
Hall, Michael C. 217, 219
Hall, Michael Keys 312
Hall, Michaela 262
Hall, Michelle T. 319
Hall, Mollie 348
Hall, Rick 207
Hall, Thomas 379
Hall, Wilson 250
Hallas, Brian 248
Hallelujah Breakdown 267
Hallett, Morgan 168
Halley, Elton P. 141
Halliday, Lynne 258
Hallqvist, Britt G. 171
Hally, Martha 355
Halpern, Jennifer 336
Halprin, Lawrence 375
Halstead, Alison 327
Halstead, Carol 261, 263
Halsted, Dana 339
Halston, Julie 164, 244
Hames, Jill 322
Hamill, Mark 321
Hamilton, Ann 245
Hamilton, Bear 350
Hamilton, Carrie 10, 140

Hamilton, George 219
Hamilton, Holli 331, 332, 333
Hamilton, Josh 192, 227, 263, 327
Hamilton, Mark Sage 260
Hamilton, Melinda Page 262
Hamilton, Nicolai Dahl 267
Hamilton, Tony 260
Hamilton, Victoria 24, 158, 159, 371, 376
Hamlet 239, 338, 378
HamletMachine 260
Hamlisch, Marvin 10, 70, 129, 149, 271, 308
Hammad, Suheir 26, 141
Hamman, Brian 326
Hammel, Lori 222
Hammer, Ben 265
Hammer, Mark 89, 200, 265
Hammerly, Rick 378
Hammerstein, Oscar II 16, 129, 136, 205, 316
Hammett, Dashiell 72
Hammond, Michael 337, 338
Hammond, Thomas H. 349
Hammond, Thomas M. 256
Hammons, Shannon 335
Hampton, Chavon Aileen 316
Hampton, Christopher 12, 158, 256
Hampton, Kate 262, 265
Hampton, Latrice 316
Hamza, Jerry 205
Hanan, Stephen Mo 30, 180
Hand, Frederic 193
Hand of God, The 112, 115, *208*
Handegard, A.J. 272
Handel, Rob 313
Handler, Evan 246
Hands 272
Handy, John 245
Hanemann, Heather 268
Hanes, Tyler 156
Hank Williams: Lost Highway 14, 30, *205*, 266, 367, 377
Hanke, Christopher J. 230
Hanket, Arthur 230, 351
Hankin, St. John 252
Hankla, Mark 256
Hannett, Juliana 146, 154, 159, 209
Hannon, Mary Ann 266
Hannouche, Cherie 249

Hanreddy, Joseph 355
Hansen, Ann-Mari Max 245
Hansen, Anna Ryan 168
Hansen, Benedicte 267
Hansen, Mark 300
Hansen, Randy 205
Hansen, Teri 134
Hanson, Alison 263
Hanson, Jeffrey K. 352
Hanson, Julie 226
Hanson, Lars 252
Hanson, Marsh 261
Hanson, Peter 135, 159
Hanson, Torrey 355, 356
Hanson, Tripp 134
Happy Birthday 259
Happy Days 237, 261
Happy New Century, Dr. Freud 346
Haqq, Devin 273
Hara, Shinichiro 250
Harada, Ann 258, 314
Harada, Tamotsu 245
Harbaugh, Brad 328
Harbaum, Bob 270
Harbour, David 255
Hardeman, Daria 179
Hardie, Raymond 262
Hardin, Russell 326
Harding, Jan Leslie
    253, 317, 336
Hardt, Paul xiii, 215, 422
Hardwick, Elizabeth 72
Hardy, K.J. 256
Hardy, Kevin 247
Hare, Jason 261, 267
Harelik, Mark
    30, 205, 266, 324
Harger, Brenda Bakker 246
Hargrove, Carla J. 317, 336
Haring, Keith 33, 198
Harlem Duet 260
Harlem Song 14, 30, 176
Harlow, Kristen 265
Harman, Paul 198
Harmon, Wynn 307
Harner, Jason Butler 197
Harnetiaux, Trish 270
Harnett, Daniel 270
Harnick, Aaron 131, 188
Harnick, Sheldon 376
Harold and Mimi Steinberg
    Charitable Trust
    iv, xii, 277
Harold Clurman Theatre 263
**Haroun and the Sea of
    Stories** 301
Harper, Francesca 196

Harper, Hill 314
Harper, Wally 193
Harran, Jacob 270
Harriell, Marcy 195, 228
Harrington, Alexander 263
Harrington, Delphi 259
Harrington, Nancy 157, 334
Harrington, Wendall K.
    155, 193, 208, 352
Harris, Alana 264
Harris, Alison 141, 315
Harris, Claudia W.
    xii, xvi, 277, 278,
    293, 422
Harris, Conrad 160
Harris, Cynthia 259
Harris, Dede 132, 184, 370
Harris, Derric 146, 196
Harris, Harriet 229, 271
Harris, James Berton 182
Harris, Jamie 254
Harris, Jared 214
Harris, Jay H. 135, 370
Harris, Jed 142
Harris, Julie 62
Harris, Kristen 202
Harris, Neil Patrick
    217, 227, 271
Harris, Paul 269
Harris, Rachel Lee 267
Harris, Rebecca 264, 322
Harris, Richard 342
Harris, Rosemary
    36, 173, 174, 377
Harris, Roy 214
Harris, Sam 227
Harris, Timothy Scott 273
Harrison, Alan 299
Harrison, Babo 247, 253
Harrison, Gregory 220
Harrison, Jordan 332
Harrison, Lanny 245
Harrison, Maryna 261
Harrison, Scott 311
Harrison, Stanley 270
Harrow, Lisa 266
Harry, Jackée 134
Hart, Caitlin 325, 326
Hart, Charles 127
Hart, Jake 264
Hart, Judith K. 355
Hart, Linda 132, 221
Hart, Lorenz 9, 134
Hart, Melissa 247, 248
Hart, Moss 69, 319
Hart, Nicolette 265
Hart, Richard 423
Hartenstein, Frank 146

Hartford Stage
    11, 41, 163, 170,
    200, 312
Harting, Carla 260
Hartley, Jan
    150, 211, 248, 308
Hartley, Mariette 218
Hartman, Karen 253
Hartman, Michael
    139, 141, 147, 149,
    153, 162, 163, 182,
    188, 189, 200, 208
Haruta, Atsushi 250
Harvey, Alec
    xii, xiii, xvi, 277,
    278, 287, 422
Harvey, Ellen 225
Harvey, Rita
    172, 226, 247, 248
Hasegawa, Kishiko 249
Hasenstab, Derek 224
Hashimoto, Kunihiko 250
Hashirigaki 14, 37, *204*
Haskins, James 346
Hassell, Dennis 304
Hassler, Stacie May 260
Hastings, Edward 261
Hastings-Phillips, Amanda
    301
Hatcher, Jeffrey 28, 189, 347
Hatcher, Lauren 335, 336
Hatcher, Robert 256, 272
Hatcher, Teri 217
Hathaway, Noelle C.K. 380
Hatley, Tim 155, 214
Hatt, Karen 249
Hatton, Luke 327
Hatzis, Georgia 334
Hauck, Rachel
    208, 258, 305, 307,
    316, 345
Hauck, Steve 249
Haugen, Eric T. 172
Haugen, Jonathan 345
Haughton, Stacey 179
Haun, Harry 376
Haupt, Paulette 313
Hauptman, Ira 301
Hauptmann 380
Hausch, Mary 321
Havana Under the Sea 247
Havard, Bernard 348
Havergal, Giles 266
Hawke, Ethan 272
Hawking, Judith
    253, 271, 272, 343
Hawkins, Peter 252
Hawkinson, Timothy 262

Hawley, J. Malia 260
Hawthorne, Nathaniel 337
Hayden, John 152
Hayden, Michael
    12, 163, 218, 319
Hayden, Tamra 226, 314
Hayes, Bill 138, 166
Hayes, Drew 262
Hayes, Elizabeth 263
Hayes, Elliot 423
Hayes, Lisa 265
Hayes, Mark D. 207
Haynes, Ed 299
Haynes, Kristoffer 248
Haynie, Jim 255
Hayon, Sarah 271
Hays, Carole Shorenstein
    153, 370
Hays, Peter 346
Hayter, Fredericka 338
Hayter, Paddy 338
Hayward, Charlie 157, 370
Hazlett, Laura 304
He Held Me Grand 328
Head, Kenn E. 328
Headley, Heather 215, 224
Heads, Talking 29
Healey, Meghan 247
Healey, Michael
    308, 311, 342
Healy, Ann Marie 262
Healy, Chris 250
Healy, Rachel Anne 324, 356
Heartbreak House 239, 268
Heat Lightning 265
Heath, Allan 304
Heath, David Cochran 304
Heath, Robin 343
Heather Brothers, The 260
Heaton, Kenneth 260
Heavy Mettle 266
Hébert-Gregory, Kimberly
    323
Heche, Anne 227
Hecht, Jessica 253, 258, 271
Hecht, Paul 214, 335, 348
Heckman, Richard 136, 212
Hedda Gabler 344, 345
Hedden, Brian 263
Hedley, Bob 347
Hedley, Nevin 149
Hedwig and the Angry Inch
    378
Heflin, Elizabeth 350
Hefti, Susan Kathryn 269
Heidami, Daoud 303
Heifets, Victor 146
Heilpern, John 367

Heinze, Roxane 269
Heird, Amanita 256
Heisler, Laura 262
Held, Jon 331
Helen 236
Helen Hayes Award 378
Helen: Queen of Sparta 250
Heller, Adam 319
Heller, Robert 163
Hellman, Lillian
    10, 47, 70–78
Hellman, Nina 253
Hellyer, John 245
Helm, Frances 316
Helms, Barbara 185, 273
Hemingway, Carol 261
Hemingway, Ernest 261
Hency, Jessica 256
Hendee, Gareth 380
Hendel, Ruth 200
Henderson, Joyce 148
Henderson, Kevin 259
Henderson, Luther 179
Henderson, Ray 180
Henderson, Stephen McKinley
    153
Henderson, Tate 264
Henderson, Tyrone Mitchell
    329, 342
Hendricks, Andrea 338
Hendricks, James J. 265
Hendrickson, Timothy 328
Hendrix, Leslie 140, 141
Hendy, Jessica 138
Henetz, Tania 304
Henk, Annie 247, 255
Henley, Beth 271, 318
Henner, Marilu 218, 219
Henning, Karl 65
Henninger, Corie 305
Hennion, Gary 264
Henrique, Paulo 250
Henry, Buck 129
Henry Hewes Design Awards
    375, 421, 422
Henry, Neil 266
Henry V 264, 265
Henry VI 265
Henry, Vincent 198
Henry, Wayne 261
Henshall, Ruthie 219
Hensley, Shuler 223, 226
Hensley, Todd 328
Henze, Sheryl 206
Hepburn, Angus 264
Hepburn, Katharine 31, 200
Her Big Chance 114, *208*
Herber, Pete 185

Herbert, F. Hugh 69
Here Arts Center 233, 263
Heredia, Wilson Jermaine 228
Herendeen, Ed 253
Herlinger, Karl 254, 264
Hermalyn, Joy 145
Herman, Darra 250
Herman, Jerry
    6, 28, 31, 197, 375
Herman, Tim 260
Herman, Tom 263
Hernandez, Jon-Michael 266
Hernandez, Juan Carlos
    174, 259
Hernandez, Omar 269
Hernandez, Oscar 243
Hernandez, Philip 223
Hernández, Riccardo
    176, 191, 195, 198,
    201, 211, 312, 334, 340
Heroes 266
Heron, Matilda 149
Herrera, Emil 338
Herrera, G. Shizuko 302
Herrero, Mercedes
    252, 254, 262, 263
Herrick, Peter 261
Herriott, Brian 223
Hershey, Lowell 206
Herskovits, David 264
Herter, Jonathan 342
Heryer, Alison 327
Heslin, George 252
Hess, Gale 213
Hess, Nancy 218, 219
Hess, Rodger 185
Hessing, Laurel 256
Hester, Richard 164
Heverin, Nathan 314
Hewes, Henry
    i, v, xiii, 375, 423
Hewitt, Tom 134, 224
Hiatt, Dan 301
Hibbert, Edward 225
Hickey, Carol A. 269
Hickey, John Benjamin 218
Hickey, Tom 264
Hicklin, Shelley 348
Hickok, John 216, 269
Hickok, Molly 262
Hicks, Bryan 252, 347
Hicks, Daniel 256
Hicks, Israel 314
Hicks, Marva 172
Hicks, Munson 342
Hicks, Sander 252, 253
Hidalgo, Allen 270
Hiding Place, The 311

Higby, Devon 315
Higgins, Clare
       11, 154, 155, 371, 376
Higgins, John Michael 311
Higgins, John Patrick 301
Higgins, Patience 179
High Priest of California
       272
Hightower, Geffri 303
Highway Ulysses 334, 378
Highwayman, The 314
Hilda 248
Hildebrandt, Erika 262
Hildreth, John 380
Hiler, Katherine 331
Hilferty, Susan 201, 256, 349
Hill, Eric 315, 335
Hill, Gary Leon 304
Hill, John 132, 133
Hill, Natalie 321
Hill, Raymond James 267
Hill, Roderick 252, 313
Hill, Rosena M.
       149, 308, 378
Hill, Ryan 245
Hill, Valerie 270
Hilliard, Ryan 266, 267
Hillman, Richard 180, 202
Hillman, Robb 145
Hillmer, Melissa 212
Hilsabeck, Rick 226
Him and Her 267
Hime, Jeanne 268
Hindman, Bill 380
Hindman, Earl 256
Hinds, Rickerby 318
Hindustan 313
Hines, John 317
Hines, Kay 250
Hines, Maurice 196
Hingston, Sean Martin 349
Hinkle, Marin 258, 303
Hinks, Alison 263
Hinners, Carson 260
Hinrichs, Renata 263
Hinton, Michael 143
Hip-Flores, Richard 269
Hippodrome State Theatre
       321
Hirata, Mikio 323
Hirota, Yuji 250
Hirsch, Barry J. 270
Hirsch, Gina 249, 261
Hirsch, Judd 7, 8, 129, 130
Hirschfeld, Al xiv, 375
Hirschfeld, Magnus 64
His Wife 271
Hitchcock, Tony 268

Hitler, Adolph 186
Hiura, Ben 250
Ho, Wai Ching 312
Hoak, Madeline 263
Hobbs, Johnnie Jr. 347
Hoch, Chris 216
Hochman, Larry 335
Hock, Robert 268
Hocking, Leah 146, 312
Hodge, Kate 343
Hodge, M. Pat 334
Hodge, Mike 252
Hodge-Bowles, Sean-Michael
       335
Hodges, Ben 263
Hodges, Jacquelyn Renae 224
Hodges, Mary 265
Hoehler, Richard 266
Hoerneman, Ethan 311
Hoey, Andy 256
Hoey, John Stephen 329, 348
Hoff, Andrew J. 265
Hoffman, Constance 312
Hoffman, Gavin 267
Hoffman, Jackie
       132, 133, 376
Hoffman, Miranda 210, 301
Hoffman, Philip Seymour
       90, 168, 200, 265, 371
Hoffman, Susan R. 202
Hofler, Robert 3, 5
Hofmaier, Mark 273
Hogan, Jonathan 255, 340
Hogan, Michael 259
Hogan, Robert 191
Hogarth, William 237
Hogue, Rochelle 153
Hohn, Amy 314
Holbrook, Curtis 198
Holck, Maile 341
Holcomb, Robin 353
Hold, Please 260, 318
Holden, Joan 307, 353
Holder, Donald
       135, 139, 153, 183,
       197, 203, 204, 309,
       326, 340, 347, 372
Holderness, Rebecca
       263, 336
Holiday, Joel 263
Holland, Greg 154
Holland, Kate 265, 337
Holland, Reece 226
Hollander, Anita 250
Hollander, Owen 163
Hollenbeck, John 245
Holliday, Jennifer 220
Holliday, Polly 348

Hollinger, Michael 332
Hollingshead, Megan 268
Hollis, Stephen 341
Hollmann, Mark 128, 271
Hollywood Arms
       4, 10, *140–141*, 371
Hollywood Reporter, The 367
Holman, Hunt 33, 176
Holmes, Davey 311
Holmes, David 193, 195
Holmes, Dyron 330, 331
Holmes, Paul Mills 329, 331
Holmes, Prudence Wright
       31, 201
Holmes, Rick 218
Holmes, Rupert
       24, 135, 335, 370
Holmstrom, Mary 259
Holsinger, Holly 249
Holt, Charles Paul 260
Holt, Shannon 331, 332
Holum, Suli 250
Holy War, Batman! or The
       Yellow Cab of
       Courage 379
Holyfield, Wayland D.
       157, 370
Home Box Office Inc.
       7, 8, 25, 26, 129
Homer 61, 170, 334
Homer, Brian 273
Homewrecker 253
Honda, Shuji 250
Honey Makers, The
       239, 246
Hong, April 309, 310
Honnoll, Tim 263
Honold, Greta Sidwell 327
Honour, Mary R. 339
Honsa, Joey 327
Hood, Cynthia 261
Hoodwin, Rebecca 256, 270
Hoogenakker, John 355
Hoover, Richard 255
Hope Bloats 245
Hope, Paul 351
Hope, Roxanna 335
Hope, Sharon 254
Hopkins, Arthur vii, viii
Hopkins, Barbara Barnes 260
Hopkins, Billy 271
Hopkins, Cynthia 248
Hopkins, Kaitlin 225
Hopkins, Karen Brooks
       171, 193, 204, 207, 244
Hopkins, Lisa 145
Hopkins, Robert Innes 186
Hopper, Tim 173, 327

Hopson, Andrew 329
Hormann, Nicholas 303, 311
Horn, Jamie 350
Hornback, Nancy 268
Hornberger, Ellen 145
Horne, J.R. 342
Horovitz, Israel
    28, 182, 269, 270, 271
Horowitz, Jeffrey 256
Horowitz, Katharine 338
Horowitz, Lawrence
    146, 161, 370
Horowitz, Susan N. 266
Horton, Damon 265
Horton, Greg 269
Horton, Jamie 312
Horton, John 225
Horton, Ward 268
Horvath, Joshua 323
Horvitz, Wayne 353
Horwatt, Linda 261
Horwitz, Andrew 269
Hosney, Doug 186
Hostetter, Curt 270, 300
Hostmyer, Tracy 307
Hot L Baltimore 380
Hot Mikado 378
Hottinger, Eric 263
Hoty, Dee 225
Hoty, Tony 300, 341
Houdyshell, Jayne
    253, 316, 317
Houghton, James
    178, 255, 313
Hould-Ward, Ann 147, 255
Hourglass, The 259
Hourie, Troy 188, 315
**House *171*, 367
House, Bob Lee 157, 370
House Committee on Un-
    American Activities 72
**House of Bernarda Alba,
    The** 305
House of Dames Productions
    353
House of Flowers
    14, 37, *196*
Houseman, John 265
**How His Bride Came to
    Abraham** 347
**How I Learned What I
    Learned** 354
Howar, Tim 223
Howard, Aimee 267
Howard, Anto 251
Howard, Arliss 334, 378
Howard, Bryce Dallas
    22, 34, 151, 210

Howard, Celia 261
Howard, David S. 130
Howard, Heidi 264
Howard, Hollie 132, 133
Howard, Jason 264
Howard, Ken 310
Howard Kleinberg Award 380
Howard, Peter 316
Howard, Rob 355
Howard, Stuart 192
Howe, Tina 265, 272, 342
Howell, Michael W. 205, 266
Howell, Sara Lee 299
Howes, Benjamin
    252, 261, 268
Howey, David 348
Howie the Rookie 378
Howland, Jason 270
Hoxie, Richmond 246, 262
Hoyle, Geoff 224
Hoyt, Lon 133
Hoyt, Tom 146
Hsu, Emily 136
Hu, Ann 260, 300
Huang, Mark 336
Huang, Wei 145
Hubbard, Jennifer 332
Hubbard, Kerrin 146
Huber, David 265
Huber, Elizabeth 338
Huber, Kim 216
Huber, Phillip 312
Hubert, Janet 191, 340
Hudson, Chuck 268
Hudson, David Stewart 301
Hudson, Scott 91, 200
Huff, Neal
    11, 107, 109, 153, 177
Huffman, Cady 227
Huffman, Tracey 250
Hughes, Allen Lee 174
Hughes, Amber 354
Hughes, Carrie 317
Hughes, Doug
    251, 270, 312, 313
Hughes, Julie 369
Hughes, Kenneth 260
Hughes, Langston 29, 179
Hughes, Ted 269
Hugo, Victor 127, 338
Huidor, Miguel Angel
    175, 320, 352
Hulce, Tom 208
Hull, Ashley 212
Hull, Mylinda 222
Humana Festival of New
    American Plays
    102, 330, 333

Humbertson, Lisa 261
Humble Boy
    14, 34, 35, *214*
Hummel, Martin 179
Hummon, Marcus 157, 370
Humphris, Caroline 193
Humpty Dumpty 309
Hunchback's Tale, The 335
Hune, Matt 350
Hung, Lyris 250
Hunt, Alva 212
Hunt, Helen 12, 158
Hunt, Mame 353
Hunt, Robert 214
Hunt, Scott 223
Hunt, Suzy 354
Hunter, Adam 145, 222
Hunter, Holly 271
Hunter-Gault, Chuma 329
Huntington Theatre Company
    197, 335
Hupp, Robert 300
Hurd, Michelle 309
Hurley, Jimmy 260
Hurston, Zora Neale 379
Hurt, Mary Beth 214
Hurwitt, Robert i
Husovsky, Peter 339
Hussa, Robyn 262
Hussein, Saddam 16
Husted, Patrick 252
Hustis, Jono 253
Hutcheson, Jessie 267
Hutchins, Amy 268
Hutchins, Reid 262
Hutchinson, Chris 265
Hutchinson, Derek 148, 244
Hutchinson, Jeffrey 324
Hutchinson, Kelly 255
Hutchison, Brian 342
Hutchison, Chris 254
Hutton, Arlene 253, 260
Huxley, Aldous 249
Huynh, Brian Lee 264
Hwang, David Henry
    16, 128, 136, 370
Hyatt, Michael 187
Hyland, Edward James 318
Hyman, Charles 252
Hyman, Shelby 324
Hypocrites, The 379
Hypothetical Theatre
    Company 264
Hyslop, David 158
Hyslop, Jeff 227

I Am My Own Wife
  xi, xv, 14, 34, *59–*
  67, 60, 63, 66, *214*
I Can Do That Productions,
  Inc. 423
I' Cook, Curtiss 224
I Just Stopped By to See the
  Man 327
I Love Myself 266
I Love New York—What's
  Your Excuse? 266
I Love You, You're Perfect,
  Now Change *169–*
  170, 222
I Sent a Letter to My Love
  423
I Want You To 268
Iacucci, Lisa 195
Ianculovici, Dana 146, 164
Ibroci, Astrit 260
Ibsen, Brian 307, 308
Ibsen, Henrik
  59, 75, 239, 245,
  261, 270, 345
Ice Cream Man for All
  Seasons, An 261
ICM Artists, Ltd 188
Idiot's Delight 77
Iggy Woo 248
Iizuka, Naomi 341
Ikeda, Jennifer 34, 210
Iliad, The 61
Ilijevich, Eric 263
Illes, Mary 351
Illian, Dan 268
Illica, Luigi 144
Illuminating Veronica 253
Im, Jennie 250
I'm Not Rappaport
  4, 7, *129–130*, 130
Imaginary Friends
  viii, x, xv, 4,
  10, 11, 69–78,
  70, 71, 73, *149*,
  150, 308
Imhoff, Gary 222
Immigrant Theatre Project,
  The 377
Impact 271
Importance of Being
  Earnest, The 264
In Arabia We'd All Be Kings
  86
In Love and Anger 253

In Real Life
  14, 34, 35, *182*, 183
In the Blood 326
In the Company of Men
  79, 80, 81
In the Realm of the Unreal
  263
In the Solitude of Cotton
  Fields 268
Incidental Colman Tod 154,
  370
Incognito 339
Indian Ink 339, 379
Indiana Repertory Theatre
  328
Infinite Ache, An 342
Informed Consent 261
Ing, Alvin 136
Ingalls, James F
  162, 201, 213, 256,
  324, 327, 334, 349
Inge, William 262
Ingersoll, James 345
Ingman, Matthew 145
Ingram, James 303
Ingram, Malcolm 342
Inkley, Fred 134, 223
Innvar, Christopher
  223, 254, 312
Inoue, Masahiro 245
Inside a Bigger Box 270
Intar 246, 264
Intellectual Memoirs 72
Intelligent Design of Jenny
  Chow, The 309, 310
Intemann, F.D. 250
InterAct Theatre Company
  345, 346
International Alliance of
  Theatrical Stage
  Employe 5, 6
International Association of
  Theatre Critics 421
Interpretation of Dreams, The
  100
Intiman Theatre Company
  307, 323, 353
Intimate Apparel
  309, 310, 332
Intimate Shift 264
Into the Woods *129*
Inventing Van Gogh 356
Invention of Love, The 72
Ionazzi, Daniel 303
Ionesco, Eugene 238
Iordanov, Krassin 268
Iorio, Jim 268
Iphigenia 273

Iphigenia in Tauris 264
Ireland, Jim 312
Ireland, Marin
  31, 188, 252, 254
Irish Arts 264
Irish Repertory Theatre
  37, 195, 201, 239, 247
Irvin, Michael 341
Irving, Amy
  239, 245, 271, 272
Irwin, Bill 9, 221, 237
Irwin, Robin 146
Irwin, Tom 327
Is There a Doctor in the
  House? 266
Isaac, Rachel 148
Isenegger, Nadine 220
Isherwood, Charles
  xi, xv, 6, 9,
  11, 51, 196, 367,
  373, 422
Isherwood, Christopher 128
Ishida, Jim 312
Ishikawa, Takeshi 250
Island Def Jam Music Group
  141, 371
Island, The
  14, 37, *207*, 377
Isler, Seth 170
Islington Entertainment 188
Isola, Kevin 175, 181
Israel, Jennie 337
Israela Margalit 258
Istel Creative Arts Publishing
  422
Istel, John i, x, xiii, xv, 79
It Just Catches 261
It's a . . . Mexican-Mormon
  250
It's a Wonderful Lie 260
It's Beginning to Look a Lot
  Like Murder! 263
Ivanek, Zeljko 35, 190
Ivanovski, Goron 263
Iventosch, Nina 197
Ives, David
  18, 146, 203, 206
Ivey, Dana
  158, 270, 271, 272
Ivey, Judith 254
Ivins, Todd Edward 348
Ivory, Paulette 215, 380
Iwasaki, Hiroshi 349
Izquierdo, Michael X. 272
Izzard, Eddie
  23, 158, 159, 371,
  376, 377
Izzo, Mary Lynne 380

Jach, Tina M.   328
Jackie Wilson Story, The
    14, 31, *207*
Jackness, Andrew   303, 348
Jacksina Company Inc., The
    185, 188, 190
Jacksina, Judy   185, 188, 190
Jackson, Anne   271
Jackson, Carter   141
Jackson, Christopher   224
Jackson, Doug   213
Jackson, Ernestine   315
Jackson, Gregory Patrick   341
Jackson, Jason   176, 212
Jackson, Kevin   309, 334
Jackson, Mark Leroy   228
Jackson, Nagle   312
Jackson, Warren   324
Jackson, Yvette Janine   301
Jacob, Lou   253
Jacobs, Amy   131, 146, 154
Jacobs, Betty   369
Jacobs, Marian Lerman   171
Jacobs, Stefan   252
Jacoby, Mark   143, 226
Jaeck, Scott   326
Jaeger, Darleen   273
Jaffe, Debbie   272
Jaffe, Jill   206
Jagannathan, Poorna   302
Jahi, Meena T.   224
Jahnke, Christopher   183
Jain, Ravi   249
Jajuan, Kimberly   316
Jakobsson, Magnus   267
Jakubowski, Peter   346
Jam Theatricals
    131, 187, 188, 370
James, Bob   308
James, Diqui   170
James, Elsie   265
James, Laurissa   261
James, Michael Guy   249
James, Nikki M.   37, 196
James, Paul   314
James, Peter Francis   196
James, Scott   318
James, Stu   228
James, Tomas   170
James, Toni-Leslie
    153, 173, 195, 196, 204
Jamrog, Joseph   272
Janaki   270
Janasz, Charles   303, 307

Janelli, Ron   164
Janelli, Ronald   136
Jane's Exchange   269
Janki, Devanand
    202, 243, 373
Jans, Alaric   379
Jarcho, Julia   314
Jardine, Luke   193, 195
Jarrow, Kyle   263
Jarvis, Brett   258, 373
Jarvis, Mitchell   185
Jarvis, Virginia   348
Jasperson, Mary   266
Jaudes, Christian   136, 164
Jay, Anjali   204
Jay Binder Casting   139
Jay, Ricky   33, 170
Jay-Alexander, Richard   185
Jazi, Esmaeil Arefian   251
Jazi, Hassan Aliabbasi   251
Jazi, Kamal Aliabbasi   251
Jazi, Majid Aliabbasi   251
Jbara, Gregory   219, 220
Jean Cocteau Repertory   264
Jean Doumanian Productions
    131, 138, 370
Jean, Nikki   318
Jefferies, Annalce
    191, 312, 377
Jeffrey Richards Associates
    197
Jeffreys, Stephen   327
Jeffries, Susan   260, 268
Jekyll & Hyde: The Musical
    378
Jellison, Marcy   249
Jenkins, Capathia   166, 167
Jenkins, Daniel   352
Jenkins, David   307
Jenkins, Jeffrey Eric
    i, iii, iv, xiv,
    xv, 3, 93, 261,
    375, 422
Jenkins, Michael A.   136
Jenkins, Vivian Cary
    i, xiv, 243, 422
Jenness, Morgan   377
Jennewein, Gigi   329
Jennings, Byron
    150, 225, 256, 257
Jennings, Mikéah Ernest   259
Jensen, Eric   338
Jensen, Erik   38, 184, 272
Jensen, Julie   258
Jensen, Sarah Jayne   164, 320
Jensen, Tim Douglas   269
Jensen, Tom   245
Jerins, Alana   253

Jermaine, Omar   262
Jerome, Timothy
    145, 146, 216, 316
Jerry Beaver and Associates
    178
Jerwich, Fanny   350
Jeske, Joel   266
Jesson, Paul   195
Jesurun, John   249
Jesus Christ Superstar   229
Jesus Hopped the 'A' Train
    87
Jeter, Derek   110
**Jew I Met on Kristallnacht,
    The**   341
Jeweler's Tale, The   336
Jews Without Money   256
Jewsbury, Lovely   159
Jhaveri, Sanji   339
Jhung, Catherine   268
Jiles, Jennifer   263
Jimenez, Carla   305
Jiménez, Robert M.   153, 177
Jitney   329
Jo-Ann, Ebony   153, 191, 340
Joe   254
Joe and Betty   265, 375
Joel, Billy   16, 138, 372
Joel, Stephanie   202
Joey Shakespear   248
Johann, Susan   178
Johannes, Mark   182
John, Elton   7, 127, 128
John Houseman Theatre   265
John, Michael Garcés   248
Johnny 23   269
Johns, Ernest   264, 265
Johnson, Addie   252, 253
Johnson, Birch   133
Johnson, Carrie A.   266
Johnson, Catherine   128
Johnson, Charles   210
Johnson, Denis   262
Johnson, Erik   311
Johnson, Gustave   313
Johnson, Harry   337
Johnson, Joel Drake   328
Johnson, Joyce   260
Johnson, Kevin   301
Johnson, Myron   352
Johnson, Natalia   303
Johnson, Natalie Joy   249
Johnson, Phyllis   317
Johnson, Royce   378
Johnson, Russell W.   338
Johnson, Tamara E.   342
Johnson, Terry   129
Johnson, Todd Alan   223

Johnson, Tom 259
Johnson, Troy Britton 321
Johnson-Chase, Michael 346
Johnston, Cara 206
Johnston, Katie 327
Johnston, Kristen 33, 175
Johnston, Laura 270
Johnston, Susan 340
Joines, Howard 136
Jokovic, Mirjana 313
Jolie, Danielle 196
Jolles, Susan 212
Jolson, Al 30, 180
Jolson and Company
   14, 30, *180*
Jonas, Joseph 145
Jonas, Phoebe 334
Jondon 204
Jones, Amanda 264, 265
Jones, Andy 328
Jones, Austin 269
Jones, Bambi 351
Jones, Bill T. 248
Jones, Billy Eugene 317
Jones, Camila 272
Jones, Charlotte 34, 214
Jones, Cherry
   11, 71, 73, 149,
   150, 308
Jones, Chris i
Jones, Christina Haatainen
   303
Jones, Christine
   178, 187, 245, 255,
   313, 317, 332, 338
Jones, Christopher Joseph
   246, 247
Jones, Cynthia 353
Jones, Delise 265
Jones, Denis 212
Jones, Fateema 171
Jones, George 375
Jones, James Earl 239, 375
Jones, Jeffrey M. 272
Jones, John Christopher
   216, 256
Jones, John Kevin 269
Jones, JV 311
Jones, Lindsay
   309, 323, 326, 332
Jones, Marie 321
Jones, Nate 246
Jones, O-Lan 304
Jones, Ora 324, 327
Jones, Robert 335
Jones, Robert Anthony 172
Jones, Rodney 176
Jones, Rolin 309

Jones, Ron Cephas
   89, 200, 265
Jones, Russell G. 91, 200
Jones, Sarah 379
Jones, Simon 206, 259
Jones, Stephanie 314
Jones, Terace 146
Jones, Toby 157, 158
Jones, Ty 261, 377
Jones, Vanessa S. 224
Joplin, Janis 30
Joplin, Laura 170
Jordan, Bruce 342
Jordan, Dale J. 315
Jordan, Don 260
Jordan, Rebecca 326
Jose Quintero Theatre 265
Joselovitz, Ernie 379
Joseph, Elbert 334
Joseph Jefferson Award 379
Joseph Jefferson Citations
   Wing Award 379
Joseph, Leonard 224
Joseph Papp Public Theater
   10
Joseph Papp Public Theater,
   The 33, 104, 154, 175,
   177, 178, 189, 198,
   202, 210, 248, 370
Joseph, Sandra 226
Josephson, Erland 171
Joshi, Abhijat 264
Joshi, Nehal 319
Journal News 367
Jovanovic, Jelena 249
Jovanovich, Brandon
   206, 207
Joy, James Leonard 350
Joyce, James 233
Joyce, Lucia 233
Jubett, Joan 268
Judge, Daniel 206
Judy, James 254
Jue, Francis 323, 349
Juhn, Paul 264, 267
Jules, Anny 198
Julia, Raul 19, 236
**Julia Sweeney: Guys and
   Babies, Sex and Gods**
   259
Juliano, Lisa 202
Julius Caesar 256, 257
Jump/Cut 252, 319
Jumper, Samantha 262
Jun, Paul 253
Junebug Symphony, The
   267
Just Us Boys 259

Justeson, Ryan 268
Jutras, Simon 150

Kaarina, Diana 223, 224
Kabatznick, Brian 207
Kaczorowski, Peter 182, 196
Kaefer, Kathleen 265
Kafele, Fatima
   193, 195, 204, 207
Kafka, Franz 265
Kagan, Diane 258
Kageyama, Rodney 302
Kahn, Gus 180
Kaikkonen, Gus
   232, 268, 347
Kainuma, Morris 146, 164
Kaiser, Joseph 146
Kaiwi, Brant 269
Kalas, Janet 154, 177
Kaling, Mindy 267
Kalke, Celise 323, 326
Kall, James 225
Kallins, Molly Grant 164
Kamal, Joseph 151, 318
Kaminsky, Jason 332, 333
Kaminsky, Sheila 250
Kamkolkar, Nikhil 339
Kamlot, Robert 369
Kamp, Robert i, 423
Kander, John
   6, 127, 128, 164, 379
Kane, David 135
Kane, Honour 253
Kane, Lyndsay Rose 259
Kane, Timothy Edward 324
Kaneko, Sumie 349
Kanes, Benjamin 349
Kang, M.J. 250
Kang, Tim 265
Kani, John 37, 207, 377
Kanor, Seth 254
Kanter, Lynn 265
Kanyok, Laurie 139
Kaokept, Adam Michael 253
Kaplowitz, Robert 178, 201
Kapner, Sara 141
Kardana-Swinsky Productions
   Inc. 205
Karel, Charles 263
Karen, Jamie 144
Karl, Alfred 192
Karl, Andy 321
Karlin, Julie 269
Karslake, Daniel 146
Kary, Michael 307

Kasbaum, Scott 331
Kashani, Dariush 271, 272
Kastner, Ron
    158, 164, 208, 370
Kata, Takeshi 209
Katigbak, Mia 264, 266
Katsafados, Thodoros 188
Katsiadaki, Maria 188
Katt, William 352
Katz, Natasha
    136, 156, 173, 193
Kauffman, Anne 248
Kauffman, Thomas M.
    335, 336
Kaufman, Daniel 261, 267
Kaufman, David 235, 376
Kaufman, George S.
    22, 69, 150, 244, 319
Kaufman, Jason 334
Kaufman, Lynne 258
Kaufman, Moisés 61, 72, 214
Kaufman, Shawn 247
Kaufold, Victor 346
Kaus, Stephen M. 244
Kauzlaric, Robert 380
Kay, Bradley 321
Kayden, Mildred 255
Kayden, Spencer 229, 312
Kaye, Howard 179
Kaye, Judy 225
KazKaz, Rana 272
Keach, Stacy 307
Keane, Brian 318
Keane, John B. 37, 195
Keany, Paul 267
Kearney-Patch, Kate 256, 349
Kearson, Anne 352
Keating, Charles 36, 183
Keating, John 247, 264
Keck, Michael 355
Keefe, Anne 141, 315
Keefe, Elizabeth 259
Keegan, Ted 226
Keel-Huff, Sandra 265
Keeley, David W. 225
Keen Company 265
Keenan-Bolger, Celia 195
Keener, Catherine
    36, 178, 217
Keepers, Nathan 339
Keesing, Darin 326
Kehr, Donnie 216
Keigwin, Larry 146
Keim, Carolyn 351, 354
Keister, Olivia 266
Keith Haring: The Authorized
    Biography 198
Keith, Larry 218, 259

Keith, Randal 222, 223
Keith Sherman and Associates
    198
Keithley, Karinne 249, 377
Kellenberg, Kurt 335
Kellenberger, Kurt 255
Keller, Greg 263
Keller, John-David 311
Keller, Michael
    144, 147, 149, 150, 164
Kellermann, Susan 44, 255
Kelley, Nambi E. 327, 328
Kelley, R.J. 134
Kelley, Robert 311
Kelley, Warren 315
Kellner, Jeff 264
Kellogg, Marjorie Bradley 342
Kelly, Alexa 269
Kelly, Daniel Hugh 307
Kelly, David Patrick 245, 312
Kelly, Dennis 331
Kelly, EC 261
Kelly, Erica 264
Kelly, George 268
Kelly, Janie 268
Kelly, Jeffrey 380
Kelly, John 236
Kelly, Kristen Lee 228
Kelly, Mickey 264
Kelly, Reade 260
Kelly, Stephen 262
Kelly, Thomas Vincent 309
Kelpie Arts 136
Kemp, Sally 268
Kenan, Hannah 314
Kendall, Rebecca 261, 267
Kendrick, Karan 322
Kendrick, Louisa 217
Kenin, Sean 266
Kenn, Dana 172
Kennedy, Anne
    318, 319, 347
Kennedy Center Honors 375
Kennedy Center, The
    303, 319, 378
Kennedy Center–Mark Twain
    Prize 375
Kennedy, Chilina 225
Kennedy, David 300
Kennedy, J. 248
Kennedy, James 262
Kennedy, Lauren 223
Kennedy, Laurie 319
Kennedy, Steve C. 133
Kennedy, York 307
Kenny, Frances 353
Kenny, Gerard 260
Kenny, Laura 352, 355

Kent, Jonathan 144
Kent, Sean 270
Kentucky Educational
    Television 121
Kenwright, Adam 321
Kenyon, Steven 212
Kenzler, Karl 151, 252
Keogh, Des 37, 195
Kepros, Nicholas 256, 349
Kerins, Rosalyn Rahn 225
Kern, Dan 346, 348
Kern, Joey 176
Kern, Kevin 223
Kernan, Ben 338
Kerouac 269
Kerpel, Gabriel 170
Kerr, E. Katherine 209, 210
Kerr, Jean 69
Kerrigan, McKenna 327
Kerrigan, Patricia 157
Kertzer, David 312
Kerwin, Brian 308
Kerwin, Patrick 328
Kesler, Ian Reed 246
Kesselman, Wendy 266
Kessler, Marc 193
Kessler, Merle 304
Kevoian, Peter 229
Key, Keegan-Michael 379
Keyes, Dave 156
Keyes, Katherine 145
Keylock, Joanna 196
Keyser, Brett 249
Keyser, Rhonda 268
Khan, Shaheen 204
Khoulenjani, Asadollah
    Momenzadeh 251
Khoulenjani, Mohammadali
    Momenzadeh 251
Kidman, Nicole 18
**Kidnapping of Edgardo
    Mortara, The** 312
Kieffer, Thomas K. 380
Kiehn, Dontee 164
Kiel, Larissa 267
Kiel, Miriam Cohen 354
Kievman, Melissa 253
Kievsky, Boris 264
Kiger, Jennifer 309, 311
**Kiki & Herb: Coup de
    Théâtre** 261
Kilgarriff, Patricia 152
Kilgore, Emilie S. 385
Kilgore, John 189
Kilian, Linda Byrd 299
Killenberger, Robert 202, 243
Killian, Scott 258
Killing Louise 260

Kilroy, Colette 311
Kilty, Jerome 316
Kim, Chung Sun 145
Kim, Daniel Dae 302
Kim, Peter 316
Kim, Randall Duk 16, 136
Kim, Susan 246
Kim, Willa 247
Kimball, Chad 201
Kimball, Charlie 355
Kimball, Dyana 266
Kimberly Akimbo
   14, 34, 35, *195*
Kimble, Phil 263
Kimbrough, Charles 255
Kimmel, Joel 321
Kimura, Donna 302
Kimura, Mami 264
Kincaid, Ken 249
King and I, The 378
**King and Queen of Planet
   Pookie, The** 261
King, Brendan 146
King, Christopher 256
King, Denis 315
King, Ginifer 164
King Hedley II 347
King, Jeffrey 345
King Lear 24, 261
King, Matthew Yang 302
King, Nicolas 140
King, Ryan 316
King, Stephen 47
King, Woodie Jr. 254
**Kingdom of Lost Songs,
   The** 264
Kinghorn, Michael 318
Kingsley, Mira 175
Kingston, Kaye 348
Kinkade, Susan 315
Kinney, Terry 327
Kinsherf, John 265
Kiracofe, Nancy 346
Kirby, Davis 134, 259
Kirk, Justin 181
Kirk, Keith Byron 204
Kirk Theatre 265
Kirkland, Dale 143
Kirkpatrick, Kelley 193
Kirkpatrick, Loralie 339
Kirschner, Alfred 65
Kirsten, Amy 250
Kirwan, Larry 247
Kishline, John 355
Kiskaddon, Walt 373
Kissel, Howard 367, 376
Kissel, Jeremiah 378
Kit Marlowe 252

Kitchen Dog Theater
   346, 350
Kitchen, Heather 300
Kitsopoulos, Antonia 145
Kitsopoulos, Constantine 146
Kitsopoulos, Nicholas
   146, 372
Kitt, Tom 187
Kitto, H.D.F. 313
Kittredge, Ann 206
Kittrell, Michelle
   155, 156, 320
Kitty the Waitress 266
Kjellson, Ingvar 171
Kladitis, Manny 186
Klaers, Michael 339
Klainer, Traci 138, 347
Klaisner, Fred D. 176
Klausen, Ray 303
Klavan, Laurence 272, 314
Kleiman, Lauren 262
Klein, Julia 258
Klein, Lauren 303
Klein, Noah 263
Klein, Randall E. 245, 329
Klein, Tanya 262
Kleinberg, Howard 380
Kleinhans, Elysabeth 263
Kleinmann, Kurt 263
Klemperer, Jerusha 269
Kliban, Ken 252
Klimzak, Michael 266
Kline, Kevin 158
Kling, Kevin 338
Klinger, Christopher 262
Klinger, Mary K. 305, 307
Klinger, Pam 217
Klonsky and Schwartz 313
Klug, Jan 249
Knable, Jim 346
Knanishu, Kristine
   326, 327, 328
Knapp, Jacqueline 329
Knapp, Jeff 341
Knapp, Sarah 341
Knee, Allan 273
Knell, Dane 315
Knight, James 252
Knight, T.R.
   151, 225, 251, 254
Knives in Hens 380
Knopf, Robert 272
Knoppers, Antonie 307
Knower, Zachary 263
Knowing Cairo 308
Knowland, Matthew 260
Knowles, Michael 260
Knox, Leila 138, 197

Knox, Paul 261
Knudson, Kurt 216
Knutson, Tom 261, 263
Koch, Jeremy 265
Koch, Ted 265
Kocher, Cynthia 153
Koehl, Coby 249
Koenig, Jack 259
Kofman, Gil 259
Kofoed, Seana 227
Kohlhaas, Karen 189
Kohn, Christian 140, 141
Kole, Hilary 170
Kolinski, Joe 262
Kolnik, Paul
   17, 132, 147, 156, 184
Koltès, Bernard Marie
   267, 268
Kolvenbach, John 313
Komer, Chris 145
Komine, Lily 245
Kondoleon, Harry 31, 174
Koniordou, Lydia 188
Kono, Ben 138
Kontouri, Niketi 188
Konyk, David 349
Kookept, Adam Michael 243
Koon, Robert 380
Koonin, Brian 149, 161
Koons, Woodwyn 329
Kopischke, Kärin 355
Kopit, Arthur 19, 160
Koplin, Russell Arden 198
Koppel, Nurit 130
Koprowski, John 268
Korbee, Thomas Jr. 198
Korder, Howard 311
Korea Pictures 144, 371
Korey, Alix 206, 207, 220
Korf, Gene 167, 370
Korf, Geoff 345, 352
Korins, David 98
Kornberg, Richard
   ix, 5, 133, 168,
   174, 176, 188, 191,
   195, 201, 211
Kornhaber, David 265
Koroly, Charles 171
Koscielniak, Lynn 327
Kosek, Kenny 247
Kosh, David 266
Kosidowski, Paul 355, 356
Kosis, Tom 137
Koskey, Monica 345
Kostroff, Gregory 188
Kosuzu, Masaki 250
Koteas, Elias 271
Kotis, Greg 128, 271

Kotler, Jill 269
Kotlowitz, Dan 314, 342
Koudal, Morten Thorup 245
Kourtides, Nick 347
Kovacs, Michelle 265
Kovalenko, Kurt 223
Kovner, Todd 267
KPM Associates 196, 213
Kraft, Kevin 259
Krag, James 323, 326
Kraine Theater 265
Krakowski, Fritz 146
Krakowski, Jane
    19, 160, 371, 376, 377
Kramer, Julie 267
Kramer, Sara 261
Kramer, Terry Allen 138, 370
Krane, David 144
Krasnow, Neil 320
Krass, Michael
    197, 206, 246, 319, 342
Krause, Matthew 323
Krausnick, Dennis
    336, 337, 338
Kravitz, Zarah 250
Krebs, Eric 29, 167, 179, 371
Kreeger, Doug 260
Kreidler, Todd 354
Kreisler, Katie 302
Kreitzer, Carson 343
Kreitzer, Scott 139
Kremer, Dan 355
Krepos, Nicholas 259
Kretzmer, Herbert 127
Krich, Gretchen Lee 252
Krinsky, Marc 266
Krishnamma, Ranjit 204
Krishnan, Sean T. 314
Kristel, Jackie 270
Kristensen, Kira 304
Kristien, Dale 226
Kristina, Amy 249
Kritas Productions 188
Kromer, Christopher 339, 340
Kronenberg, Bruce 184
Kronenberger, Louis i
Kronzer, James 378
Krueger, Rich 271
Kruger-O'Brien, Peggy 350
Krumland, Carole A. xii
Krummel, Jens Martin 270
Kruse, Mahlon 144
Krutoff, Glenn 263
Kua, Kenway Hon Wai K.
    323
Kuchwara, Michael
    xiii, 11, 367, 373, 376
Kudisch, Marc 212, 216, 229

Kuhlke, Kevin xiv
Kuhn, Dave 146
Kuhn, Judy 223, 319
Kuhn, Kevin 183
Kulasinghe, Muni 250
Kulhawik, Joyce 378
Kulick, Brian
    33, 175, 266, 352
Kulick, Elliott F. 154, 370
Kumar, Syreeta 204
Kumaran, Laxmi 323
Kuney, Daniel 267
Kung, Yufen 180
Kunii, Masahiro 245
Kunimoto, Takeharu 250
Kunken, Stephen 227
Kunze, Eric 229
Kunze, Michael 146
Kurki, Lauren 336
Kurlander, Gabrielle 260
Kuroda, Emily 302
Kuroda, Kathy 266
Kuroda, Kati 314
Kurtz, Swoosie
    11, 70, 73, 149,
    150, 308
Kurtzuba, Stephanie 349
Kurup, Shishir 316
Kuruvilla, Sunil Thomas 317
Kushner, Jeremy 215, 380
Kustermann, Margaret 327
Kux, Bill 317
Kwapy, William 175
Kwiat, David 380
Kwiatkowski, John 269
Kwon, John Woo Taak 332
Kya-Hill, Robert 270

La Jolla Playhouse
    214, 302, 303, 340, 353
La MaMa Experimental
    Theatre Club
    233, 236, 248
Labey, Russell 266
Labin, Ann 146, 164
Laboissonniere, Wade
    202, 243
LaBute, Neil x, xiii, xv,
    79–84, 238, 251,
    271, 272, 301
LAByrinth Theater Company
    86, 90, 200, 265

Lacey, Maggie
    21, 141, 265, 314
LaChanze 270
LaChiusa, Michael John
    33, 195, 271, 272
Lachowicz, Ted 192
Lacivita, Carman 262
Lackawanna Blues 353
Lacombe, Shaullanda 224
Lacy, Kevin 135
Ladd, Eliza 262
Ladies of the Corridor, The
    260
Ladies, The 248
Ladutke, Rachel Rubin 266
Lady, Be Good 263
Lady of Letters, A
    115, 117, 208
Laev, Jim 146
LaFosse, Robert 255
Lagarce, Jean-Luc 270
Laidlow, Elizabeth 323
Laing, Robin 148, 244
Laird, Marvin 164
Lake, Ricki 3
Lake, The 348
Lakeera 272
Lam, Nina Zoie 261
Lam, Serena 246
LaManna, Janine
    166, 167, 219
LaMar, Diana 356
Lamb, Arthur J. 180
Lamb, Mary Ann 206, 212
Lambert, Jason 262, 338, 339
Lambert, Juliet 223
Lambert, Mikel Sarah
    174, 265, 348
Lambert, Molly 261
Lambert, Steve 321
Lamberton, David 265
Lamberts, Heath 216
Lamb's Players Theatre 304
Lamia, Jenna 248, 314
Lamm, Alessandra Corona
    212
Lamm, Teri 270
Lamos, Mark 312
Lamparella, Gina
    149, 164, 308
Lampley, Oni Faida 260
Lamude, Terence 264
LaMura, Mark 151
Lanciers, Barb 250
Land, Elizabeth Ward 321
Land of the Dead 271, 272
Landa, Edgar 307
Landau, Elie 185

Landau, Randall 143
Landecker, Amy 262
Lander, David 62, 214
Landers, Diane 263
Landers, Matt 268
Landfield, Matthew 259
Landon, Hal Jr. 310, 311
Landon, Kendra Leigh 273
Landowne, Mahayana 266
Landwehr, Hugh
    251, 352, 378
Lane, Nathan 22, 227
Lane, William 349
Langdon, Brent 329, 331
Lange, Alyson 145
Lange, Anne 151
Langella, Frank 9, 383
Langham, Joseph 211, 339
Langlois, Danielle 348
Langworthy, Douglas 343
Lanier, Laurice 145
Lansbury, Angela 20
Lansbury, David 254
Lapine, James
    129, 138, 319, 351
Lapira, Liza 273
Laporte, Stéphane 266
Laramie Project, The
    61, 379
Largay, Stephen 181
Lark Theatre Company, The
    346
Larkin, Jennifer 262
Larkin, Peter 163
Larlarb, Suttirat 331
Larsen, Anika 202, 243, 314
Larsen, Darrell 269
Larsen, Liz 267
Larsen, Lori 352, 355
Larsen, Ronnie 28, 196
Larson, Corrine 317
Larson, Jonathan 127
Larson, Larry 322
Larson, Peter 180
Larsson, Stefan 171
Lasana, Gyavira 256
Lash, Elissa 269
Laskey, Margaux 261
Lasko, Jim 380
Lasky, Becky 256
Last Child 264
Last Day 259
Last Five Years, The 347
Last Kiss 340
Last of the Suns 266
Last One, The 271
Last Schwartz, The 380
Last Stand 273

Last Sunday in June, The
    14, 29, ***208–***
    209, 209, 269
Last Supper, The 113
Last Train to Nibroc 260
Last Two Jews of Kabul,
    The 250
Latarro, Lorin 143, 144
Late (A Cowboy Song) 262
Late Night, Early Morning
    272
Late Nite Catechism *169–*
    170
Latessa, Dick
    5, 132, 218, 221,
    371, 376, 377
Latham, Aaron 155, 320
Latham, Stan 26, 141, 371
Lathan, Tendaji 141
Lathon, Daryl 267
Latin Heat 243
LaTourelle, Adrian 265
Latreille, Laura 378
Latta, Richard 179
Latus, James 175, 189
Lauer, Leo 265
Lauren, Ellen 334
Lauren, Liz 325
Laurence, Michael 331, 332
Laurents, Arthur 20, 164
Laurino, Michael 318
Laurits, Eric 269
Lavalle, John 221
Lavan, Jonathan 346
LaVecchia, Antoinette
    195, 259
Lavelle, Robert 163
Lavender, Daniel T. 266
Lavery, Bryony 375
Lavey, Martha 326
Lavin, Linda 10, 140
Lavner, Steve 216
Law, Leslie 352
Law, Lindsay 379
Lawler, Matthew 260
Lawrence, Blake 263
Lawrence, Darrie 259
Lawrence, Joey 230
Lawrence, Megan 223, 229
Lawrence, Peter 144, 164
Lawrence, Sharon 219, 303
Laws, Heather 218
Lawson, David M. 247
Lawson, Leigh 225
Lawson, Steve 271
Layman, Terry 329
Layng, Kathryn A. 261
Lazar, Paul 262

Lazarus, Bruce 135, 370
Le Loka, Tsidii 224
le Sourd, Jacques 367
Leach, Kristina 261
Leader of the Pack 422
Leaming, Greg 314, 342
Learned, Michael
    36, 173, 174
Leavel, Beth 221
Leavengood, Bill 272
Lebby, Marsha 170
LeBeauf, Sabrina 314
LeBlanc, Shon 321
LeBouef, Clayton 254
LeBow, Will 334
Ledbetter, Mark 262
Lederle, JR 326
Ledford, Margaret M. 320
Ledger, Karen Ann 345, 346
Ledo, Elizabeth 355
Ledoux, Paul 272
Ledsinger, David 308
Lee, Annabelle M. 302
Lee, C.S. 264
Lee, C.Y. 136
Lee, Cherylene 311
Lee, China 317
Lee, Chris 347
Lee, Darren 323
Lee, Eddie Levi 322, 354
Lee, Eugene 173
Lee, Gihieh 204
Lee, Gypsy Rose 164
Lee, Heather 164
Lee, Heland 260
Lee, Hoon 136
Lee, Hyunjung 264
Lee, James Edward 267
Lee, Jeffrey Yoshi 209
Lee, Jeremy J. 343
Lee, Joyce Kim 302, 305, 307
Lee, Liz 299, 322
Lee, Ming Cho 375
Lee, Robert Isaac 302
Lee, Sherri Parker
    256, 257, 269
Lee, Shinho 313
Lee, Steven N. 302
Lee, Tina 264
Lee, Tom 250
Lee, Tuck 146
Leebove, Patricia Harusame
    249
Leeds, Jordan 222
Leeves, Jane 218
LeFevre, Adam 225
Leftfield Productions 171
Legacy Codes, The 311

Legault, Anne 260
Legg, Dori 288, 291, 319
Leggett, Wil 301
Legrand, Michel 16, 138, 370
Leguillou, Lisa 131
Leguizamo, John 379
Lehman, Ernest 129
Lehman, Jon L. 378
Lehmann, Harold 264
Lehrer, Robert 256, 263
Lehrer, Scott
    131, 183, 195, 201,
    206, 212, 256, 349
Leichter, Aaron 204
Leigh, Jennifer Jason
    217, 227
Leigh, Mercedes 163
Leigh, Mitch 142
Leight, Warren 270, 332
Leighton, John 247
Leighton, Ralph 128
Leighton, Richard 262, 268
Leiner, Matthew 141
Leipzig, Zachary 326
Leishman, Gina 258
Leitner, James 345
Lema, Julia 179
Lemay, Harding 253
Lemenager, Nancy 263
Lemmeke, Ole 267
Lemon 141
Lemper, Ute 219
Lenat, Jesse 202, 265, 314
Lencowski, Kristopher 338
Lengfelder, Bill 350
Lenox, Adriane 211
Lenz, Matt 133
Leo, Melissa 253
León, Alia 228
Leon, Kenny 326
Leonard, John 204
Leonard, Katharine 132, 133
Leonard, Robert Sean
    168, 255, 371
Leonard, Valerie 318
Leonce and Lena 262
Leong, David S. 153
Leong, Terry 256
Lepard, John 255
Lepcio, Andrea 264
Lepers of Baile Baiste, The
    378
Lerch, Sara 206
Leritz, Lawrence 214
Leroux, Gaston 127
Lesbian Pulp-O-Rama! 263
Leslie, Mark D. 299
Leslie, Rachel 342

Lesser, Sally 250
Lessing, Gotthold 268
Lesson Before Dying, A 378
Lester, Gideon 334
LeStrange, Philip 151
Letendre, Brian 155, 320
Letscher, Brian 261
Lettre, Peter 249, 262
Lettuce, Hedda 196
Leung, Telly 136
Leve, Harriet N. 152
Leveaux, David 19, 161, 372
Levee James 313
Levering, Kate 220
Levesque, Joe 269
Levin, Cynthia 346
Levine, D.C. 220
Levine, David
    252, 253, 255, 262
Levine, James 375
Levine, Jonathan 134
Levine, Laura xiv
Levine, Lawrence 260, 268
Levine, Michael
    73, 76, 150, 308
Levine, Peter 261
Levine, Rob 162
Levings, Nigel 146, 372, 377
Levinson, Brad 266
Levy, Aaron 192
Levy, Annie 265
Levy, Daniel 264
Levy, Julia C.
    134, 151, 158, 159,
    160, 166, 173, 370, 371
Levy, Lisa 264
Levy, Philip 184
Levy, Ted L. 378
Lew, Jason 268
Lewandowski, Sheila 264
Lewis, Buddy 303
Lewis, Clea 213
Lewis, Ellen 157
Lewis, Irene 332
Lewis, Jerry 6
Lewis, Marcia 220
Lewis, Michael Shawn 227
Lewis, Norm 138
Lewis, Peter 263
Lewis, Sam 180
Lewis, Shannon 166, 167
Lewis, Vicki 219
Lewkowitz, Jerry 272
Lexington Road Productions
    146
Leyden, Leo 317
Leydorf, Mark 225
Leynse, Andrew 197, 255

Leyton-Brown, Allison 264
LFG Holdings 147
Liao, Angela 265
Liao, Joanna 253
Libman, Daniel 260
Libman, Martha 254
Librandi, Geraldine 341
Library of America 421
Lieber, Mimi 130, 253, 311
Lieberman, Amy 137
Lieberman, Andrew 342
Life (x) 3   4, 11, 12, *158*,
    371, 377
Lifeline Theatre 379
Light, Judith 254
Light, Sara 157, 370
Lightcap, Brenda 211
Lightly Built Bridges 313
Lightman, Alan 263
Ligon, Tom 262
Lil Budda 314
Lillie, Brenda J. 336, 337
Lillis, Padraic 268
Lily of the Valley 261
Lim, Jennifer 316
Lim-Dutton, Elizabeth 145
Limbaugh, Rush 81
Limelight Editions iii
Lin, Jodi 267
Lina, Tess 266, 309
Lincoln, Abraham 211
Lincoln Center 422
Lincoln Center Festival
    237, 250
Lincoln Center Theater
    9, 11, 22, 36,
    128, 129, 150, 154,
    170, 183, 196, 204, 370
Lincoln, Michael
    246, 258, 313
Lindblom, Gunnel 171
Linden, Brian 268
Linden, Hal 218, 219, 220
Linder, Jason 256
Linders, Jeanie 170
Lindsay, Priscilla 329
Lindsay-Abaire, David
    34, 195, 264,
    352, 369
Lindsey, Grant 196, 213
Lindsey, Jillian 314
Lindström, Bekka 259, 260
Linehan, Rosaleen 151, 237
Lines, Sybil 270, 351
Linkas, Malina 263
Linklater, Hamish 309, 310
Linn-Baker, Mark
    19, 161, 162, 267

Linney, Romulus
    235, 246, 269, 271,
    313, 375
Linscheid, Joy 256
Lion King, The
    127, 224, 380
Lion, Margo 132, 176, 370
Lion Theatre 265
Lipitz, Ben 224
Lipner, Miriam 265
Lipp, Frieda 256
Lippa, Lou 346
Lipscomb, William 258
Lipton, Elizabeth Wittlin 255
Lipton, Peggy 271
Liquid Moon, The 379
Lisanti, John 263
Lisi, Joe 11, 153, 177
Literary Managers and
    Dramaturgs of the
    Americas 423
Little, Brad 226
Little Eyolf 270
Little Fish 14, 33, *195–196*
Little Foxes, The
    47, 71, 378
Little Ham
    14, 29, 179, *179–180*
Little, Horace A. 316
Little Matchgirl, The 272
Little Night Music, A 319
Little Shubert Theatre 30
Littman, Naomi 320, 321
Litzsinger, Sarah 138, 216
Liu, Allen 136
Liu, Jennie Marytai 268
Lively Lad, The 331
Livier, Ruth 311
Living Out 306, 307
Living Theatre 233, 240
Livolsi-Stern, Katherine
    145, 206
Livsey, Christopher 198
Llana, Jose 136, 228
Lloyd, Christopher 33, 175
Lloyd, John Bedford
    22, 151, 338
Lloyd, Todd 314
Lloyd Webber, Andrew 127
Lluberes, Michael 259
Llynn, Jana 188
Loarca, Emanuel 255
Lobby Hero 324
Lobel, Adrianne
    19, 161, 162, 370
Lobel, Arnold
    19, 161, 162, 267
Local, The 273

Lochie, Robert B. Jr. 380
Lockett, Angela 182
Lockwood, Lois 341
Lockwood, Sharon
    306, 353, 354
Lockyer, Peter 145, 146, 223
Lodato, Victor 252, 313
Lodej, Anna 260
Loder, Jim 351
Loeb, Maury 256
Loebell, Larry 345, 346
Loeffelholz, J. 220
Loeks, Barrie 370
Loeks, Jim 370
Loesel, Paul 260
Loewith, Jason 326
Loftus, Tim 262
Logan, Daniel 250
Logan, Lael 265
Logan, Leroy 262
Logan, Stacey 217
Lohbauer, Bob 337
Lohbauer, Govane 336, 337
Lohr, Aaron 198
Lollos, John 170
Lomaka, Christine 300
Lombardi, Maryann 264
Lombardi, Michael J. 270
Lombardo, Matthew 200
Lommel, Anne 377
London, Becky 252
London, Carol 249
London, Chuck 45, 255
London Critics' Circle Award
    190
London Evening Standard
    Award 190
London, Mark 248
London, Todd 252
Lonergan, Kenneth 324
Long, C. Mingo 196
**Long Christmas Ride
    Home, The** 349
Long, Damian 269
**Long Day's Journey Into
    Night** 4, 23, 102,
    167–168, 168, 370,
    371, 372, 375, 376
Long, Jodi 16, 136
Long, Quincy 311, 331
Long, Richard Edward 258
Long Road Productions 213
Long Shot, The 261
Long Wharf Theatre 303, 314
Long, William Ivey
    133, 371, 377
Longbottom, Robert 136, 372
Longchamp, Nicole 259

Loo, Jackson 256
Look, Lydia 305, 349
Look of Love, The
    4, 26, 27, *166–167*
Lookadoo, Michelle 255
Loomer, Lisa 307
Loomis, Kevin C. 354
Loos, Anita 259
López, Abigail 270
Lopez, Carlos 144
Lopez, José 302
Lopez, Michael Evans 270
Lopez, Priscilla 263
Lopez, Robert
    237, 258, 314, 373
Lopez, Sal 311
López-Morillas, Julian
    301, 302
Loquasto, Santo
    139, 168, 213, 371
Lorca, Federico García 305
Lord, Sarah 252, 255
Lordan, John 326
Lorenzo, Darren 212
Lorey, Rob 217
Lorl, Daniel 338
Lorite, Francisco 267
Lorraine, Janice 315
LoRusso, Ted 261, 267
Losing Ground 268
Lost and Found 269
Lost in Translation 253
Lost Ones 234
Lotito, Mark 150
Lotorto, Louis 309
Loud, David 134, 135, 166
Louie, Diane 303
Louie, Kevin 246
Louis, Allan 321, 352
Louiselle, Bryan 192
Louizos, Anna 204, 244, 258
Louryk, Bradford 204, 270
Love 261
Love Arm'd 268
Love Hungry Farmer, The
    14, 37, *195*
Love in a Forest 210
Love in Pieces 267
**Love in the Age of
    Narcissism** 262
Love, Janis *170*
**Love Song of J. Robert
    Oppenheimer, The**
    343
Loves and Hours 308
Love's Labour's Lost 272
**Love's Labour's Lost: The
    Musical** 259

Lovett, Lauren 302
Low, Betty 182
Lowe, Chad 269
Lowe, Janice 314
Lowe, Leopold 261, 262, 268
Lowe, Michele 342
Lowe, Todd 311
Löwensohn, Elina 268
Lowes, Katie 268
Lowney, Jeffrey 243
Lowrance, Nicole 256
Lozano, Florencia
    252, 265, 354
Lu, June Kyoko 302
Lubetzky, Yael 141
Lucas, Chris 261
Lucas, Craig
    31, 174, 261, 263
Lucas, Jan 329
Lucas, Lauren 157, 370
Lucci, Derek 316
Luce, Clare Boothe 76
Lucille Lortel Award xvi, 373
Luckinbill, Laurence 218, 258
Lucky Chance, The 262
Lucky Hans 272
Luczak, Raymond 264
Ludlam, Charles 59, 235, 238
Ludwig, Deborah 263
Ludwig, Ken 318
Luft, Caroline 267
Luftig, Hal 138, 370
Luhrmann, Baz 18, 146, 372
Luke, David 266
Lukens, Steven 141
Luker, Rebecca 319
Lum, Randall K. 309
Lumbard, Dirk
    78, 149, 150, 308
Lumpkin, William 244
Lund, Monique 225
Lundberg, Judith 327, 328
Lundeberg, Karl Fredrik 311
Lundquist, Lori 350
Lunetta, Larry 146, 164
Lunsford, Kate 260
LuPone, Patti 225
LuPone, Robert
    251, 312, 316
Luscious Music 252
Lute, Denise 265, 316
Lutzhoft, Morten 245
Luz, Michael 260
Lydon, Christopher 334
Lyles, Leslie 252, 253
Lynch, David 43
Lynch, Gary 225
Lynch, Jayne Ackley 247

Lynch, John Carroll 303
Lynch, Michael 270
Lynch, Michele 133
Lynch, Pauline 148
Lynch, T. Paul 326
Lynch, Tertia 205, 266
Lynch, Thomas
    135, 174, 201, 302,
    327, 354
Lyng, Nora Mae 138
Lynskey, Susan 318
Lyon, Rick 237, 258, 314
Lyons, Donald 367
Lyons, Jason 254
Lyons, Patty 204
Lyons, Thomas 246
Lypsinka! The Boxed Set
    379
Lysistrata Project, The 253

M, Lebo 127
M. Elizabeth Osborn Award
    173, 277, 375, 422
Ma, Jason 323
Ma Rainey's Black Bottom
    4, 22, *152–153*,
    153, 261, 371, 376
Ma-Yi Theatre 266
Maas, Penny Ayn 218
Mabe, Matthew 37, 197, 313
Mabou Mines
    233, 234, 235, 236, 251
Mac Intyre, Tom 264
Macbeth 237, 245, 316
MacCary, Meg 262
Macchiarola, Frank J. 6
MacDermott, Grant 314
MacDevitt, Brian
    131, 152, 161, 168,
    189, 190, 195, 372, 375
MacDonald, Karen 334
MacDonald, Robert David
    266
MacDonnell, Theresa 160
Macdougall, Robert 352
MacEwen, Janet 217
Machado, Eduardo
    241, 285, 321
Machalani, Michele 315
Machan, Grant 261
Machinal 379, 380
Machota, Joe 225
Mack, James 269
Mack, Victoria 252, 339, 340
Mackenzie, Marianne 267

Mackes, Steve 214
Mackey, Jennifer 334
Mackie, Anthony 153
MacKinnon, Pam 347, 350
Macklin, Albert 348
Macknin, Laura Jones 328
MacLaughlin, Sean 262
Maclay, Joanna 327
MacLean, Lara 314
MacLeish, Archibald 267
MacLeod, Wendy 354
Macmillan, Katrin 272
MacNeil, Ian 188
MacNeil, Laura 317
Macon, Peter 316
MacPherson, Greg 209, 246
MacRae, Sloan 269
MacVittie, Bruce 264
Madaras, Jody 248
Madden, Angela 264, 265
Madden, Corey 307
Madden, Marinell 273
Maddigan, Tina 225
Maddow, Ellen 249, 377
Maddow-Zimet, Anya 264
Maddox, Gloria 263
Madera, Hemky 255
Madigan, Deirdre 198
Madigan, Reese 192
Madison, Cathy 379
Madonna and Child 259
Madurga, Gonzalo 320
Mae 313
Maeda, Jun 249
Maerz, Lara 326
Maeterlinck, Maurice 264
Maffia, Roma 331
Magaw, Jack 327
Magee, Daniel 266
Magee, Rusty 323
Mages, Libby Adler
    135, 163, 370
Magic Fire, The 348
Magic Theatre 304
Magid, Larry 167, 371
Magnificent Waste 253
Magnus, Bryn 327
Magnuson, Ann 248
Magrath, Monette 318
Mags, Michael 262
Maguire, Jenny
    211, 265, 271, 349
Maguire, Kate 335
Maguire, Martie 157, 370
Maguire, Matthew 252, 253
Maguire, Michael 223
Mahaffey, Valerie
    114, 208, 377

Mahaffy, Kasey 270
Mahan, Kathleen 318
Maharaj, Rajedra Ramoon 266
Maher, Bill 25, 167
Maher, Matthew
    181, 256, 270
Mahmud-Bey, Shiek 267
Mahoney, Siobhán 252, 318
Mahowald, Joseph 223
Maidstone Productions
    154, 370
Maier, Charlotte
    150, 151, 158
Maier, Helen 209
Maierson, Eric 268
Maika, Michele 223
Major, Fred 331
Makedonas, Panos 270
Making of Americans, The
    204
Malavet, Michelle 176, 209
Malcolm, Graeme 250
Maldonado, J. 220
Maleczech, Ruth
    233, 249, 251
Malek, Rami 314
Malina, Judith 240
Malina, Stuart 17, 139, 372
Malinowski, Arlene 326
Malkovich, John 235
Mallarino, Tatiana 250
Malle, Louis 240
Mallette, Wanda 157, 370
Maloney, Griffith 245
Maloney, Peter 151, 245
Malouf, Juman 176, 187
Maltby, Richard Jr. 376
Maltese, Elena M. 317
Malvestuto, Gina 353
Mamet, David 33, 189, 383
Mamma Mia! *128*, 225
Man of La Mancha
    4, 18, *142–144*,
    143, 225, 371, 379
Man of No Importance, A
    14, 36, *183–184*,
    184, 377
**Man Who Had All the Luck,
    The** 9, *129*
Man Who Laughs, The 338
Manasse, Jon 145
Manchester, Melissa 423
Mancina, Mark 127
Mancini, Marlene 130
Mandel, Briana 254
Mandel, Ellen 252
Mandel, Frank 205
Mandelbaum, Ken 367

Mandell, Alan 311
Mangaser, Allan 323
Mangione, Chuck 97
Manhattan Ensemble Theater
    204, 205, 266
Manhattan Rhythm Kings 193
Manhattan Theater Ensemble
    37
Manhattan Theatre Club
    34, 119, 120, 131,
    171, 182, 187, 192,
    195, 198, 203, 214
Maniam, Mano 256
Manim, Mannie 207
Manis, David 308
Mankin, Joan 304
Mann, David 133
Mann, Emily
    174, 265, 340, 377
Mann, Terrence 216, 223
Mann, Theodore 369
Mann, Thomas 266
Mannarino, Luca 145
Manners, J. Hartley 248
Manning, Kate 162
Manning, Keith Lorrel 259
Manocherian, Jennifer 152
Mansfield, Karl 145, 317
Mantello, Joe 8, 11, 36, 104,
    110, 131, 154, 177,
    183, 372, 373, 376, 377
Mantle, Burns i, vii, viii, 422
Mantooth, Randolph 255
Manus, Mara
    177, 189, 198, 202,
    210, 248
Manzay, J. Kyle 261, 377
Manzi, Warren 169
Manzy, Charde 299
Maog, Victor 313
Mapoma, M. Martin 355
Marano, Vincent 267
Marantz, Ruthie 264
Marathon 269
Marberry, Craig 191, 340
March, Chris 269
Marchand, Jeff 145
Marchant, Tyler 197, 252
Marchetti, Will 317
Marchica, Ray 146
Marcos, J. Elaine 136
Marcus, Joan 12, 21, 32, 60,
    63, 66, 70, 71,
    73, 80, 82, 86,
    88, 104, 107, 120,
    123, 134, 136, 137,
    139, 142, 143, 149,
    150, 151, 152, 153,

    154, 155, 158, 159,
    160, 165, 168, 172,
    174, 175, 177, 181,
    186, 187, 189, 192,
    199, 201, 203, 210, 211
Marcus, Leslie
    181, 191, 201, 209, 214
Marcus, Valerie 189
Marden, Elysa 273
Mardikes, Tom 339
Mardirosian, Tom
    244, 246, 253
Maré, Quentin 178
**Marga Gomez's Intimate
    Details** 249
Marginal Saints 267
Margo Jones Citizen of the
    Theater Medal xvi
Margo Jones Medal 385, 421
Margoshes, Steve 147
Margraff, Ruth 271
Margulies, David 314
Margulies, Donald 311, 326
Margulies, Julianna 272
Marla Stuart 14, 36, *171*
Marie, Donna 309
Marie Stuart 171
Mariela in the Desert 248
Marien, Robert 222
Marineau, Barbara
    183, 217, 262
Marini, Ken 347
Marino, Roger 164, 370
Marinoff, Judith 182
Marinyo, Tony 323
Maris, Peter 269
Marivaux, Pierre
    265, 334, 354
Mark, Garth T. 269
Mark of Cain 270
Mark, Ryan 259
Mark Taper Forum
    136, 178, 182, 304,
    305, 306, 353
Mark, Zane
    30, 173, 176, 198
Markell, Jodie 195
Marker, Craig 301
Market Theatre of
    Johannesburg 207
Markle, Lois 273
Marks, Dana 334
Marks, Kate 270
Marks, Ken 195, 225, 261
Marks, Kristin 160
Marks, Laura 267
Marley, Donovan 312
Marley, Susanne 258

Marlowe, Christopher 266
Marmer, Joshua 269
Maroney, Kieran 263
Marquis, Dan vii
Marquis, David 31, 213
Marrero, Janio 264
**Marriage of Miss
    Hollywood and King
    Neptune, The** 318
Marrié, William 138, 139
Marriott, The 271
Marriott Theatre in
    Lincolnshire 379
Marsden, Kristie 225
Marsh, Frazier 332
Marshall, Anthony and
    Charlene 167, 370
Marshall, Ian 261
Marshall, Jennie 229
Marshall, Jim 157, 370
Marshall, Joel 267
Marshall, Kathleen
    196, 205, 212
Marshall-Money, Andrea 263
Marshall-Work, Jill 266
Marte, Fior 255
Martell, Julie 164
Martí, José 280
Martin, Andrea 226
Martin, Barrett 155, 320
Martin, Carol xiv
Martin, Catherine
    18, 146, 371, 377
Martin, Elliot 129
Martin, Jane 278
Martin, Jesse L. 228
Martin, John Jeffrey 267
Martin, John Philip 311
Martin, Kamilah 132, 133
Martin, Laura 255
Martin, Leila 269
Martin, Lourdes
    252, 255, 321
Martin, Lucy 141, 158
Martin, Madeleine 158
Martin, Matthew 317
Martin, Melissa Jane 340
Martin, Michael X. 143, 144
Martin, Millicent 351
Martin, Nicholas 36, 197, 335
Martin, Richard 248, 262
Martin, Tim 239
Martin-O'Shia, Troy A. 348
Martindale, Kelly 146
Martinez, Christopher 198
Martinez, James 271, 273
Martinez, Rogelio 245, 253
Marting, Kristin 264

Martini, Richard 371
Martone, Nicole 260
Marty 335
Marvel, Elizabeth
    31, 174, 175, 265
Marvel, James 346
Marvel, Linda 332
Marx, Bill 378
Marx, Jeff 237, 258, 314, 373
Marx, Peter 78, 149, 308
Mary of Scotland 171
Mary, Queen of Scots 171
Mary Stuart 171
**Mary Todd . . . A Woman
    Apart** 14, 37, *211*
Masaki, Rino 250
Masenheimer, David 206
Masha No Home 246
Mason, Aaron J. 196
Mason, Chris 264
Mason, Dalane 262
Mason, Doris 272
Mason, Jackie 25, 138
Mason, Karen 225
Mason, Marsha 271
Mason, Marshall W. 41, 46, 255
Mason, Tod 266
Masonheimer, David 223
Master Builder, The 240
Master Class 76
**"Master Harold" . . . and the
    Boys** 378
Masteroff, Joe 128
Masterson, Marc 329, 331
Masterson, Mary Stuart
    19, 160, 371, 376
Masterson, Peter 349
Mastrantonio, Mary Elizabeth
    18, 143, 225, 371
Mastrelli, Adam 185
Masur, Richard 268
Matalon, Vivian 335
Match 269
Mathews, David 145
Mathews, Jamie 250
Mathews, Suzanna 145
Mathis, April 272
Mathis, Stanley Wayne 224
Matic, Sean 267
Matricardi, Lisa 206
Matsui, Rumi 250
Matt and Ben 267
Matthews, Dakin 307
Matthews, Ed 211, 339
Matthews, Liesel 154
Matthews, Mia 315
Mattox, Christopher 260
Mattsun, Lars 267

Maturo, Jennifer 256
Matz, Jerry 250, 261
Matz, Peter 193
Mau, Les J.N. 332
Mauer, Gary 223, 226
Mauldin, Callie 261
Maupin, Elizabeth 278
Maurer, Kelly 334
Maxfield, Redman 262
Maxwell, Jan 182, 373
Maxwell, Richard 254
Maxwell, Robert 8, 131
May, Andrew 343
May, Daniel 136
May, Elaine 28, 192
May, Marlene 264, 265
Mayer, Jerry 240
Mayerson, Frederic H.
    132, 370
Mayerson, Rhoda 133
Mayes, Sally 155, 320
Mayhem 346
Mayhue, Carl L. 380
Maynard, Jaye 266
Mayne, John 304
Mayo, Deborah 150, 151
Mayo, Don 143
Mayor's Limo, The 265
Mays, Jefferson 34, 60, 61,
    63, 66, 214
Mays, Marshall 267
Mazur, Heather 316
Mazza, Nicholas John 262
Mazzie, Marin 225
McAdams, John
    252, 253, 255
McAllister, Elan V. 132, 370
McAnarney, Kevin P.
    196, 213
McAndrew, Kelly 255
McAnuff, Des 303
McArdle, Andrea 216, 217
McBride, Tammy Elizabeth
    315, 316
McBurney, Simon 36, 186
MCC Theater 81, 251
McCabe, Aimee 262
McCabe, Jennifer 256
McCafferty, Kathy 261
McCallum, David 254
McCallum, Davis 264
McCann, Christopher
    271, 314, 317
McCann, Elizabeth Ireland
    189
McCarter Theatre
    142, 173, 187, 191, 340
McCarthy, Donna 341

McCarthy, Ed 247
McCarthy, Jeff 216, 229
McCarthy, Joseph 180
McCarthy, Liz 352, 354
McCarthy, Mary 10, 70–78
McCarthy, Michael 223
McCarthy, Senator Joseph 71
McCarthy, Sheila 313
McCarthy, Siobhán 148, 244
McCarthy, Thomas 225
McCartney, Liz 146
McCarty, Bruce 173
McCarty, Margaret K.
    345, 347
McCasland, Meredith 260
McCaw, Tamara
    171, 193, 195, 204, 207
McClain, Johnathan F
    209, 269
McClair, Curtis 253
McClam, DeLandis 176
McClanahan, Rue 321
McClarin, Curtis 184
McCleary, Dan 337
McCleister, Tom 265
McClellan, Wendy 334
McClelland, Stephanie
    136, 172
McClendon, Afi 317
McClintock, Jodie Lynne 358
McClintock, Justin 314
McClinton, Marion
    23, 153, 271, 314, 326
McCluggage, John 308, 309
McClure, Robert 130
McColl, Hamish 157, 158
McCollough, Lynne 211
McCollum, Kevin 144, 371
McConnell, Mary Jo 217
McConville, Maria 254
McCool, Mary 349
McCord, Marianne 219
McCorkle, Steve 312
McCormack, Mary 217
McCormack, Thomas 28, 173
McCormick, Michael
    164, 172, 183
McCourt, Frank 37
McCourt, Sean 183
McCracken, Perris 303
McCracken, Timothy
    271, 341
McCrea, Corrie 265
McCrory, Helen
    193, 194, 195
McCullough, Mark 335
McCullough, Mia 327
McCune, Rod 138

McCutchen, Heather 340
McDaniel, Drucie 346
McDaniel, Justin 332
McDaniel, William Foster 255
McDermott, James T. 307
McDermott, John 174
McDermott, Sean 255
McDonagh, Donald 376
McDonald, Amber 262
McDonald, David 263
McDonald, Heather 353
McDonald, Kirk
    134, 335, 336
McDonald, Peggy 353
McDoniel, Kate 322
McDonnell, Emily 262
McDonough, Ann 150
McDormand, Frances
    31, 188, 189
McDowell, Bob 259
McElroen, Christopher
    261, 262
McElroy, Michael 172, 228
McElroy, Steven 267
McEwan, Adrienne 226
McEwan, Mitchell 262
McFadden, Greg
    259, 265, 330, 331,
    332, 333
McFadden, Heather 146
McFadzean, David 304
McFarland, Martha 311
McGarry, Chris 163, 265
McGee, Robin L. 159
McGeehan, J J 146
McGhee, Elena 254
McGhee-Anderson, Kathleen
    318
McGillin, Howard 226
McGinn, Andre 175
McGinn, Andrew 265
McGinn/Cazale Theatre 266
McGinnis, Megan 216, 245
McGiver, Boris 42, 255, 271
McGlynn, Kevin B. 312
McGoff, Michael 178, 211
McGough, Bill 326
McGowan, Tom 220
McGrane, Paul Anthony
    201, 256, 349
McGrath, Bob 248
McGrath, Katherine 36, 183
McGrath, Matt 191, 217
McGrath, Michael 244
McGrath, Monette 311
McGravie, Anne 327
McGraw, Caroline V. 261
McGregor, Patricia 149

McGuigan, Marcy 245
McGuinness, Frank 36, 196
McGuire, Jenny 271
McGuire, William Biff 340
McGuire, William Francis 309
McInerney, Bernie 214, 314
McInerny, Susy 312
McIntyre, Dennis 270
McIntyre, Gerry 315
McIntyre, Lisa and Gary 378
McIsaac, Gerard 216
McIvor, Charlotte 263
McKay, Heather 248
McKay, Robert 259, 272
McKenna, Amy 262
McKenna, Tyler 301
McKenzie, Bruce 303
McKenzie, Jacqueline 186
McKenzie, Valentina 262
McKiernan, Patrick 246
McKinley, Bryan 261
McKinley, Philip Wm. 267
McKinney, Chris
    186, 252, 314
McKinnon, Kelley 239
McKinty-Trupp, Ryan 339
McKittrick, Jamie 263
McKittrick, Ryan 334
McKneely, Joey 198
McKnight, Jenny 328
McKoy, Candice 301
McLachlan, Rod 197
McLane, Derek
    62, 166, 214, 254,
    319, 347
McLaughlin, Ellen 254, 271
McLaughlin, James 259, 260
McLaurine, Marcus 179
McLean, John 350
McLeish, Kenneth 148, 244
McLeod, Raymond 146
McLucas, Rod 265
McMahon, Caroline 201
McMahon, Cheryl 335
McMahon, Chuck 173
McMahon, Terri 345
McManne, Dihlon 307
McMichael, Lucy 267
McMillan, Colleen 348
McMurdo-Wallis, Cristine 353
McNabb, Barry 258
McNall, Sean 268
McNally, Lori 332
McNally, Terrence
    8, 36, 76, 128,
    131, 183, 271, 379
McNamara, Rosemary 260
McNicholas, Steve 169

McNiece, Ray 249
McNight, Sharon 171
McNulty, Anne 193, 195
McNulty, William 331
McPherson, Conor
    xi, xiii, xv, 35, 51–
    57, 196, 267
McPhillamy, Colin 331
McQueen, Armelia 196
McQuery, Andrew 324
McQuilken, Michael 353
McRae, Maurice 263
McSweeney, Mary Ann 149
McSweeny, Ethan 314, 348
McTaggart, Fletcher 259
McVay, Marcelle 327
McVety, Drew 218
McVey, J. Mark 223
McWaters, Debra 166, 212
McWilliams, Lue 261, 267
Me and My Girl 377, 378
Me, Georgia 141
Meadow, Lynne
    182, 187, 192, 195,
    203, 214
Meaney, Colm 262
Mears, Mark 267
Mecca, Mary Jo 321
Mecchi, Irene 127
Medak, Susan 301
Medash, Keith 339
Medea 4, 22, *148–149*,
    149, 244, 316, 371,
    372, 376, 377, 378
Medea/Macbeth/Cinderella
    316, 377, 378
Medeamachine 267
Media Medea 254
Medina, Thelma 262
Medlock, Alanna 249
Mednick, Murray 265, 375
Medoff, Kara 167, 370
Medvin, Michelle 326, 327
Mee, Charles L.
    170, 303, 304, 348, 352
Mee, Erin 304
Meehan, Thomas
    ix, 5, 128, 132,
    370, 376
Mehta, Krishen 339
Meier, Aaron
    164, 182, 187, 193,
    195, 203, 214
Meineck, Peter 36, 174
Meir, Golda 37
Meisle, Kathryn
    22, 151, 175, 371
Meisner, Vivian 261

Meister, Brian 141
Mele, Peter 252
Meleady, Billy 378
Melendez, Joseph 355
Melendez, Suzanna 262
Melich, Nancy 278
Melillo, Joseph V.
    171, 193, 204, 207, 244
Mellen, Kymberly 324
Meller, Dana 224
Mellman, Kenny 261
Mellor, Barb 255
Mellor, Stephen
    236, 255, 377
Melrose, Ron 149, 150, 347
Melting Pot Theatre Company
    266
Meltzer, Howard 192
Melville, Herman 355
Memento Mori 246
Memories of Our Women
    247
Memory of Resistance, A
    346
Mena, Chaz 255, 263
Menaechmi, The 135
Mendel, D.J. 268
Mendelsohn, Daniel 375
Mendelsohn, Eric 272
Mendenhall, Francie 351
Mendes, Brian 254
Mendes, Sam
    20, 164, 193, 195
Mendieta, Wilson 143
Mendillo, Stephen 141, 300
Mendiola, Michael 245
Mendoza, Alvaro 263
Mendoza, Paola 262
Mendoza, Zilah 306, 307
Menger, Michael 270
Menin, Geoffrey 272
Menken, Alan 127, 272
Menken, Louis 272
Menocchio 301
Menon, Kannan 256
Menopause: The Musical
    170–171
Menzel, Idina 215, 228, 271
Meola, Tony 144, 312
Mercer, K.B. 304
Mercier, G.W. 318, 322
Mercier, Mel 244
Mercurio, Gregory John 249
Mercurio, Peter 260
mercy 245
Mercy Seat, The
    x, xv, *79–84*,
    80, 82, 238, 251, 367

Merediz, Olga 143
Merkerson, S. Epatha 202
Merlis, Jack 259
Mermaids on the Hudson
    261
Merman, Ethel 7, 20
Merrick, Warren III 263
Merrill, Bob 350
Merrill, Todd 267
Merrily We Roll Along 319
Merritt, Lawrence 259
Mertes, Brian 248
Meschter, David 149, 245
Meshejian, Paul 346
Meshugah 265
Meskouris, Dimitri 332
Messalina 253
Messina, Chris 163, 188, 269
Metamorphoses *128*
Metamorphosis, The 265
Metcalfe, Stephen 308
Metheny, Russell 328
Method Skin 318
Metropolitan Playhouse 266
Metz, Janet 222
Metzgar, Bonnie
    177, 202, 210
Meyer, Douglas L. 132, 370
Meyer, George 180
Meyer, Jerry 208
Meyer, Joseph 180
Meyer, Leo B. 315, 316
Meyer, Mark 268
Meyer, Marlane 268, 273
Meyers, Andrew 300
Meyers, Larry John 342
Meyerson, Ross 185
MGM/UA 129
Mhlongo, Futhi 224
Miami Herald 277, 421
Michaell, Monnae 303
Michaels, Jay 266
Michaels, Karina 313
Michalski, Jared 260
Michalski, Mandi 324
Michel, Fritz 250
Michel-Bernard, Jack 270
Michelangelo 113
Michelfeld, Gretchen M. 264
Michelson, Eve 259
Mickenberg, Risa 311
Micoleau, Tyler 196
Middleton, Kate 335
Midgette, Monique 196
Midnight's Children
    14, *204*
Midsummer Night's Dream,
    A *170*, 267

Midtown International Theatre
    Festival 266
Midwestern Chum 272
Mighty Myths 318
Mighty Nice! 254
Miguel, Mayumi 196
Mikos, Mike 268
Milando, Patrick 143
Milanov, Rossen 348
Milazzo, Robert 248, 254
Milburn, Rob
    141, 153, 162, 324,
    326, 327
Mileaf, Maria 266
Miles, Julia 258
Miles, Shauna 262
Militello, Anne 307
Millán, Amy Levinson 303
Millán, Rene 331
Miller, Allan 311
Miller, Annette 378
Miller, Arthur
    xii, xvi, 93, 128,
    129, 277, 293, 338,
    342, 375
Miller, Betty 262
Miller, Bill 160
Miller, Brian 160, 183
Miller, Caitlin 187
Miller, Cathleen 272
Miller, Danny 146
Miller, David 145
Miller, David Don 256
Miller, David Rockwell 258
Miller, Gilbert 69
Miller, Jeffrey 314
Miller, John
    133, 135, 139, 146,
    156, 161, 166, 183, 201
Miller, Kelly 266
Miller, Lyle 207
Miller, Matthew Floyd 318
Miller, Melissa 152
Miller, R. Michael 335
Miller, Roy 129, 262
Miller, Susan 272
Miller, Taylor 328
Miller, Yusef 261
Millicent Scowlworthy 313
Milligan, Tuck 255
Milliman, Linc 161
Mills, Elizabeth 134
Mills, Jason 206, 264, 269
Mills, Peter 269
Mills, Thomas 263
Mills, Tiffany 264
Milne, Dorothy 380
Milwaukee Rep. Theater 355

Minarik, Michael 266
Miner, Ann vii
Miner, Mary Michele 307
Ming-Trent, Jacob 301
Mingione, Ernest 268
Mingo, Alan Jr. 224, 228
**Minnesota Fats Is Right
    Around the Corner**
    260, 262
Mint Space 266
Mint Theater Company
    239, 251
Mintz, Cheryl 340
-1 (Minus One) 256
Miramontez, Rick 168, 175
Mirchin, Allan 270
Mirescu, Doris 268
Mirin, Jonathan 331
Misalliance 379
Misdary, Isis Saratial 264
Misérables, Les 127, 222
Mishkin, Chase 155, 193, 320
Mismond, Daryl 163
**Misogamy, or You're So
    Pretty When You're
    Unfaithful to Me** 264
**Miss Fozzard Finds Her
    Feet** 113, *208*
Miss Saigon 379
Missouri Repertory Theatre
    339, 354
**Mistress of the Inn (La
    Posadera), The** 255
Mitchell, Brandy 152
Mitchell, Brian Stokes
    18, 143, 225, 371, 379
Mitchell, Gregory 143
Mitchell, Jerry
    73, 133, 150, 164,
    308, 372
Mitchell, Kenneth 259
Mitchell, Larry 259
Mitchell, Lauren 134, 198
Mitchell, Lizan 314, 331
Mitchell, Michael 191
Mitchell, Sinclair 176
Mitchell, Susan 268
Mitchell, Tim 157
Mitchell, William Charles 329
Mitler, Matt 249
Mittelman, Arnold 156, 320
Mittenzwei, Veronica 265
Mitterlehner, Akeime 302
Miyagawa, Chiori 271
Miyamoto, Amon 250
Mo', Keb' 172
Moarefi, Kim 185
Moby Dick 355

Moccia, Jodi 164
Mock, John 348
Mockus, Jeff 301, 308, 309
Mode, Becky 347
Modern, B. 308, 309
Modigliani 270
Modirzadeh, Leyla 249
Modjeska, Helena 171
Moe, Mechelle 380
Moen, Katie 339
Moffat, Lynn
    174, 188, 201, 211
Moffett, Annie Lee 269
Mogentale, David 272
Mohmed, Buddy 213
Mohr, Jim 326
Mohrmann, Al 339, 340, 341
Momi, Mahmood 251
Molaskey, Jessica 183
Molbert, Chandler 339
Molière
    22, 151, 152, 256, 323
Molina, Alfred 13
Molina, Carlos 247, 255
Molloy, Geoffrey 267
Molloy, Mary 268
Molloy, Susan 267
Molly's Dream 239, 256
Molnar, Paul 273
Moloney, Aedin 247
Molossi, Robert 263
Moment, The 261
Monacelli, Joey 270
Monaco, James 180
Monaghan, Megan 322, 323
Monaghan, Michele 254
Monat, Phil 192
Moncada, Raúl 308
Monferdini, Carole 299
Mongiardo-Cooper, Nicholas
    256
Monique, Cree 261
Monk, Meredith 245
Monley, Adam 321
Monroe, Jarion 302
Monroe, Josh 188
Monroe, Mary 261
Monroe, Rebecca C. 137
**Monsieur Ibrahim and the
    Flowers of the Koran**
    266
Monster 119
Montalvo, Doreen 247
Montana, Janice 190
Montanaro, Anna 219
Montano, Robert 313, 335
Montel, Max 272
Montel, Michael 260

Montell, Jermaine 198
Montezuma 311
Montgomery, Charles 272
Montgomery, Chuck 265
Montgomery, Claire 339
Montgomery, J.C. 134
Montgomery, Mitch 253
Montoya, Richard
    144, 307, 309, 317, 318
Moody, Morgan
    145, 146, 206
Moon Bath Girl, The 245
Moon Please, The 271
Moon, Suzie 256
Mooney, Declan 266
Mooney, Kathleen 315
Mooney, Nate 176
Mooney, Nell 331
Mooney-Bullock, Jesse 380
Moontel Six 313
Moor, Bill 173
Moore, Alice 262
Moore, Allison 261, 264, 346
Moore, Benjamin 353
Moore, Charlotte
    195, 201, 247, 248
Moore, Christopher 268
Moore, Christopher Liam 316
Moore, Heather Shannon
    352, 353
Moore, Jason 237, 258, 314
Moore, Karen 206, 212
Moore, Kevin 319
Moore, Lee 252
Moore, Marilyn 265
Moore, Maureen 164
Moore, Melba 207
Moore, Michael V. 256
Moore, Mikhail 355
Moore, Monica 200
Moore, Roger 27, 158
Moore, Simeon 256
Moore, T.I. 266
Moore, Todd Jefferson 353
Moore, Wiley 329
Moorer, Margo 299
Mooy, Brad 300
Morales, Alejandro 248, 253
Moran, Braden 324
Moran, Martin 183, 218
Moran, Michael P. 205, 266
Mordecai, Benjamin
    136, 152, 172, 173
More Bitch Than a Bitch
    266
Morea, Gabor 272
Moreau, Elizabeth 334
Morehead, Rozz 155, 320

Moreland, Jason 261
Moreno, Louis 247
Morer, Paul 200
Moretta, Michelle 186
Morfogen, George 268
Morgan, Abi 308
Morgan, Cass 217
Morgan, Charles 270
Morgan, Charles F. 252
Morgan, Christopher L. 179
Morgan, Edward 355
Morgan, Ian 254
Morgan, James 180, 248, 258
Morgan, Jamie 354, 355
Morgan, Michele 303
Morgan, Nathan 145
Morgan, Robert
    76, 150, 308, 312
Moriarty, Bill 348
Moriber, Brooke Sunny
    201, 352
Morick, Jeanine 218, 225
Morishita, Dina 223
Morishita, Kaname 302
Moritz, Joel 323
Moritz, Marc 267, 270
Morley, Simon 170
Morning's at Seven 9, *129*
Morris, Cherry 193, 194, 195
Morris, Colette 202
Morris, Jennifer 253, 254
Morris, Joe 355
Morris, Peter 313, 314
Morris, Richard 129
Morris, Zoie 176
Morrisey, Bob 308
Morrison, Bob 157, 370
Morrison, Christopher 304
Morrison, J'aime 251
Morrison, John-Andrew 261
Morrison, Matthew 132
Morrissey, Thomas 259
Morrow, Jenifer 343
Morse, Tom 319
Morss, James 264
Mortensen, Marianne 245
Mortenson, Cristin 226
Mortimer, Vicki 161
Morton, Amy 326
Morton, Sarah 261, 267
Moscow Art Theatre 193
Moseley, Robin 348
Moser, Elizabeth 259
Moses, Burke 206, 216
Mosley, Dennis 354
Moss, Jenny 256
Moss, Maia A. 196
Moss, Robert 342

Moss-Bachrach, Ebon 255
Mostly Sondheim 9, *128*
Mother, The 250
MotherBone 253
Mothergun 264
Motherhouse 313
Mothers Against 343, 344
Motz, Bob 329
Moulds, Steve 329, 332
Moulin Rouge 18
Mound Builders, The 235
Mount, Anson 273
Mountcastle, James 135, 158
Mourning Dove 346
Mover, Richard 270
Movie Man, The 102
Movin' Out viii, 4, 16, 17,
    138–140, 139, 367,
    370, 371, 372, 376, 377
Mowatt, Anna Cora 266
Mowers, Dave 250
Moyer, Allen 308
Moylan, Pat 321
Mozart, W.A. 338
Mr. Gallico 264
Mr. Goldwyn *170*
Mrozik, Jennifer 229
**Mrs. Bob Cratchit's Wild
    Christmas Binge** 318
Much Ado About Nothing
    270
Mudge, Grant 265
Mudge, Jennifer 270, 318
Muehlhausen, Jens 179
Mueller, Ryan 301
Muench, Rebecca 311
Mufson, Lauren 314
Mugleston, Linda 160
Muir, Keri 339
Mulamba, Gwendolyn 261
Muldowney, Dominic 155
Mulgrew, Kate 31, 200
Mulheren, Michael 314
Mullaney, Tim 324
Müller, Heiner 260
Mulligan, Kate A. 307, 316
Mullins, Carol 249, 377
Mullins, Paul 317
Mullins, Willie 261
Mumford, Peter 155, 244
Munar, Andres 269
Munderloh, Otts 141
Munk, Erika 377
Munk, Troels II 245
Munoz, Javier 266
Murakami, Kanjiro 250
Muraoka, Alan 323
Murcelo, Karmin 311

Mürger, Henri 144
Murin, David 255, 315
Murmod Inc. 247
Murney, Julia 314
Murphey, Mark 343, 344
Murphy, Amy L. 345
Murphy, Audie 83
Murphy, Ben 266
Murphy, Donna 271
Murphy, Elizabeth 341
Murphy, Jeremiah 266
Murphy, Karen 198
Murphy, Michael R. 267
Murphy, Sally 36, 183
Murphy, Timothy Ford 264
Murphy, Tom 247
Murray, Andy 309
Murray, Billy 180
Murray, Brian 251, 312
Murray, Jeff 190
Murray, Tom 379
Murray, Walter 259
Murtaugh, James 259
Museum 265
Musgrove, Brad 227
Musica, La 262
Musser, Kristina 206
Mussman, Linda 249
Mustard—It's a Gas! 266
Mustillo, Louis 31, 190
**Mutant Factor of
   Reconciliation, The**
   259
Mutation Show, The 241
Mute, The Dream 251
Mwine, Ntare Guma Mbaho
   248
My Fair Lady 44, 379
My Father's Funeral 245
My Life in the Trenches
   266
My Life With Albertine
   14, 34, *201*
My Old Lady
   14, 28, *182*, 373, 375
My Special Friend 269
Myatt, Julie Marie 332
Mydell, Joseph 148, 244
Myers, Darin 265
Myers, Don 138
Myers, Ernie 267
Myers, J.D. 255
Myers, Jake 246
Myers, Michael F. 339
Myers, Scott 190, 196, 213
Myler, Randal
   30, 170, 205, 245,
   266, 271, 272

Myrberg, Per 171
Myrin, Arden 189
Mystery of Attraction, The
   273, 377
Mystique of Fly, The 264
**Myth of Moon and Morning
   Star, The** 269

N.E. 2nd Avenue 247
Nadeau, Lise 206
Naghavi, Fatemeh 251
Naidu, Ajay 186
Naidu, Sulekha 302
Nakachi, Mari 129, 172
Nakagoshi, Tsukasa 245
Nakahara, Ron 266
Nakasone, Wayne 302
Nakayama, Yasutaka 250
Naked Boys Singing! *170*
Nalbach, John 152
Nalepka, Brian 193
Nall, Lethia 34, 210
Namkung, Wende 146
Nana 379
Nance, Kevin 278
Nance, Marcus 145
Nanes, Ezra 267, 269
Narayan, Manu 202
Narciso, Alfredo 254
Nardelli, Ray 324, 326
Nardicio, Daniel 264
Nargeskhani, Hassan 251
Naro, Tom 175
Narver, Allison 265, 352
Nason, Brian 198, 247, 322
Nassar, Mark 262, 265
Nassif, Robert Lindsey 141
Nastro, Caroline 262
Natel, Jean-Marc 127
Nathan, George Jean 423
Nathan the Wise 268
Nathanson, Michael 267
Nation, The 423
National Actors Theatre
   36, 186
National Arts Journalism
   Program 421
National Asian American
   Theatre Company 267
National Endowment for the
   Arts 279
National Medals of the Arts
   375
National Theater of Greece
   36, 188

Nattenberg, Edward 301
Nauffts, Geoffrey 230
Naughton, Amanda 308
Naughton, James
   21, 142, 212, 219
Naughton, Keira
   253, 263, 272
Navarro, Puy 263
Naylor, Rashad 132
Ndiaye, Marie 248
Neal, Andrew 186
Nealy, Milton Craig 230
Near, Timothy 308
Neary, Julia 314
Nebelthau, Alan 341
Necessary Angel Theatre
   Company 346
Necrason, Jena 262
Nederlander, Amy
   163, 189, 200, 208
Nederlander, James L.
   138, 370
Nederlander, James M.
   148, 193
Nederlander, Scott E.
   138, 144, 161, 189,
   200, 208, 370, 371
Neer, Daniel 145
Neerland, Liz 338
Neff, Travis 320
Negron, Rick 321
Nehls, David 185
Nehls, Elizabeth 321
Nehring, Carl 341
Neill, Robert 271
Neipris, Janet 313
Nelis, Tom 303
Nellis, Jeff 202
Nelson, Anne 287
Nelson, Derrick 380
Nelson, Eric 321
Nelson, Linda S. 267
Nelson, Novella 186
Nelson, Rebecca 182
Nelson, Richard
   34, 201, 256, 349
Nelson, Stephanie 327, 380
Nemetz, Lenora
   218, 230, 351
Nemiroff, Brian 332
Nester, Kathleen 143
Neufeld, Ken 341
Neulander, Jason 253
Neumann, David 256
Neumann, Frederick 251
Neumann, Kimberly Dawn
   155, 156, 320
Neumann, Larry 326

Neuwirth, Bebe
    36, 213, 219, 271
New 42nd Street 162
New Boy 266
New Brain, A 380
New Dramatists 252
New Dramatists Lifetime
    Achievement Award
    376
New Federal Theatre 254
New Georges 267
New Group 238, 254
New Jersey Repertory Theater
    341
New Line Cinema 132, 370
New Moon, The
    14, 37, *205–207*
New Rules, The 272
New School University 241
New Theatre 279, 320, 380
New Victory Theater 19, 267
New War, A 378
New York 367, 421
New York Drama Critics
    Circle xiii, xvi
New York Drama Critics'
    Circle 365, 366, 422
New York Herald Tribune,
    The 421
New York International Fringe
    Festival 30, 188, 267
New York Observer, The
    367, 423
New York Post, The 367
New York Shakespeare
    Festival
    33, 175, 177, 189,
    198, 202, 210, 248
New York Stage and Film
    Company 189
New York Sun, The 367
New York Theatre Workshop
    31, 170, 174, 188,
    201, 211, 267
New York Times, The
    ix, 5, 6, 8,
    9, 21, 25, 26,
    27, 29, 43, 71,
    78, 87, 240, 366,
    421, 423
New York University xiii, 422
New York Yankees
    xi, 10, 105
Newbury, Kevin Lee 268
Newcomer, Michael A. 352
Newcott, Rosemary 322
Newell, Charles 323
Newfield, Anthony 152

Newhauser, Tina M. 135
Newman, Fred 260
Newman, Paul
    21, 141, 142, 371
Newman, Phyllis 271
Newman, Ralph xiii
Newman, Randy 352
Newport, Elaina 171
Newsday 367, 376
Newsome, Paula 311
Newton, John 268
Newton, Veronica 264
Next Episode, The 248
Next Theatre 326, 379, 423
Next Wave Festival
    149, 237, 244
Nguyen, Qui 253
Nicholas, James Hayden
    157, 370
Nicholaw, Casey 312
Nichols, Alexander V.
    301, 309, 318, 343
Nichols, Darius 202, 243
Nichols, Jane 254
Nichols, Jonathan 311
Nichols, Margaret 259
Nichols, Michael 341
Nichols, Mike
    157, 238, 300, 371
Nichols, Peter 158
Nichols, Taylor 303
Nicholson, Jim 254
Nicholson, Paul 343
Nickel and Dimed
    306, 307, 353
Nicklaus, Jill 138
Nickole, Dwandra 336
Nicola, James C.
    174, 188, 201, 211
Nicols, Shellee 256
Nielsen, Kristine 331
Nielsen, Petra 218
Nielson, Stina 259
Niemietz, Sara 140
Nietzsche Ate Here 261
Night Bloomers 261
Night Ether 260
Night of the Iguana, The
    377, 378
Nigro, Kirsten 346
Nilsen, Chessa 311
Niman, Grant 159
Ninagawa, Yukio 237, 245
Nine 4, 19, 160, *160–
    161*, 371, 372,
    375, 376, 377
Nine Eleven 264
Nine Ten 270

9-19 272
Ning, Jackson 268
Nisei Widows Club, The 302
Nishii, Brian 271
Nita and Zita 253, 377
Nixon, Cynthia 238, 246, 272
Nixon, Marni 262
Nixon, Roz 249
Nixon, Vivian 303
**No Foreigners Beyond This
    Point** 332
No God But Yearning 248
No One You Know 271
No Place Like Home 327
No Strings 14, 37, *212*
Nobbs, Keith
    35, 53, 54, 196,
    272, 314
Noble, Anne 327
Noble, Don 225
Noel, Craig 307, 421
Noises and Voices 264
Noises Off 9, *128*, 225
Nolan, Timothy 267
Nolan, Victoria 316
Nolen, Dean 225, 331
Nolen, Terrence J. 345
Noll, Christiane
    206, 207, 255
Nolte, Bill 138, 227
Nonas-Barnes, Aurora 253
None of the Above 267
Noon, Katharine 267
Noonan, Joyce A. 247
Noone, James 156, 320
Noone, Ronan 378
Noor, Haythem 272
Nora Theatre Company 378
Nordli, Robin Goodrin
    344, 345
Nordstrom, Ben 245
Norén, Lars 267
Norman, Grant 216
Norman, Marsha 261
Norman, Sylvia 266
Norment, Elizabeth 355
Norris, Bruce 326
Norris, William J. 328
Norrup, Christina Marie 315
North of Providence 269
Northeast Local 345
Norton, Edward
    36, 178, 217, 235, 377
Norton, Jim 35, 52, 54, 56,
    196, 377
Norwood, Margaret 250
**Not Fool the Sun Or Fester
    'n Sexx** 268

Not Herself Lately 267
Notebook, The 266
Notes From Underground
  236, 255
Noth, Chris 191, 314
Nothing of Origins 270
Nottage, Lynn
  271, 272, 309, 332
Nouri, Michael 271, 272
Novak, Duke 353
Novak, Elizabeth 299
Novelist, The 267
Novick, Julius i, xii, xv, 59,
  214, 423
Nowlin, Kate 260
Noyes, Alfred 314
Noyes, Ned 323
Ntshona, Winston
  37, 207, 377
Nunez, Coco 255
Nurse, Karlie 328
Nurse! 265
Nussbaum, Mike 379
Nutter, Duncan 270
Nyberg, Pamela 173, 317

O Jerusalem 238, 263
Oates, Joyce Carol
  289, 290, 291
Oatman, Deborah E. 265
Oberhausen, Leslie K.
  331, 332
Oberle, Megan 311
Oberman, Brett 198
Oberon 261
Obie Award 377
Obispo, Fabian 314, 342
O'Blenis, Edward 252, 263
O'Brien, Abbey 212
O'Brien, Alana 163
O'Brien, Cubby 164
O'Brien, Dan 264
O'Brien, Eleanor 307
O'Brien, Jack
  76, 133, 150, 307,
  308, 372, 376, 377
O'Brien, Jacki 200
O'Brien, Michael 350
O'Brien, Tom 197
Observe the Sons of Ulster
  Marching Towards
  the Somme
  14, 36, *196–197*,
  197, 204, 367, 373
O'Byrne, Adam 316

O'Byrne, Brían F. 239, 248
O'Byrne, Jennifer 176
O'Casey, Sean 51
Ochi, Norihide 250
Ochoa, Maricela 307
O'Connell, Deirdre
  211, 273, 314
O'Connell, Didi 262
O'Connell, Eileen 268
O'Connell, Jason 261
O'Connor, Caroline 219
OConnor, David 315
O'Connor Girls, The 354
O'Connor, Jim 346
O'Day, Michael 262
Ode to a Cube 236
Odell, George C.D. ix
Odets, Clifford 129
O'Donnell, Anthony
  193, 194, 195
O'Donnell, Mark
  ix, 5, 132, 370, 376
O'Donnell, Mimi 200, 254
Odum, Henry Michael 380
Odyssey, The
  61, *170–171*, 334
Oedipus for Dummies 261
Oesterman, Phillip 155, 320
Of Mice and Men 267
Of Two Minds 246
Off the Map 260
Ofsowitz, Megan 332
Ogawa, Aya 262
Ogbuagu, Chinasa 336
Ogden, Barrett 263
Oglesby, Greta 325, 326
Ogonowski, Lisa L. 319
O'Grady, Reyna Decourcy
  262
Oguma, Olivia 253
Oh, Sandra 305
O'Halloran, Sean 254
O'Hanlon, Barney 334
O'Hara, John 268
O'Hara, Kelli 201, 271
O'Hara, Robert 263
O'Hare, Denis
  11, 109, 153, 154,
  177, 218, 254, 371,
  373, 376, 377
O'Hare, Fergus 159
O'Harra, Brooke 250
Ohio State University 421
Ohio Theater 267, 377
Ojeda, Perry 149, 308
Oka, Marc 136
Okada, Makoto 250
Okamoto, Rika 138

O'Keefe, Laurence 322
Oklahoma! viii, *129*, 226
Okulitch, Daniel 145
Okuzu, Cypriana 265
Olagundoye, Toks 322
Old Globe, The 10, 307
Old Saybrook 213
Old Soak, The vii
Old Vic Productions 148
Oldest Living Confederate
  Widow Tells All 308
Olds, Lance 260
O'Leary, Thomas James 226
Olich, Michael 308
Olin, Elissa 268
Oliva, Lauren A. 196
Oliver, Anna 301, 302
Oliver, Barbara 301
Oliver-Watts, Guy 267
Oliveras, Maria 262
Olivier Award
  11, 35, 87, 190
Olivieri, Vincent 329, 331
Olmstead, Dan 348
Olmsted, Richard 301
O'Loughlin, Orla 193, 195
Olsen, Chuck 145
Olsen, Jennifer 145
Olsen, Ralph 164
Olson, Karin 338
O'Malley, Kerry
  35, 53, 56, 196
Omnium Gatherum
  329, 330
Once in Elysium 313
Once Removed 321
One Dream Sound 172
One Million Butterflies
  14, 37, *197*
One More Time 10, 140
One Shot, One Kill *171*
O'Neil, Chris 268
O'Neil, Shaun 268
O'Neil, Tom 269
O'Neill, Eugene 19, 24, 93,
  102, 167, 270
O'Neill, Heather 247
O'Neill, Kel 267
O'Neill, Kittson 267
O'Neill, Rob 269
Ong, Han 267
Only the End of the World
  270
Onodera, Kaori 250
Ontiveros, Jesse 247
Ontiveros, Tom 185
Ontological Detective, The
  260

Ontological Theatre 234, 268
Opatrny, Matt 252
Opel, Nancy 203, 229
Open Theater 233, 240, 241
Or Polaroids (Version 2.1)
    264
Orange Lemon Egg Canary
    331
Orbach, Ron 146, 220
Orchard, Robert J. 334
Oregon Shakespeare Festival
    343
O'Reilly, Ciarán 195, 201, 247
O'Reilly, Terry 251
Orel, Gwen 299
Oremus, Stephen 314
Orenstein, Toby 378
Oreskes, Daniel
    255, 256, 258, 352
Orfeh 270
Origlio Public Relations
    180, 202, 209
Origlio, Tony 180, 202, 209
Orizondo, Carlos
    255, 283, 320
Orlandersmith, Dael
    xi, xiii, xv, 34,
    119, 119–124,
    123, 187, 252, 375
Orlando, Matt 324
Orlando Sentinel 278
Orloff, Rich
    259, 261, 267, 300, 341
Ornstein, Suzanne 206
O'Rourke, Evy 222
O'Rourke, Kevin 258
Orphan on God's Highway
    249
Orr, Laurie Ann 262
Orsini, Angelique 256
Ortado, Victor 267
Orth-Pallavicini, Nicole
    254, 260
Ortiz, Ana 311
Ortiz, April 316
Ortiz, Deborah Louise 266
Ortiz, John 86, 354
Orton, Joe 326
Osborn, M. Elizabeth
    173, 277, 375, 422
Osborn, Paul 129
Osborne, Kevin 139
Oscar, Brad 227
Osgood, K. Winston 267
Osgood, Kimberly 324
O'Shaughnessey, Katie 269
Osher, John and Bonnie
    132, 370

Osheroff, Joe 259
Oshima, Usaburo 250
Osian, Matte 186
Osorno, Jim 150
Ost, Tobin 202, 243
Ostadazim, Sheila 265
Ostar Enterprises 141
Ostling, Daniel
    244, 324, 326, 341, 353
O'Sullivan, Anne 335
Osusky, Eva 354
Other Line, The 270
Other Love 268
**Other Side of the Closet,
    The** 261
Otis, John 249
Otis, Laura 267
Ott, Gustavo 248
Ott, Sharon 353, 354
Our Lady of 121st Street
    xi, xv, 14, 28,
    85–92, 86, 88, 199,
    200, 265, 367
Our Sinatra *170*
Our Town 4, 20, 21, 43,
    47, 118, *141*, 142,
    288, 371
Ouradnik, Diane 339
Out of My Mind 264
Outer Critics' Circle Awards
    377
Over the Moon 354
Overanalysis 259
Overbey, Kellie 192
Overcamp, David 250
Overshown, Howard W.
    35, 119, 120, 123, 187
Overstreet, Karyn 206
Overton, Kelly 221
Overton, Kenneth 206
Ovid 128, 236
Owen, Marianne 353
Owen, Paul 329, 331, 332
Owen, Susan 216, 226
Owens, Dan 179
Owens, Destan 219
Owens, Frederick B.
    143, 144
Owens, Jon 134, 166
Owens, Robert Alexander
    252, 253
Oxford University 423
OyamO 271

Pabotoy, Orlando 266, 377
Pace, Lee 258
Pace, Michael 312

Pacheco, Kim 265
Pachino, Jamie 379
Pacific Overtures
    250, 323, 379
Pacino, Al 23, 36, 163, 186
Paciotto, Andrea 249
Packard, Kent Davis 250
Packer, Tina 336, 337
Packett, Kila
    171, 193, 195, 204, 207
Padding the Wagon 259
Paddywack 266
Paeper, Eric 260
Page, Patrick 217, 224, 316
Pagliano, Jeff 260
Paice, Jill 225
Paige, Amanda Ryan 243
**Painted Snake in a Painted
    Chair** 249, 377
Painter, Devon 339
Pair of Hands, A 264
Pakledinaz, Martin
    135, 162, 166, 195,
    352, 354
Pakman, Ben 145
Palillo, Ron 268
Palin, Meredith 317
Palmer, Carl 261, 263
Palmer, Saxon 309
Palmer, Tanya 329, 331
Palminteri, Chazz 186
Paltrowitz, Adam 269
Panaro, Hugh 195, 226
Panayotopoulos, Nikos 188
Pancholy, Maulik 316
Pang, Andrew 270, 332
Panic! (How to Be Happy!)
    234, 268, 375
Pankow, John 198, 199, 347
Panou, Themistoklis 188
Panson, Bonnie 147
Pantheon Theatre 268
Pantoliano, Joe 8, 221
Paoluccio, Tricia 187, 262
Papadopoulos, Peter 313
Papagapitos, Chris 248
Papaleonardos, Eleni 332
Paparelli, P.J. 351
Paper Armor 252
Paper Mill Playhouse 320
Papp, Joseph 236
Pappas, Evan 335
Pappas, Justin 253
Paradise, Grace 164
Paradise Project, The 236
Paradise Theater Company
    268
Paraiso, Nicky 250

Paramount Pictures 155, 320
Paran, Janice 340
Pardess, Yael 347
Parente, Greg 270
Parents Evening, The 261
Pareschi, Brian 161
Parham, Lennon 253, 314
Parichy, Dennis 45, 255, 329
Pariseau, Kevin 222
Parison, Richard M. Jr. 348
Parisse, Annie 265
Park, Joshua 247
Park, Mary Ellen 326
Parker, Chandler 202
Parker, Christian 190
Parker, Christina 265
Parker, Daniel T. 316
Parker, Dorothy 260
Parker, Gilbert 369
Parker, Jacqui 336
Parker, Mary-Louise 227
Parker, Timothy Britten 271
Parker, Tina 350
Parkinson, Elizabeth 138, 139, 371, 376
Parkinson, Scott 323
Parks, Suzan-Lori 33, 129, 202, 326
Parnell, Charles 253, 329
Purnell, Peter 128
Parnell, Robert 304
Parnes, Joey 189
Parra, Maya 349
Parrish, Robyne 270
Parry, Chris 208, 309, 352
Parry, Steve 157
Parry, William 164
Parsons, Estelle 23, 163, 241
Parsons, Robert 301, 304
Part-Time Gods 263
Partisan Review 71
Partition 301
Parts They Call Deep 261
Pascal, Adam 215, 228
Pascual, Christine E. 328
Pasekoff, Marilyn 335
Pashalinski, Lola 236, 303
Pask, Scott 138, 154, 161, 177
Paslawsky, Gregor 307
Pasquale, Steven 183
Pass the Blutwurst, Bitte 236
Passage Theatre Company 346
Passaro, Joe (actor) 259
Passaro, Joseph (musician) 206

Passaro, Michael J. 147, 162
Passe-Muraille", "Le 138
Passengers 271
Passion 258, 319, 378
Pasternack, Gregg 261
Patano, Tonye 331
Patch, Jerry 309, 311, 332, 352
Patchell, Debra 145
Patel, Neil 173, 192, 198, 251, 312, 323, 334, 347
Patellis, Anthony 260
Paternostro, Michael 227
Paterson, Jayne 223
Patinkin, Mandy 25, 141
Patric, Jason 80, 271
Patrick, Leslie 263
Patrick, Michelle 163
Patrick, Sean 339
Patsas, Yorgos 188
Patterson, Anne 348
Patterson, Billy "Spaceman" 172
Patterson, Courtney 322
Patterson, George Paco 207
Patterson, Jay 318
Patterson, Meredith 220
Patterson, Michael Craig 272
Patterson, Rebecca 262
Patterson, Stephen Brian 223
Patton, Fitz 159, 193, 198, 244, 332, 347
Patton, Jammie 261
Patton, Leland 162
Patton, Monica L. 179
Patton, Will 262
Paul, John 266
Paul, Meg 139
Paul, Michael B. 354
Paulsen, Larry 245, 339
Paulus, Diane 170
Pavilion, The 329
Pavkovic, Dave 327
Pavlopoulos, Lefteris 188
Paw Paw Patch 318
Pawk, Michele 10, 140, 218, 220, 371
Paykin, Lanny 206
Paymer, David 311
Payne, Herman 196
Payne, Monica 327
Payne, Robyn 224
Payton-Wright, Pamela 255, 312
Pazerski, Gayle 262
Peace Corps 423

Peaco, Bobby 198
Peacock, Raphael 345
Pearl 303
Pearl, Katie 253, 377
Pearl Theatre Company, The 239, 268
Pearlman, Dina 265
Pearthree, Pippa 173
Pease, Robert 214
Peaslee, Richard 170
Pebworth, Jason 227
Peccadillo Theater Company 268
Pechar, Thomas 322
Peck, Erin Leigh 146, 222
Peck, Jim 322
Peck, Nathan 146
Peck, Sabrina 316
Peden, Jennifer Baldwin 302, 339
Peden, William 270
Pederson, Rose 352, 353
Pedini, Rob 266
Peditto, Paul 346
Peet, Amanda 272
Peg O' My Heart 247, 248
Pegasus Players 379
Peglow, Phillip Scott 335
Peil, Mary Beth 19, 160
Peirano, Tomi 264
Peirson, Nathan 304
Pelegano, Jim 260
Pelican Theatre 268
Pelinski, Stephen 316
Pellegrini, Larry 270
Pellegrino, Susan 150
Pellerano, Micki 268
Pellick, Andy 146
Pelzig, Daniel 162, 206
Pemberton, Michael 130, 343
PEN 237
Pen, Polly 314
Peña, Ralph B. 252, 266, 377
Pendarvis, Sade 269
Pendleton, Austin 271
Penetrate the King 252
Penhall, Joe 35, 190
Penn, Kal 302
Penn, Laura 353
Penn, Matthew 271
Penn, Stephane 264
Penna, Tony 329, 331
Penner, Anne 342
Pennington, Jesse 256, 314, 349
Pennino, Anthony P. 269
Penrod, Richard and Jacqueline 326

Pentecost, Del 187
Pentimento 72
People Be Heard 311
People's Light and Theatre
    Company, The 346
People's Light and Theatre,
    The 41
Pepe, Neil
    35, 190, 196, 213, 244
Peppas, Sophoclis 188
Pepper, Rick 260
Peremartoni, Krisztina 302
Perez, Gary 252, 253, 321
Perez, Jesse 252
Perez, Luis 144, 173
Perez, Paul Andrew 265
Perez, Rosie 8, 221, 245, 271
Perez, Sonny 259
Perfect Crime *169*
Performance Space 122
    235, 236, 254
Perhaps 259
Perich, Frank 268
Pericles 263, 307, 323
Perkins, Damian 216
Perkins, Drew 205, 266
Perkins, Kathy A. 182
Perkins, Patti 183, 195
Perkins, Toi 256
Perlman, Max 214
Perloff, Carey 300, 314, 355
Perlow, Karen 337
Perozo, Frank 255
Perr, Harvey 267
Perri, Michael 265
Perrineau, Harold Jr.
    35, 190, 191
Perrotta, Joe
    158, 166, 188, 195, 213
Perry, Alvin B. 322
Perry, Eugene 244, 324
Perry, Jennifer 225
Perry, Karen 336
Perry, Lisa M. 267
Perry, Maren 355
Perry, Margarett 258
Perry, Robert
    189, 191, 244, 340
Perry, Tara 260
Perry-Folino, Jo 301
Persbrandt, Mikael 171
Persians 269
Pesce, Vince 196
Pesic, Serge 338
Pessino, Maria 245
Pessyani, Attila 251
Pessyani, Khosrow 251
Pessyani, Setareh 251

Pet Sounds 204
Pete Sanders Group
    141, 156, 175, 193
Peter and Vandy 268
Peters, Bernadette
    19, 164, 165, 371
Peters, Bill 304
Peters, Clarke 219, 220
Peters, Glenn 259, 267
Peterson, Christopher Mark
    223
Peterson, Jon 217
Peterson, Lisa
    201, 258, 305, 307
Peterson, Matt 134, 166
Peterson, Paul 308
Peterson, Richard 380
Petit, Lenard 262
Petrarca, David
    162, 195, 267, 324
Petrocelli, Richard
    87, 200, 265
Petrosino, Marc 264
Petrovich, Victoria 302
Pettigrew, Shawyonia
    185, 188
Petty, Jason 205, 266, 377
Peveteaux, April 259
Pfisterer, Sarah 226
Phaedra in Delirium 254
Pham, Linh Thanh 327
Pham, Tuyet Thi 319
Phantom of the Opera, The
    127, 226
Phèdre 323
Phelan, Aimee 268
Phelan, Andy 260
Phenomenon 264
phidias8 346
Phil Bosakowski Theatre 268
Philadelphia Theatre
    Company
    198, 347, 423
Philip Rinaldi Publicity
    183, 197
Philippi, Michael 322, 323
Philippou, Nick 273
Philipsen, Heidi E. 263
Phillip, Kathryn 256
Phillips, David 183
Phillips, Fleur 321
Phillips, Jack 254
Phillips, Jacquie 185
Phillips, Michael i, 17, 250
Phillips, Patricia 145, 253
Phillips, Siân 182
Phillips, Thaddeus 250
Philoktetes 249

Philp, Richard 376
Phoenician Women, The
    270
Picasso, A 347
Piccini, Cristy 256
Piccininni, Erica 258
Piccione, Nancy
    187, 193, 195
Pickart, Christopher 345
Pickering, James 355
Pickering, Rose 355
Pickering, Steve 355
Pickle, John 206
Pielmeier, John 271
Pierce, Cynthia 270
Pierre, Christophe 255
Pierson, Kyle 269
Pietraszek, Rita 326, 328
Pietropinto, Angela 254, 348
Pietrowski, John 341, 346
Pigg, Kendall 268
Piggee, Timothy McCuen 352
Pihlstrom, Zane 327
Pilbrow, Richard 142
Piletich, Natasha 269
Pill, Alison 267
Pilloud, Rod 352, 353
Pillow, Charles 149, 164
Pine, Larry 254
Pines, Jeff 328
Pinheiro, Ilka Saddler 267
Pinkins, Tonya 196
Pino, Joe 349, 350
Pintauro, Dan 253, 267, 270
Pintauro, Joe 261, 269, 271
Pinter, Harold 59, 237, 421
Pinter, Mark 254, 318
Pinti, Adam 263
Piontek, Michael 225
Piper, Nicholas 258
Pipitone, Vito 341
Pirandello, Luigi 59
Piraro, Dan 267
Piretti, Ron 268
Piro, Jacquelyn 223
Pisoni, Lorenzo 34, 210
Pistone, Charles 321
Pitcher, Rebecca 226
Pitoniak, Anne 75, 149, 308
Pitre, Louise 225, 272
Pittelman, Ira
    144, 182, 200, 371
Pittelman, Nancy 331
Pittenridge, Robert A. 300
Pittman, Demetra 343
Pittman, Jamet 145
Pittman, Reggie 179
Pittsburgh Post-Gazette 423

Pittu, David 244, 255
Pizzi, Jason 345
Pizzi, Paula 314
Placencia, Osvaldo 255
Plain Dealer, The 278
Plana, Tony 311
Plato 236
Platt, Jon B. 142, 371
Platt, Oliver 33, 175
Plattsmier, Amanda 254
Plautus 135
Play What I Wrote, The
    4, 26, 27, **157**,
    158, 367, 371
Play Yourself
    14, 31, 32, **174**, 175
**Playboy of the Western
    World, The** 246, 247
Plays International 421
**Playwright of the Western
    World, The** 260
Playwrights Horizons
    34, 60, 61, 171, 181,
    191, 201, 209, 214
Playwrights Theatre of New
    Jersey 341, 346, 347
Pleasant, David 191
Plimpton, Martha 33, 189
Plotkin, Tom 312
Plowright, Joan 13
Pluess, Andre
    214, 323, 326, 327,
    328, 380
Plumb, Jason 300
Plummer, Amanda 340
Plummer, Christopher 24, 187
Plummer, Joe 266
Plumpis, John 224
Plymesser, Stuart 342
Pockriss, Lee 351
Podemski, Tamara 228
Poet, Bruno 204
Poetics of Baseball, The 269
Poetri 27, 141
Pogrebin, Robin 5, 27
Pohlel, Zany 323
Poisson, Amy 353
Polan, Nina 255
Polanski, Roman 17, 146
Pole, Jane 152
Polendo, Ruben 248, 301
Polish Joke 14, 34, 35, **203**
Politically Incorrect 25
Polk, Andrew 318
Polk County 379
Polk, Matt
    135, 152, 159, 161,
    166, 174

Pollack, Charlie 229
Pollin, Tera-Lee 155, 320
Pollock, Suann 342
Polseno, Robin 143
Polsky, Eric J. 269
Polunin, Slava 250
Pomerance, Bernard 129
Ponce, Ramona 249
Pool, Carol 133
Poole, Brady 319
Poole, Russell 327
Poole, Stan 322
Poor Beast in the Rain 264
Poor, Bray 331
Pope, Manley 228
Pope, Stephanie 219
Popiolkowski, Chester 342
Popolizio, Brenton 314
Popp, Carolyn 339
Pops 272
Porch 423
Porretta, Matthew 223
Porro, Susan 269
Portantiere, Michael vii, 30
Portelance, Mariessa 335, 336
Porter, Billy 198, 314
Porter, Cole 193, 258, 261
Porter, Kilbane 250
Porter, Lloyd 263
Porter, Spence 272
Porterphiles 258
Portes, Lisa 314, 326
Portia 89, 199, 200, 265
Portnow, Richard 213
Posey, Parker 255
Posillico, Cynthia 267
Posner, Aaron 329, 345
Posner, Kenneth
    73, 133, 150, 202,
    308, 372, 377
Pospisil, Craig 273
Post, Douglas 328
Poster, Kim 152
Posterli, Tina 266
Pothier, Nancy 260
Potter, Betsey 254
Potter, Kirsten 354, 356
Potting Shed, The 259
Potts, Michael
    175, 252, 271, 334
Poulos, Jim 201, 228
Poulton, Mike 129
Pourfar, Susan
    209, 252, 269, 314, 322
Powell, Gary 195
Powell, J. Dakota 271
Powell, Janis 190
Powell, Linda 253, 334

Powell, Marcus 254
Powell, Michael Warren
    260, 271
Powell, Molly
    252, 253, 254, 258
Powell, Steve 267
Power, Alice 157
Powerhouse Theatre at Vassar
    189
Powers, Andy 261
Powers, Leslie 262
Powers, PJ 380
Prada, John 268
Prael, William 188, 258
Prasad, Shanti Elise 262
Pratt, Cynthia 328
Pratt, Nina 185
Prayer, A 271
Precious Stone 253
Preece, Lars 250
Preher, Kathy 329
Preisser, Alfred 261, 262
Prelude to a Kiss 263
Prendergast, James 259
Prendergast, Shirley 254
Pressley, Brenda
    309, 310, 334
Pressman, Kenneth 259
Prestininzi, Ken 346
Preston, Carrie 253, 314, 332
Preston, Lisa 265
Preston, Rob 312
Preston, Wade 138, 139
Pretlow, Wayne W. 196
Previn, André 348
Prewitt, Tom 248, 346
Price, Joseph 339
Price, Lonny 156, 320
Price, Mark 146
Price, Michael P. 312
Price, The 379
Price, Timothy 246
Priester, Sally 322
Priestley, J.B. 270
Primary Stages
    37, 171, 197, 238, 255
Primis, Theo 146
Prince, Akili 252
Prince and the Pauper, The
    14, 29, **171–172**
Prince, Charles 201
Prince, Faith 36, 183, 225
Prince Hal 263
Prince, Harold 10, 140, 141
Prince, Warren "Chip" 145
Prinz, Rosemary 260
Private Jokes, Public Places
    250

Private Lives *129*
Pro Bono Publico 313
Producers Club, The 269
Producers, The
    77, *128*, 227
**Project X: Before the Comet
    Comes** 353
Proof *128*, 227, 329
Prop Thtr Group 346
Prosky, Andy 268
Prosky, Robert 319
Prospect Theater Company
    269
Prosser, Peter 146, 164
Prosser, Sarah 139
Proust, Marcel 34, 201
Prouty, Deane 164
Prud'homme, Julia 254
Prugh, Niki 327
Pruitt, Jasika Nicole 260
Prune Danish
    4, 25, *138*, 371
Pruzin, M. Jason 300
Prymus, Ken 253, 270
Pryor, Peter 345
Psalmayene 24 318
Psychic Life of Savages, The
    317
Psychotherapy Live! 264
Public Relations 264
Publicity Office, The
    144, 150, 178, 181,
    191, 192, 201, 210, 214
Pucci, Peter 317
Puccini, Giacomo 144
Puerto Rican Traveling
    Theater 255
Pugh, David 157, 371
Pugliese, Frank 271, 272
Pula, Ramona 250
Pulitzer Prize xi, xii, xvi, 33,
    35, 120, 187, 277,
    279, 368, 421, 423
Pullella, Mary Ann 300
Pullman, Bill 221
Pulse Ensemble Theatre 269
Pumo, David 259, 260
Puppetry of the Penis *170*
Purcell, Douglas 206
Purchase College, SUNY 423
Purdy, Renee 315
"Pure" Gospel Christmas, A
    265
Purinton, Miles 266
Purnell, Kimberly "Q" 254
Purnhagen, Gregory 324
Purple Rose Theatre 41, 278
Purviance, Douglas 143

Purwin, Kate 355
Pusz, Christy 151
Puzzo, Michael 265
Pyant, Paul 214
Pye, Tom 149, 244
Pyle, Wayne 224
Pyretown 253
Pytel, Janice 214

QED 9, *128*
Quackenbush, Karyn
    149, 222, 308
Quackenbush, Laura 340
Quade, Vicki 169
Quan, Dori 302
Quan, Samantha 246
Quandt, Stephen 342
Quarles, Jason 249
Quartet 335
**Queen of the Remote
    Control** 302
Queen's 2 Bodies, The 346
Queer Carol, A 270
**Quick and Dirty (A Subway
    Fantasy)** 273
Quick, The 318
Quigley, Bernadette 262, 264
Quijas, Vanessa 272
Quills 60
Quinlan, Michael 249
Quinn, Ardes 259
Quinn, Kirsten 346
Quinn, Patrick 216, 270
Quinn, Rosemary 264
Quintero, Jose 265
Quisenberry, Danielle 267
Quisenberry, Karen 316, 317

Raab, Marni 226
Rabe, David 317
Rabe, Lily 271
Rabkin, Gerald 373
Rabson, Lawrence 139
Raby, Roger Allan 351
Rachel, Mlle. 171
Rachele, Rainard 259
Racine, Jean 323
Rada, Mirena 258
Rader, Wendy 329
Radiant Baby 14, 33, *198*
Radio City Music Hall 3
Radio Wonderland 264

Radnor, Josh 221
Raetz, Elizabeth 301
Rafferty, Sarah 311
Rafferty, Stephanie 250
Raffo, Heather 259
Ragland, Jim 313, 352
Rain Dance 235, 255
Raine, Michael 216
Rainer, Elizabeth 343
Raines, Howell 78
Raines, Ron 219
Rainey, DanaShavonne 176
Raiter, Frank 334
Raitt, John 7
Raize, Jason 224
Rajput, Rachel 301
Rak, Rachelle 166, 167
Rakosi, Samantha Massell 145
Ralph, Sheryl Lee 229
Ramaswamy, Vasudeva 339
Ramayana, The 301
Ramey, Nayna 339
Ramikova, Dunya 309
Ramin, Sid 164
Ramirez, Ana Tulia 247
Ramirez, Bardo S. 258
Ramirez, Rebeca 262
Ramsey, Kenna J. 228
Ramsey, Matt 335, 336
Rand, Randolph Curtis
    249, 377
Rand, Ronald 261
Rand, Tom 244
Randall, Jay 301
Randall, Tony 36, 186
Randals, Kathy 253
Randell, Patricia 260, 270
Randels, Kathy 377
Randle, Mary 224
Rando, John 17, 147, 203
Randoja, Karin 249
Randolph, Beverley 196
Randolph, Jim
    130, 138, 142, 167
Randolph, Tod 337
Randolph-Wright, Charles 317
Raphael, Frederic 148, 244
Raphael, Gerrianne 269, 273
Raphel, David 247
Rapp, Adam xi, xiii, xv, 93–
    102, 261, 269
Rapp, Anthony 101, 228, 261
Rapt 263
Raree 252
Rasalingam, Selva 204
Rash 352
Rasheed, A-men 261, 263
Rashovich, Gordana 308

Rask, Julia 208
Raskin, Kenny 216
Rasmussen, Andrew 263
Rasmussen, Benjamin Boe
    245
Ratajczak, Dave 166
Ratner, Brett 141
Rattazzi, Steven
    249, 258, 271, 272,
    343, 377
Rattlestick Theatre
    208, 209, 269
Rauch, Bill
    307, 316, 345, 378
Rauch, Matthew 42, 45, 255
Rausch, Nate 380
Ravenhill, Mark 314
Ravvin, Genna 334
Rawson, Christopher
    i, xi, xiii, xv,
    10, 103, 154, 178, 423
Ray, Bill C. 319
Ray on the Water 264
Raymond J. and Pearl Berman
    Greenwald 370
Raymond, Lisa 269
Rayner, Martin 253, 348
Rayson, Jonathan 162
Reade, Simon 204
Real Time With Bill Maher 25
Reale, Robert
    19, 161, 267, 370
Reale, Willie
    19, 161, 267, 370
Reams, Lee Roy 216, 227
Reaser, Elizabeth
    245, 253, 314
Reay, Christopher 353
Rebeck, Theresa 329, 375
Rebhorn, James
    22, 150, 151, 246
Recent Tragic Events
    xii, xvi, 277, *287–292*,
    288, 291, 319, 375,
    378
Red 349
Red and Tan Line 260
Red Hot Mama *171*
Red Press, Seymour
    136, 195, 196, 206, 212
redbird 270
Reddin, Keith
    259, 271, 322, 349
Reddy, Brian 151
Reddy, Gita 267
Redesign 271
Redgrave, Corin
    256, 257, 349

Redgrave, Lynn
    113, 118, 208, 376, 377
Redgrave, Vanessa
    24, 168, 371, 376
Redsecker, John 206, 212
Redwood, John Henry 271
Reed, GW 269, 273
Reed, Kim 267
Reed, Luke 157, 370
Reed, Maggie 254
Reed, Michael (arranger) 147
Reed, Michael James (actor)
    307
Reeder, Ana 214
Reedy, M. Kilburg
    167, 179, 371
Rees, Roger 36, 183, 184
Reese, Andrea 269
Reference Guide to American
    Literature, The 422
Regan, Suzanne 44, 255
Reichard, Daniel 198
Reichel, Cara 269
Reichgott, Seth 348
Reid, Catherine 300
Reid, Michael 245, 270
Reidy, David 273
Reiley, Jennifer 344
Reilly, Ellen 261, 263
Reilly, John C. 335
Reilly, T.L. **272**
Reim, Alyson 259
Reimer, M. Anthony 320
Reinders, Kate 164, 267
Reiner, Alysia 262
Reiners, Portia 266, 314
Reingold, Jacquelyn
    238, 246, 271
Reinhart, Charles L. 376
Reinis, Jonathan 167, 371
Reinking, Ann
    166, 212, 218, 271
Reisch, Michele 319
Reiser, Paul 36, 213
Reiter, Elizabeth
    244, 324, 326
Reiter, Stuart 380
Reith, Jeanne 304
Rella, Concetta Rose 254
Remedios, David 334
Remembrance of Things Past
    201
Remler, Pamela 164
Remo, Melissa 145
Rempe, Frank 262
Rendall, Jill 343, 345
Rene, Yves 262
Renschler, Eric 159

Rent *127*, 228
Rentmeester, Ryan 261
Repertory Theatre of St. Louis
    41
Repplinger, Jill 262
Requiem for William 262
Resa Fantastiskt Mystisk
    267
Resistible Rise of Arturo Ui,
    The 14, 36, 186,
    186–187
Resja, Reid 299
Resnick, Judith 135, 136, 370
Resnik, Hollis 223, 324
Restrepo, Federico 250
Resurrection Blues
    xii, xvi, 277, 293,
    294, 338, 375
Rettig, Shane 331
Return to the Upright
    Position 271, 272
Reuben, Aubrey 369
Reuben, Gloria 271
Reuning, Jonathan 261
Revelation Theater 37, 188
Reverend Billy 268
Rey, Melanie 270
Reyes, Erik 249
Reyes, Joselin 247
Reyes, Randy 249, 323
Reyes, Stephen 263
Reynaud, Jacques 245
Reynolds, Brett W. 261
Reynolds, Corey
    152, 222, 371
Reynolds, Graham 253
Reynolds, Jonathan 375
Reynolds, Shelley 353
Reza, Yasmina 12, 158
Rhapsody in Seth 259
Rhodes, Elizabeth 209, 245
Rhodes, Ginette 263
Rhodes, Josh 156
Rhodes, Michael 273
Rhymicity 332
Ribada, David Perez
    280, 283, 320
Ribbon in the Sky 272
Riccardi, Rose 341
Ricci, Arlette 315
Ricciardi, Paul 349
Riccomini, Raymond 160
Rice, Elizabeth Hanly 309
Rice, Tim 127, 128
Rich, Geoffrey 254
Rich, Jeremy 161
Rich, Marian 260
Rich, Shirley 369

Richard, Ellen
    134, 151, 158, 159,
    160, 166, 173, 370, 371
Richard, Judine 132, 133
Richard Kornberg and
    Associates
    ix, 133, 174, 176,
    188, 191, 195, 201, 211
Richard Rodgers Award 376
Richard Rodgers Theatre 6
Richard, Stephen 317
Richards, David 369
Richards, Devin 206
Richards, Jamie 246
Richards, Jeffrey
    163, 197, 370
Richards, Lisa 142, 300
Richards, Walker 260
Richardson, Abby Sage 172
Richardson, Cathy 352
Richardson, Desmond
    166, 167, 196
Richardson, Gisele
    259, 260, 262
Richardson, Kevin 220
Richardson, Miranda 13
Richardson, Natasha 217
Richardson, Steve 338
Richel, Stu 269
Richenthal, David 167, 370
Richmond, Robert
    36, 174, 267
Richter, Tom 266
Rickenberg, Dave 133
Rickman, Allen Lewis 252
Ricks, Tijuana T. 317
Ricky Jay on the Stem
    33, 170–171
Riddett, Cecilia 346
Rideout, Vale 206
Ridiculous Theatrical
    Company 233, 236
Ridiculous! The Theatrical Life
    and Times of Charles
    Ludlam 235, 376
Riding, Nicole 223
Riebe, Jeff 261
Riegel, Chara 301
Riehle, Richard 314
Riesco, Armando
    254, 263, 272
Rifkin, Jay 127
Rifkin, Ron 218
Rigdon, Kevin 349, 350
Rigg, Kate 250, 271, 272
Riggs, Cristeena Michelle 223
Riggs, Lynn 129
Riker, Jennifer 302

Riley, Eric 179
Riley, Rob 324, 328
Riley, Ron 252, 253
Rimers of Eldritch 47
Rinaldi, Philip
    151, 155, 183, 197, 204
Ring, Derdriu 246, 247
Ringwald, Molly 12, 163, 218
Rios, Michelle 143, 144, 249
Ripley, Alice 223
Rishard, Steven 349
Rising, Craig 270
Ristori, Adelaide 171
Rita, Rui 163, 173, 335, 349
Ritchey, Lee 267
Ritual of Faith, A 266
Riva, Amadeo 270
Rivals, The 259
Rivas, Geoff 311
Rivera, Chita
    19, 160, 219, 271,
    305, 371, 375, 376
Rivera, Clea 252
Rivera, Eileen 267
Rivera, Elan 253
Rivera, José 271, 285
Rivera, Mira 256
Rivera, Primy 256
Rivera, Thom 246
Rivers, Ben 261
Riverside Drive 213
Rives, Chelsey 308
Rizner, Russ 206
Rizner, Russel L. 136
Rno, Sung 252, 253
Roach, Dan 341
Roach, Maxine 145
Road to Hollywood, The
    312
Roads That Lead Here, The
    332, 333
Robards, Jake 141
Robbins, Blake 272
Robbins, David 185
Robbins, Emily 329
Robbins, Jerome 164
Robbins, Kurt 185
Robbins, Rebecca 206
Robbins, Rhonda 309
Robbins, Tom Alan 224
Roberson, J. 220
Roberson, Ken 176, 258
Robert Fox Ltd. 154, 370
Robertazzi, Justin 145
Roberto Zucco 268
Roberts, Aaron 350
Roberts, Alison 345
Roberts, Carolyn 337

Roberts, Chris 271
Roberts, Crystal 329
Roberts, Dallas 178, 217, 314
Roberts, Daniel 259
Roberts, Jennifer 327
Roberts, Jennifer Erin
    268, 354
Roberts, Jimmy 169
Roberts, Jonathan 127
Roberts, Jonno 154
Roberts, Judith 342
Roberts, Keith 138, 371
Roberts, Marcia 136
Roberts, Rachael 262
Roberts, Richard J. 329
Roberts, Samuel 259
Roberts, Sydney 322
Roberts, Taylor 314
Robertson, Scott 134
Robeson Tape, The 300
Robie, Wendy 326
Robin Williams: Live on
    Broadway 4, 129
Robinette, Nancy 378
Robins, Laila
    262, 294, 338, 340
Robins, Robert P. 321
Robinson, Angela 198, 255
Robinson, Audrey 250
Robinson, Claudia 345
Robinson, Dre 207
Robinson, Edward G. 202
Robinson, Fatima 198
Robinson, Hal 218
Robinson, Jo Ann 300
Robinson, Julie Anne 252
Robinson, Mark Steven 266
Robinson, Mary B. 246, 271
Robinson, R. David 270
Robinson, Rebecca 264, 265
Robinson, Reginald 309, 332
Robinson, Roger 322
Robinson, Romel 265
Robinson, Stacey 252
Robinson, Terrell 250
Robinson, William "Smokey",
    Jr 375
Rocha, Kali 225, 311
Roche, Billy 264
Roche, Paul 316
Rockaby 237
Rocker, John 110
Rockwell, David 133, 371
Rockwell, Norman 47
Rodarte, Randy 307
Rodarte, Scott 307
Rodenborn, Ted 254
Roderick, Ray 171

Rodericks, Basil 259
Rodger, Struan 148, 244
Rodgers and Hammerstein
    Organization 136
Rodgers, Kami 261
Rodgers, Richard
    6, 9, 16, 129,
    134, 136, 212, 316
Rodrigues, Tania 204
Rodriguez, Adrian 269
Rodriguez, Diane 307
Rodriguez, Enrico 202
Rodriguez, Jai
    30, 202, 203, 228
Rodriguez, Jake 300
Rodriguez, Onahoua 311
Rodriguez, Robynn 343, 344
Rodwin, David 248
Roe, Alex 266
Roe, Kate 259
Roeder, Patti 328
Roeder, Peggy 379
Roemer, Laura 270
Roeters, Kirsten 304
Roethke, Linda 323
Roff, Brian 200
Roffe, Al 86, 89, 200, 265
Roffe, Mary Lu 142, 371
Rogers, Brian 264
Rogers, Douglas R. 309
Rogers, Mac 264
Rogers, Michael 256
Rogers, Ninon 271
Roggie, John 198
Rogustad, Sylvia 311
Rohr, Beth-Stiegel 210
Roi, Natacha 340
Rojo, Jerry 348
Rolle, John Livingstone 268
Rollnick, Bill 192
Rom, Erhard 319
Roman, Carmen 313, 348
Roman Nights 262
Romance Cycle, The 323
**Romance of Magno Rubio,
    The** 266, 377
Romano, Joe 307
Romberg, Sigmund 205
Romeo and Bernadette
    320, 380
Romeo and Juliet 18, 240
Romero, Constanza 326
Romero, Elaine 258
Rommen, Ann-Christin 245
Romola and Nijinsky 255
Ronan, Brian 135, 166
Rooks, Joel 135
Room 314 260

Ropes, Bradford 128
Rordam, Jeppe Dahl 245
Rosa, Billy 267
Rosa Lublin 379
Rosario, Willie 313
Rosato, Mary Lou 245
Roscoe, Carol 355
Roscoe, Norbert 180
Rose and Walsh 303
Rose, Anika Noni 314
Rose, Erez 261
Rose, Gina 188
Rose, Ian 347
Rose, Philip 254
Rose, Richard 346
Rosegg, Carol 7, 52, 54, 56,
    112, 115, 117, 130,
    179, 191, 197, 200,
    208, 213, 244, 246,
    247, 294
Rosemary 346
Rosen, Cherie 143
Rosen, Joel 150, 308
Rosen, Lauren 254
Rosen, Robert 338
Rosenbaum, Michael 332
Rosenberg, David (producer)
    141
Rosenberg, David A. (critic)
    xiii
Rosenberg, Michael S. 245
Rosenberg, Roger 212
Rosenblum, Tamara 264
Rosenfeld, Jyll 138, 371
Rosen's Son 269
Rosenthal, Todd 326, 355
Roses in December 272
Ross, Blair 221
Ross, Jonathan Todd 260
Ross, Joye 146
Ross, Linda 313, 349
Ross, Michael 332
Ross, Stuart 33, 198
Ross, Tom 301
Rossellini, Isabella 271
Rossetter, Kathryn 260
Rossier, Mark 373
Rosswog, Joseph 264
Roth, Daryl
    148, 163, 176, 200,
    208, 262
Roth, Michael 208, 352
Roth, Sarah Hewitt 133
Rothan, Elizabeth 350
Rothe, Lisa 270
Rothenberg, Andrew 328
Rothenberg, David 246
Rothman, Alyse Leigh 264

Rothman, Carole
    176, 191, 195
Roundabout Theatre
    Company
    9, 19, 22, 23,
    25, 27, 129, 134,
    151, 158, 159, 160,
    166, 173, 208, 370,
    371, 376, 422
Roustom, Kareem 336
Routh, Marc 182, 185, 373
Rovere, Craig 270
Rowan, Tom 246
Rowand, Nada 268
Rowe, Stephen 238, 263
Rowland, John G. 378
Roy, Edward 261
Roy, Jacques 355
Roy, Melinda 156, 320, 372
Royal Court Theatre 52
Royal Dramatic Theatre of
    Sweden 171
Royal Family, The 379
Royal Hunt of the Sun, The
    380
Royal National Theatre
    11, 154, 155, 158,
    190, 207, 239
Royal National Theatre, The
    370
Royal Shakespeare Company
    38, 204
Rozell, Vicki 311
Rozenblatt, David 146
Rozie, Fabrice 350
Rozin, Seth 345, 346
Roznowski, Robert 222
Ruark, Joel K. 252
Rubald, Mark 312
Rubber 266
Rubens, Herb 254
Rubenstein Associates Inc.
    180, 196, 206, 212
Rubin, Arthur 369
Rubin, John Gould 200, 270
Rubin, Judith 369
Rubin, Tara 137, 150
Rubin-Vega, Daphne
    202, 228, 314
Rucker, Mark 311
Rudd, Paul 271
Ruderman, Jordin 265
Rudetsky, Seth 259
Rudin, Scott 148
Rueck, Fred 272
Ruede, Clay 136, 206
Ruehl, Mercedes 221
Ruf, Elizabeth 256

Ruffelle, Frances 223
Ruggles, Brian 139
Ruhl, Sarah 246, 262, 318
Ruiz, Mildred 332
Rum and Vodka 267
Runco, David 267
Rundle, Erika 248
Ruocco, John 271
Rupert, Michael 204
Ruppe, Diana 262
Ruscio, Elizabeth 307
Rush, Brian 268
Rush, Geoffrey 60
Rush, Michael S. 256
Rushdie, Salman
    38, 204, 301
Rushen, Jack 261
Rusinek, Roland 315
Russell, David 353
Russell, Jay 157, 216, 315
Russell, Kirsten 264
Russell, Mark 254
Russell, Melissa 260
Russell, Monica 262
Russell, Ricky 258
Russell, Ron 270
Russell Simmons's Def
    Poetry Jam on
    Broadway
    4, 26, *141*, 371
Russo, Dan 180
Russo, Peter 266
Russo, William
    181, 191, 201, 209, 214
Rustin, Sandy 222
Ruta, Ken 301
Ruth Foreman Award 380
Rutherford, Ivan 222, 223
Rutherford, Stanley 270
Rutigliano, Danny
    206, 207, 224
Rutkovsky, Ella 134, 166
Ruzika, Tom 321
Rx 267
Ryall, William 230, 351
Ryan, Amanda 202
Ryan, Annie 202
Ryan, Bruce 141
Ryan, Kate (1) 262
Ryan, Kate Moira (2) 32,
    211, 352
Ryan, Leah 250, 272
Ryan, Maybeth 339
Ryan, Patti 157, 370
Ryan, Rand 302
Ryan, Randy 271
Ryan, Richard 147
Ryan, Roz 220

Ryan, Thomas Jay 317
Rye, Nick 345
Rynne, Chris 308
Rzepski, Sonja 264

S-Dog 249
S., Albert 334
Saba, Sirine 204
Sabath, Bruce 263
Sabato, Patricia 345
Sabberton, Kenn 267
Sabel, Shelly 176, 187, 210
Sabella, D. 220
Sabella, Ernie 143, 220, 225
Sabin, Amy 300
Sacharow, Lawrence 272
Sachon, Peter 183, 193
Sachs, Stephen 346
Sack, Domonic 315
Saddler, Donald 315, 373
Sadler, William 186
Sadoski, Thomas 256, 349
Saed, Zohra 249
Safdie, Oren 250
Safe in Hell 311
Safer, Daniel 268
Saffarianrezai, Morteza 251
Sageworks 152
Sagona, Vincent 270
Saguar, Luis 304
Said, Najla 267
Saietta, Bob 249
Saint and the Football
    Players, The 234
Saint, David 255
Saint Joan 44, 45
Saint Lucy's Eyes 322
Saint She Ain't, A 315
Saints and Singing 266
Sainvil, Martine 131, 137
Saito, James 246, 323
Saito, Kirihito 250
Saivetz, Deborah
    252, 258, 262
Sajadi, David 314
Sakakura, Lainie 136, 379
Sakata, Jeanne 302, 305
Sakemoto, Akira 250
Salamone, Louis S. 190
Saland, Ellen 269
Salao: The Worst Kind of
    Unlucky 380
Salata, Gregory 173, 259
Saldivar, Matt 256
Sale, Jonathan 261

Salguero, Sophia 255
Salinas, Ric
    304, 307, 309, 317, 318
Salk, Susanna 315
Salkin, Eddie 134, 161
Sallid, Otis 314
Sally Smells 261
Salmen, Tania 249
Salmon, Susan 148
Salmon-Wander, Ashley 270
Salome 4, 23, *163*
Salome Sings the Blues 269
Salonga, Lea 16, 136
Salt Lake Tribune, The
    278, 422
Saltz, Amy 271
Saltzberg, Sarah 267
Saltzman, Marc 320
Salvatore, Matthew 145
Samayoa, Caesar 255, 340
Sampliner, James 198
Sams, Blair 311
Sams, Jeremy 138, 370
Samuel Beckett Theatre 269
Samuel, Peter 223, 227, 314
Samuels, Jill 264
San Diego Theatre Critics'
    Circle 421
San Diego Union-Tribune
    421
San Francisco State University
    422
San Jose Repertory Theatre
    308
Sanabria, Marilyn 266, 267
Sananes, Adriana 255
Sanchez, Alba 248
Sanchez, Alex 206, 212
Sánchez, Edwin
    260, 272, 285, 313
Sanchez, K.J. 253
Sanchez, Olga 353
Sande Shurin Theatre 269
Sander, Natalie 332
Sanders, Brian 348
Sanders, Casey 300
Sanders, Jay O. 38, 184
Sanders, Pete
    141, 156, 175, 193
Sanderson, Austin K. 255
Sands, Ben 335
Sandy, Solange 146, 196
Sanford, Tim
    181, 191, 201, 209, 214
Sans Cullotes in the
    Promised Land 252
Santiago, Maxx 259, 260
Santiago, Saundra 19, 160

Santiago, Tania 263
Santiago-Hudson, Ruben 353
Santos, Fiona 185
Santvoord, Van 247
Sanville, Guy 255
Sanz, Carlos 311
Saporito, James 161
Sapp, Robb 202, 243
Sapp, Steven 332
Sarcoxie and Sealove 252
Sardou, Victorien 75
Sargent, Mark 269
Sargent, Stacey 176, 177
Sarkar, Indrajit 259
Sárossy, Gyuri 193, 195
Sarpola, Richard 206
Sarsgaard, Peter 217
Satalof, Stu 136, 212
Satterfield, Valda 235
Saturday Night Fever 229
Saturn's Wake 264
Saunders, A. 220
Savage, Abby 270
Savage, J. Brandon 214
Savage, Sheila 312
Savages of Hartford, The
    253
Savelli, Jennifer 146, 212
Savin, Ron Lee 216
Saviola, Camille 305
Sawotka, Sandy
    171, 193, 195, 204, 207
Sawyer, Ray and Kit 131, 370
Saxe, Caroline 315
Saxe, Gareth 195, 250, 307
Say Goodnight, Gracie
    4, 24, *135*, 370, 377
Sayama, Haruki 250
Saylor, Jacob 329
Scanavino, Peter 261
Scanlan, Dick 129
Scanlon, Patricia 245
Scapin 323
Scardino, Don 308
Scarface 23
Scarlet Letter, The 337
Scarpulla, John 139
Scarpulla, Stephen Scott 164
Scattergood 251, 367
Scènes de la Vie de Bohème
    144
Scertier, Nancy 340
Schachter, Beth 263
Schactman, Ken 263
Schadt, Timothy 160
Schaefer, Paul A. 201
Schaefer-Jeske, Juliet 266
Schaeffer, Eric 319, 351

Schafer, Scott 259
Schaffner, Brooke 327
Schantz, Magin 249, 262
Schanzer, Jude 261
Scharf, Katie 262
Scharf, Kenny 248
Schatz, Jack 136, 212
Schechner, Richard 250
Scheck, Frank 367, 376
Schecter, Amy 192
Schecter, Jeffrey Howard 216
Scheib, Jay 268
Schein, Omri 265
Scheine, Raynore 326
Scheitinger, Alexander 148
Schelble, Bill 369
Schellenbaum, Tim 249, 250
Schenck, Margaret 345
Schenkkan, Robert 318
Scherr, Gina 352
Schertler, Nancy
    300, 318, 355
Schiappa, John 154
Schilke, Raymond D. 142
Schirle, Joan 316
Schirner, Buck 345
Schiro, Chad L.
    155, 156, 320
Schlackman, Marc 192
Schleifer, Mike 332
Schlossberg, Julian 192, 193
Schmidt, Erica
    34, 176, 187, 210, 261
Schmidt, Josh 327
Schmidt, Katherine 206
Schmidt, Mary Ethel 340
Schmidt, Paul 323, 334
Schmidt, Sara 146
Schmidtke, Ned 307
Schmitt, Eric-Emmanuel 266
Schmoll, Ken Rus 248
Schnee, Jicky 268
Schneggenburger, Marie 378
Schneid, Megan 188
Schneider, Michael 322
Schneider, Ted 245, 252
Schneiderman, L.J. 260
Schnirman, David 163
Schnitzler, Arthur
    239, 252, 302
Schnore, Ludis 259
Schnuck, Terry E. 163, 370
Schoeffler, Paul 160, 217
Schoenbeck, Steve 309
Schoevaert, Marion 267, 268
Schönberg, Claude-Michel
    127
Schondorf, Zohar 145

School for Greybeards 253
Schooler, Luan 343
Schraft, Micah 248
Schreck, Heidi 353
Schreiber, John 176
Schreiber, Liev
    80, 81, 82, 251, 272
Schreiber, Terry 272
Schreier, Dan Moses
    138, 198, 307
Schremmer, Troy 252, 267
Schrider, Tommy 342
Schrock, Robert 170
Schroeder, Eric 314
Schroeder, Wayne 172
Schubert, Allison 301
Schuette, James 334, 379
Schuler, Duane 347
Schulfer, Roche 324
Schull, Rebecca 270
Schulman, Andrew 265
Schulman, Arlene 266
Schulman, Craig 222, 226
Schulman, Susannah
    311, 343, 344
Schulner, David 342
Schultz, Armand 314
Schultz, Carol 268
Schumacher, Jon 267
Schuttler, Harmony 252
Schuval, Michael 264
Schuyler, Peter 250
Schwab, Edna 280, 320
Schwab, Laurence 205
Schwandt, Charles 338
Schwartz, Andrew 136, 267
Schwartz, Chandra Lee 164
Schwartz, Craig
    182, 304, 306
Schwartz, Jean 180
Schwartz, Jesse 312
Schwartz, Robert Joel 254
Schwartz, Scott 204, 378
Schwartz, Susan L. 187
Schweikardt, Michael 185
Schweizer, David 249
Schwiesow, Deirdre 269
Schworer, Angie L. 227
Scisioli, Peter 324
Scoones, Fiona 254
Scott, Adam 311
Scott, Bobbi Lynne 331, 332
Scott, Eric Dean 268
Scott, Jared 196
Scott, Jason 269
Scott, Kimberly 311
Scott, Klea 307
Scott, Les 160

Scott, Rachel 301
Scott, Seret 252, 308, 347
Scott, Sherie René
    187, 215, 228
Scott, Steve 326
Scott, Wayne 263
Scott-Flaherty, Alexa 270
Scott-Reed, Christa 178, 265
**Screaming in the
    Wilderness** 267
Scribe, Eugène 75
Scrivener's Tale, The 336
Scruggs, James 263
Scurria, Anne 349
Sea of Tranquility 311
Seagull 380
Seal, Elizabeth 335
Sealed for Freshness 268
Seamon, Edward 268
Searle, Tanya J. 299
Sears, Djanet 260
Seascape 312
Seaton, Laura 206
Seattle Repertory Theatre
    182, 353
Seattle Times, The 278
Seavey, Jordan 259
Sebesky, Don
    135, 136, 166, 193, 335
**Second Death of Priscilla,
    The** 331
Second Skin 271
Second Stage Theatre
    33, 170, 176, 191, 195
Secret Garden, The
    379, 380
Sedgwick, Rob 269
Seebald, Ed 271
Seed, The 259
Seegebrecht, George W. 380
Seehorn, Rhea 181, 314
Segal, David F. 308, 320
Segev, Rahav 42, 45, 48
Seiber, Christopher 216, 229
Seidelman, Arthur Allan 321
Seiden, Jackie 265
Seiderman, Pamela 264
Seidman, Matt 329
Seiff, Carolyn 260
Seiver, Sarah 160
SEL 132, 370
Seldes, Marian
    22, 31, 32, 150,
    151, 174, 175, 237,
    371, 373
Sella, Robert 217
Sellars, Lee 329
Sellars, Peter 334

Seller, Jeffrey 144, 371
Sellers, Barbara 312
Sellwood, Tom 263
Selma's Break 267
Seltzer, Michael 164
Selya, John 138, 371, 376
Sen, Nandana 270
Senbloh, Saycon 215
Seneca 326
Senior, Kimberly 327
Senor, Andy 228
Sensenig, E. Andrew 185
Serpent, The 241
Serralles, Jeanine 260
Serrand, Dominique
    301, 338, 339
Servitto, Matt 271
Sesame Street 237
Sesma, Thom 143, 144
Sessions, Tally 380
Setlock, Mark 209, 269
Setlow, Jennifer 301
Setrakian, Ed 163
Sevan, Adriana 311
Seven Angels Theatre 315
7-11 271
1776 379
78th Street Lab 270
Severence, Michael 254
Severine, Nicole 263
Severs, William 262
Severson, Sten 317
Sewell, Richard 268
Sexaholix . . . a Love Story
    379
Sexton, Coleen 265
Sexton, Michael 188, 331
Seyffer, Gene 380
Seymour, C.C. 268
Seymour, Nicole 259
Sgambati, Brian 336
Shaddow, Elena 160, 185
ShadowCatcher Entertainment
    189
Shaefer, Paul 314
Shafer, Margaret 206
Shafer, Scott 259
Shaffer, Henry 252
Shaffer, Jeremy
    153, 163, 173, 182,
    185, 189
Shaffer, Zach 252
Shafir, Ariel 263
Shaghoian, Vicki 317
Shaiman, Marc
    ix, 5, 132, 370, 376
Shain, Julie 260
Shakar, Martin 142

Shakespeare and Company
    205, 336
Shakespeare in Hollywood
    318
**Shakespeare, Moses and
    Joe Papp** 378, 379
Shakespeare, William
    ix, 33, 34, 36,
    135, 170, 174, 175,
    193, 210, 245, 256,
    259, 261, 263, 264,
    265, 267, 268, 270,
    272, 273, 302, 307,
    316, 323, 338, 423
Shakman, Felicia Carter 250
Shalit, Willa 152
Shalwitz, Howard 319
Shamblin, Jack 250
Shamieh, Betty 261, 271
Shamos, Jeremy
    36, 197, 314, 323
Shane, Hal 193
Shane, Tracy 218, 226
Shanet, Larry 256
Shanghai Gesture, The 268
Shanghai Moon
    238, 245, 373
Shankel, Lynne 260
Shanks, Gabriel 259, 264
Shanks, Priscilla 263
Shanley, John Patrick
    238, 265, 270, 271
Shanman, Ellen 267
Shannon, Michael 262
Shape of Things, The
    79, 80, 81, 301, 378
Shapiro, Anna D. 314, 327
Shapiro, Doug 263
Shapiro, Ronald 129
Shapiro, Steve 320, 321
Sharma, Kish 204
Sharp, Elliott 122, 187
Sharp, John 262
Sharp, Jonathan 146
Sharp, Julia 339
Sharp, Kim T. 258
Sharp, Rebecca 264
Sharp, Travis 322
Sharpe, Michael 348
Shattuck, Frank 266
Shattuck, Matthew 245
Shaud, Grant 213
Shaughnessy, Shannan 250
Shaw, David 263
Shaw, Fiona 22, 148, 149,
    244, 371, 377, 378
Shaw, George Bernard
    44, 59, 239, 268

Shaw, Jane 255
Shaw, Margery 315
Shaw, Rob 133
Shaw, Tim 223
Shawn, Wallace 240
Shayne, Sharron 265
Shayne, Tracy 219
She Stoops to Comedy
   14, 34, *209–210*,
   210, 367, 377
She Stoops to Conquer
   239, 268
Shear, Claudia 72, 348, 351
Sheara, Nicola 261
Sheedy, Jaime 262
Sheehan, Ciaran 227
Sheehan, Judy 339
Sheehy, Cam 302
Sheerin, Kelleia 155, 320
Sheffey, George 271
Sheffield, Pat 339
Sheik, Duncan 175
Shell, Roger 145
Shelley, Carole 218
Shelton, Sloane 151
ShenanArts 346
Shenker, Jenifer 202
Shenkman, Ben 227
Shepard, Matthew 223
Shepard, Sam
   93, 100, 235, 241
Shepard, Tina
   249, 250, 264, 377
Shepardson, Dia 196
Shephard-Massat, S.M. 313
Shepherd, Sarah 324
Shepherd, Suzanne 258
Sheppard, Danette E. 378
Sheppard, Julian 266
Shepperd, Drey 260
Sher, Bartlett 256, 353
Sher, Emil 346
Sheridan, Dixie 190, 251
Sheridan, Richard Brinsley
   259
Sherin, Mimi Jordan 312
**Sherlock Holmes and the
   Secret of Making
   Whoopee** 267
Sherman, Andrew 187
Sherman, Barry Del 377
Sherman, Deborah L.
   283, 320
Sherman, Elizabeth 245, 260
Sherman, Howard 313
Sherman, Jonathan Marc
   263, 267, 272
Sherman, Keith 198

Sherr, Erik 270
Sheward, David 367
Shields, Brooke 218
Shields, Charlotte Devaux
   308
Shields, Timothy J. 355
Shiffman, J. Fred 319
Shim, Eric 245
Shimban, Meera 311
Shimono, Sab 302, 309
Shin, Eddie 246
Shindle, Kate 217, 218
Shinn, Christopher
   34, 191, 267, 272
Shinner, Sandy 327, 328
Shiotani, Kipp 302
Shipley, Sandra 154, 270
Shippee, Deborah 342
Shively, Ryan 261
Shoes 269
Shooltz, Emily V. 317
Shooting Craps 341
**Shoppers Carried by
   Escalators Into the
   Flames** 262
Shor, Miriam
   44, 255, 263, 319
Short, Martin 227
Short, Melissa 262
Shorthouse, Dame Edith 146
Shotkin, Thomas E. 316
**Showtune: The Words and
   Music of Jerry
   Herman** 14, 31, *197–
   198*
Shrader, Jennifer 216, 217
Shriver, Lisa 138
Shubert Organization, The
   138, 154, 370
Shue, Elisabeth 217
Shukla, Ami 262
Shulman, Lawrence Harvey
   261
Shuman, Celia 304
Shumway, Susan 206
Shunpo 250
Shutt, Christopher 186, 214
Shyre, Paul 259
Sia, Beau 141
Siberry, Michael 340
Sicangco, Eduardo 351
Sickles, Scott C. 272
Sicular, Robert 301
Sie, Allison 309
Siegel, Ed 378
Siegel, Marv 268
Siegel, Seth M. 142, 371
Sieger, Gary 156

Siegfried, Mandy 225, 311
Sieh, Kristen 254
Sierros, John 379
Sigler, Jamie-Lynn 216
Signals of Distress 239, 256
Signature Theatre (Virginia)
   351
Signature Theatre Company
   36, 41, 178, 235,
   255, 373
Signor, Tari 251
Siguenza, Herbert
   307, 309, 317
Silberman, Adam 146
Silberman, Brian 271
Silbert, Peter 355
Silence 270
Silent Piece 273
Silliman, Maureen 308
Sills, Brian 224
Sills, Douglas 319
Silva, Donald 252, 260
Silva, Greg 327
Silva, Michael 260
Silva, Staysha Liz 316
Silva, Vilma 343
Silver, Amy 256
Silver, H. Richard 269
Silver, Matthew 201
Silver, Mort 164
Silver, Nicky 9, 134
Silver, Stephanie Ila 260
Silverman, Adam 159
Silverman, Antoine 156, 183
Silverman, David 323
Silverman, Leigh 252, 319
Silvers, Louis 180
Silversher, Michael 331
Silverstein, Jerry 157, 370
Silverstone, Alicia 221
Silvia, Marc 328
Sim, Keong 198
Simard, Jennifer 222
Simhan, Meera 302
Simkin, Toby 168
Simmons, Candy 269
Simmons, Gregory 260
Simmons, Kimora Lee
   141, 371
Simmons, Kissy 224
Simmons, Paulanne 256
Simmons, Robert Lee
   330, 331, 332
Simmons, Russell
   26, 141, 371
Simms, Heather Alicia
   153, 317
Simon, Alyssa 265

Simon, Christen 259
Simon, Dan Hendricks 262
Simon, John 367
Simon, Mark 141
Simon, Meg 369
Simon, Neil 303, 375
Simon, Paul 375
Simon, Richard 265
Simon, Roger Hendricks 262
Simonds, Dave 245
Simone 215
Simoneau, Marcel 270
Simonian, Ron 346
Simons, Lake 264
Simons, Ron 261, 273
Simonson, Eric 309, 355
Simpatico, David 271
Simpson, Cathy 329
Simpson, Herb 278
Simpson, Jim 238, 263
Simpson, Markiss 342
Sims, Bill Jr. 353
Sims, Gregory 263
Sims, Marlayna 224
Sine, Jeffrey 144, 371
Sinfully Rich 267
Singer, Brooke 351
Singer, David S. 189
Singer, Gammy 254
Singer, Isaac Bashevis 265
Singlish 269
Sinkkonen, Eric 304
Sinnott, Ethan 351
Siravo, Joseph 134, 246, 253
Siretta, Dan 350, 351
Sirlin, Jerome 351
Sirugo, Carol 272
Sissons, Narelle
    91, 197, 200, 245
Sister Week 340
SITI Company 334
**Six Dance Lessons in Six
    Weeks** 321
Six Feet Under 287
Six, Michele 254
Six of One 260
Sketches of Yucca 300
Skiles, Sophia 249
Skinker, Sherry 151
Skinner, Emily
    22, 150, 151, 201,
    212, 319
Skinner, Kate 221
Skipitares, Theodora
    236, 250
Skjaerven, Torkel 317
Skoczelas, Tracy 307
Skowron, Jeff 224

Skraastad, Danielle 348
Skura, Greg 273
Sky Over Nineveh, The 264
Skybell, Steven 191, 340
Skye, Iona 263
Skye, Robin 244
Skylab 271, 272
Slag Heap 261
Slaight, Craig 314
**Slanty Eyed Mama Re-Birth
    of an Asian** 250
Slater, Glenn 272
Slavitt, David R. 128
Slavitt, Donald 326
Sledd, Rachel 300, 340
Sledge, Logan 261
Sleepers, The 267
Sleeping With Straight Men
    14, 28, **196**
Sleepless in Seattle 69
Sleigh, Tom 266
Slezak, Victor 221, 272
**Slide Glide the Slippery
    Slope** 330, 331
**Slight Defect—A Desert
    Holiday** 346
Slinkard, Jefferson 267, 273
Sloan, Peter 263
Slonina, Jim 380
Slovacek, Randy 321
Slugocki, Lillian Ann
    271, 272
Slusar, Catharine K. 345
**SlutforArt a.k.a. Ambiguous
    Ambassador** 248
Sly Fox 422
Smagula, Jimmy 143, 144
**Small, Melodramatic Story,
    A** 347
Small Bachelor, The 354
Smart, Annie 303
Smart, Mat 314
Smedes, Tom 373
Smelling a Rat 367
Smirnoff, Yakov 25, 159
Smith, A.C. 328
Smith, Alex 270
Smith, Alice Elliott 141
Smith, Anna Deavere 62
Smith, Brad 332
Smith, Bree Sunshine 350
Smith, Catherine M. 329
Smith, Chris 262, 271
Smith, Chuck 324, 326
Smith, Craig 264
Smith, David Ryan 301
Smith, Dennis 259, 260, 272
Smith, Derek 224

Smith, Geddeth 197
Smith, Graham 331
Smith, Greg 139
Smith, Jacques C. 228
Smith, James E. 272
Smith, Jaymi Lee
    326, 327, 328
Smith, Jennifer 260
Smith, Jessica Chandlee
    270, 272
Smith, Jonathan 149
Smith, Joseph 158, 208
Smith, Juliet 205, 266
Smith, Keith Randolph 252
Smith, Kiki 249, 377
Smith, Larilu 247
Smith, Leslie L. 188
Smith, Louise
    245, 249, 299, 377
Smith, Maggie xii
Smith, Molly 271, 317, 319
Smith, Peter (1) 209, 269
Smith, Peter Matthew (2)
    132, 133
Smith, Sam 206
Smith, Selina 267
Smith, T. Ryder 210
Smith, Todd Michel 132
Smith, Virginia Louise
    151, 152, 158
Smith, Warren 179
Smith-Cameron, J. 22, 151
Smits, Jimmy 33, 175, 311
Smoots, Jonathan 356
Smucker, Matthew 352, 353
Smyth, Deborah Gilmour 304
Smyth, Robert 304
Smythe, Sally 354
Snelson, Nicole Ruth 230
Snider-Stein, Teresa 130
Sniffin, Allison 245
Snook, Dan 256, 262
Snow Angel 264
Snow, Cherene 272
Snow, Chesney 268
Snow, Daniel 267
Snow, Jon 350
Snow White 272, 303
Snowdon, Ted 179, 208
Snyder, Kelly 269
Snyder, Nancy
    44, 48, 255, 342
Soar Like an Eagle 265
Sobel, Shepard 271
Sochol, Nanci 342
Sod, Ted 253
Soelistyo, Julyana 334
Soho Rep 239, 255

Soho Think Tank 377
Solá, Martín 145
Soleil, Sky 302
Solis, Felix
        87, 200, 245, 253, 265
Solis, Meme 247
Solomon, Alisa i
Solomon, Andrew 271
Solovyeva, Ekaterina 145
Soloway, Leonard
        155, 193, 320
Solving Your Script 423
Some Like It Hot 230, 350
Somers, Asa 146
Somerville, Phyllis 246, 317
Something Wonderful Right
        Away 423
Somewhere Someplace Else
        262
Sommers, Avery 220
Sommers, Michael (critic)
        367, 376
Sommers, Michael (designer)
        323
Somogyi, Ilona
        181, 202, 211, 314
Son, Diana 271
Son of Drakula 262
Sonderskov, Robert 270
Sondheim, Stephen
        20, 25, 129, 141,
        164, 250, 271, 319,
        323, 373, 376
Sonenberg, David 146
Song, Sue Jin 272
Soni, Thandazile A. 224
Sonia Friedman Productions
        370
Sonooka, Shintaro 250
Sontag, Susan 64
Sony 176, 205
Soooo Sad 261
Sophiea, Cynthia 225
Sophocles 188, 262, 313
Sopranos, The 8
Sordelet, Rick
        130, 135, 147, 156,
        172, 198, 245, 258,
        316, 317, 320, 336
Sorenson, Erik 319
Sorge, Joey 335
Sorkin, Joan Ross 261
Soroka, Stephen 263
Sorrentini, Jamie 262
Sosa, Emilio 191, 198, 340
Sosko, PJ 270
Sothern, E.A. 149
Soto, Carlow 245

Soto, Letty 247
Soule, Samantha
        150, 268, 314
Soules, Dale 263, 345
SourceWorks Theatre 270
South Coast Repertory
        195, 309, 310, 332,
        354, 423
South, Hamilton 157, 371
South Pacific 378
Southard, Beth 226
Spain 346
Spanger, Amy 219
Spangler, Walt
        52, 141, 175, 189,
        196, 309, 332, 352
Spanish Girl 14, 33, *176*
Spano, Joe 311
Sparks, Don 248
Sparks, Johnny 260
Sparks, Paul 154, 253
Spaulding, Doug 339
SpeakEasy Stage Company
        378
**Special Price for You,
        Okay?** 272
Speckhard, Tom 339
**Spectacle of Spectacles: The
        Clairvoyant Cabaret**
        249
Speer, Alexander 329
Speier, Susanna 264
Spellman, Larry 135, 370
Spence, Barbara J. 267
Spencer, Brant 263
Spencer, David 376
Spencer, Keith 206
Spencer, M.E. 220
Spencer, Rebecca 206, 249
Speredakos, John 261, 262
Sperling, Ted 183
Speth, Uli 145
Spialek, Hans 206
Spidel, Jonah 249
Spidle, Craig 324
Spiller, Christopher M. 246
Spiller, Jennifer R. 246
Spinella, Stephen
        21, 141, 273
Spiner, Brent 12, 158
Spinghel, Radu 145
Spinning Into Butter 378
Spinozza, David 133
Spiro, Matthew 301, 303
Spiroff, Tom 339
Spisto, Louis G. 307
Spivak, Allen 167, 371
Splendour 308

Split 265
Spon, Marian 193, 195
Sposito, Dee 260
Spottag, Jens Jorn 245
Sprague, Kevin 337
Sprauer, Fred 341
Sprecher, Ben 192
Spring Awakening 269
Spring, Robert 221
Springer, Gary 186
Springer, Steve Scott 223
Springer/Chicoine Public
        Relations 186
Squadron, Anne Strickland
        167, 371
Squire, Theresa 252, 256
SRU Productions LLC 214
sss-t-o-n-e-ddd 249
St. Ann's Warehouse 23
St. Hilaire, Stephanie 260
St. Louis, David 176, 177
St. Nicholas 51
St. Paul, Stephen 253
St. Paule, Irma 265
St. Peter, Jaime 259
St. Valmiki 301
Staats, Amy 246
Stackpole, Dana 138, 139
Stadelmann, Matthew
        94, 96, 99, 254,
        261, 314
Stadlen, Lewis J. 227
Stagehill 422, 423
Stahlhuth, Gayle 340
Stalin, Joseph 71
Stamberg, Josh 314
Stamford Center for the Arts
        192, 378
Stamos, John 217
Stan, Sebastian 262
Stancati, Frank 259
Stanczyk, Laura 206
Stanescu, Saviana 250
Stanford University 421
Stanion, Karen 259, 260
Stanton, Ben 174, 201, 255
Stanton, Brooke 334
Stanton, Robert 186
Staples, Deborah 355
Stapleton, Jean 384
Star Crossed Lovers 266
Star Messengers 249
Star-Ledger, The 367
Stark, Kevin 327
Starr-Levitt, Megan 226
Starrett, Pete 154
State Theatre 278
Staton, Daniel C. 133

Staudenmayer, Edward 216
Stauffer, Scott 204
Staunton, Noel 146
Steakley, Joey 350
Stearns, Donna 266
Steele, Erik 151, 152
Steele, Kameron 245
Steele, Shayna 132, 133
Steen, Carla 338
Stefanowicz, Janus
    187, 347, 348
Steiger, Rick 198
Stein, Adam 224
Stein, Andy 193
Stein, Douglas
    256, 343, 349, 352
Stein, Gertrude 37, 204, 266
Stein, Jean 148
Stein, Navida 269
Steinbeck, John 267
Steinberg, Eric 266
Steinberg, James D. xii
Steinberg, Michael A. xii
Steinbruner, Gregory 256
Steindler, Catherine Baker
    267
Steiner, Rick 132, 370
Steinfeld, Dayna 261
Steinman, Jim 146
Steinmetz, Lynn 318, 319
Steitzer, Jeff 354, 355
Stephens, Claudia 255, 342
Stephens, Darcy 190, 196
Stephens, James A. 248
Stephens, Lamont 258
Stephens, Linda 318, 322
Stephens, Mara 262
Stephens, Spencer 322
Stephenson, Don 227
Stephenson, Tom 304
Steppenwolf Theatre
    Company
    178, 326, 423
Sterl, Tania 250
Sterlin, Jenny 252, 254, 270
Sterman, Andrew 134, 212
Stern, Cheryl 222, 262
Stern, Daniel 28, 198, 347
Stern, Edward 271, 342
Stern, Eric 319
Stern, James D.
    132, 152, 271, 370
Stern, Jenna 254, 271, 314
Stern, Kathryn 271
Stern, Matthew Aaron 163
Sternhagen, Frances
    116, 208, 271
Sterrett, T.O. 146, 202

Stesichorus 236
Stetler, Paul Morgan 352
Stetson, Wendy Rich 331
Steve 272
Stevens, Alexandra 164
Stevens, Brad 326
Stevens, Cameron 229
Stevens, Fisher 272
Stevens, Graham 259
Stevens, Jodi 155, 320
Stevens, Robert 265
Stevens, Susan Riley 329
Stevens, Wass M. 262
Stewart, Daniel Freedom 261
Stewart, Ellen 248
Stewart, Gwen 228
Stewart, Kellee 317, 336
Stewart, Michael 128
Stewart, Nicole 272
Stewart, Paul Anthony 245
Stewart, Peter 269
Stewart, Victoria 332
Stieb, Corey Tazmania 272
Stiebel, Hunter 355
Stiles, George 193, 195
Stiles, Julia 33, 175
Stilgoe, Richard 127
Still, James 328, 332
Still, Melly 204
Still, Peter John 256
Stillman, Bob 156, 370
Stinger, Laura Berlin 268
Stinton, Colin 221
Stites, Kevin 160, 161
Stith, Monica 256
Stock, Jennifer Sherron 265
Stockhausen, Adam
    336, 342, 352
Stoddard, Gerald 249
Stokes, Colin 222
Stole, Mink 196
Stoll, Jon 138, 371
Stollmack, Noele 245
Stolowitz, Andrea 308
Stomp *169–170*
Stone, Angie 220
Stone Cold Dead Serious
    xi, xv, *93–102*,
    94, 96, 99, 261
Stone, Daryl A. 255, 350
Stone, David 142, 371, 373
Stone, Doug 268
Stone, Elise 264
Stone, Fred 326
Stone, Greg (1) 156
Stone, Gregory Calvin (2) 222
Stone, Peter 350
Stoner, Ross 259

Stones in His Pockets 321
Stop All the Clocks 271
Stoppard, Tom
    72, 239, 339, 348, 421
Storace, Greta 263
Storch, Larry 230
Storey, Tella 270
Storm, Doug 146
Stoudt, Charlotte 332
Stout, Stephen 267
Stover, Laren 269
Stowe, Dennis 143, 144
Straiges, Tony 163, 200, 350
Stram, Henry 314
Strand, Ashley 263
Strand, John 351
Straney, Paul 266
Strange Attractors 353
Strange Fish 272
Stranger, The 248
Strasberg, Anna 373
Stratford, Aoise 266
Strathairn, David
    23, 163, 239, 245, 348
Strathie, Angus 146, 371
Stratton, Hank 218
Stratton, Jay 268
Strauss, Bill 171
Strauss, Georgia 264
Strawbridge, Stephen
    303, 317
Streber, Ryan 245
Street Corner Pierrot, A
    250
Street of Useful Things, The
    252
Streisand, Barbra 28, 198
String Fever 238, 246
Stripped 380
Stritch, Elaine 3, 20, 25, 236
Strober, Rena 253
Strock, Bob 249
Stroman, Susan 128
Strome, Jenny 197
Stronach, Tami 256
Strong, Caroline 270
Strong, Mark 193, 194, 195
Stronger Faith, A 346
Strouse, Charles 335
Strus, Lusia 379
Stuart Howard Associates 422
Stuart, Kelly 253, 346
Stuart, Lisa Martin 175
Stuart, Matty D. 267
Stubbings, Chuck 324
Stuckenbruck, Dale 145
Stude, Roger Dale 272
Studio 42 270

Studio Arena Theatre 341
Studio Theatre 270, 379
Stuff 300
Stuhlbarg, Michael
    175, 218, 252, 253
Stuhr, Greg 322
Stumm, Michael 268
Stumpf, T. Tyler 351
Sturch, Jennifer 349
Sturgis, Nanka 307, 308
Stutts, Will 348
Styer, Allan 266
Styler, Trudie 271
Styles, Joy 179
Styne, Jule 20, 164, 350
Suarez, Eileen 280, 283, 320
Subway, The 273
such small hands 342
Sucker Fish Messiah 258
Suckling, Jenny-Lynn
    146, 214
Suddaby, Anne 260
Suddeth, J. Allen 181, 313
Sudduth, Kohl 153, 177
Sudduth, Skipp 213
Suenkel, Michael 302
Suga, Shigeko 250
Sugarman, David 138
Sugarman, Jeff 311
Sugg, James 345, 349
Suh, Lloyd 246
Sullivan, Daniel
    7, 130, 182, 311
Sullivan, Deb 335
Sullivan, Greg 354
Sullivan, Kerry 249
Sullivan, Kim 342
Sullivan, Patrick Ryan
    216, 221
Sullivan, Susan 255
Sullivan, TJ 141
Sullivan, Yaakov 263
Sulsona, Philip James 268
Summa, Don 133, 168, 174,
    176, 188, 201, 211
Summer 336
Summerhays, Jane 218
Summerour, John 266
Summers, Lee 179
Summons To Sheffield 348
Sumonja, Drago 265
Sumption, Christine 354
Sun, Nilaja 270
Sun-Up 266
Sundance Theatre Laboratory
    10, 61, 182, 214
**Sunday in the Park With
    George** 378, 379, 380

Sunde, Karen 347
Sunjata, Daniel
    11, 104, 107, 153,
    154, 177, 371, 373, 376
Supple, Tim 204, 301
Surabian, Michael 264, 265
Surface Transit 379
Survival of the Fetus 249
Surviving Grace *170*
Susan Smith Blackburn Prize
    xiii, 375
Sussman, Ben
    214, 323, 326, 327, 328
Sutcliffe, Steven 314
Sutcliffe, William 266
Sutherland, Diane 262
Sutliffe, Joel 380
Sutton, Eric 288, 319
Svich, Caridad
    252, 253, 254, 271, 272
Svilar, Gordana 323
Swados, Liz 250
Swain, Howard 304
Swan, Matthew 267
Swanson, Sarah 380
Swansong 316
Swartz, Jerome 158
Swartz, Kraig 347
Swearingen, Dawne 340
Swee, Daniel 151, 155, 197
Sweeney, April 254
Sweeney Todd 378
Sweet, Jeffrey i, xii, xv, 111,
    208, 375, 423
Sweet, Sam 351
Sweet Smell of Success
    9, *129*
Swenson, Todd 221, 266
Swenson, Will 263, 265
Swiggum, Randal 355
Swing! 378
Swinsky, Morton
    132, 146, 147, 152,
    176, 184, 370
Sykes, Kim 259
Sylvester, Mark D. 348
Symes, Weylin 269
Synapse Theatre 270
Synetic Theater 378
Synge, J.M. 247
Syracuse Stage 329, 342
Syringa Tree, The *170*
Szász, János 334
Szczepanski, John-Paul 185
Szücs, Edit 334

T. Schreiber Studio 272
Tabb, Leni 256
Taber, Kitty 328
Tabor, Philip 210
Tabori, George 186
Taccone, Tony 301, 309, 343
Tackaberry, Celia
    331, 332, 333
Tague, Eileen 347, 348
Tahse, Martin 308
Tailor's Tale, The 336
Takahashi, Suzi 250
Takami, Janet 213
Takara, Yuka 136
Take Her, She's Mine 69
Take Me Out xi, xv, 4, 10,
    11, 14, 33, *103–110*,
    104, 107, *153*, 154,
    177, *177–178*, 366,
    367, 370, 371, 372,
    373, 376, 377
Taking Care 327
Taking Steps 380
**Taking Steps Three
    Thirteen** 248
**Tale of the Allergist's Wife,
    The** 9, *128*
Tale Told, A 47
Talen, Bill 268
Talkin' Broadway vii
Talking Band, The 241, 377
Talking Heads
    xii, xv, 14, 29,
    111–118, 112, 115,
    117, *208*, 366, 367,
    376, 377
Talley and Son 47
Tambella, Mark 250
Tammi, Tom 308
Tanaka, Anne 245
Tanaka, Sara 314
Tanaka, Yumiko 204
Tandy, Madame Pat 249
Tangelson, Dario 249, 262
Tangi, Lydia 341
Tani, Akinori 250
Tanji, Lydia 309
Tanner, Jill 163
Tanner, Vickie 258
Tanno, Momoko 338
Tanokura, Yoshinori 341
Tansley, Brooke 133
Tapper, Jeff 250
Tara Rubin Casting 137, 150

Tartaglia, John 258, 314
Tartuffe 4, 22, 151, 152,
    371, 375, 380
Tassara, Carla 266
Taste of Fire, The 378
Tatad, Robert 136
Tatarowicz, Roman 346
Tate, Katrina 207
Tatum, Bill 269, 273
Tauber, Michele 252
Taviani, Paul 322
Taxi Cabaret 269
Tayloe, Richard 261
Taylor, Andy 218
Taylor, Clifton 251
Taylor, David 351
Taylor, Dominic 253
Taylor, Elizabeth 375
Taylor, Giva 213
Taylor, Harlan 330, 333
Taylor, Jackie 207
Taylor, Jennifer 263
Taylor, Juliet 157
Taylor, Lindsay Rae 267
Taylor, Meshach 217
Taylor, Myra Lucretia 160
Taylor, Regina
    33, 191, 300, 340
Taylor, Russel 267
Taylor, Samuel 212
Taylor-Williams, Catherine
    336, 337
Taymor, Julie 127, 380
Tazel, Erika 252
Tazewell, Paul
    141, 176, 189, 323
Ta'Ziyeh of Hor, The 251
Tea at Five 14, 31, *200*
**Teaspoon Every Four
    Hours, A** 138
Tec, Roland 263
**Ted Kaczynski Killed
    People With Bombs**
    304
Teddy Tonight! 258
Tedeschi, John 266
Tejero, Lisa 328
Tekosky, Valarie 207
Teller, Keith 273
Teller, Ryan Michael 258
Telsey, Bernard
    133, 138, 144, 146,
    147, 163, 168, 174,
    190, 200, 213, 251
Tempest, The
    236, 268, 302, 379
Temporary Help
    14, 37, *188–189*

ten Haaf, Jochum
    11, 154, 155, 376
Ten Unknowns 307
Tena, Paul 196
Tennessean, The 278
Tenney, Jon 189, 190
Tennyson, John Gentry 176
Tepe, Heather 164
Tepper, Arielle 140, 147, 176
Terkel, Studs 258
Terlizzi, Ann K. 338
Terminal 241
Terrazas, Elisa 264
Territory 260
Terror Eyes 271
Terry, Beatrice 245, 264
Tesori, Jeanine 129
Testani, Andrea J. 131, 214
Tester, Hans 252
Tetreault, Paul R. 349
Tewes, Cynthia Lauren 354
Tewksbury, Stephen 223
Texarkana Waltz 265
Thacher, Andrew 259
Thacker, Kit 272
Thaler, Jordan
    154, 178, 202, 210
Tharp, Twyla
    16, 138, 372, 376, 377
**That Damn Dykstra (The
    Boxed Set)** 258
That Day in September 268
Thatcher, Ginger 162
Thau, Harold 189
Thayer, Emmelyn 307, 308
Thayer, Maria 173, 252
The Who's Tommy 422
Theater 377
Theater for the New City 256
Theater Hall of Fame
    xiii, xvi, 22, 381,
    384, 422, 423
Theater J 319
Theater on the Edge: New
    Visions, New Voices
    421
TheaterMania.com vii, 30
Theatre 3 270
Theatre at St. Peter's 270
Theatre Communications
    Group 279
Theatre Cooperative, The 378
Theatre de la Jeune Lune 338
Theatre for a New Audience
    256, 257
Theatre Forum 423
Theatre New England 278
Theatre on the Square 141

Theatre Royal Haymarket
    Productions 152
Theatre Three 350
Theatre Under the Stars 350
Theatre World Award 376
TheatreWorks 311
Thebus, Jessica 327
Thebus, Mary Ann 328
Theodorou, Andrew 195
Theophilus North 318
Theroux, Justin 36, 196, 197
Thestrup, Ole 245
Thibodeau, Marc
    144, 150, 178, 181,
    192, 214
Thicke, Alan 219
Thiel, Regan 223
Thiérrée, James 267
Thies, Howard 163
Thiessen, Vern 266
**Thieves in the Temple: The
    Reclaiming of Hip
    Hop** 268
Thigpen, Haynes 317
**Things Being What They
    Are** 354
Thinnes, Roy 269
13th Street Repertory Theatre
    270
Thirty-Fourth and Dyer 272
36 Views 341
**This Will Be the Death of
    Him** 261
Thoemke, Peter 338
Thoeren, Robert 350
Thomalen, E. 265
Thomas, Brenda 252, 260
Thomas, Cori 246
Thomas, Erika 142
Thomas, Isa 340
Thomas, Jack 200
Thomas, Jay 213
Thomas, Katrina 270
Thomas, Keith Lamelle
    176, 177
Thomas, Marlo 272
Thomas, Rasta 303
Thomas, Ray (1) 263
Thomas, Ray Anthony (2)
    329, 342
Thomas, Robert L. 207
Thomas, Sarah Megan 272
Thomas, Shelley 202, 243
Thompson, April Yvette
    184, 261, 299
Thompson, Billy 172
Thompson, David 166, 212
Thompson, E. Randy 268

Thompson, Fred 263
Thompson, Jenn 259
Thompson, Jennifer Laura
    195, 229
Thompson, John Leonard 342
Thompson, Judith 270
Thompson, Justin Ray 259
Thompson, Kent 299
Thompson, Lea 217
Thompson, Louisa 256
Thompson, Mark
    158, 193, 195
Thompson, Raphael Nash
    263, 313
Thompson, Robert 152
Thompson, Sister Francesca
    369
Thompson, Stuart 157, 371
Thompson, Timothy M. 318
Thorell, Clarke 132
Thorn, Chris 266, 270
Thorne, Callie 192
Thorne, Eric 315
Thorne, Joan Vail 258
Thorne, Stephen 349
Thornton, Christopher 253
Thornton, David 246, 259
Thoroughly Modern Millie
    7, *129*, 229
Thrasher, Mark 134, 166
Threatte, Renee 342
3 O'Clock in Brooklyn 258
3 Weeks After Paradise
    270, 271
Three-Cornered Moon 265
Three's a Family 69
Throw 271
**Thunder Knocking on the
    Door**
    14, 29, 172, *172–173*
Thunderbird 252
Thureen, Paul 270
Thwak! 267
Tiamfook, Marissa 262
Tiberghien, Lucie 270
Tichler, Rosemarie 369
Tick, Tick, Boom 230
Tighe, Susanne
    137, 158, 190, 196,
    198, 213
Tilghman, Tyee 319
Till, Kevin Scott 265
Tilley, Bobby Frederick II
    244
Tillie Project, The 339
Tillinger, John 135, 200, 347
Tillman, Ellis 156, 320, 321
Tillman, Jimmy 207

Tillman, Rochele 261
Timbers, Alex 264
Time 367
Time and the Conways 270
Time Machine 2.0 266
Time Out New York 23, 367
TimeLine Theatre Company
    379
Times Square Theatre 270
Times, The (London)
    421, 422
Timlin, Addison 164
Timperman, Erika 201
Tin Box Boomerang 380
Tindall, Blair 143, 206
Tindall, Don 299
Tindle, Jonathan 253
Ting, Liuh-Wen 134, 160
Tiny Alice 378
Tipton, Jennifer 211, 316
Tisch School of the Arts
    xiii, 422
Tisdale, Christianne 216
Tisdale, Michael 302
Titcomb, Caldwell xiii, 378
Titcomb, Gordon 156
Titone, Tom 335
Titus, Jane 265
T'Kaye, Eileen 188
To, Rodney 266, 355
Toan, Braden 143
Tobes, Bill 263
Tobin, David A. 265
Tobin, Kathleen 343
Tocqueville, Alexis de 93
Todaro, Michael J. 230
Todd, Jeffrey 259
Todd, John J. 139
Todd, Tony 314
Todd, Will 271
Toibin, Fiana 168
Tokudani, Betty 302
Tolan, Cindy 162, 186
Tolan, R.J. 269
Tolins, Jonathan 29, 208, 269
Tolley, Justin 332, 333
Tolstoy, Leo 280
Tomei, Marisa
    23, 163, 271, 272
Tomkins, Steve 351
Tomlin, Lily 375
Tomlinson, Sorrel 263
Tommasini, Anthony 6
Tommer, Michael 148
**Tommy Tune: White Tie
    and Tails** 14, 30, *193*
Tompkins, Matthew Stephen
    350

Toney, David 318
Tongue Tied and Duty Free
    254
Tonkonogy, Gertrude 265
Tony Award ix, xi, xvi, 3,
    5, 7, 9, 10,
    11, 17, 19, 20,
    21, 23, 26, 28,
    103, 109, 133, 138,
    139, 141, 146, 154,
    161, 168, 369, 372, 423
Tony 'n' Tina's Wedding
    169–170
Took, Don 311
Toolajian, Loren 178
Topdog/Underdog
    9, 33, *129*
Topol, Daniella 266, 340
Toppall, Lawrence S.
    135, 370
Topping, John 267
Torbeck, Bret 353
Torcellini, Jamie
    143, 144, 216
Toren, Nick 259, 265
Torke, Michael 245
Torn, Tony 260, 268
Toro, Natalie 229
Torres, Joaquin 245
Torres, Maria 243
Torres, Marilyn 317
Torres, Michelle 247
Torres-yap, Fay 256
Torsiglieri, Anne 335
Torsney-Weir, Maureen
    345, 348
Toser, David 195, 247, 248
Tosetti, Sara J. 185
Toshiko, Katrina 336
Totally Over You 314
Touchscape 263
Tovatt, Patrick 227
Tower, Josh 224
Towler, Lorinne 272
Town Hall 270
Towne-Smith, Nathan
    336, 337
Towns, Anne 322
Trabitz, Randee 254
Trachta, Jeff 352
Trade 261
**Trafficking in Broken
    Hearts** 260
Traina, Anastasia 261
Tran, Tricu 302, 312
Trani, Vince 321
Transatlantic Liaison 350
Transvestiten, Die 64

Trap Door Theatre 379
Trapnell, Susan 338
Trash Anthem 332, 333
Trask, Stephen 211
Travis, David 270
Travis, Ken 173, 254, 256
Travis, Michele 264
Travis, Nancy 303
Travolta, John 18, 156
Treadway, Erin 269
Treco, Gregory 243
Tree, The 269
Treick, Joel 180
Trentacosta, Joe 186
Trepidation Nation 331
Trese, Adam 254, 262
Tresnjak, Darko 307, 335
Tresty, Steve 268
Trevens, Francine L. 265
Treyz, Russell 268, 269
Triantaphyllopoulos, Kostas 188
Tribeca Playhouse 272
Trien, Cathy 164
Trinity Repertory Company 349
Trinkoff, Donna 243
Triple Happiness, The 252
Triska, Jan 334
Triumph of Love, The 265, 354
Troche, Alfredo D. 249
Trojan Women, The 254, 325, 326
Trotsky, Leon 71
Trout, Deb 352
True Love Productions, Inc. 148
True West 100
True-Frost, Jim 327
Truitt, Mark Rafael 304
Trulock, Dianne 308
Truman, Leslie 322
Trumbell, Kelly 342
Trumbo 272
Trumbo, Christopher 272
Trumbour, Mary 327
Trunell, Christopher 260
Tsangaridou, Agnes 313
Tsao, Andrew 302
Tse, Elaine 334
Tseng, Muna 248
Tsikurishvili, Irina 378
Tsikurishvili, Paata 378
Tsoutsouvas, Sam 314, 316
Tsuchigane, Sonya 256
Tsuji, Yukio 163
Tsukuda, Saori 262

Tsutsui, Hideaki 245
Tuan, Alice 248, 266
Tucci, Louis 258
Tucci, Michael 220
Tucci, Stanley 8, 131, 221, 272, 371
Tucker, Allyson 143, 144
Tucker, Jamie A. 309
Tucker, Shona 314, 318, 331
Tucker, Sophie 171
Tuesdays With Morrie 14, 28, *189*, 190
Tufino, Pablo 255
Tuft, Sarah 271
Tulchin, Ted 172
Tulk, Jere Stevens 350
Tully, Pauline 252, 273
Tumas, Sally Ann 217
Tumor 264
Tune, Tommy 19, 28, 30, 193
Tunick, Jonathan 161, 196, 319, 372
Tunie, Tamara 255
Tuomanen, Mary 314
Tureen, Rufus 253
Turgenev, Ivan 129
Turhal, Ozlem 265
Turick, Richard 341
Turley, Sandra 223
Turnbull, Laura 380
Turner, Allyson 134, 166
Turner, Charles (actor) 261
Turner, Charles M. III (stage manager) 204
Turner, David 209, 244, 269
Turner, Jerry 345
Turner, Jessica D. 261
Turner, Kathleen 221
Turner, Stephen Barker 313
Turturro, John 12, 158, 237, 271, 272
Tushingham, David 301
Tuthill, Patricia 212
Tutor, The 376
Tuttle, Ashley 138, 371
Tuva or Bust! 128
Twain, Mark 171, 172
Twelfth Night 14, 33, 37, *175*, *193–195*, 194
Twelve Brothers 272
29th Street Rep 272
21 Dog Years: Doing Time @ Amazon.com *171*
Twine, Linda 161, 173, 191, 340
Twiss, Jo 348

Twist, Basil 349
Two Loves and a Creature 248
2001: An Oral History 271, 272
Twyford, Holly 288, 319, 378
Typographer's Dream, The 262
Tyranny, "Blue" Gene 249, 377
Tyson, David 250

Uchizono, Donna 349
UE92/02 249
Uesugi, Mikiko 304
Uffelman, Jonathan 262
Uggams, Leslie 29, 172, 229
Ugurlu, Zishan 268
Uhry, Alfred 270, 312
Ularu, Nic 249, 377
Ullian, Seth 197
Ullrich, Mattie 188, 245, 254, 258
Ullrich, William 160
Ulvaeus, Björn 128
Uncle Dan 258
Uncle Vanya 14, 37, *193*, 194, 240, 264, 334, 340, 377, 378
Under the Blue Sky 302
Underneath the Lintel *170*, 353
Undiscovered Country 239
Unexpected Man, The 12
Ungaro, Joan 375
Unger, Aaron Mostkoff 249, 262
Unicorn Theatre 346
Uninvited Guest, The 266
Union City, New Jersey, Where Are You? 245
United Artists 335
United States Theatre Project 318
Unity Fest 2002 259
Universal 129
University of Massachusetts Dartmouth 421
University of Michigan Musical Society 204
University of Minnesota 422
University of Pennsylvania 423
University of Pittsburgh 423

University of Washington, The
  422, 423
University of West Alabama
  43
Unspoken Prayers 328
Until We Find Each Other
  253, 314, 327
Untitled 347
**UP (The Man in the Flying
  Lawn Chair)** 253
Updike, Jason 314
Upham, Ben 270
Urban, Carey 259
Urban Cowboy 4, 18, 19,
  155–157, 156,
  320, 370, 372
Urban, Edward 179
Urban, Ken 264
Urban Stages 272
Urbaniak, James 181, 262
Urbanowksi, Alexandra 308
Urbi, Erwin G. 323
Urgent Fury 261
Uriarte, Sarah 216
Urich, Robert 219
Urinetown
  25, 30, 77, *128*, 229
USA Ostar Theatricals
  72, 131, 138, 142,
  146, 149, 303, 370, 371
USA Today 21, 366
USA: A Reading 259
Usiatynski, Walter "Wally"
  133
Uterhardt, Geoff 322

V-Day 260
Vaaz, Shaheen 305
Vaccariello, Patrick
  146, 147, 164, 319
Vaden, Phillip 311
Vagina Monologues, The
  38, *170*
Valdes-Aran, Ching 264, 266
Valencia, Carlos 247
Valladares, Mercy 269
Valle, Miriam Colón 255
Valles, Tony 269
Valley of Decision, The
  336, 337
Valparaiso 260
Value of Names, The 423
van Cauwelaert, Didier
  16, 138, 370
Van Cleve, Emory 260

Van De Hey, Megan 380
Van Der Beek, James 255
Van Driest, Carey 264, 265
Van Druten, John 69
van Druten, John 128
Van Giesen, Nicole 347
van Gogh, Vincent 11, 155
van Itallie, Jean-Claude 241
Van Lear, Phillip 326
Van Name, J.J. 268
Van Norden, Peter 301
Van Note, Jill 273
Van Outen, Denise 219
Van Swearingen, Guy 327
Van Tieghem, David
  174, 181, 251, 312, 313
van Tonder, Michelle 249
Van Wagner, Peter 266, 312
Van Why, Artie 268
Vanda 267
vanden Heuvel, Wendy
  148, 260, 338
Vanderbilt, Kip 180
Vanderbilt University 423
Vandergrift, Deborah 312
Vanderpoel, Mark 138
VanDevender, Kate 268
Vanstone, Hugh 158, 193, 195
Vanya on 42nd Street 240
Varbalow, Jennifer 246
Varela, Andrew 321
Varga, Joseph 355
Vargas, Ovi 243
Varhola, Kim 136
Variety 3, 5, 6, 9,
  11, 16, 21, 366,
  367, 422
Varjas, Grant 260, 268
Varla, Zubin 204
Varner, Kevin 256
Varon, Susan 260
Varveris, Stefanie 265
Vasen, Tim 181, 332
Vasquez, Alden 324, 326
Vassallo, Ed 252, 266
Vassar College 71
Vaughan, Melanie 150
Vaughn, Brian 356
Vaughn, Robert 335
Vavasseur, Kevin 264
Vazquez, Michele 307
Vazquez, Tory 254
Vazquez, Yul 253
VCX Ltd. 187
Vehill, Scott 346
Vela, Christina 350
Velez, Jamie 262
Velez, Loraine 228

Velvel, Kathryn 272
Venberg, Lorraine 329, 331
Venitucci, Guido 259
Ventimiglia, John 186, 260
Ventouras, Phoebe 270
Ventura, Eliza 260
**Venus de Milo Is Armed,
  The** 299
Vercelloni, Franca 256
Verdi, Giuseppe 128
Vereen, Ben
  7, 8, 129, 130, 220
Vergel, Fulvia 255
Vermeulen, James
  87, 200, 251, 255, 353
Vernace, Kim 139
Vernoff, Kaili 262
Veronique 268
Vert-Galant 261
Vetere, Richard 171
Vichi, Gerry 230, 351
Vickery, John 224, 311
Victims/Trust 259
Victory Begins at Home
  25, *167*
Victory Gardens Theater
  327, 423
Vida, Richard 179
Vidnovic, Martin 198
**Vienna: Lusthaus
  (revisited)** *170–171*
Viertel, Jack 196, 205, 212
Viertel, Thomas
  182, 185, 313
Vietor, Marc 314, 331
Vietti, Alejo 209
Vig, Joel 132, 133
Vigorito, Nick 266
Village Theatre, The 272
Village Voice, The
  367, 421, 422, 423
Villalobos, Vanessa 267
Villanova University 423
Vincent, A.J. 351
Vincent, Christian 198
Vincent in Brixton
  4, 11, *154–155*,
  155, 367, 370, 371, 376
Vincent, Liam 304
Viner, Michael 167, 371
Vineyard Theatre, The
  237, 256, 373
Vinkler, Greg 324
**Vintage Red and the Dust of
  the Road** 380
Vinton, Chandler 329
Violet Hour, The
  309, 310, 327

Vioni, Lisa 167, 370
Vipond, Neil 173
Virgil 269
Viscomi, Jordan 164
Visit, The 379
Visitor, Nana 218, 219
Vitali, Carl 272
Vizki, Morti 270
Vlastnik, Frank 19, 161, 267
Vogel, Carlo 267
Vogel, Frederic B. 163, 370
Vogel, Paula 349
Volansky, Michele
    xv, 119, 187, 311,
    347, 423
Volckhausen, Alex Lyu 187
Vollmer, Lula 266
Volunteer, The 256
von Arnim, Elizabeth 12, 163
Von Essen, Max 146, 220
von Gerkan, Florence 204
von Hoffman, Nicholas 249
von Mahlsdorf, Charlotte
    xi, 59–67
von Mayrhauser, Jennifer 174
von Schiller, Friedrich
    36, 171, 355
von Tilzer, Harry 180
von Waldenburg, Raina 268
Vorlicky, Robert xiv
Vosburgh, Dick 315
Voyage of the Carcass 264
Voyce, Kaye
    196, 245, 323, 342
Voytko, Kathy 160, 226
Vradenburg, Trish 170
Vrancovich, Estela 320
Vreeland, Rita 328
Vroman, Lisa 226
Vujosevic, Tatjana 272
Vukmirovic, Jelena 378
Vukovic, Monique 268

Wackerman, Dan 260, 268
Wada, Emi 250
Wade, Adam 130
Wade, Kim 328
Wadsworth, Oliver 173, 254
Wadsworth, Stephen
    302, 354
Wager, Doug 311
Wagman, Nela 246, 272
Wagner, Chuck 216
Wagner, Jean 272
Wagner, Robin 136

Waite, Todd 350
Waiting for Godot 237
**Waiting For My Man (World
    Without End)** 260
Waiting for the Telegram
    111, 116, **208**
Waits, Tom 237, 245
Wakefield, Scott 355
Wakely, Richard 201
Walch, John 277, 278
Walcott, Derek 170
Waldman, Jennifer 265
Waldman, Price 256, 263
Waldman, Robert 151
Waldrop, Mark 320
Walford, Malinda 260, 263
Walker, Christopher
    182, 351, 353, 354
Walker, Erik Ian 304
Walker, Fredi 228
Walker, Gavin 269
Walker, George F. 355
Walker, Jeanne Murray
    339, 346
Walker, Jon Patrick 187
Walker, Michael 335
Wall, Marilyn A. 315, 321
Wall, Mary Ann 256
Wallace, Charles E.
    176, 177, 378
Wallace, Cynthia 141
Wallace, Deborah 262
Wallace, Naomi 258
Wallace, Peter 335
Wallace, Victor 225
Wallach, Eli 271
Wallach, Tyler 271
Wallert, James 270
Wallis, Ruth 28, 31, 214
Wallnau, Carl 37, 211, 339
Wallnau, Colleen Smith
    37, 211
Wallowitch, John 316
Walnut Street Theatre 348
Walsh, Alice Chebba
    137, 153
Walsh, Barbara 221
Walsh, Enda 239, 248
Walsh, Mary Ann 250
Walsh, Paul 300, 355
Walsh, Tina 225
Walsh-Smith, Tricia 262
Walter, Jessica 314
Walters, Travis 141
Walton, Bob 222
Walton, Debra 266
Walton, Tony 130, 142
Wands, Susan 308

Wanetik, Ric 180
Wang, Ben 332
Wang, Nathan 302, 341
Wangen, Mike 299
Warchus, Matthew 12, 158
Ward, Anthony
    164, 193, 195, 377
Ward, Bruce 252, 300
Ward, Buzz 342
Ward, Elizabeth Caitlin
    256, 323
Ward, Hilary 265, 273
Ward, Jennifer 269
Ward, Joseph 267
Ward, Lauren 206, 207
Ward, Robert 376
Ward, Steven 179
Ware, Bill 256
Waring, Dorothy 379
Warmbrunn, Erica 317
Warmen, Timothy 146
Warner, Craig 300
Warner, Deborah
    22, 149, 244, 372, 377
Warner, Neil 144
Warner, Sturgis 254, 255
Warnick, Adam 351
Warren, Amy 326
Warren, David
    193, 198, 340, 347
Warren, Harry 128, 321
Warren, Rachel 349
Warren, Sloane 322
Warren, Thom Christopher
    224
Warren-Gray, Nicholas
    259, 260
Warrilow, David 234
Washburn, Anne 248
Washington, Ajene 254
Washington College 423
Washington, Krystal L. 228
Washington, Linara 327
Washington, Louis 327
Washington Post, The 278
Washington Times, The 41
Wassberg, Göran 171
Wasserman, Dale 142
Wasserstein, Wendy 318, 319
Wassum, Debra 256
Watanabe, Kunio 250
Watch on the Rhine 71, 75
Water Coolers 14, 30, *185*
Waters, Daryl 30, 176, 182
Waters, John ix, 3, 132, 366
Waters, Les 303
Waters, Stephanie 223
Waterston, James 311

Waterston, Sam 272, 317
Watford, Myk 205, 266
Watkins, Amanda 222
Watkins, Jamie 267
Watkins, Maurine Dallas 127
Watson, Emily
    37, 193, 194, 195
Watson-Davis, Myiia 228
Watt, Douglas 376
Watt, Michael 164, 370
Wave 252
Waving Goodbye 379
Wax Lips Theatre Company
    193
Waxman Williams
    Entertainment 136, 187
Way, Adam 348
Way Out, The 267
**We All Went Down to
    Amsterdam** 326
**We Never Knew Their
    Names** 271
Weatherly, Christal 303, 378
Weaver, Casey 267
Weaver, Deke 264
Weaver, Jeremy Gram 339
Weaver, Sigourney
    80, 82, 251
Webb, Alex 175, 319
Webb, Charles 129
Webb, Daniel 145
Webb, Jeremy 258, 348
Webber, Stephen 334
Weber, Bruce 25, 29, 366
Weber, Carl 260
Weber, Jake 195
Weber, James 262
Weber, Steven 227
Weber, Suzanne 264
Weber, Theresa 267
Webster, J.D. 206
Wedekind, Frank 269
Weeden, Bill 270
Weeden, Derrick Lee
    343, 344
Weedman, Lauren 352
Weeks, Jimmie Ray 310, 311
Weems, Andrew 262
Wegener, Amy 329, 331
Wegener, Maggie 304
Wehle, Brenda
    112, 115, 208, 334, 377
Wehrle, Elizabeth
    178, 189, 198, 202, 210
Weidman, James 315
Weidman, John
    128, 250, 323
Weigand, John 263

Weigert, Robin 225
Weil, Melissa 222
Weil, Tim 202
Weill, Kurt 237
Weiman, Kate 263
Weinberger, Eric H. 263
Weincek, David 270
Weiner, David
    151, 256, 334, 343, 352
Weiner, Gregg 267
Weiner, Miriam 272
Weiner, Randy 170
Weingarten, Seth M. xii
Weinstein, Arnold 244, 324
Weinstein, Bob and Harvey
    144, 371
Weinstein, Harvey 164, 370
Weir, DeeAnn 262
Weir, The 51
Weisberg, Lois 379
Weisberg, Noah 260
Weiser, Mark 266
Weisman, Annie 260, 318
Weiss, Jeff 294, 338
Weissbard, A.J. 245
Weite Land, Das 239
Weitman, Rebecca 265
Weitzenhoffer, Max 148
Weitzer, Jim 227
Weitzman, Ira 201
Weitzman, Ken 318
Welch, Christopher Evan
    213, 252
Welch, Jane 246, 342
Welch, Rainey 268
Welden, J.R. 353, 354
Weldin, Scott 351, 356
Weldon, Charles 329
Weller, Frederick
    11, 107, 153, 177
Weller, Michael 261, 265
Weller-Fahy, Johanna 250
Wellesley College 69
Wellfleet Harbor Actors
    Theater 378
Wellman, John 262
Wellman, Mac
    236, 255, 262, 263, 377
Wells, Chris 254
Wells, Christopher Spencer
    311, 316
Wells, Matthew 269
Wells, Tom 337
Welsh, Margaret 303, 311
Welty, Tara 254
Welzer, Irving 163, 370
Wember, Asa F. 315
Wendell, Courtenay 259

Wendland, Mark 181, 202
Wendt, Roger 146, 164
Wenzel, Erin 327
Werner, Howard 135
Werner, Jennifer 159
Werner, Paul 332
Werner, Stewart 45, 255
Wernke, John 266
Werthmann, Colleen 253, 314
Wertz, Kimberlee 162
Wesbrooks, William 185
West, Ashley 259
West, Darron L.
    191, 334, 340, 349
West, Erin 327
West, Jessica Phelps 322
West, Libby 311
West, Mae 72
West, Michael 37, 201, 263
West, Patti 353
West Pier 267
West Side Story 422
West, Troy 326
WestBeth Entertainment 188
Westbrooks, Nyjah Moore
    260
Westenberg, Robert 230
Westergaard, Louise 135, 370
Weston, Jim 351
Weston, Jon 150, 161, 308
Westport Country Playhouse
    20, 21, 141, 180, 315
Westside Theatre Downstairs
    272
Wetherall, Jack 252, 264, 316
Wever, Merritt 211
Wever, Russ 205, 266
Whaley, Frank 259
Whaley, Michael 214
Wharton, Edith 336, 337
Wharton, William 258
What Didn't Happen
    14, 34, *191–192*, 192
What I Missed in the 80s
    260
**Whatever Happened to
    Baby Jane?** 351
What's Inside the Egg? 264
What's Your Karma? 269
Wheeler, E. Milton 328
Wheeler, Harold
    133, 372, 377
Wheeler, Hugh 319, 323
Wheeler, Jedediah 148
Wheeler, Nathan Thomas 301
Wheeler, Sally 273
Wheeler, Susan 206
Wheetman, Dan 205

When Grace Comes In 353
When Harry Met Sally 69
When We Dead Awaken
    261
Whidden, Amanda 343
Whinnery, Peter 345
Whisper 247
Whistler, Michael 346
Whitaker, Maggie 301
Whitaker, Paul 209, 352
Whitcomb, Margo 340
White, Al 347
White, Alice 252
White, Alton Fitzgerald 224
White, Amelia 244
White Barn Theatre 315
White, Bernard 302
White Bird Productions 272
White, Conor 246
White, David R. 312
White, George C. 272, 313
White, J. Steven
    178, 255, 256
White, Jacob Garrett 256
White, Jennifer Dorr 270
White, John P. 332
White, Julie
    198, 199, 262, 347
White, Lillias 191, 340
White, Margot 263
White, Michole Briana 202
White, Nathan 253
White, Randy 252, 253, 266
White, Rebecca 253
White Russian 264
White, Sullivan Canady 329
White, Welker 272
White-Peppers, Naeemah A.
    378
Whitehead, Charles 157, 371
Whitehead, Reggie 380
Whitehill, B.T. 245
Whitehurst, Scott 268
Whiteley, Ben 206
Whitney, Ann 326
Whitney, Barbara 334
Whitney, Belinda 206
Whittaker, Jay 324
Whittinghill, Kevin 265
Whitty, Jeff
    237, 258, 311, 314,
    324, 373
Whitworth, Paul 342
**Who Are the People in
    Your Neighborhood?**
    266
Whores 253, 314
Whoriskey, Kate 309, 332

Whose Family Values! 254
Why, The 346
Wickwire, Alexis 265
Wiens, Wolfgang 245
Wierzel, Robert
    303, 312, 313, 378
Wiese, Mike 336
Wiesenfeld, Cheryl 208
Wiesner, Nicole 323
Wiest, Dianne 23, 163
Wiggin, Tom 265
Wilber, Jason 329
Wilbur, Richard 151
Wilcox, Wayne 347
Wilde, Oscar
    23, 59, 163, 264
Wilder, Billy 350
Wilder, Matthew 259
Wilder, Susan 348
Wilder, Thornton
    20, 43, 118, 141, 318
Wilfert, Sally 172
Wilkas, Matthew 209, 269
Wilkerson, Jacen R. 216
Wilkerson, John 206
Wilkerson, Steve 300
Wilkinson, Colm 222
Wilkof, Lee 134
Wilks, Talvin 249
Will and the Ghost 266
Will, Ethyl 134, 164
Willeford, Charles 272
Willett, Mark 258
William Inge Theatre Festival
    375, 422
Williams, Bill 301, 302
Williams, Celeste 326
Williams, Christine 343
Williams, Christopher 263
Williams, Craig 271, 272
Williams, Curtis Mark 309
Williams, Denise Marie 224
Williams, Diane Ferry 379
Williams, Elaine 322
Williams, Garry 246
Williams, Hank 205
Williams, Jacqueline 327
Williams, Jim 263
Williams, Juson 260
Williams, Karl 266
Williams, M. Drue 254
Williams, Marvette 224
Williams, Mel 263
Williams, Patty Korbelic 350
Williams, Robin 7, 129
Williams, Rosalyn Coleman
    314
Williams, Ross 262

Williams, Roy 252
Williams, Shané 309, 310, 334
Williams, Tennessee 67, 421
Williams, Toby 172
Williams, Trevor 253
Williams, Virginia 273
Williamson, Jama 176, 187
Williamson, Laurie 196
Williamson, Nance 308
Williamson, Zachary 248
Williamstown Theatre Festival
    197
Williford, Steven 271, 314
Willinger, David 256
Willingham, Calder 129
Willis, Dorothy 380
Willis, Jack 186, 318
Willis, Mirron E. 345
Willis, Steve 259
Wilma Theater 348
Wilmes, Gary 254
Wilner, Jon 369
Wilner, Sheri 347
Wilson, August
    152, 261, 281, 313,
    326, 329, 347, 354, 376
Wilson, Brian 37
Wilson, Brian (musician) 204
Wilson, Brian Anthony (actor)
    347
Wilson, C.J. 168, 314
Wilson, Casey 256
Wilson, Chuck 136, 166
Wilson, Danelle Eugenia 132
Wilson, Darlene 137, 212
Wilson, Edwin xiii
Wilson, Erin Cressida 271, 272
Wilson, Jackie 28, 207
Wilson, Jessica-Snow 223
Wilson, Joe Jr. 179
Wilson, Jonathan 313
Wilson, Lanford
    x, xiii, xv, 36,
    41–49, 178, 233,
    235, 239, 245, 255,
    318, 373
Wilson, Lindsay 261
Wilson, Mary 324
Wilson, Mary Louise 218
Wilson, Matthew R. 249, 272
Wilson, Michael
    163, 191, 271, 272, 312
Wilson, Moira 189
Wilson, Patrick 226
Wilson, Robert 237, 245
Wilson, Sarah Grace 352
Wiltse, David 37, 188
Wimberly, Bridgette 322

Wimberly, Michael 322
Wimmer, Aaron 196
Winant, Bruce 220
Winchester, Richard 269
Wind Cries Mary, The 309
Windheim, Bennett 263
Winer, Linda i, 367, 376
Wing-Davey, Mark
    248, 271, 343
Winger, Debra 18, 156
Winkler, Richard 351
Winnick, Jay Brian 216
Winokur, Marissa Jaret
    ix, 3, 132, 221,
    371, 376, 377
Winslet, Kate 60
Winslow, Lawrence 261
Winslow, Pamela 217
Winston, Connie 264
Winters, Michael 352
Winter's Tale, The 239, 245
Wintersteller, Lynn 314
Wintertime 303, 352, 378
Winther, Michael 198
Winton, David 269, 272
Winton, Graham 256
Wirth, Julius Rene 136
Wischnia, Samantha 348
Wise, Birgit Rattenborg 324
Wise, Paula 155, 320
Wise, Scott 138
Wisker, Stephen 271
Wisniewski, Jim 267
Wisniski, Ron 216
Wisocky, Rebecca
    262, 331, 332, 333
Withers, Brenda 267, 268
Withers, Jeffrey 317
Witherspoon, Pilar 252
Witkiewicz, Stanislaw Ignacy
    239, 250, 261
Witkin, Stephen 376
Witten, Dean 145
Wittman, Scott
    ix, 5, 132, 370, 376
Wizemann, Bryan 268
Wodehouse, P.G. 354
Wohl, David 151, 256
Wojyltko, Chris 261
Woldin, Judd 179
Wolf, Fay 314
Wolf, Jeffrey C. 267
Wolf, Rita 263, 305
Wolf, Scott 36, 197
Wolfe, George C.
    30, 33, 34, 175,
    176, 177, 189, 198,
    202, 210, 248

Wolfe, John Leslie 319
Wolfe, Jordan 269
Wolfe, Wayne
    141, 147, 149, 162, 200
Wolff, Barbara 260
Wolkoff, Barbara 373
Wolohan, Danny 301
Womack, Cornell 187
Womack, Mark 145, 146
**Woman at a Threshold,
    Beckoning** 271, 272
Woman From the Sea, The
    272
Woman vs. Superman 266
Womble, Terence 141, 156
Women in Heat 261
Women of Lockerbie, The
    238, 254
Women, The 76
Women's Project and
    Productions
    238, 254, 258
Wonderful Wizard of Oz, The
    100
Wong, B.D. 238, 245
Wong, Eunice 253, 268, 343
Wong, Jane 332
Wong, Kevin 314
Woo, Anna 302
Wood, Frank 10, 140, 271
Wood, Greg 329, 345
Wood, Maryrose 376
Wood, Stephen Douglas 269
Woodard, Charlayne
    34, 182, 183
Woodbury, Richard
    168, 303, 324, 327
Woodhead, Mindy 334
Woodiel, Paul 134, 166
Woodruff, Loretta Guerra 265
Woodruff, Robert 334
Woods, Allie 261
Woods, Carla 378
Woods, Carol 220, 230
Woods, Harry M. 180
Woods, Terry 329
Woods, Yvonne
    256, 261, 349
Woodward, Jeffrey 340
Woodward, Joanne
    21, 141, 315
Woodward, Jonathan M. 307
Woodward, Max 319
Woolard, David C.
    191, 198, 203, 312,
    319, 340, 347
Wooley, Michael-Leon 196
Woolley, Jim 150, 164, 308

Woolly Mammoth Theatre
    Company
    287, 319, 346
Woolverton, Linda 127, 128
Wooten, Jason 146, 314
Wopat, Tom 221
WorkShop Theater Company,
    The 272
World Journal Tribune 421
World Over, The
    14, 34, *181*
World Set Free 327
World Trade Center
    x, 238, 241, 289,
    290, 292
Worley, D. Matt 301
Worm Day 263
Wormsworth, James 265
Worth Street Theater
    Company 273
Woyasz, Laura 201
Woyzeck 237, 245
Wrangler, Jack 271
Wreford, Catherine 220
Wright, Amy 260
Wright, Charles i, x, xiii, xv,
    10, 69, 150, 423
Wright, Chlöe 145
Wright, Christopher 190
Wright, Craig xii, xvi, 277,
    287–292, 318, 319,
    329, 375
Wright, Donna 322
Wright, Doug xi, xiii, xv, 34,
    59–67, 214
Wright, Erica 269
Wright, Harland 350
Wright, Lynn 259
Wright, Meredith 314
Wright, Milicent 329
Wright, Nicholas
    11, 154, 370
Wright, R. Hamilton 352, 354
Wright, Robert Allen 322
Wright, Samuel E. 224
Wrightson, Ann G. 318, 335
Writer's Block 14, 35, *213*
Writers Theatre 379
Wu, Jade 268, 349
Wu, Mia 206
Wu, Nancy 332
Wuehrmann, Nicholas 267
WWLC 164
Wynkoop, Christopher 168
Wynn, Doug 263
Wynne, Gene 254

Yadegari, Shahrokh 334
Yaegashi, James 153, 177
Yager, Jerry 197, 211, 307
Yaji, Shigeru 345
Yajima, Mineko 136, 206
Yale Repertory Theatre
    316, 377
Yama, Michael 302
Yamada, Mayu 250
Yamagata, Aja M. 256
Yamamoto, Takanori 250
Yamashita, Kosuke 250
Yamauchi, Satomi 254
Yando, Larry 224
Yaney, Denise 182
Yang, Chi-wang 249
Yang, Ericka 136
Yang, Wendy Meiling 268
Yanik, Don 354
Yankowitz, Susan 254
Yazbek, David 128
Yeager, Matt 262
Year With Frog and Toad, A
    4, 19, *161–163*,
    162, 267, 370
Yeargan, Michael 324, 340
Yee, David 143, 259
Yee, Jenny 248
Yeh, Felice 264
Yeh, Ming 145
Yellowman xi, xv, 14, 34,
    35, *119–124*, 120,
    123, *187*, 252, 375
Yeo, Gwendoline 302
Yerkes, Tamlyn Freund 166
Yershon, Gary 157, 158
Yerys, Drew 304
Yeston, Maury 19, 160
Yew, Chay
    266, 271, 305, 341,
    349, 353
Yionoulis, Evan 309
Yionoulis, Mike 309
Yionulis, Evan 266
Yntena, Sylvia 262
YokastaS 250
Yoo, Aaron 264
York, Marshall 267
York, Matthew 326
York Theatre Company 180, 258
Yorkin, Bud 129
Yoshida, Keiko 263

Youmans, James
    193, 255, 311
Youmans, James M. 340
Youmans, William 145
Young, Adrienne 260
Young, Cedric 327
Young, Eric Jordan
    166, 195, 219
Young, Frank M. 350
Young, Joe 180
Young, Karen 249, 258
Young, Nan 246
Young, Rebecca 214
Young, Sharon L. 224
Young, Steven 321
Young, Tara 147
Young, Tracy 316, 378
Younger, Carolyn 270
**Your Call Is Important to
    Me** 261
Your Friends and Neighbors
    79, 80
You've Got Mail 69
Ysamat, Uma 267
Yulin, Harris 255, 314
Yurman, Lawrence 212, 312

Zabel, William D. xii
Zacarías, Karen 248
Zacek, Dennis 327, 328
Zacharias, Emily 321
Zachry, Anne Louise 256
Zafiropoulou, Miranta 188
Zaitchik, Daniel 195
Zak, David G. 380
Zaken, Remy 198
Zaki, Antony 204
Zaloom, Joe 153
Zaloom, Paul 254
Zambri, Catherine 264
Zamore, Simone 269
Zandarski, Grace 314
Zandu Productions 129
Zane, Billy 220
Zanna, Don't! 14, 30, *202–
    203*, 203, 243, 373
Zaray, Nicole 250
Zarish, Janet 255
Zarle, Brandy 253
Zayas, David
    86, 88, 89, 200, 265
Zayas, Dean 255
Zazzali, Peter 258

Zee, Alexa 259
Zehra, Sameena 204
Zeiler, Van 260
Zekaria, Richard Ezra 260
Zellnik, David 245, 266
Zellnik, Joseph 245, 266
Zepp, Lori Ann 209
Zerkle, Greg 223
Zero Hour, The 253, 314
Zes, Evan 259
Zeus, Jared 202, 243
Zhuravenko, Richard 254
Zickel, Mather 272
Zieglerova, Klara
    122, 187, 198, 248, 349
Zielinski, Scott 245, 309, 332
Zielinski, William 345
Ziemba, Karen 218, 253, 314
Zien, Chip 134
Ziman, Richard 203
Zimet, Paul
    241, 249, 253, 377
Zimmer, Hans 127
Zimmer, Kim 258
Zimmerman, Guy 265
Zimmerman, Mary
    128, 244, 324
Zindel, Paul 264
Zingarelli, Vito 351
Zinkel, Julianna 349
Zinn, David 316, 334
Zinnato, Stephen
    171, 258, 272
Zinoman, Jason 367
Zipay, Joanne 265
Zipper Theater 238, 273
Ziter, Edward xiv
Zito, Torrie 150
Zizka, Blanka
    121, 187, 314, 348, 349
Zizka, Jiri 348
Zmed, Adrian 219
Zoetic Dance Ensemble 322
Zoglin, Richard 367
Zollo, Frederick M. 23, 152
Zombie Prom 380
Zoo Story, The 241
Zorich, Louis 152
Zorn, Danny 272
Zorn, John 264
Zuber, Catherine
    22, 31, 151, 174,
    188, 251, 256, 309,
    312, 313, 332, 343,
    371, 375
Zubrycki, Robert 145, 206
Zulueta, Ogie 302
Zuniga, Rolando 262